Halifax

Handley Page
Halifax
From Hell to Victory and Beyond

CLASSIC

An imprint of
Ian Allan Publishing

K.A. Merrick

The Author

Ken Merrick has been researching and writing about British and German aviation subjects for the last 40 years, producing around 14 books ranging from the history of individual aircraft types, through to a highly detailed history of Allied clandestine air operations in World War Two. He became particularly interested in the subject of German camouflage systems some 30 years ago and has written a number of highly acclaimed books on the subject in the intervening years.

This work on the Halifax was the first to be written by him, though not the first of his books to be published; the 1960s and 1970s were a period when only Spitfires and Lancasters were deemed of interest to the public in Great Britain and the Commonwealth countries. That changed, and in the 1980s the history of the Halifax was finally published, by Ian Allan Publishing, followed in 1990 by a revised edition from Aston Publications. Now, as his final work, the history of the Halifax has again been heavily revised and expanded, published once more by Ian Allan Publishing. Full circle.

Handley Page Halifax
© 2009 K.A. Merrick

ISBN 978 1 906537 06 7

Produced by Chevron Publishing Limited
Project Editors: Chevron Publishing Limited
(www.chevronpublishing.co.uk)

Cover and book design: Mark Nelson
© Text: 2009 K.A. Merrick
© Colour profiles: Tim Brown
Index: Alan Thatcher

Chevron Publishing would like to thank David Wadman
and Sally Forsyth for their assistance in the preparation of
this work.

Published by Ian Allan Publishing
Riverdene Business Park, Molesey Road,
Hersham, Surrey, KT12 4RG

North American trade distribution:
Specialty Press Publishers & Wholesalers Inc.
39966 Grand Avenue, North Branch, MN 55056, USA
Fax: 651 277 1203 Tel: 651 277 1400
Toll free telephone: 800 895 4585
www.specialtypress.com
Printed in England by Ian Allan Printing Ltd
Riverdene Business Park, Molesey Road,
Hersham, Surrey, KT12 4RG

Visit the Ian Allan Publishing website at:
www.ianallanpublishing.com

CONTENTS

INTRODUCTION AND ACKNOWLEDGEMENTS

ASKING for opinions from people who risked their lives as to the flying qualities of a particular aircraft often draws an inevitable endorsement, regardless of any shortcomings. It is interesting then to take an example from someone who had an outstanding flying record on both the Halifax and Lancaster and received the relatively rare endorsement of "exceptional pilot". David Leicester had a meteoric rise in rank in Bomber Command, commensurate with his exceptional abilities, which commenced with his being posted to 158 Squadron (Sqn) at Lissett on 6 May 1943 as a Flight Sergeant (Fl/Sgt) pilot. Following the disastrous Nuremberg attack of 10/11 August 1943 that cost the squadron its Commanding Officer and its navigation, gunnery, signals and engineering leaders, Leicester, as the most experienced pilot with 20 operations behind him, was promoted to command 'C' Flight – a move that saw him go from Fl/Sgt to acting Squadron Leader (S/Ldr) in a period of just six weeks and all at the age of 19. He subsequently led 'C' Flight until it became the nucleus of 640 Sqn and then took over as 'A' Flight commander and acting Commanding Officer (C.O.) Having completed 31 operations he was sent to the RAF College, Cranwell for a junior commanders course before being posted to the Lancaster-equipped 35 Sqn of the Pathfinder Force where he completed a second tour, this time of 32 operations, earning a Distinguished Flying Cross (DFC) and Bar in the process. His views on the qualities of the Halifax and Lancaster are thus valuable; the Lancaster was capable of carrying a larger bomb load and further, beautiful to fly but slower to react to the controls. The Halifax was more direct and faster in its response under the same conditions, something that Leicester credits with saving his life on several occasions. In short, there was very little to separate the two types in the bombing role.

The sheer versatility of the design capabilities of the Halifax is partly to blame for obscuring the type's success. Unlike the Lancaster, it operated in a wide range of front line duties – day and night bombing, anti-shipping operations, meteorological duties, glider towing for the major wartime airborne operations, the dangerous, low-level Special Duties operations, radar countermeasures and transport work – and saw extensive service in experimental flying with a variety of weapons and electronic equipment ultimately destined for use by Bomber and Coastal Commands and the Airborne Forces; all of which were carried out across the complete breadth of the operational areas of the RAF.

Interestingly, the performance data for both types reveals some additional facts often overlooked, with Halifax speed and range exceeding that of its compatriot in some instances. Survival statistics for both types also strongly favoured Halifax crews at 29% with 11% for Lancaster crews. Perhaps then, even more reason to view each on their respective merits rather than their wartime propaganda coverage.

As with the Manchester/Lancaster, the Halifax was a mutation of its original concept but suffered from an initial defect that was accepted as a justifiable risk at a time when the future of Bomber Command hung in the balance. The almost daily need to add extra equipment, increase bomb loads and tasks upon Bomber Command's meagre force of 'heavies' would combine with this defect to cause losses that otherwise might not have occurred; at least not in the same proportion.

This led to an assumed but false reputation that lingered long after it had ceased to be in any way true and was due in part, to the very biased personal opinion of Sir Arthur Harris. In more peaceful times, the fault would have been rectified long before the Halifax entered service and the historical record perhaps less prejudicial. Whatever its mixed reputation, the record stands a most distinguished one for all who designed and built the Halifax, maintained it, and flew in it. To all concerned, this work is respectfully dedicated.

This work was originally researched and written 45 years ago at a time when the only aircraft histories considered to be of significant interest to the public were those of the Lancaster and Spitfire. Not until the mid-1970s did the realisation spread that other aircraft had participated in the battles fought by the RAF during the Second World War and public interest grew. Well received when published in 1980, the first edition generated a flow of interest from people who expressed their appreciation that the Halifax's contribution to the wartime record of the RAF was finally receiving recognition. That belief in the worth of its contribution and the opportunity to include the volumes of information and photographs received led to an enlarged work in 1990. That, in turn, brought a second wave of information which included some personal information of the very earliest days of the Halifax's service, nothing of which survives in the official accounts. For that, and all the other personal contributions, I am exceedingly grateful.

Since then several significant historical works have been published which greatly enhanced the ability to form a detailed and more accurate assessment of Halifax operations in Europe; *The Bomber Command War Diaries* by Martin Middlebrook and Chris Everitt, provided a firm foundation for understanding the overall European air war against Germany and Italy. This significant work has since been enhanced by the series of yearly records: *Royal Air Force Bomber Command Losses of the Second World War*, compiled by W. R. Chorley. Combining those volumes made it possible to trace the bulk of the Halifax's wartime career in Europe, and I record here my deep appreciation to all three authors for their dedication. W. R. Chorley had already contributed two Halifax squadron histories of great value: *To See The Dawn Breaking 76 Squadron Operations*, and, with R. N. Benwell, *In Brave Company, The History of No 158 Squadron*, both of which gave detailed personal accounts. From a personal perspective, H. W. 'Sandy' Barr has done great service to the crews of No 38 Group with his *No 644 Squadron - Through The Eyes Of A Canadian*, giving an insight into one of the seemingly forgotten roles of the Halifax.

Among the new round of contributors, I wish to record my thanks to an old friend, the late Eric Marsden who provided a wealth of detail and photographs of the very earliest days of the Halifax's entry into service. His enthusiasm, photographs and detailed memories of that crucial period provided invaluable information on the introduction of the Halifax to operations with No 35 Squadron. Eric Balcomb is another who gave generously,

providing a unique record of his experiences with 35 Squadron in the very earliest days when bombing policies and practices with the new 'heavies' were still being formulated, often at a great cost to crews. Fred Brinton, another of those tireless individuals who, without any type training, nursed the fledgling Halifax into its Middle East career under the most trying conditions. He too provided a wealth of information and photographs.

The history of the Meteorological squadrons was not easy to determine from the rather bare bones records of the units, disguising the critical contribution gained during these often extremely dangerous operations which determined much of the air war's daily round of attacks. I am indebted to the generosity of the following for filling out, in great detail, that part of the Halifax's history: Keith McGonigal, Allan Huston, Allen Williamson, Les Lambert, Neville Beale, Glenn Traub, Cooper Drabble, Ed Aveling, Roy Turner and Winston Diamond. It is a significant part of history long ignored and long overdue for publication. The Coastal Command history was just as thin in terms of detail and Bob Doudle introduced me to the two incredibly detailed histories *U-Boat Operations of the Second World War* by Kenneth Wynn, significantly aiding in unravelling the anti-submarine and shipping operations of the Halifaxes and their crews.

The No 38 Group Airborne Forces history has been enhanced through the generous time and effort of Captain Bernard Halsall of the Glider Pilot Regiment who recorded not only the glider borne battle details, but also the extensive training undertaken to fly gliders into battle. For that insight and introduction to Captain Halsall I must record my thanks to another Halifax veteran and old friend, Emil Gillies, who was intimately involved with the glider borne attacks from the Halifax end of the tow rope. Thanks goes also to another old Royal Canadian Air Force (RCAF) friend, 'Sandy' Barr for providing his records and photographs, as well as his patience in recording his experiences, and fleshing out his final, unique operation to Norway.,

The French use of the Halifax with Bomber Command is known but little of their wartime experiences and almost nothing of its post-war use by the French Air Force, the principal foreign user of the type, has appeared in the English language. I am therefore particularly indebted to Philippe Couderchon for his extensive help in rectifying this omission by providing both extensive records and photographs. Through him, other French contributors generously added to the photographs available and I wish to thank Jean Delmas, Claude Petit, Patrick Vinot-Préfontaine, Pierre Riviére, and the family Cretin-Louvat. From another French contributor, Philippe Canonne, came two significant photographs recording the disastrous start to the Chemnitz attack in March 1945 when weather proved the deadliest enemy.

In Sweden, Mikael Olrog patiently traced further valuable information and photographs for this work from the Nils Arne Nilsson's Collection, and the Photo Archive of thenSwedish Aviation Historical Society.

In Australia another old friend, John Hopton, delved into his truly vast collection and produced some superb photographs of one of the rarest, much modified, Halifax aircraft to visit Australia, plus some of the equally rare civil machines that ended their days there.

To Phillip Moyes, Chris Cole, Bill Chorley, Dennis Davison, Pat Kimber, Ken Russell, Freddie Puttock, Jonathan Falconer, the late Chaz Bowyer, Eddie Creek, S/Ldr Les Manfield, S/Ldr Victor Kemmis, Jack Phillipson, A. J. Brogan, Betty Williams, John Eggert, W/Cdr Russell, Ken Russell, John Eggert, S/Ldr M. Miller, Jack Easter, Alan Sherlock, Brian Pickering, G/Capt David Richardson, Steve Coates, Ted Dann, Harry Hawthorn DFM, Dickie Hughes, Stuart Usher, Peter Hinchcliffe, G. V. Smith, A. C. Smith, S/Ldr Roy Smith, W. E. Miller, J. Muirhead, Jim Halley, D. F. Light, A. Davies, Roger Hayward; my sincere thanks for their sharing of their extensive information and photographs.

For the late Bruce Robertson, long time friend and mentor, a very special note of thanks for his support and guidance when writing this history first began in 1962 and continued through successive upgrading of the work. During the 1960s, he also provided information, which was still technically 'restricted' for no other reason than that the files had never been declassified, as well as photographs and some critical, very detailed help with the Airborne Forces operations. Without that assistance, both Halifax and crews would have been robbed of significant aspects of their history. He also provided two pieces of wisdom, "*the most rare item will be in the background*" and "*the rarest items will be photographs of the poorest quality*"; how right he has been proven over the last 46 years.

A special word of thanks is due to Mick Wright, a collector of Halifax photographs, all of which he so generously provided. The manufacturing process of building a Halifax was brought to life in great detail through the generosity of Peter Summerton who fortuitously rescued the photographic archive of the Rootes Securities Ltd site at Speke Airport, and made it available for this work.

To Kev Ginnane, sincere thanks for his skill as a professional photographer in turning many indifferent, but historically significant, photographs into small masterpieces.

To my life-long friend David Vincent, himself a valued author of RAAF histories, my thanks for his enduring support over 40 years and his seemingly endless ability to contribute information and resources for this work.

Finally, to my wife, Rae, who has remained a tower of strength throughout a lifetime of writing, inevitable neglect, and her essential, very direct support that has never flagged, my heartfelt thanks. This is my last work and it is time to repay some of that debt to her.

K. A. Merrick
South Australia
2009

CHAPTER ONE

FROM PROJECT TO PRODUCTION

A T the close of the First World War, the Royal Air Force (RAF) held a distinguished position as the most powerful force of its kind in the world. A unique feature of this air force was the fact that it alone had designed and organized a strategic bombing force independent of the control of the other two Services. However, within a few short years it had dwindled to a mere shadow of its former strength. The reasons were not hard to find and many were inevitable. The extreme youth of the RAF as a separate and independent entity did nothing to assist its struggle to survive and expand alongside the older established Services. Not until 1923 was the issue of its independence finally and favourably settled with the findings of the Salisbury Committee. However, its fight for expansion remained.

The ensuing years bore witness to a constant series of debates and committees to decide the exact composition of the RAF regarding the ratio of day and night bombers and fighters. A distinct lack of any urgency did little to assist matters. The continuing efforts of the League of Nations disarmament commission which began in 1925 and dragged on unsuccessfully until 1933 had its own harmful effect on the expansion; for while no positive agreement was reached, one of the sub-proposals made and accepted in 1931 stipulated that there should be no increase in armaments during the term of the conference.

In 1934, when the British Government found itself faced with the problem of reconstructing an air force that could compete with those of other European countries, the immediate prospects were far from ideal; the quality and quantity of existing aircraft were below international standards and several vital technical aspects had been neglected. Long distance navigation, particularly at night, was virtually unpractised and any forms of aids, other than those used during the First World War, were unknown. A major factor in this was a lack of research funding to which the bombing results of the first three years of the Second World War would bear sad testimony.

The immediate result of this alarming state of affairs was a five-year period of rapid expansion during which large numbers of what were to prove, in some cases, tactically unsuitable aircraft, were produced. This came about not by design but rather by necessity, since more advanced types were not ready for production, with others little more than ideas on the drawing board.

The evolution of faster, more heavily armed fighter types reflected a direct need for improving the performance of bomber types in the face of such potential opposition. Of equal necessity was the requirement for increased range – a factor that had been brought home during the Abyssinian crisis when British forces in Egypt had been forced to place their aircraft dangerously close to the frontier in order to make it possible to attack Italian bases in Libya if so required. All of these factors combined to prove the inadequacy of both the light and medium bomber as long-range offensive weapons.

Specification B3/34, which produced the Armstrong Whitworth Whitley, was less than 12 months old when, on 8 May 1935, a now far-sighted Air Ministry looking to replace the Whitley issued specification B1/35 for an advanced twin-engined bomber to satisfy Operational Requirement 19.

This required a capability to carry a 2,000 lb bomb internally over a range of 1,500 miles while cruising at no less than 195 miles per hour (mph). With the potential for war increasing, the requirement's overlying emphasis was on rapid production. Powered by two 1,000 hp service-approved British engines (i.e. Armstrong Siddeley Deerhound, Rolls-Royce Merlin or Bristol Hercules) driving variable-pitch metal airscrews, the aircraft would be fitted with Lewis or Vickers K-gun-equipped Hubbard gun turrets for nose and tail defence. It was also to have Frazer-Nash powered controls, a capability for in-flight refuelling (something that demonstrated how far Air Ministry planning had progressed), wireless and direction-finding equipment, along with cabin heating and an intercommunications system for a crew of four.

Sir Frederick Handley Page had a carefully assembled design team. G. R. Volkert had joined the Handley Page Company in 1912, becoming chief designer two years later. In 1929, the team was joined by Dr. G. V. Lachmann [1], who was put in charge of aerodynamics, stressing and slot development; the two remaining major figures in the team were Chief Draughtsman J. Ratcliffe and the Chief Aerodynamicist, R. S. Stafford. Between them, they formulated the Handley Page submission designated as the HP55 with two Bristol Hercules HE ISM air-cooled radial engines as the first power option. However, as a safeguard, alternative layouts were studied using either Rolls-Royce Merlin or Vulture engines, a decision that would later prove

The prototype Halifax, L7244, photographed at Bicester in October 1939. It was delivered to the Air Ministry on 27 March 1940 and was passed to the A&AEE on 13 September 1940. The airframe is in pristine condition, the fuselage roundels were red, and blue B-type in matt finish as specified for night bombers, in all positions, but reappearing for wing upper surfaces and fuselage sides for a short period in 1939. As can be seen in the 1940 side-view, the fuselage roundels were replaced with the so-called A-type. The matt black colouring to the rear face of each propeller blade is clearly visible. (B. Robertson)

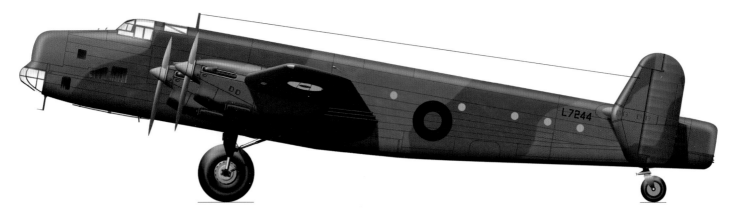

Handley Page Halifax prototype
L7244 as seen at Bicester in October 1939.

useful. The Specification limited the span to no more than 100 ft and an all-up weight preferably not exceeding 20,000 lb; the HP55 came in at 95 ft wingspan and an all-up weight of 26,326 lb.

In September, Contract No. 4411975/35 was issued to cover construction of a single prototype, allocated Air Ministry serial number K8179, and restricted to either the Hercules or S-type engines. Although several aircraft companies tendered designs, the process was overtaken by events with the mock-up stage conference being postponed and a new draft specification discussed instead. The Handley Page design was not selected. The successful tender came instead from Vickers, whose design eventually evolved as the Warwick.

Such was the increasing pace of international developments that the following year the Air Ministry was thinking in terms of a heavy four-engined bomber, which was later to emerge from specification B12/36 as the Short Stirling, and was intended to have an approximate all-up weight (a.u.w) of 55,000 lb. However, the twin-engined class had not been abandoned. Issued on 8 September, Air Staff Operational Requirement OR 41 under specification P13/36, called for what was now designated as a medium-heavy, twin-engined class with an a.u.w of approximately 45,000 lb. This specification was also far more extensive, using terms such as 'world-wide use', 'by day or by night' and 'capable of exploiting alternative long-range or heavy bomb loads aided by catapult launching in a heavily loaded condition'.

All-round defence was essential and was something that would become a controversial factor in the years to come. Power-operated turrets were required for both nose (two guns) and tail (four guns) positions. High speed was also a critical factor, the previous speed range having been expanded to a minimum of 275 mph, at two-thirds engine power at 15,000 ft. Range at that height with normal war load, including 1,000 lb bombs, was not to be less than 2,000 miles. With a 4,000 lb bomb load comprising sixteen 250 lb bombs (take-off distance having been increased from the initial 500 yards to 700 yards, the range requirement remained the same but if 'accelerated' (catapult) assistance was employed, the range was to be a minimum of 3,000 miles. A maximum load of 8,000 lb (comprising sixteen 500 lb or four 2,000 lb bombs) was specified coupled with a range of 2,000 miles. The service ceiling requirement was 28,000 ft when carrying a normal load. Added to these were size limitations imposed by the limits of available transportation facilities – thus the centre section could not exceed 35 ft in length, 9 ft 6 in in height and 8 ft in width. The remaining fuselage components were restricted to 22 ft by 9 ft by 7 ft in width; a very ambitious set of parameters indeed.

Crew requirements remained as before at four: two pilots with one to act as navigator, front gunner and bomb aimer, a second air gunner and a wireless operator with provision for an additional pilot for long-range flights. This doubling up of roles was the

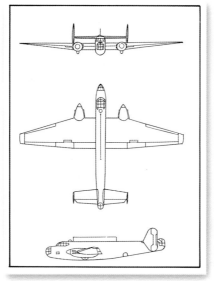

The original design concept drawing submitted for the P13/36 tender. Designated by Handley Page as their HP 56 project, it won the contract.

Major J. L. B. H. Cordes, Handley Page's chief test pilot, and the first to fly a Halifax, seen here during production testing of Hampdens.

Achilles heel in the thinking and a lingering reflection of the pre-war period of poor funding; repeated in the specification comment: "*There is a possibility of combining the Medium Bomber, General Reconnaissance and General Purpose classes in one basic design. Special consideration is to be given to the possibility of carrying two torpedoes.*" This type of requirement had hampered military aircraft design since the 1920s and precipitated the poor position of the aircraft industry.

Development contracts were issued to several firms including Handley Page, whose design team undertook a redesign of their earlier HP55 project which was close to the requirement in its existing form. This was to be an all-metal, mid-wing cantilever monoplane, powered by two Rolls-Royce Vulture engines. The new design, the HP56, was successful and the company was awarded development Contract No. 624972/37 on 30 April 1937, serial numbers L7244 and L7245 being allocated for the two prototypes ordered, each quoted at £50,000 by Handley Page [2].

Design work began immediately and progressed rapidly, including the construction of a mock-up. However, before the design was completed Rolls-Royce experienced some serious teething troubles with their 24-cylinder Vulture engine, which was essentially two 12-cylinder Kestrel engines sharing a common crankshaft. While the Merlin showed far greater promise for development, the Vulture required 50% more time to produce. With only three factories geared for production, producing both types in sufficient quantities was also problematic. Under the circumstances, the Air Ministry had little alternative but to revise the Handley Page specification and in July 1937, the company was requested to submit drawings to Specification P13/36 showing both twin and four-engine installations. The company did so, using four Taurus engines for the latter submission but pointed out the difficulties of adapting the existing design for four engines and still matching the existing Specification requirements.

The redesign began in August and by November the Merlin installation information had been received, thus allowing the installation design work to proceed. The original specification had been far too complex and the design team was somewhat relieved when the Air Ministry finally abandoned certain aspects while others, such as the catapult requirement, took direct and determined discussions between the Ministry and Handley Page himself. The torpedo and dive brake requirements were also abandoned. Interestingly Handley Page had been against a power-operated tail turret, favouring instead a mid-upper and mid-under turrets for rearward defence – a somewhat prescient suggestion as time and losses would demonstrate.

Although extensive, the design change produced only minor variations to the main contours of the wing and fuselage but saw the wingspan increase from 88 ft to 98 ft 8 in while the estimated a.u.w rose from 26,300 lb to 40,000 lb. To save time, L7244 was to be

The rear view, taken at the same time as the photograph on page 7, clearly shows the four small mast type fuel tank vent pipes on the upper wings between the engines. Also visible are the under slung aileron mass balances and the matt black rear face of each propeller blade to prevent dazzle. The only break in the clean lines of the fuselage upper surface is a glazed escape hatch set over the mid-wing rest bay section. The massive Messier magnesium alloy undercarriage box casting, the largest of its kind produced in the UK, is also clearly visible. The upper surface camouflage pattern is regulation Dark Earth and Dark Green. Initially, both type A as seen here and type B (mirror image) camouflage patterns were adopted for the initial production models but after early 1941 only Type A was used. The B-type wing upper surface roundels were regulation matt red and blue. (B. Robertson)

L7244 photographed several months into its testing cycle at Boscombe Down. The two long sections of leading edge slats are clearly visible in the open position and the undercarriage doors had yet to be fitted. The faired nose section has a small square built-in observation window similar to that fitted in the tail fairing and although present, the upper of the two windows in the side of the nose section is difficult to see in this view. Each of the engines (serial numbered 120758, 120759, 120766 and 120825) was fitted with a de Havilland duralumin two-position variable-pitch three-bladed propeller but these were not adopted for production aircraft. L7244 was loaned to 35 Squadron on 23 November to assist with conversion training and was returned to Handley Page's repair depot on 3 August 1941. Following a minor crash in January 1942, L7244 was sent to Airspeed's depot for repairs on 25 January and was then passed to the Airborne Forces Experimental Establishment on 15 March. It was transferred to No 4 School of Technical Training on 11 August 1942 as instructional airframe 3299M. (B. Robertson)

Taken at the same time and location as the previous photograph, the A-type fuselage and under wing roundels are clearly visible but the fin flashes have yet to be applied. The fuselage serial dimensions (originally applied in black but changed to red for production aircraft), were 8 in high by 5 in wide spaced 1.5 in apart with 1-in wide strokes. No serial numbers were carried beneath the wings. Aircraft under surfaces were Night (black), the low demarcation between upper and lower fuselage camouflage colours based on a 60-degree tangent line from the horizontal of the lowest surface point. Spinners and propeller blades remained in bare metal with matt black rear surfaces to the latter. Clearly visible in this view is the forward extent of the leading edge slats when fully open. The original short aerial mast aft of the cockpit was found unsatisfactory and was replaced. (B. Robertson)

Right: This air-to air view of the second prototype, L7245 provides a comparison with the previous photographs. Upper surfaces remain Dark Earth and Dark Green but the lower surface Night Black has been repainted yellow in accordance with revisions to the colours and markings for prototype, experimental and all basic training aircraft. This was a safety measure because air and ground defences were liable to open fire on aircraft of unknown type. Ironically, the first Halifax to be lost on operations would be through such circumstances. Note the wavy demarcation line sweeping up to meet the wing leading edge and the broad yellow area around the lower surfaces of the tail plane. Fuselage roundels are now type A1, being type As simply revised by the addition of a yellow outer ring but under wing roundels remain type A. Fin flashes, 24 in high by 24 in wide have been applied in three equal divisions of red, white and blue with red leading. The serial number is applied beneath each wing in black, as the Halifax was not yet a front line aircraft. Spinners and propeller blades are matt black and black rubber de-icing boots are fitted to the leading edges of the fins and horizontal tail plane. An astrodome with an internal armour plate glass panel is fitted above the flight engineer's position and the navigator's most forward window has been replaced with a teardrop-shaped blister. The radio aerial system has been finalised with a single mast in each of the fore and aft positions, a D/F loop in a streamlined housing added to the top of the fuselage and a standard Lorenz Beam Approach aerial fitted beneath the nose. A Boulton Paul C Mk I turret armed with two 0.303-in calibre Browning machine guns is fitted to the nose and an E Mk I, minus its normal complement of four Browning machine-guns, fitted in the tail position. The retractable tail wheel swung forwards for retraction.

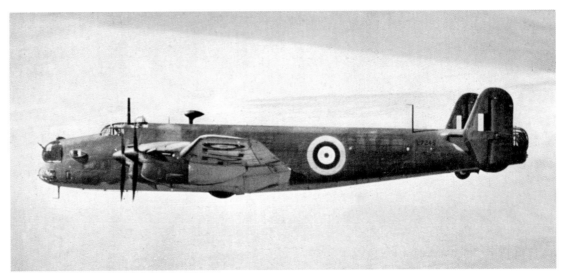

Middle: This view of L7245 shows the type A upper surface camouflage pattern more clearly. Contemporary test reports do not mention the two projections close to the fuselage on the upper wing surface, which were not fitted to production aircraft and may have been associated with airflow tests. Unfortunately, the only photographs of L7244 do not show if these were present on the first prototype. The cut-down fuselage area forward of the windscreen on the starboard side was a characteristic of the Halifax.

This three-quarter front view emphasises the clean lines of the Halifax while still giving a clear impression of its impressive bulk. The transition between the yellow under surface colouring and the camouflaged upper surfaces at the wing leading edge is evident. (B. Robertson)

Seen from a higher viewpoint, the strong lines of the design are more apparent, as is the depth of the fuselage. The horizontally mounted Lorenz Beam Approach aerial under the nose section has the fairlead for the trailing aerial projecting from just behind it. The raked-forward lower section of the engine cowlings are clearly visible and in due course, changes to the shape of this area would become diagnostic for the multitude of sub-marks of Merlin-engined Halifaxes. (B. Robertson)

completed as a pure test airframe for flying trials while L7245 would be fully equipped for complete service trials. With these alterations came a change in the company type number to HP57. In order to cover the construction of the two prototypes the original contract was cancelled and a revised one, 32/37, issued in its place on 3 September; this, in turn, was superseded by Production Specification Halifax I/P1/H.P for 100 aircraft issued on 7 January 1938, under Contract No. 692649/37, the first 50 to carry serial numbers L9485-L9534. The pressures of growing unrest in Europe had now reached the point where the Air Ministry was ordering a production run off the drawing board. To the company's credit and despite all the changes, it produced the first aircraft in 38 months. This met the requirements plus some extras, like the fuel jettison pipes that Handley Page insisted on including, rightly pointing out that in an emergency, without such a facility, an aircraft with full tanks and war load could not land safely within the first three hours after take-off.

Construction of the two prototypes began in March at the Company's Cricklewood plant but work was concentrated on L7244 and completed in the autumn of 1939. The only significant change during construction had been the abandonment of an integral fuel cell system in the wings in favour of four separate fuels tanks in each wing, an Air Ministry requirement by then. Aircraft companies tended to align themselves with specific armament manufacturers; Handley Page chose Boulton and Paul, themselves aircraft manufacturers then currently licence-building the Blackburn Roc turret fighter for the Fleet Air Arm at their Pendeford works, who also specialised in turret design. However, as the power-operated Boulton Paul C Mk I nose and E Mk I tail turrets were not yet ready for delivery, it was decided to fair over the positions rather than delay the testing process.

Fully involved from the mock-up stage, the company's chief test pilot, Major J. L. B. H. Cordes, was a man of significant skills and had been the test pilot for the development of the slotted wing. Certain of the recommendations he made, he would not hesitate to defend his position, especially in the face of comments from those who did not have to fly an aircraft. Amongst his insistences for the prototype Halifax were a revised size to the pilot's emergency exit panel in the cockpit roof and a refusal of some test aspects until they were corrected; one such example occurred during the initial ground handling tests when he reported that the hydraulic braking system was inadequate and refused to continue with the tests until Dunlop pneumatic brakes were fitted to the aircraft.

The Handley Page airfield at Radlett allowed no safety margin for the first test flight should the wheels of L7244 lock on landing. The nearest suitable airfield was that at RAF Bicester in Oxfordshire and the prototype was transported there in sections, the company's unique split construction design (introduced for its Hampden production) lending itself well to this process. With the dismantled L7244 being re-assembled in a hangar, Cordes took the opportunity to familiarise himself with local landmarks through a series of flights in a Miles Magister. On 25 October 1939 and with E. A. Wright as flight observer, Cordes took L7244 into the air for the first time, the supposedly secret flight being witnessed by a host of people whose cars lined the boundary fence of the airfield. No armament was fitted for the flight, the front and rear turret positions being faired over with metal panels.

To simulate the required weights for full and overload conditions, the fuel cells between the inboard and outboard engines were filled with water, necessitating installation of temporary fuel tanks in the fuselage bomb bay. The flight was satisfactory, but a defect developed in the hydraulic system, something that was to prove troublesome and continued to plague the aircraft during its early service career. After further testing during which Cordes and Wright reported some fuselage oscillation, on 22 November the aircraft was flown to the Aeroplane and Armament Experimental Establishment (A&AEE) at RAF Martlesham Heath in Suffolk for

completion of the test programme. Further tests conducted during early 1940 to eliminate the oscillation problem led to improvements in the wing/fuselage fillets and a lengthening of the rear portion of the inboard engine nacelles. The process was still unresolved when, on 4 June, Volkert issued a memo stating that while the matter was under investigation, production aircraft would have the horizontal tail plane set at a higher angle of incidence and the first ten aircraft were to have the

Positioning of the serial number beneath each wing is seen here, marked in black against the yellow of the under surface colouring rather than the regulation white against matt black. The introduction of four engines and the normal serial number dimensions required splitting the marking. The marking was set at 5 ft 8 in from the wing tip, each letter/numeral 3 ft 2 in wide by 5 ft 0 in high, set 6 in apart, with width of each stroke 7.5 in. Despite the poor quality of the photograph, the wing bomb cell doors are just discernible, fitted between the inboard engine and the fuselage.

Routine maintenance being carried out on L7245; note the additional small round window below the triangular window of the navigator's position, something not often visible in photographs. The presence of this modification and the reduced height of the small forward window now fitted with a teardrop blister indicate that this photograph was taken after the main production cycle had started, as this modification was not immediately adopted for the Halifax B Mk I. The opening section (escape hatch) of the canopy above the first pilot's position is also visible and the rear turret does not have its four Browning machine guns installed, although it is possible that these were never fitted to L7245. The aircraft was loaned to No 28 Halifax Conversion Flight (HCF) on 7 November 1941 where it served until the Flight was disbanded and absorbed by No 1652 CU in January 1942. L7245 was then allocated to the Airborne Forces Experimental Establishment and was struck off charge (SOC) on 24 February 1942. Permission for its conversion to an instructional airframe was obtained under the authority of AMP H 581960/E1B on 24 December 1942. It was subsequently used as a synthetic trainer with the serial of 3474M.

engine nacelles of intermediate length – as fitted on the two prototypes. Extended fairings, with the rear portion attached to the landing flaps would thereafter be adopted for the production aircraft.

The second prototype L7245, fitted out with full equipment and with Cordes again at the controls, flew for the first time on 17 August 1940 and on 11 September transferred to Boscombe Down where it joined L7244 for an extensive series of tests. More representative of the production series, it was fitted with mock-ups of the Boulton Paul C Mk I nose and Boulton Paul E tail power-operated gun turrets plus two floor guns situated in the fuselage well, aft of the bomb bay. It was also intended to supplement this armament at a future date either with beam guns or a power-operated dorsal turret. The fuselage and wing bomb cells had a total capacity of 11,000 lb for holding alternative loads comprising either fifteen 250 lb or 500 lb bombs or four 2,000 lb bombs in the fuselage and six 500 lb bombs in the wing cells. Provision was also made for the carriage of two 1,500 lb mines, plus either twelve 500 lb or twelve 250 lb bombs.

The main series of performance tests was concentrated at an a.u.w of 50,000 lb. Though designed to include leading edge slats, tests had shown that the flight characteristics were quite satisfactory with these locked shut. At an a.u.w of 50,000 lb using 40 degrees of flap, L7244 recorded a mean take-off run of 505 yards, 880 yards to clear a 50 ft screen and an unstick speed of 84 mph. Comparative figures for L7245 with the slats locked and sealed were 570 yards, 1,000 yards and 80 mph, the minor discrepancies between the figures being due almost entirely to errors in measurement and take-off technique. The aircraft was found to have a medium tendency to swing to port as the throttles were advanced, which could be countered easily by applying full rudder and, if necessary, a slight touch of brake. The control column load was high during the initial stages and almost impossible to get fully forward; however, once airflow built up over the elevators the tail could be raised easily and take-off was then straightforward, the aircraft needing no assistance to become airborne. Raising the undercarriage and flaps required very little change of trim. However, at the overload weight of 55,000 lb, a marked difference occurred and the aircraft had to be pulled off the ground.

L9485, the first production Halifax, as the type was now designated, joined the test programme in October. Having flown for the first time on the 11th of that month, it would remain with A&AEE for its working life. While externally similar to L7245 in most respects, it was distinguishable by beam gun hatches[3] fitted with a full-width handle across the top section. Not so obvious was the change from the de Havilland two-position variable-pitch three-bladed duralumin propellers used on L7244 to Rotol constant speed units with Schwartz compressed wood blades. While the latter units were not fully feathering, they were initially chosen for the production aircraft, a decision later rescinded in favour of 12 ft 6 in diameter Rotol RXF5/1 units with magnesium alloy blades[4].

The ailerons fitted to the first two prototypes were considered effective but response was sluggish over initial small angles of attack at all speeds. At speeds in excess of 250 mph, they became increasingly heavy, so, to overcome these deficiencies, the ailerons on L9485 were given a slight reflex that proved satisfactory in most respects; they still remained a little sluggish. The wooden aileron trim tabs also proved to be a source of trouble by rapidly becoming waterlogged and warping badly. They were subsequently replaced by plywood-covered tabs even though a recommendation was put forward at the same time to replace them with metal tabs. For some obscure reason, this took nearly a year to effect, the new metal tabs eventually being tested on L7245 on 16 August 1941 and found to be entirely satisfactory.

By far the most significant fact to emerge from the trials was a report concerning rudder response; at speeds below 120 mph, they gave little response but were effective at high speed. While it was thought at this point that they would probably have sufficient power to cope with asymmetric power loads, the matter was to be the subject of a special series of tests with one, and two engines cut. At speeds below 150 mph, there was a tendency for the rudders to overbalance with the application of rudder trim; this was particularly noticeable when one engine was throttled-back and rudder applied to overcome the resultant yaw. In the meantime, a modified trim tab was fitted in an attempt to overcome the problem, but this phenomenon was to linger, with fatal results.

For its unprecedented size, the stall characteristics of the Halifax were remarkably mild – straightforward with no tendency to drop a wing and allowing control to be regained quickly. Elevator control was considered light and effective up to 250 mph, the aircraft possessing sufficient longitudinal stability for those conditions. It was considered that no difficulties would be experienced when the aircraft was flying on automatic pilot or on a bombing run. In excess of 250 mph, i.e. in diving attitude, a certain amount of elevator tab was required to overcome the high control column loads as the aircraft became progressively tail-heavy. Above 300 mph, it required all of the pilot's strength to keep the aircraft in the dive and it was during these tests that airframe vibration was first encountered. Subsequent investigation isolated the trouble as being caused by the nose turret when it was offset by more than 5 degrees from dead ahead. Some difficulties were also experienced with turret rotation due to high slipstream forces, but were remedied by fitting balance flaps operated by cams attached to the turret such that either flap opened as the turret rotated away from it.

No difficulties were experienced with the landing technique and the aircraft could be put down smoothly in a three-point attitude. Full brakes could be applied at any time during the landing run without any tendency to swing. On several occasions, the tail wheel retraction jack rod was found to be slightly bent and had to be replaced; this was thought to be caused by play in the knuckle joint that, in turn, caused the tail wheel shimmy experienced from time to time. This shimmy and tail wheel failure was to recur throughout the Halifax's early service career and, with the exception of L9485, production aircraft had the tail wheel fixed down. In the event of an overshoot caused by a baulked landing, the aircraft would climb satisfactorily with no loss of control using full throttle and maximum engine rpm.

The interior layout of crew positions and equipment was considered satisfactory although subject to some minor criticisms. Communication between the navigator's compartment and the astrodome position involved crawling underneath the second pilot's controls, a task which would have proved extremely difficult in full flying kit[5]. The ammunition drums and plastic ducts for the rear turret had proved unsatisfactory under test and were to be replaced on the production series aircraft by ammunition boxes and chromium-plated steel ducts. The size and position of the drums had necessitated a shallow platform for the port beam gun position in order to allow the gunner to carry out depression shooting. The beam gun windows were easily removed and the guns could be locked on their pillar mountings quickly. Although the draught was bad, firing trials on L9485 proved that the guns could be operated at all normal speeds, i.e. up to 260 mph. Above this, a certain amount of effort was required to move the guns against the airflow but steady aiming could still be carried out. The ventral position, also armed with two Vickers K guns, proved satisfactory despite the strong draught. However, it was proposed to replace this manually-operated position with a Boulton Paul K Mk I turret, armed with two .303-in Browning machine guns with 1,000 rounds per gun, sighted by means of a periscope[6]. The main T1083-R1082 communication set was recommended for replacement with a T1154-R1155 set, this change being incorporated from the 13th production aircraft onwards.

Since aircraft performance was virtually unaltered with the leading edge slats locked shut, a recommendation was passed for their deletion with barrage balloon cutters and ramps being installed in their place. This came into effect from the 61st aircraft, the first 60 having the slats fitted but locked shut and sealed. With the completion of these modifications, the Halifax was ready to enter service.

CHAPTER TWO

INTO BATTLE

O N 5 November 1940, No 35 Squadron re-formed as a bomber squadron under the command of Wing Commander (W/Cdr) R. W. P. Collings and was attached to A&AEE, Boscombe Down as the first RAF Halifax squadron. The task was not an easy one for several reasons, not least of which was the fact that no one had any previous experience with four-engine heavy bombers, leaving the crews with little alternative than to learn as they went. This was alleviated to some degree, however, by the arrival of some experienced operational pilots and their crews to help in the process of transition to the new breed of aircraft.

A lack of aircraft, combined with a series of moves, rather retarded initial attempts at progress. On 13 November, Flying Officer (F/O) M. Henry DFC and crew collected the squadron's first aircraft, L9486 and ferried it to Boscombe Down. Although an attempt was made to begin some form of organised instruction with this aircraft, it was hampered by the squadron's move to Leeming on 20 November where it came under the jurisdiction of No 4 Group, Bomber Command. An effort to ease the training situation was made by the temporary loan – from the Ministry of Aircraft Production (MAP) – of the first prototype L7244 for dual instruction, W/Cdr Collings ferrying it in on 23 November.

Within 12 days the squadron had moved once more, this time to Linton-on-Ouse on 5 December; the only other progress made during the remainder of the month was the arrival of four pilots and one observer.

Even so, the new year of 1941 brought with it the promise of better things and the slow trickle of production aircraft commenced once more with the arrival of L9487 from 24 Maintenance Unit (MU) on 4 January. Limited as they were by a

Photographed in April 1941, L9486: B was the first Halifax received by No 35 Squadron and the first of its type to enter front line RAF service. Delivered to the Department of Technical Development at A&AEE Boscombe Down on 13 November 1940, it was ferried to 35 Squadron by F/O M. T. G. Henry DFC and crew the same day. Tests with the prototypes had shown that slats provided no significant advantage and a recommendation was issued that they be locked and sealed on production aircraft and barrage balloon cable cutters to be fitted to the leading edges. However, while slats continued to be fitted until changes could be incorporated into the wing assembly jigs, permanent deletion was to come into effect from the 61st airframe but, clearly, the recommendation was not put into immediate effect. This writer and others have previously suggested that this aircraft was L7245, photographed when serving with No 28 Halifax Conversion Unit (See Appendix I) but examination of the camouflage pattern negates this assumption. Flown by W/Cdr R. W. P. Collings, the squadron CO, it took part in the first Halifax wartime operation against Le Havre on 10/11 March 1941. In October 1941, it was transferred to No 28 Halifax Conversion Unit and later to that unit's successor, No 1652 HCU. (M. Wright)

L9490 was ferried with L9488 to No 35 Squadron on 16 February 1941 by P/Os J. W. Murray DFC and G. A. L. Elliot DFC. Both aircraft took part in the first Halifax operation against Le Havre on 10/11 March 1941, L9490: L departing at 19.15 hrs and L9488: M five minutes later. Note the change to the camouflage pattern, a characteristic of early B Mk I Series I aircraft with the matt black taken up to the horizontal mid-point as far as the roundel then gently swept up to meet the horizontal tail plane and just skirting the serial number. Other distinguishing marks of this early variant were the depth of the window immediately aft of the nose turret with no clear teardrop observation blister, the under-slung aileron mass balances and the staggered beam gun hatches with their Perspex window and narrow hinged upper section. The small round window below the navigator's triangular window remained but often had a small black curtain drawn across it, making it difficult to detect in photographs. The crew entrance hatch can be seen, just aft of the roundel, in the open position. At the time of the photograph, no armament was fitted and the squadron codes had yet to be applied. Involved in a flying accident on 17 July and initially assessed as Cat B (FA) (Repairable, Flying Accident), L9490 was later declared as Cat E (beyond economic repair) and written off. (B. Robertson)

A rare air-to-air photograph of one of 35 Squadron's early Halifaxes, S-Sugar photographed while flying over York during the winter of 1940. (Air Commodore P. A. Gilchrist via C. Bowyer)

shortage of aircraft, the squadron began a serious training programme with six crews under instruction, the programme consisting of fuel consumption flights, one hour flights at operational heights, handling at 50,000 1b a.u.w, use of the Standard Blind Approach equipment, W/T [1] procedures and auto-pilot tests. The arrival of L9489 on 12 January increased the squadron's meagre supply of aircraft to four, but within 24 hours this was reduced back to three, F/O Henry and his crew being killed when L9487 crashed in flames at Homefield Farm.

The training programme continued unhindered for the next few days but further trouble in the form of continuing bad weather reduced efforts to a minimum for the next five weeks. Other more serious delays also occurred during this period with all aircraft being grounded in mid-January and again in early February due to persistent trouble with the hydraulic system.

Simultaneously, the supply of aircraft continued at a frustratingly slow pace with only a further five, L9493: G, L9496: N, L9488: M, L9490: L and L9498: T, being received. Bad weather continued to hamper training during the remainder of February, but a steady increase in aircraft numbers managed to offset this and by early March 15 crews were under training, six of which were ready for operations.

The Halifax had entered service at a time of change for Bomber Command. Freed at last from tactical obligations, it was now able to concentrate on a strategic policy. On 15 January 1941, the Air Ministry had sent the head of Bomber Command, Sir Richard Peirse, a clear, concise and pointed directive. Synthetic oil plants were to be the prime objective of concentrated bombing for the next six months in the belief that destruction of a major portion of that industry's capacity would have direct and dire consequences for the German war industry as a whole. When oil targets could not be attacked, long lists of secondary objectives were to be bombed.

On 9 March 1941, a crisis arose and a new directive was issued; U-boats and long-range aircraft were devastating Allied shipping. For the time being, attacks on U-boat harbour facilities and production centres would take priority, but oil would still receive some attention. Unwelcome as it was, the resulting four-month diversion of effort would mask Bomber Command from its first major crisis – powerful critics who claimed, with some accuracy, that its crews could not locate and bomb specific targets such as oil installations. Some awareness of this shortcoming was already circulating within the Air Ministry for, in that same directive, reference was made to a selection of targets that lay within the congested areas of cities, the bombing of which would produce the greatest effect on German morale. Thus was the foundation of a formal policy of area bombing laid for, until some form of sophisticated bombing aid could be introduced, this seemed the most profitable way to employ the forces of Bomber Command. Crews, however, would continue to be briefed to attack specific targets within the cities and in good faith, and would report what they believed to be their relative successes.

On 10 March the squadron received a signal ordering it out on its first operation since re-forming. Seven aircraft were detailed to attack the docks and shipping canal at Le Havre, with their alternate target being shipping at Boulogne, while eight Blenheims would attack Le Havre independently. During the briefing for the raid, a signal was received from the AOC-in-C (Air Officer Commanding in Chief) Bomber Command. It read, *"Good wishes to No 35 Squadron and the heavyweights on the opening of their Halifax operations tonight. I hope the full weight of the squadron blows will soon be felt further afield."*

The six-man crews for this first operation were:

L9486: B – W/Cdr R. W. P. Collings AFC, P/O Franklin, F/O Tetley, Sgt Hill. P/O Careless, Sgt Watt.

L9498: F – S/Ldr P. Gilchrist DFC, Sgt R. Lucas, P/O E. Arnold, Sgt S. Broadhurst, P/O A. Cooper, Sgt R. Aedy.

L9496: N – F/Lt P. Bradley DFC, S/Ldr Sarsby, Sgt Collinge, Sgt Stone, Sgt Roberts, Sgt Wheeler.

L9488: M – F/Lt G. Lane DFC, Sgt Bailey, Sgt Walters, Sgt Sawyers, Sgt Turner, Sgt Hill.

L9493: G – F/O R. Warren DFC, Sgt Greaves, Sgt Wilson, Sgt Hogg, Sgt Somerville, Sgt Ogden.

L9490: L – P/O Hillary, Sgt Godwin, Sgt Gibb, Sgt Chalmers, Sgt Robinson, Sgt Willingham.

Weather conditions over England were perfect at the time of take-off; W/Cdr Collings, the squadron C.O., departed first at 19.00 hrs with the remaining five following at approximately five-minute intervals and the last, F/Lt Lane's aircraft, leaving at 19.20 hrs. The seventh aircraft, piloted by P/O J. Murray DFM, was forced to turn back soon after take-off due to the Halifax's persistent problem of hydraulic failure.

Weather conditions remained good over France and four Halifaxes successfully attacked the primary target, but shrapnel from a near miss damaged L9493: G and wounded the navigator. The radiator of the port inner engine was punctured causing it to overheat badly and Warren was forced to cut the engine. To complicate matters, a hydraulic failure allowed the port undercarriage to come down, but despite these difficulties the aircraft was brought safely back to base.

Eric Marsden, an NCO Fitter with the squadron during this early period, recalls that the lesson with the broken hydraulic line was not ignored and eventually led to the fitting of a mechanical up-lock in the form of a bolt, about ten feet long, which was inserted from the rest bay position into lugs on the main undercarriage legs. In addition, bungee cords were fitted to give lowering assistance in the event of damage to the hydraulic system – this took about 30 seconds – but in the interim, widespread hydraulic problems persisted.

Of the other two aircraft, L9496: N was unable to locate either the primary or secondary target due to cloud and bombed Dieppe instead while L9488: M, after continued attempts to locate the primary target through thickening cloud, was forced to return to base through fuel shortage, the bombs being jettisoned safely in

The bomb aimer's prone position was just forward of the navigator's table (on left). To his right are the bomb fusing and release panels, while the ammunition bins for the C Mk I nose turret flank his head and shoulders. The standard bombsight of this period was the CSB (Course Setting Bomb Sight). The gunner's folding seat is hanging in its down position. In the lower left corner of the photograph is the vertical mounting frame for the target camera, which had a circular window set in the belly of the nose section.

Above: The asymmetric shape of the cockpit glazing is clearly apparent in this wide view of the pilot's instrumentation and controls. The blind flying instruments are set immediately in front of his position with engine instrumentation in the centre behind the throttle quadrant. The inset triangular levers on the control column were for the brakes and the rather odd, anchor-shaped attachment was the ground control lock. When seated next to the pilot, the flight engineer assisted with the handling of the throttles and boost levers as required.

Above: Looking back and upward at the wireless operator in his position directly beneath the pilot illustrates the depth of the fuselage. The wireless operator was separated from the navigator's position by a bulkhead on which radio equipment was mounted. The horizontal bar is the control linkage rod to which the second pilot's controls could be fitted when needed. The bulkhead behind the pilot was fitted with armoured glass panels and the flight engineer is standing on the steps leading down to the front fuselage compartment. The flight engineer had a folding seat, part of which is visible on the left. When in use it was swung up and locked into the frame of the pilot's floor section.

Above: The flight engineer's panel was mounted on the aft bulkhead and could be viewed from either his normal standing position or from the folding seat next to the pilot. The top row contains two fuel tank gauges flanking four fuel pressure indicators while below another six fuel gauges sit above four oil pressure indicators, flanked on either side by two oil temperature gauges. Eight radiator inlet temperature gauges, two per engine, complete the upper panel. Beneath on the right are the radiator shutter controls with four propeller anti-icing control knobs. Four starter magneto switches are next, with the aerofoil anti-icing air pressure gauge for the flexible rubber de-icing boots and on the right, the two No 5 port and starboard fuel tank contents gauges. Fitted above this position was the astrodome, which contained a semi-circular armour plated glass panel, mounted on a frame that allowed it to be swung up into a near vertical position when serving as a fire control position. (E. Marsden)

Left: Looking down into the nose section from the doorway into the flight engineer's compartment shows the steep angular cut of the windshield and fuselage dorsal area, providing the pilot with an uninterrupted view to starboard that was enhanced by the fixed window in the starboard cockpit wall. The bar for the second set of controls and the upper part of the flight engineer's folding seat are seen more clearly in this view.

The rear bulkhead of the flight engineer's position was fitted with an armoured door that opened into the rest bay section set between the two main wing spars. This had seating for eight, four each side – which initially was the intended crew number – used by crew for take-off and landing. The fixed step made getting over the spar easier, a critical feature in an emergency. The dorsal escape hatch could be reached via a fixed wire ladder on the right (out of view). This example is from a B Mk II but other than for the padding, is identical to the B Mk I.

The more Spartan interior of the B Mk I looking aft over the rear spar from the rest station amidships clearly showing the pillar mounting for the starboard pair of Vickers Gas Operated machine guns with the guns in the stowed position. The roof-mounted racks for the ammunition bins for the rear turret are on the right with two flares in their horizontal stowage positions below and in front. The flare chute was just forward of the entrance door, on the starboard side. The armoured door to the rear gunner's turret, with its small window, is on the left. (E. Marsden)

the Channel. The overall success of the operation was marred by a tragic incident when S/Ldr Gilchrist's Halifax, L9489: F was mistaken for an enemy aircraft and shot down by a British night-fighter over Surrey, crashing by the small village of Normandy near Aldershot at 22.40 hrs. Only S/Ldr Gilchrist and the flight engineer Sgt Aedy were able to bale out in time; the rest of the crew perished with the aircraft.

On the night of 12/13 March, a mixed force of 88 aircraft was dispatched to attack the Blohm und Voss works at Hamburg. The heavy bomber contingent comprised just three Halifaxes and four Manchesters; the first time either type had been sent to a German target. Only two Halifaxes were successful, the third being forced to return with both gun turrets unserviceable. The following night, the same target received the attention of two more of the squadron's aircraft along with 137 others, including five Manchesters. Both crews reported a large fire burning in the centre of Hamburg, this being the main office block and two slipways on which U-Boats were being built and visible from 80 miles away during the return trip. This would be the squadron's last operation for a month but they were far from inactive, as shown by a total of 204 hours of flying training during March alone.

On 23 March, P/O E. Franklin flew L9486 to the Air Fighting Development Unit (AFDU) at Duxford for Tactical Trials, but was forced to return on the 31st due to the recurring enigma – hydraulic failure of the undercarriage, making, in the words of the squadron diarist, "... *a sad but beautiful landing on the belly of the aircraft, causing the minimum amount of damage.*" These hydraulic failures were to be a source of much frustration for some time to come. Repaired, the Halifax was sent to No 28 Conversion Flight, eventually being absorbed with its parent unit into No 1652 Heavy Conversion Unit (HCU) before a second belly landing at Marston Moor on 3 March 1942 saw it converted to Instructional Airframe 3005M.

At the beginning of March, after completing 15 operations in six months, Wireless operator/Air gunner Sgt Eric Balcomb[2] was posted in from No 78 Squadron and joined P/O Franklin's crew for air firing exercises in which the attacking aircraft were Hurricanes and Spitfires flown by experienced pilots: "*Our part of the exercises was to measure the various fields of fire from the turrets... and from the twin Vickers 'K' machine guns housed amidships on each side of the fuselage. In the rear turret (my domain) one Browning gun was replaced by a G.45 Camera gun, which recorded*

on film the length of time taken of each burst of 'fire', as well as the visual approach of an attacking aircraft. Thus, we calculated the distances at which to open hostilities.*"

On 12 April orders were received to prepare for the formation of a second Halifax squadron, No 76[3], under the command of W/Cdr S. O. Bufton DFC. Three days later, 40 airmen arrived on posting from No 10 Squadron to be trained within 35 Squadron's 'C' flight to gain operational standards and experience prior to being redesignated as No 76 Squadron[4].

That same night, 15/16 March, No 35 Squadron was back on operations, sending five Halifaxes to Kiel as part of a 96-strong force that included two Stirlings; the first time both types had operated against a target together. While still over the target area, the starboard undercarriage leg of Sgt Lashbrook's L9493 came down and he was forced to fly his aircraft back to base in that configuration but was prevented from landing by the presence of an enemy aircraft in the vicinity. While circling waiting for clearance to land, both port engines of the Halifax, damaged earlier by flak, failed in rapid succession and over-correction of the resultant downward swing ended in a forced landing near Tollerton village, the aircraft hitting a tree in the process. Fortunately, only the navigator and the tail gunner were slightly injured, the rest of the crew escaping unharmed.

At the beginning of May the squadron once more entered a period of inactivity due mainly to the aircraft being grounded by persistent undercarriage hydraulic failures. All second pilots were temporarily attached to No 58 Squadron, who shared the base with 35 Squadron, for experience on Whitleys.

Marsden states that the hydraulic problem was a combination of failure of the clutch on the hydraulic pump, which permitted unloading of the pump when pressure was not required and a defect: "*.....unknown to me and, I suspect, also to the French Messier representative who rebuilt the hydraulic system on '86 after the aircraft had been belly landed and was undergoing repair at Linton. It thus became a trials model until the civilians had the circuits to their satisfaction. The initial indication of this fault was a near crash, just averted, of an aircraft, which was engaged in circuits and bumps at*

Leeming or somewhere near when an explosion apparently occurred within the hydraulic system, perhaps in one of the larger accumulators, causing sausage-shaped formations to occur all over the hydraulic system – and a certain amount of sweat to appear on the pilot's brow." This problem and the squadron remedies were later to have an unexpected consequence when, on 17 July: *"All this led to W/Cdr Tait landing a Halifax on one main wheel – having seen his own side main leg down and two greens on the dash (one for the locked-down tail wheel) he landed a perfectly good aircraft and separated it into production components within seconds. The mechanical up-lock, not used on local flying, had vibrated into position and locked the starboard wheel up on L9495: B and nobody checked. I was nearly put on a charge by the Duty Pilot for demanding a red Very flare to give Willie a chance to discover the problem."*

On the same date as the previously related incident, a second 35 Squadron Halifax, L9490: L was written-off in a 'ground accident'. It was on a fuel-exhaustion test flight and the pilot pushed the range limit a little too far, ending up making a wheels-up forced landing at North Mimms, Hertfordshire when the fuel ran out.

The forward-retracting tail wheel was also still giving trouble. Either it would stay retracted or, when the wheels did lower, the self-centring did not work properly. Marsden recalls that tail wheel shimmy first appeared with the regular use of concrete runways, but with new aircraft using the grass strips it was rare. *"The shimmy was very severe, enough to rattle the teeth in your head when in the rear of the aircraft on landing, perhaps even alarming in the rear turret. This was probably the chief cause of tail wheel failure."* As a temporary measure, tail wheels were locked down *".....*

The door in the rear bulkhead opened into the horizontal attachment section for the tail plane, the gunner passing under the spar to reach the rear doors of his turret, the armrests being raised and locked in position for entry and egress via the two sliding doors seen here in the open position. The four 0.303 Browning machine guns were mounted on their side, their 10,000 rounds of ammunition being fed via the long ducts into a central point beneath the turret, then via spiral ducting and rollers upwards, beneath the gunner's firing controls, to each gun. The gunner's controls comprised a short control column projecting through a diamond-shaped aperture set in a near horizontal panel with the firing and turret circuits mounted on the vertical section of the panel. A high-speed switch was mounted on the left-hand side and the turret power supply switch on the right.

three or four months after the Halifaxes entered service. Certainly, the first operations were carried out with retracting wheels and I remember the comments as to loss of speed when it occurred."

During this period of operational inactivity, the squadron carried out several 'social' engagements, which included flights for the American Mission at Hatfield, S/Ldr Gilchrist flying a Halifax there on 19 April, and three aircraft participating in a fly-past for the War Weapons Week appeal while others did the same for local fund-raising appeals.

The Halifaxes may have been temporarily inactive but the enemy was not. At 01.45 hrs on 10 May, Linton-on-Ouse was subjected to a bombing attack that lasted for approximately 30 minutes. The initial stick of incendiaries hit the 35 Squadron hangars, starting multiple fires and only the prompt action of the aircraft guards and other airmen brought the blaze rapidly under control. Damage, fortunately, was light, limited to some holes in the hangar roofs, a lightly burnt main plane on one Halifax and the front fuselage of another burnt out. The loss of life, however, was not so light, 35 Squadron losing three airmen and seven others badly injured. The Station Commander, G/Capt F. F. Garraway, also lost his life conducting fire-fighting operations.

On 22 May W/Cdr Collings and P/O J. Murray DFM flew L9495 to Abingdon where it was inspected by Their Majesties and the Princesses Royal, the Minister of Aircraft Production and the AOC in C. Of slightly less 'social' nature, but undoubtedly of prime importance in the light of the squadron's first operational loss, was a joint exercise held on the East Coast where, along with other new types of aircraft, P/O Owen demonstrated L9491 to the Observer Corps. On 6 June, W/Cdr Collings flew L9506: X to West Raynham to be inspected by the Prime Minister. These engagements continued sporadically but finally petered out in July as bombing activities intensified.

Operations were renewed on the night of 11/12 June with the squadron's largest effort to date, nine Halifaxes as part of a mixed force of 80 bombers dispatched to Duisburg, which was attacked with moderate success despite 8/10ths cloud at the planned bombing height. However, Cologne, some 30 miles distant, just outside the industrial haze of the Ruhr and not on the target list for that night, was also bombed, causing much damage. The attackers may have been from a force of 92 bombers sent to Düsseldorf, but it would not be the last time that the glow of fires drew crews to the wrong target. Of the nine Halifax crews, six delivered their attack from heights between 7,000 and 13,000 ft. The heavy cloud cover repeatedly obscured the target but these crews managed to find breaks through which to attack. Two others, unable to locate the primary target, chose others: F/O Franklin's L9508: F joined the attack on Düsseldorf while F/O Murray, in L9506: X, attacked what they later reported to be Leverkusen, lying close to the north-eastern edge of Cologne. He delivered his bombing run from 10,500 ft but ground haze prevented observation of the results.

The beam gun positions were staggered with that on the port side positioned further forward and immediately above the side entrance hatch to allow room for both gunners. Twin gun mountings were used for each position with eight spare drums for the starboard gunner stowed near his knees, while the port-side gunner's drums were mounted on the half cross frame of the fuselage. The pair of dual ammunition tracks for the rear turret seen on the left each delivered a pair of continuous belts of ammunition to each pair of guns. Electrically-heated flying suits were necessary because of the intense cold once the side windows were removed to allow deployment of the guns, and the long oxygen line and intercommunication cable to the rearmost gunner stretching across to the port side must have made swift traversing of the guns a little difficult under battle conditions. The parachutes for both men can be seen on the floor behind the starboard gunner.

A veteran of early 35 Squadron operations including the first daylight attack on Kiel by Halifaxes and flown on several operations by Leonard Cheshire, L9503: P is seen here with P/O E. R. P. S. Cooper and crew at Northolt on 21 July 1941 during a visit by Prime Minister Winston Churchill together with Russian and Polish Ministers. The Perspex teardrop fitting was now standardised and fitted on each side of the nose to allow the navigator clear downward views to port and starboard. It failed to return from an attack on Hamburg on the night of 15/16 September, its pilot P/O H. Brown dying in the crash but the other six crew survived as POWs.

The remaining aircraft, S/Ldr Tait's L9492: K was unable to bomb because a blown main generator fuse could not be rectified. Fl/Sgt Holden's L9509: C was the only aircraft damaged, hit by flak, shrapnel causing a glycol leak in the starboard outer engine.

Marsden recalls that Tait was very careful with his bombs and had brought his bomb load home once or twice when the target could not be found because of bad weather. *"On this occasion, a rotten wild night, snow, sleet, the lot, he went to land normally and ended up bellying across the field with the undercarriage pushed back ... the aeroplane was still intact, surprisingly enough. Maintenance Flight was fetched out to clear the field; the aeroplane was on the far side of the field from the hangars, well beyond the main runway. It had to be raised high enough to be got on to one of those heavy, four-wheeled trolleys, about six or eight feet square, fitted with big, heavy duty, wheels.*

"The bed of the trolley was about three feet off the ground. The first problem was to get the aeroplane high enough to get the jacks under, so every available body was pushed under one wing, with Chiefy giving the word, and we worked from starboard to port; then tail-end and so on, lifting bit by bit, and resting it on sandbags at each gain of height. (We had heard of lifting bags of course, but there were none on station, unless locked up in Main Stores.) Eventually we got it high enough to require tool-boxes etc for us to stand on, and at last we were high enough to get the trolley under – at which point an armourer pressed the jettison bar, to make sure that we did not take anything untoward with us. It was pitch black and snowing, our only lights lamps on wander leads and the slitted headlights of a truck. However, when a full bomb load came bouncing down amongst us – thousand pounders, five hundreds, and from the wing bays half a dozen boxes of the big hexagonal-bodied explosive incendiaries – we all found somewhere else to be a bit sharpish, into the outer darkness. Eventually the armourers were able to assure us that all was well and all of it was safe; the aircraft safely on the trolley and sand-bagged for stability, she was towed across to the hangars for examination as to Category."

Having satisfactorily completed its training, 76 Squadron had moved to Middleton St George, from where it began operations with a joint attack on the Hüls Rubber Factory on 12/13 June. Three of the squadron's aircraft, in company with eight from 35 Squadron and seven Stirlings, delivered the first all four-engine heavy bomber attack. It was a far from auspicious start for the crews of 76 Squadron. P/O Lewin's aircraft was the last to leave but returned within the hour with engine trouble. F/Lt Hillary DFM was airborne for over five hours before he too returned with engine trouble and although P/O Richards reached the target area, he encountered bad weather, forcing him to jettison his bombs over Essen. Of the eight crews from 35 Squadron, only two located the target; however, some of the Stirlings must have succeeded because fires were started in the target area. For the two successful crews, while a faulty bomb-setting selector prevented F/O James in L9500 from bombing despite three runs over the target, P/O Lashbrook in L9503: P had succeeded, a direct hit being observed. The remaining Halifaxes, with one exception, attacked alternative targets. The exception was Sgt L. Bovington DFM, whose L9498: T suffered engine failure; he brought his bomb load back but overshot the landing and crashed, fortunately without injury to anyone on board. Two of the Halifaxes were intercepted by night-fighters on the return journey, Lashbrook's and Sgt Godwin's L9492: K; the latter reported shooting one fighter down while the other attacker broke away.

Training was a continuous task for the squadrons when not operating, and this activity inevitably contributed its own damage. On 15 June, P/O A. Lewin landed L9514 on the secondary runway at Middleton St George, veered to the right and collapsed the starboard undercarriage when the wheel dug into soft earth. This was the first aircraft casualty for 76 since re-forming as a bomber squadron.

Initially, both squadrons continued to operate independently but with increasing numbers of aircraft, 35 Squadron dispatching ten on the night of 15/16 June to attack Hanover. Heavy cloud extending from the coast to the target area

hampered the attack and while most of the small mixed force of 16 bombers delivered their attack from between 8,000 to 14,000 ft, one Halifax captain, to be certain, went down to 2,000 ft. After completing its bombing run, two Bf 109s attacked F/O Murray's L9499: Q, their cannon fire hitting the starboard outer engine and damaging the controls. Although injured, the rear gunner kept firing, driving off further attacks and allowing Murray to nurse the damaged aircraft back to make a successful forced landing at Bircham Newton. The following evening, three Halifaxes from 76 Squadron were a part of the force of 105 aircraft sent to Cologne, but results were poor. No 35 sent three to Hanover the next night as part of the 11 aircraft sent on a series of minor night operations intended to cause disruption as much as anything else; but bad weather was still a problem and secondary targets were attacked, Dortmund by two and Vechta airfield by the other.

The two squadrons operated together again on the night of 20/21 June in the first of a series of raids against Kiel. No 35 sent six and the other squadron five, in company with 47 Wellingtons, 24 Hampdens, 20 Whitleys and 13 Stirlings. The intended target of this attack was the *Tirpitz* but bad weather foiled the attempt causing the city to be hit instead. Twenty-six aircraft, Stirlings, Wellingtons and ten Halifaxes, returned on the 23/24th but again with poor results. The enemy was more fortunate; one of 76 Squadron's four Halifaxes failed to return. South-west of Hamburg a Bf 110 of the II./NJG 1 flown by Oblt. Reinhold Eckardt intercepted P/O W. Stobbs' L9492 and after a brief fight it fell in flames at Eilendorf. Only Sgt J. Lipton survived. It was the squadron's first operational loss.

The next night 47 Hampdens and Whitleys tried their luck, but without much success; then it was the turn of the heavies again on 26/27th. A single 76 Squadron machine accompanied seven Halifaxes from 35 Squadron and 18 Manchesters and 15 Stirlings back to Kiel for the first combined heavy bomber attack of the war. Weather was generally good except for the invariable ground haze in the target area which spoilt the bombing, with little damage and no casualties being recorded by the German authorities. A Bf 110 had attacked one of 35 Squadron's Halifaxes on the outward journey and with the starboard outer engine out of action L9507: W turned back, dropping its bomb load on Husum. Ground haze had again foiled the bomb aimers resulting in only light damage to the primary target for the loss of two Manchesters.

Hamburg finished off the month's night bombing for the Halifax force, two joining a mixed force of just 28 aircraft in an attack on 29/30th. The resulting damage was relatively large for such a meagre force, but cost four Stirlings and two Wellingtons, three of which fell to night-fighters over the city – the German night defences were improving. The following day Halifaxes were to be involved in a different type of attack. There had been many discussions at Bomber Command HQ as to the practicability of daylight bomber operations. The Command retained some very vivid and bitter memories of such operations during the opening phases of the war and there were strong arguments against such operations. However, the introduction of the new generation of heavy bombers, with greatly increased defensive armament, brought about a serious reconsideration – the answer to its feasibility lay in a practical test on large scale, but first it was decided to try the basic feasibility.

Thus, on 30 June Kiel received a further attack, but this time in daylight. It had been decided to trial a series of cloud-cover daylight attacks over north-west Germany; 28 Blenheims and six Halifaxes were to attack a range of targets at Kiel, Bremen, Norderney and Sylt, while 18 Blenheims carried out a *Circus*[5] operation against the power station at Pont-à-Vendin. Two flights of three Halifaxes, in 'V' formation, set out from 35 Squadron's base in conditions of excellent weather and visibility that were to continue throughout the operation. Both flights delivered successful attacks from between 17 and 18,000 ft with all bombs seen to burst in the target area, hitting the docks and starting several fires. Both formations encountered heavy and accurate flak over the target and on completing their bombing run, the

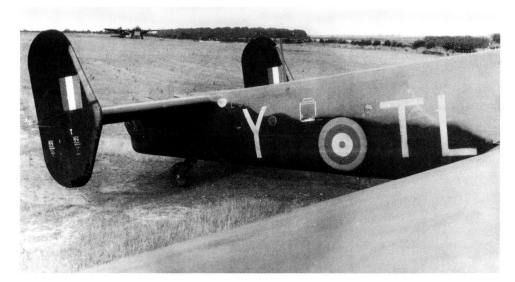

L9501: Y began taking part in operations in June, going to Kiel for all three consecutive night attacks late that month. On 30 June and piloted by F/O Owen it took part in the first daylight attack on Kiel and was damaged by Bf 110 fighters, mortally wounding beam gunner Sgt Simpson and putting the starboard inner engine out of action. Owen nursed the Halifax back to England and made an emergency landing at Docking (seen here) where repairs were made and the starboard inner engine replaced before returning to Linton-on-Ouse. The narrow style of code lettering used by the squadron at this time is clearly visible, the letters TL being positioned forward of the roundel on both sides ensuring the aircraft letter Y could be clearly seen at all times. Clearly visible in this view is the beam gun hatch, positioned further aft than that on the port side, and the rubber de-icing boots along the leading edge of each fin. F/O Owen received a DFC for the action. On 28/29th August, L9501 failed to return from an attack on Duisburg with P/O A. Adkins and crew killed. In the distance, a lone Stirling may be seen undergoing emergency engine work. (E. Marsden)

L9501: Y undergoing repair in the field at Docking, the large crate holding the replacement engine serving as a temporary sentry box for the guard. Note that an observation blister for the front window was fitted to only the starboard window. (E. Marsden)

With the defective engine removed and winched into the back of a truck, the replacement engine was installed and its wiring and supply lines connected up. The size of the Merlin X engine is clearly evident in this view and it was fortunate for the fitters that it was mid-summer and not mid-winter as these repairs would have been done in the open, regardless of the weather conditions. (E. Marsden)

A mobile crane was needed for engine removal as the height above ground and sheer size and weight of the Merlin X required heavy equipment. The engine seen here is a replacement about to be winched up and dropped into position behind the three-core radiator assembly of the port outer position. The exhaust pipe has no oxidation and the propeller shaft still has its protective cover over the spline assembly. Mobile working stands allowed a team of fitters to work on both sides of an engine simultaneously and were supplemented by the inverted 'V' ladder and platform used for minor maintenance work. LAC C. Pearce, yet another of the many ground crew forgotten or ignored by history, is working on the propeller blade of the inboard engine. New engines could have their problems and when this one was fired up, a faulty constant speed coupling failed and the propeller went into fully feathered position. Start again! (E. Marsden)

second group came under heavy attack from Bf 110 fighters, one of which was seen to fall to the guns of the formation leader, F/Lt T. Robison's L9499: Q, before it too was shot down. Only Sgt E. Harding survived from the crew of 'Q' and became a prisoner of war (POW). F/O Owen's L9501: Y was then subjected to five successive attacks by three Bf 110s that inflicted extensive damage, the starboard inner engine and radios being put out of action and the wings and fuselage badly damaged. During the attacks, a cannon shell had come up through the floor and seriously wounded one of L9501's beam gunners, Sgt Simpson, and although the crew rendered every possible aid, he died from excessive blood loss during the return journey. One of the attacking Bf 110s was believed to have been shot down.

Later that same day a signal was received from the Chief of the Air Staff congratulating the squadron on its outstanding success, which read, *"I was delighted to hear of your most successful daylight attack on Kiel today. This is a great new development, which will have far-reaching results. Heartiest congratulations and best wishes for success in future operations of the same kind."* The final seal of success was received next day with the notification of the immediate award of the DSO to S/Ldr K. B. Tait who had led the raid, and the DFC to F/O Owen. Results appeared to vindicate the view that daylight bombing was a practical proposition from all aspects. However, appearances are sometimes deceptive.

The main operations of 7/8 July were divided between Cologne, Osnabrück, Münster and Mönchengladbach, but it was the minor operations of the night that claimed another 35 Squadron Halifax. Fourteen Halifaxes and three Stirlings were sent to Frankfurt and nine other aircraft were sent to more minor targets, nothing further being heard from F/O P. Langmead's L9502: R from after taking-off at 23.01 hrs until the crew were later reported as POWs. The following night, 35 Squadron lost L9521: Z in an attack on the Leuna oil plant at Merseburg. Thirteen Halifaxes and a single Stirling had been sent to attack the plant, losing just Sgt L. Bovington DFM and his crew to a night-fighter flown by Lt August Geiger of the III./NJG 1. Although Bovington and three others survived, the Halifax crashed into a house at Mook, 10 kilometres (10 km or 6.21 miles) from Nijmegen, killing four Dutch civilians. The inclusion of a single Stirling illustrates the problems facing the nightly availability of heavy bombers for operations.

On 9 July, with the crisis at sea having been averted temporarily and German attention now firmly focused on its new Russian campaign, Bomber Command received a new directive which addressed two items: the morale of the civilian population and the dislocation of the transportation system. The futility of pursuing the oil campaign and the growing realization of the limitations facing bomber crews were beginning to have their effects on policy. Until further notice, the primary focus

would be on civilian morale, particularly that of industrial workers, and transportation. During each moon period bombers were to attack Hamm, Osnabrück, Soest, Schwerte, Cologne, Duisburg and Düsseldorf, a ring of targets around the Ruhr that contained the railway installations vital to transportation of the war materiel produced in the Ruhr. In the non-moon period Cologne, Düsseldorf and Duisburg were to be the targets, the Rhine flowing through them providing a distinct geographical feature to guide the bombers. In poor weather conditions, targets that are more distant were to be attacked such as Hamburg, Bremen, Hanover, Frankfurt, Mannheim and Stuttgart. There was to be no let up for the enemy nor, did it seem, for Bomber Command's crews. This priority of targets would remain in force well into the autumn.

Peirse now had the opportunity to use his bomber force in its main role and, it was hoped, in good weather, but the size of that force was still showing no increase in strength. New squadrons were being added, but those transferred out to other theatres of operation countered this. The new heavy bombers were still encountering technical problems, as well as the development of how best to use them. The total available during the coming period would never reach fifty. Only minor diversions would occur, to the U-Boat bases in France and the German capital ships in Brest harbour.

The campaign began well, with intensive operations against German targets and, despite adverse weather in August and October record bomb tonnages would be dropped. The now established tactic of sending larger forces during the moon period and smaller ones, to secondary targets, during the dark period, continued. Results, however, would be poor and losses begin to mount as the German night-fighter force established its presence.

During this same period, the newly formed 76 Squadron lost Halifax L9533 in a tragic accident on 21 July, P/O L. Blackwell and four others being killed when it crashed while trying to avoid a Hurricane that flew across its path as the Halifax came in to land at Middleton St George

For the next three weeks, both squadrons continued to operate at night conducting a series of attacks against Hanover, Frankfurt, Leuna, Magdeburg, Bremen and Mannheim. What is worthy of note at this juncture is that losses by both squadrons had been very light since commencing operations, with only two lost for a total of 35 sorties, both from 35 Squadron: L9502: R from the Frankfurt raid on 7/8 July and L9521: Z from the Merseburg raid on 8/9 July against the Leuna refinery.

However, the effects of German flak were nonetheless pertinent when applied to the human anatomy. Handley Page's field representative, Mr A. G. Knivett, was responsible for ensuring that any problem that arose over the Halifax was quickly and efficiently resolved. A certain pilot who complained that the Halifaxes lacked sufficient armour plate, a piece of shrapnel having penetrated the underside of his seat causing him considerable discomfort, presented him with one such problem. Ever willing to oblige, Knivett obtained some armour plate left over from when some Hampden fuel tanks had been modified. When it duly arrived, it was transported to a small workshop in Leeds where it was cut into small pieces. News spread rapidly and soon many crew members had their own personal piece of security. Unfortunately, one evening the commanding officer happened to see one of the navigators literally staggering under the weight of his green canvas navigation bag and questioned him about the contents. The result was a discreet word to Knivett to let him know that the practice had been brought to a halt because pretty soon *"... the bloody aircraft would be so heavy that they would never get airborne!"*

During these three weeks, Bomber Command had been assessing the results and merits of daylight bombing operations and it was resolved that the deciding factor in such operations was primarily one of defence. Until recently, British fighter aircraft had lacked the range for other than shallow penetration escort operations, which seriously limited the choice of targets for the bombers. However, during July the introduction of long-range tanks in sufficient quantities to equip five Spitfire squadrons had alleviated this situation to some extent. It was planned to launch a surprise attack on 24 July against the *Scharnhorst* and *Gneisenau* in Brest harbour using a mixed force of approximately 150 medium and heavy bombers. Three of the Spitfire squadrons were to escort the second wave of the attacking force, the other two following later to deal with enemy fighters that managed to refuel and rejoin the battle. At the last minute *Scharnhorst* moved to La Rochelle, some 200 miles (321 km) south, and the heavy bomber element was withdrawn from the Main Force and detailed to attack this target – unescorted! For some unknown reason the already meagre size of this force was diminished further by the withdrawal of the Stirlings. For an even more bewildering reason, those six Stirlings were sent to attack *Scharnhorst* on the evening of the 23rd, losing one of their number in the ensuing action and putting the German defences on the alert.

The following day, while the Main Force set out to attack Brest, 15 Halifaxes, nine from 35 Squadron and six from 76 Squadron, formed their 'vics' of three into two large V formations over Stanton Harcourt, having been temporarily attached to this southern station to reduce distance to the target and allow an increase in bomb load. The formation went out via Lizard Point, then across to a position 50 miles west of Ushant, whilst maintaining a height of 1,000 ft or less to avoid detection by German radar. From there they flew direct to the target, intending to bomb from 19,000 ft but, as events turned out, it was ultimately carried out from 15,000 ft.

Sgt Balcomb, Sgt Godwin's front gunner, provides a vivid account of the operation. *"Looking out in the early morning of 24 July there was a mist over the surrounding Oxfordshire countryside with a promise of an English summer's day ahead. After breakfast and briefing, the skies cleared... We were briefed to form with our section led by Flying Officer (Nelly) Owen in L9501: Y... P/O Peter James (later Wing Commander James DFC) in L9500: H was No. 2 and our pilot, Flight Sergeant Godwin at No. 3 in L9527: M ..... It was a truly magnificent sight to see in the skies some 15 Halifax aircraft ...blazing at low level across the Home Counties towards the south-west, a pre-determined course that took us over Plymouth. ...... I remember sitting in the front turret as we skimmed first just a few feet above the water with bright sunshine, and almost unbearable heat of the sun magnified by the Perspex – seeing a number of fishing vessels in the Bay..."*

Weather conditions were excellent – brilliant sunshine, no cloud and perfect visibility – unfortunately, a little too perfect. An enemy destroyer was passing near the Isle d' Yeu and believing itself about to be attacked began evasive action and opened fire. However, as soon as it was realized that it was not the target it radioed the course and size of the formation to the shore facilities, thus destroying the element of surprise.

The Halifax formations, having now climbed to bombing height, went in for the attack only to be greeted by a very heavy concentration of flak and a force of approximately 18 Bf 109 fighters from the four aerodromes around La Rochelle. As planned, the attack was carried out in echelon formation, but the intense flak barrage soon began to take its toll. Several aircraft were hit and one, Fl/Sgt C. Godwin's L9527: M, seriously damaged by flak, was attacked by three Bf 109s over the town of Angles, from where eyewitnesses later recorded the events, and went down in a slow spiral with smoke coming from one or two of its engines. Only two parachutes emerged before the Halifax crashed 15 km (9.32 miles) from the town of Lucon. *"The Halifax came tumbling to earth, crashing in the yard of a farmer known as Terrier du Four. It exploded and caught fire, showering the fields for hundreds of yards in all directions with twisted fragments ..."* The five killed were buried in Angles graveyard, three of the local people defying the Germans by following the hearse. The following morning a mountain of flowers covered the graves and the Germans immediately removed them – but the gesture had been made and respect given to the fallen crew. Balcomb's narrative picks up what had happened.

"From a cloudless sky... through the period of engagement, the grey haze from the 'flak' bursts – approximately 2,000 ft thick – left quite a scar in the sky.... Everything happened in one split second. A particularly loud explosion followed by a metallic rattle throughout the nose of the aircraft made the aircraft lurch. The front turret became smoke filled and our Observer [Navigator] having just released the bombs on the target appeared to be wounded in the legs. At the time, he was lying in the bomb aimer's position just under the front turret. It was then, when I was firing at an attacking M.E. 109 that suddenly the turret became inoperative and the guns stopped firing. The 'flak' burst earlier on had smashed some Perspex in the turret, my dark glasses (Woolworth's best at 6d per pair) were destroyed and one engine started to smoke with the threat of others becoming inoperative. I seem to recall the Skipper operating the automatic fire extinguishers.

"Before I left the turret I could hear our tail gunner [Fl/Sgt S. Shirley] *reporting attacks by the fighters – and then his dying cry. There were three fighters attacking us in turn and it is a wonder that we did not 'blow up' there and then through their cannon fire, which out-ranged our .303 ammunition. When I scrambled out from the turret over what I thought to be the prone body of the Observer, I noticed our Flight Engineer* [Sgt C. Newstead] *manning the side Vickers guns. He suffered a severe hit ... he was still alive but must have been mortally wounded. How he still stood on his feet – I don't know. What I recall of the Skipper and his second pilot* [Sgt G. Esnouf] *– it seemed they too suffered severe wounds. With difficulty, they were fighting with the controls of the aircraft, which now started to spin in. Two engines were trailing smoke and the other two engines may not have had sufficient power to control the aircraft. The Wireless Operator* [Sgt R. Rudlin] *I could not see clearly, I am not sure whether he was slumped over the set ....*

".... By now, we had no defence and were losing height rapidly. The front hatch was taken up...possibly through prior damage by 'flak' the hatch was jammed across the escape opening thus reducing the size by half. There was not time to use another escape method.. I recall helping the wounded Observer to the front hatch and stamping on his shoulders to help him through the narrow opening. Then, as he left the aircraft seeing his 'chute open and down below, the outline of a shore which appeared to spin crazily."

In helping the Observer out, Balcomb had ripped his own parachute pack and with one hand clasped over the tear, he managed to squeeze through the hatch. *"The ground was coming up very fast and after bouncing along and nearly getting caught up in the belly with the bomb doors still open, I thankfully cleared it all, released my hand clasping the 'chute which immediately opened up of its own accord. I recall seeing the smashed rear turret with the body of the tail gunner slumped over the controls, and then a fighter now turning its attention to me."*

Deaf from the explosion near his turret, he did not hear the cannon fire, but saw tracers passing near him. *"Suddenly the aircraft, which I thought to be already in flames,*

crashed below me; the heat of the explosion could be felt. I landed nearby, near a farm house – my movements became automatic. I recall trying to bury my 'chute; my limbs were aching through the jolt of hitting the hard ground – still in total deafness I could feel the percussion of cannon fire still firing as the Messerschmitt dived towards me – maybe to express his delight in his victory – or as he was missing me I will give him credit to assume that it was his way to salute a conquered enemy."[6]

Attempts at evasive action, necessary due to the heavy flak, caused further disruption of the formation. Some of the enemy fighters, paying little heed to their own flak, pressed home attacks during the bombing run. However, a concentrated attack was carried out as the Halifaxes were withdrawing, the fighters only breaking off the engagement long after the target area had been left. Those Halifaxes that had managed to stay in formation fared somewhat better than the stragglers who received most of the attention of the fighters, one aircraft sustaining twenty separate attacks. No 35 Squadron lost an additional aircraft, L9512:U; hit by flak it was finished off by a Bf 109 and left to crash in the sea, just north of the Ile de Ré, Fl/Sgt S. Greaves and his crew all surviving as POWs. No 76 Squadron lost three: L9494, was first hit by flak then finished off by a Bf 109, S/Ldr W. Williams ditching it near La Rochelle, the crew being rescued by a French fishing boat only to be made POWs[7]; P/O/ J. McKenna's L9517 was shot down by flak and also crashed off La Rochelle, killing all on board; while F/Lt A. Lewin's L9529 was shot down by fighters near Vendee at l' Aiguillon-sur-Mer.

When the reports from the survivors had been assembled, results of the operation were highly debatable. Five Halifaxes had been lost; one, L9507 of 35 Squadron, landed safely but was so badly damaged it was written-off as Damaged Beyond Repair (DBR). Five more were damaged to the extent that they required approximately three weeks to repair, while two others were damaged to a lesser degree. The remaining two suffered only superficial damage. Against this had to be weighed the damage inflicted to the *Scharnhorst*. All crews, except one whose bombs had hung-up, had succeeded in delivering an attack – but only one claimed a direct hit. In fact, five direct hits had been scored, but three were by armour-piercing bombs that passed right through the ship, each leaving only a small hole; the remaining two did explode, but caused only minor damage, thus illustrating the problems with the selection of bombs available during this period. Even so, *Scharnhorst* sailed for Brest that same evening, where better repair facilities were available – along with the security of its smokescreens, better flak protection, and fighters – with 3,000 (some reports quote 7,000) tons of water in her. These facts would undoubtedly have provided a more cheerful note for the surviving Halifax crews had they only known. Nevertheless and despite the losses, morale remained high and the gunners had displayed the highest standards of courage and skill throughout the long fighter attack, claiming five destroyed, three probables and several damaged.

Now, the two squadrons returned once more to their nocturnal operations, sending two Halifaxes out next evening to accompany seven Stirlings for a nuisance raid on Berlin, the main targets of Hanover and Hamburg being attacked by bombers from the twin-engine force. The cost of the attack was two Stirlings and one of 35 Squadron's Halifaxes. Nothing more was heard from P/O E. Cooper's crew in L9507: W, which was brought down near the target, killing the entire crew. The loss ratio was out of all proportion to the results and this frittering away of the new heavy bombers on such targets must be seen as poor policy at such a critical time.

Main target attacks continued with smaller forces going to secondary targets the same evenings. The term secondary was a relative one, for there was nothing minor about Berlin, eight Halifaxes, five Stirlings and 40 Wellingtons raiding it on 2/3 August without loss to the Halifax component. Kiel was the other minor target of the night. On 5/6th, Mannheim, Karlsruhe and Frankfurt constituted main targets with minor operations to Aachen and Boulogne plus mining sorties off the east coast of Denmark. Halifaxes were used only on the Karlsruhe attack with eleven being sent as part of the 97-strong force. No 76 Squadron lost Sgt T. Byrne and his crew in L9516 with all but one surviving when it was shot down near Tienen, in Belgium. Halifaxes also took part in the Essen attack on 7/8th, fortunately without loss, but results were poor.

A significant development occurred on 11/12 August during an attack on Mönchengladbach; 29 Wellingtons attacked a railways target, two of them fitted with a new navigational device, *Gee*, about which more will be said later. The trials continued for two more nights and were successful – then they stopped to allow mass production of the equipment to commence. In the intervening period, Bomber Command would face some very serious moments.

Berlin was targeted again on the night of 12/13 August by a force of 70 bombers, 12 of which were Halifaxes. Of this force, only 32 claimed to have reached and bombed the target for the loss of nine of their number – three Manchesters, three Wellingtons, a Stirling and two Halifaxes. The latter were both from 76 Squadron. Sgt C. Whitfield's L9531: R was shot down by a night-fighter flown by Lt Hans Autenreith of the 6./NJG 1, 15 km (9.32 miles) SSE of Bremerhaven; only two of the crew survived. F/Lt C. Cheshire's L9530: L crew fared a little better, all but two surviving when the Halifax was brought down by flak near Parnewinkel, 40 km (24.85 miles) north-east of Bremen. A *Gee*-equipped Wellington, flying with the smaller force sent to attack Hanover was also lost that night; fortunately, the Germans did not recover any of the secret equipment.

Railway targets at Magdeburg, attacked by 52 bombers on 14/15 August, cost 35 Squadron another Halifax, P/O R. Lisle's L9500: H, which crashed at Andervenne, near Lingen-Ems, killing the entire crew. Bad weather hampered many attacks

The size of Bomber Command's new heavy bombers can be seen in this photograph of L9530: L, a B Mk I Series II of 76 Squadron, the personal mount of P/O Christopher Cheshire, brother of Leonard Cheshire, which had completed four operations when photographed. The mock crest below the cockpit was that of the pilot. The small, wedge-shaped, cable cutter ramps fitted at the joint between wing leading edge and each engine cowling were designed to guide any barrage balloon cable to a small explosive-powered cutting tool mounted on each section of the wing. The device was not popular having no proven operational effect and most were removed, leaving just the ramps as seen here. L9530: L was lost during an attack on Berlin on 12/13 August 1941 when it was shot down by flak – the crew, less the front and rear gunners, baling out successfully.

Handley Page Halifax, B Mk I Series II
L9530:L, No 76 Squadron. The personal mount of P/O Christopher Cheshire, brother of Leonard Cheshire.

during this period; an attack on Kiel on 19/20th included six Halifaxes but icing and thick cloud over Bremen resulted in poor bombing results, Kiel residents suffering no casualties or damage other than that caused by an unexploded flak shell.

Luck finally ran out for P/O J. McGregor-Cheers and most of his crew on the night of the 24/25 August. They had survived an earlier crash-landing at Ashcroft Farm while returning from an attack on Berlin on 12/13 August with one of the port engines damaged by flak. Sgt Burns was the only member of the crew to be injured, suffering a broken ankle, which, in hindsight, was a very lucky break for him. He was replaced by Sgt T. McHale who would be lost along with the rest of the crew when L9572: G crashed near Chièvres, Belgium, following an attack on Düsseldorf.

The target was cloud covered throughout the attack, the bombs being dropped on its estimated position. Interestingly, a new countermeasures tactic was tried out that night, six Hampdens being used against the searchlight belt at Wesel, attacking any searchlight with a bomber in its beam with small bombs and machine gun fire.

It was a successful tactic and after twenty-five minutes, all of the searchlights in the area became erratic and some even extinguished.

The next Halifax target was Duisburg on the night of 28/29 August when, again, the Hampdens were used to suppress searchlights in the target area. For once, good weather provided clear visibility and good bombing results were claimed although local reports later stated that only 63 bombs had hit the area. Two aircraft from the six-strong Hampden force were lost along with eight aircraft from the main bombing force, 35 Squadron's L9501: Y being one of these with P/O A. Adkins and crew killed.

The following night, the first 100-plus attack was carried out against Frankfurt by a mixed force of 143 aircraft comprised of Hampdens, Whitleys, Manchesters and five Halifaxes. The main aiming points were railways and harbour facilities but, again, bad weather frustrated the attackers and although bombing became widespread, little damage was caused. However, losses were light with just three aircraft failing to return and while the five Halifaxes returned safely, L9518: P of 76 Squadron was abandoned by its crew near Pocklington airfield after running out of

In this air-to-air view of L9530: L, the twin radio masts, handrail behind the D/F loop, dorsal escape hatch and long air intake of the inboard engine are clearly visible. Beneath the nose, the aft line of the horizontally mounted Beam Approach aerial is cut by the radio trailing aerial fairlead, forward of which is the distinctive L-shaped pitot head projecting down behind the lower nose glazing. The beam gun hatch is visible immediately above the fuselage roundel, the latter being positioned further aft and lower than on very early production B Mk I Series I Halifaxes. The high demarcation line between the upper and lower camouflaged areas broke the continuous flow of the relatively paler Dark Earth and Dark Green colouring onto the wing upper surfaces, effectively breaking the image into three pieces tonally. The stubby pipe on the wing upper surface, midway between the engines, is the breather pipe for the fuel tanks which, with the aileron mass balances above each wing tip, identify this aircraft as one of the 25 strengthened to B Mk I Series II standard. The landing light beneath the wing is in the locked down position; while this produced extra drag it was deemed acceptable rather than fitting the retraction system.

fuel. Baling out at a height of some 2,000 ft, the pilot, S/Ldr R. Bickford DFC, being the last to leave the aircraft, died after his parachute became entangled on the tail unit; one other crew member also died. Bad weather conditions continued to frustrate the attacks and on the last night of the month, a 103-strong force including seven Halifaxes went to Cologne but heavy cloud cover resulted in only the estimated position of the city being bombed with few bombs falling on the city and just one person reported killed.

On the night of 2/3 September, Berlin was attacked again by a force of 49 aircraft comprised of Hampdens, Halifaxes, Stirlings and Manchesters. Although the heavy bombers were present, they were very small in number and the 32 Hampdens bore the brunt of the attack. Of the seven Halifaxes taking part, two, both from 35 Squadron, were lost. P/O D. Fraser's L9560: F was lost en route to the target with two of the crew surviving to become POWs. The second, L9508: X, was lost to the north of Berlin with all but two of the crew taken prisoner; the pilot, F/O R. James DFC was not amongst the survivors. Halifaxes were back over Berlin on the night of 7/8 September, just six amongst the force of 197 bombers sent to attack the city. For once, clear visibility greeted the attackers and bombing results were good, with most bombs falling to the east and north of the city centre, and although 15 aircraft failed to return, none of the six Halifaxes was amongst them.

The Halifax had now been in service since November 1940, but its official naming ceremony was slow in coming. On 12 September at Handley Page's Radlett airfield, Lady Halifax, wife of the Foreign Minister, performed the official naming ceremony. L9608, the last of the B Mk I Series III aircraft, its nose section emblazoned on each side with the word HALIFAX in bold white block lettering, was hit ceremoniously with a bottle of champagne. Following the ceremony, a fly-past was carried out, Handley Page taking the opportunity to include another of the B Mk I Series III Halifaxes for the official photographers.

On 10/11 September, Italy now came up on the target list, meeting the definition of 'distant target', with 76 aircraft being sent to Turin, seven of them Halifaxes. Bombing of the Fiat steelworks and the centre of the city was considered good. Five bombers failed to return, with 35 Squadron losing two. The first was L9566: R. Possibly due to faulty navigation, the last transmission given by F/O G. Williams' wireless operator gave a plot just north of Le Havre and it seems that the crew mistook the Cherbourg peninsula for the English coast and turned towards France; its crew was subsequently made POWs. The second, L9526: O, ended up much closer to home when P/O Cresswell force-landed in a field near Harling Road Station at 06.20 hrs, probably due to fuel shortage. None of the crew was hurt during the landing and although the Halifax had been landed skilfully, with minimum damage, it was eventually assessed as non-repairable and by mid-1942 was serving as instructional airframe 3034M.

On 13/14 September, Brest was attacked again by a mixed force of 147 aircraft without loss, although the results were hard to assess because of the effective

L9608 was the last production B Mk I Series III and the subject of the official naming ceremony at Radlett on 12 September 1941, performed by Lady Halifax, wife of the Foreign Secretary. The name HALIFAX was painted temporarily on both sides of the nose section in large white block letters. It had all the Series III features and an almost identical style of camouflage division as seen on L9601. Delivered to 76 Squadron it became H-Harry and eventually passed to 1652 HCU, the recipient of many surviving B Mk Is. Retaining its code letter H it was part of the HCU force used in the third 1,000-bomber raid and after completing 218 flying hours, was written off in a crash. (Flight International)

One of the nine B Mk I Series III machines, immediately identifiable by the bulge in the lower edge of each radiator cowling, carries out a low fly-past for the benefit of the official photographer. However, a difference in camouflage style is apparent with a wavy division between the upper and lower fuselage colours as seen on L9490 and L9503 of 35 Squadron, but it has a straight upper edge sweep beneath the tail plane and a straight edge division on the engine cowlings, angled steeply down to miss the leading edge of the wing. This interim stage between styles may indicate that this is possibly L9600, the first of the Series III modified aircraft. Handley Page's changes to camouflage were variable and difficult to encapsulate on a broad scale at this point of production.

deployment of smokescreens. At 02.55 hrs on 14 September, L9567 of 76 Squadron was lost to an unspecified cause when it crashed at Water End near Bedford after being abandoned by its crew, the pilot, P/O R.E. Hutchin, breaking an ankle in an awkward parachute landing. Hamburg appeared on the target list two nights later with 169 bombers being sent to attack its stations and shipyards. Conditions over the city were clear but most crews found that glare from the searchlights prevented clear recognition of the aiming points; even so, much damage was caused for the loss of eight aircraft – amongst them P/O H. Brown's L9503: P from 35 Squadron, all but Brown surviving to become prisoners.

The attacks continued in the face of deteriorating weather and although Halifaxes went to Stettin on 29/30 September, they did not take part in any further operations until the night of 12/13 October when nine Halifaxes, as a part of a force of 152 aircraft, carried out the first large-scale attack on Nuremberg. Despite optimistic reports from the crews, only a few bombs fell in the city with most dropping on Schwabach 6 km (3.75 miles) south of the target and a few on Launing some 40 km (24.85 miles) away while Lauffen, a regular decoy fire site 60 km (37.25 miles) away, also drew some of the bombs. Like Nuremberg, both latter towns sit beside wide rivers and indicate the considerable navigation problems facing Bomber Command at this time for, once started, the fires tended to draw the attention of other crews, thus compounding the problem of successfully targeting an objective. Just one Halifax was lost, Sgt Williams' L9579: P from 35 Squadron. Running low on fuel, Williams had his crew bale out before successfully crash-landing a mile north of its home base. The aircraft caught fire but no one was injured. However, Fl/Sgt E. Muttart of 76 Squadron was not so fortunate, losing his life when his Halifax L9561: H was shot down by a night-fighter flown by Lt Leopold Fellerer of the 4,/NJG 1 during the night's secondary attack, a force of 99 aircraft against Bremen. The aircraft came down near Wons, south of Harlingen in Holland, the rest of the crew surviving. Hüls, the third target for the night, was left to a force of 79 Hampdens and Manchesters.

Five Halifaxes returned to Nuremberg on the 14/15th as part of an 80-strong force which encountered very bad icing conditions and thick cloud while en route to the target. Only 14 crews claimed to have attacked the city with only one claiming to have identified the aiming point, 51 others being forced to divert to alternative targets. Although the Siemens factory was hit, only three groups of bombs were recorded as falling in the city.

October continued in this manner, small raids interspersed with others against major targets, but even then, in only relatively small numbers. The heavy bomber component was minimal, Halifaxes going only to Emden on the 20/21st, Mannheim on the 22/23rd and a minor raid on Dunkirk on the night of 31 October/1 November; the only bright point for the two Halifax squadrons was the arrival of the first of the B Mk IIs.

The bad weather conditions of October continued to hamper operations into November. No doubt, the slow pace of operations and subsequent poor results were taking their toll on Sir Richard Peirse and the planners at Bomber Command, who were battling their critics as well as the weather. Whatever the cause, Peirse now made a fateful decision.

L9601, the 77th production Halifax, was a Series III aircraft fitted with Merlin XX engines, enlarged oil coolers and increased fuel tankage – all features that would be incorporated into the B Mk II Series I production aircraft. The revision to the oil coolers produced a distinctive central bulged 'lip' to the lower edge of the cowling, making it possible to identify the nine B Mk I Series III aircraft. Note also the change to the camouflage, relatively straight demarcation lines on both engine cowlings and fuselage instead of the original undulating style of division line. The revised shape of the nose window, shallower than before and covered by a Perspex blister, cable cutters with ramps in the join between wing and engine cowling on the wing leading edges and the repositioning of the aileron mass balances above the wing were all Series II modifications. The retractable dual lens landing light underneath the wing is in the locked down position. Delivered to the RAF on 2 October 1941, it was issued to 76 Squadron and as MP: F it took part in most of the squadron's early operations, including the daylight attack on Tirpitz. It eventually passed to No 78 Conversion Flight where it finally succumbed to a crash on 23 August 1942 at Middleton St George, swinging on landing due to a flat tyre, which caused the undercarriage to collapse.

CHAPTER THREE

EXPANDING THE HALIFAX FORCE

THE Halifax had already undergone a series of minor improvements during its brief front line service as feedback from operational use was evaluated. The first had occurred in June 1941 when 25 airframes were stressed to allow an increase in a.u.w by 5,000 lb to 60,000 lb. Designated B Mk I Series II, they retained their existing Merlin X power units. Externally, little distinguished them from the earlier model: the most significant changes, although not directly related to the strengthening, were the repositioning of the aileron mass balance above the wing and a reduction in the size of the fuselage window immediately behind the front turret.

Some of the additional weight lifting capacity was sacrificed, however, for increased range and was addressed by replacing the Hampden fuel tanks, normally fitted in the fuselage rest bay, with an additional permanent tank in each mid-wing section, raising the total fuel tankage by 88 gal. Total capacity was thus raised from 2,242 to 2,330 gal, this last modification being introduced on the last nine B Mk Is of the initial Handley Page contract (L9600 to L9608 inclusive). Initially Merlin Xs were retained but some airframes were subsequently fitted with Merlin XXs. Engine overheating also had been experienced and to overcome this, larger diameter oil coolers were introduced. With these modifications to the fuel system and engines, the type designation was changed to B Mk I Series III.

While these modifications were being introduced to improve performance of the existing basic model, the Handley Page design team were already looking further ahead and L9515, the 31st production machine, had been set aside for development trials. Again, the emphasis was on two major points, increased range and improved performance. The first was met by the installation of an additional 123-gallon tank in the outboard wing section, this No 6 tank, as it was designated, being connected to the No 5 tank to produce a 245-gallon unit. This increased standard fuel capacity

from 1,640 to 1,886 gallons and maximum fuel capacity to 2,576 gallons, raising optimum range from 1,700 to 2,000 miles – thus finally reaching the range requirement set in the original specification.

The second point had been achieved by installing Rolls-Royce Merlin XX engines in place of the existing Merlin Xs. By a very ingenious piece of engineering, Rolls-Royce had managed to produce an engine of almost identical external dimensions, delivering 1,280 brake horse power (bhp) at 3,000 revolutions per minute (rpm) for take-off as compared with the 1,075 bhp of the Merlin X; all for the relatively small increase of 8.5% in the dry weight. The new engine had a considerably improved performance over its predecessor, both with regard to the maximum power available and the altitude at which it maintained this figure. At 3,000 rpm, the Merlin X produced 1,010 bhp at 17,750 ft while the appropriate Merlin XX figures were 1,175 bhp at 21,000 ft. Perhaps the most significant feature of all was the fact that both engines were interchangeable, which meant that the new engine could be introduced on to the production lines without any delay.

Fitted with these engines, L9519 had begun a series of six tests, carried out between 18 and 31 August 1941. These were made at an all-up weight of 60,000 lb and, apart from the lack of beam guns and the additional tankage, the aircraft was representative of the standard B Mk I Series III model. The improvement in performance was sufficient to warrant a series of bomb door tests at 23,000 ft on 4 September. Speed tests had already been made at heights up to 26,000 ft and the aircraft had been operated continuously at 23,000 ft for a period of 65 minutes.

Handley Page's original contract for 200 B Mk I Halifaxes had been amended on 29 January 1940 and from L9609 onwards, airframes were produced as B Mk II Halifaxes. Similar revisions were made with the other contractor, English Electric, who had received their production contract approval on 15 May 1940. Mass

L9485, the first production Halifax B Mk I was retained by the A&AEE and fitted out as the trials aircraft for the Boulton Paul C Mk V mid-upper and ventral K turrets. The latter is visible below the lower line of the fuselage with its pair of 0.303-in calibre weapons pointing aft; the rectangular shapes visible on its lower edge distinguish it from the later R turret design. It also served as the trials aircraft for a wide variety of tests at the A&AEE including exhaust flame damping, its starboard engines being fitted with the bulky asbestos exhaust shrouds when this photograph was taken. Damaged in early July 1942, it was returned to Handley Page on 8 July for conversion into Instructional Airframe 3362M and was issued to No 4 School of Technical training on 15 September 1942.

The interior of the Boulton Paul K turret with guns and cupola removed is shown here in the fully extended (lowered) position. It was mounted on a circular frame attached to the floor of the aircraft. The gunner's electro-hydraulic gun operating control column that controlled azimuth and depression angles is at the centre between the extended metal containers for the ammunition boxes. Two 0.303-in Browning machine guns were fitted in the semi-circular quadrants projecting from either side of the position of the gunner's head. The drag penalty incurred by this turret in the lowered position likely had some bearing on the decision to stop production soon after it started. Drag not only slowed an aircraft down but also reduced its operational height and radius of action, factors that would have influenced the Air Ministry assessment.

production requirements were beyond the capacity of a single company and sub-contracting was already an established practice in the aircraft industry. Handley Page were thus the only ones to build the B Mk I, and, as recorded in Chapter Two, their last machine, L9608, was made subject of the official naming ceremony carried out at Radlett by Lord and Lady Halifax on 12 September.

Externally there was little to distinguish L9515 from a standard B Mk I apart from the revised engine cowlings. The radiator bath had been reduced in frontal area as much as possible, resulting in two semi-circular apertures with a dividing, central lower lip. Less conspicuous was the change to 12 ft 6 in diameter Rotol, three bladed RXF 5/1 propellers. The first few production B Mk II aircraft followed this pattern until the introduction of a Boulton Paul C Mk V mid-upper turret to replace the hand-operated beam guns, this bulky item clearly establishing the identity of the B Mk II Halifax. These collective changes did not produce any change to the existing B Mk II designation, the Series I designation only emerging later after further changes produced the designation Series I (Special), as noted further on.

The first production Halifax, L9485, had been retained for armament trials and fitted simultaneously with a Boulton Paul C Mk V dorsal turret and a Boulton Paul K Mk I ventral turret, the two hand-operated ventral guns fitted to L7245 never having reached the production aircraft. While the C Mk I turret had been designed specifically for the Halifax, the Air Ministry requested a variant suitable for the mid-upper position for Hudson aircraft being supplied from America. This was achieved by redesigning the C Mk I with a domed cupola providing additional headroom as the guns could be depressed to 30° on the Hudson. As the C Mk V with 45° depression angle, it was adapted for the Halifax. The K turret had also been designed specifically for the Halifax, albeit via another idea. On 27 June 1938, the Air Ministry had instructed Boulton Paul to proceed with design studies for a low-drag ventral turret for the Halifax, the requirement being revised in November for a two-gun retractable turret, which eventuated as the K Mk I. Mounted on two vertical guide

rails, it could be retracted until almost flush with the fuselage belly. Fully equipped it weighed 6,421 lb and, like all Boulton Paul turrets, was electro-hydraulically driven and operated, azimuth being continuous while the guns could be depressed from a minimum angle of 30° down to 90°. Despite a production order being placed for 104 units on 4 January 1939 and a further 114 being added soon after, it was cancelled on 3 September 1939, only two prototypes surviving the cuts. The turret, in extended position projected 32.2 inches and no doubt would have caused considerable drag and that may have caused further consideration of its employment once the Halifax had entered service. However, the cancellation was not based on that premise and a pattern of erratic decision-making was to be repeated throughout the war years. L9485 was still flying with the K turret as late as mid-1942, though for what purpose is not clear.

Cancellation had barely been implemented when the original concept was raised again, this time the MAP specifying that the gunner be entirely enclosed within the aircraft, aiming to be done via indirect means (periscopic), a 360° rotation capability, armour plate and incorporating the Boulton Paul electro-hydraulic mechanism. The design designation was to be Type R. Mk. I. A prototype was completed by mid 1941, installed in R9486 at Boulton Paul's Pendeford Flight Shed and flown to Boscombe Down for testing. The subsequent report on 28 August 1941, concluded, *"The R.Mk.I turret is acceptable for service use, subject to incorporation of the modifications listed in Appendix I."* The latter were mostly minor except for those relating to feed chutes

Tested in April 1941, the Boulton Paul R turret had a much slimmer external profile; optically sighted via a periscopic system from within the fuselage, armament again was a pair of Browning 0.303-in machine guns. Tested on L9485 and found satisfactory, this more promising design was not adopted, the Frazer Nash FN 64 being chosen instead. This latter turret also encountered problems in service and was removed by most squadrons.

and ejection system, and all were implemented. Further testing followed with another report on 23 November stating that the modifications were successful.

However, during the intervening period, the MAP had requested a series of changes to the second prototype, significant enough to have the designation changed to Type R Mk II; in fact, the request involved an almost complete redesign. Despite the high priority placed on this work, extended delays ensued, caused in many instances by Boulton Paul being unable to get specific machine tools, and sub-manufacturers reluctant, in the face of restrictions on materials, to proceed until....etc, etc. Consequently, by March 1942, the frustration was mounting with MAP placing urgent orders for production of the turret with Joseph Lucas Ltd[1], Boulton Paul being requested to assist Lucas by supplying that company with drawings.

On 11 February, Boulton Paul was requested to produce a third prototype – just when they had finally obtained the materials for the second. This meant starting all over again with the sub-contractors to get supply of a second set of one-off items. And so the process dragged on; the first Mk II turret was completed in July 1942 and successful ground test firing took place, the only problem being one of synchronization between the gunsight and the two machine guns. On 25 August the company was reminded how urgent it was to have the turret installed in the Halifax and air-tested – then on 15 September they were told completion was no longer a matter of urgency and that a decision was pending on whether production would proceed. The air tests were finally carried out, though no firing was undertaken and the results reported as satisfactory – no further work would take place; the Frazer-Nash FN 64 ventral design being favoured instead.[2]

In the meantime, the addition of the mid-upper turret had gone ahead with the beam guns being deleted, although many early production aircraft retained their beam gun hatches or had them faired over until existing fuselage jigs could be replaced or modified. Shortly after introduction of the C Mk V turret, the rearmost aerial mast was deleted and the aerial leads attached to the inboard face of each fin. Production aircraft were also fitted with two different sizes of Rotol three-bladed, fully feathering wooden propellers. Both types, either 12 ft 9 in diameter R7/35/54 or 13 ft 0 in diameter R7/35/55 were fitted and it was not uncommon to find a combination of both on a single aircraft.

*   *   *

On 25 October 1941, 35 Squadron received its first two B Mk II Halifaxes, R9364: M from Handley Page and V9979: E from English Electric. As recorded, October and November had been a period of reduced activity for Bomber Command and the Halifaxes because of the terrible weather conditions, reducing major operations to just five, with one split between two targets. However, it was the second, on 7/8 November that was memorable for all the wrong reasons.

Its origins lay first with a very damning assessment of the first two years of the RAF bombing campaign, compounded by the Butt Report. This analysed the photographic results of the bombing for June and July and, released on 18 August 1941, only enhanced the earlier report. That assessment recorded, in part, that the equivalent of the entire front line strength of the command had been lost in a four-month period and for little success, despite the courage and determination of crews. Not surprisingly, crew morale was declining. It made sobering reading for Sir Richard Peirse and his senior commanders; of those bombers that reached and bombed their target[3], only one-third got within five miles of the actual aiming point, even in the best of weather and on moonlit nights. It was clear that unless matters improved, the enemy would never suffer sufficient damage to seriously hamper its war effort, while those at home opposed to the independence of Bomber Command were being provided with ammunition to campaign for its disbandment, with its forces dispersed to Army and Naval control for tactical use.

Thus, the heavy bomber force had to find a means of improving the accuracy of both navigation and target identification; simply increasing the number and weight of bombs dropped was not enough – they had to be on the target. Peirse's reaction was to mount a major effort against Berlin on the night of 7/8 November 1941 and he did so in the face of the knowledge and clear warnings from his specialist planning staff that weather conditions would be extremely bad, with storms, thick cloud, icing and hail along the routes to and from Berlin. Conditions were so bad that Air Vice-Marshal Slessor of No 5 Group had objected strongly enough against Berlin to be allowed to withdraw his forces and send them, instead, to Cologne. In all, some 392 aircraft were to take part, a record effort for Bomber Command, and probably the maximum number of serviceable aircraft available that night.

Of the 169-strong mixed force of Wellingtons, Whitleys, Stirlings and Halifaxes sent to Berlin, 12.4% were lost[4], most succumbing to the appalling weather conditions. Final radio plots for several aircraft came from positions over the North Sea, the heavy winds and deadly icing conditions simply exhausting the fuel of many aircraft, sending their crews to a freezing and lonely death. Only 73 were assessed as having reached the general area of Berlin, but only fires on the outskirts were claimed, cloud denying crews any meaningful assessment of where their bombs had fallen. The Berlin report of that night records scattered bombing with just 14 houses destroyed and eleven people killed. This was to be the last major attack on the city until January 1943.

The attack on the secondary target, Cologne, by a force of 61 Hampdens and 14 Manchesters, produced little better results but did so without loss. A force of 53 Wellingtons and two Stirlings attacked the third target, Mannheim, where, despite

enthusiastic crew reports of the starting of a large fire, the Mannheim report recorded that no bombs had fallen in the city at all although seven Wellingtons were lost. Another 30 Halifaxes, Hampdens, Wellingtons and Whitleys were out on 'rover patrols' to Essen and other targets, losing a Halifax, two Hampdens and two Wellingtons. The Halifax, L9603: P from 35 Squadron, was shot down by a night-fighter flown by Oblt Herbert Lütje of the III. /NJG 1 and crashed in the Imbos Forest near Rozendaal, Holland.

Twenty-eight other aircraft went to Ostend, and 22 to Boulogne losing none of their number, while to the north 13 Halifaxes laid mines off Oslo. Overall, the night's 392 sorties had cost 37 aircraft, a 9.4% loss and more than double the previous worst figure. It compounded Peirse's refusal to cancel the operation in the face of strong warnings, a decision ultimately deemed indefensible, especially in the face of his back-down to Slessor that pointed to him understanding the situation clearly enough; he would leave his command on 8 January 1942[5] and be temporarily replaced by Air Vice-Marshal J. E. A. Baldwin. The change of command, however, did not result entirely from the terrible losses of the Berlin raid. In the interim, the War Cabinet had met to discuss the losses and results and an instruction to strictly limit Bomber Command operations 'for the immediate future' pending a review of current policies, was issued on 13 November.

Despite the disaster, or perhaps because of it, Peirse had not hesitated to send out his dwindling force the next night, 54 going to Essen with another 18 on minor raids. In contrast to the previous night, only two aircraft were lost. The following night, 9/10 November, Hamburg was targeted by 103 aircraft for the loss of one while elsewhere 21 others carried out minor operations, also for the loss of one aircraft. Minor operations resumed on the 15/16th, 13 of which had been mounted prior to the next major attack, planned against Hamburg for the night of 30 November/1 December. Of the 182 aircraft sent, 122 claimed good results, something confirmed by the Hamburg damage report. Wellingtons, Hampdens, Whitleys, Halifaxes, Manchesters and Stirlings had taken part, losing 13 of their number. No 35 Squadron's L9582: T failed to return, but all but one of Fl/Sgt J. Hamilton's crew survived. A second Halifax loss happened closer to home when L9604: W of 76 Squadron crashed on returning to base, fortunately without injury to the crew[6]. A further fifty bombers had targeted Emden while another 15 carried out minor actions.

Aachen was next on 7/8 December, targeted by 130 bombers, but local reports stated that only about 16 aircraft had attacked the city, with some flying as low as 400 m (1,200 ft). Only five high explosive bombs were recorded (two of which failed to explode) and nine incendiaries. Sixty-four crews claimed to have attacked; some clearly made every effort to do so in difficult weather conditions but even so, many bombs fell in open ground north of the city and damage was slight. Only two aircraft were lost, neither of them Halifaxes. However, the failure rate of British bombs was still cause for concern and crew morale would have suffered had they known that their battles to reach the targets were occasionally frustrated by such faults.

Brest, the secondary target for the night, was attacked by 23 Wellingtons and seven Stirlings – but Stirlings with a difference. Drawn from Nos 7 and 15 Squadrons they carried out the first operational trial of *Oboe*. This ground-controlled blind bombing device provided great accuracy; above 30,000 ft at speeds over 300 mph it had an error of just 300 yards – even less at lower heights. Its deficiency was that it required two ground stations transmitting signals to the aircraft to give the interception release point and could only handle 18 aircraft per hour. The navigator used *Gee* to reach a specific point ten minutes before the *Oboe* system was initiated. Preliminary operational trial results were good, but more work would be needed. The operational trials continued with raids on Brest in December, but introduction to operations on a full-time basis was still a year away.

Small operations continued with another Halifax lost during an attack on Cologne on 11/12 December with P/O H. Buckley's L9600: U from 35 Squadron presumed to have come down in the sea off the Belgian coast. There were no survivors. Meanwhile, Bomber Command had been assessing the merits of the first daylight operations – despite the heavy losses and damaged aircraft, the attack had forced the *Scharnhorst* to remain in harbour for repairs that would extend to a four-month period. The results were considered inconclusive and, in some quarters, it was felt that improved defensive armament might yet make such operations practical. Night attacks were also proving ineffective; six Stirlings had been sent on 18/19th, then 11 Halifaxes and seven Stirlings on 25/26th followed by 23 Wellingtons and seven Stirlings on 7/8 December. A cloud cover attack mounted on 12 December was abandoned and other targets attacked by the six Hampdens sent; then 18 Wellingtons and six Stirlings tried again that night, with a further 22 Hampdens and six Stirlings trying again on 14/15th, all with negligible results.

With additional production output, a third Halifax squadron joined the ranks in December 1941, No 10 Squadron relinquishing its Mk V Whitleys in favour of B Mk II Halifaxes. Its first operation coincided with Bomber Command's decision to explore further daylight bombing against the German capital ships at Brest – but this time with a heavy bomber force. *Operation Veracity I*, set for 18 December, was to use a mixed force of Halifaxes, Stirlings and Manchesters against *Scharnhorst* and *Gneisenau*. A strong fighter escort would provide cover for both the actual bombing attack and the withdrawal. The preceding night, 121 Wellingtons, Hampdens and Whitleys were sent against the ships, losing a single Hampden; 80 crews reported having bombed the approximate position of the German ships, but for such a target

No 10 Squadron blooded its Halifax B Mk IIs for the first time in Operation Veracity I on 18 December 1941. L9619: E was the eleventh B Mk II delivered from Handley Page. Externally, there was nothing to distinguish it from a B Mk I Series III as it retained beam gun hatches, both tall radio masts and no mid-upper turret. Kilfrost de-icing paste was spread on the de-icing boots on the leading edges of each fin and horizontal tail plane. What looks like a white 'T' marking on the fin is actually two small rectangular aluminium data plates, the one set at right angles recorded the airframe data while the hazy white patch immediately below was a stencilled standard W/T marking. The colour of the aircraft serial number has been changed to dull red. Although hard to see and an idiosyncratic feature of this production batch, the serial number is positioned in line with the top of the beam hatch window and extending back over the small circular window aft of it, the top horizontal stroke of the 'E' stopping just short of touching the letter L. After running out of fuel returning from the St Nazaire raid of 15/16 February 1942, Fl/Sgt E. Lloyd ordered his crew to bale out, leaving the Halifax to crash at Angram, south of Keld and just 28 miles short of its home airfield at Leeming. All the crew survived.

'approximate' was not good enough for accurate bombing. Daylight seemed the only answer.

Despite intense cold and heavy frost, the weather was excellent and having formed up into two sections, No 35 Squadron's six Halifaxes, V9979: E, R9367: G, R9377: B, R9372: O, R9364: M and V9978: A, were joined by the other two Halifax Squadrons. For 10 Squadron, which had started operating Halifaxes just four days earlier, this was their first operation, sending L9619: E, R9368, R9369, V9369, V9984, R9370 and R9371. W/Cdr Tuck's Halifax immediately developed hydraulic trouble, making it impossible to retract the starboard undercarriage leg and he aborted, leaving command to S/Ldr Webster who swung the remaining five into position behind the 35 Squadron formation. They were followed by the six – L9617: A, V9980: B, R9379: L, L9375: T, L9620: O and R9373: W – from 76 Squadron, which took up station at the rear of the formation. The route to the target was Lundy Island to Lizard Point then to Lanildut on the French coast and then Brest. The attack was to be carried out from 16,000 ft at 12.38 hrs but, despite the detailed planning, some difficulties were encountered.

Marshalling of the entire force was to be done at a point some five to ten miles north of Lundy Island, but when the Halifaxes arrived ten minutes early, there was no sign of either the Stirlings or the Manchesters. At this point, R9379: L from 76 Squadron jettisoned its bombs and withdrew with engine trouble as the remaining Halifaxes commenced a wide left-hand orbit. Halfway around the orbit, the Stirling formation was seen approaching from the east and, despite the fact that there was still some five or six minutes to go before the scheduled departure time, proceeded in the direction of Land's End. Caught off guard, the Halifaxes turned in behind the fast disappearing Stirlings that were now only just visible with two stragglers well to the rear. Apparently, the timing error was discovered because the Stirlings suddenly swung west of track; the Manchesters were nowhere to be seen.

Having reached Land's End, the Stirlings turned south for Brest but then made another surprise move by suddenly starting to climb, forcing the Halifaxes to swing to starboard to avoid overtaking the Stirling stragglers and closing in on the main

formation. Finally established correctly, the two formations proceeded to the target where the Stirlings attacked first.

The Halifaxes were in perfect formation, each squadron in sections, in V-formation and close in to each other. At a predetermined point, the leading squadron went into line astern formation and made for a point just inside the coastline from where the final run-up to the target was made. Heavily engaged by flak and a few fighters, some Stirlings broke to the right as the Halifaxes, in tight formation, came in on a course directly at right angles to the two battleships lying in dry dock. Despite the heavy and accurate flak, the Halifaxes held their formation, bombed, and withdrew to their original starting point. As they did so, the late-arriving Manchesters appeared approaching the coast in tight formation.

The leading Halifax, V9978: A, was hit in the port wing by flak that riddled both engines with splinters and set them on fire. W/Cdr Collings was unable to feather the propellers but did manage to extinguish the fires. Despite the drastic reduction in airspeed, now in the region of 110 mph, his two wingmen managed to hold formation with him until he ditched the Halifax in the sea some 60 miles off the English coast. It continued to float for 20 minutes and Collings re-entered the aircraft twice during this period, the second time to look for his favourite pipe. The entire crew was rescued that same evening.

Halifax R9367: G in the second section of the 35 Squadron formation also sustained flak damage to two engines and immediately after leaving the target area, the port inner failed and was feathered only with difficulty. Shortly afterwards the starboard outer also failed and caught fire but was easily extinguished. In spite of the damage, it reached Boscombe Down safely with the other two Halifaxes of the section holding perfect formation all the way, again at a drastically reduced air speed.

Apart from a small amount of shrapnel damage to some aircraft, the only loss had been Collings' Halifax from their portion of the attacking force (four Stirlings and a Manchester were also lost in this attack). Damage to the battleships could not be assessed accurately, but bomb bursts were clearly observed on the stern areas of both.

The month of December ended badly for the Halifax force with five lost in two days. On the 29th, two from 10 Squadron were carrying out night training when L9614 collided with V9981 being flown by W/Cdr Tuck, the squadron C.O., killing Sergeants W. Tripp and W. Green in L9614. Tuck was uninjured but his aircraft was damaged beyond repair. Then Brest loomed large again.

Heartened by the success of the Brest operation, Bomber Command ordered a repeat performance on 30 December. However, due to unfavourable weather conditions in the No 3 and 5 Group areas, the three Halifax squadrons were left to carry out *Operation Veracity II* unassisted. Fighter escort was provided by a Polish Spitfire Wing to cover the Halifaxes from five minutes before the attack right through to the withdrawal. The three bomber squadrons used the same formation as before, but this time with six Halifaxes of 35 Squadron leading followed by four from

Taken during the bombing attack against Brest on 18 December 1941, the camera caught these bombs as they left the wing bomb cells; the main bomb bay doors were also open and the first bomb was just leaving its rack. The twin barrels of the machine guns mounted in the beam hatch on the port side are just visible.

No 10 Squadron[7] with six from 76 Squadron bringing up the rear. Just before beginning the bombing run the port outer engine of the lead Halifax cut causing it to swing, momentarily upsetting the tight formation, but they recovered in time to bomb as planned.

The German defences were well alerted this time and the flak gunners put up a concentrated, accurate barrage. S/Ldr Middleton's V9979: E went down after being hit in the port wing, crashing in the target area; L9615: X, hit during the actual bombing run, was seen to dive away from the starboard side of the formation. Gliding out to sea with smoke coming from the starboard outer engine it finally ditched some 20 miles from the coast. Two Spitfires protected it from further attack as it went down but P/O D. King and his crew all perished.

The withdrawal was intercepted by a strong force of enemy fighters, which was immediately engaged by the Spitfire escort. One 10 Squadron Halifax, R9374, was already badly damaged by flak, which had smashed the port outer engine. Unable to keep in formation, it was attacked by a Bf 109, which riddled it with cannon fire from dead astern, killed F/Lt R. Roach and put both inboard engines out of action. Fl/Sgt Whyte managed to ditch the crippled Halifax safely in the sea 80 miles south of Lizard Point, the surviving crew members being rescued by a Royal Navy MTB[8] some five hours later. P/O Hacking's R9370 was also attacked by a Bf 109 that made the mistake of passing directly over the tail of the bomber, only to be promptly shot down by Sgt Porritt, the rear gunner. He then drove off a second Bf 109 and the Spitfire escort shot down the next two that attempted to attack the Halifax. Although slightly wounded in the face and hands during these attacks, Porritt still managed to drive off yet another Bf 109.

The results of the raid were not encouraging at first glance; three Halifaxes and two crews were lost and most aircraft had suffered extensive flak damage. However, it had been realised that the Halifaxes were the sole attacking force and had withstood the worst of the very extensive, well-alerted defences.

In early January 1942, news reached the War Cabinet that *Tirpitz* had arrived in Aasen Fjord. This was bad news; *Tirpitz* was considered the most powerful battleship extant and British naval forces were stretched to the limit with the launching of the Japanese attacks in the Pacific. Churchill however had no doubts; *Tirpitz* was the most important target and should be attacked immediately *"....both by carrier-borne torpedo aircraft and with heavy bombers by daylight or at dawn."*

Two detachments from Nos 10 and 76 Squadrons were secretly sent north to Lossiemouth on the Moray Firth for this operation. As the closest point possible, it was still over 600 nautical miles (nm) to the target and at the extreme limit of the Halifax's loaded range and there were almost no navigational aids available for the mainly featureless journey. With the ship estimated to be anchored only about 50 ft from the shore, it would be possible to roll some special spherical mines down the sloping side of the Fjord and into the water beneath it. Fitted with hydrostatic fuses, the mines should then detonate beneath *Tirpitz* and rupture the relatively vulnerable lower hull. Starting at an altitude of 2,000 ft the Halifaxes had to descend during a timed run in order to reach the dropping point at a height of 200 ft. Each aircraft was loaded with four of the special 1,000 lb mines that would not quite fit into the main bomb compartment, the Halifaxes having to fly with the bomb doors partly open[9].

The force, which included seven Stirlings, attacked on 29/30 January 1942, taking off just after midnight, but poor weather severely hampered the operation with 10/10ths cloud covering most of Norway. The four aircraft from 10 Squadron all failed to locate the *Tirpitz*, being forced back by diminishing fuel, as did four of the five from 76 Squadron.

Of the latter, L9581: Q, lost a port engine during the return flight and even after jettisoning the mines, the pilot was forced to ditch three miles off Aberdeen through lack of fuel, the crew fortunately being rescued by the Aberdeen Lifeboat. The remaining Halifax also failed to identify the target positively but assumed that it was the source of the flak and bombed accordingly. No 149 Squadron lost one of its Stirlings which, returning to its base skidded on the ice, hit a trench and collapsed the undercarriage.

On 22 February, Air Chief Marshal Sir Arthur Harris arrived to take over Bomber Command; he would remain its leader until war's end. Eight days earlier, the new policy had come into effect and he took stock of his forces; just 378 serviceable bombers, of which only 82 were heavy bombers; 29 Halifaxes, 29 Stirlings, 20 Manchesters and four Lancasters, nothing greater than had been available a year earlier to his predecessor. The policy was based around a shift to greater bomb-carrying capacity and better navigational aids, though both were still in the embryonic stage. Russia was now fighting the Germans on land but Britain could only assist from the air until an invasion of Europe became possible – something that was a little more than a long-term objective. The Air Ministry had selected 43 major German cities housing industrial capacity and collectively 15 million people – these were to be subjected to continuous air attack. The first obstacle was that an estimated 4,000 bombers would be needed to achieve the desired destruction; the second required reliable navigational aids to guide the bombers to the target.

While the aircraft industry increased its heavy bomber production, the first boost to improve navigation had already arrived and right at the critical moment,

Photographed at Hurn airport on 27 March 1942, V9977 was already fitted with its distinctive H2S scanner housing, but fitting of the scanner and associated electronic equipment was still to be done. It was lost in the catastrophic accident described in the text, taking with it most of the H2S scientific team. (Sir Bernard Lovell)

with the introduction of the TR1335 electronic navigational aid. Code-named *Gee*, it had already undergone operational trials in August 1941 just as the findings of the Butt Report were being absorbed. Reports of the results from raids where *Gee* was used had boosted confidence all round and raised the expectations of the Air Staff to an unprecedented and perhaps unsustainable level as the spring offensive was to be based around this new equipment.

The most experienced crews were selected and tasked to use *Gee* to mark targets with incendiaries, the technique being code-named *Shaker*. If, as often happened, the target was obscured by cloud, they were dropped blind using *Gee* fixes (*Sampson*). In both forms of attack, the Finders (as they were termed) attacked in waves to keep the target illuminated throughout the raid. Results varied; the technique was tried in the attack on the Renault Works on 3/4 March 1942 and was very successful. Other attacks were less rewarding as accuracy declined with distance thus making it less reliable; it was also realised that it could, and eventually would, be jammed over Europe. However, morale, which had been declining within Bomber Command, was again climbing. While results over Germany were at times questionable, crews now had a system that gave the navigator, rapidly and with relative simplicity, a precise fix of the aircraft's position by using two intersecting radio beams. Over England, it was very precise and it became a particularly significant aid to returning aircraft, some of which inevitably were in desperate need of finding an airfield quickly – and it was independent of weather conditions.

Enemy jamming was anticipated but already more sophisticated devices were under development; what was required was a self-contained blind bombing device carried by each aircraft and not reliant upon ground stations in England. One such device was already under development and had been air-tested on 1 November 1941, fitted in the nose of V6000, a Blenheim Mk IV of the Telecommunication Flying Unit (TFU).

Initially fitted with a 9 cm Air Interception (AI) system, normally used for air-to-air searching and interception by night-fighters, the beam in this case was tilted downward to try to record ground responses. As the results showed distinct promise, at a meeting on 23 December 1941, the Secretary of State had directed the Telecommunications Research Establishment (TRE) to commence test flights of the device[10]. He further added that development should proceed with the highest priority as it was intended for use in the new four-engined Stirling, Halifax and Lancaster heavy bombers currently in the process of replacing the twin-engined Wellingtons[11], Whitleys and Hampdens. Such was the urgency for this equipment, that immediately following this meeting, Electrical and Musical Industries Ltd (EMI) were contracted to manufacture 50 complete units, now code-named *H2S*. To complete the contract, EMI added their best engineers to the project, headed by A. D. Blumlein, a pioneer in television development and widely regarded as one of the finest electronic engineers in the country.

Following the meeting, two representatives of the TRE visited A&AEE at Boscombe Down to inspect the three types, selecting the Halifax as it had more alternative positions for the scanner and its housing than the other two. Having just been placed in charge of the development programme, Bernard Lovell[12] visited the Handley Page works on 4 January 1942 to discuss the installation. Interestingly, Sir Frederick Handley Page and his design team were opposed to the idea of fitting a device in the position designed for a ventral gun turret, adding that it and its external scanner housing would reduce bomb load and speed[13]. In spite of objections, the programme was not allowed to stall. After a week of anxious waiting, Halifax B Mk II V9977 landed at Hurn airport on 27 March. This was the first of the English Electric-built B Mk IIs and was standard in every aspect other than for the scanner housing underneath the fuselage and only the forward radio mast. It retained the beam gun hatches and had no mid-upper turret. Delivered to the RAF on 5 September 1941 it was then sent to the TFU, which had moved to Defford, Worcestershire in May 1942 having already received the Halifax. Between then and its arrival at Hurn airport, a teardrop-shaped Perspex housing had been fitted over the ventral gun position and painted black to conceal the rotating scanner housed within it. The housing was vacuum moulded from two sheets of Perspex but unfortunately, the identity of the company which designed or produced this first example is unknown. The design never changed and production would eventually be common to all manufacturers producing aircraft that required the fitting. It was attached to an L-shaped skirt riveted to the belly of the aircraft, removable bolts being used around the edge to retain the Perspex fairing. Nash & Thompson, who had produced the spiral scanner set used in V6000, also manufactured the hydraulic scanner for the Halifax. Metropolitan Vickers had also been drawn into the programme to manufacture an electrically operated scanner of the same dimensions as a back-up. It was subsequently fitted to Halifax B Mk II R9490, when it joined the flying programme three weeks later.

The operational requirement for the developed system specified a range of 30 miles from an altitude of 18,000 ft for navigation and target approach, with a clearly defined image at short range for bombing. However, the current ability was limited to five miles and gaps appeared in the image shown on the cathode ray tube of the Plan Position Indicator (PPI) of the display unit. The staff at TRE doubted that the lower powered klystron system would ever work sufficiently. Both magnetron and klystron systems were centimetric radars using a 10 cm wavelength, but power was the problem and use of the more powerful magnetron system was causing concerns lest it fall into the wrong hands if used over enemy territory. In contrast, German scientists, with reports on its development having been published there in 1939, already knew about the klystron valve. The other complication was that centimetric Air to Surface Vessel (ASV) used many of the same components, including the magnetron, and was nearing readiness for manufacture; if the magnetron-powered *H2S* fell into enemy hands the Allied advantage in the war at sea also would suffer. Finally, a compromise was reached, allowing both klystron and magnetron systems to develop in parallel. To this end, the allocation of a second Halifax at the 4 January meeting had been made good with the arrival at Hurn airport of R9490 on 12 April. While V9977 was fitted with the magnetron equipment, R9490 had the klystron equipment, both using the same form of Perspex housing under the fuselage.

Tests continued, but with disappointing results. In May, Lovell recorded that the picture on the display tube was extremely bad, while by early June the lower powered klystron equipment was encountering an endless repeat succession of troubles. The desperate urgency for this equipment is, perhaps, reflected best by the revised operational requirement that came from the Air Staff meeting of 19 May, which stated in part

"That the system should be accurate enough to guarantee that bombs would fall within an industrial or other area selected as the target.

That the Air Staff would be satisfied in the first instance if the range of the device enabled the aircraft to home on to a built-up area from 15 miles at 15,000 ft."

The pure navigational aspect was to be deferred lest it delay further development, and could be introduced retrospectively. The TRE team saw in these revised figures a hope of achieving the required results sooner rather than later. Then disaster struck.

In the last days of May, bench testing of the equipment was finally producing good results; the two Halifaxes had been transferred to Defford and allocated for the use of the TRE. The EMI engineers were testing their klystron equipment in R9490, and were still encountering poor range results, but the magnetron equipment in V9977, based on the 25-30 mile range achieved with the Blenheim tests, was expected to give the decisive result. On 6 June, Lovell and his colleague Geoffrey Hensby, the radar operator, flew in V9977 and immediately saw that ranges were now greater than any previously achieved. The next day the EMI team decided to see the improved results for themselves and the Halifax took off at 15.00 hrs for a short demonstration flight. On board were the EMI team of Blumlein, C. O. Browne and F. Blythen, along with Hensby and P/O C. E. Vincent of the TRE team, S/Ldr R. J. Sansom, a Bomber Command Liaison Officer on loan to the TRE and an RAF crew of five: P/O D. J. D. Berrington, pilot, with F/O A. M. Phillips acting as second pilot, Flt/Sgt G. Millar, navigator/observer, Leading Aircraftsman (LAC) B. D. C. Dear, flight engineer and wireless operator Aircraftsman II B C. F. Bicknell.

At 19.35 hrs news reached Defford that the Halifax had crashed. This was confirmed an hour later and that all on board had been killed. Important members of the TRE group, along with the key EMI personnel had been lost in one swift blow. The *H2S* equipment was destroyed, the magnetron being the only recognizable fragment. The official report into the accident established that the aircraft had caught fire at 2 to 3,000 ft between Newport and Chepstow, lost height and crashed. The starboard outer engine had failed in flight and subsequently caught fire, the aircraft crashing from a height of 500 ft. The cause of the fire was put down to the fracture of an inlet valve stem, resulting in a fire when the pilot attempted to restart the engine, possibly to provide power for the equipment under test as the alternator for the *H2S* equipment was driven by that engine. The fire extinguishers failed to operate and the bottles were found to be empty, probably having left the manufacturers in that condition. Interestingly, the matter stayed there until a former engineer with TRE's successor, RSRE, W. H. Sleigh, decided to investigate further in 1984/5. His findings record some differences.

An eyewitness to the crash, Mr. Onslow Kirby, was working on the family farm in the Wye Valley, eight miles south-west of Ross-on-Wye. He first sighted the Halifax when the starboard wing was on fire at about 350 ft above the River Wye; then the starboard wing broke off, the Halifax rolled onto its back, and crashed only about 300 yards from where he was standing. The last, brief radio message had been received when the aircraft was still at 2 to 3,000 ft, sufficient height for the crew to parachute to safety but it was speculated that with eleven personnel on board it is likely that the civilians were not familiar with the parachute procedures or possibly not enough packs were carried. (Bomber crews used a clip-on pack, each stowed in a specific place when not needed.) Last minute unanticipated changes to the civilian members who were aboard attests to the likelihood that none were wearing standard RAF parachute harness, each of which would have needed to be adjusted by a ground staff member prior to departure, but there is no mention of this happening in the witness statements[14]. The remaining three engines were certainly enough to have gained sufficient height and time had the engine fire not developed as rapidly as it did, leaving Berrington little choice but to attempt a wheels-up landing. He was close to achieving that when the fatal moment occurred.

Sleigh's investigation, aided by Rolls-Royce engineers, led to the conclusion that the cause of the fire originated through human error. The Merlin XX engine (198341) was checked after every ten hours of running, all four having been checked between 25 May and 1 June during the normal 30 hour inspection cycle, a replacement engine for the port inner position having been fitted on the 25th. It was later thought likely that a single tappet nut, one of the 48 on the engine and thus one of 192 that needed such attention, had not been locked down during the last inspection. This subsequently allowed the fatigue failure of an inlet valve stem to develop between then and the day of the crash. Combustion gases had then ignited the mixture in the induction and carburetion system, causing a major fire, which then burnt through the engine bulkhead and ignited the wing fuel tanks.

The old moral about the battle being lost for the want of a nail, etc., had a grim echo – but for the want of a nut being tightened, the urgently needed *H2S* development had been all but destroyed at the moment of Bomber Command's greatest need.

While remaining somewhat uninformed as to the success achieved with the equipment on the day before the crash, Churchill continued to apply relentless pressure to have the equipment brought to operational use immediately. Another B Mk II, W7711, arrived at Defford on 26 June, as a replacement for the ill-fated V9977, but the klystron/magnetron debate continued and was not resolved, in favour of using the latter, until mid-July. By working day and night, another magnetron set was completed and installed in W7711 and the trials recommenced at the end of the first week in July. Eventually, with both R9490 and W7711 fitted with the more powerful magnetron equipment, results began to improve. Testing of the system was to be done at the Bombing Development Unit (BDU), which worked in close conjunction with TFU, and where RAF navigators would be trained to use the first production prototype equipment. On 30 September, W7808, fitted with the first EMI-produced apparatus which produced an improved PPI picture, was flown to the BDU. The main drawback was poor serviceability of the equipment, being described by the experienced BDU navigators as hopelessly bad; even so they thought the system was valuable, both as a navigational and target-finding aid. Built-up areas showed as a white ill-defined mass, but open countryside gave a less solid return and water gave none at all; but it took skilled interpretation to make the best of this imaging system.

The main problem was now to meet the target set on 24 July – to build and fit *H2S* sets to 24 Halifaxes and 24 Stirlings by 31 December. (Harris, at that meeting, had complicated matters by insisting that he wanted sets fitted to Stirlings). Churchill had demanded two full squadrons equipped with the device by October, but had been persuaded to accept the lesser target. Even then, the scientists saw it as an almost impossible task. By 31 December, despite the superb effort of the EMI staff, there were just 24 sets available, all produced by them. The target had been to supply 50 with the Radar Production Unit, the special organization created in association with TRE, to build and supply an additional 150 sets by that date; they had produced not a single set. No 35 Squadron at Graveley had 12 of its Halifaxes fitted with *H2S* while 7 Squadron at Oakington had 12 Stirlings similarly equipped. Permission was finally given to begin using the new equipment as from 1 January 1943. However, that was still in the future and we must now return to operational events at squadron level as they had developed during this same period.

* * *

Despite poor weather conditions, 35 Squadron had been active on five occasions during January 1942. Snow and ice caused considerable trouble for the ground crews, who had to keep the aircraft free from these dangerous accretions. Such was the intensity of the cold that several aircraft had trouble with turrets freezing up in flight, and one, L9584: L mysteriously became uncontrollable 45 minutes following take-off but was able to be landed safely. Eventually, it was established that the pitot head had frozen up and the aircraft had been flown in a stalled condition. Fortunately for all on board, the stall characteristics of the Halifax were very mild.

Bomber Command had continued with night attacks on Brest, but without any success. Then January closed with a significant piece of information for Allied Intelligence – *Scharnhorst, Gneisenau* and *Prinz Eugen* were likely to break out from Brest harbour and make a dash through the Channel within the very near future. The subsequent break-out by the three capital ships on 11 February has been described in great detail many times before. Amongst the Bomber Command forces employed were four Halifaxes from 35 Squadron, all of which failed to attack due to

This view of engineering staff servicing the starboard Merlin engines illustrates the number of fittings that needed to be removed, checked and replaced with each engine adjustment, exemplifying what led to the fatal crash of V9977. The fitter nearest the camera has removed the rocker cover and is adjusting the tappets. The fishtail shape of the actual exhaust manifold is clearly visible. (via M. Wright)

the foul weather conditions prevailing at the time. One sighted the force for a brief moment but lost it again almost immediately. The seven Halifaxes from 10 Squadron had similar poor luck, six returning to base without even sighting the ships. The seventh, R9366 flown by S/Ldr Thompson, caught a momentary glimpse of a large ship through a break in the clouds and released all its bombs in one stick from 9,000 ft but the crew were unable to observe the results.

The 'Channel Dash' episode had brought further severe criticisms to bear against Bomber Command and it was in the midst of this situation and change of policy that Harris promptly took up its defence in characteristic fashion. On 3/4 March, using an unprecedented concentration in time and space, a highly successful attack was carried out by 235 bombers against the Renault works at Billancourt, near Paris. Only a single Wellington was lost and the raid established a number of records – for numbers employed and concentration in time over the target, averaging 121 per hour, plus the heaviest bomb load dropped. The attack also employed the mass use of flares with selected experienced crews opening the attack – a tactical move that would develop into specialist form during the coming months.

The Halifaxes' contribution was restricted to a relatively small force, 20 drawn from Nos 10 and 76 Squadrons, principally because all three Halifax squadrons had been screened from operations at the beginning of the month to allow the Halifaxes to be equipped with *Gee*, the new radio navigational aid. There was, however, one drawback in that the equipment could not be fitted retroactively and squadron aircraft had to be replaced by new ones specially modified during assembly. This problem was partly to blame for the delay in No 102 Squadron becoming operational after it had begun to re-equip with Halifaxes during December. A shortage of *Gee*-equipped Halifaxes on 102 Squadron was finally overcome by exchanging W1047, W1048, W1049, W1050, W1051 and W1053 for six fully-equipped Halifaxes R9441, R9442, R9446, R9449, R9488 and R9494, from 35 Squadron on 9 April. The other three Halifax squadrons had not been inactive during this period having all moved north to Scotland from where they carried out another attack on the *Tirpitz* in Aasen Fjord starting on the night of 30/31 March.

The previous problems of weather and distance had not changed since the earlier attempt. The Halifaxes crossed to Norway at 1,000 ft to avoid detection by German radar and visibility remained good until the target area was reached; 10/10ths cloud and fog again foiled all attempts to locate the *Tirpitz*. The Halifaxes remained in the target area as long as their marginal fuel reserves would allow but they were eventually forced to abort the operation. Most of them jettisoned their four 1,000 lb mines in the Fjord while three donated theirs to the local flak and searchlight batteries, which promptly ceased to operate. Losses were relatively high, six of the 34 Halifaxes failing to return. Fuel problems were acute and most aircraft

landed with virtually dry tanks while R9453: K of 76 Squadron was known to have ditched in the sea, presumably 16 miles south of Sumburgh in the Shetlands, but the crew were never found. There is little doubt that fuel starvation accounted for most, if not all, of the other missing Halifaxes that night – two from 10 Squadron (W1043: F and W1044: D) and three from 35 Squadron (R9438: H, R9496: L and W1015: P).

Improved tactics to start the attacks using aircraft fitted with *Gee* was carried a step further on the 8/9 March attack on Essen. Always a difficult target, the newly devised *Shaker* tactic was carried out. The 211-strong force was split into three: Illuminators, Target Markers and Main Force, each Illuminator carrying 12 bundles of triple flares in addition to its bomb load. Each was to make a run along the upwind side of the target area, dropping flares every ten seconds, the aim being to maintain a line of flares approximately six miles long, which would drift across the target and its approaches, keeping the ground illuminated for 12 minutes. The markers would do their part and the Main Force would then bomb. Despite the planning and a fine night, the ever-present industrial haze prevented accurate bombing, producing poor results for the loss of five Wellingtons, two Manchesters and a Stirling. The *Gee*-equipped aircraft were unable to define the target sufficiently and the main aiming point, the Krupp factories, was not hit. However, the new technique had been proven and would be further refined for use on other targets.

Improved navigational aids were not the only new items introduced by Bomber Command during the early months of 1942. The 8,000 lb high capacity (HC) bomb also made its initial appearance at this time.

L9485 had been used for trials with this large type of bomb, which was of such proportions that it could not be contained entirely within the fuselage bomb bay. It projected below the fuselage for about one quarter of its depth, the bomb doors having to remain partly open.

Mr Knivett, the Handley Page representative, had assisted with the first trial installation of the 4,000 lb version of this weapon. While one of the installation party was working in the cramped confines of the bomb compartment wiring up the new bomb rack, Knivett was inside the fuselage with two of the bomb winches still in place. Four times one of the technicians asked if he could remove the winches, and each time Knivett declined saying that there was still plenty of time. A short while later, one of the ground crew, who had nothing to do with the bomb installation party, connected the aircraft's main power supply.

The whole Halifax suddenly shook as the huge bomb dropped from its rack and hung on the quivering strands of the winch cables, about a foot below it. During the routine servicing checks, someone had left the jettison bar of the bomb selector box pulled down! It is extremely doubtful if the bomb would have exploded had it broken free and struck the ground, but the experience was nonetheless sobering.

L9485 had continued its trials work with various forms of armament and, on 11 April 1942, tested the first double 4,000 lb bomb installation. As with the single 4,000 lb 'block buster', the bomb projected into the airflow, forcing the Halifax to fly with the main bomb doors partly open. While this had no effect on handling qualities, the drag factor was increased and when used operationally, a doped strip of heavy canvas was used to fair the weapon in at the front end. The Lorenz Beam Aerial and the trailing aerial fairlead can be seen upper right.

The trials were carried out with both a single 8,000 lb installation and a double 4,000 lb combination. Despite the bulkiness of the loads, the results showed no measurable adverse effect upon the take-off performance and general handling characteristics. To ease the drag as much as possible, a doped canvas strip was used to cover the end of the bomb and the partly open bomb doors. At 00.25 hrs on 11 April, the first 8,000 lb bomb was dropped – on Essen – by R9487: A of No 76 Squadron. Despite the Halifax being badly damaged by flak, the captain, P/O Renaut, returned to report one very large explosion, with a momentary glow of dull red and orange colour, on the north-west side of the target area. This was but the first of many such attacks with these large bombs.

Knivett was also involved with Leonard Cheshire in an unofficial bombing experiment, fitting a gunsight to a Halifax so that Cheshire could attempt 'precision' dive-bombing. The results were spectacular – but far from promising, because insufficient allowance was made for bomb clearance and relative dive angle. Cheshire returned with damage to the front bulkhead where the bombs had passed through them.

No 102 Squadron operated its Halifaxes for the first time three nights later, 14/15 April, sending two to Dortmund as part of a force of 208 aircraft. Its second night of operations, the 27/28th, brought the squadron's first losses. W7653: A, one of two sent as part of a mixed force of 97 aircraft to Cologne was shot down on the outward leg by Oblt Reinhold Eckardt of the 7./NJG 3, crashing near Hamois, 6 km NNE of Ciney, Belgium. Twelve aircraft had also been sent to Dunkerque to lay mines, the second 102 Squadron loss occurring when R9528 failed to return, shot down by flak in the target area, along with a second flak victim, W1017: T from 10 Squadron which crashed while taking evasive action. The other three Halifax squadrons were also active that night, but against a far more distant target – *Tirpitz* in Trondheim Fjord.

Two of the squadrons, Nos 10 and 35, as on the previous raids, were briefed to attack with mines, but 76 Squadron was armed with conventional bombs and ordered to bomb the defences. Twelve Lancasters were also added to the attacking force this time. Thirty-two Halifaxes set out from their temporary Scottish bases with one aborting soon after take-off. Visibility was slightly better on this occasion but so also were the defences, active and passive. Several aircraft later reported dropping their mines from the prescribed 200 ft near the target, but others had their attempts frustrated by the billowing smokescreens. The defences did not have it all their own way and 76 Squadron made a considerable impression on them with its bombing attacks; but no hits were scored on *Tirpitz*. The raid cost four Halifaxes and one Lancaster. W1048: S and W1020: K were lost from 35 Squadron, the former having sustained flak damage which started a fire in the starboard wing. P/O MacIntyre managed to retain control and made a crash-landing and, with the exception of Sgt Stevens who had broken his leg, all evaded capture. No 10 Squadron lost W1041: B, a brand new aircraft which was being flown by 10 Squadron's new commanding officer, W/Cdr D. C. T. Bennett, and W1037: U. Three of the crew evaded capture and escaped into Sweden and Bennett himself was back in command of the squadron five weeks later; by August, he would be commanding several squadrons. W1048 was also to return, albeit 31 years later when it was recovered from the lake at Hocklingen into which it had sunk through the shattered ice of the surface. Regrettably, the Imperial War Museum chose to leave the aircraft unrestored despite its very intact state. It would take others great effort and many years to finally bring two more Halifaxes back to near original condition as a tribute to the design and its crews.

Determined to make maximum use of the force while it was still available, a repeat attack was mounted the following night by a now depleted number of Halifaxes. The operation cost 35 Squadron two of its nine Halifaxes (W1053: G and W7656: P) but the other two squadrons operated without loss. P/O Whyte very nearly became a casualty when his W1057: X sustained heavy flak damage, which caused the flaps to come down. The return journey was made at 110 mph and Whyte was just able to reach Sumburgh on the southern tip of the Shetland Isles.

A fourth Halifax-equipped squadron, No 78, carried out its maiden attack on 29/30 April, as a part of a raid on Ostend while the Main Force, 88-strong, went to Paris to attack the Gnome & Rhône factory. F/O R. Shattock's W7663 left Croft at 21.03 hrs but nothing further was heard from them. No 405 (RCAF) Squadron also joined the Halifax ranks in April as the slow process of conversion began to gather pace. By year's end six more squadrons would be added, Nos 76, 460 (RAAF), 103, 408 (RCAF), 77 and 419 (RCAF).

Despite the success of the Billancourt operation and a series of very well executed raids on Cologne, Rostock and Lübeck during April and May, Bomber Command was still the subject of criticism to those who wished to see it disbanded and its forces dispersed to support the needs of the Army and Navy. The use of *Gee* had greatly aided the accuracy of these raids and the new tactic of concentrating the attack within a short time period had proved most successful, the defences being swamped. Harris decided the time had now come to demonstrate Bomber Command's potential to the full with a display of force greater than any seen before. Three more squadrons had been stood down during April and May to convert to Halifaxes and two of these, Nos 78 and 405 Squadrons, became operational in time to participate in the first of Harris's mammoth raids.

After careful consideration, Cologne was chosen as the target for 1,046 bombers on the night of 30/31 May. The first wave of the attacking force consisted of Gee-equipped Wellingtons and Stirlings of Nos 1 and 3 Groups which acted as 'pathfinders' by using a high percentage of incendiaries to mark the main aiming points. The second wave followed in the next hour, while the third, composed entirely of Halifaxes and Lancasters, attacked during the last 15 minutes of the raid.

One hundred and eighteen Halifaxes, drawn from Nos 10, 35, 76, 102 and 405 Squadrons and 1652 Heavy Conversion Unit (HCU), took part in the raid, which proved to be an outstanding success. It left a deep impression on most crews, a wing commander from 35 Squadron stating in his report: *".... enormous fires burning in the target area, visibility good, no cloud. Bombs dropped in the target area. The whole centre of the town was in flames and dense smoke from the fires reached up to 9,000 ft. The fires were visible from 100 miles after leaving the target area."* A 76 Squadron pilot reported intense opposition at the coast and the defended belt but over the target itself both searchlight and flak appeared to have been put out of action by the previous attacks. Typical of the bomb loads carried by the heavy bombers were those of 76 Squadron, their 21 Halifaxes delivering 61 x 1,000 lb HE bombs, 16,380 x 4 lb incendiaries and 488 x 30 lb incendiaries.

Losses for the operation, wave by wave, made an interesting comparison. The first suffered 4.8%, the second 4.1% and the last, which was the most concentrated, 1.9%. Halifax losses, from all causes, amounted to the remarkably small figure of four. The first to fall was L9605: GV-Y from No 1652 HCU, which contributed no less than 13 Halifaxes to the raid. F/Lt Wright was an experienced pilot but his scratch crew were all on their first operational flight. Just south of the night-fighter airfield at Venlo, a fighter attacked from astern, its first burst shattering the tail unit and damaging the starboard aileron. Wright jettisoned the bomb load and ordered the crew to bale out, just as the fighter attacked again. With the fuel tanks in one wing blazing, the aircraft went into a spin at 15,000 ft and Wright only managed to pull out at 6,000 ft, having seen the air speed indicator hit 400 mph in the process. The aircraft now zoomed uncontrollably, going over in a loop. Then, as it began its second loop, stalled and plunged, Wright managing to bale out at the last minute. Three others also survived.

Indicating just how much work was carried out in unsheltered conditions, this view shows B Mk II, BB194: E of 10 Squadron undergoing servicing with two engine fitters working on the port outer Merlin. On the right are the engine cowlings from one engine, the bottom one showing its interior to the camera with the rear lower cowling to its right. The positioning of the serial number, approximately on the midline of the roundel just forward of the aircraft letter, was highly unusual. This aircraft served first with 10 Squadron and then its Conversion Flight before being passed to 1658 HCU. It was written off on 3 February 1943 after overshooting when landing at Melbourne and was burnt out. (E. C. Darby)

Night-fighters were out in strength and several other Halifax crews later reported determined attacks but Sgt Moore's 10 Squadron Halifax, W1042: T, was less fortunate and was shot down by a night-fighter 16 km SE of Eindhoven. It was probably a collision with a Lancaster of 61 Squadron that brought down W7707: K of No 405 Squadron. However, for 78 Squadron, the cause of the following loss was not in doubt. F/O Foers' W1013 emerged from a rain cloud at 2,000 ft over the English countryside unaware that Hampden P5321: GL-P3 from No 14 OTU, also returning from the raid, was directly underneath. The subsequent impact tore away the Halifax's starboard outer; the starboard inner burst into flames and the two aircraft crashed within two fields of each other at Plantation Farm in Huntingdonshire. Only the Hampden pilot, S/Ldr Falconer, survived from his crew, having been flung clear and able to parachute to safety. Three of the Halifax crew, including Foers, who was badly injured, survived. The cumulonimbus cloud that had masked the Halifax from the Hampden almost claimed another victim, a 78 Squadron Halifax being flown by the new Commanding Officer, W/Cdr Lucas. Caught in the terrible violence within the cloud, Lucas ordered his crew to bale out at 3,000 ft but, unable to reach his own parachute, he was forced to stay at the controls and at less than 1,000 ft he managed to get the aircraft out of its spin. Unsure of his whereabouts and unable to lower the undercarriage or flaps, he eventually made a wheels-up landing at RAF Wittering.

Never one to waste an opportunity, Harris launched two further 1,000-plus raids during the next three weeks. The first of these, on the night of 1/2 June, targeted Essen, the industrial heart of the Ruhr and home of the Krupp factories. A permanent industrial haze, combined with a constantly recurring ground mist, always made this target an extremely difficult one. Accordingly, seven of the 22 Halifaxes from 76 Squadron were briefed to attack the precise aiming point, a large shed in the middle of the Krupp works. Twenty Wellingtons were to pinpoint their position and then release flares to illuminate the entire target area for the fire raisers of the marker force. The remaining 120 Halifaxes were to join the Main Force attack.

The target-marking force had great difficulty finding the aiming point due to haze and a layer of low cloud and results were poor, with bombing scattered over 11 other towns as well; Oberhausen and Duisburg suffered more casualties than Essen, where damage was relatively light. Thirty-one (3.2%) of the attacking force were lost, including nine Halifaxes: No 10 Squadron's L9623: O, which ditched off the Dutch coast, and W1098: W. W1064: J of 76 Squadron which lost its starboard inner engine and was then attacked and shot down over Belgium by Oblt. Heinrich Prinz zu Sayn-Wittgenstein of the III./NJG 2; four crew members survived and two evaded capture to return to England. No 78 Squadron lost three: R9364 crashed into the sea after flak caused rudder stall and a flat spin, W1143: F crashed 25 km (15 miles) SW of Rotterdam and W7698 collided with a German night-fighter at 14,000 ft over Bucholt and crashed at Winterswijk in Holland with three of the crew surviving. No 102 Squadron lost R9529: H, which crashed near Düsseldorf. No 405 Squadron's W7713: T crashed near Krefeld, while No 1652 HCU's R9372: K was shot down approaching the Dutch coast near Ijmuiden, with all the crew surviving.

Thirty-eight Halifaxes returned to Essen the next night, part of a much smaller force of just 195 aircraft, but the results proved just as elusive and bombing was just as scattered, only three high explosives being recorded in Essen for a loss of 14 aircraft, two of them Halifaxes. Both were from 102 Squadron, R9491: N crashing in

the sea off Harwich while the second, R9532: D, lost control on final approach to base, crashed heavily and was written off but the crew survived. Bombing attacks continued at this more usual level of activity until the night of 25/26 June when Harris sent out his third and final (for the time being) mass attack, this time against Bremen.

This third attack, on Bremen, followed much the same lines as the Essen attack with 76 Squadron providing eight Halifaxes for the marker force. The problems of target identification and night-fighter opposition encountered on the Essen attack had been carefully reviewed; Bremen, on the banks of the River Weser, should be clearly distinguishable if the weather co-operated. Compressing the attack into 65 minutes combined with shallow penetration of the night-fighter belt was expected to reduce the casualty figure of 3.2% from the 956 aircraft used against Essen. The assembled force was initially under the 1,000 mark, Bomber Command having only 960 aircraft available from all sources even by once again drawing heavily on the Operational Training Units (OTUs) and HCUs. The final force was the most diverse ever used for an attack and included an additional 102 Wellingtons and Hudsons from Coastal Command, which brought the final figure of aircraft dispatched that night to 1067 and larger than the Cologne force. The hopes for good weather failed and cloud shrouded Bremen throughout the attack. Results, however, were much better than at Essen and the use of *Gee* allowed fires to be started, giving some guide to the other bombers. Results were better than those for the second mass raid with 696 aircraft making confirmed attacks on the city and a rising wind aiding the spread of fires, destroying and damaging over six and a half thousand homes. Nonetheless, damage to industrial areas was less extensive.

Losses, however, were high[15] with 48 aircraft failing to return, four of which were able to ditch just off the English coast with nearly all crew members rescued. This was the heaviest loss of any raid, exactly 5% of the attacking force of which almost half was amongst the crews from the OTUs whose aircraft were older — 23 out of 198 Whitleys and Wellingtons, a loss ratio of 11.2%. Coastal Command lost five. Of the 124 Halifaxes dispatched eight failed to return. No 35 Squadron lost W1105: N to flak near Oldenburg, W7747: G from 76 Squadron was lost without trace, while Uffz Heinz Vinke of the II./NJG 2 shot down 78 Squadron's W1067, which crashed in the Ijsselmeer. No 102 Squadron was again hardest hit, losing V9987: U from its Conversion Flight, R9446: F and W7654: Q were presumed to have been lost over the sea, while W7759: L was lost without trace. F/O Bradbury's DG225: H, one of the four that ditched and the first Halifax loss for No 158 Squadron since converting from Wellingtons, was one of the luckier ones. The aircraft was put down in shallow water less than a mile off Scarborough Pier when its fuel ran out, the extra 200 miles of the round trip and search time at the target being a significant factor.

Three other Halifaxes were lost during preparations for the raid. W1155: U from 10 Squadron and R9482: D from 76 Squadron were lost during air tests and No 76 Conversion Flight lost R9378 to fire caused by part of the incendiary load falling from the aircraft and igniting while being prepared for the operation. These losses were not included in the raid statistics.

It was the Command's worst loss figure for the war to date, but deemed acceptable because of the factors involved. While the results of the three raids varied, their effect was undeniable; Bomber Command had now demonstrated its potential

No 405 was the first of the RCAF squadron to operate the Halifax, re-equipping with B Mk IIs in May 1942 and commencing operations with an attack on Cologne on 30/31 May. W7710: R was among the initial batch of Halifaxes issued to the squadron and was soon adorned with nose artwork; a small cartoon train pulling coaches, with 'Ruhr Valley Express' painted in white letters under the train track. The defences of the Ruhr were a constant reminder of how difficult this target was. Accompanied by W/Cdr Fauquier in 'J-Jig', S/Ldr Thiele flew 'Ruhr Valley Express' on 3 August in one of Bomber Command's fortunately brief experiments with 'cloud cover raids'. W7710 was lost during the raid on Flensburg on 1/2 October 1942 with F/O E.C. Olsen and his crew perishing when it crashed at Liehuus, 6 km from the target and virtually on the German/Danish border. The squadron lost two others that night, W7780: Q in the target area and W7802: T, which crashed at Bohlberg, both crews being killed.

removing anything from a crashed enemy aircraft, this provides an insight into German assessment of what they thought the Halifax possessed in terms of structural and technical innovation at that time.

The mass raids produced an interesting, if unsuccessful, experiment by S/Ldr Cheshire to find a quicker method of getting his squadron airborne. A fighter type take-off was adopted with four Halifaxes in a diamond formation, the experiment taking place on a day when no operations were scheduled. Everything went well until the formation just became airborne and the leading pilot selected bomb doors open instead of undercarriage up, causing the Halifax to lose speed quickly and Cheshire, flying the rearmost aircraft, found himself rapidly approaching its stern. He quickly throttled back and in doing so, his Halifax momentarily touched down on its partly retracted undercarriage. The lead Halifax pulled away almost immediately enabling Cheshire to open up the throttles again, but not before he had bent the undercarriage retraction jacks, jamming the wheels halfway up. The rest of the formation landed safely and Cheshire put his Halifax down on the grass as gently as possible; when Group HQ received the subsequent damage report, they were understandably less than impressed.

With the completion of the three 1,000 bomber raids, the squadrons turned to an intensive campaign against targets in Germany, which received a large proportion of 4,000 lb and 8,000 lb bombs. Carrying bombs of this size produced some very dangerous situations as typified by the experience of W7761: N of 35 Squadron. Over the target, the bomb aimer pressed the release for the two 4,000 lb bombs but the forward lugs on the front one failed to release. Unable to jettison the now precarious load, the pilot was forced to fly back to England with it, but because of the large shift in centre of gravity, the aircraft was very difficult to control and was finally abandoned by the crew near Harrogate. During its final plunge, it rolled onto its back and caught fire, the tenacious bomb being wrenched free in the process to fall within half a mile of the aircraft. The subsequent Court of Inquiry recommended a modification of the emergency release gear.

In contrast with the mass raids of May and June, ten Halifaxes, including two each from Nos 102 and 405 Squadrons, were dispatched to attack Hamburg on 3 August. The attack however, was to take place in daylight using cloud cover to provide an element of surprise.

In view of Hamburg's formidable defences, it was perhaps fortunate that all cloud cover ceased at the Dutch coast and the raid was aborted – albeit with some reluctance by W/Cdr J.E. Fauquier, the C.O. of No 405 Squadron who spent

sufficiently to silence most of its critics. The new tactics used were mostly successful and would be built upon until eventually between 700 and 800 bombers would pass over a target in less than 20 minutes. Despite the losses, crew morale had risen and remained high when Harris decided to cut back on the practice of easing new crews into the night bombing role with an introductory leaflet raid prior to their going on to main operations. In the coming years, this practice would be viewed less favourably by newcomers.

The crossing in and out of Europe frequently fed bombers over Holland and it became a killing ground for German night-fighters for much of the war. An interesting aside developed from this carnage; Hank Volker, a schoolboy at the time, recalls, *"About 1942 the Germans presented a Technical College in our neighbourhood (H.T.S, Kleverlaan, Haarlem) with the remains of a Halifax for study purposes."* Given restrictions on civil populations in occupied countries

W7773 was a standard B Mk II fitted with a C Mk V mid-upper turret with the antenna mast removed and the aerial leads attached to the inner face of each fin. One of a batch produced and delivered between 8 June and 4 August 1942, it was being test-flown by F/Lt R. Talbot, Handley Page's Chief Test Pilot when photographed, probably around the middle of July. The bulky asbestos exhaust shrouds introduced after testing on L9485 was completed at the A&AEE are clearly visible in this photograph. Their unpainted state emphasises their bulkiness and possibly suggests that they were a recent addition into the production cycle. Along with W7774, W7775 and W7776, this Halifax was issued to 138 (SD) Squadron. It was lost on an SOE flight into Poland – an arms drop and insertion of three Polish Army agents on 29/30 October 1942. The International Red Cross later confirmed that P/O F. Pantowski and his crew had all perished when the Halifax was shot down between Helleren and Refsland in southern Norway. (Rolls-Royce)

90 minutes cruising up and down the coast waiting for cloud to increase before eventually abandoning the operation. Eventually this type of raid was left to the Mosquito force and the heavies kept for the night assault.

Mainz was attacked for the first time on 11/12 August by 154 aircraft, 25 of them Halifaxes. For No 78 Squadron it was to be a bleak night with four of its Halifaxes lost. WO2 W. Lunan RCAF was flying W1061; coned by searchlights in the target area it was severely damaged by flak, which destroyed both port engines and wounded several of the crew. Subsequently attacked by a night-fighter it crashed at Wommelgen, near Antwerp with five of the crew surviving. Lunan was not amongst them but four evaded capture thanks to the Dutch underground. Flt/Sgt J. Fleetwood-May's W1233 was lost without trace, presumed down in the sea while F/O D. Kingston's W1245: B was brought down near Méan, 18 km north-east of Ciney, Belgium with two crew members surviving to become POWs.

Pat Kimber, flying in W1115, was among the crews lost that night, his Halifax crashing at Igstadt, 5km east of Wiesbaden, killing Sergeants J. Peart and J. Mitchell RCAF, the mid-upper and rear gunners.

"We were shot down by flak, after we had bombed, somewhere near the target area. We were trying to unload one bomb, which was hung up. Fortunately, when we were hit the aircraft did not dive so that all five of us up front got out safely. The rear gunner baled out but was killed as he landed, hitting the side of a bridge. The mid-upper went down with the plane.

"Of the six aircraft sent out by No 78 Squadron, one returned early and four were lost (W1061, W1115, W1233 and W1245: B). Apart from our five, a rear gunner from another survived, and a wireless operator from a third managed to escape[16]*. We culled the information from subsequent POWs. The squadron were given a week's survivors' leave, we heard. Our initial reception on the ground, two of us were brought into a village police station, was quite good. We were a nine-day wonder. Four Luftwaffe guards then escorted us by bus, train and tram to the internment camp at Oberusel. On Wiesbaden station the situation was rather ugly, but the guards were conscious of their orders and protected us with hands on revolvers. On the tram ride we went through Mainz and saw the results of the bombing (or at least some of it)."*

A fifth Halifax, W7748: D from 405 Squadron was brought down at Duisberg-Nuenkamp. An additional Halifax was also lost on minor operations, 16 aircraft going to Le Havre, from which 35 Squadron's W1242: G failed to return. A second attack carried out the next night was equally successful, again doing much damage, but Mainz would not be targeted for another large-scale raid until 1944.

The success of the *ab initio* target-finding techniques used initially during the Billancourt raid on 3/4 March had continued to grow with Bomber Command using raid leaders to try and improve target finding. This had led to the suggestion of gathering the experienced crews charged with such duties into a cohesive single force to lead the main bomber force. The concept was presented to Harris when he first took command but he dismissed it, as he strongly opposed the formation of an elite force, preferring instead for each squadron to retain its experienced crews as support for the newer ones. An additional suggestion that six squadrons be grouped in close proximity so that they could exchange ideas on target-finding tactics was also refused. After many delays over the summer months, on 11 August 1942 Harris received a direct order from Sir Charles Portal[17] to form a special force of squadrons to help Bomber Command find its targets. Harris had no choice but to comply and after refusing the title 'Target Finding Force' agreed to 'Pathfinder Force' (PFF) instead. The squadrons were to be selected from each bomber group; the final selection came from just three: Nos 7 and 156 from No 3 Group (Stirlings and Wellingtons), 35 Squadron from No 4 Group (Halifaxes) and 83 Squadron from No 5 Group (Lancasters).

By 15 August, the four squadrons were at Graveley, Oakington, Warboys and Wyton. Already at Wyton and contrary to published reports, 109 Squadron was not initially part of the new force although that would change when it replaced its Wellingtons with *Oboe*-equipped D.H. Mosquitoes. Determined not to lose a moment of available bomber time, Harris ordered the new force to be ready for operations on the evening of 17 August. While he may have opposed the force, he fought to have its members promoted by one rank while they remained active to compensate for the higher danger level. The force did not have Group status, working instead directly under the planning staff at Bomber Command HQ, with orders passed via No 3 Group – an arrangement that lasted only a short time. G/Capt D. C. T. Bennett, whom Harris personally admired, was appointed to the overall command of the squadrons, a position he would retain until the end of the war. Officially, five squadrons were beyond the command rank of a Group Captain and the force remained under direct control of Harris. However, it remained a 'Cinderella' force for some time, having little power to gain the necessary supplies and manpower that it required, while the expectation that superior crews would have been chosen over others had been watered down as entire units had been transferred. Nevertheless, Bennett, like Harris, was not to be stopped.

As described in the text, W1245: B had only been with 78 Squadron for about a month when it became one of four that failed to return from the Mainz attack on 11/12 August 1942. It was shot down near Méan, Belgium with only two of the crew, Sgt J. Stewart and Sgt R. Kendall RCAF, surviving. (via P. Kimber)

With no specialised equipment and still trying to formulate techniques, the task was difficult enough, but it also came at a time when the German defences were forcing the bombers higher and higher and deception tactics were increasing. The first operation for the force came with an attack on Flensburg on 18/19 August with 31 crews from 7, 35, 83 and 156 Squadrons being sent to mark the target for 87 bombers. Unfortunately, forecast winds proved inaccurate and the bombing drifted north into part of Denmark. From the force dispatched, two Wellingtons, a Stirling and a single Halifax, W1226: J of 35 Squadron, failed to return. Sergeant J. W. Smith's crew gained the unenviable distinction of being the first loss of the new Pathfinder Force. Fortunately all baled out safely to become POWs.

The attack on Nuremberg by 159 aircraft on 28/29 August saw participating crews ordered to attack from as low an altitude as possible. The fledgling Pathfinders found their aiming point and marked it with great accuracy, using on trial for the first time a new marking device known as 'Target Indicators'. This initial experiment marked the start of a series of refinements that would eventually become very sophisticated.

Adapted from 250 lb bomb-casings, the new markers were filled with 60, 12 inch-long, pyrotechnic candles available in three colours: red, green and yellow. The candles, each with their own igniter, were ejected from the casing, the ejection height being controlled by a barometric fuse in the nose of the bomb casing. Each candle burned for three minutes and the pattern of the spread was approximately 100 yards in diameter. Having proven their worth they were approved for production, their first full-time operational use being the attack on Berlin on the night of 16/17 January 1943.

Main Force crews reported a very successful attack but post raid reporting from the city claimed that only about 50 had actually bombed the target. Losses were high at 15.1% with 20 falling to flak and night-fighters, a further four being lost to crashes during take-off or on landing following the operation. Of these losses, three were Halifaxes, two Pathfinders from 35 Squadron; Sgt D. John's crew were all killed when W7676: P was hit by flak and crashed into the Westerschelde off the Dutch coast; and P/O F. Taylor's W7700: C, came down near Montcornet north-east of Laon, also killing all on board. The third, Sgt H. R. Dryhurst's BB214 from No 103 Squadron, was shot down by a night-fighter with him and two of his crew surviving.

A second attack carried out that night on Saarbrücken was an experimental one, the Pathfinders not being used for the force of 71 Wellingtons, 24 Halifaxes, 17 Hampdens and a single Stirling. With the moon four-fifths full and the target just inside Germany and relatively undefended, it was thought that the heavier raid on Nuremberg would draw off any of the night-fighters. It was a mistaken assumption. Bombing was widely scattered and four Hampdens, a Wellington and two Halifaxes failed to return, No 78 Squadron losing Sgt J. Marshall and his crew when W7809 crashed south-east of Brussels, and three surviving from WO1 R. Telfer's crew when BB204 of 103 Squadron was attacked by a night-fighter at 12,000 ft over Ostend and set on fire, Hptm Wilhelm Herget of the II./NJG 4 claiming the kill. A third Halifax from 102 Squadron encountered severe icing, forcing it lower where flak near Ostend shot away the port aileron and punctured the No 5 tank. One of the crew, Sgt W. Storey, was badly wounded by flak splinters and died shortly after W/O F. Schaw crash-landed W7712: S[18] at Honington.

Saarbrücken was attacked again on 1/2 September by 231 aircraft, but this time Pathfinders were used and marked what they thought was the town. Main Force crews delivered a very concentrated attack but unfortunately, the Pathfinders had marked Saarlouis, some 13 miles to the north-west and situated on a similar bend in the River Saar. P/O H. Sherwood was killed when W1244: D from 76 Squadron was shot down south of Woumen, Belgium by Hptm Wilhelm Herget, but Sherwood's crew of six survived to become POWs. P/O K. Stinsons and his crew

Above and opposite page top: This fine air-to-air study of W7676: P illustrates all the features of the B Mk II and retrospectively what would be termed a Series I Halifax. Two dorsal escape hatches were now standard, positioned between the rear of the D/F loop and the front of the bulky mid-upper turret and by the time W7676 appeared around April 1942 the beam gun hatches had been eliminated from the production jigs. Positioning of the forward radio mast, offset to port, is more clearly shown in this view; the rear mast having been deleted and the aerials slung to the inside face of each fin. The demarcation line between the upper and lower camouflage colours had now reached a point of refinement after the variations of the first year of production. The square red marking on the port wing was the sealing tape around the stowage for the main dinghy, which could be released from within the aircraft if the aircraft had to ditch – assuming it did so safely. The linear effect produced by air pressure along the rear part of the fuselage is apparent and the serial numbers, now applied in decal form on Halifaxes, occasionally produced a slight, oblong sheen under certain lighting conditions, making them difficult to read. The large 'rams horn' style of exhausts produced a very visible bright exhaust and would become the focal point of much discussion and future development time. Produced at the end of April, W7676 failed to return from Nuremberg on 29 August, one of two from 35 Squadron lost that night, Sgt D. John and crew perishing when it crashed near Westerschelde, off Zeeland after being hit by flak. The squadron's second loss, W7700: C, crashed near Montcornet, north-east of Laon, killing all of P/O F. Taylor's crew.

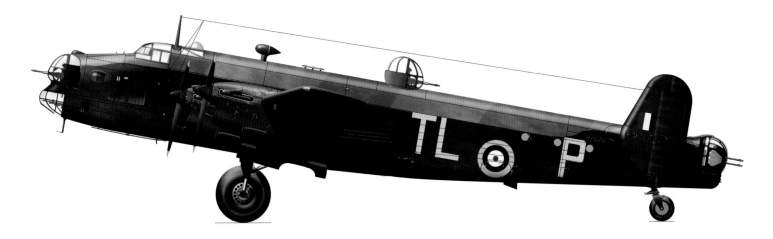

Handley Page Halifax, B Mk I Series II
W7676: P of 35 Squadron was lost on the night of 29 August whilst on a raid to Nuremberg.

escaped injury when their 102 Squadron Halifax developed a serious glycol leak in the starboard outer during the return flight; before Stinson could make an emergency landing the remaining three engines cut, forcing him to crash-land W1248: O seven miles from York. Sergeant N. MacKenzie however, was not so fortunate. He had only been airborne 41 minutes when the port outer engine caught fire as they were crossing the east coast. Although the blaze was brought under control, the port wing began to fail and MacKenzie ordered the crew to bale out

before the Halifax plunged into the sea off Skegness; only three of the crew survived. Additionally, a Lancaster, Wellington and Stirling failed to return with a further two Wellingtons lost in crash-landings on their return.

On the night of 4/5 September, a new Pathfinder technique was tried for an attack on Bremen by a force of 251 aircraft with the aircraft of the PFF split into three specific sections. The 'Illuminators' would use white flares to illuminate the area, the 'Visual Markers' would drop coloured flares when and if they identified the

J. Hartshorn's W1167: J of 102 Squadron overshot the Pocklington runway, stalled and crashed, he and his crew fortunately surviving. A decoy fire had been lit some distance from Kiel and the flak batteries had initially held their fire to aid the deception leading almost half of the attacking force to drop their loads on open countryside. Even so, the remainder bombed Kiel and caused wide-ranging damage. None of the Pathfinders from 35 Squadron was lost.

The sixth Halifax squadron to be formed, No 103, was also part of the attacking force that night. Its career with Halifaxes however, was as short as its operational activity was intense. Commencing operations on 1 September, it attacked 14 major targets in Germany and Italy before its last Halifax operation on 25 October. Under the new policy of concentrating aircraft types into Groups for maintenance and logistic purposes, this lone Halifax squadron of No 1 Group then converted to Lancasters. The tenacity of its crews is exemplified by S/Ldr C. Saxelby's experience in W1219 during the costly raid on Nuremberg on 28/29 August. During

aiming point and the 'Backers-Up' would drop all-incendiary bomb loads onto the coloured flares. This arrangement would form the basis of most future PFF marking techniques with specifically designed pyrotechnic target markers and various electronic aids being added as they were developed. The attack was highly successful with clear weather aiding the Main Force crews as well as those of the PFF. Twelve aircraft were lost but this was deemed a satisfactory ratio for the damage inflicted. When all of the factors worked well results could be extremely good but such odds were rare, and the PFF would have its continuing failures, as both techniques and equipment were refined. One such example was the 8/9 September attack against Frankfurt when PFF crews could not locate its position accurately, with most bombs falling to the south-west of the city, spreading back to Rüsselsheim some 25 km (15.5 miles) away, producing little damage for a loss of 2.8% of the 249 bombers involved.

Two nights later, the attack on Düsseldorf on 10/11 September saw the PFF employ a new target-marking weapon. Christened 'Pink Pansy', it was based on a 4,000 lb bomb casing filled with pyrotechnic material that burnt with a reddish glow and would become a standard weapon in the PFF inventory. Reports from crews of the 479 aircraft taking part in the attack were enthusiastic, a local report confirming the extensive damage caused to most of the city; 33 of the attacking force failed to return.

And so the pattern continued, some good results and some bad and occasionally, some with indifferent bombing as the PFF crews refined their skills. The weather was now becoming a more significant factor; on 13/14 October twelve PFF Halifaxes were assigned to the attack on Kiel – five as 'Finders' to lay sticks of marker flares across the target area or, if the aiming point was definitely identified, to act as 'Illuminators' and to drop their flares over the aiming point; three, as 'Illuminators', to light the target area from zero hour-plus one to 17 minutes; and the remaining four carried five 1,000 lb GP bombs and were to attack with the 288-strong force. Sixty-six other Halifaxes took part in the raid, which cost 15 Halifaxes, Lancasters, Stirlings and Wellingtons, eight to enemy action and the remainder to crashes back in England.

No 10 Squadron's W7870: G was lost without trace, W7766: H of 158 Squadron was badly damaged by flak over the Selenter See, east of Kiel, but Sgt W. McAlpine nursed the Halifax back to base, crash-landing just beyond the East Moor airfield boundary. One of the crew later succumbed to his injuries. Forced to return early because of serious problems with the radio and starboard inner engine, Flt/Sgt

the first bombing run, Saxelby's bomb aimer clearly identified the aiming point and pressed the bomb release but no bombs were released. It was then discovered that the bomb doors had not opened and the crew spent some 13 minutes outside the target area while the doors were pumped open by hand. A second bombing run was made at 8,200 ft and all the bombs released – or so it was thought but a visual check to be certain showed a single 1,000 lb bomb still in the racks which the navigator, putting his hand through the inspection hole in the bomb bay floor, eventually released manually. A further 20 minutes was then spent trying to close the bomb doors but just as the pilot reported them shut, the gauge blew off the top of the hydraulic accumulator, partly blinding the wireless operator and covering the other two crew members with oil. Only the rapid response by the flight engineer prevented further loss of oil and the potential for consequent hydraulic failure.

Of the 159 aircraft dispatched to Nuremberg that night, two Halifaxes from 103 Squadron, BB204 and BB214, three Stirlings, four Lancasters and 14 Wellingtons

Caught by the evening light, W7710: R of 405 Squadron RCAF shows off the well-proportioned lines of the Halifax. This was the fully revised configuration of the B Mk II, with mid-upper turret and rear radio mast removed. (RCAF)

The prototype installation of the Dowty lever suspension undercarriage installation on L9520, the B Mk I that served as the test aircraft for the B Mk V version of the Halifax.

failed to return – 14.4% of the attacking force. This figure did not include losses occurring in the UK amongst aircraft returning to their respective airfields. Nuremberg seemed to be a nemesis for Bomber Command, which would return to savage it again.

Just as Bomber Command had striven to increase its efficiency with new aids, so had Germany been building up its defensive system, both passive and active. Before the May 1940 campaign, a string of early-warning *Freya* radar sets had stretched in a line that ran from the Danish to Swiss borders, some 120 km (75 miles) in depth. Its weakness however, was that control was divided between several commands. The fledgling German night-fighter force, initially equipped with Bf 109 Ds (expanded later to include Dornier Do 17 Z-10s, Bf 110s and Junkers Ju 88s), all guided by the rudimentary data provided by *Freya* early-warning radar, had increased its potential. *Freya* information was relayed to the night-fighter pilot and, aided by a skilled ground operator, could bring interception distance down to as little as about 50 m (165 ft). The first successful interception using this system occurred on 2 October 1940 and, by the late summer of 1941, an additional 48 had been recorded. However, slow delivery of *Freya* sets hampered the effectiveness.

On 17 July 1940, General Josef Kammhuber had assumed control of tactical development and deployment of the night defence system; three days later the I./NJG 1 had been formed with 23 Bf 110s and was rapidly followed by the formation of the II. Gruppe equipped with 20 Ju 88 C-6s. In October, three night-fighter zones were established around the Zuider-Zee and Rhine estuary; each was 90 km (56 mls) long by 197.14 km (122.5 mls) in depth and lay along Bomber Command's approach routes to the Ruhr. A line of searchlight sites was also placed across the approaches used by British bombers entering Germany that extended from Liège in Belgium north-eastward to the Danish border with Jutland. Night-fighters and flak batteries operated in the dark area extending from the coastline back to the searchlight line, using ground control information to make interceptions. The difficulty was that German aircraft carried no form of Identification Friend or Foe (IFF) equipment, making interpretation of data by radar personnel difficult; and the early warning Würzburg sets had a limited range, only about 30 km (19 mls).

The illuminated belt exposed the bombers in a flak-free zone for approximately two minutes, during which time night-fighters could make a visual contact and attack before the bombers then slipped into the dark region beyond. The small amount of time proved to be the weakness as it was rarely long enough for a successful interception. The top speed of the Bf 110 C and D models was also less than that of the bombers, and bomber crews negated the process to some degree by flying around the end of the line, or diving to gather speed before reaching the illuminated zone, then speeding through it before climbing into the darkness on the other side. In the summer of 1941 Würzburg-Riese sets, with a range of about 80 km (50 mls) entered production and deliveries started in the autumn, which helped with earlier warning. The extent and depth of the coverage of the line was

extended in stages and by the closing months of 1942 it stretched from south of Paris to northern Denmark.

* * *

In October 1942, a second RCAF squadron, No 408, converted to Halifaxes, but Halifaxes with a difference. In late 1941, the Ministry of Aircraft Production had expressed doubts about the continued supply of the imposing British Messier undercarriage units being able to keep pace with the expanding Halifax production. Tests were then made to see if it would be possible to adapt a Dowty lever suspension undercarriage for use in its place, using L9520, a B Mk I that had been set aside for this purpose. Fitting the Dowty undercarriage required some redesign of the existing hydraulic system but otherwise the conversion was fairly straightforward. Tests carried out in January 1942 showed the new undercarriage to be superior in certain respects to the Messier type. Its main advantage was smoother operation over uneven ground, improving handling during take-off. This change in design resulted in a change in designation to B Mk V and allotted the Company type number HP63. In all other respects, the type was identical with the B Mk II series. Despite its slim proportions the Dowty undercarriage and its associated hydraulic system was heavier than the British Messier installation. The latter's bulk was deceptive, the large hollow box housing acting as a strengthener to the undercarriage elements. It was one of the largest magnesium castings in regular production and weighed in at 260 lbs.

Tail wheel shimmy, a long-standing problem with the Halifax, had appeared during the crosswind landing tests. Accordingly, a converted Dowty tail wheel unit was fitted to L9520 and was tested a few days later but did not entirely eliminate the problem. However, the results did recommend that further anti-shimmy damping be provided. This recommendation was dealt with immediately, a new damping device being manufactured and fitted to both production and existing service aircraft within the space of two months.

Production of the B Mk V was handled by just two firms, Rootes Securities Ltd and Fairey Aviation, the first production aircraft, DG231, leaving Rootes' factory on 12 August 1942 with the first from Fairey, DJ980, following on 27 October. Production would continue at both plants until October 1943, by which time a new version of Halifax had entered the production cycle. With few exceptions, nearly the entire initial batch from Rootes went to No 408 Squadron, RCAF, while the first part of Fairey's production batch went to No 77 Squadron.

No 408 Squadron received its first two B Mk V Halifaxes on 11 October and by the end of the month had thirteen on charge, but lost DG238: Q on 9 November when it crashed near Hornby during a fighter affiliation exercise. However, the squadron was not to retain its B Mk Vs for long, an order for their replacement with B Mk IIs being received on 30 November. Twelve of the B Mk Vs were ferried to 18 MU, Dumfries, where they were to be modified to a new standard – for some obscure reason a single B Mk V remained on 408 Squadron's charge for several months. The withdrawal of the B Mk Vs was only a temporary measure and they would reappear within the space of a few months, but in modified form.

The origin of the modifications lay in a general review of the Halifax's performance made during the autumn of 1942 which revealed, in the words of the official report, 4. *". . that deterioration in performance of the Halifax II aircraft, consequent upon progressive application of external equipment, has augmented to such an extent that the aircraft has become incapable of meeting concurrently the operational requirements of both high loading and high-altitude cruising."* If somewhat verbose, the meaning was still quite clear – the situation was critical.

Reasons for this fall-off in performance were multiple. Since the introduction of the B Mk II Halifax into service, engine power had remained static while weight had crept steadily upwards due to constant additions to internal equipment and the airframe, such as the bulky C Mk V turret. Attempts had been made to increase the performance by a series of trials with different types of propeller, carried out between February and April 1942, on R9387, W1008 and L9515. A second round of tests were conducted on W1009 between March and April, using Rotol R.S. 5/18 propellers but with no better results; all failed to produce any major improvement. The dorsal turret was removed from W1008 for some tests and results showed that the turret reduced top speed by 2 to 3% (5 to 7 mph).

During the early months of 1942, three major changes had been made to the external condition of the Halifaxes then in service. The installation of large asbestos tunnel shrouds over the engine exhausts, introduction of RDM 2A special rough night black finish on the sides and under surfaces of the aircraft, and the regular operational carriage of two 4,000 lb bombs with the bomb doors only partly closed. Between August and October a series of other trials were performed and the results have already been stated above. However, the details are worthy of closer scrutiny. Systematic tests were begun in August using W7801 to measure the effects of flying with large bombs and partly open doors, and the large flame damping exhaust shrouds, 'elephants ears' (as the asbestos shrouds were called in some reports). Results confirmed that the aircraft could no longer be operated within the present weak mixture cruising limitations at altitude, requiring the use of the F.S. gear supercharger setting.

During the same month a fully equipped operational B Mk II aircraft from No 78 Squadron, DG221: A, manufactured by Rootes Securities early in April, was also thoroughly flight-tested and examined. Operational aircraft had a harder life than test aircraft and the rationale was that the former were more representative of

Subject of the official investigation into declining performance, DG221: A was a fully equipped and operational B Mk II of 78 Squadron which, manufactured early in April 1942, had completed ten operations when selected for testing at the A&AEE in August of that year. The bulky exhaust shrouds had been removed when these photographs were taken. It was returned to 78 Squadron and then passed to I658 HCU, finally being written-off in a landing accident when the undercarriage collapsed at Riccall on 30 November 1943.

current Halifax conditions. This was borne out as it was found to have some small additional items of equipment and showed evidence of bad workmanship and poor servicing. In addition, it had a particularly rough coat of RDM 2A black finish[19].

This aircraft, DG221, was test-flown with and without the large asbestos tunnel shrouds and the airflow behind these examined with the aid of wool tufts. Results showed excessively turbulent flow over the inboard engine nacelles and wing section, causing considerable vibration of the wing trailing edge. In addition, the aircraft showed a marked lack of directional stability. Take-off tests were made without the shrouds fitted, at an a.u.w of 60,500 lb and ground runs lasting from 33 to 37 seconds were recorded. After fitting the shrouds, the take-off became critical, the final test run taking 42.5 seconds, and the aerodrome boundary being cleared with difficulty only after two previous attempts to become airborne.

In an effort to regain some of the lost performance, in collaboration with a Handley Page representative, further tests were made on another operational aircraft. Accordingly, a B Mk II, W7776, from 138 Special Duties (SD) Squadron was chosen and subjected to a clean-up process. On arriving at A&AEE, the front turret was removed and faired in, Tollerton Aircraft Services [20] manufacturing the new fairing panel, its compound curves requiring rolling equipment and experience with aluminium welding. Additional work and testing was undertaken during August and September, during which time further significant changes were made and progressively tested. The mid-upper turret, one wireless mast, one navigation blister, handrail on top of the fuselage, fuel jettison pipes, fairing in front of the flare chute, barrage balloon cable cutters and ramps, tropical air intakes and their Vokes air cleaners, and the large exhaust shrouds, were all removed. The Kilfrost paste was cleaned off leading edges of fins and tail plane, all engine nacelle and body leaks were sealed and extended radiator shutters fitted to all four engines.

The net gain of these removals was just sufficient to compensate for the speed loss incurred by the use of the RDM 2A finish![21] A new B Mk V, DG237, camouflaged with standard D.T.D 308 finish was flown back to Rootes Securities plant at Speke aerodrome and given an additional, carefully applied, coat of RDM 2A. Results showed that even a careful application of one coat of this rough night finish over the ordinary smooth black finish reduced airspeeds by an average of 4 to 5 mph and increased the time to 20,000 ft by four minutes. While appearing small, such speed losses on operations could be enough to be the deciding factor in some situations. Over an eight-hour journey, the speed loss alone could add 30 to 40 minutes to the flight time, during which time the aircraft could come under attack.

The inadequacy of the radiators to cope with engine temperatures had been amply demonstrated during the preceding months. It had been found necessary to keep the radiator flaps partly or fully open during operational flights, thus causing a speed loss of 9 mph (True) at 15,000 ft which, in turn, affected the operational ceiling of the aircraft. Rolls-Royce suggested increasing the radiator exit area and introducing a cruising boost limit of 6lb/sq in. However, some squadrons had already been applying their own remedial action by cropping the radiator flaps to increase the effective exit area when fully closed.

The results of the trials with W7776 saw a series of immediate proposals put forward embracing the modifications. Further immediate cleaning up of the airframe was to include better sealing of the wing and fuselage bomb doors, removal of the second navigation blister, provision of bomb doors capable of completely enclosing large bombs and fitting of a retractable tail wheel. Long-term modifications provided for the introduction of Merlin 23 or 61 engines and adoption

The fifth production B Mk V from the first batch of the type built by Rootes Securities, DG235, provides a further time frame for the introduction of the asbestos exhaust shrouds. Produced in June 1942, W1245: B, pictured earlier, lacked these shrouds, suggesting an introduction date of late June even though they were retroactively fitted to all Halifaxes over a short period of time. DG235 was issued to 408 Squadron (RCAF) in October, but then had a period of transfers including some time spent on trials work. (Rolls Royce)

of dropped inboard engine nacelles which, although designed for Merlin 61 engines, could also be used for Merlin XX engines.

Results of these trials were sobering in the extreme. In No 4 Group between March and August 1942, 109 Halifaxes had been lost from 1,770 sorties, a 6.2% casualty rate. August had been the worst month with 10.1% losses, and in the light of that, all squadron operations were drastically reduced for a period of three to four weeks while the aircraft were modified. During this period, crews received a welcome rest and underwent additional training. Analysis of the rising casualties among Halifax crews during the Autumn of 1942 had revealed that the number of sorties made before failing to return was directly related to the number of trips made as second pilot before becoming a captain of a crew, countering Harris's premise and subsequent reduction of this extra operational training experience. Statistics showed that those pilots who had done less than three trips as a second pilot only completed an average of two main target trips before being lost; those who had completed six

These two views show W7776, which served as the prototype for what would become B Mk II Series I (Special) Halifaxes. The prototype Tollerton fairing did not include a Perspex window and blanked off the upper half of the fixed lower glazed section. In the side view, removal of both nose and mid-upper turrets distinctly cleaned up the lines of the airframe but there was still more to be done, as recorded in the text, and much that caused the problems was not readily visible. After tests were completed, it returned to 138 (SD) Squadron in its refined aerodynamic form. The triangular projection just forward of the tail wheel was standard for its operational role with 138 (SD) Squadron and prevented the static line becoming entangled in the wheel when an agent or container was dropped by parachute. It was lost on 1/2 October 1942 returning from a Special Duties flight to Poland when, low on fuel, Fl/Sgt S. Klosowski made a forced-landing two miles south-west of Goldsborough in Yorkshire, fortunately without injuring anyone on board.

trips as second pilot averaged eight operations. Consequently, Halifax pilots were given a series of cross-country exercises and two or three mining operations as second pilots before assuming command of a Halifax and crew of their own. It was perhaps cold comfort, but another survey showed that figures for crews who survived being shot down were relatively more favourable for Halifax crews at 29% against 17% for Stirlings and 11% for Lancasters.

At squadron level, modifications were not instituted to a specific pattern which, for many months, resulted in Halifaxes being seen in varying stages of metamorphosis. For instance W7922:L, a 78 Squadron Halifax flown in for

W7922: L was one of the operational B Mk II Series I (Special) Halifaxes selected for testing at Boscombe Down in December 1942. Seen here on a typically misty winter day, it illustrates the interim status that ensued with the Series I (Special) modification programme. The asbestos shrouds were replaced with close-fitting saxophone exhausts, navigation blisters, handrail on the fuselage top, fuel jettison pipes have all been removed as have the balloon cable cutters and ramps between each pair of engines but the four cutters and ramps outboard and inboard of the engines remained, as did the C Mk V mid-upper turret. The engines retained their ice guards and normal air intakes but had their radiator flaps cut back to a chord of 12.5 in. The landing light was retracted and the hole for the retractable tail wheel (locked down on all production aircraft) sealed. The airframe was given a smooth black finish with Kilfrost de-icing paste applied to the leading edges of ailerons, elevators, rudders, and trimmer surfaces. The date of the testing was 18 December and provides a reference as to when the Tollerton fairing reached its final design stage incorporating the horizontal Perspex window and upper section of the original fixed glazing. After testing, it returned to service and later transferred to 102 Squadron where it was destroyed in an accidental fire on 14 February 1943.

examination and testing at Boscombe Down on 18 December had been cleaned up by squadron personnel and had most of the modifications applied to W7776, including the fitting of a Tollerton fairing. It had a considerably improved performance; maximum operational height had been increased slightly, the service ceiling raised by 1,000 ft and the time to 20,000 ft reduced by two minutes. This, however, was not the total benefit possible as it retained the mid-upper turret, some barrage cable cutters, carburettor ice guards and Kilfrost de-icing paste on the leading edges of the control surfaces. This Halifax also was used to test the increased cruising boost limitation of 6 lb/sq in and locked mixture control for its Merlin XX engines as suggested by Rolls-Royce. This greatly improved the cruising capabilities over the height range from 15 to 18,000 ft as well as improving the cruising speed on high supercharger setting by approximately 20 mph up to the full throttle height of 17,400 ft. It also raised maximum operational height to 19,000 ft.

The degree of modification was by no means limited to the official recommendations. No 76 Squadron's dynamic commanding officer, W/Cdr Leonard Cheshire, had done a little extra stripping of his own, amounting to practically everything removable including the armour-plated door of the flight engineer's compartment. Removal of the mid-upper turret was not strictly innovative for some squadrons had already decided that the speed loss caused by its bulky shape did not warrant the additional protection it provided. Most night-fighters attacked from astern and below with the bomber silhouetted against the relatively lighter night sky, and many crews had expressed concern at the vulnerability of this totally blind area beneath the belly of their aircraft. Sergeant G. Coates and LAC F. Layton of 76 Squadron with the enthusiastic backing of W/Cdr Cheshire, produced their own answer to this problem in the form of a Perspex blister, fitted over the ventral well hatch position of W7650 [22].

One recommendation that did not find acceptance was for bulged bomb doors to enclose the 4,000 lb and 8,000 lb High Capacity bombs, which could not be entirely enclosed by the existing bomb door system. The Halifax had a series of bomb bay doors that slid inside each other as they opened but a revised configuration was tested on V9985, the tenth from English Electric's first B Mk II production run. It had been issued to 10 Squadron and as 'V-Victor' had taken part in the daylight *Tirpitz* attack in Aasen Fjord on 30 January 1942 and the subsequent night attack on 30 March and was fully representative of current operational B Mk II Halifaxes. Handley Page had designed a set of bulged doors with fixed streamlined ends and V9985 transferred to A&AEE for them to be fitted. The tests were satisfactory, but the complications versus benefit involved with production

The metamorphosis of the Tollerton fairing may be followed from these two photographs. Like some others, B Mk V Series I (Special) DG235, seen here awaiting delivery from Speke aerodrome, had only a single horizontal window – in this case fitted just above the point where the metal fairing met the horizontal arc of the original Perspex nose structure. Compare this with the posed official photograph of a B Mk II Series I (Special) with two horizontal windows, neither of which is in the same position as on DG235, one set high, the other incorporated into the upper area of the normal fixed glazing. As DG235 was produced before DG249 this points to the retroactive modification of Halifaxes still awaiting delivery from the factory. Allocated to 408 Squadron, DG235 then went to 1659 HCU before returning to the squadron, at least on paper, before being sent to Rolls-Royce for propeller tests. It finished its service life with 1667 HCU and it was struck off charge on 1 November 1945. (Rootes Securities)

A very early production B Mk V Series I (Special), DG249, photographed at Speke aerodrome. It still retained the bulky asbestos exhaust shrouds, tall radio mast and ice guards, C Mk V mid-upper turret, but the Tollerton fairing was identical with the prototype design tested on W7776 in August 1942. Rootes Securities Ltd started producing B Mk Vs with batch DG231 - DG253, which were delivered between 12 August and 11 October 1942, and so judging by this photograph, implementation of the revisions at production centres had taken effect very quickly, possibly by very early September. This may be the first one fitted with the Tollerton fairing modification. (P. Summerton)

V9985: V served with 10 Squadron before being transferred to the A&AEE for use in testing bulged bomb bay doors. The side view shows the extent of the experimental door system with both ends streamlined. The doors reduced drag but were not put into production; the initial order for 50 sets was cancelled, their complication in fitting and removing for changing operational conditions militating against their widespread use – and other refinements were already in hand with the clean-up process that produced the B Mk II Series I (Special) configuration.

eventually weighed against adopting the new design. However, the work was not wasted, as recorded later in this book. (see Chapter 14)

No 77 Squadron had also converted to Halifaxes during October, receiving B Mk II Series I that were soon recalled and replaced with what were now designated as B Mk V Series I (Special) Halifaxes. The production cycle had begun incorporating the recommended changes in October, the revisions producing the suffix 'Series I (Special)'. This designation made retrospective changes to designations seen in some documentation, where the original Mk II and V series were now referred to as Mk II Series I and Mk V Series I, just as the Series II and Series III suffixes had retrospectively produced the Series I designation for the original B Mk I Halifax.

With the introduction of the B Mk II and V Series I (Special) Halifaxes, losses dropped markedly and the type was in time to participate in the offensive in support of *Operation Torch*, the Allied invasion of French North Africa in late 1942. Italian ports were central to reinforcements for Rommel's Afrika Korps forces but only the long autumn and winter nights could provide adequate cover of darkness for such long-range operations. No 5 Group sent 112 Lancasters to Genoa on 22/23 October 1942, accompanied by Pathfinders of the newly created force, tasked with marking targets for Main Force attacks.

On 23/24 October, it was the turn of the rest of the Main Force when 122 aircraft returned to Genoa, 53 of them Halifaxes. No 78 Squadron lost W1018 while 158 Squadron lost W7862: D, which also failed to return. From the latter squadron, Sgt M. Caplan found the defences more accurate than he had anticipated. Having attacked, he was intercepted by two single-engine Italian night-fighters near Turin, which fired several long bursts of cannon fire at DT521: O, damaging the radio equipment and wounding the rear gunner, Sgt M. Danban. The night's light losses, two Halifaxes and a Stirling, were marred by a return flight collision between two aircraft of 102 Squadron landing away at Holme-on-Spalding Moor. W1181: D had

burst a tyre on landing and DT512: O, landing a minute later, collided with it, killing both the pilot, W/Cdr S. Bintley DSO, DFC, and crew member F/O A. Graham.

Milan was next on the target list, first in a daylight operation by Lancasters on 24 October, then again that night by a mixed force of Halifaxes, Stirlings and Wellingtons. The weather, always a threat, was bad and the force was scattered en route with only 39 crews claiming to have attacked the target. Four Wellingtons and two Stirlings failed to return. Italian targets were off the bombing list after that until 6/7 November, when No 5 Group sent 72 Lancasters to Genoa.

After a break, on 7/8 November, a mixed force of 175 aircraft attacked Genoa again, losing six aircraft, among them four Halifaxes. DT515: T of 76 Squadron was hit by flak crossing the French coast on the outbound leg and the crew baled out near Chaumont. No 78 Squadron lost W1063, but only after a major effort on the part of its crew. One engine had failed en route but the crew elected to continue and managed to reach and bomb the target. It was then found impossible to gain enough height to re-cross the Alps and the navigator gave F/Lt A. Dowse, DFC, a course for Gibraltar but it was just too far and Dowse had to ditch the Halifax five miles off Valencia. Rescued by the Spanish, the crew were interned briefly before repatriation to England, via Gibraltar, by early February 1943. The extraordinary tenacity of crews on these long flights was outstanding. Fuel exhaustion was a significant concern during these operations. Fl/Sgt J. Newcombe's crew, from the same squadron, also ended up ditching safely, but this time the Halifax, DT516, came down 65 miles off Newcastle; their return was swifter than Dowse and his crew. P/O D. Beveridge's 158 Squadron aircraft, W1253: M also ran low on fuel and ditched in the River Humber nearly eleven hours after taking off. Two of the crew baled out before ditching but drowned and one other was killed in the ditching.

Bomber Command did not return to Genoa again until the night of 15/16 November, the 40 Halifaxes, 27 Lancasters and eleven Stirlings attacking

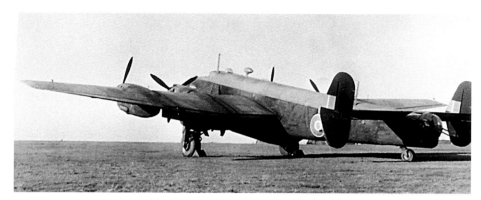

The angle of the light has highlighted the ZA code letters and aircraft letter V (just visible immediately below the vertical line of the rear radio mast) painted out when V9985 was transferred from 10 Squadron to the A&AEE as a test aircraft. It had all the operational features of the standard B Mk IIs then in front line service. After completion of the bulged bomb bay door tests it was retained and used for other test work. It was finally disposed of to No 48 MU at York and struck off charge on 28 February 1944.

Photographed in October 1942, 'M-Mother' a B Mk II of 405 Squadron's B Flight, gets its servicing done as usual – in the open. The tubular frame work stand had adjustable leg sections and two large wheels and when tipped it could be manoeuvred into any position using the large handle and the feet lowered to secure it. They provided three working levels as well as allowing access to the wing upper surfaces; the heights involved were not inconsiderable and a fall usually meant serious injury. Removing large engine panels in strong winds required dexterity and considerable care when standing on such open platforms. The portable A-frame ladder seen on the left was generally used by a single person for minor work while the long tubular frame with two small wheels seen at the front of the photograph was used for guiding the aircraft with the tail wheel when needed.

without loss, but 78 Squadron's DT522: B ran low on fuel and Fl/Sgt R. Martin ordered his crew to bale out near Martlesham Heath, one of the crew unfortunately drowning in the River Debden. A second casualty was the redoubtable P/O Beveridge, who was flying W7859: T. Trying to land at Gatwick airfield on return the aircraft crashed just west of Haywards Heath, fortunately without loss of life. Two members of the crew had been with him just a week previously when he ditched in the Humber. Bomber Command considered he had done enough and he was rested from operations. No 158 Squadron also lost DT558: H, the crew being forced to bale out over Sussex when almost home – fortunately without loss of life.

As can be seen, defences were only part of the danger. W/Cdr B. V. Robinson, DSO, DFC of 35 Squadron located and bombed Turin on the night of 18/19 November, but on reaching the Alps one of the four flares which had failed to release burst into flames causing a fire in the bomb bay. The fire appeared to be spreading and he ordered the crew to bale out but before he had time to leave the aircraft himself, the fire abated and finally extinguished itself so Robinson brought DT488: S home alone, crash-landing at Colerne and receiving a bar to his DFC for his tenacity. Italian radio later reported that his crew were safe and prisoners.

Engine failures were an ever-present threat and W/Cdr W. Fletcher of 158 Squadron lost the starboard engine of W1091: W shortly before bombing Turin.

To complicate matters, 40 x 4 lb incendiaries failed to release. Unable to gain sufficient height to cross the Alps, Fletcher turned the Halifax south-west to the Rhone valley; from there he flew it across France to a point west of Le Havre and then back to base where he landed with visibility down to 500 yards. This effort earned him an immediate DFC and the navigator, Sgt H. Kay and flight engineer, Sgt R. Lewis, each a DFM. Sergeant S. Beneford from the same squadron was not so fortunate; having been hit by flak while homeward bound and about 35 miles south east of Paris, he and his crew were forced to abandon BB209: G over England, the aircraft crashing near Grantham. The crew all baled out safely.

And so the year drew to a close. Turin continued to draw occasional attacks, interspersed with attacks on German targets and mining operations though weather conditions were now severe. The long battle by Bomber Command to keep its strength intact, despite demands for assistance to other services over the preceding three years, was finally to pay off, albeit still subject to the occasional urgent diversion of its forces. In addition, new electronic aids were to flow into its arsenal over the following year and a half.

R9376: D, the fourteenth B Mk II built by Handley Page and delivered at the end of 1941, makes an interesting comparison with the photograph of L9619: E manufactured on the same production line about a month earlier. The two production batches, (L9609 - L9624, delivered between 3 October and 6 December 1941 and R9363 - R9393, delivered between 20 October and 17 January 1942) overlap and the introduction of the C Mk V mid-upper turret occurred during this time, most probably commencing with the R9363-production batch at the beginning of October. Initially, the rearmost radio mast was retained when the mid-upper turret was introduced into the production cycle. Camouflage style remained unchanged but squadron code letters were now marked in red rather than white to provide better concealment during night operations. The engines of the Halifax from which the photograph was taken show the flaking of paintwork that occurred around the front of the engine cowls on some early Halifaxes. R9376 had a mobile existence for a while; starting with 10 Squadron it was loaned briefly to 138 (SD) Squadron, then back to 10 Squadron again before moving to No 10 CF for a while and then back to its parent unit. It lasted almost a year before a propeller failed and broke loose, resulting in a crash-landing near Melbourne on 14 November 1942.

Halifaxes of 35 Squadron prepare for departure for a night sortie. Ground staff stand ready to pull the wheel chocks away once engines have been started while the pilot watches out of his side window as another of the ground staff points to the No 1 engine (starboard outer) indicating ready for start-up. The Halifax taxiing out in the background has beam gun windows and two radio masts with the tip of the rearmost one barely visible. The scalloped division between upper and lower surface camouflage appeared first on the preceding batch of B Mk Is from Handley Page but this very high demarcation line with smaller scallops was characteristic of just part of B Mk IIs of the R9363 to R9540 serial blocks. Upper surface camouflage was now reduced to a strict plan form when viewed from above. The manner in which the company changed camouflage styles during the early period is intriguing and was possibly an ongoing process to achieve the optimum balance between upper and lower surface colouring. As far as can be established, this was the only batch of Halifaxes to use this more refined and distinctive transition style indicating that at least the Halifax in question was a B Mk II Series I. In the distance, 'K-Kitty' stands at its dispersal point. The weather and a scarf around the neck of one of the men in view indicate that the photograph was taken late in the year.

CHAPTER FOUR

FINDING THE TARGET

TESTS to find a suitable replacement for the bulky C Mk V turret were continuing when a Boulton Paul T Mk I turret arrived at Boscombe Down on 22 September 1942 and was fitted to R9436. This was a compact turret mounting two Browning No 2 Mk II 0.5-in machine guns that weighed 1,404 lbs fully equipped. Although a successful series of trials were undertaken during October, a far more promising turret was already under test and the T Mk I did not enter production, the prototype being sent to America instead. This other turret, the Boulton Paul A Mk VIII, was fitted to HR679 for a series of tests. Some eight inches shallower and five inches smaller in diameter than the C Mk V it was equipped with four Browning 0.303-in machine guns, 550 rounds of ammunition for each gun and 7.5 lbs of 12 mm armour plate and weighed only 586 lb fully equipped. As such, it entered the production cycle as Mod 421[1].

Initially, a surplus of Boulton Paul A Mk II turrets, left over from the Defiant turret-fighter production, were modified to this new standard and designated A Mk VIII (Special)[2]. Although the turret required a built-up metal surround for a gun interrupter track, when installed and tested in R9375 during October, it proved most successful. The only drawback was that, until the final production turret became available, it would require the built-up surround as tested on R9436 instead of the usual Boulton Paul electro-mechanical interrupter system to prevent damage to the aircraft. However, this raised track position produced as much drag as the C Mk V turret, the only real advantage being provided by the four rather than two machine guns. By mid 1943, the stock of surplus A Mk II turrets was exhausted and the production A Mk VIII turret began entering the system, its lower position considerably reducing the drag penalty.

At the beginning of 1943, Bomber Command was almost ready to begin a sustained offensive against Germany when the U-boat crisis in the Atlantic forced a temporary diversion of the bomber effort to relieve the situation by attacking the U-boat pens and their facilities in the occupied French ports of Lorient, St Nazaire and La Pallice. Air Marshal Harris believed this to be a gross misuse of his carefully husbanded force because the pens themselves contained all the necessary facilities and were virtually bomb-proof. However, left with little or no choice, Harris dispatched 3,170 sorties between 14 January and 6 April, all of which were concentrated against Lorient and St Nazaire. The two largest attacks, mounted during February, saw 466 aircraft attacking La Pallice on the 13th and 437 targeting St Nazaire on the 28th. During the St Nazaire raid, eight Halifaxes from No 35 Squadron formed part of the attacking force and the old problem of engine overheating manifested itself once more.

S/Ldr Dean's W7877: Q lost its port outer engine at 13,400 ft and despite being forced down gradually to 9,000 ft, the bombing run was continued on three engines. Just after leaving the target area, the starboard inner engine failed and with flames shooting out of the air intakes, the Halifax slowly lost height down to 3,000 ft. As the aircraft continued its flight through heavy cloud and preparations were made for ditching, the English coastline fortunately came into view and a homing was established to Harrowbeer airfield. Unfortunately, its flare path was extremely feeble and Dean, landing halfway along the 1,100ft runway, overshot and collapsed the undercarriage on rough ground where the Halifax finally came to rest without any casualties amongst the crew.

The campaign, comprising 14 raids, cost Bomber Command 38 aircraft with nine others destroyed in accidents over England. Yet, Harris's point had been proven for, despite the destruction of much of the towns of Lorient and St Nazaire, the U-boats pens, their facilities and the U-boats themselves remained virtually unscathed. Even so, this diversification had not prevented the remainder of Harris's forces from being used against Germany in a series of attacks as a prelude to the planned major offensive in March.

For the first time since 1941, Berlin was attacked on 16/17 January 1943. A notoriously difficult and dangerous target and well beyond the range of available navigational aids, including *Oboe*, the Pathfinders, who were to mark the target, had to rely on dead reckoning navigation. Three Lancasters were to drop flares in the

The Boulton Paul T Mk I turret was fitted to R9436 in late September 1942. Armed with a pair of 0.5-in calibre machine guns it promised heavier hitting power and longer range against the cannon-armed Luftwaffe night-fighters. Despite successful trials, the Air Ministry rejected it in favour of the Boulton Paul C Mk VIII fitted with four 0.303-in calibre weapons. This Halifax was converted into Instructional Airframe 4204M in October 1943.

target area two minutes before zero hour, and by their light, five Halifaxes and five Lancasters were to identify the aiming point visually and drop Target Indicators to guide the Main Force. This attack marked the first use of production manufactured Target Indicators which had undergone modification since their trial introduction. At this time, *Oboe* marking had a limitation of five minutes minimum between the attacking aircraft due to the system of control used by the ground stations in England and because of this, the burning time of the bundle required extending. This extension was achieved by restricting the initial burst to just 20 candles with a further 20 following two and a half minutes later and the final 20 five minutes after that[3]. This extended burning time to about seven minutes but reduced the intensity of illumination. To counter German efforts to douse the candles, up to 30 of them were fitted with explosive devices to discourage the effort. Ground Markers backed these up, tripling the area illuminated, and most salvos dropped usually included a Long Burning Target Indicator.

Unbroken cloud covered the route across Europe to within ten miles of Berlin, making navigation extremely difficult; Berlin itself was covered with a thick haze. The 201-strong Main Force attacked, aiming on the Target Indicators with a large portion of the force achieving some very concentrated bombing. No 76 Squadron provided 14 Halifaxes, *"the cream of the squadron"* in the words of their diarist, for this raid and all returned safely. Returning crews reported that the damage done by HE and incendiaries dropped in and around the concentration of Target Indicators was devastating and fires could be seen concentrated over the entire target area, the glow being visible from as far away as Hanover during the return journey. The reports were correct, but the area illuminated so thoroughly by the Target Indicators lay in the Tempelhof district and the remainder of the force bombed a widely spread area of the southern suburbs. A single Lancaster failed to return from this attack.

The next night, 187 bombers returned to Berlin, inexplicably by the same route, both outward and homeward, but results were virtually no better. Unfortunately, the same could not be said for the losses, 25 aircraft, with an additional 30 damaged, almost 12% of the attacking force. This use of the same route had enabled the German night-fighter force to successfully intercept the bomber stream and 21 of the 170-strong Lancaster force were lost to enemy action, with one more crash-landing at its home base on returning. Of the 17 Halifaxes taking part, three were lost, including W7886: C, one of 35 Squadron's target marking force with the remaining two, DT569: C and DT647: P being from 76 Squadron. The experimental use of Lancasters and Halifaxes dropping Target Indicators against Berlin was now suspended pending arrival of a new navigational aid.

Essen received six small visits from Bomber Command during January, but the Hamburg raid on the night of 30/31 January was to be unique[4]. The new *Gee* equipment had made a significant contribution to solving the navigational problems that had beset Bomber Command since the earliest days of the war. Unfortunately, it was singularly a navigational aid and an analysis of bombing errors had pointed out a desperate need for some form of blind bombing aid. As recorded earlier *Oboe*, though a dedicated blind bombing aid required two control stations for each aircraft and required the aircraft to fly straight and level for several minutes during the final stage of the bombing run. The equipment was also 'line of sight', limiting the range and thus targets against which it could be used. It was first used to carry out ground marking[5] for the Pathfinder Force against Düsseldorf on the night of 27/28th. Had this aid not been available, the thin layer of cloud cover over the target could have resulted in failure, but as a result the bombing had been very concentrated for a cost of three Halifaxes and three Lancasters.

The attack on the night of 30/31st was carried out under moonless conditions and poor visibility in the target area made visual identification almost impossible. Six Halifaxes of 35 Squadron, in company with seven Stirlings from 7 Squadron, were to mark the target for the Main Force. Three of 7 Squadron's Stirlings aborted early in the raid due to *H2S* unserviceabilities with 35 Squadron faring little better; W7875 aborted with mechanical failure while W7872, W7873, and W7874 suffered *H2S* failures. However, the remaining two aircraft, W7851 and W7878, succeeded in marking the target using *H2S* and, of equal significance, conducting their navigation solely by its aid.

F/O Brown, pilot of W7851: N, reported afterwards: *"There was thin strato cumulus cloud over the target with tops at 5,000 - 8,000 ft, as a result of which no ground detail could be seen. The target was identified, however, on special equipment and at 0237.30 hrs, four red flares were dropped at 52° 50' North 09° 09' East from 21,000 ft. At 03.04 hrs four green flares were placed as instructed from 20,000 ft followed three minutes later by 16 red/green star flares from the same height. In poor conditions no photograph was attempted and very little was seen."* In fact, the bombing was scattered over a wide area with many bombs falling in the River Elbe's adjacent marshes. Even so, a considerable number of fires were started.

Two further trial raids were carried out in quick succession, Cologne on 2/3 February and Hamburg on the night of the 3/4th. Target markers were dropped on Cologne in cloudy conditions using both *Oboe* and *H2S* but again results were disappointing with the bombing scattered widely across the city. Hamburg received its second attack, this time from 263 aircraft and the first 200-plus attack mounted for more than two weeks; the terrible weather with icing and dense cloud over the North Sea forcing many crews to turn back. Over the target, the Pathfinders were unable to produce concentrated and sustained marking and the bombing was again scattered with results no better than in the previous attack. Nonetheless, the bad weather did not deter the German night-fighter force, the combination of weather and defences claiming four Halifaxes, eight Stirlings, four Wellingtons and a Lancaster, a devastating 6.1% of the attacking force. No 78 Squadron lost W7938: Y while 102 Squadron lost W7921: M, 408 Squadron DT680: D and 419 Squadron DT630: T. One of the 35 Squadron Pathfinders, W7923: D, was hit by flak and suffered undercarriage failure on landing, fortunately without loss of life, but was written-off.

The operational introduction of *H2S*, albeit in small quantities, had occurred at a most opportune moment for a directive had reached Bomber Command HQ on 4 February, which stated the main Allied aims were: *"... Primarily the progressive destruction and dislocation of the German military, industrial and economic system and the undermining of the morale of the German people to a point where their capacity for armed resistance is fatally weakened."* It was accompanied by a selection of targets to be attacked, weather and tactical considerations permitting comprised of U-boat construction yards, the aircraft industry, transport, oil plants and other targets allied to the war industry. In addition, Berlin was to be attacked on occasions when it was likely to have the most effect upon German morale as a whole, or, conversely, whenever it would boost Russian morale. Harris interpreted these instructions in the best interests of his force and its abilities, namely the destruction of the industrial heart of Germany. The time for the first great offensive was not quite right but Bomber Command continued to increase its tempo of attacks and perfect the techniques associated with the new blind bombing aid and the Pathfinder target marking.

There were still minor problems involved as shown by a report from S/Ldr P. Fletcher of 158 Squadron. He was flying W7865: G over Nuremberg on 25/26th February and the Pathfinders were late. *"Within a few moments of the first target indicator markers going down everyone sitting around the target pounced on it and you could see everything going down at once. The yellow flares at Speyer were dropped over a wide area. Weather to and from the target was awful."* Of the 337 bombers sent to attack, nine were lost, amongst them a single Halifax from 158 Squadron, DT668: R, which crashed in Belgium – lower losses than previous attacks.

The success of the system was proven, but it would take time and practice for the full benefit of *H2S* to become completely effective. However, production difficulties

would delay introduction of the new bombing aid in quantity for several months; by the end of May, the maximum number of *H2S*-equipped bombers to operate on any one raid would not exceed eighteen. These problems would eventually be overcome and 840 sets produced by August. Yet, while production was one aspect, fitting the equipment into the aircraft was another; by 12 October only 155 Halifaxes, 225 Lancasters and 70 Stirlings had been equipped and delivered to Bomber Command. During that period, the normal attrition rate had already accounted for 70 Halifaxes, 50 Lancasters and 29 Stirlings but despite these delays, Bomber Command continued its attacks.

By early March, Harris was finally able to open his sustained campaign against Germany; the concentration of forces against specific targets was his mantra. Spring was coming and with it shorter nights, making distant targets like Berlin impractical. The Ruhr was the logical choice; rich in bituminous coal to the extent of 75% of all coal produced in Germany, and the home of the most important heavy industries and metallurgical factories. Its geographical situation was perfect, lying as it did at the hub of the transcontinental road, rail, river and canal routes. It had ready access to major seaports through a network of waterways, but it also lay nearer to England than almost any other part of Germany, a point well appreciated by the Germans who provided it with formidable defences; its notoriety earning it the title of 'Happy Valley' amongst the aircrews.

Bomber Command stood ready to pit its much improved force against those formidable defences, which included a comprehensive early warning radar system of *Freya* and *Würzburg* radars for the tracking and local plotting associated with ground controlled interception techniques. Radio Counter Measures (RCM), in support of Bomber Command, had begun in December 1942 when crews were notified that they were allowed to use their IFF sets to jam the *Würzburg* equipment. To jam the *Freya* sets a device, code-named *Mandrel*[6], was fitted to Bomber Command aircraft, Nos 158 and 408 Squadrons being among the first Halifax units to be so equipped. Thus armed, Bomber Command began the Battle of the Ruhr, as it would become known, on the night of 5/6 March 1943 with an attack on Essen.

This city had been raided many times before, accounting for 10% of Bomber Command's total effort during 1942. F/Lt K. Reynolds of 158 Squadron was flying DT700: S that night, and his description of the attack is most vivid: *"After the first target indicator marker was dropped Essen seemed swamped with Halifaxes. Pathfinder yellow marker was dead on time and the first red target indicator flare burst just after passing over the turning point. Searchlights were in greater numbers than I have ever seen previously. The whole sky leading in to the target was criss-crossed by beams. At first the searchlights were in very large cones and the heavy AA was bursting in the intersections but as the attack developed the searchlights were badly disorganised and useless and the flak less effective. The target was blazing with incendiaries and the flashes from the HEs lighting up the long buildings. I think Krupps really got a pasting."* Photographic reconnaissance later confirmed that some 300 acres of Essen had been severely damaged, the Krupp works suffering some 10% damage, an encouraging start after so many failures. The cost aspect was also encouraging at 3.2%. Of the 442 aircraft dispatched, 4 Lancasters, 4 Wellingtons, 3 Stirlings and 3 Halifaxes were lost. Of the Halifaxes, BB282: R of 76 Squadron was lost without trace, HR687 of 78 Squadron was shot down by Hptm. H. Lütje of the III/NJG 1 and DT646:C of 419 Squadron was hit by flak over the target and then attacked by a night-fighter, all but one of P/O R. Graham's crew becoming POWs.

Harris sent a message of congratulations to all crews, which included a reference to *"... giving it a second barrel without pause."* However the old enemy, weather, prevented this follow-up blow for a week, but when it did fall on the night of the 12/13th, it was equally devastating. The German defences were as tenacious as ever and 23.5% of the 457 bombers failed to return. Crews however were enthusiastic about the success of the raid, 58 Squadron's diarist recording, *"It is reckoned by experienced members of the crew that this was the most damaging raid that they had ever seen."* Later bomb damage assessment reports estimated that 27% of the Krupp factory complex had been badly damaged.

Although not actually lying within the confines of the Ruhr Valley, Nuremberg, Stuttgart and Munich in southern Germany were, along with similar locations, included on the target list. This achieved a wider dispersal of the German defences and thus indirectly aided the Ruhr offensive. No 77 Squadron, recently converted to Halifaxes, suffered its first casualties during one of these raids when JB795: H and DT734: J failed to return from Munich on 9/10 March; the latter had been forced back with glycol problems and fell to the guns of a night-fighter over Belgium. All but one of S/L R. Sage's crew survived, with three evading capture.

Stuttgart was the target the next night but it was a failure, the bombing force arriving late and with the Germans employing dummy target markers for the first time to mislead crews, most of the bombs fell in open country and the fringe suburbs of nearby towns; the game of countermeasuring the new Pathfinder tactics had begun in earnest.

Of the 314 aircraft dispatched, 11 failed to return including six from the 109-strong Halifax force, most to night-fighters and one, DT492: H of 76 Squadron, was abandoned by its crew over Sussex on return. Of the remaining two, 158 Squadron's DT748: J and 405 Squadron's W7803: B crashed in France and three from 405 Squadron fell victim to night-fighters. BB212: U was shot down en route to the target with all but one of the crew surviving; BB250: E reached the target but fell to the guns of a night-fighter and crashed at Mondrepuis, France. (Oddly, there were eight crew members on board – two were killed, five evaded capture and one was taken

No 10 Squadron's BB324: X, photographed in April after completing four sorties, was typical of a B Mk II Series I (Special) 'cleaned up' at squadron level. This was one of the production aircraft tested at A&AEE around mid-February and at which time it still had its C Mk V mid-upper turret. Below the cockpit is a cartoon of a terrier dog's head wearing an RN sailor's cap, with 'Wings For Victory' marked below in white. Produced by L&PTB around mid February 1943, it had probably left the production line with the Tollerton fairing fitted but retaining its mid-upper turret. The somewhat rough repainting of the panel fitted over the resulting aperture was indicative of a squadron change, rather than a factory one, and its twin landing light remained locked down.
(E. Darby)

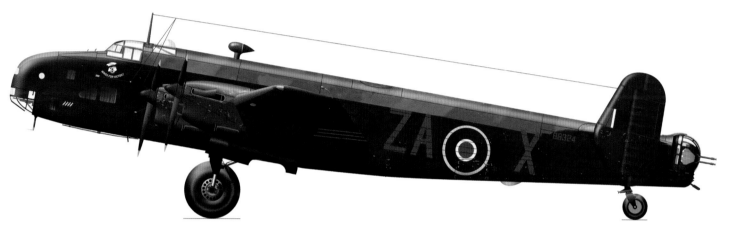

Handley Page Halifax, B Mk II Series I (Special)
BB324: X, No 10 Squadron.

In this view of BB324, the fuel jettison pipes have been removed from beneath the wings and a small Perspex blister (Modification 639B) added below the rear fuselage. The dipole aerial protruding below and aft of the rear turret (Mod 385) was for the Monica equipment that warned of approaching night-fighters. Unfortunately, it did not discriminate well enough to distinguish between other bombers in the bomber stream and its almost continuous series of warning pips in the pilot's headphones often led to it being switched off – perhaps fortunately. Unknown to Bomber Command, from the late autumn of 1943 the Luftwaffe had introduced FuG 227 into the night battles; this could home into the emissions from Monica at a range of 100 km and under ideal conditions sometimes twice that distance. Once locked on, no matter what manoeuvres the bomber carried out, the night-fighter could keep contact, ultimately closing in for an attack. BB324 started service with 76 Squadron before passing to 10 Squadron; it did not enjoy a long life, failing to return from the Mülheim attack of 22/23 June 1943, Sgt R. Pinkerton and his crew all perishing when their aircraft was shot down by a night-fighter over the North Sea 25 km west of The Hague. (E. C. Darby)

prisoner). The fourth, DT745: V was shot down south-west of Châlons-sur-Marne and again eight were on board, all escaping by parachute. Two evaded capture, one of them, Sgt P. Dymtruk RCAF joining up with the Maquis only to lose his life in a ground action on 9 December.

Essen was attacked next, on the night of the 12/13th at a cost of 23 aircraft from the 457 sent, seven of them Halifaxes. Weather conditions then restricted major operations until the 22/23rd when 357 aircraft were sent to attack St Nazaire, losing a single Lancaster. Duisburg was attacked on the 26/27th by a force of 455 aircraft. Sergeant G. Vinish, the pilot of DT784, later made the following report, which is

interesting as an example of the gradually developing use of the Pathfinder techniques: *"Bombed primary target at 02.22 hrs from 19,000 ft on red target marker and a timed run from yellow markers. Visibility fair and bombs were thought to have fallen near red target marker. A good number of fires noted in the target area. Moderate flak encountered but six groups of searchlights were operating in and around Duisburg."*

A single Halifax, W7931: J from 78 Squadron, was among the six bombers that failed to return. The single Mosquito loss, DK318: B of 109 Squadron, was one of the *Oboe*-equipped Pathfinder Force, the first of its type to be lost.

Berlin had received a heavy attack on 1/2 March that resulted in concentrated bombing and an apparent saturation of the enemy defences. In view of this result, the raid by 396 aircraft of 27/28 March was something of an anti-climax, most bombs falling in open country and a large proportion failing to detonate. The Pathfinders had established two separate marked areas, but both were well short of the city and damage was relatively light. Some crews found the target area and received a very warm reception by the defences. Coned by searchlights over the target for eight minutes, Sgt C. Surgey of 158 Squadron released his bombs and took violent evasive action during which flak near-miss caused W1221: H to roll on its back and enter a spin. Although the engines cut, he was able to regain control and restarted them at 7,000 ft. During the spin, the escape hatch had opened and sundry equipment and personal effects, including the wireless operator's watch and silk gloves and the bomb aimer's gloves were lost. Perhaps the most keenly felt loss was the contents of the smashed thermos flasks. Nine aircraft were lost, four of them Halifaxes; one W7907: M, a 35 Squadron Pathfinder machine, was a victim of the intense flak. HR753: B of 158 Squadron was brought down by flak in the south-west suburbs of Bremen with five of the crew surviving while 408 Squadron lost BB332: H and 419 Squadron lost DT634: E. The former was also a victim of flak near Hanover, but even with both port engines dead and fuel tanks holed, Sgt R. Batchelor managed to nurse the crippled machine to Sweden where it crash-landed at Blindberg. The crew survived and although temporarily interned, were back in England in April. The remaining Halifax, flown by F/O C. Porter, had also been hit by flak south-west of Bremen but continued on to the target and bombed; but on the homeward leg it was shot down by a night-fighter north of Hamburg with all but Porter baling out safely to become POWs.

St Nazaire was raided the following night and Berlin again on 29/30th. Extremely bad weather severely hampered the operation and results were again disappointing with 21 aircraft lost out of the 578 dispatched – 11 Lancasters, seven Halifaxes and three Stirlings. Adding to the severe icing and inaccurately forecast winds, the target marking, although concentrated, was too far south and the bombing force arrived late with most of the bombs falling in open country yet again. Further attacks on Berlin were deferred until crews could utilize the security of the autumn nights. Meanwhile attacks, interspersed with minor operations, were carried out against Essen, Kiel, Duisburg, Frankfurt and Stuttgart. Two new squadrons had joined the Pathfinder Force during the month, No 405 Squadron with Halifaxes, and No 97 Squadron with Lancasters.

Part of the routine checks conducted by the A&AEE was random testing of production aircraft. During the period from January to May 1943, seven had passed through the establishment. Five B Mk IIs, DT744, JB857 and JD145 from English Electric, BB324 from LPTB and HR784 from Handley Page, plus two B Mk Vs, DK128 and EB238, from Fairey Aviation and Rootes Securities respectively. The summary of the condition[7] of each was interesting. They were compared first with W7922, tested for climb and level speed performance on 18 December 1942 as detailed in Chapter III (smooth black finish, Tollerton fairing etc). BB324 was the only one to retain its C Mk V mid-upper turret during these tests with the exception of HR748, the rest having the A Mk VIII (Special) type with high metal surround. The saxophone exhaust shrouds had been removed from six, but HR748 had close fitting shrouds. Excluding the latter, all were Series I (Special) Halifaxes with D.T.D. 83A(c) cellulose finish. The other point that emerges is that, even allowing for the addition of 544 lbs for the Dowty undercarriage, a variation in tare weight of up to 1,100 lbs existed. Five aircraft were fitted with 12 ft 9 in diameter Rotol variable pitch R7/35/54 propellers and the other two 13 ft diameter Rotol R7/35/55 propellers. Even so, performance varied little, all stalling at between 78 and 82 mph with flaps and undercarriage down. Interestingly, of the seven test results, BB324 had the best all-round performance, even with its C Mk V turret in place, at 260 mph and a service ceiling of 21,700 ft.

The inclusion of HR748, produced in mid-March, plus the comment that with its exception *"... all were Series I (Special) aircraft, i.e. with Tollerton fairing"* provides an approximate date for the start of introduction of the Series IA modifications because both JD145 and EB138 were built around the start of May, well after HR748. As would be expected, as the parent firm, Handley Page had designed the changes and introduced them into production before any of its sub-contractors. The time difference however is interesting, illustrating just how long it took to provide the new jigs and tooling for those changes. It also illustrates the confusion about what constituted precise parameters for a Series IA classification. HR748 had the extended fuselage with Perspex nose modification, an A Mk VIII turret in the low position with simple fairing, shallow astrodome, main aerial mast deleted and aerials attached to the D/F loop housing, and stack pipes on the wing upper surfaces eliminated and replaced by venturi vents fitted below each fuel tank. However, despite being the only one fitted with Merlin 22 engines, it retained Gallay radiators and old-style cowlings – technically still a Series I (Special) by Air Ministry standards. The external finish was also new, synthetic D.T.D. 314S replacing the usual D.T.D. 308(c) cellulose finish used on many Halifaxes *"... Presumably on account of the supply situation. The synthetic finish appears dull in comparison with the cellulose finishes."*

Other less well-defended distant targets continued to be attacked including the docks at La Spezia, Italy, which, it is believed, allowed damaged aircraft to fly on to Allied airfields in North Africa for the first time. Then, on 16/17 April, 327 bombers were sent to the Skoda armament works at Pilsen in Czechoslovakia while 271 aircraft carried out a diversionary raid on Mannheim that cost nine Wellingtons, seven Stirlings and two Halifaxes – 6.6% of the attacking force. However, despite this costly diversion, the Skoda raid was a complete failure that cost 18 Lancasters and 18 Halifaxes[8]. In a complicated plan carried out in full moonlight, the Main Force was ordered to confirm the location of the target visually, the Pathfinder marking being intended only as a general guide. Regrettably, a large asylum seven miles from the target was mistaken for the Skoda works and the factory was not hit, only six crews returning with photographs showing bombing within three miles of the actual target.

The full moon conditions contributed to the many losses with a number occurring over France on the outbound leg, several due to night-fighters but most to flak, but as usual the crews showed great determination. With his aircraft badly damaged in a night-fighter attack at 9,000 ft on the outward leg, Sgt J. McCrea elected to attack an alternative target but when homeward bound at 7,000 ft, DT690 was hit repeatedly by flak, forcing the crew to bale out near Laon. Although landing inside the Laon-Athies airfield perimeter, Sgt D. Jones managed to escape; he and two of the crew evaded capture, while the remainder became POWs. Crews seem to have been flying relatively low, possibly because of the moonlight conditions. F/Lt A. Dowse DFC was an experienced pilot on his second tour but his aircraft, DT773, fell victim to a Bf 110 at 12,500 ft; Dowse died but his crew baled out successfully. Outbound at 12,000 ft, F/Lt E. Mortenson's HR659 was shot down near Trier in a combined attack by a Bf 110 and Bf 109, the altitude confirming the height level set by the squadron for the operation. Five baled out of Mortenson's aircraft and survived. Homeward bound at 9,000 ft, HR663 flown by S/Ldr Lashbrook DFC, DFM was attacked by a night-fighter that set fire to the port wing and both engines. The crew baled out and the Halifax plunged to earth south of Maubeuge in France. Six of the crew survived, one becoming a POW while the rest evaded capture. F/O J. Sergeant's DT752 also fell to night-fighter attack, Hptm. Ludwig Meister of the I./NJG 4 shooting it down over Belgium. This time all perished[9].

Despite this disaster, there were successes closer to home. Stettin, some 600 miles from England, was attacked on 20/21 April, 339 bombers being sent out. Despite the loss of 13 Lancasters, 7 Halifaxes and a single Stirling, the raid was the most successful attack launched beyond the range of the *Oboe* marking system during the Battle of the Ruhr. For once visibility was good and target marking perfect. Approximately 100 acres of the city was devastated, much of it industrial buildings. Once more, a diversionary attack was mounted at the same time with 86 Stirlings going to the Heinkel works at Rostock during which the Halifax of P/O W. Sherk of 35 Squadron was almost added to the losses. Five minutes after marking the allotted target, it was struck by incendiary bombs, one of which smashed through the pilot's escape hatch and set his seat on fire before exploding in the flight engineer's compartment. With the aircraft out of control, the pilot gave the order to bale out, but moments later he regained control and cancelled the order. Seconds could mean the difference between life and death and JB785: F returned to base minus two of the crew who had abandoned the aircraft during those first vital moments. It returned to operations after repair as TL-Q and was later lost with a different crew, shot down by a night-fighter near Rotterdam, while returning from an attack on Münster on 11/12 June.

The battle between new measures and countermeasures was now getting into its deadly stride and new German night-fighter tactics were being encountered during these raids. Sergeant J. Currie of 76 Squadron was piloting DT698: W to Stuttgart on 14/15 April when, over France, a Ju 88 approached with all its lights on. The rear gunner hit it with a well-aimed burst that sent it spiralling down with one engine aflame. Immediately a second Ju 88 riddled the Halifax with a long burst of fire, mortally wounding one of the crew. These decoy tactics were frequently repeated, usually with less favourable results for the victim.

Minelaying, a secondary and usually far less hazardous occupation in times past, was assuming increased importance and Bomber Command launched some quite large sorties. On the night of 27/28 April, 160 aircraft were sent to lay 458 mines along the Biscay and Brittany coasts and into the Frisian Islands for the loss of a single Lancaster. The following night, 207 aircraft were sent out to drop 593 mines off Heligoland, in the River Elbe and in the Great and Little Belts. Poor weather forced most crews to low level and flak took its toll, 22 aircraft being lost, two of them Halifaxes – HR773: A of 158 Squadron and JB923: Q of No 419 Squadron. Although this was the greatest minelayer loss for the war, it also saw the highest number of mines laid in one night.

* * *

A further change to the Halifax's external lines occurred around May when the first of the B Mk II and V Series IA aircraft were issued to squadrons. Following the review of the Halifax's performance which produced the critical report of late 1942, a series of tests had been carried out on two aircraft, L9515 and HR679, incorporating some recommendations made in the report.

It was known that the Tollerton fairing modification was only an interim measure and L9515 was subsequently modified to flight-test the mock-up of a proposed revised nose shape of superior aerodynamic properties.

The report stated that the aircraft had been 'super cleaned up'; the front turret had been removed and replaced with a metal fairing mock-up of the revised nose shape for the definitive version of the B Mk II. Previously all nacelles, body apertures and tail wheel housing had been sealed and other drag-producing elements such as

These two photographs show L9515 as it appeared in December 1942 fitted with the mock-up of the definitive nose shape for the Mk II and V series aircraft. The airframe has been greatly cleaned up with most modifications recommended for the Series I (Special) but it retains the close-fitting saxophone exhaust shrouds. It had both inboard engine nacelles extended as part of the trials to try to remedy the aerodynamic flow problems over the inboard engine nacelles. (Flight International)

the top handrail, fuel jettison pipes and ice guards removed. At the end of that process, tests had shown that all benefit achieved by those actions could be negated by a rough application of RDM 2A and a further clean up was recommended so, by the time L9515 was required for the testing of the new nose design, most had been implemented. In addition to the experimental nose cone, an A Mk VIII mid-upper turret, with shallow surround fairing and shallow astrodome had been installed and the rudders fitted with Mod 413[10]. Upper surface camouflage now extended to the lowest line of the fuselage with all lower surfaces painted yellow in keeping with the aircraft's experimental status.

Turbulent flow over the inboard wing section had been a prime source of concern and was not entirely the fault of the bulky exhaust shrouds. The positioning of the inboard engines caused a portion of the turbulence and it had been recommended that the engines be dropped relevant to the wing chord. As this would have involved major structural changes and disruption to production, an attempt was made to overcome the airflow problem by extending the existing nacelles well aft of the wing trailing edge.

Having flight-tested these modifications on L9515, they were then incorporated on to HR679, which was then further modified to become the prototype B Mk II Series IA Halifax. The mock-up nose section of L9515 was replaced by a small extension of the fuselage and terminated in a Perspex nose cone, increasing the overall fuselage length to 71 ft 7 in. The criticism about the marginal power was overcome by installing Merlin 22 engines, rated at 1,480 bhp at 12,250 ft, in place of the Merlin XX engines; the Gallay radiators and oil coolers, which had proved troublesome, were replaced by Morris single-block radiators with series oil cooler. This produced a revised radiator bath shape similar to that fitted to the B Mk I, but with a raked-back chin. The tail wheel was also made fully retractable.

Thus equipped, HR679 was extensively test-flown between December 1942 and May 1943, some of the equipment and modifications being added as the tests progressed. On 28 February, it had been flown to Boscombe Down, where armament trials were carried out with a single Vickers Gas Operated machine gun fitted in a gimbal mounting to the nose transparency. Test results were very good with most of the modifications tested recommended for incorporation into the production lines. The extended inboard engine nacelles, however, dropped relative to the wing chord and including doors that totally enclosed the main wheels, were not included due to the marginal benefit gained compared with the production problems involved. The tail wheel also remained non-retractable. With the introduction of the new marque the bad weather vision panel in the cockpit starboard quarter light was deleted.

Due to the inevitable supply problems and speed with which the modifications

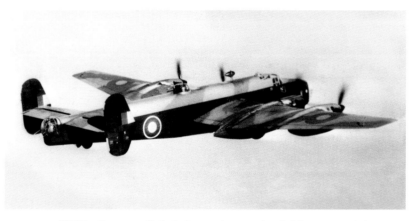

HR679 had been set aside for further tests incorporating all of the recommended modifications from the earlier tests with L9515 and, fitted with a glazed nose and slight nose extension, it became the prototype B Mk II Series IA. This air-to-air view shows the main features including the extended inboard engine nacelles; however, these were not adopted for the production Series IA aircraft.

could be incorporated onto the production lines, many of the early Series IAs were fitted with Merlin 22 engines but retained Gallay radiators with their characteristic cowlings[11]. This produced something of an anomalous situation for, while they were fitted with the lengthened fuselage and new engines, they were still officially Series I (Special) Halifaxes, an Air Ministry order specifically stating that the Morris radiator modification was essential to the classification Series IA. To complicate matters further, albeit less frequently, some late production Mk II Series I (Specials) were also fitted with Morris block radiator modification (presumably attached to Merlin 22 engines), thereby producing an enigma within a conundrum in terms of designations. Such subtleties do not appear to have reached the squadrons, who continued to refer to their improved charges as Series IA Halifaxes.

*   *   *

As April turned to May, weather conditions were still middling and between minor operations, crews returned to German targets; Essen on 30 April/1 May, Dortmund on 4/5 May, Duisburg on 12/13th, and a dual raid against Bochum with Pilsen as the secondary target on 13/14th. The attack commenced well but decoy markers soon drew the Main Force away from the target and losses were relatively high at 5.4%. The Pilsen attack, against the elusive Skoda works, again failed to produce damage; target-marking proved difficult and most bombs were dropped in open country north of the target. Although circumstantial evidence had been accumulating since April, it was at Bochum that positive evidence was gained that the Germans had developed and were using dummy Target Indicators. Fired from the ground, they burst at a lower height but were convincing enough to draw the attention of some of the bomber force. The sophistication of these would gradually increase as the Germans developed a series of decoy systems, sometimes using them singly, or in conjunction with decoy fires in open country or with smokescreens.

Perhaps one of the greatest fears was that of mid-air collision for, with literally hundreds of aircraft within the vicinity of a target, the chance was always there. During the early hours of 1 May, Sgt M. Smith of 158 Squadron was guiding HR752: T in for a blind bombing attack on Essen. With 9/10ths cloud over the target, the Pathfinders had marked the track into Essen with red and green Target Indicators and then released sky markers for the Main Force to bomb on. Smith's bomb aimer released the bombs and the Halifax turned away, only to collide with a Lancaster at 18,000 ft. The impact ripped two blades from the port outer engine, which burst into flames and damaged the wing. Smith was lucky; he managed to extinguish the fire and limp back to base. Luck, however, finally ran out for this Halifax during a raid on the Peugeot works at Montbeliard when a night-fighter shot it down north-east of Dijon on 15/16 July with all but three of Sgt R. Deans' crew losing their lives.

Enemy night-fighters also interdicted the bomber streams and often used many ruses in their tactics, an unusual example being the experience of F/O R. Fitzgerald's No 77 Squadron crew who were part of a force sent to attack Duisburg on 12/13 May. En route to the target, another aircraft was seen approaching on a parallel course and was eventually identified as a Halifax. On closer examination, it was seen to be devoid of nose and mid-upper turrets and was painted black all over with no national markings visible. The mystery Halifax slipped nearer to Fitzgerald's JD110: P, its speed being some 25 mph faster. No exhaust flames were visible, which, in itself, was unusual for a Halifax and no lights were showing. The captain's suspicions were aroused and he turned into and under the nose of the black Halifax which immediately straightened out as if trying to bring its rear turret guns to bear. Fitzgerald turned his Halifax in again and the other aircraft broke away to port and disappeared towards the coast. Immediately afterwards a Ju 88 was sighted, also painted black, but there was nothing to suggest definitely that the two were working together although the black paint rendered observation of both very difficult. No surviving German records confirm this use of a captured Halifax and, while consistent with a variety of experiments conducted by the German night-fighter arm as it grappled with the increasingly heavy RAF night attacks, it may well have been just a case of mistaken identity. The mystery aircraft's changes of flight attitude were what would be expected from a British bomber in a bomber stream although a black overall finish was also still in use for some German night-fighters.

Night-fighters, however, were only a part of the rapidly increasing defences; heavy calibre flak guns were brought into action capable of sustained fire up to 21,000 ft. Sergeant G. Beveridge of 10 Squadron had a narrow escape from these weapons during the early hours of 14 May. One of 12 Halifaxes and 150 Lancasters sent to attack the Skoda Works in Pilsen, his Halifax was flying at 18,000 ft, between Düsseldorf and Cologne, when searchlights caught it. During his subsequent violent evasive manoeuvres, a near miss from a flak burst caused the rudders to overbalance and the aircraft turned over on its back. The nose dropped and the aircraft plunged to 7,000 ft before Beveridge could regain control and level out but the mid-upper gunner, no doubt thinking the aircraft doomed, had baled out. Again, the searchlights locked on to HR695: D and shortly afterwards Beveridge jettisoned the bomb load to escape the blinding fingers of light. At 12,000 ft over the Zuid Beveland the rear gunner, Sgt Compton, sighted a Ju 88 some 500 ft above them and some 600 yards to port and astern with a searchlight in its nose. Just at that moment another Ju 88 was sighted 300 yards away on the starboard quarter and Beveridge swung the Halifax to port as the second Ju 88 attacked, causing it to miss. Compton returned the fire from 100 yards range and thought he hit the Ju 88 in the starboard wing. The evasive action caused both Ju 88s to be momentarily lost from sight, but within a few seconds both attacked again from the port and starboard quarters. Compton exchanged fire with the attacker from the starboard quarter, neither finding his mark. A few moments later one of the Ju 88s attacked from the port beam and closing to 300 yards fired a short burst. This time Compton saw his own fire register on the port engine and nose of the Ju 88 causing the former to smoke. In a well-timed attack, the other assailant struck from the starboard beam, also closing to 300 yards. Two further attacks were made from the port beam and quarter, but the Halifax eventually evaded its pursuers and returned safely to its base. Damage was only moderate, being confined to the port tail plane, elevator, rudder, the outboard fuel tank in the port wing and one gun rendered unserviceable.

Dangers were not restricted to enemy action alone. Sergeant J. Sugden of No 158 Squadron felt two heavy thuds on HR721: S, which he took to be near misses from flak bursts. The whole aircraft shuddered and the rear gunner reported a large hole in the port elevator. After landing, the base of a 4 lb incendiary bomb was found jammed in the hinges of the tail plane. Repaired and given the code letter 'J', and wearing the name 'My Gal Sal', the Halifax was eventually abandoned, due to fuel shortage, over Sussex, returning from a raid on Nuremberg on 10/11 August, 1943. The crew baled out but unfortunately their parachutes were carried out to sea with only one, F/O T. Walker, surviving to be rescued.

Between 12 – 24 May, 30-plus Halifaxes failed to return from operational sorties due to various reasons. In operations on 12/13th, No 51 Squadron lost four: HR786: J to a night-fighter over Holland; JB806: J was hit first by flak and was finished off by a night-fighter; and DT645 and DT685 to unknown causes. No 77 Squadron lost DT632: Z and JB865: J, the latter crashing close to home at Bishop Wilton, killing two of the crew while JB799: E of 102 Squadron did not make it home across the North Sea. Flight Sergeant J. Palmer's JB861: C from 419 Squadron was a victim of a night-fighter, the crew dying in the crash near Zuidland am Putten while a second 419 Squadron aircraft, JB791: X, was hit by flak over the target and finally crashed at Bedburg-Hau in Belgium, the pilot, W/O G. McMillan being killed. During the attack against Dortmund on 23/24th, 18 Halifaxes failed to return amongst which two members of F/Lt J. Sale's crew were killed when Oblt August Geiger of the III/NJG 1 shot down DT801: A of 35 Squadron over the Dutch German border.

The largest raid of the month was mounted against Dortmund on 23/24th by 826 aircraft. This was the biggest force employed since the three '1,000 bomber raids' a year previously. The weather was clear and Pathfinder marking accurate; the ensuing attack was very successful, large areas in the north and east of the city being destroyed, but it would be exactly one year before Bomber Command attacked the city again.

The most notable raid of the month had been the famous Dams Raid, but that was an operation outside the norms of Bomber Command attacks. Düsseldorf was attacked on 25/26th but unlike the Dortmund attack, it was a failure, with two layers of cloud obscuring the target and making accurate target marking extremely difficult with decoy markers and fire sites compounding the poor results. Of the 759 aircraft sent, four Halifaxes, nine Lancasters, eight Stirlings and six Wellingtons were lost. No 35 Squadron lost W7825: P which crashed in the target area, testifying to the determination of the Pathfinder Force crews; HR853 of 51 Squadron was lost to unknown causes; W7813: C of 77 Squadron was reputedly shot down by Oblt William Telge, from the Stab/II./NJG 1, the Halifax falling at Gruitrode in Belgium. However, a more disastrous end attended 77 Squadron's other loss, Sgt R. Lewis's JB837: D. Hit by night-fighter fire, it exploded with such force that it brought down two Stirlings, EF361: MG-B of 7 Squadron and 15 Squadron's BF534: LS-L, both crews being killed. Night-fighter attacks and successes were mounting and the losses of the night were in no small part due to them.

Even during this period of intense operational activity, some squadrons were called upon to meet certain public obligations. No 77 Squadron, affiliated with the City of Lancaster, had been ordered to take part in the city's 'Wings for Victory' parade on 22 May. Fifty members of the ground personnel participated in the march past while four of the squadron's Halifaxes flew overhead in tactical pairs. Even so, such events made no impact on the nightly battles in the skies over occupied Europe.

Essen was next, attacked on 27/28 May, the 158 aircraft losing 23 of their number for limited damage to the target. Weather conditions were poor and the Pathfinders had to use sky marking, resulting in scattered bombing results, many crews undershooting. The final raid of the month against Wuppertal brought better results and was the outstanding success of the Battle of the Ruhr campaign. Target marking and the attack itself were particularly accurate and large areas of fires developed in the narrow streets of the city. Approximately 1,000 acres were destroyed, some 80% in the targeted Barmen area, along with five of the six major factories and some 211 other industrial sites for a cost of 33 of the 719 aircraft sent to attack.

* * *

Losses were the product mainly of enemy defences but a lingering problem from the very first test of the first prototypes continued to catch the unwary or, perhaps, the unfortunate pilot caught in the heat of battle. Perhaps the most critical report directly related to the Halifax's design, rather than the inevitable operational stresses produced by pushing aircraft beyond their original design limits, appeared in May 1943. It starts:

"The incidence of accident rate on the Halifax Mk II aircraft increased during 1942 and an analysis of these incidents showed a large number to be the result of rudder overbalance – a feature which has been present in the type since its introduction into the service." (32nd Part. Report No A&AEE 760/a prepared and issued April/May 1943)

As already recorded in Chapter I, the first instance of rudder overbalance occurred during the trials with L7244. During propeller feathering tests with L7245 in December 1940, the test pilot had reported that the factor limiting the speed at which the aircraft could be flown straight with two propellers feathered on one side was overbalance of the rudder (4th Part, Report A&AEE 760/-). If the angle of the rudder trimmer was reduced to avoid overbalance, the force on the rudder bar became excessive.

Initially, it was thought that this feature of the vertical tail surfaces was, to some extent, inherent in the design, making a complete cure improbable using a simple modification which could be applied retrospectively. Nevertheless, further flight tests were required to more fully explore the motion of the aircraft subsequent to rudder overbalance and hopefully result in a means of reducing the accident rate. Comprehensive asymmetric test flights were conducted by Carr and Unwin and the results briefly reported (2nd Part, Report A&AEE No 760/a) on 22 November 1941. In it, various modifications were recommended. While the test flights failed to indicate a simple means of eliminating rudder overbalance, without making the rudder too heavy for asymmetric flight conditions, the handling characteristics subsequent to the overbalance could be improved by reducing the angular deflection of the rudders.

The initial test flights showed that a reduction of 3° in the design rudder angle partially reduced the tendency for the rudder to overbalance and orders for the retrospective modification of all service Halifaxes were issued. The benefits of this temporary expedient were negated largely by two other factors brought to light by the same trials. The limit stops for the rudders were made of a rubber block sandwiched between two metal plates, which were gradually deformed by the rudder forces until the rubber was permanently compressed. This allowed the rudder to move over a greater angular distance than originally intended and aggravated the stall condition associated with the overbalancing. The metal limit stop arm, which struck the limit stop, also tended to wear at the point where it was attached to the rudder by a bracket, again allowing the rudder more angular deflection than desired. It should be realised at this point that the forces involved here were quite considerable. An accident occurred during sideslip tests in which the top half of one of the rudders broke away due to the force with which the rudder overbalanced and struck the limit stop. Throughout this detailed and extensive report the terms rudder locking and rudder overbalance were deemed to be synonymous.

An attempt was made to rectify the overbalance problem by adjusting the range of movement of the balance tab on each rudder. This created some difficulties since the tab was a combined balance-trim tab. Satisfactory adjustment could be made to the balance range, but the resultant trim range was insufficient and further improvement became imperative. Wind tunnel tests were made on a complete 1/10th scale model and a partial 1/3rd scale model to examine this problem. These revealed that directional instability due to fin stall occurred at about 20° of sideslip, and associated with this was a reversal of rudder force required to maintain directional trim due to rudder overbalance. Various modifications were tried, including the use of leading edge slats to delay the fin stall, but no substantial improvement resulted. The set back rudder balance was cut back and trailing edge cords fitted, as well as tests with three different sizes of horn balance, but again with negative results. Finally, various modifications to the rudder balance showed that some form of shielded horn appeared to produce the most promising results. This was achieved by thickening the nose of the rudder to give a bulbous nose effect to that part of the balance that protruded into the slipstream at large angles of attack.

The bulbous noses were fitted to the rudders of L7245 and a series of tests carried out. Since the airscrews rotated clockwise, the resultant torque produced a tendency for the aircraft to roll to the left. Under normal circumstances, this was not noticeable and even with the starboard engines shut down and feathered, no difficulty was encountered flying on the remaining two engines. However, the most critical condition obviously occurred when the port engines were cut, the natural tendency for the port wing to drop, aggravated by the torque, and it was under these circumstances that rudder overbalance occurred. The early tests with L7245 were made with the starboard engines running at the normal cruise setting and both port engines switched off. At 170 mph, the rudders began a slight oscillation and violently

This view shows Mod 413, the bulbous nose additions to the top and bottom of the rudder leading edge introduced as the first round of change during the attempts to find a permanent solution to the rudder stall problem. It was only partly successful.

overbalanced at 160 mph, remaining hard over to starboard. Control could not be regained by increasing the speed; at 180 mph the starboard engines were throttled back and only then could the rudders be centralised.

For normal flying, the bulbous noses had the effect of making the rudders sloppy at all speeds up to 260 mph. They were then transferred to L9515, which also had the balance tab movement reduced by 50%, thus reducing the available trimming range by 30%. The tests were carried out at 50,000 lb a.u.w, with only the port outer engine shut down and the propeller feathered. Full trim range to starboard was required to keep the aircraft straight at 178 mph; at 150 mph control could be comfortably maintained if 10° of bank were used, but below this speed the foot load on the rudder pedals became excessive. There was no sign of overbalance at speeds as low as 130 mph, although this speed could only be held for a short period. With both port engines off and full trim, the foot load became excessive at 140 mph.

The overbalance problem had almost been solved, but it remained clear that the trim problem had not. A further series of modifications and tests produced a

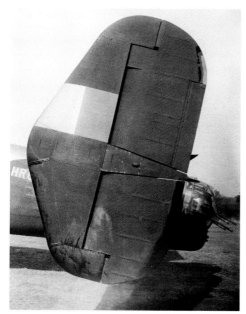

The standard fin condition existing at the time of the further experimentation incorporating Mod 413 is shown here on the vertical tail surfaces of HR679, this assembly being designated Type B. The pale patch around the upper portion of the fin resulted from attempts to use doped lengths of fabric of various chord to provide trim changes.

The modified Type C tail assembly tested on HR727 had the Mod 413 changes removed and the fin leading edges cut back two inches, a narrow strip of metal being added to the fin where it overlapped the rudders. It also incorporated Mod 670 which reduced rudder travel by 3 degrees but, again, tests showed no improvement.

A series of drastically altered experimental fins, Types E, F and G were tested on R9534 before a modified Type C with a significantly enlarged fin of approximately 50% more area finally solved the problem. This was the Type D variant and entered production under that designation as Mod 814.

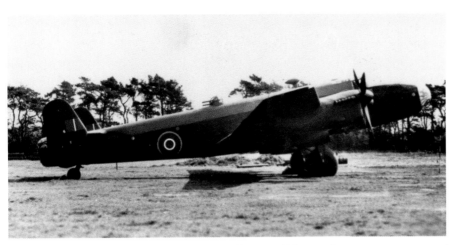

HR756, the prototype B Mk II Series II exhibits the principal features which were to be included in the projected B Mk IV. It had dropped inboard engines with nacelles extending aft beyond the wing trailing edges, six-way exhaust shrouds, deep radiator baths, a fully enclosed main wheel door facility and Beaufighter-type spinners.

trim range, which allowed the aircraft to be flown on the starboard engines only, at 140 mph with 10° of bank and full right rudder, the foot load being zero under these conditions. The rudders, however, remained sluggish at low speeds and further improvement was still considered desirable. It was suggested that some increase in fin area would overcome the sluggishness at low speeds as well as improve the asymmetric handling characteristics. Meanwhile, as a palliative, the bulbous noses, officially Handley Page Modification 413, were introduced on to the production lines, but a considerable delay was experienced in incorporating them retrospectively.

Meanwhile, the accident rate continued and subsequent analyses indicated that rudder overbalance was a contributory factor and further investigation was recommended. The earlier tests had shown that overbalance might be cured by fitting a larger fin; however, in view of the delays involved in such a major modification, further tests were made on HR679 and another B Mk II Series IA aircraft, HR727, in an effort to find a stop-gap palliative. The latter aircraft was fitted with modified triangular fins of slightly increased area. The bulbous noses were removed from the rudders, which also had their leading edges cut back two inches and the resulting gap filled in with additional fin area. However, results of the tests served only to show that no simple means of eliminating rudder overbalance was to be found.

A drastically modified fin assembly was then fitted to R9534, currently under test as the prototype B Mk III (See Chapter 10 for fuller details). The rudders were standard units without Mod 413, but the leading edge of each fin had been built up to produce a broad rectangular shape, the increase in area being approximately 40%. Side-slip and asymmetric flight tests were carried out with these between 1st and 19 June, care being taken to repeat the same programme already carried out when the aircraft was fitted with the original triangular-shaped fins.

The new fin and rudder assembly was considered satisfactory, although somewhat heavy on controls at the high end of the speed range, between 250 and 300 mph. Under normal conditions of zero bank with two engines cut, the rudder power was insufficient to allow turns to be made against the working engines at the best climbing speed, or in straight flight. However, for asymmetric flight at minimum cruising speed for comfortable continuous cruising, i.e. approximately 150 mph Indicated Air Speed (IAS), the rudder was sufficient to enable straight flight and turns against the working engines, particularly if ailerons were used to assist the rudder. Side-slip tests showed that there was no longer any need to restrict the range of the rudder movement, and even when using the trimmers the

rudders did not lock over. An identical set of fins and rudders was then fitted to DK145, a B Mk V Series I (Special), and a similar series of tests carried out. These produced an equally satisfactory set of results, the only adverse comment again being the fact that the rudder control was a little heavier than usual for the type.

The new fin and rudder assembly, officially Mod 814, was introduced onto assembly lines as rapidly as possible, the production version varying only slightly from the prototype. The overall height of the fin was increased by two and a half inches, due to the top and bottom leading edge corners being filled out slightly, and the combined trim-balance tab was increased in chord by approximately one inch. Retrospective modification of Halifaxes already in service presented a major problem, but this was overcome largely by the magnificent efforts of the working party from 13 MU at Henlow. Composed of a warrant officer, five senior NCOs and 36 other ranks, they travelled from airfield to airfield modifying 225 Mk II and V Halifaxes in the remarkably short period of three and a half months. Within the next two months they modified a further 277, and in March 1944, moved to St Davids where they modified a further 60 Halifaxes for Coastal Command.

While the squadrons continued to operate their modified Series I (Special) Halifaxes, tests also continued to try to improve performance even further. HR756 was set aside for these tests and incorporated the recommendations that had resulted from the Series IA trials. The most radical modification was dropping of the inboard engines, the nacelles being extended aft of the wing trailing edge. The nacelles were then fitted with modified undercarriage doors, which completely enclosed the main landing wheels when retracted. The air intakes for the cabin heating system were removed from the top of the inboard engine cowlings and fitted underneath each wing, near the root. The four Merlin 22 engines incorporating Morris block radiators, thermostatically controlled radiator flaps and six-way exhaust ejector stubs were fitted, and the propellers were three-bladed Rotol, Type XHF53/W units. These were basically standard R7/35/54 blades with their root shape slightly modified to allow Beaufighter-type spinners to be fitted. Apart from a fixed tail wheel and engine modifications, the aircraft was externally similar to HR679, the prototype B Mk II Series IA aircraft.

The prototype B Mk II Series II Halifax, as HR756 was now designated, was thoroughly tested between April and May 1943. Cruising speed was only 9 mph faster than the standard Series IA aircraft, but the cruising ceiling had been greatly improved, to over 19,000 ft. The Series IA Halifaxes fitted with Merlin 22 engines had their boost limitation increased to +7 lb for weak-mixture cruising and gave a cruising ceiling of 16,000 ft; above that height, with throttles fully open, the boost fell off until at 20,000 ft it reached +4 lb. The significance of this improvement becomes clear when it is realised that the Series IA aircraft, fully laden, were unable to operate in the weak-mixture range because of insufficient power to maintain the minimum speed of 155 mph above 18,000 ft. They were thus forced to carry out the flights in the rich-mixture range, with engines set at 2,650 rpm and +6 lb boost, resulting in a very high fuel consumption rate. There was very little improvement in the climbing speed, but the service ceiling was some 500 ft higher and the maximum speed, using +9 lb boost, was 264 mph at 18,000 ft.

Short of putting the Series II Halifax into production there remained only two other alternatives to improve the operating ceiling of the

Handley Page responded to Specification B1/39, which called for a super-heavy bomber. However, the drastic wartime developments of 1940 brought the construction of a prototype to a halt but the company was encouraged to enlarge the existing Halifax design under the designation HP 60A. It would have incorporated most of the B Mk II Series II features and received the company designation B Mk IV.

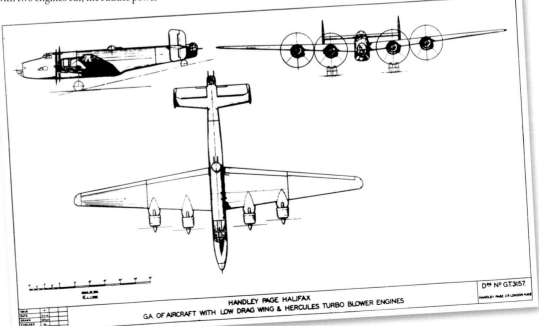

HANDLEY PAGE HALIFAX
G.A. OF AIRCRAFT WITH LOW DRAG WING & HERCULES TURBO BLOWER ENGINES

Series IA aircraft. Either the airframe could be further cleaned up, such as removal once more of the mid-upper turret, or engines would have to be fitted that gave more power at altitude for weak-mixture cruising. Production of the Series II aircraft was considered impractical in view of the trials being carried out with the prototype B Mk III and its impending introduction on to the production lines. Further cleaning up of the Series IA aircraft offered little scope for the necessary improvement, and the growing menace of the German night-fighter force ruled out removal of the mid-upper turret. This narrowed opportunity for improvement down to the engines, and HR756 was fitted with Merlin 85s in June. These were later exchanged for Merlin 65s, but by the time that the tests had been completed the B Mk III had made its operational appearance and retrospective introduction of the more powerful Merlin engines was no longer of any practical advantage.

Specification B1/39 had been issued in 1939 for a super-heavy bomber, but the emergency issues of 1940 had drastically delayed the development associated with this project. Although construction of a prototype was stopped in May 1940, the Air Ministry and MAP encouraged Handley Page to enlarge their existing Halifax design and the company designation HP60A was allocated to this project. Most of the B Mk II Series II features were to have been included in the B Mk IV, as it was designated, along with a new strengthened fuselage floor and an enlarged bomb compartment. However, like the Series II Halifax, its necessity was precluded by the production of the B Mk III.

Merlin 24 engines were tested on V9985 during July and a series of comparative take-off trials made in conjunction with DK145, a B Mk V Series I (Special). The use of V9985, originally transferred from 10 Squadron for the bulged bomb bay tests, was somewhat unusual as it retained all the features of the very early B Mk II Halifaxes: nose and tail turrets, beam gun hatches, two wireless masts, two navigational blisters, long chord radiator shutters and triangular fins. The rudders, however, by then did have the bulbous nose modification. By comparison DK145 was representative of the late Series I (Special) aircraft, having been cleaned up and fitted with an A Mk VIII turret in a raised surround, cut-back radiator shutters and the new 'D'-shaped fins. Because of the drastic physical differences between the two, results of the trials were all the more interesting.

The Merlin 24 engines had a boost limit of +18 lb compared with the +12 lb of the Merlin XX engines fitted to DK 145. In spite of using a higher boost figure of +14 lb, achieved by using the boost control cut-out, DK145 took 1,010 yards to become airborne and 1,330 yards to clear a 50 ft screen (the standard height used to test all aircraft). Using the same take-off weight, 60,000 lb, V9985 became airborne after only 540 yards and cleared the 50 ft mark after 890 yards. The unstick speed was also 12 mph slower.

Other attempts to increase performance were made by trying to improve propeller efficiency. A B Mk II Halifax was fitted with two sets of Wellington Mk VI four-bladed propellers, but these caused a reduction in the cruising performance. Further tests were required to establish the climb and level speed performance using a full set of four-bladed propellers. DK145 was again used as the test aircraft, being fitted with four sets of 13 ft diameter Rotol XH54 propellers, which had an identical blade shape to the standard R7/35/5 5 propellers. Prior to this test DK145 had 12 ft 9 in R7/35/54 units on the inboard engines and R7/35/55 units on the outboard engines. Results showed no appreciable difference in level speed figures, but weak-mixture cruising speed was increased by 2-4 mph. The rate of climb, at low altitude, remained unaltered, but there was a gradual increase of up to 70 ft/min at higher altitudes and the service ceiling was raised by 1,000 ft.

Four-bladed Rotol Type R7/14B5/4 propellers were adopted for use by service Halifaxes and allocated principally to the B Mk Vs, regardless of which Command they were serving, (a former No 408 Squadron flight engineer FL/Sgt F. Puttock, commenting that when the first example arrived it raised eyebrows). However, their use on Mk II Halifaxes was restricted mainly to a few Coastal Command aircraft. Rolls-Royce used DG235, a B Mk V Series I (Special) for further tests with four-bladed propellers, these units being later transferred to a B Mk II Series I (Special) Halifax, W7783.

Another feature adopted with the Series IA aircraft was close-fitting exhaust shrouds. Flame-damping trials, with a variety of shrouds, had begun with a series of tests on L9485 in September 1941. The normal, unshielded, exhaust emitted a feathery orange flame approximately four inches long from the fishtail, while the rest of the exhaust pipe glowed a cherry red. The bulky asbestos tunnel shrouds (which were to have such a marked effect on performance), were also tested, fitted to the starboard engines for comparative purposes. Their adoption and subsequent removal has already been related; however, their replacement was another matter. With the knowledge of earlier tests on unshielded exhausts, it was obviously necessary to find a substitute as rapidly as possible and two B Mk II aircraft, DG221 and W7823, were tested in October 1942 with anti-glow paint and a venturi flame-damping extension respectively. Both items failed to achieve the desired result. A multi-blister, four-fishtail manifold was tried on a B Mk V, DG281, in May 1943, but despite a slight improvement of the flame-damping qualities, the type did not meet the required conditions of invisibility. The same aircraft was also used to test a set

The venturi-aided exhaust system tested on W7823 during trials to find an answer to the night visibility problem. The telltale glow from aircraft exhaust systems was almost impossible to eliminate and it aided night-fighters on both sides of the conflict. The outline of the large asbestos shrouds fitted previously provides some scale to the changes in the palliative measures tried.

The saxophone exhaust solved the dilemma but manufacturing problems caused much trouble until standards were rigorously enforced. The three shown here were found during routine testing of production examples at Boscombe Down. At the top is an oversize example from JD304, in the centre a standard version from HR679 and at the bottom a grossly oversize example from DK256. The latter was so large it had to have a butt strap riveted along its horizontal mid-line. How such production anomalies were allowed to pass inspection is bewildering.

of close-fitting shrouds that followed the outline of the exhaust manifold. These had already been fitted to HR679 and achieved the desired result, but had a marked effect on performance. The maximum level speed was reduced by 2% and maximum economical cruising speed by 3%; rate of climb was reduced by 50-l00 ft/min, the time to reach 20,000 ft increased by seven minutes and the service ceiling reduced from 21,000 ft to 19,000 ft. In view of other tests being conducted to improve performance figures this was counter-productive.

Regardless of the drawbacks, use of the shrouds was unavoidable and they entered production immediately. It was possibly because of the rapidity with which they were placed in production that tolerances slipped and badly oversize shrouds crept into the production lines. It was standard procedure for production aircraft of all types to be selected at random and tested at the A&AEE. Two such aircraft, a B Mk II, JD304, and a B Mk V, DK256, were received for testing in July and in both cases, the exhaust shrouds were found to be grossly oversize. Those fitted to DK256 had a butt strap riveted between the half sections of each shroud, which increased the circumferences of the outlet branch by approximately one and a half inches. Both

A 78 Squadron B Mk II Series I (Special) photographed at its dispersal, running up its engines. 'M-Mike' was typical of the final standard with the forward tall radio mast now eliminated and the aerial leads slung from the top of the D/F loop housing. It still had an A Mk VIII (special) mid-upper turret with the raised surround but these were not replaced retroactively when the production version, set lower and without the raised surround, entered the production cycle.

Halifaxes were thoroughly test-flown and the effects of the oversize shrouds carefully measured. DK256 fitted with its oversize shrouds, then with normal-size shrouds and, finally, without any shrouds, respectively, recorded the following rates of climb to 16,000 ft: 360 ft/min, 400 ft/min and 430 ft/min. The appropriate service ceiling figures were 18,900 ft, 19,400 ft and 19,900 ft.

Steps were taken to prevent the abnormal shrouds being issued to production lines and the problem was rapidly eliminated, although a few still slipped through. A B Mk V, LK729, received for routine testing in November 1943 was fitted with abnormal shrouds. The subsequent report stated that the sub-normal performance of the aircraft was due entirely to the shrouds. Without them the aircraft had a better than average performance.

These difficulties were finally eliminated with the introduction of a four-way ejector shroud design (Mod. 487); these were fitted to later production Merlin-engined Halifaxes, and greatly improved performance once more.

* * *

Meanwhile, the Halifax force had continued its steady expansion; No 6 Group had become operational on 1 January 1943, composed exclusively of RCAF squadrons and B Mk V Halifaxes, at last available in quantity, were issued in mid-year principally to this mixed Halifax-Lancaster Group. This eased maintenance problems as the Dowty landing gear was common to both types. There was, however, the inevitable exception; No 76 Squadron at Linton-on-Ouse and within 4 Group, was also equipped with the type, based on its B Mk II Halifaxes having been withdrawn in May and replaced by B Mk Vs. However, the following month the station itself was transferred to No 6 Group, thus solving the problem.

In June, the Pathfinder Force was expanded as the size of the attacking force continued to grow with Nos 105 and 139 Squadrons joining No 8 Group[12]. The number of Halifax squadrons also increased, No 427 RCAF having joined in May, followed by 428 and 434 Squadrons RCAF in June, with a fourth Canadian Squadron, No 431, joining during July. The number of bombers now being sent out was increasing and it was hoped that concentrating time over target would enhance both the bombing results as well as reducing losses. However, the best planning was always subject to chance to some degree – it could never be otherwise. During the raid on Düsseldorf on 11/12 June, one of the Oboe-equipped Mosquitoes of the Target Marking force inadvertently released its markers 14 miles north-east of the city, which drew some of the Main Force bombing. Even so, the attack was successful, delivering the most damaging attack of the war on this city.

Again, a large force had been assembled for the attack, but so had the Luftwaffe night-fighters, which were active in large numbers, shooting down many of the 38 of the 783 bombers dispatched. The battle was not entirely one-sided however, and several crews claimed kills that night. Flight Sergeant Williams, a veteran Australian rear gunner of 35 Squadron, was badly wounded in the body and legs by the opening burst from one of two night-fighters which attacked his Halifax. Despite intense pain, he was able to pass directions for evasive action when the second fighter attacked. The turret rotation mechanism had been destroyed in the first attack but Williams managed to open fire on the second attacker, which exploded in the air. The first night-fighter then resumed its attack and promptly met the same fate as its companion. Williams remained at his post until HR798: A landed back at its base where the turret had to be cut away to release him. For his courage and gunnery skills, he received an immediate award of the comparatively rare Conspicuous Gallantry Medal.

Others were not so fortunate. Of the 16 Halifaxes that failed to return, three were definitely confirmed as having fallen to night-fighter attacks. DK170: C, one of two lost by 76 Squadron, fell to Oblt Walter Barte of the II./NJG 1, 77 Squadron lost JD168:T to the guns of a Bf 110 G-4, flown by Hptm Eckart-Wilhelm von Bonin of the 6./NJG 1, while W7932 of No 78 Squadron fell to Maj Werner Streib of the I./NJG 1. Given the crash sites of several others, it is quite possible that they, too, fell victim to the night-fighter force although flak did its deadly best with the remainder.

A subsidiary raid to Münster had supported the main attack, not only to hopefully split the defenders but also to test an all-H2S force attack. Just 72 aircraft of the No 8 Group Pathfinder Force took part; thirty-three carried target markers or flares, with the markers joining the remainder as the bombing force. It was all over in ten minutes with much damage inflicted on the railway installations – but at the cost of five aircraft. NJG 1's night-fighters were present, Hptm Eckart-Wilhelm von Bonin claiming 35 Squadron's DT805: Y at 0143, which crashed near Doetinchem in Holland, killing F/Lt S. Howe DFC, with the remainder of the crew parachuting to safety and captivity. Just four minutes later, von Bonin shot down a second Halifax, from the Düsseldorf force, as recorded above.

The attack on Bochum the following night of the 12/13th provided a test for the Oboe- equipped marking force, complete cloud cover extending over the target. Despite this, the 503 Halifaxes and Lancasters bombed accurately, causing severe damage to the centre of the city. The heavy cloud cover had screened the bombers from the worst of the flak, but the night-fighter force claimed a high proportion, at least 12 of the 4.8% of the force lost – 14 Lancasters and ten Halifaxes.

Homeward bound, near the border of Germany and Holland, a new B Mk II Series IA Halifax of 158 Squadron, JD246: R, was attacked by two Bf 110 fighters. In the ensuing action, two bursts of cannon fire hit the Halifax, one shell going through the port side of the fuselage. Glancing off the control rods it passed between the pilot's legs, went underneath the instrument panel and hit the leads to the Gee and IFF sets causing their emergency destruction detonators to explode. It then struck the bomb aimer, Sgt Dunning, a glancing blow on the scalp before smashing its way out through the Perspex nose cone. The rear turret guns were out of action at this stage and the only defensive fire came from the mid-upper turret, while the rear gunner called out evasive manoeuvres to the pilot. One attacker became a little too enthusiastic and nearly rammed the Halifax, earning itself a good solid burst from the mid-upper turret guns. It broke off the engagement and disappeared. The other Bf 110 continued to press home attacks from dead astern and underneath, repeatedly hitting the Halifax. Then it suddenly changed tactics and stood off, trying to hit the Halifax when it was about halfway down each corkscrew manoeuvre, forcing Sgt C. Robinson to apply 40° of bank to avoid the enemy fire. After approximately 15 minutes of this, the Bf 110 broke off the fight (possibly short of fuel) and the Halifax was able to regain its original course for home. Robinson received an immediate DFM for his efforts.

JD246, however, would not be so lucky. A night-fighter shot it down 7 km (4 miles) south of Trebbin during the Berlin attack of 31 August/1 September, killing Sgt K. Ward and two others.

Flak was now intense and bomber crews had to face concentrated fire on the approach to, above and beyond each main target. Chances of mid-air collision were increasing, but other dangers also existed in the now crowded skies over the target. Flight Sergeant D. Cameron's HR837: F of 158 Squadron had just released its bomb load over Cologne in the early hours of 29 June, when it was struck simultaneously by a cannon shell from a Ju 88 and a 1,000 lb bomb from another aircraft above.

The sturdy construction of the Halifax could take considerable damage and keep flying. Built around the middle of May, HR837 was taken on charge by 158 Squadron on the 20th. As 'F-Freddie' it flew eleven sorties, the last as part of the attack on Cologne on 28/29 June 1943 when it was hit by a bomb dropped from an aircraft higher up. The bomb passed right through the fuselage but Fl/Sgt D. Cameron and his crew made it safely back to base. The mid-upper gunner was possibly the luckiest man on board, as can be seen from the damage. Sent for repair, the aircraft was allocated to 1656 HCU on 12 April 1944 where it remained until struck off charge on 11 January 1945.

Although the bomb passed through the fuselage and port wing, leaving a hole four feet square in the fuselage near the mid-upper turret, the Halifax returned safely to base.

The Ruhr campaign drew to a close with a series of attacks on Cologne, four being made between 16/17 June and 8/9 July. The first attack, by a mixed force of Lancasters and Halifaxes, this time with 16 of the Pathfinder Force using *H2S* to mark the target, was frustrated by a combination of bad weather and technical difficulties. Cloud covered the target and problems with some *H2S* equipment reduced the target marking ability carried out using sky markers. The marking was late and meagre, and only 100 Lancasters bombed, the rest of the force turning back. The resulting damage was scattered and a dubious result for the loss of 14 Lancasters. However, the next three were all very successful and Cologne lay virtually devastated from end-to-end. Yet even this was to be nothing when compared with what lay in store for Hamburg.

The *H2S*-equipment problems had marred the marking potential and further refinement of this process would be needed. A new variation was to be attempted against Le Creusot on 19/20 June for, while Germany remained the main focus of attention, a series of smaller raids was launched against small targets in France, employing different techniques. The intention was to destroy key industrial targets with precision attacks and thus avoid civilian casualties. On the night of 19/20 June, a force of 290 bombers – 181 Halifaxes, 107 Stirlings and two Lancasters – had set off to attack the Schneider armaments factory and the Breuil steelworks Le Creusot. The Pathfinder force dropped only flares, by which light the Main Force crews were expected to identify their targets and make two runs from between 5,000 and 10,000 ft, dropping a short stick of bombs each time. The results were not good, the crews later complaining that the smoke from the many flares which had been dropped, obscured the target and for crews now conditioned to bombing a glowing target marker, the task must have been extremely difficult, as the results showed. However, S/Ldr Earthrowe's crew took a very successful series of photographs of the raid from DK190 of No 427 Squadron, this, as far as is known, being the first time a daylight camera had been used at night. A later, similar attack on the Montbeliard factory, in

the French town of Sochaux on 15/16 July, saw more terrible results. An all-Halifax force of 165 aircraft had attacked in clear conditions from between 6,000 and 10,000 ft and in view of the results of the earlier operation, this time the Pathfinders dropped markers, but these fell some 700 yards beyond the factory and most bomb loads hit the town causing many civilian casualties. This underscored the difficulties of employing Main Force crews against small targets in occupied countries.

While innovative, it was a retrograde process, in that by this stage of the war Main Force crews were used to aiming at Target Indicators and had little skill in visual identification of small targets. The results brought this home; while most bombs fell within three miles of the targets, only about 20% hit the factories. No 10 Squadron's JD109: Y was the only loss to enemy action of the raid but 77 Squadron lost JB863: V after take-off when it crashed soon afterwards near No 4 Group HQ, south of Heslington. Even so, there might have been more; twenty Halifaxes of 51 Squadron were waiting to be bombed up for the attack when an explosion took place in the bomb dump at approximately 13.30 hrs. Incendiaries caught fire and all personnel were forced to take cover until 17.00 hrs. During this period, a large number of heavy calibre bombs blew up killing 18 people. With no bombs available, transport was rushed to RAF Holme to obtain the necessary supplies. In spite of considerable difficulties, by the joint efforts of the ground and aircrew of all ranks, 14 aircraft were bombed up in time for the operation.

The attacks against main German targets were less benign and on the night of 21st/22nd, of the Krefeld force of 705 aircraft, 44 of the attacking force – 6.2% – were lost. The moon period had not finished and good visibility aided the Pathfinders in attaining almost perfect marking; again, *Oboe* was used to good effect, backed up by ground marking. Most of the 619 bombers that attacked dropped their bombs within three miles of the aiming point. The whole city centre, approximately 47% of the built-up area, was destroyed but the clear skies and moonlight produced a grim result, night-fighters claiming a large number of the 35 aircraft brought down. The Pathfinders suffered heavily with 12 being lost, six from No 35 Squadron – W7878: J, BB361: V, BB368: H, HR685: X, HR799: R and HR848: Q – the latter three victims of the night-fighters.

The design of the Halifax with its split construction modules often allowed major repairs to be carried out on site by specialist mobile working parties. DT643: V of 77 Squadron was delivered to the RAF at the end of November 1942 and had the initial modifications of the B Mk II Series I (Special), a Tollerton fairing and Mod 413 to the rudders, but retained the tall radio mast, high profile astrodome and probably its C Mk V mid-upper turret. It had completed ten operations when photographed and had suffered some major damage to its rear section, which appears to have been replaced; the camouflage was being made good along with its serial number being painted by hand. Serial numbers were normally applied in decal form at the aircraft's point of manufacture but as each set of decals was a one-off item, when damage occurred it was back to basic sign-writing skills, as seen here, albeit in a different style to the usual regulation spacing and thickness of strokes. The replacement rear section was most probably a section recovered from another damaged airframe delivered to the Rawcliffe centre in Yorkshire where more major repairs and rebuilding took place.

After five heavy raids on Duisburg, Bomber Command considered that sufficient damage had been caused to allow attacks to be concentrated on the two important satellite towns of Oberhausen and Mülheim. The latter was the primary focus for the 557-strong force dispatched on the night of 22/23 June; the attack included a new tactic. A thin layer of stratus cloud made marking more difficult but the resultant bombing was intense. The civil defences of many cities were now finding that the ensuing intensity of fires brought inevitable interruptions to the fire-fighting, and during the latter part of this raid target marking was shifted northwards, cutting all road and telecommunication connection with neighbouring Oberhausen, to which Mülheim was linked for its defences, and the bombing spread into the eastern edges of Oberhausen. Damage was severe to both cities, 64% of Mülheim being devastated. It was now becoming a war of attrition between the attacker and the attacked. Of the 35 bombers lost, 12 were Halifaxes, but this time none was from the Pathfinder Force; damage to others was not light. Sergeant F. Mathers was one of the 77 Squadron pilots in the attacking force and had just released his bombs from 19,000 ft when a flak burst put the starboard outer engine out of action. Three minutes later, a second flak shell hit the port inner engine and he managed to feather both damaged engines and subdue the fires only to learn that several petrol tanks had also been holed. The mid-upper guns were jettisoned after half an hour due to the severe loss of height. Undaunted, he headed for base, deviating from the set course to avoid the heavy defences of Amsterdam and Rotterdam. Shortly after crossing the enemy coast, an hour and a quarter later, he and his crew were beginning to feel that their luck might have changed for the better. A sudden burst of fire from a Bf 110 changed their minds, JD110 being raked from stem to stern. The rear turret, its ammunition tracks and the intercom were all damaged. The Bf 110 made three more attacks before the rear gunner shot it down into the sea. Having finally reached base the crew found that the hydraulic system had also been hit and Mathers had to make a wheels-up landing, fortunately without injury to anyone. It was an outstanding piece of flying.

In view of the rising night-fighter menace, crews initially welcomed *Monica*, a tail-warning radar set that produced an audible signal in the pilot's headphones if another aircraft approached from astern. Aircraft fitted with the device were distinguished by a small dipole aerial, protruding rearward from beneath the rear turret; however, it would turn out to be a doubled-edged sword, as related in the next chapter.

During July, the third of four major attacks was launched against Cologne on the night of 3/4th by 653 bombers with the east bank section of the city as the primary target due to the amount of industry located there. The *Oboe* markers were backed up by equally accurate target markers and the resulting damage was heavy with 20 industrial sites hit and some 2,200 houses being destroyed. The night was also important for the introduction of a new form of night-fighter tactics. JG 300 commenced its *Wilde Sau* (Wild Boar) operations, employing single-engine fighters which relied on the illumination from the attack to guide them to the bombers. Flak was restricted to specific levels to ensure that the fighters had a free area for their attacks. As the bomber crews had previously only rarely encountered fighter attacks right over the target itself, the new tactic had an additional element of surprise,

No 405 Squadron, now part of the No 8 Group Pathfinder Force, assisted in marking. On the way into the target Sgt J. Phillips' NA179: B was attacked by a single-engine night-fighter whose first burst tore into the starboard tail plane and severed the control rods. Unable to take any evasive action, defence rested solely with the gunners and an accurate long burst of 800 rounds by Sgt Kohnke, the rear gunner, damaged the night-fighter sufficiently to drive it off. Meanwhile, Phillips was having great difficulty in preventing the Halifax from stalling because it kept trying to climb. This was partly overcome by tying the control column to the rudder bars with the dinghy rope, but pressure still had to be maintained to hold it forward. In addition to damage to the starboard elevator and tail assembly, a cannon shell had passed through the starboard wing causing internal damage. The fuselage and the bomb doors had been hit, as also had the astrodome and the mid-upper turret, the gunner being wounded. Despite the damage and control difficulties, Phillips continued his run in to the target but the bomb doors failed to open due to the damaged hydraulics. Sergeant McLean, the flight engineer, tried to pump the doors down by hand but they would not move, but during the return journey the doors finally freed themselves and the crew were able to jettison the three 1,000 lb and eight 500 lb HE bombs. One 1,000 lb bomb had already been jettisoned by hand-release, passing through the closed bomb doors, but the Target Indicator flares were brought back, the Halifax landing safely, albeit with considerable difficulty, at its home base.

JG 300's pilots claimed 12 victories from the night's action, but the same number was claimed also by the flak defences, leaving results uncertain. In all, thirty bombers were lost – ten Halifaxes, eight Lancasters, eight Wellingtons and five Stirlings.

From the Halifax force of 182, nine of the ten lost fell to night-fighters. No 10 Squadron lost DT784: M to Lt Johannes Hager of the 6./NJG 1, crashing in Belgium on the way to the target, while JD2262: J of 51 Squadron fell to Oblt Ludwig Meister of the I./NJG 4 on the homeward leg, again over Belgium. A Pathfinder from No 35 Squadron, HR6773: B also fell to night-fighter attack and was claimed by Hptm Siegfried Wandam of the I./NJG 5 who died within the hour, the victim of one of his targets. HR734: P from 158 Squadron, also fell to Ofw Reinhard Kollack of the 7./NJG 4 and crashed near Brabant in Belgium. A night-fighter probably brought the second 405 Squadron Pathfinder Halifax, HR813: H down as it also fell near Brabant. No 408 Squadron lost two: JB796: C, which crashed in France, and JB913: F, a definite night-fighter victim, which was claimed by Hptm Walter Milius of the III./NJG 3 over Belgium on the outward leg of the operation. JD159: Y of 419 Squadron was shot down by what was possibly a Bf 109 single-engine night-fighter – possibly a second victory that night for Ofw Kollack of the 7./NJG 4 – the Halifax crashing near Antwerp.

Accounts of combats with night-fighters were prolific during this period of intense activity; some were unusual. During the Montbeliard raid of 15/16 July, F/O M. Sattler's 405 Squadron crew had encountered what both gunners positively identified as a Do 217 night-fighter. Both also recognised British-style camouflage and national markings on the aircraft that attacked them eight times. Sattler carried out a series of violent corkscrew manoeuvres but the Do 217 hit the Halifax several times, shooting away one of the bomb carriers, piercing several fuel tanks and wounding the mid-upper gunner, F/O W. Anderson, in the left arm. Anderson and the rear gunner returned the fire and eventually the Do 217 went into a shallow dive and one engine burst into flames before it hit the ground and continued to burn. While the crew's description of the camouflage possibly could be accounted for by the German shift from all-black to two shades of grey (often applied in large patches, reminiscent of RAF-style camouflage), their identification of British roundel markings is harder to dispute. However, for what purpose such markings would have been useful at night is puzzling.

CHAPTER FIVE

THE BATTLE INTENSIFIES

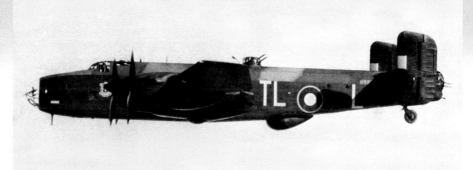

DESPITE its growing pains, Bomber Command was making its newfound strength felt. Between April and June 1943, approximately 11,000 sorties had gone to the Ruhr and the Rhineland, a figure equal to the entire effort of all the heavy bomber raids made during 1942. The coming autumn offensive was now aimed at a deeper penetration into the heart of Germany, Harris already having decided his next campaign objective long before the Cologne raids which ended the Battle of the Ruhr. This in itself meant that precise target identification and navigation depended entirely upon *H2S* equipment. The first major blow was therefore directed at Hamburg which, in addition to its importance as a target had the secondary benefit of providing a well-defined radar response on *H2S* equipment.

Between late July and early August, it would be subjected to four major attacks within the space of 10 days that would see approximately 8,000 tons of bombs dropped and an additional aid tried out; strips of coarse black paper exactly 27cm (10.62 inches) long and 2cm (0.787 inches) wide, with thin aluminium foil stuck to one side. Trials had shown that if used in sufficient quantity, this simple device would swamp the *Würzburg* radar sets that fed the German ground control for the night-fighter force, flak batteries and the airborne *Lichtenstein* sets of the night-fighters. Having been ready since April 1942, its use was held back for fear that the Luftwaffe would copy it and use it in their bombing attacks against Britain[1] – an unrealistic and expensive position to adopt, given the losses to Bomber Command in the ensuing 14 months and the known weakness of the German night bombing force when the majority of its Kampfgeschwader were heavily engaged on the Russian Front. It is estimated that between 100 and 130 bombers were saved by its use during just the Hamburg series of four attacks.

Hamburg, the largest European port and second largest city in Germany, had been on the target list since late May and attacked almost one hundred times before, but without causing significant damage. Well beyond the range of *Oboe* it was, however, theoretically ideal for an *H2S* attack given that it adjoined the sea; the distinctively shaped coastline also lent itself more to accurate navigation using this equipment. Also home port to *Bismarck*, it housed important dockyard facilities and four U-boat construction yards[2], but these were not targeted – the primary focus of the four major raids over a period of ten nights was the destruction of the work force. The USAAF was also to join the attack with B-17s bombing by day after the first night attack (though the devastating night attacks caused so much smoke that it obscured the city for days). Contrary to post-war writings, the amount of incendiaries carried was less than normal and the resulting firestorm was not intentional.

Seven hundred and ninety-one bombers launched the opening attack[3] on 24/25 July 1943 with *Window* being dropped from each aircraft at the rate of one bundle every minute. This produced responses equivalent to a force of 12,000 aircraft and

Two photographs of S/Ldr Alec Cranswick's HR926: L of 35 (PFF) Squadron photographed in the summer of 1943, with his family crest painted on the port side of the nose below the cockpit. It failed to return from an attack on Kassel on 22/23 October, one of 25 Halifaxes lost that night. A pilot of exceptional talent, Cranswick was an outstanding exponent of PFF techniques. He was killed on the night of 4/5 July 1944 flying Lancaster ND846 on his 107th sortie and his fourth tour of operations. (C. Cole)

effectively swamped the German equipment while masking the genuine echoes. Yet, this did not completely nullify the effectiveness of the night-fighters as the glow from the fires started in the city served to illuminate the bombers long enough for some to be visually intercepted.

Losses among the 246 Halifaxes were very light with only four being lost. HR940 of 51 Squadron was shot down by Oblt Günter Köberich of the IV./NJG 3, near Sonderborg, Denmark; DK187: M of 76 Squadron came down in the North Sea; JD316: X of 102 Squadron was another night-fighter victim; and HR941: A of 158 Squadron was brought down near Schleswig by Lt Böttinger of the II./NJG 3. One of the Pathfinder Halifaxes from 35 Squadron, HR803: P, had crashed just after take-off when both outer engines failed, fortunately without injury to any on board.

Total losses to enemy action for the whole operation were only 12. This figure of 1.5% was remarkable, previous percentages for Hamburg averaging out at 5.4% over the past 18 months. The effect of the next two raids by 787 and 777 bombers respectively could not be assessed until August when photographic reconnaissance revealed that some 74% of Hamburg's closely built-up residential areas had been heavily damaged.

The attack of 27/28 July again resulted in low losses, only 11 aircraft; but on the ground, unusual atmospheric conditions contributed to the development of a horrific firestorm. The highly concentrated bombing produced an intense conflagration, its extremely high temperatures producing a furnace effect, which

B Mk II Series I (Special) DT792: O of 10 Squadron illustrates just how sturdy the Halifax was. Subjected to repeated attacks by a Ju 88 night-fighter during the attack on Hamburg on 2 August 1943, F/O J. Jenkins and his crew were lucky to survive the encounter and return flight with limited control from the elevators. The central panel of the rear turret is open, some gunners preferring to endure the piercing cold to ensure that their vision was not impaired. DT792 was declared as being beyond economical repair and written-off.

Below: Two Halifax B Mk II Series IAs, NP-P and NP-M of 158 Squadron, photographed in May 1943. 'M-Mother' had artwork and approximately ten sorties marked on its nose and, given its configuration and number of operations completed, was possibly HR719. Issued to the squadron on 19 March 1943 it completed 17 operations before being lost over Düsseldorf on its 17th sortie on 11/12 June 1943. 'P-Peter' was possibly HR734 which served with the squadron from 24 March until lost on the Cologne operation of 3/4 July 1943, its 19th operation. (B. Chorley)

Below: HR861 seen here prior to delivery to 35 Squadron was produced near the end of May 1943; it was representative of the B Mk II Series IA configuration, but retained the close-fitting saxophone exhaust shrouds. As 'T-Tommy' it was lost in the attack on Nuremberg on 10/11 August 1943 with only F/Lt E. Ware DFC and three of his crew surviving. The Pathfinders had attempted to ground-mark the target but most markers were obscured by cloud. Even so, a useful attack developed causing considerable damage to central and southern Nuremberg. Six other Halifaxes, six Lancasters and three Stirlings also failed to return.

sucked everything into its raging centre.[4] Seven hundred and seventy-seven aircraft returned on the 29/30th and although fires were widespread and the damage extensive, the firestorm effect was not repeated[5]. This time 28 aircraft, 11 Halifaxes, 11 Lancasters, four Stirlings and two Wellingtons, failed to return.

The final raid of 2/3 August, however, was a failure. The German defences had been defeated but nature was not to be subdued. Severe electrical storms and icing conditions badly disrupted the mixed force of 235 Halifaxes, 329 Lancasters, 105 Stirlings and 66 Wellingtons, forcing many to jettison their bomb loads over north-west Germany or attack other targets. Enemy opposition was negligible and there is little doubt that the majority of the 30 aircraft that failed to return that night had fallen victim to the elements, yet some crews still encountered the ever-tenacious German night-fighters. F/O J. Jenkins of 10 Squadron heard a warning from the *Monica* set which had detected a Ju 88 stalking his Halifax. Moments later the fighter swept in to make several rapid attacks before Jenkins' gunner, Sgt R. Hurst, shot it down in

flames. The enemy fighter had scored several times during the brief encounter, severely damaging the Halifax's tail unit and shooting away portions of both elevators. Cannon shells had ripped through both wings, the port side of the fuselage and the bomb doors. In spite of the damage, Jenkins brought the Halifax back safely, crash-landing DT792: O *Farouk* without injury to anyone. For his actions, Jenkins was subsequently awarded a DFC while Hurst, credited with destruction of the night-fighter, the DFM.

Hamburg, however, was just part of the new round of attacks by Bomber Command and the month of August would later prove to be the most intensive period of 1943. Halifaxes were back in action as part of the forces sent against Mannheim and Nuremberg on the 9/10th and 10/11th by 457 and 653 aircraft respectively and again in the five subsequent raids against Italian targets aimed at hastening Italy's departure from the war[6].

Then, on 17/18 August while the moon period was still available 596 bombers, 324 Lancasters, 218 Halifaxes and 54 Stirlings, carried out a special attack against the German experimental research station at Peenemünde on the Baltic coast. Ironically, few if any of the crews knew the real reason for the attack because German rocket research was still highly secret. Code-named *Operation Hydra*, this was the first major

A harmony of contrasts, 77 Squadron's DT807: R having its port inner engine checked forms a background to the autumn harvest of 1943. A semi-nude with the name 'Rita' adorned the Tollerton fairing and 20 sorties were recorded below the cockpit; the eleventh one was marked in colour for some unknown reason, the remainder appearing in white. Produced in the last week of March, the aircraft was lost in the attack on Kassel on 3/4 October 1943, brought down at Wernswig, 5 km south-west of Homberg with only two, Sergeants R. Searle and D. Griffiths, surviving from Sgt H. Cracknell's crew.

raid to employ a 'Master Bomber' to supervise the target marking[7]. Both 35 and 405 Squadrons were among the Pathfinder Force that night. F/Lt Davidson, flying HR897: F of 35 Squadron later reported that the fires were visible for a distance of 150 miles after leaving the target. Visibility was excellent, the railway lines clearly seen and one block of the buildings split open and burning furiously. Another of the squadron's Halifaxes, JB787: G, was being flown by F/O J. Jagger who captured the atmosphere of the raid in the brief phrasing of his report. *"Visibility good but smoke-screen down west side of perimeter. Identified by red and green target indicators. Red target indicators went down first and flares, white, with them. Two greens went down a little later followed by more greens. These were all well grouped between aiming points F and B. Own*

B Mk V Series I (Special) DK148: G 'bar' (there were two Halifaxes coded 'B-Baker' on the squadron, this one distinguished by a horizontal bar painted above the 'B') again illustrates the sturdiness of the Halifax. On 25/26 July F/Lt C. Shannon's crew participated in the raid on Essen, this Halifax's 16th sortie. Over the target, a wooden propeller blade on the port inner engine failed and smashed into the side of the fuselage, cutting deeply into it in a ragged line. Shannon ordered the crew to bale out but only Sgt E. Waterman reacted before control was regained and 'Johnnie the Wolf' was nursed back to 76 Squadron's home base at Holme-on-Spalding Moor. Sgt Waterman became a POW but the remainder of the crew survived the subsequent crash-landing. The damage caused by the disintegrating propeller blade is evident in both views, the resulting vibration tearing the entire propeller assembly out of the engine, taking the reduction gear with it. Produced in late March 1943, DK148 exhibits the standard configuration for a B Mk V Series I (Special). (RCAF)

More details of the damage to B Mk V Series I (Special) DK148: G 'bar' after its crash-landing on 25/26 July 1943. (RCAF)

Artwork showing teeth became popular with some crews flying the Series I (Special) variant, the area around the upper horizontal Perspex window quite literally giving extra depth to the illusion with the angled lines of rivets around the window (marked here in white) providing a clear guide for ground crew if and when applying such artwork. The Aircraft Inspection Department Inspector, who checked over each aircraft after completion, marked with white chalk rivets requiring replacement; more are visible on the front section of the fuselage, the longer chalk lines leading back to the triangular window and around its front section highlighting sealant problems. This late production B Mk V Series I (Special) is fitted with Morris block radiators, which required a different lower cowling shape similar to that of the original B Mk I. Engine Fitters and Flight Engineers routinely attended training courses at the relevant manufacturer's plant and this group were photographed at Rootes Securities factory at Speke inspecting changes to the engine coolant system. This Halifax was probably from their last B Mk V batch from which deliveries commenced mid July 1943. (P. Summerton)

greens found this group and then two yellows came down almost immediately after right on this group. HE bang on the target indicator flares. Would have been useful but for the smokescreen. Woods well alight to south-west of aiming point F. Fires close amongst buildings. One big sheet of flame went up about 00.22 hrs and also 00.25 hrs with billows of flame."

The attack achieved its aim at the cost of 40 bombers, among them ten Halifaxes from No 6 Group, three from No 4 Group and two from No 8 Group. The seemingly endless war of decoy fires and pyrotechnic devices entered a new phase during this raid, which saw the first ever use of Red Spot Target Indicators. The usual 250 lb bomb casing was filled with cotton wool soaked in a solution of metallic perchlorate dissolved in alcohol that burned on the ground for 15 to 20 minutes as a deep red single-spot fire. (A green version would enter service later). Unfortunately, fire and smoke from the bombing often rapidly obscured them and gradually they became reserved for only small precision targets or as route markers for the Main Force.

This raid marked the opening of the offensive against the V-weapon threat, now taken far more seriously following very direct evidence provided by Polish agents; the evidence had been reviewed by British Chiefs of Staff on 12 April and a plan to disrupt such work formulated. Even so, following the Peenemünde attack little would be done other than the Kassel raid of 22/23 October when the Henschel works were badly damaged. As they were producing V-1s this was a significant blow, but may have been a serendipitous gain. The specific targeting of flying bomb sites did not start until 16/17 December when 26 Stirlings and 9 Lancasters, with 12 Mosquitoes to do *Oboe* marking, attacked two sites near Abbeville on the same night as a Main Force attack on Berlin. The Stirlings sent against the Tilley-le-Haut site failed due to the *Oboe*-aided marking getting no closer than 450 yards from the small target. The nine Lancasters from 617 Squadron sent against the Flixecourt site fared no better for, although they also dropped on their marked aiming point accurately, it was again

Two views of HR782: V, one of twenty Halifaxes from 51 Squadron sent for the attack on Mönchengladbach and the neighbouring town of Rheydt on 30/31 August 1943. As recorded in the text, it collided with a Lancaster from an HCU but with a very skilled piece of flying made it home and was landed safely. The helical slicing effect from the Lancaster's propeller produced spaced, vertical gashes and shows how close it came to cutting off the port horizontal tail plane surfaces; the leading edge has two visible dents in it. Had the rotation of the propeller been a fraction of a second later it would have cut the tail plane spar along its length. The shock damage caused by the momentary compression of the rear turret shattered all of the Perspex panels. The thin pale line separating the upper surface camouflage from the black-painted surfaces was a distinguishing feature of Handley Page-built Halifaxes. The pale oblong of the serial number produced by the carrier film of the decal is clearly visible.

some 350 yards short of the target. Thus, the attacks against the flying bomb sites began but they would not develop into a steady rhythm until mid-1944.

Bombing emphasis now swung back to Germany. Leverkusen was targeted by 462 bombers on 22/23rd for the loss of just two Halifaxes and three Lancasters and on 23/24 August, 727 bombers launched the first of three heavy raids against Berlin; the steady increase in the number of heavy bombers making it possible to prosecute a winter campaign against the German capital at last[8]. However, the results were not encouraging. The first attack met with only partial success and dummy Target Indicators dropped by German aircraft to mislead the bombers were just one factor.

Between 23 August and 4 September, Harris launched three attacks against Berlin in what was a tentative start to a long campaign that developed during the winter months. However, poor results and high losses turned his attention elsewhere while waiting for the improved version of H2S, which was better suited to inland targets. W/Cdr C. K. Lawrence and his crew were preparing for one of the Berlin attacks when photographed here in front of JD173: V of 78 Squadron. Produced in May 1943, this English Electric-built B Mk II exhibits the refinements of the Series IA excluding the Morris double-block radiators and probably Merlin 22 engines. It also retains the tall radio mast. It survived to be passed to 1658 HCU and then to No 1669 where it served until struck off charge on 22 February 1945. (M. Wright)

Built by Fairey Aviation in late September 1943, aside from the saxophone style exhausts, LK640: Q of 431 Squadron exhibits all of the attributes of a final production B Mk V Series IA. In particular, the paintwork around the engines shows the very smooth, slight gloss associated with the cellulose DTD 308 finish. Photographed after its first three operational sorties had been completed, it had already acquired artwork with the name 'Queenie' plus crew names added at each location: 'Dave' the bomb aimer, 'Lorne' for the navigator's wife or girlfriend, 'Bob' the wireless operator, 'Bill' the pilot, 'Mac' the flight engineer, and two others for the gunners. As seen on many Halifaxes on RCAF squadrons, a white disc containing a red Maple Leaf forms a part of the bomb log decoration. The aircraft was lost on the Mannheim attack on 18/19 November, crashing into the Channel and killing all of F/O G. Carefoot's crew. A check of names indicates that this was not the same crew recorded here. (J. Falconer via B. Robertson)

The Pathfinders had been unable to pinpoint the centre of the city by *H2S* and despite the use of a Master Bomber to direct marking, the southern area was marked instead. The Main Force arrived late and despite the use of flares dropped at points to mark the route and keep the Main Force both on track and concentrated, many crews, trying to make up time, approached from the south-west instead of the specified south-south-east route, resulting in many bomb loads falling in open country. The defences were extremely strong and claimed 7.9% of the bombers, the Command's heaviest loss in the war so far with 56 of the 727 bombers failing to return.

As already recounted, night-fighter attacks from the region of the blind underbelly of RAF bombers had prompted the 76 Squadron experiment of late 1942. By mid-1943, the growing menace of such lethal attacks prompted other squadrons to take matters into their own hands and, during August, 419 Squadron modified their B Mk II Halifaxes to carry a single 0.5-in calibre hand-operated machine gun in the old fuselage-well position. They installed a seat of the type used for both front and mid-upper turrets and a bracket to hold the machine gun and though it was a very cold and semi-exposed position, the crews felt that they were no longer so open to blind attacks from below. This modification was made outside of official tests to find a suitable ventral defensive fitting and is perhaps an indication of the frustration of the crews that led the squadron to carry out its own unofficial modifications on such a scale[9].

Between the first and second Berlin attacks, Nuremberg was targeted on the 27/28th and Mönchengladbach and the neighbouring town of Rheydt on the 30/31st. This was the first major attack on Mönchengladbach since 11/12 August 1941 and of the 660 aircraft sent against the two targets, 25 were lost, eight of them Halifaxes. HR782: V from 51 Squadron had survived the raid and the crew were starting to relax after crossing the English coast and the pilot started his let-down procedure; but at 4,000 ft, ten miles south-east of Ossington, he saw something on the port bow closing head-on and very fast. He pushed the nose down but the collision swung the Halifax 60° off its previous heading and a violent vibration started in the port wing. Trying to reduce speed further the rudder suddenly locked

to starboard, stalled and the starboard wing dropped, the Halifax going into a spiral. About to order his crew out, the speed slowly began increasing and he was able to get the Halifax back on a normal heading. The collision had set off the destruction charges in the IFF and *Gee* sets, which caught fire and filled the interior with smoke. The top of the rear turret had been pushed in, momentarily stunning the otherwise lucky gunner. The fuselage had gashes in it and the flight engineer reported that the port tail assembly appeared to be missing.

Experimentation soon established that the Halifax would not respond at less than 180 mph IAS unless full port aileron and rudder trim were used. Only three engines were working, the flap actuator accumulator had been knocked adrift and was leaking oil making the flaps inoperative and the undercarriage pressure gauge was reading zero. The pilot then made a low approach using full throttle on the two starboard engines, cutting them as they crossed the airfield boundary. The starboard wing dropped just before touchdown and an attempt to pull it level again produced a swing which took the Halifax off the runway and risking all, the pilot opened the throttle on the starboard engines and got the aircraft running parallel with the runway before stopping a hundred yards short of the airfield boundary. It was later established that a Lancaster from an HCU had been the culprit and had survived to make a safe three-engine landing. Damaged propellers, two feet missing from the outer set, and one foot from the port inner set, had produced the vibration experienced in HR782's port wing. Although damage was substantial, HR782 was repaired and returned to 51 Squadron, continuing on operations as 'A-Able' until shot down by flak, homeward bound from the attack on Leipzig on 3/4 December 1943. It crashed 10 km east-south-east of Boppard, killing Sgt S. Ainsworth and one of his crew, Sgt S. Tarrant, but the other five survived.

The following evening, 622 bombers again set out for Berlin. Crews later reported less interference from ground defences going to and from the target and relatively moderate flak in the target area itself, but night-fighters were present in large numbers and had introduced a new tactic using flares. Dropped from approximately 20,000 ft the flares served to illuminate the bomber stream, and received a particular mention in the post raid analysis. *"... consisting of continuous illumination of the skies above the target by intensely bright white flares. Crews were of the opinion that they were dropped by aircraft in clusters of a dozen or more at the corners of the target area with a double strip apparently dropped by rapidly moving aircraft around the perimeter of the area and igniting at about 17.000 ft and lasting for several minutes. Enemy night-fighters were very active ...*" Searchlights were also plentiful and went into action before the attack actually commenced. Again the raid was not successful – cloud in the target area combined with *H2S* difficulties and, perhaps, the ferocity of the defences, caused the Pathfinder markers to be dropped well south of the centre of the city; most bombs fell ten miles or more south of the city, some as far as 30 miles back along the approach route.

The loss of 47 bombers – 20 Halifaxes, 17 Stirlings and 10 Lancasters – was even more depressing when the results of the raid were analysed, little material damage being achieved for the loss of about two-thirds of these bombers to night-fighters over or near Berlin. No 158 Squadron had dispatched 19 for the raid, four of which failed to return, HR937: P, JD246: R, JN903: C with the fourth, Sgt W. Kidd's HR738 'Zombie's Zephyr', shot down by two night-fighters near Paderborn with only two of the crew surviving. Four had baled out of Sgt K. Ward's JD246, another victim of night-fighter attack, the Halifax falling at Märtensmühle, south of Trebin. The flight engineer, Sgt H. Simster then made a remarkable escape. Having landed in the Berlin suburbs, he hid for the rest of the night and then set out for the coast, stealing two bicycles during his long journey. At one stage, he almost made a fatal mistake by entering the Heinkel works at Rostock. At Lübeck, he tried to gain passage on a ship but after being refused twice, headed for Hamburg on one of the stolen bicycles. Helped to mend a punctured tyre by local German workmen, he eventually peddled off to Holland. There he was helped to get into Belgium where the local underground took charge of him and he reached Switzerland. Tiring of his forced retirement he moved back into France, joined the Maquis and was eventually flown to Tunis courtesy of the USAAF and then back to England just one year after being shot down. His tenacity in escaping from so deep within enemy territory won him an award of the Military Medal.

The final Berlin raid of 3/4 September made by a comparatively small number of 316 Lancasters and four Mosquitoes achieved only slightly better results. The high casualty rates amongst the Stirlings (16% of their force) and Halifaxes in the previous attack had prompted their absence: an action that would lead to other restrictions. Although the Mosquitoes dropped 'spoof' flares well away from the bomber stream to attract the night-fighters, 22 Lancasters were still lost. While material results were meagre, the psychological effect on the German population was most marked and the panic evacuation following the initial raid of 23/24 August was comparable to that experienced in Hamburg. Despite the minor target damage achieved by the three attacks and the panic evacuation, Gauleiter Dr. Josef Goebbels[10] felt concerned enough to order the evacuation of all children and adults not engaged in war work in Berlin. The intent of Bomber Command was now clear.

By September 1943, stocks of the A Mk VIII (Special) turrets finally had been used up and the production model A Mk VIII introduced onto Halifax production lines. This version was readily distinguished when the improved B Mk II Series IA Halifaxes entered service. The large metal fairing, with its contour track for the interrupter gear, was gone and the turret lowered some five inches; a simple metal skirt faired it into the fuselage and the standard Boulton Paul electro-mechanical fire interrupter gear system was again used.

September 1943 saw the ranks of Halifax-equipped squadrons increase again. Nos 429 and 433 Squadrons RCAF were joined by No 466 Squadron RAAF; they had arrived at a time when operations were slowing against the Ruhr but there were plenty of opportunities to use their new heavies on other targets. No sustained offensive was maintained against Ruhr and Rhineland targets during the actual autumn period but a variety of industrial targets were attacked at intervals. Kassel, an important engine-manufacturing centre, was one such target that received two heavy raids during October. Fl/Sgt McPhail of 102 Squadron took part in the first of these on 3/4 October flying Halifax, JD467: V, which had suffered flak damage during the operation. While circling to land back at Pocklington, the port inner engine fell out of the aircraft but McPhail still managed to make a safe landing. Fortunately, such occurrences were rare in the extreme.

Others were not so fortunate; the long haul to and from the target and nervous tension from the fighting all took a steady toll to which was added crew fatigue, an ever-present threat which all too often cost lives in the final stage of the night's operation. On 4/5 October a force of 406 aircraft had targeted Frankfurt, losing ten of their number – five Halifaxes, three Lancasters and two Stirlings plus a USAAF B-17[11]. Now another Halifax was about to be added to the list. Sergeant Fenning of 51 Squadron was returning to Snaith in HR727: V in the early hours of 5 October, after it was damaged over the target area, when a night-fighter set the port inner engine on fire and Fenning had corkscrewed the Halifax down to 9,000 ft before shaking off its attacker as well as putting out the fire. Fenning feathered the engine while Sgt Lane the flight engineer checked the petrol situation and, finding that the number 2 tank was obviously holed, he ran all three engines from it rather than waste what was left of the 64 gallons of fuel (to transfer fuel from the port to the starboard wing tanks required cutting the locking wires that held the valve switches and normally prevented accidental transfer).

Having done this, Lane recalculated the fuel situation and estimated that they had four hours flying time left. He passed that information to the navigator and then checked which accessory services would have to be operated by hand now that the No 2 engine and its auxiliary systems were not available. Finally, Beachy Head was sighted and the Halifax continued its northwards flight but as it did so, it ran into bad weather and the wireless operator found reception from Snaith extremely poor. The signal continued to fade and finally died away completely. The Halifax was now in bad weather, on three engines, with no weather reports or radio bearings for the navigator and no visual contact with the ground since passing over Reading. Already to port of track, the navigator could only estimate the winds and consequent drift; Snaith was calculated to be 15 minutes flying time distant.

Fuel was now running low and time would be needed in the circuit to check out everything before making the landing with one dead engine. At 2,000 ft the Halifax was still in cloud but if they could get below the cloud base then they might be able to follow the *Pundits*[12] to their own base. Fenning warned the crew and began his last descent – and flew straight into the ground at Blackden Moor in Derbyshire. Three survived the crash, but one died while the rescue team was on its way. The bomb aimer and the rear gunner were the lucky ones. The subsequent court of inquiry placed the blame on Fenning for breaking cloud when uncertain of his position! The flight engineer was also criticised for failing to keep an adequate check on the fuel situation and for failing to warn of the impending fuel shortage. Flak and night-fighters were clearly not the only enemies that exhausted crews had to contend with!

Completed at the end of June 1943, this B Mk V Series I (Special) EB214 passed to 427 Squadron RCAF with whom, from the bomb log marked on its nose section, it had a successful run of operations before being transferred to 1664 HCU where it soldiered on until 1 November 1945. Photographed on 16 November 1943, the nose art of a large apple was a play on its own identity of 'A-Apple', the letter being repeated on the front face of the Dowty undercarriage. Twenty-one white bomb symbols were displayed when this photograph was taken. Its Canadian 'ownership' is displayed in the form of a red Canadian Maple Leaf on a white disc below the cockpit, a feature common to many RCAF Halifaxes. (RCAF)

JD300:G of No 158 Squadron was fitted with Merlin 22s but retained the original Galley radiators with their distinctive nacelle shape – officially a B Mk II Series I (Special). During the raid on Nuremberg on 10/11 August 1943, its gunners claimed a Do 217 destroyed, 25 miles NW of Ludwigshafen. Between 30 June and 24 December it completed 28 operations with the squadron before being transferred to No 51 Squadron. It was later used briefly at Boscombe Down to test a ventral gun installation during the continuing trials work with the fixed Preston-Green cupola. It then passed successively to No 78 Squadron, No 1663 HCU and then No 1652 HCU, before being struck off charge on 8 February 1947 – a long and successful career for any World War Two bomber of early 1943 vintage. (G. V. Smith)

By November 1943, Bomber Command had expanded its heavy bomber element sufficiently to allow the long awaited sustained campaign against Berlin to get underway. Quantity production of *H2S* had now been achieved and over 90% of the force was fitted with this equipment. Mid-November marked the beginning of Harris' long-awaited campaign against not only the heart of Germany but also the entire German system. He believed that this campaign would open the final, fatal cracks in German morale thus meeting the joint Allied directive, which had called, in part, for the breaking of the morale of the German people and their capacity to continue the war. With few exceptions, for the following four and a half months, Harris would be allowed to use his bomber force as he saw fit. During this period, 32 major attacks would strike Germany, half against Berlin and the remainder against other major cities. However, the crews who flew those sorties did not care for pedantic distinction – to them it would be known as the Battle of Berlin while for Bomber Command it would become as much a life and death struggle as for the German people. Pathfinder aircraft were equipped with a newer version of *H2S*, but this device, good though it was, was limited against a sprawling city such as Berlin in that it offered little specific target discrimination. *Oboe's* range limitations would allow only one of the 32 major targets to be marked with this far more accurate aid. The German night-fighter force had also made a significant and deadly recovery from its recent period of decline caused by the introduction of *Window*. It was perhaps ironic that *Window* had brought about the demise of the old controlled box system, which had favoured a relatively small percentage of the force – the experts who had, by their skill, run up large personal scores.

The German night defensive system was also in transition and the *Wilde Sau* system expanded. Twin-engined night-fighters were sent to freelance amid the bomber stream – a bomber stream that until now had protected the individual aircraft from identification on night-fighter radar screens behind the snowy mass of the *Window* responses. Even so, that electronic snowstorm marked the bomber stream and allowed Ju 88 reconnaissance aircraft to fly towards it to try to determine

the actual bomber stream as early as possible while night-fighters assembled over radio beacons to await instructions. As these moves were underway, Ju 88-equipped illuminator units stood by to fly above the bombers and drop strings of flares to draw the night-fighters to them. The German control system meanwhile was collecting information from its ground observer plots and broadcasting a continuous stream of information to the night-fighters while attempting to determine the final destination of the bombers.

This brought many more night-fighters into contact with the bomber stream than under the old system and results were significantly higher despite the concentration of the stream. When introduced in 1942, the bomber stream system saw the bombers stretched over an average distance of 300 miles but that was now reduced to 70 miles and the number of individual aircraft increased significantly. Even so, time over the target was cut back repeatedly until some 800 could bomb in less than 20 minutes. To counter the increase in night-fighter activity under the new German system, Fighter Command increased its Intruder operations against German airfields but more sustained help came from the specialised No 100 (Bomber Support) Group, which formed in November 1943[13]. Several of Fighter Command's night-fighter squadrons joined the Group and its specialised radio countermeasures (RCM) aircraft and would join the battle during the next phase.

Treacherous weather conditions and the necessity to restrict raids to moonless nights limited the number of operations during November and December to eight and it was following an attack on Ludwigshafen on 17/18 November that a new device came into use. Returning crews often fell at the last hurdle trying to land a badly crippled aircraft and so in August emergency landing facilities had been set up at RAF Woodbridge. This airfield had a very long runway system, which was also fitted with another recently introduced system called *FIDO*[14]. This system burned a channel of fuel oil along each edge of the runway for use when fog, as so often happened, otherwise closed many bases to returning aircraft. But it was fuel shortage, not fog that brought the first emergency landing by a bomber when LK918: F of 431 Squadron landed at Woodbridge, Fl/Sgt King having attacked Ludwigshafen earlier in the evening and landed, short of fuel, at 23.20 hrs.

The first November attack on Berlin was carried out on the 18/19th by a 440-strong all-Lancaster force while, in an effort to split the opposing night-fighter forces, a mixed force of 395 Halifaxes and Stirlings raided Mannheim. The ruse was successful and few night-fighters attacked the Berlin force, concentrating instead on the Mannheim attackers, which cost 12 Halifaxes, nine Stirlings and two Lancasters. Like Berlin, cloud obscured much of the target and although 248 Halifaxes, 114 Stirlings and 33 Lancasters carried out the attack, bombing was scattered. Even so, it did cause some major damage; the Daimler-Benz car factory suffered a 90% production loss for what the post-raid German report described as "an unknown period", four industrial buildings were destroyed and another 11 seriously damaged in the northern part of Mannheim. Four army barracks at Sandhofen airfield were among the long list of buildings damaged. This was the last major attack on Mannheim for the next 15 months.

Despite the success of the split-attack ploy, Berlin escaped relatively lightly in return for the loss of nine Lancasters. Completely cloud-covered, sky marking had to be employed but was hampered by the fact that the flares rapidly sank from sight into the cloud and the *H2S* equipment was only serviceable in eleven aircraft of the Blind Marker force. For bomber crews this was to be a very hard period, with most targets distant ones, very bad weather and a reorganized German night-fighter force.

Leverkusen was attacked on 19/20 November by a mixed force of 266 aircraft – 170 Halifaxes, 86 Stirlings and ten Mosquitoes – but a combination of *Oboe* equipment failures amongst the Mosquito marking force and bad weather brought very poor results for the force. In fact, Leverkusen recorded only one high-explosive bomb dropped but 27 other towns, mostly to the north, were hit. The bad weather extended back to England and two Halifaxes crashed on return, bringing Halifax losses to six for the night. Four Halifaxes from 35 Squadron escaped a similar fate when landing at Graveley where the first operational use of *FIDO* – described by one grateful pilot as "like landing between the gates of Hell" – was made that night.

The bombers returned to Berlin on 22/23 November, 234 of the 764 being Halifaxes, the largest force sent to Berlin to this date. Bad weather again kept the German night-fighters grounded and only 26 bombers failed to return – ten Halifaxes, eleven Lancasters and five Stirlings, just 3.4% of the force. Target marking and bombing were accurate despite the target again being completely cloud-covered. Several firestorms, aided by the dry atmospheric conditions caused by the freezing weather, broke out and smoke columns stretching up to 19,000 ft were still visible next day. It was the most effective raid yet on the city and for the Stirling force, their last operation against a German target.

It was a different story the next night when 383 bombers were again sent to Berlin, alarmingly along the same route as the previous attack. German controllers were quickly in command of the situation and had assembled the single-engine night-fighters over the city by zero hour with others arriving minutes later. However, these preparations were partially confounded by German-speaking British-based controllers passing fake instructions to the night-fighters while Mosquitoes dropped fake night-fighter flares north of the bomber stream. These countermeasures undoubtedly helped keep down the losses, but 20 Lancasters failed to return from the mixed force. Despite cloud, the Pathfinders marked the target quite accurately using the *Wanganui* method with sky markers and a well-developed attack ensued with many crews able to bomb by using the glow from the previous night's attack as the aiming point.

During November 419 Squadron carried out some experiments to try to improve their Halifax mid-under gun positions against the intense cold encountered at high altitudes. A few nights later, on the 25/26th, the squadron took part in a raid on Frankfurt-am-Main and one of their Halifaxes encountered a major 'cold' problem that affected all the crew. Halifax LW243: Y was attacked by a night-fighter that severely damaged it and forced the captain to jettison the bomb load. The port rudder and the bomb bay doors were damaged but the starboard wing took most of the night-fighter's cannon shells. The inboard engine was hit and the undercarriage doors blown off along with a large piece of the wing. More serious though, was the damage to the forward fuselage, the Perspex nose cone being blown off, destroying most of the navigator's equipment. The navigator guided the aircraft home using an old map that he had in his bag but had to lay on the floor of the rest station amidships to shelter from the icy blast that roared through the length of the fuselage.

No 102 Squadron also took part in the operation. HX153: P, one of 22 dispatched, removed part of the airfield boundary fence with its undercarriage but went on to bomb the target. On returning to base, the Halifax swung badly to port during the landing but P/O Eddy managed to retain control and pulled up without further damage. This attack was virtually an all-Halifax effort, 230 of them along with 26 Lancasters. The route into the target had been a direct one and the German controllers had correctly identified the destination. With flak restricted to a height of 15,000 ft the night-fighters had a free hand and 11 Halifaxes and one Lancaster were brought down.

The next night, the 26/27th, the Main Force headed for the same target again but split into two sections, the Lancaster force going to Berlin while 157 Halifaxes and 21 Lancasters continued on to Stuttgart. Again, the ruse worked and the night-fighter force wasted a considerable amount of time laying flares over Frankfurt-am-Main and by the time they realized that the main target was Berlin they were only able to intercept the last bomber wave. Even so 6.2% of the force failed to return – 28 Lancasters, with 14 more crashing on return to England. The Stuttgart force losses were 3.4%, all of them Halifaxes.

The weather throughout December was appalling. The Berlin attack of 2/3 December was a complete failure due to winds varying greatly, both in strength and direction from those forecast, particularly on the return flight, exposing the bombers to further night-fighter attacks. Additionally, no diversions were used, the force making a direct line for Berlin. The German controllers identified the target 19 minutes before the bomber stream arrived and positioned their night-fighters accordingly. Unlike the first Berlin raid, losses were heavy with 40 (8.7%) of the 458 bombers failing to return. Of the 15 Pathfinder Force Halifaxes that took part in the operation two were lost, these being HR876: S and HX167: C of 35 Squadron. Thirty-seven Lancasters and one Mosquito also failed to return.

Halifax losses were heavier the following night when Leipzig was the target. The 527-strong force was again sent on a direct route, seemingly heading for Berlin before turning for the real target, while Mosquitoes carried out a spoof raid on the capital, a ruse which drew the attention of most of the German night-fighter force. The majority of the 15 Halifaxes and nine Lancasters that failed to return were brought down before the bomber stream turned for Leipzig, where they delivered the most successful raid of the war against that city.

Foul weather over England again caused a heavy loss of life on return from the next Berlin raid, an all-Lancaster attack on 16/17th. It was the first use of *Serrate*[15] patrols by the British night-fighters of No 100 Group[16], marking the beginning of a long battle within a battle. The raid was also marked by a straight in and out route, which the German controllers accurately plotted and exploited. With weather conditions so bad Bomber Command could not risk diversions and for its crews it was a lose-lose situation in many cases and results were poor.

Frankfurt again received the attention of Bomber Command on 20/21st when it was attacked by 257 Halifaxes, 390 Lancasters and three Mosquitoes. This time the German control system accurately plotted their course from the English coast all the way to the target. A diversionary raid on Mannheim failed to draw off the German night-fighters until the main attack had finished; losses were 27 Halifaxes (6.3%) and 14 Lancasters. Nevertheless, and despite a decoy fire site and use of dummy Target Indicators and an unpredicted 8/10ths cloud cover, the bombing results were effective.

Berlin was attacked again on 23/24 December by 379 Lancasters, eight Mosquitoes and seven Halifaxes. Casualties were lighter than on previous recent attacks, possibly because the night-fighters encountered difficulties with the weather conditions and partly by the deception of the German controller by a spoof raid against Leipzig by the Mosquitoes. An additional twelve Mosquitoes sent to Aachen and a further nine to Duisburg plus an additional four *RCM* sorties added to the confusion. Berlin was again covered by cloud and *H2S* failures amongst the first wave of Pathfinders led to scattered marking and bombing, achieving little for the loss of 16 Lancasters.

The last operation against Berlin for 1943 was that carried out by 252 Halifaxes, 457 Lancasters and three Mosquitoes on 29/30 December. A long route was chosen, first passing south of the Ruhr and then to within 20 miles of Leipzig, while Mosquito spoof attacks were made on Düsseldorf, Leipzig and Magdeburg to add to the dilemma of the German controllers. Bad weather, for once an ally, also helped to screen the bombers on their inbound route and losses from all causes were encouragingly low at nine Halifaxes and 11 Lancasters and, while crews claimed a concentrated attack, actual results failed to substantiate this.

No 76 Squadron crews reported 10/10ths cloud over the target, but 19 of their 20 Halifaxes released their bombs on the sky markers dropped by the Pathfinders. With the night-fighters lured to Leipzig and Magdeburg, the flak defences were more active than usual but bundles of *Window* disrupted the radar prediction equipment and forced the flak batteries to resort to firing box barrages. Fl/Sgt Burcher of No 10 Squadron had one engine of his Halifax set on fire by flak but held his bombing run for two minutes. Having completed his bombing run he then extinguished the blaze and turned for home, only to lose a second engine before finally reaching an emergency airfield, where he landed safely.

Disruption of the original *Lichtenstein* night-fighter radar by *Window* caused the Germans to intensify their development of its successor, *Lichtenstein SN2*. The old equipment worked on a wavelength of 53 cm and had a very narrow search beam of 24°; the new equipment was far superior, with a beam width of 120° and a wavelength of 330 cm, the latter not being jammed by *Window*. Range was also greatly improved, but there was one drawback – minimum range was 400 yds and beyond the distance at which visual contact was normally made, but further refinement on later models remedied this. FuG 227 *Flensburg* was another radar device that could home on to the emissions from the *Monica* tail warning sets. Able to make contact at 100 km, under certain favourable conditions, that distance doubled. It enabled the night-fighter crew to home onto the bomber with deadly accuracy and no amount of violent manoeuvres would break the contact. The only thing that would ultimately save bomber crews from this deadly trap occurred when bomber streams became heavily saturated and pilots, unable to make sense of the almost continuous warning signals, switched the *Monica* set off. Nevertheless, that was still in the distant future and, in the interim, many crews would perish. A third device, FuG 350Z, *Naxos*, homed on to *H2S* emissions and was able to detect them up to a distance of 50 km. Equipped with this formidable array of radar aids, the German night-fighter force would enter into a pitched battle with the forces of Bomber Command in the New Year.

Berlin drew the bombers back again on 1/2 January 1944 but this time the German night-fighters were homed onto the Lancasters at an early stage and took a significant toll, with 28 of the 421 sent shot down. It was poor reward for the fight against weather and a cloud-covered target where accuracy of the sky marking had quickly deteriorated. Very little damage was done.

Not surprisingly, Halifax losses began to rise during January 1944. No 76 Squadron which had, until the end of the previous year, suffered virtually no losses for several months, lost six in the first two operations in January plus two more through crashes. No 102 Squadron had an equally black start to the year, losing 11 aircraft in the first month, seven of them in one night. The attack on Magdeburg of 21/22 January by 648 aircraft saw 57 (8.8%) fail to return, the 35 losses from the Halifax component of 224 representing a loss percentage of 15.6%. Halifax losses in No 4 Group reached an all-time peak during January with 11.4% missing out of 544 sorties against German targets and an overall loss of 10.1 % out of 613 sorties against all targets. For the individual Halifax squadrons, No 434 was the hardest hit with a 24.2% loss rate, followed by 102 Squadron at 18.7%, 76 Squadron at 16.7%, 77 Squadron at 15% and 427 Squadron at the lowest with 13.9%. Amidst this rising toll, the Halifax force took part in another statistical first when 891 aircraft were sent to Berlin on 15/16 February. Not only was this the largest force ever sent to that city,

When not called on for major attacks, squadrons were added into the minor operations of the night, often as a draw to split the enemy defences. Mining had been used to ease new crews into operation before Harris became C in C Bomber Command but not long into his term of office he had stopped the practice for front line units, leaving OTU crews to carry out the duties. The problem was that the German defences became very good at inflicting casualties as the minefields required relatively low-level, precision dropping. Eventually, the task once more became shared more broadly. A bomb train had delivered a load of sea mines, each with their parachute pack attached to one end, ready for loading in to 'T-Tare', but first the fuel tanks were topped-up by mobile bowser. (M. Wright)

but it was also the largest force assembled and sent to any target since the 1000-bomber raids of 1942. To all intents and purposes, this raid marked the ending of the Battle of Berlin.

On 19/20 February a force of 823 bombers, 255 of them Halifaxes, were sent to Leipzig. It was an ill-fated operation from the outset with only a part of the German night-fighter force being drawn off by a diversionary raid on Kiel Bay. As the Main Force crossed the Dutch coast, it came under night-fighter attacks which increased as the fighters were joined by those sent to investigate the Kiel raid. Harassed all the way to the target by night-fighters, the bombing force arrived over the target early due to incorrect wind forecasts and was forced to orbit while waiting for the Pathfinders to mark the aiming points. Flak brought down about 20 aircraft and four others were lost in mid-air collisions. In all, 34 Halifaxes and 44 Lancasters failed to return, a staggering 9.5% loss rate. For the Halifaxes, the loss figure was 14.9% of those that reached the enemy coast. Overall figures for Halifax losses against German targets during February now stood at 10.8% from 269 sorties, the overall figure being halved at a loss rate of 5.1% from 644 sorties against all targets.

The indications were quite clear and following the Leipzig raid, an order was issued that permanently suspended all B Mk II and V Halifaxes from operations against German targets, although B Mk IIs serving with the Pathfinder Force were permitted to continue. While much has been made of this restriction, in fact it affected just four squadrons, Nos 10, 77, 102 and 419, the remainder having already converted to the more powerful B Mk III version which had no such restriction placed upon it. The ban only affected 10 Squadron for about two weeks as it began operating B Mk IIIs in March. Nos 102 and 77 Squadrons continued to operate their Merlin-engine Halifaxes until May and June respectively, while No 419 Squadron exchanged its charges for Lancaster Xs in April. One 419 Squadron Halifax was apparently a little reluctant to leave. In the early hours of 22 March JD468: W ditched in the sea; the crew was rescued three and a half hours later with their Halifax still obstinately floating near by, gunfire having to be used to sink it.

Others fell victim to simpler things, such as birds. One of 434 Squadron's Halifaxes, LK907: M and a veteran of 18 sorties, was being air-tested during the late afternoon of 25 February. On board were the crew and three airmen. At about 11,000 ft a bird, thought to be a seagull, hit the windscreen directly in front of the pilot, shattering it and causing P/O J. Pollard some severe and painful cuts and bruises around the eyes. Unable to see, he lost control of the aircraft and F/O R. James, the bomb aimer, took over and flew the Halifax back to base. Although given the opportunity to bale out, those on board elected to stay. With virtually no forward vision and hampered by the strong windblast in his face, James had to rely upon F/O Rowe, the navigator, sitting next to him to guide him in while the pilot assisted by passing instructions over the intercom from the rest-bay position. The Halifax touched down and bounced high in the air but James kept the wings level until it touched down again. Bouncing twice more it then swung off the runway, careered across the grass, over the perimeter track and a dispersal site before finally coming to rest on a pile of rocks, where it started to burn around the starboard inner engine. All on board were able to clamber out of the wrecked aircraft unharmed. F/O James received a well-deserved and immediate DFC for his efforts.

The four squadrons affected by the ban did not remain inactive and concentrated instead on French targets and minelaying. The latter had been carried out more or less continuously since the outbreak of war and had been mainly a Coastal Command function until 1942 when heavy bomber groups were gradually equipped with minelaying gear. Mines suitable for this type of operation had been in production since 1940 and reached a monthly output figure of approximately 1,200 by the beginning of 1943, of which 95% found their way into enemy waters. *Gardening* operations, as they were code-named, required a high degree of precision for the actual drop and in the early days this meant making a timed run at low-level from a known geographic point. Initially, losses were low but as the dropping zones became known, the defences took a steadily increasing toll. Each zone received its own code-name, some of which reflected the overall *Gardening* code-name while others were more prosaic; when the operational orders were issued, the code-names were included in the Telex message, these being:

Alderney	*Hostile Zone*
Arcona-River Dievenow	*Willows*
Bordeaux	*Deodars*
Brest	*Jellyfish*
Cherbourg	*Greengages*
Den Helder	*Limpets*
Dunkirk	*Cypress*
Flushing	*Iris* *
Frisian Islands	*Nectarines*
Guernsey	*Hostile Air*
Haugesund	*Bottle*
Heligoland	*Rosemary*
Heligoland Approaches	*Eglantine, Yams*
Hook of Holland	*Iris* *
Ile d'Ouessant	*Sultana*
Kattegat	*Yew Tree*
Kattegat Areas	*Silverthorns*
Kiel Bay	*Radishes, Wallflowers, G Forget-me-Nots*
La Rochelle	*Cinnamon*
Le Havre	*Scallops*
Lim Fjord	*Krauts*
Little Belt	*Carrots*
Lorient	*Artichokes*
Morlaix	*Upas Tree*
Oslo	*Onions*
Oslo Fjord Approaches	*Tomatoes*
Rostock and Arcone Light	*Sweet Peas*
Skagerrak	*Polyanthus*
Spiekieroog	*Young Yams*
St Malo	*Hyacinth*
St Nazaire	*Beeches*
Texel South	*Trefoils*
The Sound	*Daffodil*
Zuider Zee	*Welks*

* Admiralty records show the same code name for both locations.

During trials carried out during 1943 it was found that it was possible to drop a standard mine from as high as 15,000 ft. However, prior to this and due to the need for the minefields to be laid accurately, the aircraft flying these sorties kept to the relatively low altitudes of 5 - 6,000 ft. The widespread introduction of *H2S* that year, coupled with the ability to lay mines from a greater height, gave minelaying crews considerable tactical freedom and on 4 January 1944, six Halifaxes successfully laid mines off Brest Harbour from a height of 15,000 ft. This technique went one step further with 10 Squadron dispatching 13 Halifaxes on a minelaying sortie on 25/26 February, three of them marking the route with flares and then illuminating the dropping zone before laying their own mines.

The intensity of mining operations may be gauged from the following facts. During 1943, 13,776 mines were sown in north-west European waters and were followed by another 11,415 in the first six months of 1944. Aircraft losses were 2.1% for all sorties dispatched in return for which Germany lost 175,000 tons of shipping over an 18-month period. The subsequent loss of vital supplies from Norway and Scandinavia forced Germany to increase its night-fighter forces in Jutland at the expense of its home defence network.

Withdrawal of the Merlin-engine Halifaxes from Bomber Command by no means meant the end of their front line duties and before returning to Bomber Command and its final offensive in Europe, we must make a diversion in time and location to follow their history.

CHAPTER SIX

OPERATIONS IN THE MIDDLE EAST, NORTH AFRICA AND ITALY

THE land battles of the Middle East, ever fluid in nature, had taken a serious turn for the worse by June 1942. Tobruk, symbol of British tenacity, was tottering under the relentless blows of Rommel's Afrika Korps. In an effort to glean additional aircraft with which to bolster the already overtaxed Allied squadrons supporting the ground forces, Air Chief Marshal Tedder scoured the Mediterranean while Casey, the Minister of State in the Middle East, again sent a signal to Churchill asking for more heavy bombers. By 22 June, it was agreed to dispatch two squadrons of Halifaxes to the Middle East as rapidly as possible.

While the reply stated 'squadrons', the actual response from Bomber Command was to send 'detachments' of 16 aircraft from each of Nos 10 and 76 Squadrons to Aqir in Palestine. Great secrecy was attached to the move and even the squadrons involved were given false information. The 10 Squadron diarist recorded that the force was being dispatched for *Operation Barefaced*, which was to be completed within 16 days, while the CO, W/Cdr D. Bennett (later to command the Pathfinder Force) was told that the squadron was to be used to bomb the Italian fleet. The fact that no one in the Middle East apparently knew of the 'operation' leads one to surmise that *Barefaced* was not entirely an inappropriate title. Upon arrival, the two squadrons-cum-detachments were to form No 249 Wing of No 205 Group.

On 4 July, 10 Squadron dispatched an advance party in two Halifaxes, W/Cdr Seymor-Price flying W1174: G and W/O Peterson W7756: L. Seven more[1] left the next day, staging through Gibraltar to Aqir via Kasfareet in Egypt and were followed by the remaining seven[2] two days later. That same day, 6 July, a conference was held at No 249 Wing HQ at which it was decided to combine 10 Squadron with 227 Squadron and 76 with 454 Squadron for maintenance purposes.

The initial move was not without incident. Just after taking off from Gibraltar on 8 July, F/Lt Hacking was forced to turn back and crash-landed; the crew was

Halifax B Mk II Series I W1176: Z was a part of the original 10 Squadron detachment and was taken over by 462 Squadron when it formed in September, absorbing both Nos 10 and 76 Squadron's aircraft and personnel. It was lost in a crash-landing on 29 September while en route for Tobruk. (F. Brinton)

unhurt but W1178 was a write-off. Warrant Officer O'Driscoll was equally unfortunate the following day; unable to locate a landing ground and short of fuel, he was forced to ditch W7695 in the sea off Alexandria. The crew, ground crew and passengers completed their journey to shore by dinghy and then proceeded overland to Aqir. Three unserviceable Halifaxes, W1170, W1171 and W7679 remained at Gibraltar and were still there when the squadron settled at its new base on 11 July. The previous day the first eight Halifaxes[3] of 76 Squadron had left Middleton St George led by S/Ldr Iveson and followed four days later by the remaining eight[4] under the leadership of W/Cdr Young.

On arrival at Aqir, all personnel were warned to prepare for an indefinite stay, which produced a certain amount of dismay. Apart from domestic arrangements,

W1170: U of 10 Squadron's Middle East detachment is caught in the harsh glare of the Chance Light at the end of the runway as it readies for take-off on a bombing sortie. After arrival in the Middle East the squadron code letters were painted out for security reasons (nor were unit codes applied when 462 Squadron formed, absorbing the two Halifax detachments) but W1170 retained its original aircraft letter. Under the strong light and although recently over-painted with black paint, the 'ZA' part of the code is still visible. Seven operations were marked in vertical white oblongs below the navigator's triangular window. It survived the harsh operating conditions to be struck off charge in March 1944 when 462 Squadron was renumbered at its Italian base at Celone as 614 Squadron.

impending weddings, etc, some personnel were not even medically fit for overseas service. Despite these problems, the Wing began operations on the night of 11/12 July with a lone attack on Tobruk by a 10 Squadron machine. On 13/14 July, the squadron lost its first aircraft to enemy action following a raid on the same target by four aircraft and although P/O Drake managed to crash-land the flak-damaged W1171: X at Almaza, where it subsequently burnt out, several Egyptian firemen were killed when a bomb exploded in the wreckage.

Tobruk was to remain the main target for the next few months and the Afrika Korps, already hard pressed for essential supplies, were to be denied the use of harbours. Benghazi and Tobruk were the key ports in the forward supply line and while American Liberators attended to the former, Wellingtons and Halifaxes battered Tobruk.

The sudden, and to squadron personnel at least, unexpected prolonged stay in the Middle East brought problems in the form of a continuous stream of unserviceabilities of one type or another. Hydraulic failures abounded and kept the ground crews busy trying to overcome a variety of problems with the minimum of equipment and spares.

In spite of the almost regular nightly raids on Tobruk, losses remained low. No 76 Squadron suffered its first operational loss when W7762: D was hit by flak in a port engine. Out over the Mediterranean some 160 miles from Alexandria, one of the starboard engines packed up but the pilot was able to coax the Halifax over the coast at 1,300 ft near Aboukir. He then ordered the two gunners to bale out and they eventually found their way back to base with the assistance of guides from the local population. Unable to locate the airfield at Burg el Arab, the pilot was forced to crash-land near LG 09[5], fortunately without causing any casualties.

The attacks on Tobruk were moderately successful, but haze prevented any definite assessment of damage on most occasions. Engine overheating problems were another headache for the already hard-pressed ground crews and on 5/6 August, Sgt DeClerk's 10 Squadron Halifax was lost because of this type of problem. Flak damage over Tobruk had put the starboard inner engine out of action and then, during the return journey, the port outer engine had to be feathered and W7757: B began to lose height. The remaining engines began to overheat and DeClerk was eventually forced to ditch the aircraft, the crew fortunately escaping by dinghy. Engine trouble also claimed W7754: F of 76 Squadron on 30 August, the aircraft crash-landing en route to the target, but again fortunately without loss of life. For these operations the Wing was allocated two advanced landing grounds at Kilo 40 and Shallufa (LG 224), the former being manned by Sgt Farrimond and the latter being permanently manned by Sgt F. Brinton, a fitter-armourer, and 24 airmen.

Brinton recalls "... we, as ground crew, worked very long and very hard in the heat and dust of those desert conditions, but it was all done in such a wonderful spirit of camaraderie; a carry over, I like to think, of the work, spirit and standards of the pre-war Royal Air Force. As regards engine trouble on those aircraft, I well remember a fellow Sergeant (Fitter, Engines) telling me at that time, the No 107 MU at Kashfareet kept two Spitfire squadrons grounded to keep the Middle East Halifaxes flying." Whether or not this last statement was founded on accuracy, it does give an indication of the value of the Halifaxes to the land battle.

September augured well for the Commonwealth armies with the failure of Rommel's offensive. Fuel, the lifeblood of any mechanised army, was critical and the Axis did everything in its power to improve its supplies. Crete was a most convenient staging point for both men and supplies, a fact not overlooked by the Allied planners. Heraklion airfield was a tempting target, heavily congested as it was with both transport and fighter aircraft and 249 Wing was ordered to attack it in daylight on 5 September. For some of the 76 Squadron crews it must have reawakened unpleasant memories of the *Scharnhorst* raid. Each squadron was to provide six aircraft, but unserviceabilities rapidly reduced the available numbers.

One of 76 Squadron's Halifaxes failed to take off due to a glycol leak and another, W1183: M, lost its starboard outer engine shortly after take-off and returned to base. No 10 Squadron also lost one of its number before take-off but the remainder eventually joined the four from 76. The formation arranged itself in sections of three with three from 76 Squadron leading, one from 76 and two from 10 Squadron in the middle and the remaining three from 10 Squadron in the rear. Engine failure reduced the number once more, one of the 10 Squadron aircraft from the second section having to jettison its bomb load and turn for home. The remainder made a straight and level run up to the target in perfect half-span formation with their bombs seen to burst amongst the dispersed aircraft and across the runways, causing several fires. The flak defences opened fire but failed to hit any of the aircraft in the first section. The reduced second section carried out their attack from 9,000 ft and F/Lt J. Bryan's Halifax, W1114: Q was hit, going down in flames with only two of the crew escaping by parachute. Two Bf 109 fighters attacked W1174: G shortly after it released its bombs but W/Cdr Seymor-Price managed to evade their second and third attacks successfully despite the extensive damage caused by the first. Cannon shells had ripped open the wing between the starboard engines while flak had punctured the tail wheel and starboard main wheel, torn several holes in the fuselage and shattered the hydraulics, rendering the bomb doors and flaps unserviceable. In spite of the damage, Seymor-Price brought the crippled Halifax back to Fayid.

The leading Halifax of the third section, W7679: C, went down shortly after bombing with the starboard outer engine on fire. The fire spread along the wing and several parachutes were observed before it hit the ground to the south-east of Castelli Padiada. The loss of S/Ldr Hacking and his experienced crew was a severe setback to the squadron as they had accumulated 137 operations as well as being credited with destroying two Bf 109s and damaging a third. Both of the remaining Halifaxes suffered minor damage from flak and fighters but returned safely.

The following day instructions were received from 205 Group HQ to amalgamate the 10 and

The remains of W7672: E, which crashed on 29 September 1942 following engine failure during an air test. The crew escaped unharmed. (F. Brinton)

76 Squadron detachments into a new squadron, No 462 RAAF under the command of W/Cdr D.O. Young, DSO, DFC, AFC. The 76 Squadron diarist recorded the following comments before the unit lost its identity *"... since the arrival in the Middle East of No 76 Squadron ... the 16 aircraft which comprised the squadron have completed 154 sorties without replacement aircraft and the whole squadron, both air and ground crews, are to be congratulated on this fine achievement."*

The squadron number may have changed but the priorities had not and Tobruk appeared on the target list with monotonous regularity. A particularly heavy attack was made on 13 September in support of a combined army and naval offensive. Fourteen Halifaxes took part without loss, some attacking from as low as 8,000 ft with one making 16 runs over the target. The ground and sea forces were not so fortunate and suffered heavy losses.

Engine failures still took their toll, and two Halifaxes were lost on 29 September from this cause. The first, W7672: E was being air-tested during the morning and crash-landed after the pilot was forced to feather a port engine and, although the aircraft was burnt out, the crew escaped. The same day, W1176: Z left in the late afternoon for an attack on Tobruk but lost its port outer engine at 50 ft. Then, at 150 ft, the port inner failed and F/Lt Murray successfully crash-landed in the desert five miles north-west of Fayid. The first news the squadron heard of the crash was when Murray walked into the watch office to report it.

October brought an addition to the target list and the squadron turned its attention to Crete once more. During one of these attacks on 10 October, S/Ldr P. Warner's Halifax, W1183: M, sustained a near-miss while over the target. The shell burst very close to the nose of the aircraft, riddling it with splinters that severed all electrical services in the forward fuselage and put both outboard engines out of action. The navigator F/Lt F. Collins was also seriously wounded but continued with his duties after receiving first-aid treatment. The Halifax continued to lose height and was down to 1,100 ft before the bombs in the fuselage could be released by hand. Warner managed to coax the port outer engine back to life and by jettisoning all the surplus equipment possible got the aircraft back up to 3,900 ft, at which height he managed to reach the North African coast. However, the port outer engine failed again and he decided to head for Abu Sueir but, again, the Halifax steadily lost height because of the weight of the bombs, which were unable to be jettisoned from the wing cells. Following a successful forced-landing some 12 miles from Dikirnes, from which the crew escaped without further injury, Collins received an immediate DSO for his courage.

The stranglehold on Rommel's precious sea-borne lifeline never ceased and between 6 September and 24 October, the Halifaxes carried out 183 sorties against Tobruk. The historic battle for El Alamein began on 23 October and in common with other desert bomber squadrons, 462 were allotted battle area targets in support of the ground forces. The first of these attacks, which were to continue for the next four nights, came on 5/6 November. Enemy motor transport concentrations were the target and the squadron celebrated Guy Fawkes Day[6] in traditional style. Fuka, Matruh, Sidi Barrani, Sollum, Buq-Buq, Halfaya, Capuzzo,.... the list of target areas was almost as endless as the targets themselves. Flying in their unprecedented bomber-cum-ground strafing role on a nightly basis, the Halifax crews flew lower and lower. An indication of their enthusiasm was that bombing heights, which had

Tuesday, 29 September 1942 was a lucky day for F/Lt Murray of 462 Squadron. Having to force-land W1176: Z en route for an attack on Tobruk, the accompanying view of the front end of 'Z-Zebra' shows just how fortunate Murray and his crew were to escape serious injury. In the rear view, the painted out ZA code letters are just discernible as darker patches on the fuselage ahead of the roundel. (F. Brinton)

W7671 was one of the B Mk II Series I aircraft of the 76 Squadron detachment and originally coded 'H'. The Halifaxes arrived in the Middle East in standard night bomber camouflage, the green of the upper pattern gradually being changed to mid stone as appears to be the case in this view of 'W-William'. This aircraft had originally served with 78 Squadron before passing to 76 and then out to the Middle East, so it is possible that it had undergone a recent major overhaul and change of camouflage as the paintwork was still quite crisp. Retention of front and mid-upper turrets and full armament were features that gradually disappeared from these Halifaxes as night-fighter opposition failed to materialise. Suffering from battle damage, W7671 was lost in a crash-landing on Malta on 7 November 1943. (J. Stanley)

W1183: M, one of the original aircraft of the 76 Squadron detachment, photographed banking over the North African coast. Broken only by a dusty road, the absence of significant ground features in the open, endless expanses of sand of the North African desert provided little assistance for navigation. These conditions were a constant concern if an aircraft got into difficulties, as happened with W/O Vertican's crew as related in the text. (F. Brinton)

Oudref and Wadi Akrit areas. The Halifax engine failure problems continued to escalate and W/Cdr Warner began to look for finding ways to reduce not just weight but drag also. With all armament removed from the front turret and all apertures sealed, the entire turret was now covered in doped fabric to provide a more streamlined nose section, giving the Halifax something of an aggressive profile.

In the meantime, the first B Mk I Series I (Special) Halifaxes were reaching squadrons in the UK with a few starting to trickle through to Middle East Command, the first arriving in April, so both unit modified and Series I (Special) Halifaxes remained on strength.

During April, an unusually high number of engine failures gradually impaired the squadron's operational efficiency. Replacement engines were not available on the squadron and on many occasions, engines were switched from one Halifax to another in an attempt to maintain a reasonable number of serviceable aircraft. Plainly there was a limit to this process and the point was eventually reached where it was not possible to do any more switching and some 60% of the Halifaxes were finally transferred to 61 RSU (61 Rear Servicing Unit) to await replacement engines. Towards the end of the month, the supply situation improved and the squadron was brought up to strength again. However, there was deep concern about the comparatively short life of locally overhauled and rebuilt Merlin engines, amongst which failures during the first 40 hours were common. In an attempt to ease the strain put on the engines, W/Cdr Warner suggested the removal of the front and mid-upper turrets to decrease weight, permission to do so being granted later that month.

Attacks during May focused mainly on troop and motor transport concentrations in Tunisia, with a second Halifax squadron joining the ranks during the latter part of the month. No 178 Squadron, based at Hose Raui, already operating Liberators, had recently begun re-equipping with Halifaxes and launched its first Halifax operation on the night of 31 May /1 June 1943[7]. No 462 Squadron moved into the same base at the end of May and commenced operations with 178 Squadron against Italian targets. W/Cdr Warner, 462 Squadron's very popular CO, was lost during this period when his Halifax was shot down over the Mediterranean. The aircraft exploded and only the flight engineer survived, being rescued by a British destroyer almost immediately after landing in the sea.

Warrant Officer Vertican and his 462 Squadron crew were more fortunate. On the afternoon of 6 May, DT501: J and W7847: F were readied for an attack on the main roads converging on Tunis from Bizerta plus those from the west and the south; the retreating Afrika Korps were to be pursued to the end. The weather was poor but the operation went ahead with Vertican's Halifax departing at 22.55 hrs.

begun at 9,000 ft, had dropped to 5,000 ft near the end of their first series of operations, decreasing rapidly as time passed. Some crews, not satisfied with 2,700 ft went so far as to press home their attacks from 1,200 ft.

The squadron's activities were interrupted by a series of moves, first to Kilo 40 (LG 237) from where it carried out a few attacks against Crete and Tripolitania after an enforced period of inactivity due to dust storms. Further moves took it to El Daba (LG 09) then to Bir El Baheira (LG 167) in Libya from where it again attacked Crete before moving back to LG 237 on 17 December. It then became temporarily non-operational while tour-expired aircrews, about 90% of its strength, were sent home and replacement crews brought in. Thus, partly replenished, the squadron moved to its new operational base at Solluch in January 1943.

Targets and priorities had changed somewhat in the intervening period and Sicily now received the squadron's attentions. Six Halifaxes opened the new tour of operations on 29/30 January by dropping 29,000 lbs of bombs on the rail ferry terminal at Messina. Seven Halifaxes made a repeat attack two nights later with 40,000 lbs of bombs being dropped.

During a lull in the land battle, General Montgomery began building up his forces for a further offensive and, in keeping with the policy of establishing local air superiority, the desert bomber forces began a series of systematic attacks against German-held airfields. From 23 to 26 February, No 462 Squadron attacked Gabes-West airfield each night. Reconnaissance showed that large enemy troop movements, mainly reinforcements, were being made in the Mareth area south of Gabes and the squadron turned its attention to these concentrations of armour and motor transport, with similar attacks being carried out against the El Hamma,

During the height of the engine failure problems, W/Cdr P. Warner DSO, the 462 Squadron CO, initiated a series of changes to reduce weight and drag. Taken on 4 March 1943, this photograph shows the progression in trying to streamline the Halifaxes by covering the entire front turret with doped canvas. Pulled forward to meet the fixed glazing of the bomb aimer's window structure and emphasising the characteristic chin profile, it gave the impression that the turret had been removed. The mid-upper C Mk V turret was still retained at this stage. (W/Cdr W. Russell)

With the guns removed and the entire front turret sealed with doped canvas, W1169: S of 462 Squadron lands amidst its own personal dust storm and gives a better idea of the problems encountered when operating Merlin engines under such harsh conditions. One of the original 76 Squadron detachment aircraft, it had completed 50 operations by September 1943 and was struck off charge along with a number of the other, older Halifaxes when the squadron re-formed as 614 Squadron in March 1944. (J. Stanley)

B Mk II Series I (Special) Halifaxes began joining the Middle East air war between late March and early April 1943. Built in mid-February, BB325: P of 462 Squadron was photographed at Fayid on 17 April 1943. Fitted with a standard Tollerton fairing it retained its C Mk V mid-upper turret, tall radio mast and high astrodome but lacked the under wing fuel dump pipes. The hydraulically operated landing lamp under the port wing is in the retracted position. After returning safely from a bombing sortie on 20 July, the aircraft was involved in a ground accident later that day and subsequently written-off. The reduced size of the individual aircraft letter as seen here became a common feature of squadron aircraft. (G. Carver)

Right: In May 1943, a second Middle East squadron, No 178, began converting to Halifaxes. BB331: S, seen here resplendent in its camouflage of mid-stone and dark earth with black under surfaces had arrived in the Middle East in May 1943 and was issued to the squadron at Hose Raui. However, a sudden revision of policy saw the squadron retain its Liberators, the Halifaxes being withdrawn in September and later transferred to the newly-formed 614 Squadron. Photographed after completing 28 operations and indicating the lack of night-fighter opposition, the rear turret armament of BB331 had been reduced to two machine guns and the nose and mid-upper turrets deleted. It was struck off charge in February 1945 when the squadron converted to Liberators. (G. Carver)

On 6 May 1943, W/O Vertican and crew were flying in DT501: J when they encountered severe engine problems outward bound for an attack on a major road junction between Bizerta and Tunis. What followed was an epic ten-day saga of survival after ditching the Halifax some 20 miles out to sea. Modifications to remove the front and mid-upper turrets had not been carried out when this photograph was taken, dating it perhaps to earlier in 1943. (J. Halley via R. Hayward)

As soon as an aircraft landed, the inboard engines were shut down with taxiing being carried out using the two outboard engines for both maximum turning ability and to reduce the storm of fine sand thrown up by the propeller wash. (W/Cdr W. Russell)

Navigation throughout was by dead reckoning and on the last leg as they flew north over Tunisia, the starboard inner engine developed a glycol leak, rapidly began to overheat and had to be shut down. With the British Army spread out somewhere beneath, Vertican could not jettison his bombs safely and, despite decreasing altitude, called for a course to the nearest point on the coast, some 40 miles distant. As the Halifax reached 9,000 ft, the coast appeared below them allowing the bombs to be jettisoned and course set for base but shortly afterwards the port inner engine also developed a glycol leak and had to be shut down. As the high ambient air temperature taxed the remaining two engines, Vertican called for a course to Castel Benito airfield and ordered the crew to jettison everything possible, including the parachutes. The Halifax finally held height at around 1,000 ft but this caused concern because the ground around Castel Benito reached to nearly three times that height. Now over the sea and unable to distinguish anything, Vertican held his course until the coast was estimated to have been crossed; then he turned out to sea again to await the fast approaching dawn. The Halifax was holding a steady altitude now that it was much lighter but about 20 miles out to sea the port outer engine also developed a glycol leak. Vertican immediately cut the engine, put the nose down and ordered the crew to their ditching stations. Emerging from the cloud base he successfully put the Halifax down on the sea and the crew got into the dinghy; 90 minutes later the Halifax finally slid from view leaving the crew to face a tortuous 10-day saga at sea before they finally reached the shore some 15 miles west of Homs on the North African coast. Sergeant C. Curnow, the flight engineer (one of the first trained in the Middle East) had struggled tirelessly to keep the Halifax's engines operating and he now proved just as tireless in keeping morale up as he and the rest of the crew lay under the blistering heat, rationed to one-seventh of a pint of water a day. Awarded

A 462 Squadron Flight Sergeant navigator already wearing his Mae West, ground-checks his equipment in preparation for an operation. The fold-down seat for use by the flight engineer when seated alongside the pilot is on the left; the horizontal bar extension to the first pilot's control column cuts across the photograph just above it. Navigation in this theatre of operations was very much a case of 'back to the basics' and required a high degree of skill, there being few ground aids other than radio fixes to work with. (W/Cdr W. Russell)

The degree of clean-up applied to the B Mk II Series I (Special) Halifaxes supplied to the Middle East was just as vague as in the UK. The Tollerton fairing was standard but retention of the mid-upper turret appears to have been arbitrary – but in this instance it had been removed. The open coastal arid conditions are visible and even without the dust, just working on metal aircraft in the daily temperatures of the hottest part of the year must have made loading wing bomb cells even more arduous than seen here during a relatively cooler part of the year. The large differential winch was used for both wing and fuselage bomb bays. (RAAF)

The use of a small mobile crane was sometimes required to deliver bombs, the finned tail cones for each being fitted before bombs were hoisted into the bomb bay by means of the large differential hand winch and cable. The wearing of battledress jackets and jumpers indicates that this photograph of 'B-Beer' was taken during a cooler part of the year, possibly early Spring. (RAAF)

the DFM, he later rose to the rank of Flight Lieutenant, serving with 102 Squadron.

The move to Hose Raui was not particularly popular and conditions, already primitive, were further aggravated by torrential rain. The continuing engine failures were also beginning to create a morale problem and W/Cdr W. Russell, who took over command at this crucial period, recalls the seriousness of the situation in the following words:

"We even had aircraft which, on being collected from the MU after a major overhaul, arrived at the squadron on three engines – one had packed in on the delivery flight.

"Operating over the Mediterranean under these conditions was not conducive to a happy, carefree existence. Invariably the flare path party remained on the scene for an hour after the last take-off to be ready for an early return due to engine failure. With a full load, on hot nights, if an engine packed in there was only one thing to do – unload and return. If you didn't it was a pretty good bet that the added strain on the remaining three engines would cause even more trouble. I still remember one night listening to one gentleman who progressively lost one, two and three engines. He was on his way back and there were a lot of anxious blokes on the ground, as well as in the air, before he limped into an airfield up the road having restarted a second engine to enable him to complete the last few miles successfully."

In spite of these difficulties, the Halifaxes continued to operate regularly. One from 178 Squadron had a spirited fight with a Ju 88 on the night of 26 July. On the way into the target, the Reggio di Calabria aerodrome, the Ju 88 attacked from astern, its first burst raking the fuselage of BB385: Q, damaging the intercom and wounding the wireless operator. Continuing its attack, it fired a second and third burst, inflicting further damage and jamming the port elevator down. The rear gunner fired a short burst, registering strikes on the Ju 88. Then, as it closed in for the kill, the rear gunner fired one long burst and the Ju 88 blew up, falling in flames into the sea. The Halifax managed to limp into Malta, where it landed safely; subsequently repaired, it was later passed to No 614 Squadron.

Night bombing operations in the Middle East had been handicapped to a large degree by the almost total lack of navigational facilities. For the most part it was back to the 1939/40 methods of dead reckoning, plus astro-navigation whenever possible. These problems had been a source of discussion at HQ Middle East for some time and W/Cdr W. Russell rapidly put into practice the ideas that had been formulated.

Selecting about four of the best crews, he made them concentrate on their navigation techniques and on every raid two of them would carry nothing but flares. They were required to locate the target and illuminate it continuously for the duration of the raid, which usually lasted from five to ten minutes. Aircraft times over the target were also concentrated into this time bracket and crews now took a photograph of the aiming point, more to assist with the navigation post-mortem than for target damage assessment. Results, and the squadron morale, improved rapidly. This applied also to the ground crews, some of whom had been in the desert for 18 months without a break, working under the worst possible conditions. Anyone who served on 462 Squadron at this time will recall the unofficial, but very effective remedial measures instituted by W/Cdr Russell. Squadron personnel were given leave whenever possible and flown to Cairo in one of the Halifaxes. Had a single one of them failed to return on time Russell would have been in serious trouble with HQ, but, as he said, not a single man ever let him down; a very fine tribute to a very fine C.O. Another measure of rising morale was an unofficial squadron badge that also emerged during this period, a very pugnacious bird wearing boxing gloves.

The continuing Merlin engine problems had finally reached a critical point and a representative from Rolls-Royce, having visited the Squadron, instituted changes at the MUs, which greatly improved the overhaul of the engines. One of the main problems discovered had been with the local manufacture of big-end bearing shells made from white metal, which simply rapidly deteriorated and caused endless problems with the Merlin XX engines. Other relief in this quarter came with the arrival of replacement Halifaxes fitted with Merlin 22 engines, 13 being taken on charge by the end of September. Some of them came from 178 Squadron which had ceased its Halifax operations on 7/8 September and returned to Liberators. The Merlin 22s produced an immediate improvement in operational efficiency and a rapid decline in engine changes. Unfortunately, one of the new aircraft was found to have a defective fuel tank, a similar fault affecting the entire batch of Halifaxes in the BB-serial range. Modified tanks were fitted at 161 MU and by the end of the month eight Halifaxes were back and operating regularly. For every rule, there is usually an exception and W1169: S was just that and had completed its 50th sortie during September. It was one of the original 76 Squadron machines and due to the keenness and efficiency of its ground crew, retained its clean appearance and

JP228, one of the fully-equipped B Mk II Series I A Halifaxes with Merlin 22 engines with late model exhaust flame dampers, H2S and other refinements that began to reach the squadron after its move to Italy when it re-formed as 614 Squadron in March 1944. Delivered to 45 MU on 3 February, it was transferred to 32 MU on the 16th, to No 1 OADU on the 28th and then on 12 March to 301 FTU from where it was ferried out to Italy on 28 April, arriving the same day. This process from manufacture to delivery at a squadron's location gives some idea of the time factor involved. Marked as 'P-Pip', JP228 was lost on operations on the night of 21/22 August 1944.

reputation for reliability right through to its last operation. It survived until March 1944 when it was finally struck off charge with age and not the enemy having caught up with it.

The squadron spent the remainder of the year carrying out its new illumination and bombing policy with attacks being concentrated against Italian and Greek aerodromes during October and November, with December marking the beginning of diversionary raids to cover mining operations around Greece and Crete, plus some anti-shipping raids against Suda Bay and Piraeus.

Christmas festivities were barely over when orders were received to move from Terria, the squadron's base since late September, to El Adem. The move was hampered by a shortage of road transport, but squadron personnel rose to the occasion in true style. In most theatres of war, captured enemy vehicles were usually taken over by a central authority but with 462 Squadron, it was a case of 'finder's keepers' and its road convoy was almost endless in its variety of 'privately owned' German and Italian vehicles. During this move, Corporal (Cpl) J. Stanley, an instrument fitter responsible for maintaining the automatic pilots fitted to squadron Halifaxes 'acquired' the first permanent workshop the instrument section had ever had. A mobile caravan-type workshop had been abandoned on the side of the road because of the loss of its wheels. Stanley happened to be driving a semi-trailer with some space left on it; the next vehicle in the convoy was a mobile crane so a quick inspection, an equally quick conference, and the instrument section had a workshop at last.

Bad weather severely restricted operations and only 46 sorties were flown during the seven raids mounted in January. Preliminary advice was also received on 19 January 1944 of an impending move to Italy where the squadron would change its role to one of target marking, thus becoming pathfinders for the entire central Mediterranean night bombing forces. Several crews had been sent to England to learn the new technique thoroughly and the first of these returned during January, bringing with them a Halifax fitted with *H2S* and a Mk XIV bombsight.

February 1944 was hectic in every sense of the word with only 21 sorties flown on diversionary bombing and leaflet dropping but this was no measure of the actual activity. An intense ground instruction course was implemented to teach crews to handle the new equipment and between this and the operations, the squadron began its move to Celone, Italy. The move was completed by 1 March and two days later, the squadron was renumbered as No 614 Squadron, its original number being allocated to a new RAAF unit in England. Ironically, this change back to an RAF

identity came at a time when the squadron was more Australian in numbers and character than it had ever been.

Large quantities of *H2S* and *Gee* equipment were on hand when the squadron arrived at its new base and it lost no time in becoming operational again. Seven Halifaxes attacked the marshalling yards at Genoa on 11/12 March and despite the bad weather, all bombed from 16,000 ft. However, the next operation on 15/16 March was disastrous; four of the nine Halifaxes sent to bomb the marshalling yards at Sofia failed to return, among them JP227, BB382 and BB446. Very bad weather was encountered and one crew baled out while a second Halifax crashed, the remaining two presumed to have been shot down. Three more bombing operations were carried out, during which BB415 was abandoned by its crew near Melfi while returning from an attack on Sofia. The Squadron then stood down to concentrate on training. Its new policy was outlined in the following directive: *"The squadron will become the target marking force for No 205 Group. It will consist of two operational flights of eight H2S-equipped aircraft, each with a training flight consisting of two dual, non-H2S, aircraft and four H2S aircraft. Squadron will be brought up to establishment in equipment and ground personnel, non-essential bomber aircraft will be removed and training flight will supply replacement crews. These will be above average No 205 Group crews with experience in night operations and they will be converted on to Halifaxes and trained in target marking techniques on the squadron."*

While training continued, the first marking operation was carried out on 10/11 April, when eight Halifaxes successfully marked and illuminated the Plovdiv marshalling yards. Similar tasks followed at a steady pace and successes were enhanced by an extremely low loss rate; JP108 on 22 April and JP111 failing to return from an attack on Bucharest on 8 May.

During mid-May, the squadron moved to Stornara from where it continued its run of successes against a wide variety of targets. Oil was the top priority during June and July, no effort being spared to deny the enemy this vital commodity. On 1/2 July, three of the squadron's Halifaxes acted as route markers for minelaying operations in the Danube, a method very successful in slowing the movement of oil by river transport. Five nights and 10 operations later 614 Squadron was called upon to mark Fürsbrunn airfield for a mixed bomber force of Wellingtons and Liberators. Nineteen enemy aircraft were destroyed and the remaining 50 immobilized by the heavy cratering of the runways and surrounding area. The raid was not without loss, and in addition to 10 Wellingtons and two Liberators, a single Halifax, JP287, fell victim to enemy night-fighters. The next day the American Fifteenth Air Force

Non-airworthy or damaged airframes were frequently stripped of components; this B Mk II Series IA had broken its back at the join of the fuselage front and mid-sections and had had most useful items removed. The location of the wreck is unknown but with a Beaufighter and a Stirling in the distance, and the photograph known to have been taken after 462 Squadron re-formed as 614 Squadron, the likely location is thought to be Celone, Italy. The first two letters of the serial number appear to be JP, the bulk of 614's Halifaxes being supplied from that production block.

encountered no opposition in that area and General Twining sent a message of appreciation to 205 Group.

Despite the original policy statement, 614 Squadron began operating a few of its Halifaxes on purely bombing duties accompanying the Pathfinder Halifaxes. Target allocations moved northwards, spreading gradually east and west during August and on 3/4th, eight Halifaxes marked the marshalling yards at Valence, France, for a force of 55 Wellingtons and 22 Liberators. A few nights later the squadron aircraft were active over the infamous Ploesti oil refineries in Rumania, an operation that cost two Halifaxes, JP225 and JP282, and several other crew casualties.

Operation Dragoon, the invasion of southern France, opened on 15 August 1944 and the Mediterranean Allied Strategic Air Force (MASAF) was heavily committed in support of this battle. As a preliminary to the operation, 614 Squadron marked the docks at Genoa and Marseilles on the 13th and 14th respectively. The next day it marked the Valence aerodrome but the resulting attack was a failure due to thick haze covering the target. Firmly established, the ground forces made no more immediate demands upon the MASAF and 614 Squadron turned its attention to other targets. The last five operations of the month were in direct support of the Eighth Army in Italy with three attacks on German divisions at Pesaro and two on marshalling yards, Bologna and Bovenna, in the battle area.

Losses were not restricted to operations; JN912, on a training flight from Catina, developed a fire in the port inner engine and was forced to ditch in the sea. The Halifax turned on its back and the dinghy failed to inflate, so one of the passengers, LAC Isaacs, and the wireless operator, P/O Homes, swam for the shore, some 20 miles distant. Isaacs staggered ashore 19 hours later and alerted Italian Marines who rescued Homes, who had accompanied Isaacs to within one mile of the shore, but he died from sheer exhaustion immediately after his rescue.

During September, the squadron received its first four Liberators and all 205 Group squadrons would be converted to the type over a period of several months. It was a changeover dictated by compatibility of maintenance supplies and the fact that the Liberator would be more compatible with the numerically superior USAAF element of the MASAF. Halifax operations continued unabated and on 16 October, the squadron's first mixed Halifax-Liberator force marked the Zagreb East marshalling yard. Recognition for the squadron's Pathfinder duties finally came through during the month with authority received for selected crews to wear the distinctive PFF badge.

On 31 October, two Halifaxes were detached to assist the Balkan Air Force (BAF) by marking dropping areas for Special Operations Executive (SOE) flights operating over Yugoslavia. This was the start of a series of operations in support of the Balkan Air Force either by marking or by dropping supplies. These in turn progressed to attacks on troop concentrations and aerodromes and daylight bridge-busting operations. Typical of the latter was an attack by three Halifaxes and a Liberator on the main bridge and a subsidiary pontoon bridge at Matesevo on 19 December. The bombing was carried out from between 7,000 and 8,000 ft and Halifax JP134 made six runs across the target, dropping a 1,000 lb bomb each time. The third bomb fell alongside the bridge on the eastern side of the river while the sixth hit the entrance to the bridge on the south side, removing part of the approach; the remainder hit the road, badly cratering it. Sweeping in from 3,200 ft the Halifax's gunners sprayed over 2,500 rounds of machine gun fire into a line of 50 camouflaged motor transports strung along the road, three of which burst into flames and several others were damaged. The same night six more of the Squadron's aircraft, five Liberators and a Halifax, attacked the marshalling yards at Sarajevo West, again without loss.

The rapid tempo of operations gave 614 Squadron little opportunity to operate in its intended Pathfinder capacity except for three very accurate marking operations against bridges in northern Italy in late December. Duties varied mainly between bridge busting and the odd supply drop and the squadron rapidly developed a great talent for the former. Bad weather kept the aircraft grounded for 12 days during late January 1945 but at the first opportunity they were again out in force with a successful attack on the Udine marshalling yards. The next few weeks were spent attacking targets in northern Italy: the Naval Ammunition Dump at Pola, twice, Verona West marshalling yards four times, the oil refinery and naval fitting-out basin at Fiume, Trieste Naval Dockyards, the Graz marshalling yards and the marshalling yards at Padua and those at Brescia. Additionally, the squadron carried out supply drops to Yugoslavian partisan groups, 13 Halifaxes flying dropping sorties on 18 January.

Finally, on 3 March 1945, JP280 carried out the Squadron's last Halifax operation, an attack on Port Marhamo oil storage depot, as part of a diversion for some mining operations. While Merlin-engined Halifaxes had been withdrawn from German targets at the beginning of 1944, they had given continuous valuable service in this and other theatres of operations.

CHAPTER SEVEN

SPECIAL DUTIES OPERATIONS

THE Special Operations Executive was formed to promote and organize sabotage against the enemy from within his own territories and the supply of the manpower and the means to achieve this end was largely the responsibility of the RAF. From August 1940, this task was carried out most successfully by 419 Flight[1] with its few Lysanders and twelve months later, increasing demands for its unique talents led to its expansion into a full squadron[2], the Lysanders forming 'A' Flight while Whitleys formed the new 'B' Flight.

Among the urgent requests received by the SOE was one from the Polish Home Army (PHA) who wanted supplies and equipment to be dropped to them. This posed a problem since the distances

involved were far beyond the practical range of a Whitley. To overcome this, two B Mk II Halifaxes plus one reserve aircraft were allocated to the squadron in October 1941. They were to be modified at RAF Ringway[3] near Manchester with L9612 being the first to be sent. It is perhaps indicative of the value that some saw in the squadron's activities that these Halifaxes should be allocated at a time when they were still in short supply. Predictably, Air Marshal Harris fought the allocation of any bomber aircraft for what he considered, in colourful language, as a wasted effort. He was to oppose expansion of the SD[4] squadrons *per se*, refusing to acknowledge either the need for, or the value of their work. He also dismissed the idea that a bomber crew could fly, unaided, to a specific field in occupied territory, and there drop personnel and materiel at a time when his Main Force crews were having difficulties locating an entire city.

The initial Polish volunteer crews began to arrive early in October 1941 following completion of their conversion course at Linton-on-Ouse where they had received instruction from S/Ldr Tait and F/Lt Franklin of 35 Squadron. The first crew, drawn from Nos 300 and 301 Squadrons, was headed by navigator F/O S. Krol with F/O Jasinski and Sgt Sobkowiak as first and second pilots[5]. The three Halifaxes, L9611, L9612 and L9613, were modified by the Airborne Forces Establishment as a trial lash-up upon which the official Handley Page modifications could be based. As requested by the Directorate of Technical Development (DTD) and the Directorate of Operational Research (DOR), the first aircraft to undergo conversion, L9612, was completed by 28 October. The modifications included the fitting of a circular hatch in the fuselage well, a winch to retrieve the parachute static lines and a short, faired mast fixed to the underside of the fuselage just forward of the tail wheel to deflect any containers that were swept back as they entered the slipstream. To protect the tail wheel and prevent the static lines from becoming entangled with it, a simple sheet metal fairing was wrapped around the front and both sides.

Operation Ruction, the first of many clandestine trips to Poland, was flown under the command of W/Cdr Rudkowski on the night of 7/8 November 1941 but because 138 Squadron had no technical personnel trained on Halifaxes at Newmarket, the Polish crew took L9612 back to Linton-on-Ouse for the operation. The load consisted of three instructors, Bidzinski, Segiera, Piwnik[6], and their equipment, which were to be dropped to a reception party from the Polish Home Army at a point west of Warsaw. The Halifax left at 18.15 hrs but encountered a 50 mph wind blowing from the west coupled with 10/10ths cloud up to 11,000 ft. Not far from the Polish border, F/O Jasinski took the Halifax down to 6,000 ft, sighting the ground for the first time since departure and, finding their first pinpoint soon after, turned for the dropping point. Icing had already taken its toll and the hydraulic system had burst at 7,000 ft allowing the undercarriage to drop down. At 22.25 hrs, a signal was sent to the reception committee and after receiving their reply, the three men and their equipment were dropped. The combined effect of the strong west wind, now blowing at about 60 mph, and the drag from the undercarriage had reduced the ground speed of the aircraft to about 75 mph. Over Denmark at 04.15 hrs with only one and a half hours fuel remaining, it was realised that England was beyond range so a course was set for Sweden. At 05.20 hrs with the Halifax now down to 400 ft, a suitable site for a forced landing appeared and Jasinski did not hesitate. As they touched down the

L9612 was both the first B Mk II Halifax and first Special Duties Halifax to be lost on operations and had just flown the longest operational flight of the type so far in the war. These photographs show the burnt-out wreckage of L9612 photographed on the morning of its crash near Tomelilla in Sweden. At first, the crew had difficulty in setting fire to it but persisted, determined to leave no evidence of the parachute and dropping well fittings or anything to reveal the nature of their flight. The Halifax had been modified at the Airborne Forces Experimental Establishment. (Nils Arne Nillson collection via M. Olrog)

undercarriage was torn off, then the aircraft hit a low stone wall and slithered to a halt in an open field at Tomelilla, near Ystad in southern Sweden. The crew escaped injury but the aircraft had to be destroyed to cover its modified state. The crew tried, but it did not catch fire and finally getting it to do so took some effort. This was the first B Mk II Series I Halifax to be lost. Fortunately, the Swedish authorities were most polite and did not ask too many difficult questions; the crew were eventually repatriated and Rudkowski and Krol were back with the squadron early in the New Year.

While the Halifaxes were used for Polish operations, they were also involved in other operations along with their Polish crews, the scope of which gradually broadened over the next few months. On 28/29 December, F/Lt R. Hockey took L9613: V to Czechoslovakia with three parties aboard: two communications and training squads plus the team who were to assassinate Reinhard Heydrich, the Gauleiter of Czechoslovakia. The Halifax left Tangmere at 22.00 hrs and, crossing the French coast a short time later, headed for Darmstadt.

Shortly afterwards a night-fighter appeared astern on the port quarter and dropped two flares but fortunately did not attack despite shadowing the bomber for some 20 minutes. Pinpointing Darmstadt, Hockey headed for the selected dropping point but with snow beginning to fall and visibility decreasing, Hockey had no option but to keep the Halifax descending steadily to keep the ground in view. Although the flak batteries at Pilsen eventually pinpointed their position, the first party successfully parachuted in. Shortly after, the second dropping point was located and despite some difficulties, the agents were dropped in from 800 ft, later being followed by the third team, which unfortunately was dropped 12 miles from

S/Ldr R. Hockey's veteran L9613: V photographed at Fayid in December 1942, a year after he had used it to drop the Heydrich assassination team into Czechoslovakia. The short ventral mast and sheet metal fitting just forward of the tail wheel was added to prevent parachute static lines from becoming entangled with the tail wheel assembly. This was one of the three Halifaxes specially modified at Ringway; produced in October 1941, it served for a long period on Special Duties operations then passed first to 1661 HCU and then to 1662 HCU. It was written off following a belly-landing at Blyton on 20 April 1944. (H. Levy)

its preferred dropping point[7]. Flak opened up on the Halifax during the return flight and no navigation pinpoint could be obtained until Brussels put up more flak. Shortly after crossing the French coast, the escape hatch in the pilot's canopy blew open and jammed, requiring the second pilot to stand by Hockey and hang on to it for the remainder of the flight. Had it broken free, it could have fouled the elevators and although speed was reduced to 140 mph, the Halifax landed safely at Tangmere at 08.19 hrs.

The early operations flown to Poland followed a route across the North Sea to Denmark then along the Baltic coast to a point between Danzig and Kolobrzeg before turning inland on a southerly heading. The shortest distance involved was approximately 800 miles to a dropping zone in Pomerania while to Warsaw itself was 1,000 miles. The 2,000-mile round-trip Warsaw flights were barely within the Halifax's range, even with long-range tanks if a margin for emergencies was to be allowed. Because of this, payloads were reduced to a maximum of approximately 2,400 lb.

Artwork was almost non-existent on 138 (SD) Squadron. S/Ldr R. Hockey, seen here, was an extremely experienced pre-war pilot and Flight Commander and had this mock heraldic shield attached to L9613: V, his usual mount for operations. The combination of a heraldic shield, possibly related to the Hockey family and their Scottish heritage, plus the play on his name with the hockey stick and trombone made an interesting device and, painted on a sheet of duraluminium, was riveted to the fuselage. The Latin motto translates roughly as 'By braving we shall overcome'. The geometry of the curved section of the windshield with its opening bad weather panel, not usually seen in detail, are shown clearly in this view. (R. Hockey)

The other Flight Commander, seen here, was another very experienced pilot, S/Ldr Alan Boxer who led the Polish flight within No 138 Squadron; a New Zealander, he chose the traditional Maori greeting Kia Ora for his artwork. Post-war, Boxer was knighted and stayed in the RAF until retirement. (Sir Alan Boxer)

P/O F. Pantowski and his crew were killed when W7773: S was shot down on 30 October 1942 when carrying a supply of arms and three Polish agents for the Polish Wrench network. The Halifax crashed between Helleren and Refsland in southern Norway.

Typical of the extremes involved was the Polish attachment's third operation to Poland on 6 January 1942. Foul weather persisted for most of the journey and the round trip took 14 hours, the Halifax landing with its tanks almost dry. On 25 January, the Halifax strength of 138 Squadron was increased to five, without any reserves, to be allocated and issued as required. In addition to its aircraft, the squadron received several more crews including their first Czech one. February was accompanied by its usual winter savagery and on several occasions, crews were forced to return early due to severe icing conditions. The weather improved in March and operations commenced again and continued until May when a temporary halt was imposed with the onset of shorter nights.

During March the squadron had moved, along with its Polish detachment, to Tempsford, in company with the second Special Duties Squadron, No 161, which had formed in February, the nucleus of its personnel having gained their initial experience with 138 Squadron. The operations flown by the Polish detachment were not confined solely to PHA needs as they also carried out supply drops to Norway, Austria and Czechoslovakia. It was during an operation over Austria on 20/21 April that the Poles lost their first crew. W/Cdr Farley, the CO, flew V9976 with a mainly Polish crew who, unknown to them, were to drop a Russian NKVD[8] team as the result of an agreement between the British and Russian governments. Unfortunately, while flying in dense fog on the way to the dropping point, the Halifax flew into a hill at Kreuth in Bavaria killing all on board leaving Hockey, the other veteran, to take command of the squadron. It was a bad night for the squadron as Whitley Z9158: V had also been lost. Sent out to drop leaflets in the region of St Etienne it had returned to find thick mist covering Tangmere. Diverted to land at Boscombe Down, it crashed at Porton and caught fire, killing all but one of the crew of five.

In September, the longer nights allowed a resumption of supply flights to Poland. The suitability of the Halifax for SOE operations was to be exploited further as soon as sufficient aircraft could be diverted from the priorities of Bomber Command. On 6 October, 161 Squadron received its first Halifax, W1046, which was followed by two more on the 18th. On 24/25 October, a most unusual SD operation was flown by 138 Squadron's F/O Wodzicki to carry an agent to Estonia in W7773: S – the only such operation flown to that country from the West. The agent was Ronald Seth[9] who, although soon caught, survived. October's longer nights also signalled the return to Poland, Czechoslovakia and Norway. On 29/30th, both squadrons flew operations to Poland, Holland and Denmark with one of the two Polish sorties, code-named *Brace*, probably being the longest ever SD flight made from England. F/O Walczac took off at 17.45 hrs and landed back at Bircham Newton at 08.00 hrs, a round trip of 14 hours 15 minutes. The second Polish operation was unusual for other reasons. F/O Krol's crew had intended to bomb the Gestapo HQ on Szuch Avenue in Warsaw and although a long-hoped-for operation, it was unfeasible when only the Whitleys were available. The Polish crew found the building, but after several bombing runs it was clear that it was not possible to achieve a precision attack at night with a Halifax. Even a slight error would have caused Polish civilian casualties; the population of Warsaw was already suffering

enough. As an alternative, the German-occupied airfield at Okecie was chosen, the attack severely disrupting the night-flying in progress. This was the only bombing attack carried out on Poland by an RAF bomber during the Second World War. On the return flight some 50 miles west of the Danish coast, two Bf 110 night-fighters caught up with W7774: T and damaged it sufficiently for W/O Klosowski having to ditch it near the English coast. The crew scrambled out into the spare dinghy carried inside the aircraft for use by agents in an emergency and as an SOS had been sent off before they ditched, they were soon rescued.

A further duty fell to the Poles. The fighting in North Africa had swung back and forth since 1940 but the decisive final battle was about to begin at El Alamein. As Rommel's forces approached Montgomery's defensive line, the build-up of material to support the coming battle was reaching a climax and an urgent call went out for any aircraft capable of shifting supplies to North Africa in support of the forthcoming offensive. The Liberator-equipped No 511 Squadron had formed in October 1942 as a transport squadron just at the critical time but as there was a shortage of Liberators, the two SD squadrons were attached temporarily to fill the gap, the capacious fuselage of the Halifax being ideal for the task. Both squadrons sent Halifaxes and crews on attachment to 511 Squadron at Lyneham[10] with P/O Szrajer flying the first load out from Hurn in W1229: A on 4 October. Nevertheless, this diversion of valuable SD aircraft and highly experienced crews was to cost dearly as the flights shuttled back and forth; a process that continued after the battle of El Alamein had ended and transport aircraft remained in short supply. On 15 December, F/O L. Anderle's L9618: W failed to arrive at Malta during a return flight and it was later learned that it had been shot down on the Cairo-Malta leg. Anderle, the longest serving Czech in the squadron was a very experienced pilot. Each Halifax used for these transportation duties carried two ground staff tradesmen to look after the essentials while en route and on this occasion both Cpl Chandler and AC1 Hutchinson were lost with Anderle's crew.

Laid low with sand fly fever at Malta during his return flight the now W/Cdr Hockey later recalled, *"Since I was kept in hospital with no time schedule I decided to send the remainder of the force on, but via Gibraltar. We had some passengers from Cairo for the UK; on the first leg I had Lord Apsley and Air Marshal D'Albiac – so redistributed these and off they went. Dobromirski had Lord Apsley on board and returned after taking off at night, only to crash on the aerodrome, killing all aboard. There was a court of enquiry in which I gave evidence from my hospital bed."*

There were seventeen on board F/O K. Dobromirski's DT542: Q when he took off in the evening of 17 December, the subsequent report stating that the Halifax crashed at the Luqa airstrip, just beyond Zeitun. In addition to the six crew and two ground staff there were seven more RAF personnel and two Army majors; Major Lord Apsley DSO of the Royal Armoured Corps and Major A. Millar attached to the Indian Army. The day had not started well for the squadron as W1002: Y had crashed earlier in the Western Desert, near LG 224 outside Cairo, but no details appear to have survived as to the cause of the crash or any casualties. Hockey found Malta a rather hectic location to be caught at for any length of time. *"We had been bombed most days but the crew had kept the shrapnel holes in L9613 repaired."* Released from hospital on the 20th, he carried out a quick test flight and left for Gibraltar immediately. Having landed there, he discovered that F/Lt Sutton's aircraft had not arrived; he had lost his bearings, drifted south and force-landed at a strip near Fez and returned to Tempsford on 21 October, unharmed.

For extreme long-range operations, 138 Squadron Halifaxes were fitted with extra tankage thus giving them the largest fuel capacity for the type at 2,752 gallons as compared to the 2,572 gallon maximum for a standard Mk II or Mk V filled with the full complement of auxiliary tanks. Even so, the very long-range sorties to Poland pushed fuel capacity to the limit. Earlier, on 1/2 October, Fl/Sgt S. Klosowski of 138 Squadron had made the long round flight to supply the *Chisel* network; running low on fuel on return he had to make a forced-landing two miles from Goldsborough, fortunately without injuring anyone on board. On 29/30 October, the squadron lost two more Halifaxes on the long Polish route. P/O F. Pantowski's W7773: S, carrying a supply of arms for the *Wrench* network as well as three Polish agents, was shot down over southern Norway between Helleren and Refsland. Klosowski, now promoted to Warrant Officer, was also over Poland that night on the same operation. Running short of fuel, he had to ditch W7774: F off Sheringham in Norfolk. Fortunately, the coastguard saw them ditch and they were rescued unharmed by the lifeboat 'Foresters Centenary'. Klosowski later reported that they had been attacked by night-fighters, causing damage to the control surfaces and some of the fuel tanks. Given the small number of Halifaxes available for these clandestine operations, October had been a bad month.

SOE operations by 161 Squadron using the Halifaxes of 'B' Flight started on the night of 14/15 January 1943 when F/Lt Prior flew DG245: W to a dropping zone (DZ) in Belgium near its border with Holland for an operation code-named *Sexto*. On board were two agents plus cartons of coffee[11] and pigeons. Pinpointing his route across Belgium, he passed near Givet before changing course for the DZ but now ran into thick cloud that extended almost down to ground level and he was forced to abort the operation for, without being able to see the usual hand-held torches that

marked the DZ, it was pointless to continue. These frustrations were never absent and were hard on crews who spent most of their operational tour of duty flying continuously at very low level, alone across enemy-held territory, to locate a few people holding torches in a field. It is all the more remarkable that so many flights were successful. The normal operation periods each month were restricted to those of the moon when its light helped with a navigational process that relied very much on eyesight and good night vision rather than any artificial aid.

P/O Wynne also had Belgian DZs for his *Gibson I* and *Mistletoe* operations and carried two agents, one for each DZ, in DG286: Z plus some coffee. Identifying Guise, he flew on to Hal and then on to the first DZ but unable to locate it, he flew back to Hal and tried again, this time with more luck. Identifying the woods south of Torneppe, he was able to drop the *Mistletoe* agent north of the woods as required. He then set course for the *Gibson I* DZ but poor visibility foiled the attempt and the agent was brought back. The summary for the month of January is fairly indicative of the normal type of SOE and SIS operations and the margin of success involved; out of 16 operations, three were completed, five partly completed, five not completed due to no reception committee at the dropping point, two abandoned and one Halifax failed to return. Each trip usually involved more than one task and the composition of the loads varied greatly. Failures were not infrequent because of the factors involved; sometimes the lack of a reception committee meant they had been stopped from arriving by German patrols, or worse, captured. Nevertheless, crews went to extreme lengths to complete each operation in what was, basically, a very lonely war.

On 25/26 January 1943, F/Lt Prior carried out a double operation (*Crab 12* and *Designer/Stationer*) to France in DG245: W, which left Tempsford at 22.03 hrs with a load of six containers, leaflets, two agents[12] and a package. They crossed the French coast at Cabourg at a height of 2,000 ft and set course for the Loire area and having located it, map-read to Givors and from there to the appointed dropping point. The reception party flashed its coded signal; the Halifax released its six containers from 1,000 ft which were seen to drop close to the ground party. Phase one of the mission

DG253: F of 138 Squadron is seen here at its foggy, wet dispersal site at Tempsford. F/Lt 'Dick' Wilkin RCAF used this aircraft on a number of operations. It was written off on the evening of 18 August 1943. Airborne at 20.14 hrs, P/O K. Brown had turned back soon after when a strong smell of fuel pervaded the aircraft. Making his approach too fast, he touched down at 20.29 hrs and careered on into scrub off the end of the runway, damaging the Halifax beyond economic repair but without injuring anyone on board. (R. Wilkin)

F/Lt R. Wilkin DFC, MC (Czechoslovakia), MID, RCAF (thumbs in pocket) photographed with his crew and ground crew at 138 Squadron's home airfield at Tempsford. He regularly flew this B Mk V Series I (Special) DG253: F. He and his crew were killed on 19/20 September 1943 when flying a different Halifax, DG252, which was shot down by flak into the sea just west of Harlingen during a dual SOE operation code-named Catarrh 14/Leek 9. Wilkins' crew of five was a very experienced and highly decorated one: P/O G. Berwick DFM, F/O H. Brown DFM, F/O H. Burke DFM and Fl/Sgt A. Hughes MC (Czechoslovakia). Hughes was reported as continuing to fire from the rear turret until impact. A second Halifax from the squadron, BB317: N, also on a dual drop into Holland, was damaged by flak on its way out over the coast and forced to ditch in the North Sea. Two of Fl/Sgt N. Sherwood's crew went down with the Halifax and a third was washed out of the dinghy before a German boat rescued the survivors four hours later. (R. Wilkin)

completed, Prior headed DG245 towards the next dropping point, map-reading at low level all the way. Having positively identified it, the 'Joes' and the parcel were dropped from 800 ft. The Halifax landed back at base at 05.28 hrs after a trip of nearly seven and a half hours, mostly at low level over occupied territory and relying mainly upon the crew's ability to map-read at night.

No 161 Squadron's first loss also followed what was to become a familiar pattern. P/O H. Readhead's DG285: X departed for France on the night of 15/16 January with a load of four containers, one parcel, 20 pigeons and some leaflets for *Ker/Crab*. The next day a message was received from the French underground that a four-engine bomber had been burnt out four miles south of Rennes. The bodies of the seven crew members were amongst the wreckage. It was not determined whether the Halifax had fallen to flak or fighters, but in either case, the low altitude at which the aircraft operated gave little hope of escape by parachute. It was the first operational loss of a B Mk V Halifax.

Operations to Poland were always fraught with problems because of the extreme distances involved, but all crews pushed themselves to the limit to complete them. On 13/14 March, six sorties to Poland all succeeded, a notable achievement marred only by the losses of the following night. The long-range priority was still in force and four Polish and two Czech operations were flown in addition to five to French DZs. The returning Halifaxes from these sorties were diverted to several airfields; two would succeed but two would not. F/O S. Smith's DT620: T failed to return while trying to carry out a sortie to a DZ named *Wrona 614* of the *Slate* network in Poland, the Halifax having been shot down near Store Heddinge in Denmark on the outward flight killing all on board. S/Ldr C. Gibson had been heading for a DZ north of Brno on a sortie to the *Bronze* network in Czechoslovakia but BB281: O was shot down near Munich on the outward flight with only Sgt M. Hudson surviving before succumbing to his injuries three weeks later.

No 161 Squadron also lost two crews that night. Five aircraft had been scheduled for Czech and French operations. F/L A. Prior's DG245: W was brought down over Germany while heading for Czechoslovakia and a DZ for the *Iridium* network. F/O G. Osborn and three of his crew were a little more fortunate when DG283: Y crashed due to engine failure at Fawley 30 minutes after take-off for a *Director34* drop in France. The Halifax caught fire and Osborn showed exceptional courage in pulling most of the injured clear, an action for which he was awarded the George Medal.

As noted, the triple disaster claimed three of No 138 Squadron's Halifaxes on 16/17 December 1943. F/Sgt J. Watson's crew were returning from a drop to the Detective 3 DZ in France, when weather closed in and, while trying to land at the emergency airfield at Woodbridge, LL115: A (seen here awaiting delivery at Speke airfield) collided with trees and crashed at 05.30, at Capel Green, killing all but three of the eight crew.

Halifax B Mk V Series IA, LL119, photographed while awaiting delivery from the Rootes Securities airfield at Speke. It was issued to 138 Squadron in December but was lost on the 17th of that month when extremely bad weather created havoc among returning bomber crews with 29 crashing at their respective bases as a result. No 138 Squadron lost three Halifaxes, possibly the heaviest losses suffered in one night by either of the two Special Duties squadrons. (P. Summerton)

He had done something similar when he had pulled his Observer/Navigator clear of a burning Whitley at an OTU, receiving such severe injuries that he was hospitalised for six weeks.

There were two more losses for the month, one from each squadron. On 19/20 March, F/O H. Wynne DFM was heading for Norway in DG244: Y for a drop to a *Vega 3* SIS network, but nothing further was heard of the aircraft. F/O E. Clow's 138 Squadron crew fared better when HR665: L ditched in the Ijsselmeer off Enkhuizen while heading for Holland on a double sortie, *St John/St Andrew* for SIS and *Leeks 5/Catarrh 11* for SOE. All of the crew were rescued and taken prisoner but one of the two Dutch agents on board, Gerbrand, was rescued by a fishing boat and evaded capture. The second agent, Bergman, was the only fatal casualty of the ditching.

Because of these heavy losses, the old route to Poland was abandoned and a more northerly one over Sweden selected. This increased the distance involved by up to 160 miles, which meant that only during exceptionally good weather, and with great difficulty, could the Polish-manned Halifaxes keep up their hazardous supply runs.

However, other hazards always lurked and a triple disaster claimed three of 138 Squadron's Halifaxes on 16/17 December 1943 to the old enemy – the weather. Fl/Sgt J. Watson's crew were returning from a drop to the *Detective 3* DZ in France, when the weather closed in and, while trying to land at the emergency airfield at Woodbridge, LL115: A collided with trees and crashed at Capel Green at 05.30 hrs, killing all but three of the eight crew. F/O R. Watson and crew in LL119: F were also caught by the terrible weather when returning from a *Wheelwright 36* drop in France but all managed to bale out safely over Suffolk, the Halifax being left to crash into the sea off Felixstowe. Fl/Sgt T. Tomas's crew were also returning from France after a drop to *Marc I* DZ when four of them were killed when LW280: K crashed into the sea off Harwich.

Early 1943 also brought a small expansion of the SOE force with the formation of No 1575 (SD) Flight at Tempsford on 21 May. Formed around a nucleus of officers from 161 Squadron, it was equipped with four Halifaxes and two Venturas and posted to north-west Africa to undertake operations in the Mediterranean area. The first of two Halifaxes, EB140 and EB141, departed for Maison Blanche on 11 June; EB142 and EB143 followed eight days later, by which time the other two Halifaxes had carried out the unit's first operations over Sardinia and Corsica on 13/14 June

respectively from their base at Blida. Although the unit confined its operations mainly to Corsica, Sardinia and Italy, occasional trips were made over southern France, EB141 making the first of these on 19/20 June.

On 6 August, EB141 crashed, fortunately without loss of life, and just one month later, on 7 September, Ventura AE881 failed to return from an operation. Two further Halifaxes were lost in crashes during the brief life of this unit, EB197 on 9 September and EB188 on the 20th, again without loss of life. Two days later the flight was disbanded and all personnel and aircraft posted to the newly formed No 624 (SD) Squadron.

Another SOE squadron already in existence in the Middle East was No 148, a Wellington-equipped bomber unit that had four Liberators on its charge, AL510: W, AL506: X, AL509: Y and AL530: Z. These were engaged in SOE operations and continued their task as an independent unit after the squadron disbanded in December 1942. No 148 Squadron was then re-formed in the SD role and reacquainted with the four Liberators, the first Halifaxes arriving on 18 February 1943. By 13 March, the squadron had moved to its new base at Gambut and dispatched its first sorties, HR680: D and Liberator AL510: W, three days later. The Liberators were to prove a useful addition since the squadron had an establishment of only ten Halifaxes and a replacement priority of one per month.

Another move on 3 April 1943 took the squadron to Derna from where a very successful series of operations was carried out over Greece and the Balkans. Reports received from the partisan forces gave high praise to the almost uncanny accuracy of these supply drops.

As for most Middle East-based squadrons, living conditions for 148 Squadron personnel were poor and the supply of spares, containers, parachutes, etc, was far from satisfactory. Not to be overcome by such difficulties, ground crews became very adept at working near-miracles to keep the precious supply of Halifaxes

W/O C. Fortune's name was propitious when on 10 December 1943, BB344: C was caught in foul weather flying through mountainous country. In the act of changing places with the second pilot, the Halifax entered a vicious down-draught which turned it over on its back. What followed was a nightmare and the crew were lucky to survive; this photograph was taken before the near fatal occurrence.

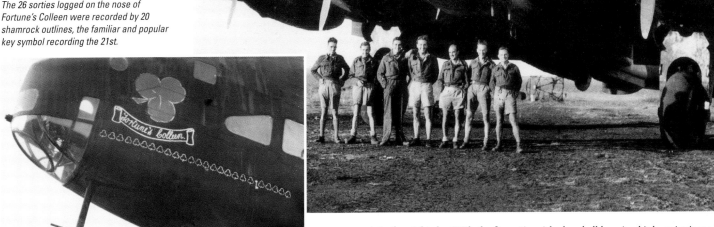

The 26 sorties logged on the nose of Fortune's Colleen were recorded by 20 shamrock outlines, the familiar and popular key symbol recording the 21st.

available. The following account, by no means an isolated case, is typical of their ingenuity. On 15 June, a Halifax was brought in with damage to the fuselage, wing and tail plane on the port side. The main box formers had been damaged and normally the aircraft should have been transferred to 161 MU at Fayid. This would have meant losing the Halifax for at least a week at the peak of the moon period, which was the time of maximum activity. The engineering officer, P/O Fuller, undertook to have the aircraft serviceable within three days. The ground crew were very keen to tackle the job and rigged up temporary lights using old car headlamps and starter batteries. New stringers were made from sheet metal and, as no salt bath was available, the metal was normalised by blowlamp and oil. A rudder was taken from another Halifax that had already lost its engines to keep three other Halifaxes flying. The repairs to the fuselage and wing took 863 rivets, and by working double shifts, day and night, the Halifax was fully serviceable within 36 hours, the normal routine 40-hour inspection having also been carried out at the same time.

Despite such problems, the squadron kept up a steady series of operations and during August delivered to the partisan forces 1,957 containers and 2,079 packages plus 70 agents. The total weight of supplies was just short of 264 tons. Allied intelligence placed considerable value on these operations, estimating that to counter them 50,000 Germans were immobilised in Greece, Albania and Yugoslavia.

After moving to Tocra on 1 September 1943, 148 Squadron's activities for the month consisted of leaflet raids over Tripolis, Novplion, Argos, Xylokastron, Lamia, Volos, Larissa, Salonika and Athens. While the danger from night-fighters and flak was less acute in operations over Greece and Yugoslavia, crews faced additional hazards from both weather and terrain. Accurate drops to partisan forces often meant flying into deep valleys between mountain peaks and W/Cdr Blackburn had a particularly frightening experience on 19 October whilst dropping containers at low altitude in the Greek mountains. One container hung up, but the parachute opened pulling HR680: D into a sudden nose-dive. Blackburn managed to pull the Halifax's nose up in time and turned away out over the Gulf of Corinth where the parachute finally pulled both the container and the bomb rack free but the parachute then became briefly entangled in the tail unit before finally parting company. Undeterred, Blackburn returned to the dropping point and completed his mission.

Dangers from weather were always present. Warrant Officer (W/O) C. Fortune was flying BB344: C through mountainous country in foul weather on the night of 10 December and just as he was changing places with the second pilot, the Halifax entered a vicious down-draught that turned it over on its back. The entire crew ended up on the roof along with some incendiary flares, which burst into flame and set fire to the surrounding kit bags and fuselage. Fortunately, the mid-upper turret was not fitted with any armament and the fire blew itself out. Grabbing the control column, Fortune heaved back on it as best he could from his unusual position. As speed built up, he forced full aileron on and managed to roll the Halifax out of its inverted dive at a height of 4,000 ft; the surrounding mountains towered another 4,000 ft higher

into the night sky. With the fire extinguished and all burning kit bags jettisoned, Fortune continued on to the dropping zone but failed to locate the reception committee. Jack Easter, the Wireless Operator, recalled that Control then wanted to divert the Halifax to a landing ground code-named *Berka 2* because of the strong crosswind at a base, but because of the condition of the aircraft, and the low fuel status, Fortune insisted on returning direct to their home base. On landing, the strong crosswind caught the Halifax, causing it to swing badly and veer off the runway and because of the change of attitude and lack of petrol, the port engines did not respond – the Halifax ran off the runway, collapsed the undercarriage, pulverised a parked Spitfire and both aircraft burst into flames. Miraculously, the crew escaped without serious injury. Easter is of the opinion that if proper fire fighting facilities had been available, the Halifax might have been saved. The crew stayed together and finished their tour of operations.

The Middle East-based SOE force gained strength with the arrival of No 1586 (SD) Flight at Tunis in November. This unit, with its establishment of 10 crews, three Halifaxes and three Liberators, was Polish in its entirety and had formed at Brindisi in southern Italy at the beginning of October. The Polish element of 138 Squadron at Tempsford had received a boost when No 301 (Polish) Squadron was disbanded on 7 April 1943 and some of its personnel transferred to No 138, which provided sufficient crews for the Poles to form a new unit, No 301 (SD) Flight, in July. The difficulties of operations to Poland were partly alleviated in October with the

Photographed at Blida in North Africa, W/O Reagan's JP205: K of 624 Squadron had a close call off the Corsican coast on the evening of 18 March 1944 after being hit by flak, which caused the starboard main tyre to burst, blowing a large hole in the top of the wing. On board were three agents and an American general along for the ride. As the Halifax lost height, Reagan ordered everything except personal gear to be jettisoned including large bundles of leaflets to be dropped as cover for the agent drop but, unfortunately, one of the crew cut the strings holding a bundle together before throwing it out and filled the interior of the Halifax with paper! Despite the crisis, two of the crew saw the humour in it but their passengers failed to appreciate the moment. Levelling the Halifax off at 1,500 ft Reagan was able to nurse it back to its base for a crash-landing without injuring any of those on board. (F. Tunesi)

LL385: H of 148 Squadron displays its full load of 15 containers, three in each wing cell and nine in the fuselage bomb bay. The outboard engines were fitted with four-bladed propellers, a not uncommon occurrence where extra power absorption for long-range flying was required. On the left in the distance is EB196: E. (M. McKay)

Free-drop supplies lined up by the crew entry hatch of BB338: M waiting their turn to be loaded. This view also shows the varying style of code lettering applied to some of the squadron's aircraft. The packing sequence was critical to the dropping requirements for each specific DZ so great care went into the order in which items were loaded and stowed. The dispatchers often had to handle the cumbersome loads in almost total darkness and ensure the rapid dropping necessary on each run over the reception site. BB338 was lost when it crashed into the sea returning from a supply drop in Yugoslavia on 5 November 1944. (M. McKay)

allocation of three Liberators, which had greater range than the Halifax; but this small number was insufficient to cope with the workload and the Flight was transferred to Italy where the Allied invasion had made suitable bases available. For security reasons the number of the Flight was changed to 1586.

No 1575 Flight's successor, 624 (SD) Squadron had formed at Blida on 7 September 1943 and began operations on the night of 22 September with EB154: A going to Italy and BB444: D and EB196 going to Corsica. The squadron dispatched a detachment to its advanced base at Protville on 1 October where three Halifaxes from 138 Squadron joined them to carry out a very special secret mission before returning to England on 11 October. On 15 October, two ground crews moved to Malta with EB197 for an operation over Czechoslovakia but it was replaced two days later by EB154, the former being due for an inspection.

On 16 October a 624 Squadron detachment moved to Sidi Amor and continued to operate from this base until the whole squadron finally moved to Brindisi, via Tocra in Cyrenaica, in late December, sharing the airfield with 1586 Flight as part of 334 Wing. Operations resumed on 4 January 1944, 93 sorties being flown by the end of the month, 72.5% of them successful. Operations were a mixture of leaflet drops over Yugoslavia, Albania and Italy plus some agent and supply drops. The squadron suffered its first loss on 1 February when BB444 crashed at the Albanian dropping point, with only the rear gunner surviving.

A change of policy during February saw 624 Squadron ordered back to its old base, the first aircraft leaving for Blida on the 8th. Once established there, the squadron concentrated on operations over France for the remainder of its war. Its place at Brindisi was filled by 148 Squadron, which had moved in from Tocra on 22 January. In conjunction with 1586 Flight, it concentrated its operations over the Balkans and central Europe, with arms drops into Poland being made in increasing numbers.

One of 148 Squadron's earliest operations from Italy involved a large supply drop to partisan forces in Yugoslavia. However, things were very fluid on the ground; the Germans overran the original dropping point late in the day, and a new one was nominated 15 miles away. Eleven Halifaxes were dispatched and the first six completed their task successfully. P/O Leleu was next and, having guided JP239: C up to the dropping point, began unloading his containers when he saw other parachutes showering down on the target accompanied by coloured parachute flares. Looking up he saw several aircraft overhead with their navigation lights on. It was only then he realised that he was caught in the middle of a German paratroop attack and, in his own words: *"got the hell out of there fast"*. The remaining Halifaxes reported no reception lights when they arrived.

During the early part of 1944 most of the SOE squadrons began to receive Mk II or V Series IA Halifaxes to replace their ageing Series II (Special) machines. The majority of Halifaxes used for special duties sorties carried reduced crews, but those operating with 1586 Flight were drastically reduced to two pilots, a navigator and a dispatcher in an effort to keep payloads as high as possible. Loads varied, but on

average, the gross disposable load was from 7,000 to 7,400 lb compared to 5,000 lb for the Liberators. A typical load is shown broken down as follows:

15 containers	4,624 lb gross	2,824 lb net
29 packages	2,058 lb gross	1,458 lb net
Nickles (leaflets)	230 lb gross	230 lb net
Total disposable gross load 6,912 lb		

The number of agents carried averaged two or three and occasionally was as high as five, but more could be accommodated for shorter sorties; for example, operating over France 624 Squadron carried up to 15 personnel at a time.

During the early months of 1944, 624 Squadron increased its activities over France, the number of sorties per night varying between 12 and 14 and occasionally going as high as 19. The loss rate remained encouragingly low. It also undertook a series of paratroop tasks for the USAAF during May, which earned a letter of appreciation from General Ira C. Eaker.

On 15 July, the Squadron learned that it was to convert to Stirlings and the C.O. W/Cdr Stanbury collected the first of these from 144 MU on the 28th. By 18 July, eight Stirlings were on charge but despite conversion training, the Halifaxes continued to operate regularly over France. However, as new Stirling crews arrived, surplus Halifax crews were transferred to 148 Squadron. The first mixed

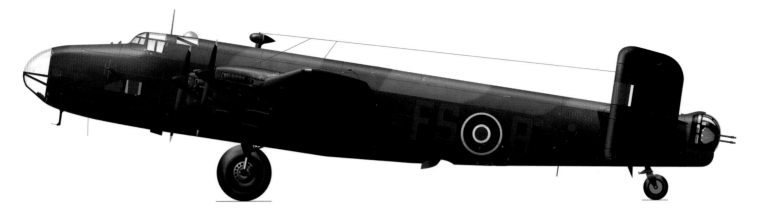

Handley Page Halifax, B Mk V
JP246: B, 148 Squadron, Brindisi, Italy July 1944.

Routine maintenance being carried out on JP246: B of 148 Squadron. The shadow of the Rebecca aerial, the airborne half of the Rebecca/Eureka system, can be seen on the side of the aircraft's nose. In the background to the right is C- Charlie also undergoing maintenance but minus its rudders, while EB196: E, with the old-style triangular empennage, is visible beneath the fuselage of JP246 and the tail of another, with triangular fins, is visible on the left. The oval window under the nose of the Halifax at the top right of the photograph was for the target camera which was mounted just forward of the navigator's station. The ban on Merlin-engined Halifaxes in Bomber Command in the UK did not apply to MAAF squadrons and Mk II and V Series IAs with Merlin 22 engines were supplied to squadrons as older aircraft were replaced. (M. McKay)

Stirling/Halifax operation was flown on the night of 29 July and by August the Squadron was fully operational with Stirlings. The last Halifax sortie was flown on 13 August by F/O F. Driscoll in JN896 which, unfortunately, failed to return,.

The short summer nights had restricted the activities of the Brindisi-based Halifaxes with drops made only to Yugoslavia and northern Italy. On average, losses were normally very small, although 148 Squadron lost four Halifaxes on 3 July. After this, losses – still small in number – became consistent and were related directly to the increased Axis defences and the steadily worsening weather conditions. But worse was yet to come.

On 1 August 1944 the Warsaw uprising began and the Polish Home Army, which had come out into the open, seized a large section of the city from the occupying German forces. This action caught the SOE forces off balance at first and it was not until the night of the 4th that a major supply effort could be made. Both 148 Squadron and 1586 Flight flew seven sorties to Warsaw that night. Conditions were catastrophic; dense smoke from the burning city billowed up, obscuring the flares at the reception points. The close proximity of the German and Polish forces also made it essential to use absolute precision when dropping the supplies. This, in turn, meant that the aircraft were forced to fly at between 300 and 400 ft and 148 Squadron lost four Halifaxes on the first night: EB147: K, JP276: A, JP181: X and JP162: S.

To add to the disaster, LW284: Z, borrowed from the Polish Flight, was forced to return early because the rear turret, the only armament carried, was unserviceable. A tyre burst as it landed, the undercarriage collapsed and the Halifax burst into flames. The crew were lucky to survive. The port inner engine of another Halifax, JN897: T failed, leaving a runaway propeller which forced the pilot to jettison the load. The other aircraft, JP295: P brought its load back having been unable to find any reception at either the primary or the secondary DZ. Of the Polish crews, three succeeded, two into Warsaw and one into the woods at Kampinos. Among those operating that night was the veteran pilot F/O Szrajer in JP252: L; it was his 100th operation and the last of his third tour of duty.

Air Marshal Slessor, Deputy Air C-in-C MAAF,[13] refused permission for further operations convinced that it was suicidal and a waste of experienced crews and would do nothing to affect the fate of Warsaw. However, political pressure was brought to bear and Slessor was forced to allow Polish crews to resume operations but refused to let British crews operate again until the last quarter of the moon. Understandably, the Polish crews had begged to be allowed to continue and on 8/9 August recommenced limited operations. Eventually the tragedy drew in SAAF[14] Liberator squadrons who paid an equally devastating price in aircraft and crews.

As the battle progressed, the German flak defences were increased along the route that the supply aircraft were forced to follow, culminating in a very heavy concentration over Warsaw itself. Crews were sometimes forced to fly as low as 100 ft to get below the lines of fire from the flak batteries. Losses were heavy and one pilot from 148 Squadron reported seeing five aircraft shot down over the city itself during his mission. Halifaxes that returned were usually so badly shot-up that they required extensive repairs; some had bullet holes inflicted from above, caused by machine guns mounted on higher ground around the city, testimony to the determination of crews, some of whom navigated to their dropping point using individual streets for identification. On 16 August, the following message was received by 334 Wing, from the GOC Warsaw, General Bor-Komorowski. *"The gallant effort of your airmen has enabled us to continue our struggle. Fighting Warsaw thanks heroic airmen and sends them her highest appreciation. We bow with deepest reverence before fallen crews."* A message was also received from Air Marshal Slessor praising the courage of the 334 Wing crews.

Due to the attrition rate suffered in previous operations over Yugoslavia and Italy, the Polish Flight had been in the worst possible position when the uprising began. This applied not only to crews but also to aircraft and 148 Squadron lent any Halifaxes that it could spare. However, its own losses prevented more than a token effort and the cumulative losses of this period exhausted the general Halifax reserves in the Mediterranean area. On receipt of an urgent request from the PHA HQ, the Air Ministry ordered ten Halifaxes to be withdrawn from Bomber Command and transferred immediately to 334 Wing. Unfortunately, these were equipped to Bomber Command requirements and needed to be stripped of a considerable amount of equipment. It was also necessary to modify the interior to take static line attachments for freight dropping through the fuselage well hatch. All this took time and the first nine arrived at Brindisi between 30 August and 1 September. Despite this, during August, 148 Squadron carried out 116 supply missions and 1586 Flight, 80.

Further supplies of aircraft to 334 Wing were held up through the dispatch of some Mk V Halifaxes, which, on arrival at 144 MU, were found to be due for major overhaul and inspection. They were also fitted with Merlin XX engines, which had to be changed for Merlin 22s before they could be cleared for operations.

Tragically, despite crews literally navigating street by street across the burning city at little more than rooftop height, less than half of the precious supplies dropped reached the PHA, the Germans and the raging fires consuming the remainder. Bad weather set in during late September and by the time it had cleared the Polish forces had capitulated. Only then did Rossokovsky's army start to engage German forces around the city; for Stalin, the Germans had eliminated his main political problem – there would be no pro-Western forces left when the Russians finally 'liberated' Warsaw.

Earlier, in October 1943, a decision had been taken ultimately to withdraw the Halifaxes from Nos 138 and 161 Squadrons and replace them with Stirlings. The latter had been withdrawn from bombing sorties because of their altitude performance problems but were otherwise very good aircraft. By withdrawing the Halifaxes, the Stirlings would find very useful employment in conditions where heights rarely exceeded 1,000 ft and in return, the Halifax saving would be diverted into Main Force bombing requirements. The process was initiated, but it was some considerable time before Halifaxes left service with the two squadrons. In the interim operations continued at an intensive pace.

By now, the two squadrons had established a balance between SIS and SOE requirements, with 161 Squadron concentrating more on the former establishment's needs. In addition to the decision to phase out the Halifaxes, changes in operational requirements also added some impetus. No 161 Squadron found that there was considerable economy to be gained for some operations where only one or two agents were carried and Hudsons were brought into wider use. Because of these factors, the Halifaxes began to be concentrated in 138 Squadron from January 1944.

Although not known to the crews, the New Year heralded the beginning of the build-up for the invasion of Europe and drops to Germany began to appear on the operations list. Lt Hysing Dahl dropped two agents in the Schwarzwald, between Stuttgart and the Swiss border, from his 161 Squadron Halifax on 6/7 January. That same month, the squadron found itself short, not of Halifaxes, but of crews as tours were completed and it saw personnel transferred in from 138 Squadron to help balance the operational needs during February.

The mounting operational pressure took its toll as SOE, SIS and the American OSS now increased their flow of agents into Europe. All SD units, both home-based and abroad, were kept very busy and losses were not light. The number of individual sorties per night was far removed from those of two years previously. Typical of this period was the night of 9/10 April; 138 Squadron had 16 Halifaxes out, while its sister squadron sent out seven plus three Lysanders for pick-up operations. No 90 Squadron, which had some crews and aircraft on temporary secondment, mounted 17 Stirling sorties while 38 Group sent out 18 aircraft from its various squadrons.

On 15 August a decision was made not to re-equip 161 Squadron with Stirlings until sufficient numbers were ready for a complete changeover. This decision was to have been reviewed in September. Meanwhile, the only modified SD Stirlings so far supplied were allotted to 138 Squadron and held as surplus until sufficient were available for the proposed changeover. As part of this arrangement, five of No 138 Squadron's 17 Halifaxes were transferred to 161 Squadron and held as immediate replacement for operational losses. With Halifaxes now being phased out of this specialist task, replacement aircraft, modified to SD standards, were no longer available.

This precaution was, however, eroded by events over Warsaw, which had resulted in the urgent request for replacements for 148 Squadron and 1586 (Polish) Flight. Eight from 138 Squadron and five from 161 were sent initially, but the scale of losses forced a revision of the original 11 September changeover date for 161 Squadron. As the Warsaw situation steadily became more critical, the date was brought back to the 3rd and the eight Mk V Halifaxes of 161 Squadron were made immediately available for transfer to Brindisi. The aircraft left the following day, the squadron having flown its last Halifax sorties on 1/2 September to Holland, Norway and Germany. F/Lt Kidd flew the latter operation, dropping the first OSS agent to go into Germany in what was a joint SOE/OSS operation. The last Halifax loss for the Squadron had occurred just days earlier on 28/29 August when F/Lt P. Green's LL388: W had been shot down, fragments of 20mm shell (indicating that a night-fighter crippled the Halifax) wounding W/O N. Slade, and killing Kroon, one of three Dutch agents on board for operations *Hendrik* and *Stalking*. The Halifax was on its way into Holland when shot down, crash-landing between Engelen and the Maas River. The crew were captured and Slade later died from his wounds but the remaining two agents, Buitendijk and Van der Meer, fortunately were able to escape; there would have been no POW status for them. This was the last Mk V Halifax lost by the Squadron.

No 138 Squadron also flew its last Halifax sorties that month and Lt Nevin, a South African, flew this last Halifax sortie as part of a mass drop by ten aircraft to a French DZ. Shortages amongst the Stirlings had necessitated using one of the few remaining Halifaxes at Tempsford, where they were awaiting redeployment[15].

In October, 148 Squadron received instructions that daylight operations would be permitted whenever possible. Flying conditions were much harsher during the day due to the turbulence caused by the sun heating the barren mountains. Towering cumulonimbus clouds, magnificently beautiful but dangerous in the extreme, were also a daily feature of the landscape. However, most crews considered that the increased accuracy of the drops justified the rougher conditions. One drawback was

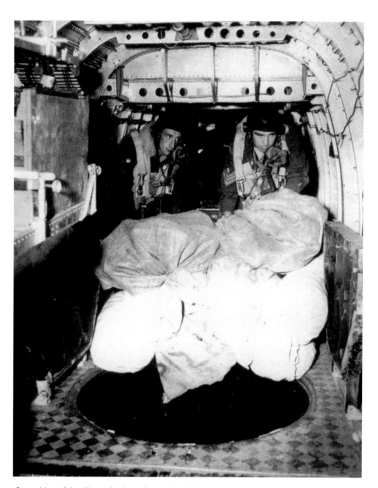

Some idea of the dispatcher's task may be obtained from this picture of two Flight Sergeants about to push a free-drop load through the dropping hatch during a daylight operation. Both men are watching the panel containing the lights for the dropping sequence, yellow for 'ready', green for 'drop' and red for 'stop dropping' which was operated from the bomb aimer's position. The two half-shell doors that covered the well position when not in use are open and locked back against each side of the fuselage. The diamond patterned aluminium floor has a non-slip finish common to most Halifaxes. The only armament carried by the special duties units were those in the rear turret, the ammunition boxes for which are visible on the left of the photograph, which also gives a good appreciation of the width of the Halifax fuselage.

that the dropping point markers were harder to distinguish in daylight, but eventually this was overcome by using 'SOE Operations' smoke flares. The increased accuracy can best be judged by a message received during October from a Balkan partisan group thanking the crew for dropping the supplies right in the yard of their headquarters. Another message, somewhat tongue in cheek, wished to remind the Halifax crews that it was only necessary to drop the supplies in the area marked by the smoke flares and not to extinguish the individual smoke flares with the containers.

The one member of the crew who definitely preferred daylight drops, despite the rougher ride, was the dispatcher. His duty was to push the supplies through the well hatch and, since they were stacked in the rest bay during take-off, he had to move them aft for dropping after the Halifax became airborne. On night operations this meant working in almost total darkness so that no light showed through the hatch. To prevent the chance of falling out he was usually attached to the static line rail by a rope from his parachute harness. Timing was critical, and all the packages had to be stacked near the hatch ready to be thrust out with a minimum of delay. Because bags dropped without a parachute had a longer trajectory, they were dropped first. As soon as the green light illuminated on the dispatcher's panel, the parachute-equipped containers were pushed out as rapidly as possible until the light went out. The Halifax was then out of the area and had to make another run if there were any supplies left. Often, odd-shaped bags would not go through the hatch cleanly and the dispatcher would have to jump on the particular article to push it through. A good dispatcher and his assistant, usually the wireless operator, could drop half a ton in three seconds. The actual final run up to the dropping point was the responsibility of the bomb aimer. The Halifax would begin its run over the target with the bomb doors open, flaps partly down and engines throttled back while the bomb aimer called out corrections and finally released the containers in the bomb bay. It was on his signal that the dispatcher dropped the fuselage load.

The Poles continued their night operations to Czechoslovakia, Austria, Yugoslavia, Bulgaria and Crete plus 20 drops to the Polish Home Army operating

Some of the RAAF personnel on 148 Squadron were used for a sequence of photographs showing a crew kitting up for an SD operation and helping load the aircraft. Standing in front of DG357: O they are, from left to right, F/O R. Eisenhauer, F/O K. Walker, Fl/Sgt W. Hodgins, W/O V. Murphy, W/O L. Shannon and F/O O. Mason. The Halifax carries nose art of a flying caped woman with blonde hair dropping lightning bolts. Although not shown in this photograph, an interesting markings feature peculiar at the time to MAAF aircraft, was the addition of C 1 type roundels beneath the wings which would not be seen in European skies until 1945, and never on black-camouflaged under surfaces. (M. McKay)

P/O Sollin's LL484: H of 148 Squadron photographed after its crash at San Vito on 26 December 1944 when the port outer engine had to be shut down during take-off causing the aircraft to crash, killing the navigator. A former 138 Squadron aircraft, it was fitted with four-bladed propellers and the mid-upper turret had been removed. (H. Walker)

Right: An undated view of two Halifaxes, with JP259 in the foreground and behind it another Special Duties Halifax operated by the Polish unit based in Italy. In addition to the Pegasus and Polish emblems, the latter Halifax carries a record of 32 parachute drops. Both aircraft were undergoing complete engine changes at the time, plus other repairs; JP259 was delivered on 12 March 1944 and issued to 1586 (SD) Flight, remaining on strength when that unit became 301 (Polish) Squadron on 7 November 1944 and serving until 28 February 1945. Records show that it then passed to 614 Squadron but that must have been for a very brief period, possibly only a paper entry, as that squadron had ceased Halifax operations on 3 March. The two Halifaxes were likely with either 1586 Flight or under its new identity of 301 Squadron when photographed.

behind German lines. On 7 November, the strength of 1586 Flight was finally up to that of a full squadron and it was renumbered as 301 (SD) Squadron. Its last supply drop to Poland was made on 28 December because further flights were banned by the SOE due to the Soviet offensive in Poland. What German forces had been unable to accomplish was thus achieved by politics.

No 148 Squadron received a couple of Stirlings during November and then, in December, received orders that it would be converting to Liberators. As none of these had arrived, the squadron continued to use Halifaxes, making a particularly successful drop to the Russian forces in January 1945, leaving the Russians highly impressed. Despite the winter conditions, operations continued throughout January

and several agents, some female, were dropped along with a jeep and supplies to partisans in northern Italy.

Because of the rapidly declining requirements of the SOE, on 28 February 301 Squadron was transferred to transport duties, thus reflecting the general situation in Europe. No 624 Squadron had disbanded on 24 September 1944, leaving only 148 Squadron which now found itself acting in direct support of the final army operations in Italy, which kept it occupied until VE day. Its first peacetime operation was to dispatch five Halifaxes to Yugoslavia to evacuate POWs. Finally, on 23 May 1945, 148 Squadron made its long overdue conversion to Liberators and the Halifaxes were ferried to 144 MU at Maison Blanche in North Africa.

CHAPTER EIGHT

COASTAL COMMAND

Photographed off the Welsh coast near St Davids in 1944, HR744/G was amongst the early Halifaxes issued to 58 Squadron. Produced in March 1943, the Mod 412 nose and Type D fin and rudder assemblies had been added by the time this photograph was taken about a year after it joined the Squadron. Despite the time lapse and changes at production centres, it retained Merlin XX engines fitted with three-bladed propellers plus Gallay radiators – a mixture of Series I (Special) and Series IA features. It also shows the consistency of markings used at this stage; coded 'O' with a small but more broadly marked figure '1', the 'O' being repeated in miniature on the nose. Built by Handley Page, the style of camouflage demarcation varied around the area forward of the cockpit from that on Halifaxes produced by other manufacturers. The original nose-mounted Vickers machine gun has been replaced by a 0.5-inch Browning, the Perspex nose cone being reinforced with four bracing rods. It was struck off charge on 23 November 1944. (via M. Wright)

I N 1942, Coastal Command began a much-needed expansion of its long-range anti-submarine force with the Sunderland squadrons, which for so long had withstood the worst of these duties, to be augmented at last by American Liberators. To boost this meagre force further, detachments from the Halifax and Lancaster squadrons of Bomber Command were temporarily transferred to Coastal Command. Nos 51 and 77 Squadrons sent detachments to Chivenor, in Devon to operate with 19 Group, doing so from 7 May until October. Although neither squadron recorded making any attacks during that period, their principal function was patrol and escort work to act as a deterrent to the U-boat force. They were replaced on 24 October by aircraft and crews from Nos 158 and 405 Squadrons, which had received orders to forward operational detachments to RAF Beaulieu, again under the command of HQ Coastal Command. These detachments were completely self-sufficient, 158 Squadron sending five B Mk II and 405 Squadron 15 Halifaxes. Within three days of receiving its orders, 405 Squadron had commenced operations and three of its Halifaxes were already carrying out an anti-submarine patrol in the Bay of Biscay area. In addition to such patrols, the Halifaxes were also responsible for convoy escort work and anti-shipping strikes both at sea and in ports along the enemy-held coast. The transition from night bombing to varied day duties does not appear to have presented any great problem to the crews.

Lack of sightings was not just restricted to the Halifax force; Coastal Command's own aircraft, fitted with *ASV*, were having a similar problem at this time. Unknown to the British, the Germans had produced the *Metox* receiver[1], which detected *ASV* signals and produced a buzzing noise in the headphones of the German operator. With a good crew able to submerge in 30-35 seconds, it made any attack extremely difficult as signals from the *ASV* set were detectable at a range of more than 30 miles[2]. By September, those U-boats fitted with the *Metox* receiver were escorting their comrades across the Bay of Biscay but by the end of the year, nearly all U-boats would be so equipped.

September also marked another unwelcome development for Coastal Command crews. Admiral Dönitz had requested that Heinkel He 177s replace the aging Focke-Wulf Fw 200s used for long-range maritime operations but was denied by a combination of slow production and teething problems with the new aircraft and the demands of the Eastern Front. Instead, a Staffel of Ju88 C-6s were placed under his control, followed by a second Staffel in October and two more in November, collectively forming the V./KG 40 and based at Bordeaux-Merignac. With their superior performance over the Liberators, Sunderlands and now Halifaxes, they proved a deadly foe and in October alone, 16 of these aircraft were lost to their predation.

November proved to be a busy month for 405 Squadron and on the second day one of their Halifaxes[3] sighted a submarine, but much to the crew's frustration it submerged before they could attack. On 11 November, two of the Squadron's Halifaxes were on patrol in the Bay of Biscay when one of them surprised two motor vessels refuelling a submarine. Bringing his Halifax down to 9,000 ft, P/O Colledge attacked with machine gun fire and bombs. One salvo fell short, but the rest found their mark and Colledge's gunners added to the chaos with a steady stream of fire until one of the motor vessels eventually raised a white flag.

A surfaced submarine was sighted on 24 November but crash-dived before 405 Squadron's Fl/Sgt Stovel could attack it; however, Sgt Wober from the same squadron was to be more fortunate two days later. Sighting two destroyers escorting two motor vessels he carried out a determined attack and though their heavy defensive fire made accurate bombing impossible, his gunners were given ample

opportunity to saturate the targets with machine gun fire. That same day, Sgt Symes, also of the same squadron, sighted two submarines but these proved elusive and both crash-dived. Shortly afterwards one engine failed and Symes was forced to feather the propeller and turn for home. A second engine then began to lose power and Symes was barely able to reach St Eval airfield where, as he attempted a forced landing, W1094: F bounced off the runway and burst into flames. As the crew made their escape they saw that Sgt Farnum was trapped in the mid-upper turret; with complete disregard for their own safety, Symes and Sgt Nichols, the flight engineer, made their way back into the blazing aircraft. After considerable effort, they managed to extricate Farnum and escaped by cutting a hole in the side of the fuselage with the crash axe moments before the aircraft exploded.

The month's activities for 405 Squadron ended on the 27th with a very determined attack on a U-boat and its two escorts by F/Lt C. Palmer and his crew. This was U-263, which had left Kiel on 27 October for operations in the Atlantic when, on 8 November, news reached her captain, Kapitänleutnant Kurt Nölke, of the Allied landings in North Africa and he was ordered to divert to the area west of Gibraltar. There, U-263 sank two ships and came close to sinking a third before being damaged by a Hudson of 233 Squadron on the 24th. Two days later a Fortress from 59 Squadron had found and attacked her and then, in the early hours of the 27th, Palmer's Halifax appeared. Bringing the Halifax down to 50 ft, he attacked out of the low morning sun with a stick of six depth charges. These fell short and he turned the Halifax in for a second attack. This time he straddled U-263 with three depth charges, but concentrated fire from the escort vessels prevented him from making an accurate assessment of the damage; he was nonetheless awarded a DFC for his determined attack. U-263 reached La Pallice two days later and remained there for a year and, along with eight others, was converted into a flak-boat. She left port on 19 January 1944 but was lost with all hands the following day during a deep diving test in the Bay of Biscay.

Occasionally, daylight attacks were carried out against French harbours, mainly at Bordeaux and Gironde and, while little more than nuisance raids, their value could not be ignored. The 158 Squadron detachment returned to Bomber Command in December 1942, but that from 405 Squadron would remain with Coastal Command until March 1943, although in January its Halifaxes were grounded for a week with what was described in the unit records as *"....serious engine breathing difficulties"*.

Coastal Command, however, already had two Halifax-equipped squadrons of its own. No 58 Squadron had a detachment at St Eval, but shared its main base at Holmsley South with No 502 Squadron, both units being initially equipped with Whitley Mk VIIs. The latter were now relinquished for GR Mk II Halifaxes, the first going to 58 Squadron in December 1942 with 502 Squadron following suit in January 1943 with type conversion taking place at Holmsley South. By 23 February 1943 both squadrons were operational, with detachments again based at St Eval from where they resumed patrols in the Bay of Biscay.

The Halifax had entered service with Coastal Command at a time when improved radar aids were at last becoming available. Servicing crews began fitting 10cm *ASV* Mk III search radar to the Halifaxes in February 1943 with most being equipped by May. With it, an operator could detect a convoy at 40 miles and, more significantly, a surfaced submarine at 12 miles. It was the *H2S* land version of this equipment that caused the Air Ministry such concern where it was felt that the chances of a set falling into German hands was more likely in a bombing attack over occupied territory than at sea; and that could significantly cost the war against the U-boats. The decision went against Coastal Command's view but even though an *H2S* set had fallen into German hands in Europe in February 1943, it was eight months before a countermeasure appeared in the U-boat war in the form of the receiver – but by then another, fatal blow had befallen Dönitz's force.

An additional radar aid code-named *Boozer* was also fitted which indicated whether the aircraft itself was being picked up by enemy search radar. Much of the advantage gained from the original 1.5m *ASV* equipment had been nullified by the introduction of the *Metox* system to the U-boat fleet and it was hoped that the new equipment, combined with *Boozer*, might offset this, the new frequency being one that *Metox* equipment could not detect. In the ensuing cat and mouse game U-boats, if fuel allowed, tried to counter this new menace by making a dash at 16 to 18 knots on the surface, across the Bay of Biscay at night.

One of the earliest tasks was to establish practical operational duration parameters and P/O J. Davey's crew from 502 Squadron undertook the task. With the aircraft fitted with the standard three 330 gallon long-range tanks it was flown to its limits, returning after a flight of 14 hours 7 minutes duration. From this, an operational endurance of 11 hours was established with the extra time accounting for variations in flying conditions plus a safety margin, a figure later extended as more tests were conducted.

On 29 March 1943, P/O Davey was sent out to meet a convoy and to carry out an anti-submarine sweep in its vicinity. The weather was deteriorating and, unknown to Davey, the convoy had already sent a signal about the suspected presence of a U-boat and it was hoped that the presence of HR688: K would keep the enemy at bay. Arriving over the convoy, Davey contacted the convoy leader and then commenced a square search pattern from a point 10 miles ahead. He then turned away, flew to a point 30 miles astern of the convoy and conducted another square search pattern. Having found nothing the Halifax was now positioned on the rear starboard quarter and Davey was about to break off the patrol when a fully surfaced U-boat was sighted two miles behind the convoy. The Halifax was 10 miles astern of the submarine when it began its attack run, dropping down to 50 ft to drop a perfect straddle with the depth charges on the surfaced U-boat. Leaving the convoy to pick up the survivors from the U-boat, Davey turned for base only to find that the weather had now closed right down. Several diversions were attempted but after five hours they had still not broken free of cloud and the crew were finally forced to bale out while the Halifax, which had been airborne for 12 hours 14 minutes, crashed at Wiveliscombe, in Somerset. The identity of the submarine was not established.

This was the squadron's second loss. The first, BB314, had failed to return from convoy escort duties on 22 March as related here. As the convoys neared the end of their battle-weary journey, U-boats began to return across the Bay of Biscay to their French ports, something anticipated by Coastal Command and 19 Group which, with assistance from 16 Group, mounted a special effort for the last eight days of March. U-665 was the first to be attacked and sunk by a Wellington of No 172 Squadron in a successful Leigh Light[4] assisted night attack. The second, Kapitänleutnant (Kptlt.) Manfred Kinzel's U-338[5] which had sunk four ships and damaged another, had been badly damaged in a depth-charge attack on the 19th by a Fortress of 220 Squadron. She was limping back to port on the 22nd when a Halifax from 58 Squadron spotted her. Kinzel decided to stay on the surface and fight, his gunners shooting down F/O L. McCullock's BB314 on its approach to attack. The only survivor from McCullock's crew was the flight engineer Sgt J. Taylor who was picked up by the U-boat and taken to St Nazaire.

Three days later, HR683 was written off following an accident during take-off when it swung and ran off the runway. This was followed by another more serious crash just after midnight on the 26th when HR689 stalled on approach to St Eval at the end of a patrol and hit a parked B-17 (42-29647) killing the pilot of the Halifax.

While the main U-boat operations were centred in the Atlantic, it was realised that the key to their operations lay in the Bay of Biscay. While the new *ASV* re-established the balance in Coastal Command's favour, another German tactic not so easily countered was the introduction of long-range fighters, which began operating in increasing numbers over the Bay of Biscay from late 1942. In early April, a 58 Squadron Halifax was out on a lone patrol at 2,000 ft over the Bay of Biscay when the captain sighted seven Ju 88 fighters about one mile off to starboard and some 500 ft lower. Having spotted the bomber, the Ju 88s quickly manoeuvred themselves between it and its escape route and closed in for the kill. The captain jettisoned the depth charges and climbed to 3,000 ft in an attempt to reach what little cloud cover was available. For the next 47 minutes, the Ju 88s kept up a ceaseless series of attacks with some coming in one at a time from different sides while others made feints to draw the Halifax's fire. Three times the fighters pressed home their attack in force and each time ran into the controlled and concentrated crossfire put out by the Halifax gunners. Two departed, each trailing thick brown smoke from an engine and a third broke away after machine gun strikes were seen to register on the engine cowlings. The remainder either lost heart or were running short of fuel for they also broke off the engagement. After landing, the crew examined BB276: F and found that the only damage was a bullet hole through the tail plane and three dents on one of the turret fairings.

The German Command had been struggling since early 1941 to create new weapons to maintain the U-boat advantage and March 1943 had been the high point of the hoped-for U-boat renaissance, with over 100 boats at sea. However, May marked the defining period in the decline of the U-boat force with U-boat sinkings rising to almost catastrophic levels and saw Admiral Dönitz shift his dwindling resources away from the convoy routes in the North Atlantic.

May was thus a very active period for both Squadrons, with 58 Squadron attacking eleven U-Boats while 502 attacked five others. On 7 May 58 Squadron lost a crew when Sgt N. Robertson RAAF attacked U-228, which was sighted at 10.50 hrs crossing the Bay of Biscay. At first driven off by heavy anti-aircraft fire from the U-boat, Robertson then attacked again towards the bow, laying down fire from the single machine gun in the nose position while six depth charges were dropped, but overshot and detonated about 25 metres astern. Severely shaken and with two of his crew wounded, Kptlt Erwin Christophersen crash-dived the boat to avoid further attacks. Some of the gun crew reported having seen strikes on the Halifax (misidentified in the German report as a Lancaster) and smoke coming from it. The damage must have been fatal as Robertson's BB256: A failed to return.

Another U-boat was lost on 8 May; U-663[6] had sailed from Brest on 5 May, heading out for the Atlantic but was intercepted and attacked two days later by a Sunderland of No 10 Squadron (RAAF) 250 miles west-south-west of her home port. The damage from the attack may have damaged her hull severely because after radioing in on 8 May nothing further was heard. The post-war Admiralty analysis of the war at sea records attributes the sinking of U-663 to 'S-Sugar' of 58 Squadron on the 7th[7]. The radio message on the 8th would appear to conflict with the evidence unless the Halifax attacked after the Sunderland departed, inflicting what would become fatal damage the following day[8].

On 6 May, the Type VIIc U-666[9] set out from St Nazaire for an Atlantic patrol but was intercepted in the Bay of Biscay on 9 May by a 58 Squadron Halifax flown by Fl/Sgt J. Hoather who attacked it immediately. The U-boat defences responded rapidly and the Halifax only had time to use its single forward machine gun to suppress the anti-aircraft fire before having to turn away. Hoather made a second run but this time HR743 was hit in one of the port engines. As he turned back to attack for a third time, Hoather appeared to lose control of the aircraft and it crashed into the sea. Only slightly damaged in the attacks, U-666 was able to continue its patrol.

In view of increasing air attacks, U-boat anti-aircraft armament had increased substantially by the mid-war period. Revisions to their existing weaponry had started in the autumn of 1942 and went through a slow metamorphosis that resulted in enlargement of the existing gun platform to hold two twin-20 mm cannon plus the addition of a lower platform for more defensive armament. A 37 mm gun initially chosen for the latter position was not available and saw a quadruple 20 mm fitted in its place. Coastal Command crews pressing home attacks at low level and in a straight line against this formidable array of weapons required great nerve and it is little wonder that a number of the attacking aircraft were shot down.

On 11 May, P/O J. Stark's crew in BB268: D of 58 Squadron attacked U-528[10]. Sent to attack a convoy in the North Atlantic, bad weather made it difficult to close with the merchant ships and on the 28th, a United States Navy (USN) Catalina damaged the boat in an attack south-west of Iceland. She was heading back to Kiel on the surface when Stark's attack further damaged her north-west of Cape Ortegal. Unable to dive, the sloop HMS *Fleetwood* then attacked her with depth charges. Now severely damaged and with eleven of her crew dead, the captain ordered the boat to be scuttled.

A U-boat pack had been pursuing convoy SC 129 to the south-east of Newfoundland but the attack had faltered after HMS *Biter* joined the convoy's escort on the 14th and that night as U-266[11] was heading away she was spotted some ten miles ahead of the convoy by W/Cdr W. Oulton DFC of 58 Squadron. Running in for the attack, Oulton dropped a new Mk 24 '*FIDO*' homing torpedo from his Halifax '*M*', sinking the U-boat, the first to be destroyed using this weapon.[12]

On 16 May, Oulton scored another kill when he sank a grey and brown camouflaged U-boat off Cape Ortegal. Approaching out of the sun, he swung

HR746: M around to starboard and began his run-in from 1,000 yds while the navigator opened fire with the 0.5-inch nose gun[13]. Six Mk XI Torpex depth charges were dropped and the Halifax's gunners raked the U-boat with machine gun fire. The depth charges were well placed and as the spray subsided the U-boat suddenly jerked upwards and the whole forepart rose vertically out of the sea as a large light blue oil patch appeared ahead of the bow of the stricken vessel. Two minutes later, U-463[14] slid beneath the sea. The next day the crew of HR774: R intercepted and sank the Italian submarine *Tazzoli*.

U-boats did not always succumb so readily as U-463, as Oulton discovered on 31 May while flying HR774: R. At 15.50 hrs, the flight engineer sighted an indistinct wake some six miles distant. Oulton, who had just taken over the controls from the second pilot, confirmed the sighting with binoculars as being a surfaced U-boat travelling on a course of 270° at 12 knots. Having sighted U-563[15] he began stalking it, turning the Halifax to starboard, using the 5/10th cloud cover to bring the aircraft into a position for an attack before finally breaking cloud at 3,000 ft, four miles from the target. It was only then that a second U-boat was sighted dead ahead, but within seconds it had crash-dived. Oulton never hesitated and went straight for U-563, his navigator opening fire with the nose gun at 1,000 yds and recording strikes on the conning tower with a second burst from 600 yards seen to penetrate it. With the U-boat now yawing, Oulton swung to starboard making his final run in at an angle of 30° to the U-boat's track and dropping six depth charges across it. As the spray subsided, Oulton brought the Halifax in again from dead astern, the navigator again laying down concentrated fire from the nose position as three more depth charges were dropped. As the spray plumes from the depth charge explosions subsided, the boat was seen to be lying beam-on to the sea surrounded by a large oil slick and a great deal of wreckage. As Oulton circled the U-boat weaving and varying height, the gunners raked U-563 with machine gun fire, cutting down members of its crew manning a cannon mounted just abaft of the conning tower. By now, U-563 was moving slowly in small circles with a heavy list to starboard. Twice more the Halifax's gunners raked it with machine gun fire, but it was still obstinately afloat when Oulton received the recall order 70 minutes after he had sighted it.

As he turned the Halifax for home another of 58 Squadron's Halifaxes, DT636: J, appeared and dived to attack the crippled boat and though Oulton tried to warn P/O Hartley to take his time, he was unable to make contact. The depth charges dropped from Hartley's aircraft fell short but produced a fresh gout of oil and white vapour. Finally, Oulton summoned the assistance of a 10 Squadron Sunderland to finish the kill which, joined by a No 228 Squadron machine, finally managed to sink U-563.

Of a slightly more passive nature during the month was a leaflet drop to Spanish fishing vessels carried out by three of the Squadron's Halifaxes on 20 May. The presence of these reputedly neutral vessels so close to Allied shipping movements into and out of Gibraltar could not be risked. The leaflets carried the warning that after 31 May any vessels found other than close to their own shores would be liable to attack; it was a threat that was carried out on at least one occasion.

It was not only aircraft structural modifications that had been taking place in the first half of 1943 for, on 8 January, an official order had been issued that all Halifaxes diverted for Coastal Command duties would henceforth be camouflaged Extra Dark Sea Grey on upper surfaces in place of the Dark Green and Dark Earth finish of Bomber Command. This was amended on 1 February by an order stipulating that the main colour was to be white with the upper surface camouflage reduced to a strict plan view in the temperate sea scheme of Extra Dark Sea Grey and Dark Slate Grey. On 9 February, the MAP issued an expanded order stipulating white for all front and side views including engine cowlings and spinners but upper surfaces could now be just Extra Dark Sea Grey. This was amended yet again just a few weeks later to just Dark Sea Grey. Serial numbers were to be Light Slate Grey with codes in red. To sort out the ensuing confusion, a further ruling was now made – all aircraft operating over the North Sea, Western Approaches and Bay of Biscay would have matt white side surfaces and glossy white under surfaces. Needless to say, this confused the matter even further until 10 June when all Coastal Command aircraft finishes were standardised as all white except for the strict plan view which would be Extra Dark Sea Grey and applicable to Fortress, Halifax, Hudson, Liberator, Ventura, Warwick, Wellington and Whitley aircraft. Roundels were not required on aircraft with white under surfaces. As with the changes to structures, the camouflage changes were slow to be implemented on some production lines and considerable variation lingered for some time; at unit level, the confusion also appears to have lingered with marking of code letters in colours varying from light grey through red to black.

No 58 Squadron lost a crew on 1 June when BB257 failed to return from its patrol[16]; that no word was heard from the crew indicated that events had rapidly overwhelmed them. U-boats were tough opponents and not easily sunk. U-455 was three days out from St Nazaire and bound for the Atlantic when she was attacked twice on 2 June, first by a Beaufighter of No 248 Squadron and then Fl/Sgt Johnson's crew in a 58 Squadron Halifax; both attacks appear to have left her undamaged, and she continued her patrol[17].

Halifaxes now frequently carried three of the new 600 lb anti-submarine bombs as an alternative to the standard depth charge load but this weapon still suffered from some minor technical problems and P/O Davey volunteered to take part in some live tests. As a precaution, only his flight engineer P/O H. Barrett accompanied him to the dropping site on 6 June, where a smoke flare marked the position of a rowing boat containing a live goat moored 200 yards away. (Live goats unfortunately seem to have been the preferred animal in most bomb tests conducted during the war.) The stick of three bombs was dropped from 1,000 ft with satisfactory results but the unfortunate goat was killed by the shock wave.

Single aircraft patrols by both Halifax squadrons were still being carried out and it was during one of these on 15 June that P/O Davey encountered three surfaced U-boats. The Halifax was carrying the new 600 lb anti-submarine bombs, which he immediately dropped, damaging two of the submarines so effectively that they could not immediately dive. One also had steering damage and could only keep station with the others by alternately using power, then drifting with the current to make good its course while the undamaged U-boat maintained a protective circle around the other two. Circling at 1,000 ft, Davey sent out a *Sombrero* signal to summon nearby naval vessels – this pre-arranged signal was part of the new joint tactics developed between Coastal Command and the Royal Navy. The U-boats kept up a heavy defensive fire while the Halifax crew did their best to disrupt repair work by diving into the circle to allow the rear gunner, Archer, to spray the decks with fire. Four or five such attacks had been made by the time five naval vessels arrived in line abreast to attack; at that point, Davey broke off the action and returned to base having been airborne for just less than 12 hours.

June had also heralded a change of tactics by both Squadrons; *Operation Musketry* introduced shipping searches by three aircraft in formation, the idea being that any attack could be followed up immediately and it also countered the enemy change of tactics, with U-boats now travelling in packs of three as had been reported by P/O Davey on 15 April. Throughout April, May and June a steady series of changes had been forced on U-boat transit practices. No longer able to traverse the Bay of Biscay submerged during the day and on the surface by night, they had been ordered to fight their way out into the North Atlantic on the surface. Fitted with twin and quadruple defensive 20 mm cannon the boats now travelled in packs for mutual protection. These tactics were successful at first and Coastal Command had to revise its own to overcome this temporary enemy advantage. Thus, a closer co-operation was developed between Coastal Command aircraft and the special Naval Escort Groups which quickly saw improved results.

In the meantime, it had come to the notice of Bomber Command that Coastal Command Halifaxes were operating at over the permissible maximum all-up weight of 60,000 lb and a request was made, via Coastal Command HQ, for a report on the handling characteristics. F/O McClintock carried out the test from St Eval on 11 June using a 502 Squadron Halifax that had had its engines modified to give +14 lb boost. Despite a take-off weight of 61,400 lb, McClintock found the handling characteristics no different from normal and made a favourable report, yet HQ 19 Group considered their own views and authorised the removal of certain items of armour plate to keep the weight within the 60,000 lb limit.

On 25 July another test was carried out using HR815/G[18] of the Coastal Command Development Unit (CCDU) to establish the Halifax's maximum endurance. The engines were again modified to give +14 lb boost and 350 lb armour plating was removed, reducing the all-up weight to 61,570 lb. W/Cdr J. Halley was instructed to fly the aircraft at the lowest possible engine revolutions of 1800 at an indicated airspeed of 140 knots (kts), and to land with two hours' fuel remaining in the tanks. All normal operational equipment was retained and a full crew and a fuel load of 2,732 gallons. The Halifax landed at Boscombe Down 14 hours later where the remaining fuel was carefully measured. As the results gave a maximum endurance figure of just over 16 hours, it was recommended that 13 hours should be the normal operational endurance for Mk II Halifaxes fitted with long-range tanks, and 12 hours for those fitted with only three additional tanks in the bomb bay. During October, CCDU carried out further tests from Gibraltar, the Halifax remaining airborne for 18 hours.

Patrolling over the Bay of Biscay on 13 July, F/O A. Clutterbuck's 58 Squadron crew spotted three U-boats, U-445, U-607 and U-613[19], travelling together and heading out for a patrol in the Central Atlantic. At almost the same time that a patrolling Sunderland from 228 Squadron arrived, Clutterbuck swung his Halifax in to attack U-445 but she and U-613 dived in time to avoid being damaged. U-607 was not as fast and was sunk by the Sunderland.

U-558, in company with U-221[20], was moving independently towards the coast of Portugal where they were to patrol when a Wellington of No 179 Squadron attacked U-558 off Cape Roc on 15 July. The boat's gunners drove off the attack and U-558 escaped by diving; two days later, she was attacked again and damaged by a Liberator of No 224 Squadron. Two days after that she had her final, fatal encounter north-north-west of Cape Ortegal, being sunk by depth charges dropped from F/Lt G. Sawtell's 58 Squadron Halifax 'B' and those from a Liberator of the 19th Anti-Submarine Squadron of the USAAF.

Between anti-submarine patrols, crews were sometimes called on to search for survivors. On 25 July, F/O Davey's crew were sent to search for a dinghy but finding one small yellow dot in the vast ocean was always a difficult practice and although finding no dinghy, they did find 12 Ju 88s. The fine, sunny day that moments before had been an asset in their search task now became a severe handicap and it turned into a chase between HR693: O and the attackers. Fortunately, Davey managed to find a lone patch of cloud in time and he kept the Halifax inside it until the Ju 88s gave up their attack. The Halifax landed safely back at Holmsley South after an eventful 11.5-hour sortie.

On 30 July, the newly introduced system of co-operation produced what was perhaps the most outstanding action of this phase of the war at sea. A Liberator of

JD212 was one of the many B Mk II Series IA Halifaxes that retained Galley radiators and Merlin XX engines. Delivered in mid-June 1943, it passed first to the A&AEE where it was fitted with two stub-frames, one on each side of the lower forward fuselage, slung slightly lower than the fuselage bottom line and braced to each wing. Each held four rocket rails and tests were carried out to see if this installation could be used for GR Halifaxes engaged in anti-submarine and shipping attacks. Although successful (and also tested on GR Liberators), the installation was not approved for Halifax use. JD212 then passed to Nos 429 and 419 Squadrons before finally ending up with 1666 HCU. Returning to Wombleton from a cross-country exercise on 17 July 1944 it swung on landing, buckling the wing.

No 53 Squadron sighted three U-boats[21], one of about 540 tons and two of about 1200 tons. In accordance with the new policy, the Liberator began to home in other aircraft. A Catalina arrived on the scene shortly afterwards and was dispatched to lead the naval 2nd Escort Group to the scene. Within a short period, further aircraft, two Halifaxes of 502 Squadron, another Liberator and a Sunderland, joined the Liberator. The Halifaxes were carrying the new 600 lb bombs, which could be dropped at higher altitude than the depth charges and with the aid of the normal bomb sight.

The U-boats maintained a steady evasive action, keeping close together at all times, and put up a very determined defensive barrage. F/O Biggar took his Halifax down to 1,600 ft and burst through the wall of cannon fire to deliver his attack, but the bombs fell wide. The Halifax's elevators were damaged by flak and Biggar was forced to withdraw and return to base. F/O Van Rossum took his Halifax in for an attack out of the sun and dropped three bombs from 3,000 ft from dead astern. One exploded close to U-462 and it began to circle slowly to starboard with smoke billowing from abaft the conning tower. Meanwhile the No 461 Squadron Sunderland attacked and sank U-461 while the U-boats were concentrating their fire on one of the Liberators, which made a very gallant, low-level attack. Shortly

afterwards Van Rossum made another attack on U-462 causing further damage and 15 minutes later it settled on an even keel and sank, leaving 64 survivors in the sea. The remaining U-boat, U-504, fell victim to the Naval Escort Group, which arrived in time to join the battle.

Patrols in the Bay of Biscay were always subject to attacks by Ju 88s, sometimes in packs and other times by lone aircraft. On 31 July, F/O Davey's Halifax had been flying just above the surface of an extensive cloud layer in the early dawn light when a lone Ju 88 emerged from the cloud immediately behind it. It opened fire hitting the Halifax in the wing and putting an incendiary bullet into one of the fuel tanks that fortunately did not explode. Armstrong, the second pilot, was at the controls and immediately dropped the aircraft into the safety of the cloud layer below. The rear gunner had his guns still set at 'safe' and had had no time to return the fire. The patrol was continued once the Ju 88 had been shaken off but that other enemy, weather, was now closing in rapidly and it was decided to check just how low the cloud base extended. The aircraft broke clear at 50 ft; to the amazement of P/O Barrett, who was in the nose cone watching, ready to warn Davey of signs of the sea, a U-boat appeared directly ahead[22]. The navigator, Finlayson, scrambled to the bombsight and Davey carried out an attack, dropping all three anti-submarine bombs, but the results went unobserved as the aircraft had to be immediately pulled back up into the cloud. Back at base, the damage from the Ju 88 attack was examined and found to be just a line of holes in one wing. During repairs, the ground crew found the incendiary bullet in one of the petrol tanks. For some reason, despite the tank being only partially full when hit and thus holding a good amount of fuel vapour, it had not exploded.

Then, in early August, a sudden and dramatic change occurred in U-boat tactics. They no longer attempted to fight their way out on the surface, but reverted to their earlier policy of lying submerged by day and surfacing for essential functions only at night. Coastal Command had inflicted crippling losses on the U-boats during the preceding weeks, losses that could not be sustained indefinitely.

This interesting GR Mk II exhibits a combination of features spanning the transition between the Series I (Special) and the Series IA, the most unusual being the retention of the tall forward radio mast, a feature deleted when production changed to the Perspex nose Mod 452 configuration. Fitted with Galley radiators and three-bladed propellers it has a nose-mounted 0.5-in Browning machine gun in a strengthened, braced mounting and the landing light made retractable. While difficult to see, the mid-upper turret appears to be in the high position, though that would accord with an early production date and, as outlined in the text, the Type D fin and rudder assemblies were fitted retroactively by mobile working parties. The code letter 'V', repeated on the front face of each Messier undercarriage casting and repeated on the nose in miniature, had a small 'I' marked beside it. If this was JD178: V then it had been produced in the last week of May 1943, which may account for some of the features mentioned. Initially on the strength of 502 Squadron, it was later transferred to 58 Squadron where it was written off in a belly-landing at Brawdy after the undercarriage failed to lower on 6 August 1944. (S/Ldr T. Fairburn via Chaz Bowyer)

It was not just a war against submarines; shipping was attacked whenever opportunity presented itself and one of 502 Squadron's crews opened its shipping kills with the sinking of a German auxiliary vessel VP420, *Alcyon* on 2 August. Nevertheless, such targets were relatively rare and it would not be until 9 December that the Squadron would sink its next ship, *Le Duperre*, a 337-ton French vessel.

The usefulness of the rocket projectile as an anti-shipping/submarine weapon was not overlooked as a possibility for the Halifax (and also the Liberator) and between late September and early October JD212, a Mk II Series IA, underwent compatibility trials at Boscombe Down. Four rocket projectiles were fitted to a strut-braced carrier, one each side of the fuselage. The results showed a reduction of 6-8 mph on the maximum speed and 5-7 mph on the cruising speed, but otherwise no deleterious effects on handling; however, despite the results, they were not issued to the Halifax squadrons.

The increasing size and frequency of the Ju 88 packs met with some success during August. Losses for the two squadrons had been reasonably low to date and 58 Squadron had lost only five between January and July. August, however, changed all that. On the night of the 15/16th, F/O Grant's HR745: S was patrolling when it was intercepted in the early dawn by four Ju 88s and shot down over the Bay of Biscay; HR746 failed to return from the same area after a night patrol. On the 18th, because of engine failure, BB279 was unable to maintain height and ditched in the North Sea and on the 20th, weather was the killer when HR774 crashed into a hill 10 miles south-west of Salisbury while returning from a patrol.

The U-boats were now under great pressure, preferring to hug the French and Spanish coasts when not transiting the Bay of Biscay – an activity where neutrality was not always observed, especially when the neutral country was a friend of Germany. On 17 October, F/O Davey and his 502 Squadron crew spotted a U-boat in a Spanish coastal inlet. Assuming that neutrality had already been breached, they made a single attack, dropping one depth charge, not remaining in the area to see what, if any damage they had achieved. The squadron lost a crew next day when HR682 failed to return from a patrol and on the 24th, DT636 failed to return, a last message from the crew stating that they had made contact with 14 Ju 88s; against those odds, they stood little chance. These losses were offset to some degree by the sinking of U-221 on 27 September by one of 58 Squadron's Halifaxes. Having sailed from St Nazaire on 20 September, she was heading out across the Bay of Biscay for an Atlantic patrol when F/O E. Hartley spotted her on the 27th some 800 miles south-west of Ireland. Hartley attacked, dropping eight depth charges and U-221 slid backwards into the depths but not before the U-boat's gun crew had hit HR982 in the starboard fuel tank, which caught fire. Flak had also killed both the wireless and *ASV* operators. Hartley successfully ditched the Halifax and the six survivors climbed into the dinghy (among them G/Capt R. Mead, station commander of Holmesley South airfield, who had been acting as second pilot to gain experience). What followed was a terrible ordeal, adrift for eleven days before being rescued by the destroyer HMS *Maharatta*. Hartley was awarded the DFC and F/Sgt K. Ladds, the mid-upper gunner, the DFM.

The aggressive attitude of the two squadrons was not limited to shipping alone. On 8 October HR983: R of 58 Squadron was on a routine patrol when the pilot spotted a Blohm und Voss BV 222 flying boat.

He brought the Halifax in for an attack from the port quarter, allowing the navigator to open fire at 600 yds with his single machine gun in the nose. The Halifax then broke away to port, giving the rear gunner an opportunity to fire, and then dropped astern. Moving over to the starboard quarter, the mid-upper gunner and the navigator opened fire. Throughout this activity, the BV 222 maintained a steady course and took no evasive action, returning the fire with cannon from the two dorsal turrets and each beam position. Strikes were seen on the fuselage and hull of the enemy flying boat, which was painted duck-egg blue all over. Finally, with its rear upper turret position silenced, the BV 222 increased its power and drew away from the Halifax.

Both squadrons had been operating from either St Eval or Holmsley South during 1943 and on 5 December they were notified to move to St Davids, in Pembrokeshire. The reason for the move was to concentrate three Halifax squadrons in one area under a single station organization.

A third squadron, No 517, already at St Davids since 25 November 1943, would move to that station's satellite airfield at Brawdy as from 1 February 1944. This was a meteorological squadron formed on 11 August 1943 from No 1404 Meteorological Flight, equipped with an eclectic mix of Hampdens, Hudsons and Fortresses. However, it was 1 December before its first Met Mk V Halifaxes arrived, each of them then being sent to Gosport for modification by Cunliffe-Owen. The aircraft also had their Merlin XX engines replaced with Merlin XXIIs, being rotated through Handley Page's works at Radlett, flown each way, single-handed, by women pilots of the ATA.

Allen Williamson was a navigator who joined the squadron in February 1944. *"Initially on 517 Squadron we had Gee for navigation for the first 200 miles out, but the rest of the trip was done by dead reckoning and astro navigation. When we were eventually posted to 518 Squadron Loran sets were installed and these were a Godsend for the poor harassed navigator. At least the other crew members had a relief, but the navigator was flat out all the time."*

However, No 517 had not been the first Halifax-equipped Meteorological Squadron. In 1943, the units responsible for these duties were increased to squadron strength and No 518 Squadron had formed at Stornoway in July, equipped with Met

Mk V Halifaxes. The first two, DG288 and DG250, arrived on 7 July and operations began on 15 September; ten days later the squadron moved to Tiree in the Scottish Inner Hebrides.

Meteorological flights over the sea had begun in 1940 and in 1941 were placed under the control of Coastal Command. These flights were critical to the prosecution of the war in the air, particularly over Europe. Reconnaissance flights were sent out to the west and south-west over the Atlantic from the western seaboard, north from Scotland, south from Iceland, west from Gibraltar and out over the North Sea from the east coast of England. Their purpose was to obtain barometric pressure, temperature and humidity readings, plus weather, cloud and wind velocity data – all vital to air operations planning. Until the end of 1942, the navigator was responsible for taking the meteorological observations. The limitations of such an arrangement were eventually recognised in the face of the mounting scale of Bomber Command operations and had required a rapid expansion of this critically valuable service. The expansion brought with it the need for trained meteorological observers and late in 1942, the Meteorological Air Observers Section was promulgated and training began early in 1943. Within two months, the first five Met. Observers were posted to their units and nearly 100 had been trained by the end of the war. Upon the skills of those few men and the crews who flew them, much of the successful prosecution of the air war against Germany depended. The ground crews who kept the meteorological aircraft flying with almost monotonous regularity are among the least remembered members of that system, yet their contribution was out of all proportion to their numbers. Keith McGonigal saw extensive service with No 518 Squadron. *"My thoughts often were with, and return to, those brave souls who maintained our Halifaxes. The western gales in winter can be cold, wet and miserable and to be mounted 15-20 feet above ground on an engine nacelle, making an intricate adjustment to a complicated V12, large supercharged engine which has a rev drop of 50+ on one of its two ignition systems, at 02.00 hrs in the dark, wind and rain must have made life miserable at times. If I remember correctly the engine would still be running and its propeller adding to the icy blast."*

The 517 Squadron crews flew a triangular pattern code named *Epicure B* from Brawdy while those from 518 flew a straight out and back track code named *Mercer*, a single Halifax setting out each day on a track of 265 True to a point 700 nm from base. Positions along the track were given station numbers at 50 nm intervals and the aircraft would fly a series of step climbs and descents, crossing each station at a predetermined height, or more correctly pressure level. Sea-level pressure readings were taken every 100 nm and at the end of the 700 nm leg a circular climb would be made to approximately 20,000 ft. It was crucial that the pilots fly the aircraft at exactly the right height and follow the other instructions given by the meteorological observer on board. As the weather pattern was constantly changing, it was essential that the observations be transmitted back to base every half-hour. This was done as a series of five coded groups, consisting of five five-figure sets. Allen Williamson recalls *"... the flights provided by 517 and 518 Squadrons were normally 1,400 nautical miles in duration. They were scheduled to arrive at the terminal point at midday and midnight when the vertical ascent took place."*

This schedule meant that crews had to fly every day and every night throughout the year regardless of weather conditions. When the additional triangular meteorological flight, code-named *Bismuth*, was added to 518's schedule, four flights each day became necessary. Keith McGonigal recalls this gruelling routine. *"The original flight, Mercer, was 270° straight out from Tiree with 14 positions, each 50 nm apart at 1000 millibars (mb) (1500-2000 ft)... Take-off was at about 02.00 hrs to get to Position 14 by first light. At that point we climbed to 500 mb level (about 20,000 ft) levelling off at 100 mb level on the way up, then heading for home. At each 4th or 5th position sea-level pressure was estimated by authorised but at times daunting low-level flying."* [Salt spray on the windscreen would sometimes reduce visibility.]

"The westerly winds could be fierce and nights stick in my mind when we would be tossed around for almost seven hours to reach Position 14 and what we might see of the sea brought no comfort. Occasionally we did a 'Bismuth' – a triangular track with its apex near Iceland ... the squadron mounted two Mercers and two Bismuths per day, taking off at 02.00 and 14.00 hrs each day."

Allan Huston, who joined the squadron in 1943 and initially flew as McGonigal's second pilot, recalls how the squadron expanded. *"We started off with nine crews and built up to about 28 ... Our main enemy was the weather. We had to fly every day and during the 20 months I was with the squadron, we only missed two days' flying. Once, on a rare occasion, we were under snow* [LK966: P was scheduled for the normal 04.30 hrs departure, but the sortie was scrubbed twice due to ice and snow. It was rescheduled for 11.00 hrs, but after two attempts to get airborne, both of which ended with the Halifax skidding off into the frozen grass, the mission was finally called off.]; *the second was a gale which broke the rudder controls on the aircraft trying to take off. We would take off not knowing where we were going to come home to. I was personally diverted, because of bad weather, to a number of other airfields – Ballykelly and Limavady and Aldergrove in Northern Ireland, Banff, Kinloss and Skitten in Scotland and Benbecular in the Hebrides."*

"We carried a radio altimeter (300 ft to zero) for descending to sea level at night or in bad weather (the aneroid barometer in the normal altimeter could be out by 600 ft due to the different pressure readings over the distances we flew). The radio altimeters were notoriously unreliable and we used to test their accuracy by flying level with a lighthouse, on an island in the Outer Hebrides, at 160 ft. Mostly it was a regular run, we would fly on ops every four days and every three months we would get 10 days' leave, when we would

LK966: P, a Met Mk V Series IA, was issued to 518 Squadron in January 1944. Between October 1943 and February 1944, the squadron provided training to 58 Halifax crews before returning to operations, flying Mercer sorties and Bismuth trials, continuing to fly both for the rest of the war. LK966 was transferred to 502 Squadron at Gibraltar and, marked as 'Q-Queen', was lost following multiple engine failure off Portugal on 24 November 1944, the crew being rescued unharmed. (W. Diamond)

catch a boat to Oban and journey on to London. There was no town on Tiree, just a store." Huston completed 60 operations during his 20 months.

Cunliffe-Owen at Eastleigh carried out special modifications to the Mk V Halifaxes equipping the meteorological squadrons. To a certain extent, these modifications were the products of experience. No 518 Squadron had sent the first of its Halifaxes to Eastleigh for additional special modifications in December 1943. Eventually a standard modification was established which promised a degree of accuracy previously unknown in meteorological flying. However, the very urgency of the task in hand coupled with the reduced manpower available, forced the squadrons initially to accept limited modifications. As a result, fully modified Halifaxes were not available in quantity until early in the summer of 1944. To help overcome the delays already mentioned, some equipment was made at Gosport and supplied direct to the squadrons. Gosport also undertook the major inspections and it became the practice for crews going on leave to ferry the Halifaxes down at the same time.

A well-equipped station in a Halifax provided the meteorological observer with comparative comfort. The nose gun was removed and the additional instruments fitted in the nose section forward of the navigator's position. Radio altimeters enabled measurement of sea-level pressure to be made both by day and by night while a special instrument, a psychrometer[23] mounted on the starboard side of the nose section, recorded air temperature and humidity – essential for predicting the dew point and thus when cloud would form and at what height. On fully modified Met Mk V aircraft, a small window was added immediately behind this instrument adjacent to the specialist meteorological observer's position. *Gee*, or *Loran*, and an air-position indicator greatly assisted the high degree of navigational precision required and allowed measurement of high-level winds above cloud. Low-level wind measurement became more accurate with the introduction of a B3 drift meter and bad-weather homing facilities were improved by the fitting of *ASV* Mk II.

While equipment was steadily improved, location was another matter as Allen Williamson records: *"Tiree was of course an exposed island (actually also treeless) with almost perpetual rain and an average wind speed of 30 mph. Consequently, all rain blew horizontally. The island had one virtue, it was free of fog and being in the Gulf Stream was surprisingly free of frost and ice on most occasions. These conditions meant that aircraft could always take off: in fact, the rule was in Met. Squadrons that if you could see the end of the runway you took off. On many occasions subsequently the British Isles became fog-bound (or covered with very low cloud), all aerodromes were closed and Met. crews were simply told that they would be informed on return if there was an aerodrome open. We nearly always had one open, but some of the approaches and landings were pretty nerve-wracking."*

Glenn Traub has similar recollections. *"If it appeared that the weather at base would be bad at take-off time, the aircraft and crew would be sent beforehand to another station where it was expected that the weather would be better for beginning the sortie. I recall that for our 16 July 1944 night trip, in LL393 of 517 Squadron, we were sent to Pershore to begin the flight and on return were diverted to Exeter. The diversions were usually always due to weather at base and frequently not much better at the place we were diverted to."*

It was not always the weather that caused problems on a diversion; Alan Huston's crew came back from a sortie on New Year's Eve 1945 to find that they were diverted because of bad weather at Tiree. *"We had immense trouble with the radio as they apparently had changed all the codes and after crossing the mountains at the top of Scotland we located the marker Pundits on the ground. However, they were all flashing different codes to our list and we could not determine our position. I flew out over the North Sea and let down below cloud, then came back in, still not sure where we were. A May Day on the radio finally brought a response from a little airfield near Wick which turned on its lights for us to land."*

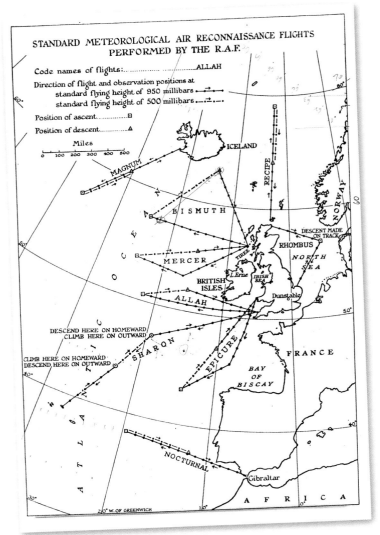

The Standard Meteorological Routes flown each day to bring back the necessary accurate weather data for the air offensive over Europe show just how far each crew had to venture, regardless of weather conditions, 365 days of the year. A dangerous, monotonous and often fatal occupation that has had little attention paid to it in post-war histories. This is a wartime copy with pencilled marks made by the navigator. (E. Aveling)

As the information from the various aircraft was received it was correlated with local observations and the results passed to all commands via the teleprinter link. It was based on this information that the weather predictions were made for Bomber Command's operations over Europe. The work was seemingly unspectacular and it was only by realising the crucial importance of the information obtained that crews retained the very high standards required.

The third meteorological squadron, No 520, which had formed at Gibraltar in September 1943, had not received its first Halifax, LK997, until February 1944. The unit flew a meteorological patrol code-named *Nocturnal*, a straight out and back track similar to *Mercer*.

A new type of meteorological flight began on 24 February 1944, when LK692: M set out to fly a triangular course code-named *Bismuth*. The first leg was a track of 270(T) from base for 550 nm, then on to a track of 045(T) for 400 nm and descents made at the various points. This trial flight was also used to measure the increase in performance with the mid-upper turret removed. The squadron continued to fly both flights for the remainder of the war.

Losses from enemy action were, with one possible exception, nil, but all squadrons lost aircraft and crews to the elements and mechanical problems. Take-offs and landings were always the most critical times for any aircraft and a proportion of losses occurred then. No 518 Squadron's first loss, DG288 on 7 November 1943, had resulted from a stalled landing ending in a crash. Its second, on 4 December, involved DG316, which crashed into the sea half a mile from the end of the north/south runway after an engine had caught fire on take-off. Fortunately, the Navy was on hand and very promptly rescued F/Lt Green and his crew who were all unharmed. Fuel shortage took LK704: L on 23 January 1944; it hit the edge of a cliff at Tullenstrand, Donegal, and crashed into the Bay. Operating from Northern Ireland had its own unique consequences, LL145 from 517 Squadron having to make a forced landing in Eire on 21 April 1944, thus becoming a technical loss as it was impounded for the duration; the crew were more fortunate. Sometimes aircraft were pushed to the limits of their endurance just waiting for weather to clear

A post-war view taken at York of LK688: H with full squadron codes applied. Delivered from Fairey Aviation in late October 1943 and allocated to 518 Squadron for meteorological duties it has all of the attributes associated with a Met Mk V Series IA aircraft, including the four-bladed propellers introduced for Halifaxes of Coastal Command and No 38 Group. The squadron was taken off operations a short time later to act as the training squadron for Meteorological units. Originally coded 'D-Dog', LK688 was sent to Gosport for installation of A.Y.D. and radar and in February, used for performance tests with the mid-upper turret removed. By 10 February 1945 when the squadron had returned to operational status, coded as 'H-How', LK688 had begun flying Mercer sorties with the ASV installation removed. Just visible on the original print is the square metal fairing over the previous location of the original beam gun hatch, a lingering feature of some production aircraft as noted in the text. (P. J. R. Moyes)

No 518 Squadron's LK998: L, a Met Mk V Series IA, the psychrometer fitting on the nose section clearly identifying its role, the shadow of the psychrometer making the observation window behind it appear much deeper than it was. It met its end on 24 February 1944 when it broke up in mid air during a fighter affiliation exercise, diving into the ground at St Edrens, in Pembrokeshire. (K. McGonigal)

so that they could land. No 517 Squadron's LK962 was found wrecked in the sea after a meteorological sortie on 14 November 1944, after just such a wait. The extremes of structural stress imposed on the airframe were more pronounced on Meteorological Halifaxes where the requirements of the task did not allow the freedom to fly around bad weather. Lightning strikes, although infrequent, were frightening to experience. Traub, on 518 Squadron, recalls a nasty experience on 8 November 1944:

"This occurred at night after flying for some time through incredibly turbulent, pitch black conditions and followed shortly after by the appearance of St Elmo's fire at the tip of the propellers. The rear gunner reported sparks jumping between the gun barrels of the rear turret... It was difficult to realise the importance, at times, of the Met. sorties and many of us longed for postings to another type of endeavour."

Allan Huston, from the same squadron: *"We were hit by lightning twice, but we suffered no damage, apart from all the outside aerials being blown off."*

Another of the squadron's Halifaxes, LK688 (now coded H), set out on a routine sortie on 10 February 1945, spending the first hour flying through very unstable air temperatures with clear ice collecting on the wings at 1,000 ft. The ice continued to thicken, the cockpit canopy turned opaque, and electrical discharges began to weave their fantastic patterns over all the protrusions on the Halifax. Two hours later a great flash lit up the aircraft followed immediately by a loud explosion as lightning struck. Despite a fuselage full of

smoke, no major damage was seen except for the starboard undercarriage, which was hanging down, and the total absence of the trailing aerial. The rear gunner reported a flapping noise in his vicinity, which turned out to be the main aerial, no longer fixed to the DF fairing but flapping between the fins. The weather continued to deteriorate, severe hail was experienced at 18,600 ft and the aircraft passed through a constant series of dangerous cumulonimbus clouds. Overcome by the severity of the conditions, the Halifax was eventually forced to turn back, one engine failing en route to base. The crew were luckier than those in LK998: L of 517 Squadron. During a fighter affiliation exercise on 24 February 1944, the aircraft broke up and dived into the ground at St Eldrens, Pembrokeshire. Airframes would take just so much stress.

Even routine air tests could kill. Two of 518 Squadron's Halifaxes, LL186 and LL296: S, were lost in a mid-air collision over their own airfield on 16 August 1944. The cloud base was 100 ft and one aircraft was being flight-tested, the other was returning from a meteorological sortie and broke cloud directly into the path of the other Halifax. Both crashed and burned and one came down close to the mess where 800 men were sitting down to dinner. The second pilot on one of the aircraft was F/Lt Revilloid, a cousin of the Czechoslovakian president of the government in exile.

While some improvement was obtained in engine reliability, the problem was never entirely overcome. Keith McGonigal recalls: *"Merlin engines were not designed for the work we asked of them on Met. recces – a long slog at high boost, low revs for range, then a rapid climb to about 20,000 ft. They would frequently protest after the climb by 'boost surge' – one, two, three or all four engines surging from -6 to +6 boost without warning for a short period, which seemed like hours. The Rolls-Royce representative could not explain it. The Merlin 22s were less prone to internal glycol leaks than the earlier XXs, but even in the cool climate of the UK we had problems of engines overheating or oiling up if we were stuck tail to wind for too long waiting for take-off. The surge problem always occurred after about seven hours' flying and the climb to height at the limit of the recce. It may well have been that the engines were having a busy time transferring fuel from the long-range tanks in the bomb bay."*

Drabble flew 65 meteorological sorties and on 15 of them he returned with only three engines working. However, it was not always the engine that caused the problem as Huston recounts. *"One night when climbing under full power a terrific vibration shook the aircraft. Every instrument was shaking like crazy and it was impossible to pinpoint the problem. Fortunately we were at 8000 ft and I throttled right back and slowed down. We plugged in the Aldis lamp and flashed it around outside looking for structural damage. I noticed one of the spinners, over the constant-speed unit, was missing. I feathered the engine to find one prop blade broken in half. We flew 600 miles home on three engines and received a Green endorsement for the effort. Initially I had thought that the dinghy in the wing had automatically inflated, popped out and damaged the tail unit. There had been a bang in that area, but later we found that the metal spinner had been driven through the side of the aircraft. I sent out a SOS when it first happened as I thought we were gone. Ten minutes in the waters of the Atlantic in winter and you were dead from hypothermia. We never wore parachute harness for that reason, no point in jumping."*

No 517 Squadron crews had a slightly better survival chance if they ditched on the *Epicure B* sorties, which took them into relatively warmer waters.

LL296: S of 518 Squadron photographed over the Caledonian Canal on 14 July 1944 from McGonigal's LK706: F while returning from a Mercer patrol, the return flight being diverted because of bad weather at the squadron's home base; when McGonigal landed 'F-Fox' at the end of this flight he was tour expired. LL296 was lost in a mid-air collision with LL186: G over their home base on 16 August. (W. Diamond)

Two views of F/O E. Aveling's crashed LL485: S, which he flew into the ground on the night of 27 August 1944 when an incorrect altimeter pressure setting gave a reading 50 ft higher than the actual ground height. Given the state of destruction and subsequent fire, it is remarkable that the crew walked away from the wreck. The view of the starboard side shows that squadron codes were still not being applied to 517 Squadron aircraft at this time. The upper camouflage was restricted to the strict plan view and the wing tip upper surfaces were finished in white. The faired-over starboard beam gun hatch is visible just forward of the top corner of the 'S' and was unique to Rootes Securities-produced Mk IIs.

F/O E. Aveling's LL144: K was out on a sortie near the Azores on 6 June 1944 gathering critical weather information for the invasion of Europe, which was just getting underway, when one engine caught fire and the Halifax had to be ditched. Ed Aveling recounts what happened: *"The port outer lost hydraulic pressure on one side of the constant-speed unit and the propeller went into full fine pitch and the revs ran away. The Rev counter wound itself off the stops and ended up collapsing into the bottom of the instrument case. The engine caught fire, but we were able to put it out with the extinguisher system. While this was being done the vibration set up shook the aircraft so badly that the oil line to the port inner engine cracked and we started losing oil and the engine temperature began rising rapidly; so we had to shut the engine down. The port outer was now windmilling and we had no means of stopping it. With both port engines out and the drag from the windmilling propeller, I could not keep the Halifax straight, even with my second pilot putting his full weight on the controls. So we gradually flew around in large circles, losing height, until I decided to ditch."* The weather was warm and fine and the crew clambered into the dinghy to await rescue while the Halifax floated nearby – something it continued to do for nearly seven hours. A signal had been sent out at 07.33 hrs advising that the aircraft was turning back; this was followed by a series of dots and dashes, which finally faded. At 12.30 hrs, the aircraft was presumed overdue and the probable ditching plotted to a point approximately 700 miles off Land's End and 400 miles west of Cape Finisterre. Dispatched to search the area, LL295: H was forced to return because of engine trouble, but the search was continued by another Halifax from the squadron, assisted by Catalinas of No 202 Squadron from Gibraltar.

"Everything went OK and a No 202 Squadron Catalina found us straight away and kept up a standing patrol overhead until relieved by one of our own squadron aircraft." The Catalina had found them at 10.00 hrs on 7th June and No 19 Group immediately requested the diversion of a naval vessel to rescue the crew. At 21.29 hrs LL220: F from No 517 Squadron made contact with the dinghy and dropped six Bircham Barrels and two dinghy radios, which were retrieved by the crew. Half an hour later another Catalina joined, circling with the Halifax, and continued the lonely vigil after LL220: F left for base at 23.30 hrs. At 03.10 hrs on the morning of the 8th it was joined by another Catalina and both aircraft circled ceaselessly until the first aircraft was finally forced to leave. Rescue, in the form of a Destroyer, arrived and retrieved

the crew at 08.25 hrs. *"It eventually transferred us to the American aircraft carrier with which it had been working on anti-submarine patrols, and we spent three weeks onboard while it finished its task and docked at Norfolk, Virginia. I went to Washington, to the RAF Delegation, and reported in to a Squadron Leader, who then interviewed me. He kindly arranged for me to go home to Canada, where I spent another three weeks waiting for a convoy back to England. When we finally reached the squadron again we had been away for 11 weeks, having started out for what was to have been an 11 hour patrol."*

Aveling's return nearly ended in total disaster. Unfortunately, they were given the wrong pressure reading to set the altimeter for their first sortie since returning. Coming in to land that night their real height was 50 ft lower than the altimeter showed and LL485: S was literally flown into the ground. Nobody was killed, but some of the crew were injured (others walked into breakfast next morning). However, two crashes were enough risk for anyone and it was decided to disband the crew. Their earlier rescue, some 700 miles out from base, was reputed to be the furthest successful search and rescue operation of the war.

This crew were the fortunate exception in both cases. No 518 Squadron's LK706: F disappeared on 10 November following engine trouble and although an SOS was received, no trace of the aircraft was ever found. The later CO of the squadron, W/Cdr Morris, was lost on 21 January 1945, in appalling weather conditions as Williamson recalls *"There was a particularly tight low pressure system west of Tiree, about 100-150 nm out. This wintertime low had particularly low temperatures and severe icing conditions were predicted. Group Command advised the CO that in view of these conditions the Met. flights could be cancelled at his discretion. Morris decided to go, but unfortunately, not having his own permanent crew, he flew with the scheduled crew captained by F/Lt Bacon [in LL123: N]. This was a late-afternoon take-off so they would have departed in darkness and passed through the centre of the low at night. Next morning a search and rescue operation was mounted which included our crew. The search consisted of flying square legs, expanding on each leg, and is pretty tough on the navigator initially as he has to track and calculate course changes every few minutes. During the search, we ourselves began to ice up and had to get out of the area immediately abandoning the search. No trace was ever found; it was pretty clear that the aircraft went down weighted with ice. The chances of ditching the aircraft were very small."*

Losses, however, could result from relatively simple things. Prior to the loss of W/Cdr Morris' aircraft, McGonigal had had such an experience with LK692: M on 27 June 1944: *"I was taking off for an air test at Tiree, full starboard rudder applied to counter the swing to port, when the rudder remained jammed on. Being near to lift-off things moved fast and to abort seemed the only possibility; but with throttles slammed shut, full right rudder and about 90 kts on the clock, we careered hastily across the grass to starboard and finished up on our belly with undercart, propellers and heaven knows what else written off. We all walked away and my impression was that a parachute, or the like, had obstructed the torque rods to the rudder.*

"I was greatly relieved that our CO, W/Cdr Morris, found the cause. The thin metal attachment of the leather stirrup at the outer end of the rudder bar had bent sufficiently under the pressure of my boot-slipping to the right and had jammed behind the throttle pedestal and was firmly locked there. Our Flight Commander at No 1674 HCU had a similar experience on landing. I wonder how many of the 'rudder stall' accidents may have been due instead to this."

While the meteorological units kept up their ceaseless flow of information, the anti-U-boat war had continued unabated. The change of tactics introduced by U-boats in late 1943 had been rapidly met and countered by Coastal Command. Equipped with parachute flares, the two general reconnaissance Halifax squadrons, Nos 58 and 502, had continued their war against the U-boats – at night.

As recorded earlier, shipping was also attacked by the Halifaxes when the opportunity presented itself, or intelligence gave forewarning; news that a blockade-runner had been sighted heading out into the Bay of Biscay brought seven Halifaxes, mustered from both squadrons, into a search on 24 December. S/Ldr Davey was in charge of the joint search and was to co-ordinate the attack if the vessel was located. When the enemy were located, they turned out to be two merchant vessels flanked by ten escort vessels, some of which were *Narvik* class destroyers. Sun and cloud made some approaches impractical for the Halifaxes and one paid the price, being shot down immediately while attacking from 2,000 ft. A second attack at 4,000 ft resulted in heavy damage to another of the Halifaxes. Davey then sent two more in, one to draw off the enemy fire while the second bombed. The ploy worked but the bombs missed and Davey then attacked as his was the only remaining aircraft still with bombs. His tactical advantage now almost exhausted, he came over the cloudbank and then nosed the Halifax straight down at the target. The fire from all

JP165/G of 58 Squadron (the G suffix indicating that the aircraft required guarding while at dispersal because of its secret ASV installation) photographed from HR792 during a patrol. Delivered from L&PTB in late December 1943, aside from the saxophone exhausts fitted to its Merlin engines, it was a GR Mk II Series IA in every respect. No squadron codes were carried during this period but the individual aircraft letter 'D', has a small figure '1' to its right. Each squadron Flight had reserve aircraft marked with a small figure '2' where an existing aircraft code letter had to be utilised. The aircraft letter was repeated in miniature just aft of the Perspex nose, which is fitted with a Vickers GO 0.303-in machine gun in a gimbal mount. Both GR squadrons later replaced this light weapon with 0.5-in Browning machine guns, which required the additional bracing of two upper and two lower struts angled back to the first fuselage frame. Despite numerous revisions to the camouflage instructions, upper surfaces were clearly still in two shades with the code letter marked in red and the serial in Light Slate Grey – that part at least being in accordance with the markings regulations. When the two GR squadrons changed to night attacks using ASV, replacement aircraft were received in standard Bomber Command colours. This particular Halifax was lost in a fatal crash into mountains, five miles south-south-west of Tarbet Harris on 9 April 1945. (K. McGonigal)

ships was intense and there was no time for finesse. Barrett, who was acting as second pilot for the attack, waited for Davey's[24] signal and both hauled back on the control column as the bombs were released, turning the Halifax immediately into the cloud cover. No assessment of their attacks had been possible but a later sweep by Hampden torpedo-bombers sent to follow up with another attack reported that one of the transports was on fire.

After her escape from an attack by a 58 Squadron Halifax and a Sunderland in July as recorded earlier, U-445 had carried out her patrol in the Central Atlantic but had not sunk any shipping. Having left St Nazaire for her next patrol on 29 December, U-445 was spotted north-north-east of Cape Ortegal by a 58 Squadron Halifax flown by F/O T. Griffiths. Griffiths subsequently made a very determined attack on the U-boat and damaged it enough that its crew, after making running repairs, was forced to take the boat back to St Nazaire where it arrived on 10 January and stayed in port until 1 February. For this action, Griffiths received a DFC.

The year ended with a coup that would spell the end of the U-boat as a major force. At Bletchley Park, the Kriegsmarine ciphers were finally broken and from then on the Admiralty were able to read German signals traffic between its bases and sea forces – in particular its submarines. Dönitz's iron control over his command was about to become its Achilles heel. Every outward-bound boat had to report clearing the Bay of Biscay; those leaving from Norway or the Baltic had to advise crossing the 60° North line. Regular position reports were demanded and no boat Commander could change his patrol plan without requesting permission, giving details of the new route and receiving approval. If boats were required to form a wolf pack for a specific convoy attack then that change also had to be acknowledged. All were required to advise of their date and expected time of arrival back from a patrol and no U-boat could return without the requisite exchanges; no deviation from this procedure was allowed. What followed was the steady destruction of the U-boat force's potential. The Schnorkel equipment would have solved the problem, allowing boats to remain submerged, but that equipment arrived too late to be a significant factor in what followed. Naturally, Coastal Command found this information too valuable to reveal and details were fed in a manner that, if detected by German sources, would not compromise the source.

On 2 January 1944, U-415[25] was returning to Brest after a successful patrol having intercepted the escort vessels of convoy OS 62 in the early hours of 24 December and sinking the Havant class destroyer HMS *Hurricane* north-east of the Azores. Early on 1 January, F/Lt I. Christie's 58 Squadron crew located her south-west of Lorient and carried out a night attack, damaging the U-boat; but it reached Brest on 6 January.

The following account by S/Ldr J.B. Grant[26] gives an idea of the difficulties encountered with this type of attack.

While carrying out a night patrol at 1,000 ft on 14 February 1944 Grant made an initial radar contact at a range of 12 miles, only to lose and regain it several times during the next few minutes until a steady contact finally appeared after dropping

down to an altitude of 600 ft. Closing to just under two miles, parachute flares were dropped and showed a surfaced U-boat travelling at approximately 12 knots at a range of one and a quarter miles. At the crucial moment radar contact was again lost and forced Grant to take HR741: H down to 200 ft as the U-boat gunners opened fire on the flares in an attempt to extinguish them before turning their fire on the fast-approaching Halifax. Grant's navigator gave a spirited reply with the single nose-mounted 0.5-in machine gun and six depth charges dropped from a height of 100 ft. Explosions were seen to occur along the starboard side of the U-boat and one minute after the attack began it had stopped moving although sporadic fire continued to come from the U-boat and was returned by Grant's mid-upper and rear gunners. Fourteen minutes later contact was lost and despite dropping five more flares, no further trace of the U-boat was found. The official Admiralty comment for this action was 'Insufficient evidence of damage.'

F/O F. Culling-Mannix RNZAF of 502 Squadron made an equally frustrating brace of attacks on the night of 28/29 January. Having picked up a radar contact, a timed run was made, two parachute flares dropped and, after a further 20 seconds, two 600 lb anti-submarine bombs. The radar operator assessed that the target had passed slightly to port but before any action could be taken a second contact appeared. Successfully homing 'S-Sugar' onto the second contact, Culling-Mannix dropped more flares and illuminated another surfaced U-boat, which he attacked. Two more bombs were dropped, this time using the Mk VII bombsight and, while they possibly straddled the boat, nothing further was seen after the attack.

U-boats were not just difficult to locate at night but also just as dangerous as ever. U-763 had slipped out of Kiel harbour on 14 December and into the North Atlantic where she acted as a weather-reporting vessel. Returning across the Bay of Biscay on 5 February, F/O Culling-Mannix's crew located her and attacked, but this time the U-boat's gun crew shot the Halifax down. There were no survivors.

Another German Auxiliary, M.4405, *Marie Anne* was caught off the Biscay coast by a 58 Squadron crew on 7 March and sent to the bottom. Patrolling closer in to the coast was developing into a better hunting ground for these smaller vessels but opportunities still appeared further out in the Bay of Biscay and another Auxiliary, *Per C.C.*, a French vessel, was sent to the bottom on 14 March, this time by a 502 Squadron Halifax.

Attacking any type of vessel was dangerous; HX225: L from 58 Squadron failed to return from patrol on 11 March and on the 25th, BB277 also failed to return. Yet, it was not always enemy action that killed crews for, on the 26th, 502 Squadron's HX223 inexplicably crashed into the sea on fire some 1,500 yards off St David's Head. The long patrols were hard on both aircraft and crew and with weather always a random player, fuel management was not always easy to judge, one of No 58 Squadron's crews being forced to ditch when JD176: W ran low on fuel returning from a patrol on 27 April. Nevertheless, shipping targets were attacked whenever possible and another German Auxiliary, V.606, the 258-ton *Fladengrund*, had been caught near the Biscay coast and sunk by a 502 crew on the 25th.

Photographed off St David's Head in the summer of 1944, Handley Page built GR Mk II Series I (Special) HR686:J2 of 502 Squadron exhibits the metamorphosis of this series. The engines, while Merlin 22s fitted with the revised multi-exhausts, retain Gallay radiators and three-bladed propellers. The Tollerton fairing and A Mk VIII (Special) mid-upper turret in its high surround were all features of the first revision introduced with the Series I (Special) classification. Squadron aircraft were modified as and when opportunity allowed but many features, such as the high astrodome and Type A fin and rudders seen here, remained unchanged from their original production status. As usual, the individual aircraft letter was repeated in miniature on the nose section. This particular Halifax failed to return from an anti-submarine patrol on 3 October 1944. (M. Wright)

No 58 Squadron lost another Halifax and crew to enemy action in May; U-846 had left Kiel for the North Atlantic on 29 April but while crossing the Bay of Biscay she was found by HR741: H on 2 May, which attacked but was in turn shot down by the U-boat, killing all on board.

With the invasion of Europe approaching, it became more and more important for the two squadrons to close the Channel to U-boats operating from the French Atlantic ports and this became their principal focus. Three U-boats were attacked by 58 Squadron in June, one of them in harbour at Guernsey. The invasion triggered an immediate reaction within the U-boat ranks. The late evening of 6 June saw U-413 and seven others ordered out to patrol the area between the Lizard and Harland Point to operate against ships of the Allied invasion fleet heading for the Channel. Ordered to proceed at top speed, the U-boats were forced to run on the surface and almost immediately after their escort left, all seven came under air attack; four were damaged and forced to turn back. The remaining three were told to proceed submerged from dawn. U-413[27] had an advantage, being fitted with a Schnorkel-system, but her next attack came during darkness while she was surfaced, a 502 Squadron Halifax crew having located her. F/O J. Spurgeon attacked and although the boat's gun crews put up a strong defence and hit one of the Halifax's port engines, the damage had been done and, having driven off her attacker, the damaged U-413 was forced to turn back for Brest harbour.

Encounters with U-boats were now becoming more dangerous as the crews put up strong defensive fire against the attacking aircraft; but in the see-sawing process of advantages, on 6 June two new weapons were added to the anti-shipping Halifaxes' armoury, the 250 and 500 lb medium-case bombs. Fitted with an airburst pistol, these caused both material damage and casualties from the shrapnel effect of near misses. The two squadrons used these weapons against their entire range of targets and they proved highly effective for night anti-shipping attacks. The replacement of the old Mk VII bombsight by the more sophisticated Mk XIV also greatly improved the accuracy of the attacks.

U-228, still under the command of Kptlt Christophersen, was one of 19 non-Schnorkel U-boats ordered out of La Pallice on 6 June to prevent their capture should Allied forces trap them there. They were to lie in a double line, 200 metres down, between Brest and Bordeaux; later they moved closer to port and held at 100 metres depth ready for a more rapid response to any invasion forces approaching that area of the coast. Even at that depth, they could be detected and were constantly attacked by aircraft when they rose to the surface at night. U-288's crew claimed to have shot down one of their attackers on the night of 10/11th, possibly 58 Squadron's JP167, which failed to return from its patrol that night. With the threat of a local invasion past, the U-boats were recalled to port on the 12th and U-218 docked at St Nazaire on the 16th. Activity, however, remained intense along the invasion front and JP168 of 502 Squadron may well have fallen foul of the enemy, failing to return from its patrol on 23 June.

By July, Nos 58 and 502 Squadrons were carrying out three types of operations: anti-submarine patrols in the English Channel and the Bay of Biscay mainly by night,

anti-shipping strikes along the French Biscay coast and anti-shipping and armed reconnaissance in the Channel Islands in support of the armies in Normandy. Between 18 and 30 July, the harbour of Granville was attacked three times as enemy reinforcements from St Malo were believed to be passing through it. Several U-boats were also attacked during the month, 502 Squadron attacking four of these as well as seven surface vessels along the northern and western coastal areas.

Throughout late July and August, the focus shifted and the two squadrons were primarily engaged in anti-shipping patrols in the Bay of Biscay and along the northern coast of Brittany. At the same time, Beaufighter strike wings severely harassed the enemy's small forces of destroyers, Sperrbrechers[28], auxiliaries and torpedo boats that plied these waters desperately trying to escort the German supply convoys. Forced almost to a standstill by day, the enemy sought the cover of darkness to mask its movements, only to be singled out by the lone Halifaxes and attacked under the very noses of the shore defences. On 28 June, two vessels were sunk by 502 Squadron, VP.627 *Elisa* and M.4457 *C. P. Andersen*, both of which were German auxiliary vessels caught close into the Biscay coast.

The audacity of these Halifax patrols is exemplified by F/Lt D. McLeod's action on 3 August. His 58 Squadron Halifax set out for an anti-shipping patrol close inshore along the coast of Brittany. Successfully avoiding fire from the coastal batteries at Les Minquiers, south of Jersey, McLeod's *ASV* operator eventually picked up a radar contact, which, in turn, led to a visual sighting of five E-boats. Sweeping in to attack, he released his stick of bombs across the formation scoring a definite hit on one. The attack, however, was not entirely one-sided and the Halifax returned with a 10-inch hole in its port wing.

The heavily armed 997-ton Sperrbrecher, Sb134 *Falke* was sent to the bottom in coastal waters in a determined attack by one of 58 Squadron's crews on 8 August and the French tug *Jannick*, sent to assist another vessel, met the same fate in a joint attack by Halifaxes from both squadrons on the 10th.

Two days later, 502 Squadron scored a rare U-boat success; U-981 had left Lorient on 7 August, transiting to La Pallice in company with U-309. The two boats were approaching the rendezvous point with their escort, south-west of La Pallice, when U-981 hit a mine. Unable to dive and with both engines out of action, her captain, Oberleutnant zur See Günther Keller called for an immediate escort – but F/O J. Capey's *ASV* operator had found the two stationary boats, and the Halifax swept in and dropped flares. At that moment U-981's engineers managed to get the electric motors restarted and the U-boat moved off slowly. Capey brought the Halifax in again and this time dropped an anti-submarine bomb at exactly the same moment that the U-boat struck a second mine. Capey then attacked again with more anti-submarine bombs and twenty minutes later Keller ordered his crew to abandon ship and as the U-981 sank, U-309 reappeared to pick up the survivors.

On 21 August 58 Squadron lost a crew when JP296 crashed into the sea, north-west of Bordeaux while carrying out an anti-submarine patrol; the cause was unknown but may possibly have been to enemy action. Encounters with the enemy were now growing fewer and the closing days of August proved somewhat of an anti-climax as suitable targets were seldom found in French waters and as a result, both squadrons were transferred to the control of 18 Group. Accordingly, the two squadrons moved to Stornoway in the Outer Hebrides from where they would carry out anti-submarine patrols between Iceland and the Norwegian coast. No 58 moved first, arriving in August, with 502 Squadron joining it in September and maintaining a detachment at Wick until war's end; but September passed slowly, without incident.

Despite the low rate of contact with the enemy, October opened with a loss for 502 Squadron on the 3rd when HR686:J2 failed to return from an anti-submarine patrol.

However, a distinct rise in morale was noted when, next day, the two squadrons were notified that they would be concentrating on night anti-shipping duties in future. Their general patrol area would cover both the Skagerrak and the Kattegat; their main area of concentration was to be the shipping lanes between Oslo, Kristiansand South and the Danish ports. These shipping lanes were not only Germany's last important sea routes for bringing in urgently needed supplies of raw materials, but were also those bringing troops from Norway to the western front.

October was a busy month and Nos 58 and 502 Squadrons, now operating in conjunction, made 27 attacks but, as was usual with night operations, results were hard to assess. On 12/13th, the MV *Havenstein* was caught and sunk by a 502 Squadron Halifax in the Skagerrak and on 15/16th a 58 Squadron crew sank the Swedish-flagged *Concord*, a 150-ton vessel, in the same area. On 22/23rd, the Norwegian-flagged *Irania* went to the bottom off the Skagerrak, setting off a run of successes for 502 Squadron. On 25 October, when one of 58 Squadron's Halifaxes set a merchant vessel and its escort on fire with a single stick of bombs, the flames were still visible at a range of 20 miles. While identification of the target was usually not possible in such attacks, three ships were positively identified and the results confirmed for the Squadrons involved. One other item of significance during the month was receipt of approval to operate the Halifaxes at an increased all-up weight of 63,000 lb. As a result, the standard bomb load was increased from five to six 500-lb medium-case bombs.

A final U-boat kill for the Halifaxes occurred on 27 October. U-1060[29] was employed on torpedo-transport duties between Kiel and various Norwegian ports and had made seven return trips in the previous nine months; but this time she was caught a day after leaving Bodø for Bergen by Fireflies of No 1771 Squadron from HMS *Implacable*. Damaged, she ran aground off the island of Fleina off the Norwegian coast. Two Liberators from No 311 Squadron and two Halifaxes from 502 Squadron found her later in the day and her fate was sealed with S/Ldr H. Holderness and F/Lt W. Powell taking the honours for the Halifaxes. During the attacks U-1060 keeled over and slid into deeper water; she had 55 on board, having picked up 28 survivors from U-957, which had been badly damaged in a collision with a German steamer a week previously. Forty-three survived the sinking.

The increasing pressure placed on their already strained shipping supply lines forced the Germans to attempt stronger countermeasures against the Halifaxes and a marked increase in night-fighter activity was soon noted. To counter this, the Halifax crews began flying at lower altitudes and after some experimentation, 200 ft was settled on as the optimum altitude. Although sighted as low as 500 ft, the German night-fighters showed an understandable reluctance to attack at these lower altitudes, preferring instead to shadow the Halifaxes and await more favourable opportunities.

In the course of the 44 sorties carried out during November, nineteen attacks were made for the loss of two crews; JP319 from 502 Squadron failed to return from its patrol on 26 November and on the 29th, the indomitable McLeod and his 58 Squadron crew in JP333: O were killed. A radio report was received from the aircraft stating that they had just attacked a 4,000-ton ship in the Kattegat estimating two hits, but nothing further was heard from them again. No 502 Squadron lost a crew in the same area just a month later when JP320 failed to return from an anti-shipping patrol on 26 December. Recorded successes by 502 Squadron amounted to damage to a German-flagged MV *Palos*, attacked in the northern Kattegat on 4/5th November, the sinking of the MV *Kiel* on 21/22nd in the Kattegat, and damage to the German-flagged MV *Borbeck* off Oslo Fjord on 24/25th. Damage could also mean that vital supplies did not reach their destination or were destroyed – either way, it was a success.

The weather, always a fickle ally, occasionally prevented normal anti-shipping patrols from being carried out during December but even so, 21 were still flown. Not to be deprived of their prey, the Halifaxes used these opportunities to attack shipping anchored at Kristiansund and to bomb Aalesund, along the central Norwegian coast. With German shipping losses being supplemented by impressed vessels, three of the six identified vessels attacked during the month were Norwegian: MV *Korsvik* sunk in the Skagerrak on the night of 30 September/1 October, MV *Molla*, damaged while off Aalesund and MV *Orion* caught and damaged northeast of Skaw, the latter by a 502 Squadron crew. The other three vessels, all German, were damaged in combined attacks by both Squadrons; MV *Winrich von Kniprode*, MV *Ulanga* and MV *Stahleck* were all caught in the eastern Skagerrak on 30/31 December.

January 1945 opened with a 502 Squadron sinking of a German Auxiliary, M.5610, *KFK 128* off western Norway during the dark period[30]. Another Norwegian-flagged MV *Vaga*, was located in the Skagerrak during the dark period on 13 January and sunk by an aircraft of 58 Squadron, but another of the Squadron's crews were faced with a different situation that same evening.

Occasionally the Halifaxes became victims of their own style of tactics as F/Lt Davison of 58 Squadron found out that night. At about 19.40 hrs at a point 20 miles north-west of Gothenburg in neutral Sweden, his Halifax was suddenly illuminated from above by four parachute flares and simultaneously coned by intense light flak from several ships. He immediately dropped JP329: Z down to 450 ft and turned to port, but a quick succession of flak strikes on the port engines caused a sudden loss of power, resulting in a violent sideslip. Davison managed to level the aircraft out, but it continued to sink and the rear of the fuselage struck the sea, tearing off the *ASV* cover, the lower half of the starboard fin and rudder and a portion of the port fin and rudder.

Thinking that a ditching was inevitable, he closed the throttles, but the Halifax rebounded into the air and the second pilot slammed the throttles and pitch levers fully open. Frantically re-trimming the aircraft, Davison somehow managed to keep it flying on an even keel. The radar operator reported that an explosion had occurred in the *ASV* set, blowing a large hole in the top of the fuselage and starting an intense fire that spread rapidly from the mid-upper turret to the rear escape hatch. While the wireless operator transmitted an SOS and turned the IFF to the distress setting, the radar operator tackled the blaze and finally extinguished it after five hectic minutes.

Davison had managed to coax the battered and badly vibrating Halifax up to 1,000 ft when the blaze broke out again with increased severity. Both gunners, the radar operator and the flight engineer spent 10 minutes trying to get the blaze under control; the rear gunner finally extinguished it with the contents of the Elsan toilet. Meanwhile the navigator had given the pilot, somewhat optimistically, a course for base but the Halifax again ran into a hail of flak. Taking what evasive action he could, he finally broke clear and nursed the Halifax up to 1,500 ft where a closer inspection was made of the damage. The port inner engine was feathered and the port outer fluctuating badly with falling oil pressure. The radio transmitter, *Gee* set and *ASV*

No 520 Squadron's LK960: L, with an additional small number '1' added to the right of the letter as photographed at Gibraltar in late 1944. This is a standard Met Mk V Series IA which, like many meteorological Halifaxes, has dispensed with its exhaust shrouds. The dark vertical oblong on the nose section is the window with the psychrometer set externally into its frame. Behind 'L' is LL518: K, the first figure 2 of the unit code 2M is just visible, thus giving an approximate date of the reintroduction of unit codes for the meteorological Halifax squadrons.

were out of action, as also were the DR compass, the airspeed indicator and the artificial horizon.

The situation was critical and Davison, having gained another precious 500 ft of altitude, turned the Halifax towards Gothenburg and the relative safety of Sweden. The reception was a hail of flak, which prompted the jettisoning of the bomb load and the firing of the distress cartridges. Unable to locate an aerodrome, Davison turned JP329 out to sea once more but the port outer engine failed completely and the aircraft began to break up. Ordering the crew to bale out, Davison turned the Halifax away from the lights of the town of Landvetter and just managed to clear the top of a hill, but hit some high-tension wires, struck a tree and plunged into a river, breaking the ice on impact. Miraculously he survived, but four of the crew did not.

No 502 Squadron claimed a definite sinking in western Norwegian waters on 25 January during the dark period, the 2,998-ton German MV *Perganon*. During February, the first of the GR Mk III Halifaxes began to arrive and the two squadrons were quick to exploit the advantages of the new aircraft which featured, amongst other things, an increased bomb load capacity to nine 500 lb bombs. The Met Mk III version, however, did not reach the meteorological squadrons until March and they continued to soldier on with their Met Mk Vs; but there was still plenty of work for the existing aircraft. The first operational sortie by 518 Squadron with a Met Mk III took place on 7 March, RG390: A 1 leaving from Tiree, followed by NR198: X 1 two days later. Flying training on the new marque was carried out using RG421: E, which was soon joined by PN337: J, PN187: N, RG414: V 1 and RG417: B while the Merlin-engine Halifaxes continued their patrols. However, the replacement process was not rapid and by the end of May, for example, 517 Squadron would still have eight Mk Vs on charge and only 12 Mk IIIs while for 520 Squadron on Gibraltar, Met Mk IIIs would not reach them until July 1945.

On the night of 20/21 February, JP174: C of 58 Squadron was out on a night patrol over the Skagerrak when the *ASV* operator reported making a radar contact. The pilot was then homed onto the contact – six merchant vessels on an easterly course – and he attacked a 3,000-ton vessel, later identified as the 6,105-ton *Porto Allegro*, scoring a direct hit with a single 500 lb bomb on its bows; this was followed by flames and smoke and the Halifax's crew left the ship blazing. Less than an hour

Handley Page Halifax, Met Mk V Series IA
Y3-L, (serial unknown) No 518 Squadron, Tiree, Inner Scottish Hebrides, May 1945. Meteorological flights did not stop with VE Day;
the ever-necessary meteorological information was as important as ever, though the aircraft is now wearing its full squadron code.

later, F/Lt F. Rush of 502 Squadron sighted a 6,000-ton ship with four other vessels 40 miles east of Kristiansand South. He attacked immediately claiming four hits on the ship, which became engulfed in flames with ammunition exploding inside it. An hour later, when 'G-George' left the area the ship was still burning fiercely and sinking at the stern. Shortly after midnight the following night, 'Y-York' from 58 Squadron homed onto a radar contact in the Skagerrak sighting two merchant vessels on an easterly course, one estimated at 4,000 tons, the other 3,500 tons, travelling at about 10 knots. The Halifax aimed for the larger vessel and direct hits were scored with 500 lb bombs on its stern; it slowed and then stopped, emitting clouds of dense black smoke. No 502 Squadron had one of its attacks during the dark period on 25 February later identified as the German MV *Astersturm*, which it sank in the Skagerrak.

As the war entered its final weeks, the volume of traffic increased as the enemy attempted to withdraw troops and equipment from southern Norway and both Halifax squadrons found themselves heavily engaged during this period with No 58 Squadron carrying out 55 attacks during March alone. JP172: U carried out an attack early in the day on the 2nd, while 502 Squadron damaged the 9,026 ton MV *Isar* during the dark period, in the Skagerrak; combined attacks by both Squadrons that night damaged the MVs *Kattaget* and *William Blumer,* both caught off southern Norway. The dark period saw the Norwegian-flagged MV *Betty* attacked in the eastern Skagerrak on the 5th by a 502 Squadron Halifax and on the 8th, the Dutch-flagged MV *Hoendeep* was caught in the Skagerrak by 58 Squadron, the dark period offering her no protection from *ASV* search. Three days later the same fate befell the MV *Theda Fritzen,* when 502 Squadron caught her in the same area. The 58 Squadron crews also had a run of successes, starting on the 12th with the sinking of the MV *Rolandseck* in the Kattegat during the dark period and followed by the German Auxiliary UJ.1105 *Wilhelm Loh,* attacked and damaged in the eastern Skagerrak during the dark period of the 16th. On the 20th, a 2,500-ton ship was hit with one bomb by one of the squadron's aircraft leaving the ship badly damaged and during the dark period of the 23rd, the German MV *Ostra* was sunk in the Kattegat. No 502 Squadron rounded off the month by sinking the German MV *Priamus* in the Kattegat.

April produced an all-time record of 101 attacks from the combined efforts of both squadrons, which cost the enemy some 5,998 tons of shipping sunk for the loss of four Halifaxes. This same month 502 Squadron received a message of congratulations from the AOC Coastal Command for the sinking of more than 25,000 tons and damaging 50,000 tons of shipping since January. Even allowing for discrepancies in accurately assessing the shipping tonnages, the figures are still impressive. It was estimated by the Ministry of Economics that the combined efforts of both squadrons operating over the Skagerrak and Kattegat had severely reduced Germany's imports from the Scandinavian countries at a most crucial time. Nevertheless, these successes had not been achieved without cost. No 58 Squadron had lost six Halifaxes to enemy action between February and April: JP173: H on 20th and HX224: P on 25 February, and three, JP336: X, JP299: J and JP330: 0, between 23 and 26 April. Nothing further was heard from any of the crews, but JP336: X was later reported to have crashed north-west of Anholt in Denmark. By contrast, No 502 Squadron had lost only PN402, one of its new GR Mk IIIs on 11 April. Identified shipping attacked and either damaged or sunk during April were MV *Gertrude Ohlrogge,* sunk by 58 Squadron in the eastern Kattegat on the 3rd and two days later the MV *Feodsia,* both occurring during the dark period. On the 8th, 502 Squadron caught and sank the German MV *Carsten Russ* in the Skagerrak and on the 10th, 58 Squadron sank a German T.13 class motor torpedo boat in the Kattegat, with 502 Squadron adding the MV *Hansa* to the tally in the same area. Three days later, also in the same area, a 58 Squadron Halifax attacked and damaged the MV *Ostland.*

On the 19th, M.403, an M Class minesweeper, was intercepted in the Kattegat by 502 Squadron and sunk, the MV *Dammator* following it to the bottom the same day after being attacked by a 58 Squadron Halifax. Also found in the same area next day, the MV *Treuenfels* was damaged by a 58 Squadron aircraft with a 502 Squadron crew adding the Norwegian-flagged MV *Trondheim* also on the same day. Then, during the dark period of the 20th, the minelayer *Ostmark* was sunk in the same area, the victim of a 502 Squadron crew. Further attacks carried out that night saw the same squadron damage the MV *Schleswig* off southern Norway and sink the MV *Neukuhren* (a former Greek owned ship) in the Kattegat. The following day, again during the dark period, 502 Squadron sank the Danish-flagged MV *Nordstern* in the northern Kattegat, later sharing the sinking of MV *Tubingen* with 58 Squadron in the same general area.

May commenced with the same tempo of operations and then, suddenly, the war was over. Both squadrons had scored their last successes on 3 May, 58 Squadron sinking the 1,600-ton cargo vessel *L. M. Russ,* and No 502 the 750-ton M Class minesweeper *M.301,* both caught in the Kattegat during the dark period favoured by the Halifaxes. However, while the more lethal aspects had been removed, operations continued at the same pace with both squadrons engaged on unarmed anti-shipping reconnaissance in their old hunting grounds, 58 Squadron carrying out 41 operations during the period 9 to 23 May. The object of the flights was to report, by wireless, to the NOIC[31] at Copenhagen, all enemy shipping movements so that the navy could check on the large number of German ships known to be fleeing from Russian-held territory.

This traffic was as diverse as it was numerous; small craft of all descriptions were sighted ranging from barges to houseboats packed to capacity with troops. Except for one isolated incident, none of the Halifaxes was fired upon although two from 58 Squadron experienced engine trouble and landed at the formerly German-occupied aerodrome at Aalborg West, in Denmark where another of the squadron's Halifaxes joined them. On 15 May the squadron engineering officer, W/Cdr Ingle, arrived by air with a maintenance party and spares and the three Halifaxes returned to Stornoway via Grove, in Denmark, on 18 May.

Both squadrons were disbanded at Stornoway with effect from 25 May 1945, their role no longer having any immediate operational value. No 58 Squadron received a final tribute from the AOC 18 Group in which he expressed his sincere appreciation of the *"... magnificent work carried out by your squadron against the main supply of the enemy between the resources of Norway and the battle zone on the Continent."*

It would be easy to undervalue the work done by all the Coastal Command crews if only a simple cost benefit analysis is applied, such as hours flown versus enemy ships and submarines sunk. Thousands of hours were flown and seemingly, relatively few enemy vessels sunk; but diversion was as valuable as destruction, and the primary role of crews was to keep the enemy away from Allied shipping. If, in the process, an enemy vessel was put out of action, or sunk, that was an additional, welcome bonus. A detailed review of all U-boat histories, set out in two large volumes in Kenneth Wynn's massive, two-volume work *'U-Boat Operations Of The Second World War'* reveals the other side of the equation – just how many thousands of patrol miles were travelled by each U-boat, often for no return. There were several factors, but interception by air and naval craft were the major ones. With the exception of *Operation Musketry,* the Halifaxes (and other Coastal Command types) operated alone throughout the war years at sea. It was a very dangerous occupation, making their results even more remarkable.

The Halifax had disappeared from Coastal Command as an anti-shipping weapon, but it was to continue for many years in the meteorological role.

CHAPTER NINE

AIRBORNE FORCES OPERATIONS

DURING the early months of 1940, the Wehrmacht had amply demonstrated the value of glider support and airborne troops as an instrument of war and the British Government was quick to appreciate the lesson. In October 1940, a Flight was formed for glider and parachute experiments and for what the Airborne Forces Development Unit (AFDU), as it was officially named, lacked in experience was made up in enthusiasm and a wide variety of aircraft types that included Hectors, Tiger Moths, Whitleys, a Wellington and a B.A. Swallow. Specifications for four military gliders were issued that same year and the first of these, the General Aircraft Ltd. Hotspur I, was test-flown by F/Os Davie and Kronfeld on 21 January 1941. The second and third Hotspurs joined the test programme in February and March respectively.

During January, mock-ups of the Slingsby Hengist and the Airspeed Horsa were inspected and four months later on 28 May, a very significant conference was held at General Aircraft Ltd. The subject was the mock-up of the Hamilcar tank-carrying glider. The rapid increase in size from the eight-seat Hotspur to this giant in so short a time posed problems with regard to a suitable towing aircraft. Clearly, it was beyond the capabilities of the Whitley and F/O Pitkethly visited Boscombe Down on 5 June to make a study of the Manchester, Lancaster, Halifax and Liberator aircraft as potential tugs. The choice soon fell to the Halifax, the capacious interior and power of it proving superior to its rivals.

The Development Unit at Ringway received its first Halifax, R9435, on 12 October 1941. Used for paratroop dropping trials, it was modified by the fitting of a circular hatch in the bottom of the fuselage well originally designed to house a mid-under turret. The first drops, using dummies, were made on 23 October but the parachute static lines proved troublesome, one damaging the dropping aperture when the line and its pack streamed back and jammed under the tail wheel during the landing. The Whitleys had experienced similar difficulties and in November three of them were fitted with tail wheel spats while another, K7220, was equipped with doors to close over the static line attachment. However, while the spat was adopted for the Whitley neither modification proved suitable for the Halifax.

General testing and modification continued but the Halifax proved the most difficult for retrieving the static lines and led to the development of a special winch to overcome this. One further modification was made that would become the distinguishing feature of this version of the Halifax, a semi-circular windshield fitted around the forward edge of the dropping aperture. This projected downwards into the slipstream and provided a region of still air to allow paratroopers to exit the aircraft cleanly before the slipstream took effect. With this refinement added three RAF parachute instructors successfully carried out the first live drop from R9435 on 10 December 1941. For existing Halifaxes modified in this manner a new marque was created with B Mk II being changed to A Mk II.

Just when this designation was implemented for existing Halifaxes modified in this manner is not known as no document has been located specifying this. However, with the introduction of the full glider tug modifications onto production lines, the 'A' designation was formally adopted.

During November, three more Halifaxes had arrived at the Airborne Forces detachment at Ringway with a fifth, R9443, arriving the following month. All were modified for glider towing with the necessary equipment installed beneath the rear fuselage aft of the tail wheel and anchored to frames 45 and 47. In January 1942, it was decided to transfer the Horsa glider test-flying programme to Snaith in Yorkshire where the manufacturer's trials with the Hamilcar were also to take place. Service trials would be carried out at Newmarket. The prototype Hamilcar arrived at Snaith on 29 January and test-flying commenced almost immediately.

By the end of May, the Halifax-Horsa trials were almost completed, as were those with the Hotspur, the latter including double and triple towing by R9443. On 7 June, two more Halifaxes, W7719 and W7720, joined the trials programme as the emphasis now gradually shifted to Hamilcar towing. However, it would not be long before the results of the Horsa trials were put to the test.

At the time of the German invasion of Norway, the Norsk Hydro Plant at Vermok was engaged in the production of deuterium oxide, better known by its more common name of heavy water, a necessary adjunct to development of atomic power. Within one month of the occupation, Norway's new rulers were demanding a substantial increase in the output of this valuable commodity. By 1942 their demands had more than trebled, a fact the Allies could not overlook for, if they were to maintain the initiative in the field of atomic research, then Germany had to be deprived of this valuable source of heavy water.

An attempt was made to destroy the plant with a bombing attack but the nature of the terrain surrounding the plant and its difficult location made this almost impossible. Accordingly, it was proposed that a glider assault force aided by Norwegian guides would be used to destroy it. This force was composed of 16 volunteer parachutists from the 9th Field Company Royal Engineers (Airborne) and a similar number from the 261st Field Park Company (Airborne). The tug aircraft came from a 38 Wing detachment specially formed for this operation with a complement of two crews and three Halifaxes. The glider crews were chosen specifically for their experience with two, Staff Sergeant M. Strathdee and Sergeant P. Doig, being members of the Glider Pilot Regiment[1] while the other two, P/O N. Davies RAAF and P/O H. Fraser RAAF, were air force pilots. Both parties were to be independent of each other and either was capable of completing the task.

Considerable practice was devoted to long-distance towing exercises with fully laden gliders and this provided valuable experience for the operation. In addition, accurate radar homing aids in the form of *Rebecca-Eureka* sets were to be used, with the sets being placed in their appropriate positions by Norwegian agents prior to the operation.

Given the code-name *Operation Freshman*, the personnel and aircraft, three Halifaxes and three Horsas, moved to Skitten in Scotland on 17 November 1942. G/Capt T. B. Cooper, DFC was in charge of the operation scheduled for the night of 19/20 November, or the next suitable night during that moon period. Weather conditions were reasonable at first on the night in question but the possibility of a deterioration stopping the operation during that moon period made it essential to go ahead according to schedule. A near-crisis occurred at the last moment when the additional flight engineer failed to arrive; this was rectified by the station Medical Officer who volunteered to fill the vacancy, and S/Ldr Wilkinson handed him a copy of the appropriate instructions and then guided him around the Halifax. Half an hour later the MO joined F/Lt Parkinson's crew and the operation got under way, Strathdee and Doig flying Horsa DP349 and the RAAF crew flying HS114.

S/Ldr Wilkinson's combination was scheduled to leave at 17.50 hrs, followed 20 minutes later by the second, each individually setting course across the 340-mile North Sea crossing. The first combination made landfall on the Norwegian coast and headed on to the target with some difficulty, the *Rebecca* set having become unserviceable shortly before and patchy cloud making map reading very difficult. Unable to find the target on the first run in, Wilkinson attempted another search despite the fact that he was flying in thick cloud and unable to climb out of it.

With the small fuel reserve diminishing rapidly the combination was forced steadily lower and lower by the severe icing conditions until, just north of Stavanger, the tow-rope of DP349 snapped through icing. Wilkinson managed to nurse his Halifax[2] back to Skitten, where he landed with his fuel supply nearly exhausted.

The Horsa was less fortunate and crashed on top of snow-covered mountains at Fylgjesdal, overlooking Lysefjord. The landing, carried out in a snowstorm, killed eight of the party, including the two Army pilots and seriously injured five of the survivors. Subsequently captured, the surviving members of the team were taken to Stavanger Hospital where the Gestapo murdered four of their number[3]. The remaining five survivors were then taken to the Grini concentration camp where they were kept in solitary confinement until January 1943 when they were taken to the Trandum forest and shot by members of the Gestapo[4].

F/Lt Parkinson's combination came to grief immediately after crossing the coast and its Horsa, HS114 flown by Davies and Fraser, crashed two and a half miles north-east of Lensmannsgard, icing having forced the combination lower and lower until the tow-rope broke, forcing a crash-landing and killing both RAAF pilots and one of the soldiers. The remainder of the party were captured and executed by firing squad near Egersund that same day[5]. The Halifax tug, W7801: B managed to clear the first range of mountains only to crash into a second range further south at Helleland, killing the entire crew. This was the first Halifax lost on airborne operations[6].

The operation had been a hazardous undertaking from the start, with a long sea crossing and a landfall in difficult and unknown terrain at night. Weather conditions were bad and had hampered both the navigation and actual target identification. The operation was a bitter failure. In conjunction with members of the Norwegian resistance movement, SOE agents eventually destroyed the plant.

Amongst the early squadrons established for glider-towing operations was No 295 Squadron, formed at Netheravon under No 38 Wing of Army Co-operation Command. It was equipped with Whitleys and a mixture of Hotspur and Horsa

Operation Beggar gets under way. EB139: NN, an A Mk V Series I (Special) of 295 Squadron, gets airborne with Horsa LG723 from Portreath on 3 June. This was the second combination to leave and the Horsa ended up in the sea following tow-rope failure. On the return flight to the UK on 25 September, the Halifax ditched 100 miles east of Gibraltar.

gliders, the Whitleys being used alternatively for glider towing, parachute dropping, leaflet raids and normal bombing duties.

In February 1943, Halifaxes began slowly to replace the elderly Whitleys of 'A' Flight, taking part in *Exercise Owl* on 1 March, each equipped with 14 containers. They operated for the first time on the night of 19/20 February when two were dispatched from Netheravon to attack a transformer station at Distre, in France. Despite flak damage to the port engine and rear turret, DK122 successfully attacked the target and returned safely to Thruxton but DK123 failed to return from the operation. This first small operation was a lonely introduction as Bomber Command was not operating that night, the two Halifaxes being the lone attackers. It was also not very helpful in getting the number of Halifaxes up to establishment level as supply was very slow which, matched by a similar deficiency in flight engineers, limited operational activity. A further six aircraft arrived on 21 April and on the 22nd, 'A' Flight became the first all-Halifax section on the Squadron.

On 1 May the squadron carried out a successful full-scale operation airlifting the entire unit, including ground personnel, to its new base at Holmsley South in the New Forest, thus allowing normal training to resume by 3 May. Basic glider-towing training employed a fairly simple but precise technique. For take-off, the tug aircraft moved forward until the tow-rope was taut and the combination then moved off down the runway in unison. The glider became airborne first at approximately 70 mph with the tug still on the runway but once both elements were airborne, the glider took up station either just below or above the tug to avoid its slipstream. Whilst on tow, the captain of the tug was in command, communication between the two aircraft being by means of an intercom wire woven into the tow-rope.

Drawn from all ranks of the army, glider pilots held the unique distinction of first having to pilot their glider and its load into the battle area and then reverting to their normal army role. They were trained to full operational standard by the RAF and the recollections of Captain Bernard Halsall MC, a very experienced army glider pilot who took part in most of the major engagements, provide an interesting insight into this training. He followed the standard RAF training route, first at an Elementary Flying Training School (EFTS) on Tiger Moths before graduating to Miles Magisters and going on to complete some 200 hours of instruction at various training airfields around Oxfordshire. Having graduated and received his RAF wings, he was then posted to the Glider Training School at RAF Skellingford where he underwent 30 hours of instruction, including night flying, on Hotspur gliders and for his final tests had to complete both day and night landings with a full load of 11 personnel with full equipment. The focus then turned to the 'crash-landing' technique, an operational requirement for most battle situations. Most gliders would descend at about 1,000 ft per minute once released, so over unknown territory the pilot had only a little time to make his decision about line of approach, landing spot, wind direction and the welfare of his human cargo and equipment, which had to be delivered in fit state for battle. If a tow-rope broke at, say, 2,000 ft, the glider pilot had two minutes maximum to get all of these factors right. The giant Hamilcar, despite its proportions, was light on the controls when flown 'empty' with about 5,000 lbs of sand bags for ballast. It became airborne at about 90 mph and rode just above the runway until the tug was airborne, after which it would be flown in the high position, just above the slipstream of the tug aircraft. Fully loaded, at between 20 and 21 tons, the controls were sluggish and the rate of descent in free flight quite substantial, even at about 500 feet per minute or less depending upon conditions. It was a substantial training regime and a great responsibility, General Hackett remarking that graduates were "The complete soldier".

While preparations for the invasion of Sicily were in progress, the first Horsa gliders began to come off the production lines in substantial quantities and because they possessed a greater carrying capacity than the American Waco, the decision was made to employ as many of the former as could be flown out to North Africa in time for the operation. This move, known as *Operation Beggar*, involved towing the empty gliders 1,200 miles across the sea, including crossing the Bay of Biscay, to Rabat-Salé in Morocco and then a further 1,000 miles across the North African mainland to the area of Sousse in Tunisia where the glider squadrons were assembled. The only available aircraft capable of the task was the Halifax and, if not interrupted by either the enemy or bad weather, it was estimated that the combination should just be able to reach the coastal area of North Africa. As 295 Squadron was the only unit equipped for the task, it fell to them.

EB139: NN, probably photographed at Kairouan in transit to Rabat-Salé after the accident with LG723, had towed Horsa HL974 out from Portreath on 6 June, returning to tow LG994 on its second ferry trip on 14 June. It came close to being destroyed taking part in Operation Fustian, the last airborne assault of the Sicilian campaign.

Accordingly, the crews were sent off on 10-hour cross-country towing exercises to provide some training for the operation but even this was not without risk; on 16 May, DG390 crashed and burnt at Sopley, Hampshire after suffering engine failure and on 11 June EB132: KK was lost when it flew into a hill at Portlock Weir in bad weather. Meanwhile, a working party from No 13 MU had arrived at Hurn on 8 May to modify 23 Halifaxes to glider tug configuration by 1 June, which, despite the loss of the two Halifaxes, was completed on time. Also resident at Hurn was the Heavy Glider Maintenance Unit that prepared the Horsas for the operation which, when ready, were collected by 295 Squadron and towed to Portreath on the Cornish coast. The position of the airfield at Portreath presented a somewhat nerve-wracking situation since the runway ended on the edge of the cliffs. This, combined with the fact that the Halifaxes were loaded to capacity with fuel and ammunition, produced some rather hair-raising take-offs with each combination disappearing from view and reappearing when some two to three miles out to sea, straining to gain height.

Operation Beggar began on 3 June with four combinations leaving for Rabat-Salé led by DK130: EE towing Horsa DP574, which was soon forced to return when the glider became unserviceable. The second combination, EB139: NN flown by G/Capt Cooper from H.Q. 38 Wing and three other crew fared little better with the tow-rope parting and the glider LG723 ending up in the sea, the crew being rescued by the Royal Navy some ten hours later, none the worse for their experience. The other two combinations reached their destination safely.

After these incidents, the operation proceeded smoothly with 14 combinations having reached Rabat-Salé by 14 June. Considering that the towing was carried out in daylight – a night operation over the distances involved was considered too hazardous – and involved flying within 100 miles of the German air bases in south-west France, the combinations had been fortunate in avoiding interception by enemy aircraft for so long. However, on that same date, the luck of the combinations ran out when two Focke-Wulf Condors of the 7./KG 40[7] intercepted DK130: EE and its Horsa 100 miles north-west of Cape Finisterre. Despite a gallant effort on the part of the Halifax's rear gunner to defend the combination, the glider was forced to cast off and ditch in the sea and its tug was shot down shortly after, killing W/O Bill McCrodden and his crew. German radio later confirmed the details of the action. This time the Royal Navy was not on hand and the unfortunate glider crew drifted for 11 days before being picked up by a Portuguese fishing boat. By a twist of fate, two of the survivors were part of the crew that had ditched on the opening day of the operation.

Apart from the standard modifications to all glider tug Halifaxes – removal of the nose and mid-upper turret, local strengthening of the rear fuselage and fitting of

Heat and sand; a 295 Squadron Halifax moves forward to take up the slack in the tow-rope and covers the Horsa behind it in dust. The location was possibly Rabat-Salé and probably taken during one of the training sessions while awaiting the arrival of all the Horsas.

the towing rig – the only additional item fitted for this operation was a set of wire gauze filters to try and prevent the engines ingesting too much of the notoriously fine North African sand. Although these worked reasonably well, DK197 spent several days languishing in the blazing August heat due to a badly fitted filter. Small items could cause large problems.

While some of the Halifaxes plied back and forth between England and North Africa, others remained to assist in training the Horsa crews. The dynamic G/Capt Cooper, not content with supervising the action from England, had flown out to Rabat-Salé again on 2 July in DG388: WW, towing DP343. On arrival, he learned that a Horsa had broken its tow during the trip from Rabat-Salé to Kairouan and landed in a ravine where it was considered a write-off due to its inaccessibility. Knowing the enormous risks taken by his Halifax crews to provide these precious gliders, Cooper obtained a Wellington and a volunteer crew for both aircraft and after landing in the narrow confines of the ravine, he successfully towed the Horsa out. Then, on another occasion, when one of the Halifaxes was declared unserviceable, he found a volunteer to act as flight engineer and flew the aircraft back to England, doing his own navigation while the autopilot kept it on course.

Only one other combination was lost by the time the 21st and last Horsa had been delivered safely to Salé on 28 June; EB135: XX went missing, along with its Horsa LG833, on the penultimate ferry flight on 27 June. Four Halifaxes had set out that day, EB139: NN towing LJ171 and the one that was lost, plus DG396: QQ and DJ994: UU without gliders. The last Horsa LG287, towed by DG392: DD, arrived at Kairouan only eleven days before the invasion of Sicily, allowing little time for training with this type.

On the night of 9/10 July, a combined Anglo-American force was launched against Sicily from the six airfields at Kairouan, towed by seven Halifaxes and 28 Albemarles of Nos 295 and 296 Squadrons of 38 Wing, and 109 Dakota aircraft of the USAAF Ninth Air Force[8]. Conditions were far from favourable, with 30 mph winds sweeping across the path of the force. Coupled with the lack of experience of most crews and the difficult nature of the final approach, the force faced disaster. Of the 137 gliders released, 69 came down in the sea as the inexperienced Dakota crews, unused to flak and misjudging the distance, dropped their tow and turned away too far out to sea, most of those in the gliders drowning; a further 56 were scattered far and wide along the south-east coast. Only 12, part of the force towed by the 38 Wing tugs, reached the landing zone and one, a Horsa, came to rest within 300 yards of the vital Ponte Grande Bridge across the Syracuse canal[9].

For the next few nights a small number of Special Air Service (SAS) and reinforcement operations were carried out by 38 Wing tugs, but an attack on Augusta was cancelled at the last minute, just as the crews were preparing for take-off. Last-minute cancellations were always a strain, but particularly so in this case as the Halifaxes had been laboriously refuelled by hand, using four-gallon petrol cans!

Mounted by British forces, *Operation Fustian* was the last airborne assault of the Sicilian campaign; its objective was to seize and hold the Primosole Bridge over the River Simeto. This again was a combined operation using 107 Dakotas and Albemarles to drop paratroops, while Halifaxes towed six Wacos and 11 Horsas, the Albemarles carrying supporting artillerymen and their 6-pounder guns. Only five Halifaxes were available, as F/O Cleaver's aircraft had been written off and another was unserviceable.

The force set out on the evening of 13 July – a date that retained its bad reputation for, due to a breakdown in communications, the glider force flew straight

through the balloon barrage protecting the troop ships off the coast. A short while after, flak began to burst around the formation, claiming at least two of the Albemarles. As the second of these spiralled down in flames, its glider turned for the safety of the coast, narrowly missing a collision with Halifax EB139: NN. These losses were a tragic mistake for the flak was coming from Allied naval vessels which were being attacked by Ju 88s just as the glider force passed overhead, while in the target area enemy flak also claimed several victims. Just after releasing its Horsa, EB139: NN was hit by flak, holing the starboard inner fuel tank and putting the port inner engine out of action. Almost simultaneously, a Halifax directly ahead disintegrated into a ball of flame from a direct hit. This was the only Halifax lost that night; the pilot was the veteran S/Ldr Wilkinson.

The operation met with mixed success, the gliders achieving the best results with 13 of them landing in their correct zones, although one of these crashed. The other four failed to reach the dropping zone, either through damage at take-off or coming down in the sea. Losses were light and, apart from Wilkinson's Halifax, only ten Dakotas and three Albemarles were lost. The bridge was secured on 16 June thus facilitating the advance of the US Seventh and British Eighth Armies in their drive across Sicily.

Although not a success from the airborne side, valuable lessons were learned that were to be applied in future operations over Europe. No 296 Squadron remained in North Africa and Sicily for a further three months for training purposes, while on 4 August 295 Squadron began its return to England for *Operation Elaborate*.

The glider-ferrying operation to North Africa continued for the next two months during which time, although several gliders were lost through various causes and two landed in Portugal, there were only two occasions involving fatalities. The flight between Gibraltar and Portreath was obviously a dangerous section of the transit trip with DK131: DD lost in unknown circumstances on 19 July, followed by DK391 on the same section two days later. The crew of EB139: NN ditched 100 miles east of Gibraltar on a return flight to Portreath on 25 September.

The other direction also took its toll and on 17 August DJ994, towing DP329, went missing on the Portreath-Morocco run. Even when a combination reached Rabat-Salé, danger was ever-present such as on 22 August when, right at the end of its ferry flight, DG393: GG crashed on the approach to the airfield. The UK end also presented dangers, EB130: EE hitting the control tower at Portreath while landing crosswind on 10 September while others just simply disappeared, as happened to EB178 and its crew on 30 October on their return flight after having delivered LH135 on the 15th.

Others came very close to being lost, such as occurred on 18 September when DG396: QQ had set out for Rabat-Salé with Horsa HS102 on tow plus the now usual Beaufighter escort. Three hours later the clear blue sky over the Bay of Biscay appeared to be empty, the Beaufighters having returned to base. P/O J. Stewart-Crump, the flight engineer, was moving forward from the rest bay section when he sighted some tiny specks in the distance ahead. For several agonising minutes, the crew watched as they grew in size and number until they became identifiable as Ju 88s.

Just as the leading Ju 88, prominent by its red spinners, fired a red and yellow Very cartridge, the Halifax's navigator spotted four more Ju 88s at sea level. The nearest flight of four banked around to starboard while the second group of four climbed away to port, gaining height for an attack on the combination from astern. The glider pilot very gallantly requested permission to cast off knowing that this would be the only hope for the Halifax. However, F/O Arthur Norman was

LL218: T, an A Mk V Series IA of 298 Squadron, photographed early in 1944. As with 295 Squadron, unit codes had not been marked on the aircraft, the 40 Halifaxes on strength using individual letters from A to Z then double letters commencing with AA. The individual aircraft letter is clearly visible on the front face of the undercarriage as is the windshield for the ventral dropping hatch beneath the rear fuselage. The number chalked on the side of the fuselage was to help with marshalling aircraft and glider for the mass airborne exercises, the relevant glider carrying the same number; this same system was employed for all major airborne operations into Europe. LL218 survived the war. (J. Stewart-Crump)

The last combination left for Salé on 23 September and the squadron began to wind up its Halifax operations in preparation for converting to Albemarles. During October, the conversion was completed and the last Halifax, DK199, operated with the squadron on the 10th.

The expansion of 38 Wing into a Group, originally suggested in August 1942, had been turned down. A further recommendation for this expansion was tabled in early February 1943 by the AOC-in-C Army Co-operation Command, who controlled 38 Wing, but was again rejected on the grounds of expense in personnel. However, when the results of the Sicilian operations were assessed it became painfully clear that the suggested expansion was indeed necessary along with a considerable reorganisation in order to provide the required facilities for training.

It was finally agreed that 38 Wing would be expanded to Group status with a structure of nine squadrons, four with Albemarles, four with Stirlings and one with Halifaxes. This latter squadron, No 298, formed at Tarrant Rushton on 4 November 1943 with an initial establishment of 17 A Mk V Halifaxes and seven Horsa gliders. Ten crews from 295 Squadron were posted in to form 'A' Flight, while 12 crews from 297 Squadron formed 'B' Flight.

Although training began with Horsa gliders, the squadron's main involvement would be with the new Hamilcar glider. The largest Allied glider to be used operationally, it first appeared at Tarrant Rushton in November 1943 where training with this giant began under the guidance of G/Capt T. Cooper DFC and Maj A. Dale DFC. Specifically designed for transporting heavy equipment, the Hamilcar spanned 110 ft and was over 20 ft in height. With an empty weight of 18,500 lb – nearly 3,000 lb heavier than the a.u.w. of a Horsa – it was capable of carrying a disposable load of 17,500 lb within its capacious 1,920 cu ft interior. Its loaded a.u.w. was 36,000 lb.

Developmental work with towing this giant had been continuing at the Development Unit of the Airborne Forces Experimental Establishment and on 19 August 1942, full load tests were flown at Newmarket by DP206 (the first prototype) with F/Lt Kronfeld and F/O Tuck piloting the glider. A week later tests were carried out with both the Halifax tug aircraft and glider at their maximum all-up weights and were followed on the 29th by jettison tests of the glider's undercarriage from a height of 150 ft, a process later modified by the addition of parachutes to arrest the fall of the undercarriage and tested on 4 September. Four days later DP206 was damaged during the last full-load test when the undercarriage collapsed while taking off from Newmarket. It was replaced by the second prototype, DP210 and DR851, the first of a batch of 10 pre-production Hamilcars. Test-flying continued into the New Year with the Halifax tug carrying out dive tests with a fully loaded Hamilcar from 10,000 ft on 30 January 1943 but, after landing, the Hamilcar's hinged nose door opened prematurely and was ripped off causing substantial damage to both the wing and fuselage. It was the first serious damage throughout the extensive trials with this huge glider. On 26 February, the contractor's trials were flown by the Halifax-Hamilcar combination.

In addition to the glider trials, Halifaxes also took part in those involving the development of a range of equipment and techniques that would be put to use in 1944. Containers were also found to be an effective way to supply ground forces and

determined not to lose his charge while the remotest chance remained and ordered the glider to remain on tow. A distant cloudbank had appeared ahead and the Halifax made a bold run for it just as the Ju 88s turned in for their first attack.

It was clear that the combination had no chance of making the cloud cover but Norman still refused to abandon the helpless glider crew. Moments later however, the decision was taken out of his hands by the unselfish action of the glider crew who released the tow[10]. As the Horsa dived for the sea, the first Ju 88 opened fire from the port beam while a second came in from the port quarter and a third from the starboard bow. Aware that the Horsa had cast off, Norman immediately began to throw the Halifax around in a series of violent evasive corkscrew manoeuvres while still attempting to reach cloud cover. Although the Horsa had cast off, Norman had allowed the tow-rope to remain streaming out behind the Halifax hoping that it might deter close-range attacks. As he kept up the violent evasive manoeuvres, the flight engineer called out the attacks and the rear gunner kept up a steady defensive fire. So violent were the evasive manoeuvres that the flight engineer was hurled bodily in all directions, at one moment pinned against the fuselage by the g-force only to smack his head up against the astrodome in the next, as the Halifax dropped out from underneath him. He also had a fleeting view of the wing tips flexing most pronouncedly upwards, only to reverse their aspect as the aircraft shot upwards again.

The tactics were effective and most of the enemy fire missed its mark. The enemy flight commander must have felt that the situation called for drastic measures for moments later he carried out a head-on attack, the high closing speed forcing Norman to hold his course for fear of a collision if he should break away in the same direction as the Ju 88. At 600 yards, the enemy aircraft opened fire which struck the Halifax as the Ju 88 swept by in a blur of speed. A length of the starboard inner propeller smashed through the fuselage, shot past the flight engineer's legs, hit the gyro units and dropped on to his platform. An enormous gaping hole appeared in the starboard wing, revealing twisted ribs and the collapsed side of the main fuel tank. Petrol poured out, leaving a white trail behind the wing, while the stumps of the three propeller blades rotated jerkily. A moment later the engine cowl broke loose and disappeared astern, baring the damaged engine which, miraculously, did not catch fire. It was obvious that the wing was severely damaged, but Norman was forced to continue his violent evasive manoeuvres. A second burst of fire penetrated the fuselage and burst inside with bright red and orange flashes followed by choking fumes. A large gaping hole in the roof helped to evacuate the offending fumes to reveal the devastation. Emergency rations were scattered, a yellow dinghy pack cover streamed out like a flag and dozens of tufts of woolly material from the upholstery of the shattered rest bay seats littered the floor, sticking to patches of hydraulic fluid from the burst header tank.

The next moment the area of blue sky visible through the hole in the fuselage turned opaque as the Halifax slid into the protection of the cloudbank. A quick check of the damage ruled out the chance of a landing at Gibraltar with its short, crowded runways and, as the flight engineer's parachute was shot to ribbons, the only course open was to head directly for Salé. After a while Norman edged the battered Halifax out of the cloud and the crew were relieved to find themselves alone except for one of their attackers wallowing on the surface of the sea about three miles distant. The Halifax eventually reached Salé and Norman received a well-earned DFC for his efforts and Sgt Grant, the rear gunner, a DFM.

While of poor quality, this is a historically important image showing LK665 of the Airborne Forces Experimental Establishment dropping a jeep and two containers during trials held in 1944. This was also the first Halifax to conduct jeep and gun parachuting tests. Manufactured as a production B Mk V Series I (Special) in October 1943, it was subsequently modified to A Mk V standard, but retained its A Mk VIII (Special) mid-upper turret with its high metal surround. The glider-towing rig behind the tail wheel and ventral parachute dropping hatch, minus the usual windshield, can be seen in silhouette. (M. Wright)

during January, as the Halifax-Hamilcar trials continued, the resident Lancaster carried out experiments with a 2,000 lb version. On 18 March, trials were held with the Halifax tug pulling the Hamilcar off the ground minus its undercarriage because recovery of the gliders was considered essential and it would not always be possible to fit a replacement undercarriage under battle conditions.

Another factor was addressed on 24 April when photographs were taken of the Halifax-Hamilcar combination for recognition purposes as new aircraft types often posed identification problems where friendly fighter forces were involved. Several weeks after the photographic session a new item had made its appearance in the Halifax test programme. On 8 June LK665, the A Mk V, carried out handling trials with a combination comprising a jeep and 75 mm gun slung in the bomb bay. The next day further flight tests were carried out with this combination while another of the Halifaxes continued with the Hamilcar towing to test the automatic release of its undercarriage. Two days later on 11 June, the jeep and gun combination underwent their final dropping trial from LK665 at Stapleton.

On 17 June, dropping tests were carried out from a Halifax using a mixed load of containers and dummies and although both were already in frequent use by the Special Duties squadrons, the airborne forces requirement was somewhat different. For this latter duty, the two had to be dropped in quick succession and involved a large number of personnel rather than the one or two associated with agent drops. The initial tests for these progressed to a mixture of live and dummy drops at Stapleton over the two-day period of the 21st and 22nd. A 500 lb container was test-dropped on the 29th and followed the next day by another new combination that involved live drops over Stapleton, but this time while towing a Horsa glider. This latter process had increased in proportion by 12 August when a stick of 20 paratroops was dropped from a Halifax-Horsa combination over Sherburn-in-Elmet. Five days later the number of paratroops had risen to 30.

By October 1943, the Hamilcar trials were almost completed and the Halifaxes were now focusing on the container and jeep/75 mm gun drops, the well-used Mk II and Mk V aircraft having been joined earlier that month by another A Mk V, LK988. The 75 mm gun drops were carried out at Sherburn-in-Elmet starting on the 14th and the number of container drops also rose steadily, with 14 dropped on 18 October and 15 on 6 November. The poor weather of January 1944 did little to impede the development programme with the Halifaxes engaged in trials with a pannier which on the 7th, was test-dropped along with dummy parachutists for the first time. Dropping trials of collapsible motorcycles[11] commenced on 9 March and were followed on the 18th by a 4,000 lb container drop. On 9 May the jeep and gun combination were trialled with six live parachutists and on 29 July a mixture of 15 containers and one stick of paratroopers were dropped, along with a 75 mm gun. By then the war in Europe had reached a very active stage.

Bad weather and other problems had delayed 298 Squadron's flying programme and by the end of January 1944, only a limited number of flights had been made. However, some idea of the operational efficiency achieved during this limited training may be judged from the take-off time accomplished in *Exercise Co-operation*. During early February, 11 Halifaxes carrying paratroops were airborne in 4 min 30 sec, followed by three Stirlings and 10 Halifaxes, each towing a Horsa in 9 min 55 sec.

On 5 February, a third flight 'C' was formed, raising the squadron's crew strength to 40 by the end of the month; the additional crews however, were to form the nucleus of a new squadron. The weather, which had hindered training, finally cleared early in the month and allowed for the introduction of a 24-hour flying schedule. Progress increased rapidly and in the two-month period ending in March 1,200 flights had been carried out including 400 at night. By 6 June, this figure had risen to 2,800.

On 16 March No 644 Squadron was formed from 298 Squadron's 'C' Flight with half of the latter's 40 crews and Halifaxes transferred into the new squadron, providing an establishment of 18 aircraft and two reserves for each unit. The new Squadron was divided into two Flights, 'C' and 'D' (the other resident squadron having 'A' and 'B' Flights), with code letters '2P' used for the former and '9U' for the latter.

Though the date for the invasion of Europe was still an unknown quantity, it was recognised that to get the assembled force of gliders airborne into a compact stream would require much practice as well as for the massed landing aspect. Among the pilots posted to 644 Squadron was Fl/Sgt H. Barr RCAF who recorded the increasing work with the Hamilcar in May. "*Mass Hamilcar lifts were carried out at dusk on the 13th and again in the morning of the 14th. Eight combinations of tugs and glider lifts were achieved in the morning of the 15th, and again in the evening of the same day...... At dusk on the 18th, a mass take-off of 24 combinations of Halifaxes and Hamilcars took place. Half of these crews were from 644 and half from 298 Squadron...... May 22nd, a mass Halifax-Hamilcar take-off, with 30 combinations taking part today, appeared to be a great success. It was once again a combined effort by both Tarrant Rushton squadron crews. The only mishap was an undershot approach by the last glider down. All combinations were off in 22 minutes. Not bad.*" The accident rate was almost nil, but one fatality occurred on 26 May, when a daytime mass take-off was cancelled because of low cloud. The weather cleared late in the day and individual crews were scheduled for two-hour Hamilcar towing sessions at night. One of the RCAF pilots Fl/Sgt A. Wood and his crew began their scheduled two hours at 22.00 hrs, to be followed by Fl/Sgt Barr's crew from midnight until 02.00 hrs. The latter had just climbed aboard their Halifax to do the checks and warm up the engines when news came that Wood had crashed. The subsequent inquest and findings angered some of the

crews as they ignored essential details. Wood had been allotted the east-west runway, the shortest one at Tarrant Rushton and as the wind died down to almost nothing, he found it more and more difficult to get enough speed for take-off and made several requests, all of which were refused by the senior control tower officer, for a change to use the longer runway. That information failed to be included in the subsequent inquest, which found that "*a very difficult towing job*" was in progress and "*none of the crew were strapped in.*" Wood, as pilot, was wearing his full Sutton harness, the rear gunner was in his turret, and the others on board at their stations as normal. Tarrant Rushton sat on the crest of a hill and the Halifax had ended up crashing below the airfield level, indicative of the low lift factor, killing Wood and Wolf, the gunner; Stewart, the bomb aimer, died of his injuries next day. Two others survived with minor injuries.

One positive consequence of this event was that Barr, a friend of Wood's, while having a quiet drink in a local country pub the next day met a Land Army girl who presented him with a small bundle of fur, a Beagle puppy. Having cycled back to base with it in his battledress, Barr and his crew examined the puppy and Barr named him Flak (he was white with splashes of black and brown). He soon had the run of the station and became not just Barr's dog but the squadron and station mascot; he was to have an interesting operational career, as noted further on.

Halsall, now at Tarrant Rushton with 'C' Squadron of the Glider Pilot's Regiment, commanded by Major Alex Dale DSO, recalled, "*Working towards D-Day the training was concentrated on mass landings and take-offs as the tighter the 'trains' were going down the runway, the easier it was to keep close during flight. We often had four 'trains' going down the runway at one time.*" The practice would pay off handsomely on D-Day.

One of the new techniques evolved for glider warfare was the use of a few specialist crews trained to land in extremely confined areas near key points to obtain a tactical advantage. A special training programme for selected Horsa and Halifax crews was established for this purpose at Tarrant Rushton under F/Lt T. Grant, DSO. The technique involved the tug's navigator working out the course for the glider pilot to fly once released, the only additional equipment fitted to the glider being a gyro-compass; although simple in essence, the required degree of perfection could only be achieved through constant practice. During this working up period in preparation for the impending invasion of Europe, the 38 Group aircraft were fitted with the additional navigation aids, *Gee* and *Rebecca Mk II*. Because the serviceability rate of the Merlin 22 engine was approximately four times that of the Merlin XX, a decision was also taken to re-equip the Group's Halifaxes with the later marque of engine. Unfortunately, a shortage of Merlin 22 engines slowed down this programme and by March only 23 of the 40 Halifaxes had been refitted.

The mass of aerial activity during the weeks leading up to D-Day could hardly have been kept secret but every effort was made to deny watchers from gaining any significant information. One method used by the crews was to integrate their mass air exercises with Special Duties operations dropping supplies to Resistance groups in France, Belgium and Holland on specific nights. Five days before D-Day the tug and glider crews were taken to an undisclosed location where, records Barr, "*We were shown a model layout of the landing area with every detail set in place; bridges, roads, towns, pubs, rivers, even hedgerows and farm buildings. Two bridges in particular, one over the Orne River and the other over a canal, were laid out. A motion picture was shown giving a graphic picture of a simulated glider approaching the target landing area. On our return to base we were confined to the station.*"

Nos 38 and 46 Groups, without the benefit of further information, were ordered to requisition for special black and white paint and the matter raised little interest. Although the reasons behind this order would become clear at the beginning of June, the first possible inkling about why this paint was to be requisitioned came in an Official Instruction issued on 3 February 1944. This stipulated that the marking of the centre section of the lower wings of Tempest and Typhoon aircraft with black and white recognition bands[12] would cease from first light 7 February. Subsequently, on 3 June, an order was issued that all aircraft were to be marked with black and white stripes for recognition purposes. However, when bad weather caused a postponement of the landings the order was cancelled and an IMMEDIATE-SECRET signal sent out again on 4 June. This notified that from first light on 5 June, aircraft could be seen with black and white striping but no aircraft so marked was to approach within 20 miles of the enemy-held coast. A combination of five stripes, three white with two black dividing them, were specified and concise details for multi-engine aircraft were 24-inch wide stripes, placed one stripe's width outboard of outer engine nacelle on wings and 18 inches forward of leading edge of tail plane, encircling the fuselage. National markings and code letters were not to be compromised. These markings did not apply to Bomber Command aircraft.

The speed with which these markings were applied and the number of aircraft involved resulted in some relatively rough applications, not that that detracted from their purpose. Nevertheless, the tragedy of the aerial operations over Sicily had not been forgotten and all gliders and tugs were identified most positively. However, as it was realised that once aircraft were so marked security would be compromised, the instructions for their application to aircraft within 38 Group were timed for D minus 1, the day before the scheduled landings in Europe.

Three principal glider operations were planned for *Operation Neptune*, the airborne phase of *Operation Overlord*. The first involved the specialist *coup de main* force that was to capture, intact, two bridges, one over the Orne River and one over the Caen canal. These bridges were vital to the success of the main operation as they

A summer afternoon at Tarrant Rushton showing the preparations for Operation Mallard, the final phase of the D-Day airborne assault by Nos 298 and 644 Squadrons using two Horsas, 30 Hamilcars and 32 Halifaxes. All 32 Halifaxes are visible and on the runway with F/O Blake's LL402: 9U-F hitched to the first Horsa. From the front, on the right is 298 Squadron's 8A-J then 644 Squadron's LL331: 9U-K (both still fitted with three-bladed propellers), LL301: 9U-R, LL352: 9U-Q, LL328: 9U-Y, LL342: 2P-L; then 298 Squadron's 8T-G, 8T-H and 8T-K. All Halifaxes and gliders are wearing the full invasion markings applied the evening before. LL402 would fall victim to flak over Dordrecht while on an SOE operation on 2 October.

would provide communication for the 6th Airborne Division with the left flank of the beachhead forces. For *Operation Deadstick* six Halifaxes, LL335: G, LL355: K, LL406: T of 298 Squadron and LL344: P, LL350: Z, LL218:2P-N of 644 Squadron, each towed a Horsa carrying the troops responsible for securing these objectives. The force attacked shortly after midnight and the gliders were released at about 6,000 ft; they then flew for a determined number of seconds on one bearing, then another and so on until their targets came into view. Meanwhile the Halifaxes, three carrying small bomb loads, continued on their original course with two dropping their bombs on a large cement factory in Caen to mask their real purpose while the third, encountering cloud, was forced to bring its bombs back[13]. Achieving complete surprise, the gliders landed on the approaches to the bridges where, after brief and bitter fighting, they were both captured intact, despite the fact that the Orne bridge force was one glider short. It had landed eight miles away on a bridge over the Dives River.

The main glider operations of the day involved a force of 350, the responsibility for towing them being divided equally between Nos 38 and 46 Groups. For their part in *Operation Tonga*, the first major assault of the day, both Halifax squadrons provided an identical force of 17 aircraft to tow two Hamilcars and 15 Horsas. The Horsas carried mostly six-pounder guns and jeeps, their tug aircraft each carrying nine containers, while the Hamilcars carried 17-pounder guns and Morris tractors of a Royal Artillery anti-tank unit. The gliders and their tugs had been marshalled on the runway adjacent to that used by the *coup de main* force.

Weather conditions were bad with low cloud and heavy rain but began to moderate over the Channel and improved steadily as the force approached the French coast, even though patches of cloud were encountered well below the release height of 1,500 ft. No 298 Squadron lost three of its gliders during the early stages with two landing in England and a third in the Channel. Heavy flak from the German coastal defences cost them Halifax LL348: K, but fortunately the crew survived; C. Anderson, the pilot thought he had counted all the crew baling out and then made his own escape but the flight engineer was still in the Halifax when it crashed, fortunately on a fairly even keel and he only suffered a fractured pelvis. The rest of the crew returned safely to Tarrant Rushton. No 644 Squadron fared a little better, losing only two Horsas, both of which landed in England. The remaining gliders all reached their correct landing zones despite one releasing three and a half miles short and another breaking loose six miles short.

Operation Mallard, scheduled to reinforce all of the troops dropped earlier, was the third and final phase of the day's airborne assault, the largest daylight operation ever attempted up to this time, the success of which vindicated the exponents of daylight tactics. A force of 256 gliders was used with 17 fighter squadrons flying escort, its principal aim being to reinforce all the airborne troops already in France. The composition of the gliders for this phase was reversed with each of the Halifax

squadrons towing 15 Hamilcars and one Horsa. As with the earlier operations, the Halifaxes towing the Horsas each carried an additional load of nine containers to be released in the dropping zone. As for the earlier mass operation, the Halifaxes were assembled along each side of the main runway and one Halifax from each alternatively moved across, was hitched to its glider and immediately moved off; the long hours of training had paid off handsomely.

This time all of the gliders reached the dropping zone safely where a 100% release was achieved. However, enemy tanks were sufficiently close to hit the tugs and 298 Squadron lost a second Halifax that day. Barr, in 2P-Q, provides an eyewitness account of the incident, which is interesting as it attests to the low altitude at which the Halifaxes were flying. *"We were fairly well in line astern formation heading for home, when I noticed a German tank...set up on the rise of a hill, so that its gun could be elevated to fire at our low flying tugs. The aircraft in front of us was hit, and shortly smoke began to pour from the fuselage. The tank fired at us as well but never scored a hit. Following the smoking kite down towards the Channel, we observed the ditching* [of LL407:H] *Following proper procedure, we circled the downed plane several times, at the same time turning on our distress call over the Wireless, and also firing off Very Pistol colours of the day. We observed the crew exiting the plane, and as it remained afloat, they stood on the wings and waved. After about 20 minutes of circling and distress call, we observed a small navy ship making a bee-line for the ditched aircraft. Assured that they would soon be picked up, we headed back to base, after cancelling our distress signal. It turned out to be a Canadian pilot, R. I. 'Chippy' Carpenter and crew of 298 Squadron in 8T-H-Howe. They were all back at Tarrant Rushton in a few days.*

"On return.... Carpenter and crew reported that a single small cannon shell from a Tiger tank had ignited two wheel covers that were in the parachute well area of the fuselage. Wheel covers protected the brake shoes from the dripping oil and grease from the....engines, and they had been thrown into the aircraft by the ground crew. This practice was certainly frowned upon. The crew, with their small fire fighting equipment, were unable to extinguish the fire, and the only solution....was to ditch in the English Channel."

Thus, neither squadron lost a single man during the invasion operations.

Four days later both squadrons were again active over the invasion area with six Halifaxes from each carrying out resupply missions to the British airborne troops. Each aircraft carried in its bomb bay a jeep, a six-pounder gun and six containers, all being successfully dropped from 1,000 ft. Experiments with this unique type of load had begun almost exactly one year previously at Stapleton. The two Halifax squadrons maintained these resupply missions until 27 June, carrying out several specialist operations during the period. These included one by 298 Squadron on the 17th when four of its Halifaxes dropped a mixed force of paratroops, jeeps and containers to SAS troops in France. Another worthy of mention was a solo effort by 644 Squadron's LL326: 9U-N, which towed a Hamilcar, flown by Capt Halsall MC, loaded with Spitfire wings to Airstrip B on the beachhead on 4 July. Halsall remarked that the take-off from Airstrip B2 for the return flight was "*very dodgy*" and not repeated. These 'airstrips' were not much more than a cleared strip of ground and far from ideal for such a large glider and its tug, even when unladen.

With the end of the resupply missions both Halifax squadrons returned to their former occupation of training, mixed in with a fairly large proportion of SOE, SAS and tactical bombing operations. On 14 July LL402: 9U-F of No 644 Squadron set out for an SOE mission, crossing the Channel just before 18.00 hrs. S/Ldr Norman sighted a V-1 flying bomb coming towards him and altered course to pass close to it on a reciprocal track. Alerting Sgt Grant, the rear gunner, he ordered him to train his guns beam-on and fire on command. Just before the V-1 passed them, Norman gave the order to fire hoping to lay down a field of fire through which the missile would have to pass. Regrettably, it did just that, without visible effect.

Some idea of the weight of work undertaken by the Halifaxes can be assessed from 298 Squadron's monthly report for August 1944. In addition to other commitments, it carried out 156 SOE and SAS missions, delivering 999 containers and 146 packages for the loss of three Halifaxes. One 644 Squadron pilot came up with an idea for increasing the payload on SOE missions; by keeping the bomb cell doors open in the wings, a double load of containers could be carried strapped together, one on top of the other. The idea worked and was soon put into practice.

The two squadrons undertook intensive Hadrian towing training and operated together again with their first sorties with the type on 5 August. On this occasion, six Halifaxes from 298 Squadron LL347: J, LL406: M, LL361: F, LL271: B, LL401: T and LL346: U and five from 644 Squadron LL326: 9U-N, LL402: 9U-F, LL301: 9U-R, LL400: 2P-T and LL218: 2P-N each towed Hadrians to Brittany as part of an SAS operation. Each glider carried a jeep plus three men and ancillary equipment. The only trouble occurred when a 298 Squadron tug was forced to turn back immediately after take-off at the request of the Hadrian pilot after a panel on the glider had come loose and was blown off; otherwise the mission was successful.

It was during one of 644 Squadron's SOE operations on 8 August that 38 Group very nearly lost one of its dynamic leaders. F/Lt Cleaver had been scheduled to carry out a drop but his bomb aimer and flight engineer fell ill at the last moment. G/Capt Cooper volunteered his services as a bomb aimer and F/Lt Stewart-Crump stood in for the flight engineer. The flight went smoothly until they reached the dropping point where some doubt was expressed as to the accuracy of the signal from the ground party. Cleaver left the decision to Cooper who finally elected to go in for the drop only to be greeted by searchlights and a hail of flak from the trap. By sheer luck, Cleaver managed to get LL312 away without too much damage and reached base safely.

The Allied armies continued to fight their way across north-west Europe and by late September, the First US Army had advanced as far as the Siegfried Line, while the Third US Army had established a bridgehead over the Moselle and the British Second Army occupied a line along the Albert and Escaut canals from Antwerp to Maastricht. The enemy had behind them three natural lines of defence in the Maas, Waal and Lower Rhine Rivers plus the Maas-Waal canal to ensure against any northern thrust by the 21st Army Group. Field Marshal Montgomery planned to advance over these three rivers and secure a crossing over the Rhine itself and into the Grave-Nijmegen-Arnhem area. The 1st Allied Airborne Army was given the job of capturing and holding intact the main river and canal crossings. *Operation Market Garden* was about to be launched.

Nos 38 and 46 Group aircraft carried out all the Airborne Pathfinder paratroop drops and glider towing, plus resupply missions in the Arnhem sector. The US IX Troop Carrier Command undertook all the main parachute drops and in the Nijmegen-Grave sector, they were responsible for all tasks except towing the British Airborne Corps Headquarters, this being left to 38 Group. The Eindhoven sector was also the sole responsibility of the US IX TCC.

Briefing and the marshalling of aircraft at Tarrant Rushton was completed by 18.00 hrs on 16 September and at 10.20 hrs the following morning the first combination rolled down the runway followed by the rest of the assembled force at 45-second intervals. The formation, split into three parallel streams spaced one and a half miles apart, consisted of seven Hamilcars and 13 Horsas from 298 Squadron and seven Hamilcars and 14 Horsas from 644 Squadron. Both squadrons suffered minor mishaps; engine trouble forced a 298 Squadron combination to return after 20 minutes while a 644 Squadron Halifax lost its Hamilcar through tow-rope failure but the glider managed to reach the coast. Weather over the target area was fair but hazy near the ground but the gliders from both squadrons were seen to land on the north bank of the Rhine. Two of the Hamilcars overturned on the soft ground, causing the loss of their 17-pounder guns. Little or no flak was experienced and the Halifaxes returned safely.

Bad weather caused a three-hour delay on the second day of the operation when 298 Squadron towed eight Hamilcars and eight Horsas, and 644 Squadron seven Hamilcars and eight Horsas. Flak was more intense this time and 298 Squadron

The comparative size of Hamilcar to Halifax can be judged in this airborne view of a combination during a training exercise, the Hamilcar having a broader wingspan.

suffered damage to one of its Halifaxes, the navigator being injured. No 644 Squadron escaped flak damage but lost two of its gliders over the Channel, only one of them reaching the coast. This glider, flown by Capt Halsall crash-landed at Andover after casting off its tow when an engine on the tug aircraft caught fire.

The third day's operations were plagued by increasingly bad weather which delayed the Halifaxes for nearly five hours. Finally, at 12.10 hrs, the first combination was airborne on the final phase of this disastrous operation. No 298 Squadron was towing 10 Horsas as the five Hamilcars that were to have been used were stood down, while 644 Squadron was left to tow a lone Hamilcar[14], in company with 10 Horsas. Weather conditions over the Channel had deteriorated slightly and although they began to improve over the Continent, a persistent haze made visibility poor.

By now, the enemy defences had improved greatly and German fighters appeared in strength. Because of a misunderstanding, there was no fighter escort for the glider force and some of the 298 Squadron crews later reported seeing several gliders shot down; but fortunately, there were no losses amongst its own charges. Despite damage to two of the Halifaxes, all of the gliders were released over the correct dropping zone. No 644 Squadron encountered very stiff resistance during the final run-in, and several Halifaxes were damaged by flak and three gliders failed to reach the dropping zone, two through broken tow-ropes. The third combination had reached the Group Rendezvous point but a flak hit near the tail caused the Horsa to dive towards the ground. The tug pilot, P/O McConville, dived LL305: 2P-A with the glider in an attempt to hold its nose up but the tow-rope snapped under the strain and the Horsa went straight into the ground. Elsewhere in the area, Bernard Halsall was not having much luck but was determined to get to the battle so he crash-

A view showing a jeep and six-pounder artillery piece loaded into the bomb bay of one of the Halifaxes. The jeep was loaded facing backwards and had its giant parachute pack fixed in the rear seat area while the artillery piece faced forwards. In this instance, eight containers had been loaded into the two inboard bomb cells in each wing using the double load method with doors left open. The amount of drag this form of non-aerodynamic load produced had little effect on the Halifax's performance. (S. Crump)

Halifax A Mk VII, 'N-Nan' seen while being loaded with a jeep and what appears to be a six-pounder artillery piece with the huge parachute pack for the jeep attached to the rear section seat area. Crash panniers were fitted to both the jeep and artillery piece where wheels or gun trailing arm touched the ground. When photographed, the Halifax carried no squadron codes but the aircraft letter 'N' can be seen on the front face of the Messier casting of the undercarriage. (D. Vincent)

landed the glider in Belgium, unloaded the lorry and anti-tank gun and its crew and drove to Nijmegen but was prevented from going any further. The battle for Arnhem is frequently referred to as a tragic failure and the ground battle is outside the scope of this work; however, with all things considered, the airborne side of the operation was not a failure despite the final outcome. During the battle, the main glider force lifted 4,500 men, 95 guns and 544 jeeps to a position some 60 miles to the rear of the enemy lines and achieved this with a considerable degree of success and relatively few losses.

One of the unlisted participants in the Arnhem operation was F/O Barr's earlier mentioned dog, Sergeant Flak. Soon after being given to Barr, he became a fixture with the crew and on the Squadron flew on operations with Barr's crew. "He was not exactly crazy about the long trips that we did, particularly if it was cold; although we did not fly very high it got pretty damn cold and on more than one occasion I saw him lying down below me on the steps near the navigator and wireless operators position shivering. I knew he was cold but there was not much I could do about it. He went to Arnhem with us and did quite a few ops with us." With Flak having become part of an operational crew, Barr reckoned he was entitled to be at least a Sergeant and while he may not have enjoyed the cold, he loved the flying and went on operations and training flights with other crews. Just how many operations Barr never discovered but a number of other crews casually mentioned having taken him.

While the Arnhem operation was in progress, one of the Albemarle squadrons, No 296, was withdrawn to convert to Halifaxes with the crews being detached in batches to No 1665 HCU. Their glider-towing training with Halifaxes commenced in October when the first of the A Mk Vs arrived from Tarrant Rushton; these were surplus as 298 and 644 Squadrons were in the process of re-equipping with the more powerful A Mk III. The other Albemarle squadron at Earls Colne, No 297, also converted to Halifaxes, again using A Mk Vs from Tarrant Rushton.

Both these squadrons continued their training programme interspersed with SAS, SOE and bombing missions. On 28 September, an A Mk III Halifax had been attached for experimental purposes to 298 Squadron then, in October, as noted above, both 298 and 644 Squadrons began converting to the more powerful A Mk IIIs. No 298 Squadron was the first to take its new charges into operations, ten being used for resupply operations on 4/5 November, with 644 Squadron joining operations again on the 10/11th, flying on SOE and resupply sorties.

SOE operations were dangerous in the extreme as the aircraft was alone and had to stay at very low level throughout. Finding the right small spot and then getting the agent or stores dropped accurately called for great skill and nerve. On 1 October, three SOE drops were scheduled and although one was cancelled at the last minute, the two crews left for Holland as planned. F/O Vince Blake's crew left first in 9U-F for a Nico 1 drop just east of Rotterdam. They found the reception committee and dropped 15 containers and two packages just as light flak opened up from all sides, forcing Blake to dodge his way at low-level across Rotterdam while the damage was assessed. The port inner had been hit and the rear gunner reported his turret

hydraulics were not working but the most serious problems were in the nose section, the navigator's area being badly damaged, all maps and equipment destroyed and the navigator, F/O F. Darling, wounded. F/O Darling recalled: "I had just left my navigator seat and had climbed the steps up to the small landing beside Vince. My back was to my vacated seat and I was looking out of the starboard window when I was hit in the backside with shrapnel. I guess I immediately blacked out, for some time. I regained consciousness in the rest bay."

Seeing the navigator collapse, F/O W. Deacon, the wireless operator, despite his own injuries, left his position and, calling to Fl/Sgt H. Harris to help him, managed to get Darling back to the rest bay area between the main spars. Meanwhile Blake had managed to inch the Halifax up to 1,500 ft and Deacon returned to his wireless set and sent out a Mayday call to the emergency landing field at RAF Woodbridge. They received permission for a straight-in landing but that was still an hour's flying time away. Once clear of the enemy coast the rear gunner came forward to be ready to help Fl/Sgt E. Gillies, the bomb aimer, get Darling out of the aircraft immediately. Arriving over Woodbridge Blake found that fog had formed and the FIDO system was lit and, seeing that the runway was clear, went straight in for a landing. However, the hydraulics had been damaged and the starboard main wheel just dropped but the port one appeared to have locked down. With the flaps and one engine also inoperable, a fast landing had to be made at about 120 mph. Aiming to keep the Halifax level on just the port wheel for as long as possible, Blake managed to keep the starboard wing up but eventually, at about 60 mph, the wing lost its lift and began to drop. Meanwhile, Gillies had jettisoned the escape hatch over the rest bay and was standing half out, ready to lift Darling clear when Smith held him up. Then, the port undercarriage collapsed under the load and the Halifax careered on to a stop, having demolished part of the FIDO installation while throwing Gillies about and dislocating his shoulder – but they were down and safe. Darling was sent for immediate surgery and made a complete recovery but Blake missed the debriefing because of his own injuries, loss of blood and shock.

Interestingly, the other crew sent out were also hit by light flak while making their drop on Rummy II about a dozen miles north of Rotterdam. The port inner engine was hit and was shut down but the crew escaped injury. For his determined effort, the pilot of this aircraft received the DFC. As for Blake's efforts .... the manner in which awards were given remains one of the greatest mysteries of the Second World War!

Part of the constant cycle of crew training was that of fighter affiliation exercises. For the Tarrant Rushton crews this was done with the Spitfires based at Henstridge airfield, one of which was later stationed at Tarrant Rushton to facilitate this training. The Halifax crews sometimes felt they were being sent on training exercises simply to keep them occupied and the Spitfire pilots seem to have felt a little restless themselves at times. On 4 December F/O Barr and crew were on a fighter affiliation exercise over Bodmin Moor in Cornwall when after half an hour of attacks and evasion tactics the Spitfire pilot called them and asked if they had had enough... and

The mixed force of A Mk IIIs and VIIs of No 298 Squadron with No 644 Squadron's A Mk IIIs at Woodbridge on 24 March 1945, for Operation Varsity. On the runway are 48 Hamilcars with 12 Horsas at the far end. On the left are No 298 Squadron's NA344: 8T-Q, 8A-M, NA347: 8A-J, NA568: 8T-E and MZ966: 8T-K. Unlike the gliders, none of the Halifaxes now wore invasion markings as it was not intended that they should operate from bases in Europe and the markings were detrimental to the bombing and Special Duties drops that were being flown at night.

would they like to do a bit of low flying instead? Barr was happy to oblige and the two aircraft went off across the moor at about 50 or 60 feet and low enough for Barr to have to ease the nose up when a tree appeared. Suddenly, he was astonished to see the Spitfire appear from under the nose of 2P-Y, going in the same direction and completing a slow roll that he had started as he reached the rear of the Halifax. Barr had just about got over the sight when he was summoned to W/Cdr Archer's office the next day regarding a complaint about a low flying Halifax and Spitfire the previous day. Archer remarked that Barr's Halifax was the only one that could have been there and asked if he had seen any other aircraft, and if so, had he by chance noted its code letters? Barr said he had not seen another aircraft and Archer, a very popular senior officer, smiled and dismissed him. However, the point had been made – no more low flying.

With the last of the A Mk Vs having been replaced by December, the newer A Mk III Halifaxes were proving popular with their increased power and the introduction of the Mark IX automated bombsight, which computed much of the data that had previously to be entered by the bomb aimer. It also aided in determining wind drift for the navigator, something that was invaluable on low-level work where wind direction near the ground could and did vary from the predictions for the higher levels.

The arrival of the New Year saw the routine of constant training, Special Duties and SAS operations, plus some bombing, continue unabated with Norway now included on the list of dropping zones being serviced. Typical of SOE operations was the dropping of an agent near Rotterdam by a 296 Squadron aircraft in February. To cover up for the presence of a lone heavy bomber at low altitude, a bridge in the city was to be bombed as a diversion by the Halifax immediately after dropping the agent. Unfortunately, the DR compass toppled at the critical moment leaving the Halifax to fly along the river and through the city at 50 ft before the compass began to operate again.

In February, a few A Mk VIIs began to appear on both 298 and 644 Squadrons to supplement the A Mk IIIs, with both squadrons continuing their mixture of tactical bombing and SD sorties while awaiting the call for the final major airborne operation of the war. In March, the long-awaited Rhine crossing was launched and all four Halifax squadrons readied themselves for what was to be their last wartime mass glider operation. The squadrons were paired off, with 296 and 297 Squadrons operating a force of 60 Halifaxes from Earls Colne while 298 and 644 moved to Woodbridge for the operation, also with 60 Halifaxes.

The object was to land elements of the 6th Airborne Division on four landing zones near Wesel in company with US Airborne forces to enlarge the bridgehead expected to have been established by the ground forces the previous night. Remembering the lessons learned from previous operations, every possible aid was provided to identify the various dropping zones precisely with *Eureka* and compass beacons set up at the various turning points. Additionally and immediately prior to crossing over the Rhine, *Eureka* beacons and coloured strips with distinctive letter panels were set up as a guide for the airborne component of the crossing.

The Woodbridge squadrons were split into two flights for the operation, W/Cdr Law-Wright DSO, DFC leading 12 Horsa combinations and W/Cdr Archer AFC of 644 Squadron, leading 48 Hamilcar combinations. Nos 296 and 297 Squadrons towed a combined force of 60 Horsas between them. On the night before the operation, 50% of the combinations had their tows in place and were lined up along approximately one-third of the length of the runway at Earls Colne while the remainder lined its perimeter from where they were fed into the take-off sequence.

Weather conditions were favourable and all combinations were dispatched on time with the massed formations of 1,500 aircraft and 1,300 gliders presenting an awe-inspiring sight to those watching the armada from below. Complete Allied mastery of the air, so vital to an operation of this nature, was evidenced by the fact that the German fighters were conspicuous by their absence. Two tugs of the Woodbridge force returned early with engine trouble and one glider broke loose soon after take-off. With the Channel safely behind them, a further two Hamilcars parted company with their tugs because of broken tow-ropes, one over France, the other near Brussels, while near Goch a Hamilcar lost its tail unit, went out of control and crashed.

Despite the laid-out aids, a smokescreen along the Rhine's east bank made it difficult for the glider pilots to pick out their correct landing zones. However, the main danger was not flak, which nevertheless claimed quite a few victims, but rather the trailing tow-ropes and the risk of collision. Apart from one glider of the Woodbridge force, which landed prematurely on the west bank of the river, the remainder released correctly and for once, luck favoured Bernard Halsall who landed his Hamilcar, loaded with a lorry and anti-tank gun and its crew, safely in the landing zone. Five Halifaxes were lost to flak and three others were damaged. No 298 Squadron had the distinction of operating the first seven A Mk VII Halifaxes to go into action during the operation. Some pertinent points about resupply missions had also been learned from Arnhem and this time, instead of one dropping point, six were chosen. Additionally, three Halifaxes were specially equipped with extra radio facilities and acted as master supply aircraft to direct these operations. *Operation Varsity* was undoubtedly a success and marked a fitting end to a type of operation developed to a high degree of efficiency through the long and bitter lessons of experience.

The liberation of Norway finally achieved; A Mk VII NA338: 9U-D of No 644 Squadron's 'D' Flight in the foreground was part of the force that, finally, landed after cessation of hostilities, bringing SAS troops and other personnel to secure the airfields and major military objectives. (H. Barr)

F/O H. Barr's crew pose for the photographer with their mascot and frequent operational companion, Sergeant Flak, in front of MZ159: 2P-T. It was this crew that landed at Gardermoen on 8 May. From left to right are, Fl/Sgt J. Sanders, Fl/Sgt A. Basnett, Fl/Sgt W. Howlett, Fl/Sgt T. Smith holding Sgt Flak and Fl/Sgt J. Greenstock. (H. W. Barr)

The remainder of the war in Europe was spent on SOE operations, mainly to Norway and Denmark. However, two final, if somewhat peaceful, operations awaited the Halifax squadrons. On 8 May, the day hostilities in Europe ceased, personnel and equipment of the 1st Airborne Division were landed at Copenhagen by a force of Halifaxes, Stirlings and USAAF C-46 Commandos; No 38 Group maintained subsequent resupply missions at intervals throughout the remainder of the month.

The final airborne operation of the war, aptly titled *Doomsday*, involved the transfer of 7,000 troops and 2,000 tons of equipment and supplies to Norway by No 38 Group. The object was to land Allied troops immediately following the German surrender to occupy Oslo, Stavanger and Kristiansund; planned to be carried out in four phases between 9 and 13 May, the weather, as so many times before, proved unfavourable and the operation was delayed 36 hours.

A rapidly approaching storm front caught 644 Squadron's Halifaxes just before they reached Norway, forcing all but two to turn back. One landed at Gardermoen, but the other ended up at Fornebu, about four miles south-west of Oslo. F/Lt H. Barr, the pilot, recalls, *"We had a jeep in the bomb bay and half a dozen soldiers on board. As we approached Norway, we could see heavy cloud and knew from our previous dropping operations at night just how hazardous this country was. If we were going to get into Gardermoen we were going to be lucky as the cloud base was down to about 1,500 ft."* This was lower than the surrounding peaks and Barr was now becoming concerned about the fuel situation. He decided to make his way up Oslo fjord hoping to find a break in the overcast, purposely keeping low. *"With the drag of the jeep below the bomb bay and the doors open consumption was higher, and Norway was on the limit of our endurance under normal conditions. I decided to try and get away from the west coast and*

the bad weather and fly up Oslo Fjord . . . Once in the fjord it got narrower and narrower and I was still down very low. I knew that the war was over but was not so sure that the Germans did, so I kept in a position where if they opened fire they would hit the other side of the fjord. In the Oslo area, I climbed a little, but the cloud base was just as low and there was no way to reach Gardermoen. We spotted an airfield to the south and I decided to try and get in there... so I called the tower on the Darkie (emergency) frequency, identifying who we were and asking permission to land." The reply was in German so Barr made it very clear that he wanted an English-speaker on the microphone. The next voice was speaking perfect English with a proper British accent.

That accomplished, he was cleared to land but the airfield, which sat in a cup-shaped depression, had one short runway. He asked for a green flare to indicate the runway to be used – and got the short one. *"I had to approach downhill and get on to the strip just as fast as I could because I was pretty well loaded and I did not think that I could carry out an overshoot... I touched down about a quarter of the way down the strip with full flap on, but I was still rolling very fast when I saw some glasshouses at the end of the strip. I had to stop or turn or do something before we hit them. During training I had once ground-looped an aircraft [W1173 of 1659 HCU] through turning too fast and collapsed the undercarriage: I thought 'Oh boy, here goes another undercarriage, and if that goes the jeep gets wrecked.' I started to swerve to the left and around the buildings, everything shuddered but the undercarriage hung on and I was pleased when we stopped safely. I left the Halifax almost where we pulled up because I did not know what kind of reception we were going to get now that we were on the ground."*

In the odd twilight atmosphere that now existed, Barr was met first by Norwegian resistance men who then took him to meet the German reception party. After exchanging formal salutes, he was taken to the control tower where the English-speaking German appeared, a very large man in full uniform. After a frustrating attempt to reach Gardermoen by telephone, Barr eventually ordered the jeep to be unloaded and left it with the Army personnel he had been carrying, while he and Willie Howlett, his navigator, went by car with some of the resistance men to Gardermoen. As he drove off, he saw the Army personnel giving everyone, including the Germans, rides around the airfield in the jeep. Passing through Oslo, crowds four to six deep were cheering the passing cars, and the one Barr was travelling in had a Home Front banner on it. When they were stopped by the crowd they were mobbed with cheers and handshakes; it was a marvellous experience. Having made his report he waited until the next morning before flying the Halifax back to England. It was a nice personal end to his glider towing, SAS and SOE operations with No 38 Group.

When war finally ended, Barr was determined to smuggle Flak aboard ship for the journey back to Canada. The last staging camp was at Torquay but while there Flak, who was unused to city traffic, was killed by a bus; he was buried on the beach by a fellow Canadian who then broke the news to Barr. *"I sat down and cried. I think of him often. I'm sure there is a dog heaven, for a great friend to all Tarrant Rushton airmen and women who remember him."* Barr had completed 29 wartime operations and Flak had flown on many of them.

CHAPTER TEN

ENTER THE B MK III

A
MONG the Halifaxes retained by Handley Page for development work was B Mk II R9534, which left Handley Page's production line as a standard B Mk II in the third week of March 1942. Allocated to the A&AEE it underwent a series of modifications, the first being those associated with the extensive changes to Series I (Special) configuration. In this instance, the Tollerton fairing was identical with that used on W7776, which served as the prototype for the Series I (Special) in having no horizontal Perspex window in either its upper half or lower section where it joined the existing fixed glazing of the bomb aimer's position. Initially it retained the C Mk V mid-upper turret but the A Mk VIII production model with the aerodynamic fairing later replaced this. The most noticeable change occurred with the fitting of four Bristol Hercules VI engines with two-speed superchargers rated at 1,615 bhp for take-off. This installation required a redesign and some strengthening of the rear boxes of the wing centre sections with continuous stringers. Flight-testing began in October, at which stage R9534 still had standard triangular Type A fin and rudder assemblies.

During sideslip and asymmetric flight trials, the normal rudder deficiencies were noted as well as some aileron snatch and to overcome the latter, the aircraft was fitted with a set of experimental ailerons. The Type A fin and rudder assemblies also proved inadequate for two-engine asymmetric flight conditions and to counter this, some variations to the fin and rudder dimensions – under testing for the B Mk II Series II – were fitted. The first combination tested were the Type E fin and rudder assemblies, which differed in having the fin area increased by about 50%, combined with the Type C rudder which did not have the bulbous Mod 413 nose fittings. Although these cured the rudder power problem, rudder overbalance continued to occur at large angles of deflection. Finally, Type D fin and rudder assemblies were fitted in May 1943 and proving successful, saw test-flying begin on 1 June. Four days later the prototype Halifax B Mk III, as R9534 was now designated, was involved in an unfortunate accident as it was prepared for a morning test flight. Having run up the engines, the pilot signalled for the chocks to be removed but the starboard one jammed and one of the RAF ground crew moved to release it but misjudged the distance and was seriously injured when the propeller struck him.

The new fin and rudder combination was also found acceptable for Mk II and V aircraft – introduced for Series I (Special) and I A Halifaxes as Mod 814 – but, because of peculiarities associated with R9534, the rudder was found to be rather heavy with the existing aileron controls. The ailerons themselves were too heavy to allow any appreciable bank at high speed and the rudders on their own were too heavy to be of much assistance in putting on bank. In view of this, the ailerons were redesigned with a bulbous nose modification similar to that applied to the original rudders[1] while an additional geared trim tab was fitted to the starboard aileron and a broad-chord geared trim tab replaced the fixed balance tab of the port aileron. On 17 July, a Type 6256 retractable tail wheel was fitted immediately prior to commencement of intensive flying tests. The aircraft had already completed 85 hrs 40 min of flying when these trials began and was flown for an additional 67 hrs during which time some trouble was experienced with the airframe because of general deterioration.

Two views of the prototype B Mk III Halifax, showing its rather pugnacious appearance in its hybrid form. R9534 had left Handley Page's production line in mid-March 1942 as B Mk II (the Series I designation would be retrospectively added), and was allocated to the A&AEE. The original A Type fin and rudder assembly was still fitted when these photographs were taken but the C Mk V turret had been replaced by the A Mk VIII production version. The Prototype marking, introduced for all such test aircraft, was marked in yellow, in this instance 4 feet high overall, with circle thickness 2 inches wide, the 'P' 2 ft 9 in high and marked in 4in-wide strokes. Camouflage had been brought down to the lowest level in side view and all under surfaces painted yellow. It was finally retired, converted to an instructional airframe as 4813M in June 1944.

HX227, the first production B Mk III flew for the first time on 29 August and, after having completed only 3 hrs 55 min of flying, was delivered to Boscombe Down on 12 September where, prior to commencing test-flying, the *H2S* blister was removed and the engine air intakes replaced by a strengthened type. Equipped to full operational standard, it retained the non-retracting tail wheel and was powered by four Bristol Hercules XVIs, which differed from the Hercules VI engines only in having fully automatic carburettors.

Two crews from operational squadrons were attached to the A&AEE to carry out routine and intensive flying while ground crews, also on attachment from operational squadrons, took care of the maintenance requirements, while additionally both test pilots and pilots from No 4 Group occasionally flew R9534. While being flown by No 4 Group crews between 27 August and 7 September 1943, R9534 spent most of its time away from its home base, its routine 150-hour inspection being carried out in the field. After 44 flights during which it logged 66 hrs and 35 min flying time, it returned to Handley Page for examination and rectification of the wing structure.

Between 14 September and 22 October, HX227 flew 45 flights, logging 150 hrs 10 min in less than five and a half weeks. The official report was most enthusiastic. It read "... *the aircraft was far better as regards maintenance and reliability than was expected from previous experience of four-engined aircraft and the intensive flight trials were completed in less time than has been taken for any other four-engined aircraft.*'"

Experiments carried out with two types of air scoops during September saw the Bristol Open Scoop-type replaced by the Vokes Modified Internal Tunnel-type, which bestowed a relatively meagre 3 mph to the weak-mixture cruising speed but added a very significant 1,000 ft to the cruising ceiling. The all-up weight was cleared to 63,000 lb although a portion of this was taken up by additional fuel, the total capacity having been raised to 2,688 gallons. Each wing still contained six fuel tanks but the No 2 tank was transferred to the centre section of the wings and provision made for additional long-range fuel tanks in the outermost wing bomb cells. The main six tanks held 1,806 gallons, the two new tanks 96 gallons each and each of the three long-range fuselage tanks 230 gallons.

Some minor difficulties with vibration had occurred and were traced to the rear turret balance flaps and partially cured by packing out the deflector flaps. Movement of the turrets, especially the rear one, affected the controls considerably and a large amount of trim had to be used to keep the aircraft straight. In violent evasive actions at speeds below 190 mph, response to the controls was good although the rudder was heavy. At high speeds, the rudder and aileron heaviness experienced with R9534 was again encountered. The modified bulbous nose ailerons, which cured the condition, were not available for the initial production aircraft and these machines were delivered with standard ailerons.

The Mk III was originally intended to be an interim model in the process of developing the Mk IV Halifax but the high-altitude variant of the Hercules engine ran into difficulties and eventually further development was abandoned; thus, by default the Mk III became the next variant and ultimately the most mass-produced. However cancellation of development of the Mk IV resulted in a number of its structural and aerodynamic improvements being incorporated into the Mk III. The MAP also insisted that all Mk III Halifaxes be fully tropicalised during the production stage and that the original design feature of the Type 6256 retractable tail wheel assembly be fitted as standard. The wing strengthening fitted to R9543 allowed for a higher all-up weight of 65,000 lbs and was to be introduced into Mk III production before the twentieth airframe, but delays with some components initially limited this figure to 63,000 lbs. The subsequent success of the Mk III development programme effectively killed off the proposed and refined Mk II Series II variant.

Use of the more powerful Hercules engines completely restored the Halifax's performance and production of the Mk III got rapidly under way. In addition to HX227, three other production Halifaxes were retained for trials work, HX226, HX229 and HX238; the latter three differed only from HX227 in having a retractable tail wheel.

The first batch of B Mk IIIs was issued to four squadrons in November 1943 amongst which was the oldest Halifax unit of all, 35 Squadron, now based at Graveley. Mr A. H. Atwood was the chief servicing engineer for Bristol at the time and had the task of lecturing to the pilots, both in the air and on the ground, on throttle-handling techniques, which differed markedly from those associated with the Merlin engines. Cabin heating provided some problems; whilst the inboard engines provided ample quantities, its distribution was difficult to control. The final version was christened with the station name, becoming known as the Graveley Heating System.

No 466 Squadron received its first B Mk IIIs on 3 November 1943 and four days later HX244 crash-landed after the undercarriage locked halfway up due to the aircraft sinking back on to the runway during take-off. No 433 Squadron also suffered an early disaster; the first Mk IIIs to be lost. Shortly before noon on 19 December, HX345 took off with a new crew on board, turned over on its back and plunged down on to HX277 parked at dispersal. Both aircraft burst into flames, killing all five crew along with three of the four ground personnel working on HX277, LACs[2] W. O'Connor, S. McEvoy and P. Butler.

By mid-1943, the MAP had issued their aircraft production programme covering from July to December, which included a decision that one-third of total Halifax production would have *H2S* fitted. Existing squadron aircraft would be fitted retroactively and a mobile *H2S* fitting party visited the four B Mk III-equipped

squadrons during December, fitting sets at the rate of one a day. Modified Vokes air intakes were also fitted during this same period by the unit ground crews. One oddity included in the MAP revisions was reference to the *H2S*-equipped aircraft having standard bomb doors while the other two-thirds of production aircraft would have large bomb doors and no *H2S*. This caused some consternation within MAP as the decision to proceed with fitting large bomb doors, as tested on V9985, had been rescinded before the initial 50 sets had been manufactured and reinstating during production could not start before July. This small insight into what had developed from the A&AEE tests is interesting given the otherwise lack of information on any response to the success of the tests. While the doors did not go back into manufacture for Bomber Command use, results of the tests were incorporated into later design modifications.

No 466 Squadron began operations with the new type on 1 December, 12 of its Halifaxes joining 19 Stirlings to lay mines off Terschelling, two of the Stirlings being lost. Four of 35 Squadron's new B Mk III Halifaxes took part in the Frankfurt raid on 20/21 December as part of the PFF marking force for the 650 bombers sent to attack. The Pathfinders had prepared their attack based on predicted clear weather but found 8/10ths cloud cover over the city. German tactics also helped to confuse the resulting bombing with decoy fires being lit five miles south-east of the city and dummy Target Indicators also being used. Ironically, the inevitable bombing creep-back from the decoy site caused more damage than was at first assessed from the post raid report sent to Bomber Command. Twenty-seven Halifaxes and 14 Lancasters were lost, among them several of the new B Mk IIIs, 35 Squadron lost HX270: M, which crashed just east of St Truiden in Belgium. The other, HX238: J occurred at the last moment when a Target Indicator exploded in the bomb bay as it was preparing to land. S/ Ldr J. Sale, DSO, climbed the burning Halifax to 2,000 ft and baled out five members of the crew. The mid-upper gunner, F/Lt R. Lamb was unable to jump as his parachute had been destroyed in the fire so Sale calmly landed the burning aircraft and then taxied it off the runway. The Halifax finally exploded when Sale and Lamb were 200 yards away. The only casualty from the incident was the rear gunner who fractured one of his ankles after baling out. For his cool-headed action, Sale was awarded a bar to his DSO. These were the Squadron's first B Mk III losses.

Such losses were, of course, not the fault of the aircraft and crews were impressed with the performance of the new Mk III. No 466 Squadron joined in the Berlin offensive with 15 of its improved Halifaxes on 29/30 December, completing its part in the operation without loss.

* * *

Improved aircraft were not the only additions to the Halifax squadrons; from December 1943 onwards, supplies of *Visual Monica*, more popularly known as *Fishpond*, became available. Fitted to the left-hand end of the wireless operator's narrow bench, beneath the vertically mounted main equipment, this new version of the tail-warning device, as the name suggests, gave a visual indication on a cathode-ray tube, rather than the original aural signal. It was the W/OP's responsibility to keep watch for aircraft approaching the centre of the screen (the Halifax) that was on a different course and moving faster. Its development was a serendipitous offshoot of the *H2S* research and it was introduced into production swiftly.

The old version of *Monica* had lost much of its effectiveness because the high concentration of aircraft within the bomber stream activated it almost continuously[3]. Meanwhile, Professor Lovell at TRE had come up with the idea of using a second plan position indicator operated from the *H2S* set which gave a radar picture of any aircraft nearby. Other bombers, since they were moving at approximately the same speed, appeared as slowly moving blips on a roughly parallel course but fighters were readily discernible by their relatively more rapid movement and angle of approach across the screen. Within two weeks of formulating the idea, a working model was produced for bench testing and shortly afterwards a test set was ready for installation in an aircraft. Within three weeks, the set was installed in Halifax B Mk II BB360 and tests begun. By July *H2S* Mk IIB, code-named *Fishpond*, was in production.

However, and as recorded earlier, during 1941 investigations had been made into drag problems associated with Halifaxes. Part of the report made a study of methods of increasing the all-up weight and stated that 63,000 lb could be achieved without further structural modifications. However, to increase this figure to 65,000 lb would necessitate an increase in wingspan to keep the take-off distance and cruising ceiling within reasonable limits. To achieve the increased span it was proposed to extend the wing centre section, but this would have entailed a considerable amount of redesign work and production delays, something not acceptable at the time. The solution eventually proved to be relatively simple, the additional span being achieved by extending the wings at the tips. These were tested at Boscombe Down on R9534 and the B Mk II Series 1A Halifax, HR845. By increasing the span to 103 ft 8 in the rate of climb was increased by 70-120 ft/min, service ceiling by 800 ft, maximum weak mixture cruising speed by 7-10 mph and cruising ceiling by 1,700 ft.

The additional weight involved in extending the wing tips added 60 lbs, the thickness of the aluminium skin being increased from 24 to 22 gauge. Added to the extra strengthening of the rear box of the wing centre section, plus the retraction gear for the tail wheel, this brought the total additional weight to 110 lbs while the

After a four-Halifax mining operation on 2 January 1944, No 433 Squadron sent 10 of its B Mk IIIs to Magdeburg on 21/22 January, two failing to return. HX283, seen here being air-tested and still fitted with Bristol Open Scoop air intakes, which took part marked 'R-Robert', was one of them. F/Lt A. Jira and his crew were lost without trace. The other crew, F/Sgt J. Wilson and his crew in HX289:T were also lost without trace. The replacement for HX268:R, by contrast, survived 62 operations before diving into the sea off Fife on 17 May 1945, one of the sixty Bomber Command aircraft that would be lost between the end of the war in Europe and that in the Pacific. (C. Cole)

introduction of the extended wing tips into the production cycle entailed manufacturing new jigs and changes to the relevant existing ones. The first batch appeared in late November or very early December 1943 and not surprisingly from Handley Page's lines, the earliest one definitely identified to date being HX318. Interestingly, examples of the original short span wings, with squared-off wing tips, were still coming off the Handley Page line as late as February 1944, two such examples being LV833 and LV857. This probably points to existing stocks of outer wing panels being used up to keep production rates running to schedule until the new extended wing tips were introduced exclusively. Even then, the modified wings were not produced sequentially (see reference to HX339 below). English Electric appears to have started its extended wing production in late April 1944. The extensions could be fitted retroactively during major overhauls and although this was done whenever possible, during the intense nightly air battles of 1944 it was not a frequent occurrence.

The first production B Mk III to undergo routine testing by A&AEE personnel was checked over between 4 and 9 January 1944. HX339 was representative of the very earliest production aircraft having short-span wings and B Mk II-type ailerons. The aircraft passed all tests satisfactorily but the oil coolers proved to be a little too efficient so seven-inch circular blanks, made from dural[4] plate backed with felt, were fitted to the centre of the forward face of each cooler. Without the blanks being fitted, the oil congealed causing temperatures to rise, with a corresponding drop in oil pressure. This modification became standard for all B Mk IIIs and in some instances, it became necessary to increase the size of the blanks.

Meanwhile, experimental work with the B Mk IIIs continued and tropical tests showed that engine temperatures were excessive. To overcome this, spinners and fans were fitted to the port outer and starboard inner engines of HX226. Attached to the spinner back plates, the 18-bladed fans revolved at the same speed as the de Havilland Type 55/18, semi-flared propellers. The tests were only partly successful and in July 1944, a fully operational B Mk III, LW125, was sent to Khartoum for tropical trials. Produced at the end of April, it had already completed 40 hrs 20 min flying time with the A&AEE before being sent to Khartoum, returning via the Cape as part of a goodwill trip combined with a rigorous series of tests, adding another 49 hrs 35 min to its flying time in the process. It had the extended wing tips modification and while the majority of the test-flying was done at an all-up weight of 55,000 lbs, some were conducted at 63,000 and 65,000 lbs.

*   *   *

Restrictions applied to the old Merlin-engine Halifaxes had had only a limited effect on operations, as some squadrons were already being re-equipped with the new B Mk III aircraft[5] and would be completed in July when No 347 (*'Tunisie'*) Squadron of the Free French Air Force (FFAF)[6] received its new mounts. Expansion of the B Mk III Halifax force was relatively rapid and by mid-January 1944, nine squadrons were operational with the type and for some, this was their first experience of a four-engine type. Prior to receiving its Halifaxes, 466 Squadron had operated Wellingtons and apart from three or four B Mk Vs for training purposes, it was equipped with B Mk IIIs from the start. In other squadrons, the transition

was slower and they operated a mixture of B Mk IIs, Vs and IIIs. No 35 Squadron sent ten B Mk IIs and a lone B Mk III to Berlin on 20/21 January 1944, but the next night sent nine B Mk IIIs and four B Mk Vs to the same target. By contrast, 51 Squadron received sufficient B Mk IIIs for its C Flight to form the nucleus of 578 Squadron while 158 Squadron went through a similar process to form 640 Squadron from its C Flight.

The changeover inevitably brought accidental losses, although relatively few and the pace of change was swift. 466 Squadron received its first on 3 December and by the end of the month had 20 B Mk IIIs on strength; its first operational loss occurring during the Frankfurt operation on 20/21 December. No 433 Squadron followed a similar pattern with five aircraft readied for its first operation on 2/3 January but only four were used, joining 22 others on mining operations off the Frisians and the French ports. It then sent nine on a major attack to Magdeburg on

No 466 Squadron's 'D-Dog' is prepared for its night sortie in crisp winter weather conditions. Ground staff and armourers were loading incendiary canisters from the bomb trolley using the bomb carrier beam system that was lowered by means of cables, and then winched back up into the bomb bays. The long rod-like central support of each container can be seen on the ones in the immediate foreground. Incendiary to high explosive ratio was biased now in favour of the former in the area attacks being conducted against Berlin. The engine fitters working on the starboard inner engine give some scale to the height above ground and the consequences of slipping in such icy conditions.

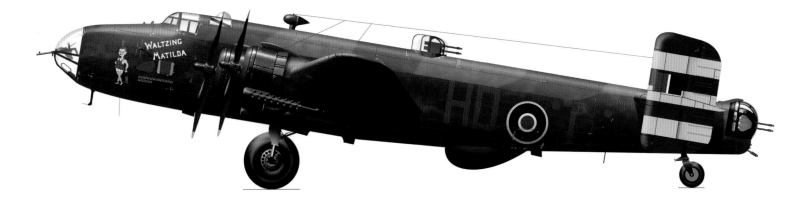

Handley Page Halifax, B Mk III

NR169: T, *Waltzing Matilda* of 466 Squadron RAAF. The aircraft completed 51 operations and is seen here in daylight tactical markings. It later became the first Halifax to join the civil register and was flown to Australia in 1946 (see page 172).

21/22 January, losing all F/Lt A. Jira's crew in HX283: R with Fl/Sgt J. Wilsons' crew suffering the same fate in HX289: T, the Squadron's first losses since converting to Halifaxes.

Magdeburg was a difficult target for the 684 bombers sent, and this was the first major attack on this city. The German controllers had followed the progress of the bomber stream across the North Sea and many night-fighters were fed into it before it crossed the German coast. The controllers were slow to identify the target but the night-fighters stayed with the bomber stream all the way, adding to the 8.8% losses. The *Wilde Sau* tactics had worked reasonably well but the weather conditions and lack of sophisticated navigation aids made results less certain than those of the *Zahme Sau*[7] which saw twin-engined night-fighters circle a radio beacon until receiving detailed assistance from the ground stations vectoring them into the bomber stream. The best crews were placed over the most favourable beacon sites but the irony was that *Window* had negated this box system and all night-fighter crews now competed on an even footing, as they now had to freelance along the bomber routes, using their own skills to make interceptions. At the time *Window* was deployed, the night-fighter arm was at the peak of its success; after that its superiority began to decline, but it was a slow process and many crews would lose their lives in the process.

The increasingly larger forces dispatched to a single target inevitably resulted in greater losses; fifty-seven were lost on the Magdeburg operation of which 35 were Halifaxes and 22 Lancasters with as much as 75% of these falling victim to night-fighters. Other squadrons also lost B Mk IIIs in the attack. Three were lost from 35 Squadron in its PFF role: Fl/Sgt W. Hill's HX317: M fell to a night-fighter in the target area, S/Ldr J. Jagger DFC was killed with three of his crew when a night-fighter shot down HX324: B near Hanover and F/O P. Bales' LV787: K was lost without trace. No 51 Squadron also lost three of its new aircraft: LV744: B over Holland with only one crew member surviving, LV775: G shot down over the target by a night-fighter with two of the crew surviving and LV779: L, also shot down by a night-fighter over the target, but all the crew baled out safely. No 158 Squadron lost just a single aircraft, HX335: P, which came down on the outskirts of the city with four of its crew baling out safely. No 466 Squadron lost one to a night-fighter with only two of Fl/Sgt C. Johnston's crew surviving when HX312: K was shot down over the German-Dutch border. Distance and battle damage also took their toll; 578 Squadron's LW468: J had to ditch on the homeward leg and although Sgt H. Melville successfully ditched his Halifax some 50 miles off Flamborough Head, the North Sea in January was merciless and hypothermia rapidly took its toll. Two of the crew died when exhaustion defeated their attempts to reach the dinghy and a third died from exposure before an RN Destroyer rescued the remainder. No 640 Squadron also lost a B Mk III when W/O2 J. Sironyak ditched LW459: W about seven miles east of Flamborough Head, but there were no survivors.

The heavy losses were a high price to pay for poor results. Some Main Force aircraft fitted with *H2S* had arrived before the PFF markers, a change in wind speed aiding their early arrival and 27 aircraft had bombed before the marking commenced. Post raid analysis brought a claim from the PFF that these early fires had added to the deception produced by some very effective decoy markers thus reducing the bombing concentration resulting in most bombs falling outside the city.

An improved version of *H2S*, the Mk III with a wavelength of 3 cm, was slowly reaching the Pathfinder Force where its greater capacity for discrimination was welcomed, but it was still up to the operator to determine the detail.

Another addition to Bomber Command's Halifaxes also appeared with the B Mk III. The long delay in approving any ventral turret design had ended with an MAP decision to produce the remotely controlled and sighted Frazer Nash FN 64, which had already been introduced on to Lancaster production lines. However, weight and problems with the sighting mechanism and limited field of view led to its removal by many squadrons. Boulton Paul, equally frustrated by the endless indecision, had attempted to interest the Air Ministry in a simpler solution; a 24-in deep ventral turret with the gunner laying curled on his right side beside twin 0.5-in machine guns with 1,000 rounds of ammunition stowed in the fuselage. There was a sitting position, but for use only as a rest position and effectively redundant for most operational trips. It was designed to fit the standard 36-in ventral aperture although the actual turret was 48-in wide and increasing its width by just one inch would have allowed a reduction of its depth to 20 inches. The field of fire was 80° of azimuth and 360° horizontally but the MAP showed no interest; then came the Preston-Green solution.

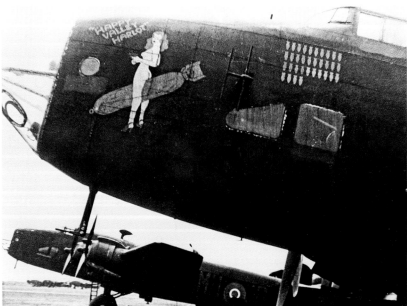

Squadrons were particularly keen on the Preston-Green fixed ventral cupola introduced on Mk II and Mk V Halifaxes and fitted to B Mk IIIs until the sufficient supply of H2S sets forced its deletion. This often coincided with a change from B Mk III to B Mks VI and VII Halifaxes and squadron diaries frequently record the reluctance of many crews to give up this additional defensive position, photographs of which are elusive and usually taken from a distance. This view of the nose of Happy Valley Harlot of 51 Squadron and her bomb log of 34 sorties also shows B Mk III MH-D, possibly LW461, complete with Preston-Green cupola with the light showing through the two small side windows which flanked the open rear section for the single 0.5-in Browning machine gun. (via M. Wright)

By comparison, it was even simpler; no elaborate sighting system, no electrical or hydraulic power systems and thus a large saving in weight – just a fixed metal bowl-shaped cupola, armed with a hand-operated single 0.5-in machine gun. A Bell adaptor anchored the weapon firmly but gave free movement, the weapon having a rearward facing lateral traverse 30° each side of the centre line of the aircraft, limited by the aperture parameters, with an elevation of 45° up on the beam, and 90° downwards. Two hundred rounds of ammunition were carried in a box with 50 rounds in the duct that fed the gun, the weapon being sighted with a free movement Mk III reflector gunsight. The gunner sat in an aft-facing bucket seat with a tilting backrest and could stow the gun at an angle of 30° on the beam to provide a clearer view for keeping watch, a rapid-release toggle immediately allowing the gun full movement. A small Perspex window either side of the open aperture allowed the gunner some lateral view. The cupola was 49 inches in diameter and fitted the existing ventral well aperture common to all three heavy bombers thus no major modification to airframe structures was needed, but the addition of this much-needed ventral defensive position required an extra crew member to man it. Gunners remarked that while not cramped, it was cold and draughty, having an open section facing directly aft to allow free movement of the gun. It was relatively easy to vacate in an emergency; two quick-release pedals, one either side of the weapon, could be stamped on hard, making it fall away, leaving a relatively large aperture through which the gunner could escape.

Little information, even at squadron records level, has survived regarding the actual date of the Preston-Green entering into operational service; some Operational Record Books (ORBs) make comment on the ventral fitting, but others seem to have taken it in their stride. The presence of an eighth crew member in casualty lists offers tentative tracking of which squadrons received Halifaxes armed with the cupola, but the practice of new pilots flying as second pilot distort that data, making it unreliable. The only positive sources are fragmentary records found in the various ORBs; for example the 76 Squadron ORB record for operations on 18/19 March 1943 states: *"19 aircraft dispatched to Frankfurt, Five aircraft*[8] *carried mid-under gunners. This was the first time mid-under gunners have been carried by this squadron."* The Squadron had begun receiving B Mk III Halifaxes in February 1944 with most being from the LW-serial range, which may offer an insight. Chorley's history of 76 Squadron *'To See The Dawn Breaking'* carries a description by a former gunner of both the position and its machine gun installation. In a similar vein, French author Jules Roy's biographical account *'Return From Hell'* contains a diary entry for 28 August 1944 of the fitting of a 12.6 mm (0.5-in) machine gun to the ventral position on his 346 Squadron B Mk III Halifax, which makes this a very late installation date. Interestingly and in contrast to the trained gunners mentioned by the 76 Squadron diarist, Roy recounts that when questions were asked as to who would man the position, the crew were told the flight engineer on the outward journey and the bomb aimer on the return flight. That the crew were only informed about the installation at the operational briefing and no training had occurred implies that fitting was done at squadron level and in fairly short time, no doubt aided by the fact that the cupola had no moving parts.

The only official reference to the addition occurs in a Boscombe Down report 16/760/b of 29 February 1944 when LW650, the second production B Mk III from English Electric, was subjected to routine random testing. The report included a description of the aircraft's equipment and noted, *"Blister for an 0.5" gun fitted at site of ventral turret (but no gun fitted). Stowage of the 0.5" gun appears to be rather unsatisfactory as the gun is some 45° on the beam and must present some unnecessary drag."* A note about this was sent to RDL2(c), dated 13.3.44 Ref. AAEE/CTO/3708/1/Eng. This has been interpreted in some writings that the Preston-Green fitting was being tested; however it appears more likely to refer only to the method of stowage. Other than for that comment the aircraft and its performance were declared normal for its type. Nothing in company production photographs shows any aspect of the ventral fitting so these may have been added post-production when aircraft routinely were delivered to MUs prior to delivery to individual squadrons.

The test flight was conducted at Leconfield, home to the newly formed 640 Squadron to which LW650: S had been issued. It was badly damaged by flak during an attack on Frankfurt on 22/23 March but Fl/Sgt R. Crockett brought it back to base where, after being inspected, it was declared as being beyond economical repair and written off. Significantly, it was carrying a crew of only seven so, as in Roy's account, one of the crew was expected to double up as the gunner. It will be noted that LW650 fell within the production batch on strength with 76 Squadron mentioned earlier as being fitted with the ventral gun position. Checking their fates reveals some extra detail. LW627 survived the war, as did LW646, which had been transferred from 78 Squadron to 76 Squadron. LW648, flying as 'Q' was lost on the Bochum raid of 4/5 November, but again was carrying only seven crew. Also transferred from No 78 Squadron, LW655: V failed to return from Frankfurt on 18/19 March but Fl/Sgt D. Joseph's crew comprised eight and the loss record notes that the mid-under gun position was manned by Sgt L. Makins. Yet LW695: M, shot down during the Russelsheim attack of 12/13 August, had only a crew of seven.

Looking across the LW-range encompassed by those already listed as having a Preston-Green cupola, LW634: P of 158 Squadron was carrying a crew of eight when shot down on 30/31 March yet LW635: K from the same squadron had only seven on board when shot down during the Trappes raid of 2/3 June. LW640: J of 640 Squadron had a crew of eight on board when it was shot down during the Düsseldorf raid of 22/23 April. No 76 Squadron's LW647: W and LW696: X lost on the Nuremberg raid were carrying crews of seven and eight respectively, while LW657: G, another transferred from 78 Squadron and lost on the Stuttgart attack of 15/16 March carried only seven. No 420 Squadron RCAF lost LW692: V over Lens on 20/21 April with seven on board. A very mixed bag but it is impractical to draw any firm conclusion as to the extent of fitting the Preston Green cupola. They were spread across several squadrons, some of which employed an eighth crew member, while others utilised one of the regular crew of seven as related in Roy's account. It is not even possible to determine if this practice alternated within a single squadron depending to some degree on the availability of spare air gunners.

The arrival of *H2S* in quantity in 1944 would eventually see the cupola replaced by the scanner and its housing, which was seen by some crews as a retrograde step. Not that the presence of a ventral gunner meant that attacks by night-fighters from the dark region below no longer succeeded as some missing Halifaxes were so fitted and how many survived because of its presence remains unknown. Yet, given the speed and accuracy with which German night-fighters were able to deliver fatal attacks, any means of deterrent must have been invaluable to many crews, even if only psychologically. Official records claim that by mid-1944, some 90% of Bomber Command aircraft were fitted with *H2S* yet the Preston-Green cupola was still being fitted to some new B Mk IIIs late into 1944[9], posing something of an enigma within the official claim. Photographic evidence confirms that some Coastal Command Mk Vs were also fitted with the cupola; LL469, the last of the batch LL437 to LL469 produced between 15 May and 7 June 1944, was one such aircraft and serves also as a reminder that the Merlin-engined Halifaxes were still in production in mid-1944.

* * *

A new target had appeared on the bombing list for minor operations – flying bomb sites were to be attacked by small numbers of bombers when conditions allowed. While the Main Force had gone to Braunschweig on 14/15 January – again for poor results and the loss of 38 Lancasters, many to night-fighters, which harried the bomber stream right back to the Dutch border – 82 bombers had attacked flying bomb sites at three French locations without loss.

The new B Mk IIIs were already reversing the trend of the previous months and Halifax losses gradually dropped[10]. Yet even while the war of electronic countermeasures was in full flow, the more basic elements of defence were still being entertained. Some squadrons made further modifications to improve the efficiency of the position. No 429 Squadron found that removal of the canvas seat improved the gunner's field of vision greatly, while 431 Squadron reputedly went a step further when they received their B Mk IIIs in March and installed twin machine guns.

On 2 March, LV907, the second B Mk III to be tested from the Handley Page initial production batch, was checked over and passed as up to standard for workmanship, but slightly above average in performance. Perhaps this helped in its subsequent operational career for it went on to complete 128 operations and survived the war. Delivered to 158 Squadron in March and marked as 'F' – 'Friday the 13th'[11], it reached the 100 mark with an attack on Gelsenkirchen on 22 January 1945 and finished the war with its 128th and final sortie against German coastal gun installations at Wangerooge on 25 April. Four other B Mk IIIs are known to have completed 100 or more missions although many others came very close to the magic figure; 578 Squadron's pair, LW58 (104) and MZ527(105), celebrated their 100th jointly with an attack on Kamen on 3/4 March 1945 while LV937, an ex-578 Squadron Halifax, completed its 100th with No 51 Squadron.

* * *

At this point, it is necessary to take a small diversion back in time to bring the countermeasures war into focus. British radio countermeasures had begun in 1940 with the primary task of disrupting the German radio navigational beams used to guide their bombers to British targets. From these small beginnings a never-ending and expanding countermeasures struggle was to grow. On 10 December 1940, a small unit known as the Wireless Intelligence Development Unit[12] was raised to full squadron status and redesignated as 109 Squadron, and for the next two years used its Wellingtons and Ansons in the development of radio countermeasures and radar aids. When the Squadron was sub-divided in July 1942, 'A' Flight became 1473 Flight[13], 'B' Flight became 1474 Flight and 109 Squadron proper re-equipped with Mosquitoes to become the first *Oboe* specialist squadron in No 8 Group.

By January 1943, the work by 1474 Flight had increased sufficiently to warrant its expansion to a full squadron. Accordingly, on 4 January, the Flight was re-formed as No 192 Special Duties Squadron and equipped with seven Mk 1c, one Mk III and nine Mk X Wellingtons, three Mk IV Mosquitoes and a Tiger Moth. Officially, the Wellingtons were to be phased out and replaced by Halifaxes, but shortages at that critical stage of the war delayed the process; two Mk IIs, DT737 and DT735, were received on 9 and 15 January respectively but it was July before the next, DK246, arrived. In the interim, the Halifax's capacity and long-range capabilities were used to ferry ground crews out to the Squadron's detachment at Blida, in North Africa.

The first Halifax operation proper took place on 22/23 June 1943 when DT735 carried out a patrol of the Dutch coast in the area of the Hook of Holland near Alkmaar. An eighth crew member known as a 'special operator' was carried on the sortie to monitor the electronic search equipment installed in the aircraft. A second

Seen here undergoing an air test, JP121 was the last B Mk II Series IA lost on a major German target, and was the last of its marque to be lost by the Pathfinder Force's 35 Squadron when shot down during the attack on Stuttgart on 20/21 February 1944, its crew surviving as POWs. Delivered to 35 Squadron on 15 November, it had flown for a total of 144 hrs 35 min when lost and while featuring most of the final refinements applicable to the Series IA, it retained the original rudder assembly and the dual landing light remained in the locked-down position. (C. Cole)

sortie on 12/13 June took DT737 to a point south-west of the Scilly Islands to search the ether for German radio signals. Several operations were also flown over the eastern approaches of the Bay of Biscay to the Brest Peninsula and to Nuremberg and Düsseldorf. On missions over Germany, the Halifaxes joined the main bomber stream to search for German radar and radio signals with the special operators logging each intercepted signal, noting its basic characteristics or, if necessary, making a recording of it.

The Halifaxes continued their patrols for the next few months and when Norway came under surveillance during this period, a detachment of one Halifax and two Wellingtons was sent to operate from Lossiemouth in Scotland. Although no major co-ordinated radio countermeasures system was directly supporting Bomber Command at this time, the Main Force groups were already using two individual defensive aids, *Monica* and *Window*. The latter could be used freely without losing too much of its value but by its nature, *Monica* was an individual device.

To aid the bomber forces, the specialist aircraft continued with their passive radar-radio listening, while from bases in England, German-speaking personnel[14] broadcast false directions to German night-fighters, which in turn was supported by the use of jamming devices[15] tuned to the German R/T frequencies and carried by Lancasters of No 101 Squadron. These aircraft, which also carried bombs and formed part of the attacking bombers, also carried a German-speaking crew member who broadcast false information to confuse the night-fighter crews. In 1943, these multiple resources were finally brought together to form No 100 Group[16].

Having already moved to Feltwell from Gransden Lodge in April, on 7 December 1943 192 Squadron joined 100 Group and moved to Foulsham by which time the squadron had lost its first Halifax in an accident. On 18 November, F/O L. Israel and crew were detailed to join the main bomber force targeting Ludwigshafen but because of a delay, they were too late and were recalled 47 minutes after take-off. During the landing something went seriously wrong and DK244: Q crashed, burst into flames killing three members of the crew immediately with three more succumbing to their injuries over the next few days.

A lack of aircraft, which had long delayed the squadron's expansion was finally overcome early in January 1944 when Mk III Halifaxes began to arrive, but the Wellingtons, however, would linger on.

*   *   *

Bomber Command continued its intensive bombing campaign throughout the remainder of February and March. Stuttgart was attacked on 20/21 February by a force of 460 Lancasters and 126 Halifaxes amongst which were included some of the few remaining Merlin-engined Pathfinders. A diversionary raid on Munich had drawn off the night-fighters and just seven Lancasters and 3 Halifaxes were lost, of which one of the latter, JP121: U of 35 Squadron, was the last B Mk II to be lost on a German target and the last of its type lost by the squadron. All but one of Fl/Sgt J. Leslie's crew, Sgt F. Paisley RCAF, had baled out safely when their aircraft was shot down. Paisley, however, had stayed with the Halifax and survived the crash to join his crew as a POW.

Schweinfurt and Augsburg were attacked in rapid succession between 20 and 25 February. The Schweinfurt operation introduced a new tactic with the 734-strong force split into two waves with the first wave of 392 aircraft followed two hours later by the remaining 342. Diversions drew up part of the German night-fighter force and the first wave lost 22 aircraft, but losses for the second were half that figure of which only four were believed to have fallen victim to night-fighters. Overall, seven Halifaxes failed to return. However, damage to the target was light with under-shooting of some of the target markers and bombing creep back being seen as the main causes for this. By contrast, the Augsburg raid of the following night and the first

major attack on this target was a spectacular success; over 60% of the target was devastated by this one raid for a cost of 21 of the attacking force, four of which were lost in collisions. Again, the attacking force was split into two waves, reducing casualties. The attack destroyed nearly 3,000 houses and damaged 5,000 more in the industrial suburbs but regrettably, some 80 million pounds worth of art was lost with the destruction of the beautiful old centre of the city. Compounding the destruction by fire was the fact that the River Lech had frozen over and many fire hoses were frozen. For the German Government, however, it was a propaganda victory and was publicised as an extreme example of 'terror bombing'. This gave rise to a feeling of fear that would later cost some crews their lives when the population occasionally turned on parachuting survivors.

Stuttgart received two further visits in early March, followed by two against Frankfurt, and then, on the night of the 24/25th, Berlin was attacked for the last time in the current campaign. The same long Baltic route was used as on the previous raid and diversionary sweeps were made to confuse the night-fighter controllers but again, an unforeseen strong northerly wind badly upset navigation and scattered the bomber force over a wide area. Berlin was a very difficult and dangerous target under any conditions and because of its sprawling suburbs gave a very poor definition on the *H2S* sets. Those aircraft not fitted with *H2S* found conditions practically impossible and another sudden, unpredicted wind change caused many aircraft to stray into the heart of the Ruhr defences on the return trip. Later analysis indicated that of the 811 participating aircraft some 50 of the 72 that failed to return were lost to flak while 14 fell victim to night-fighters in the target area. Of the 216 Halifaxes participating 28 were lost. This was the last major attack of the war on Berlin.

The end of the Battle of Berlin left crews exhausted and battered with high losses and very poor results to show in return for their determination. The main causes were the savage winter weather, the long flight to and from Berlin and the inability of Bomber Command planners to use much flexibility in the routing of the bomber force. Undeterred, Harris saw no reason to show weakness and sent his remaining crews back into the attack with a raid on Essen on 26/27 March. The Ruhr was home to many difficult targets and this was one of them. Seven hundred bombers were dispatched but fortunately, the swift change of target focus caught the German controllers off guard and only three Halifaxes and six Lancasters failed to return. For the bomber crews the raid brought about a lift in morale when *Oboe*-equipped Mosquitoes accurately marked the target through cloud to allow a successful attack to develop.

Diversionary raids were now becoming part of the countermeasures employed to confuse the German night-fighter controller's ability to predict the target. The Berlin attack of 27/28 January had been aided by diversionary operations by 80 Stirlings and Wellingtons minelaying along the Dutch coast, while 21 Halifaxes carried out a similar task near Heligoland. This was an extension of the long-standing process of sending inexperienced crews on such operations to give them experience, which was now being developed in a more sophisticated manner as part of broader deception tactics. On some occasions small numbers of Mosquitoes would attack main targets far from the real one while in other instances, the real target would be bombed by a few Mosquitoes hours before the real raid to add to the German controller's dilemma in deciding if the attack was real or a feint. On 28/29 January, 63 Stirlings and four Pathfinder Halifaxes had laid mines in the approaches to Kiel harbour just five hours before the main attack on Berlin and it was the first time that Pathfinder aircraft had assisted with this task. Then, four hours before the main attack, six Mosquitoes swept over Berlin and dropped bombs while four others attacked Hanover and a further 18 attacked night-fighter fields in Holland. However, even if diversions were unavailable or not so elaborate, it was becoming very much

A brand-new B Mk III from Handley Page, LV857, being air-tested. It left the factory production line at the beginning of February 1944 and initially was issued to No 35 Squadron then to No 10 Squadron, but finished up with No 51 Squadron; these rapid changes of allocation are emphasised by the fact that it was lost on the infamous Nuremberg raid of 30/31 March – the worst night's losses ever suffered by Bomber Command. Flying as 'H2' (there were several other extra aircraft from the Squadron on the raid, marked with the distinctive '2' suffix) F/Sgt J. Binder was shot down before reaching the target, intercepted by Oblt Martin Becker of I./NJG 6 flying a Bf 110. The Halifax crashed 400 metres south of Rossbach, killing all the crew. (Handley Page)

a cat and mouse situation for the German controller as diversions became more and more sophisticated.

Then, on 30/31 March, the last heavy raid of the winter saw a force of 795 bombers sent to Nuremberg. It was a memorable last raid for it precipitated the largest night-fighter battle of the war and the worst reverse suffered by Bomber Command. Normally this would have been the stand-down moon period for the Main Force, especially for such a distant target, but the initial forecast predicted high cloud on the outbound route when the moon was up, with cloud clearing in the target area. This was countered by a report from a Meteorological Flight Mosquito which carried out a reconnaissance, reporting that cloud was unlikely to be present en route and likely to be encountered over the target, the opposite of the earlier forecast. However, the raid was not cancelled, uncomfortably reminiscent of the circumstances that had seen Sir Richard Peirse lose his command.

Weather conditions over the North Sea precluded the use of any large-scale diversion, but 50 Halifaxes laid mines in the Heligoland Bight in the hope of drawing some of the night-fighter force away from the target area. However, these were ignored, the German controllers instead grouping their forces at Bonn and Frankfurt-am-Main where they were well positioned to intercept the bomber stream. An unpredicted high-velocity wind at altitude – a jet stream as it later became known – upset navigation badly and saw the bomber stream spread out in a broad band north of the actual track. High cloud cover, predicted to cover most of the route, disappeared over Belgium exposing the bombers to the light of the half-moon and silhouetting them against the lower cloudbanks.

The high scores achieved by some German night-fighter crews have been frequently questioned, but it does not take much imagination to see how they could be achieved. Lt Martin Beker of the I./NJG 6 was airborne in his Bf 110 that night and just after midnight made his first radar contact, a group of Halifaxes east of Bonn. Ten minutes later the first Halifax fell to his guns and within the space of the next 30 minutes, he shot down a further five. Short of fuel, he was forced to land, but took off again later and shot down a seventh bomber over Luxembourg.

It is estimated that at least 50 bombers had been shot down before reaching the target and one RAF crew counted at least 30 burning wrecks between Aachen and Nuremberg. Out of the 214 Halifaxes dispatched that night, 32 failed to return, as detailed here. Except where noted, the remainder were all victims of night-fighters. No 10 Squadron; LV881: V. No 51 Squadron; LV777: F2 (flak), LV822: Z2, LV857: H2, LW537: C2, LW544: Q2 and LW579: V which crashed south-east of Oxford on

the return flight, killing all on board. No 76 Squadron; LK795: P, LW628: J, crashed on landing at Tangmere after sustaining heavy damage in a night-fighter attack, LW647: W and LW696: X. No 78 Squadron; HX241: P, LK762: Z and LV899: Q. No 158 Squadron; HX322: B, HX349 (flak), FW634: P (flak) and LW724: S. No 424 Squadron; LV879: A and LV944: U (flak). No 425 Squadron, LV429: R. No 427 Squadron; LV898: D, LV923: W, collided with Lancaster ND767: D of No 622 Squadron and LW618: E. No 429 Squadron; LK800: N and LK804: Q, which ditched in the English Channel with one member of the crew drowned. No 432 Squadron; LK754: Z and LW682: C[17]. No 433 Squadron; HX272: N. No 578 Squadron; LK797: E, LW478: S which had six of the crew killed when the aircraft crashed while landing in poor visibility[18] and MZ508: N. No 640 Squadron; LW500: Z (flak), LW549: B and LW555: L.

P/O C. J. Barton was flying his 19th operation that night at the controls of LK979: E, a 578 Squadron Halifax when, seventy miles from the target, a Ju 88 night-fighter attacked putting the intercom out of action with its first burst of fire as an Me 210 then joined the attack and damaged one engine. By this time, all of the Halifax's turrets were out of action and the night-fighters continued to press home their attacks. With the intercom out of action, the bomb aimer, navigator and wireless operator all misinterpreted a signal and baled out. Despite the loss of these essential members of his crew and cut off from the remainder, Barton continued to Nuremberg where he released the bombs himself. As he turned for home, the propeller of the damaged engine flew off and at about this time the flight engineer discovered that two petrol tanks were damaged and leaking fuel. Without any navigational aids and hampered by the loss of one engine and strong headwinds, Barton successfully circumnavigated the heavily defended areas and crossed the English coast 90 miles north of his base. With petrol almost exhausted, two of the remaining engines cut, leaving him with only one running and at too low an altitude to allow his remaining crew to bale out. Ordering the flight engineer and two gunners to their crash stations, he made a last attempt to clear the houses over which he was flying, but crashed near Ryehope Colliery, Sunderland. Barton died in the crash but his three companions survived, the only other fatality being a passing miner killed by flying debris. Other miners from the nearby colliery helped to free the survivors. The only other loss was a house, demolished by a wing, but the occupants escaped unharmed. For his tenacity and courage, Barton was posthumously awarded the Victoria Cross, the only member of a Halifax crew to receive this rare award.

The sheer scale of some RCAF artwork was very impressive, as was its quality when former commercial artists were on hand to apply it. Cartoon characters from popular comic strips were often immortalised in this manner and this photograph of B Mk III HX318: O of 424 Squadron drew on the 'Popeye' strip, which included Oscar as one of its regular characters. Photographed in full with 57 operations marked up showed good service since being delivered in early December 1943. The usual addition of crew names or nicknames was absent other than for 'Guthrie's Gut Bucket' marked in red below the wireless operator's window. The significance of the musical notes separating the last two names is unfortunately unknown. Fate eventually caught up with Oscar over Karlsruhe on 24/25 April 1944 when it was hit by flak on the run in to the aiming point at 20,000 ft and exploded moments later, ejecting F/O G.S. Coleman and Fl/Sgt H.E. May, the only survivors from F/O W. Hugli's crew. (Public Archives of Canada via D. Wadman)

The entire operation had cost Bomber Command 95 aircraft with 11 others damaged beyond repair, 31 of them Halifaxes. This was Bomber Command's heaviest numerical loss of the war; overall losses amounted to 11.9% in percentage terms although ironically, it was smaller than the 14.5% losses incurred against the same target on 28/29 August 1942. On that occasion only 159 aircraft had been sent out, of which 24 failed to return. To the crews flying these dangerous sorties, numbers or percentages all spelled out the same stressful factor – the odds were long indeed for surviving a tour of 30 operations.

The results were even more tragic when it was realised that the attack was so scattered that little damage had been caused. Despite the disaster and the reasoning behind sending the force out, Harris was not openly censured, but the moon period stand-down from deep penetration targets was then enforced and a shift in priorities, outside of Harris's control for the time being, prevented him from pursuing his intense bombing policy.

Unlike the statistics quoted above, Chorley, in his 1944 volume of *Bomber Command Losses* provides a more accurate and chilling analysis of just what the entire winter campaign against Berlin had cost in aircraft and aircrew lives. It also includes those aircraft lost when returning bombers crashed in the UK or at their bases. For the Halifax, 135 were lost with 583 crew members killed and 255 made POWs; for the Lancaster 459 were lost, 2,435 crew members were killed and 481 became POWs; for the Stirlings five were lost, 23 crew members killed and eight made POWs; for the Mosquitoes, seven were lost with six crew members killed and four became POWs. Over six hundred aircraft and 3,047 lives lost – no wonder Harris was known to his Bomber Command crews as 'Butcher' Harris. It was a ruthless war and Harris fought it ruthlessly, to do less would have been to brook failure, but some of his decisions must remain questionable in the face of losses and expenditure of trained crews versus achievements.

Ten weeks before the Allied invasion of Europe, there was a necessary shift from strategic to tactical targeting, at least for the immediate future. Harris's forces were to begin a campaign against clearly defined targets as part of the softening up of

enemy forces in and behind the invasion front and although an official date for the change was set at 14 April, Harris had already started at the beginning of the month. For Bomber Command crews, the move to less well-defended targets and the much shorter flying distances came as a welcome relief after the heavy fighting of the previous winter. The primary intent was to isolate German forces in Normandy from reinforcement by rail along with the destruction of ammunition depots, munitions factories, airframe works, repair facilities, and troop camps. Just prior to the invasion, radio and radar stations, plus coastal batteries, were to be attacked and in order to disguise the intended landing areas, it was necessary to attack such targets in France and Belgium well away from the real areas of interest. Additionally, a massive deception plan was orchestrated to lead the German planners to the conclusion that the actual landings would take place in the area of the Pas de Calais, some 150 miles away from the real landing sites. Fortunately, the terrible winter weather that had plagued the deep penetration raids began to wane and a season of successes against French and Belgian targets began.

German targets may have been denied to Merlin-engined Halifaxes but they were out again in strength against the Trappes railway yards on 6/7 March, the first of the raids against such targets. The all-Halifax force of 261 aircraft was drawn from Nos 4 and 6 Groups with six Pathfinder Mosquitoes to mark the target. Weather improved steadily as the target area was approached and many crews reported later that after crossing the French coast it was possible to see the earlier stage of the attack by No 6 Group taking place. By the time that the No 4 Group crews reached the target, the Target Indicators for their attack were going down with the first cluster falling right on the aiming point. Visibility was so good that the lake some 700 yards to the north of the aiming point could be seen clearly. A highly concentrated attack developed with the majority of the bombing being carried out from between 12 to 15,000 ft with all loads dropped within a seven-minute period; more Target Indicators were dropped for the late arrivals. With very few exceptions, all crews brought back photographs showing that the attack was well concentrated in and around the aiming point. The last aircraft cleared the target 20 minutes after zero hour and its photograph showed the engine sheds partly clear of smoke and heavily damaged. Later analysis concluded that enormous damage had been done to the tracks, rolling stock and installations. Trappes had received 1,258 tons of bombs and remained out of action for approximately five weeks. Defences, both in the air and on the ground, were negligible with only one crew reporting an inconclusive contact with a night-fighter. No aircraft were lost.

The success of this type of operation had become obvious by the end of March and the Allied Air Forces' planners selected the 80 most important rail centres for attack. Thirty-seven were allocated to Bomber Command with the remainder divided up between the USAAF 9th Air Force, British 2nd Tactical Air Force and Air Defence of Great Britain (ADGB) fighter forces. The principal objective was to reduce the capacity of the complex French railway system to the minimum, thus denying the German forces the tactical mobility that would be so essential for defence against the Allied landings.

By 11 April, rail targets had been attacked on 13 occasions, involving 2,513 heavy bomber sorties with the majority being carried out by the Halifaxes of Nos 4 and 6 Groups. In order to create the maximum amount of damage possible, bomb loads consisted of a mixture of 500 lb and 1,000 lb bombs, e.g., on these raids the normal bomb load of a B Mk III Halifax not fitted with *H2S*, was nine 1,000 lb and six 500 lb bombs. Losses remained almost negligible in most of the 36 operations involving Halifaxes. Overall, 4,428 individual Halifax sorties were flown during the campaign for a cost of 99, a less than 0.5% loss. However, there were five attacks that resulted in significant losses. The Tergnier raid on 10/11 April, one of five railway targets attacked that night, cost 10 Halifaxes from a force of 157 but the railway yards were seriously damaged. Night-fighters are known to have accounted for at least four of these. LV880: C of 51 Squadron was attacked head-on by a night-fighter, setting fire to the port wing. Fl/Sgt H. Hall tried to extinguish the blaze by diving but moments after ordering his crew to put on their parachutes, the Halifax exploded and crashed near Montdidier with only three of its crew surviving. Railway yards at Tours, Laon, Aulnoye and Ghent also came under attack that night, the latter an all-Halifax attack that caused extensive damage for no loss to the bombing force.

Multiple attacks were carried out again on 18/19 April against railway facilities at Rouen, Juvisy, Noisy-le-Sec and Tergnier. All targets were heavily damaged with small losses to the Halifaxes, four being lost over Noisy-le-Sec and six at Tergnier where the majority of the bombs fell in a housing area south-west of the aiming point. The damage to the housing areas at Noisy-le-Sec, which resulted in heavy casualties amongst French civilians, was not completely repaired until six years after the war. Railway yards at La Chapelle, Ottignies, Lens and Chambly were attacked on 20/21 April with the first involving a new target-marking technique developed by No 5 Group using both high and low-level marking. Additionally, the bombing was split into two parts with a one-hour interval. The Ottignies and Lens attacks carried out by an all-Halifax force produced much damage for no loss. The last was a test for the new *G-H* blind bombing technique, 14 Stirlings carrying out the experimental attack.

The split attack timing was used again on 22/23rd against railway facilities at Laon, the 69 Halifaxes, 52 Lancasters and 48 Stirlings being guided to the aiming point by 12 Mosquitoes. Two Halifaxes, three Stirlings and four Lancasters failed to return with six known to have fallen to night-fighter attack. The Lancaster carrying the Master Bomber directing the attack, W/Cdr A. Coseuns of No 635 Squadron,

was amongst the other losses. When the night-fighters managed to intercept they were as deadly as ever. One of the two Halifaxes lost, LK710: S of 77 Squadron, was brought down in this manner from 7,000 ft after being raked from below by cannon fire, which killed S/Ldr K. Bond. The remainder of the crew parachuted to safety and the bomber crashed about 25 km south-west of Laon.

Aulnoye and Montzen railway yards were attacked on 27/28 April and in both cases mixed forces were used but, while bombing was concentrated on the former, for the loss of one Halifax, the attack against Montzen was far from successful. The attack was made in two waves and German night-fighters intercepted the second, shooting down 14 Halifaxes and one Lancaster for only a small section of the target being damaged. Nevertheless, the attacks continued: St Ghislain, Malines, Chambly, Mantes-la-Jolie, Haine-St-Pierre, Courtrai, Dieppe, Ghent, Lens, Lille, Boulogne, Hasselt, Trouville, Louvain, Boulogne again, Orléans Amiens, Tours, Le Mans..... Nearly all caused major damage for very low losses. By the time the invasion got underway 51 of the targets had been heavily damaged, 25 severely damaged and four only superficially damaged.

The use of *RCM* aircraft, even in seemingly very small numbers, belies their value. No 192 Squadron dispatched five sorties on 1/2 May: Mosquito, DZ376:M, was sent to Mannheim, a Wellington, LN398: A, patrolled off the northern coast of France between Boulogne and the Cherbourg peninsula, and three Halifaxes undertook radio-radar searches in co-operation with Bomber Command attacks on railway targets in France and Belgium. Halifax LW624: T went with the bombers to the area south of Malines, LW613: W made a lonely trip to a point 70 miles north-west of Toulouse, while the Main Force attacked the aircraft assembly plant and MZ501: P accompanied 75 Lancasters to Lyons for an attack on the Berliet motor works.

Aachen was attacked on 24/25 May by a mixed force of 442 aircraft. More on a scale associated with Main Force targets, the much larger number of aircraft committed to these particular railway yards, linking Germany and France, reflected the importance of their location – something mirrored by the stronger defences. The planners were correct in their expectations and 18 Halifaxes and seven Lancasters were lost; but again much damage was done to the target. Interestingly, 10% of the high explosive bombs dropped failed to explode. The old problem of faulty bomb fuses still lingered.

By coincidence, the last attack in the series, mounted by 105 Halifaxes, 19 Lancasters and four Mosquitoes on 2/3 June was against Trappes marshalling yards. However, unlike the first in March, night-fighters were waiting over the target and, aided by brilliant moonlight and flares, attacked the bombers. Losses were the highest suffered for the whole campaign; 16 Halifaxes and a single Lancaster failed to return, 12.5% of the force.

The attack cost 10 Squadron two, 76 Squadron three, 158 Squadron six, 466 Squadron two and 640 Squadron three aircraft. A third from 466 Squadron was severely damaged by an Me 210. F/Lt J. Stevens managed to nurse the battered Halifax back to base despite losing height until almost at ground level at one stage of the journey. P/O B. Bancroft of 158 Squadron had his Halifax even more extensively damaged by a Ju 88 night-fighter, the cannon fire from which tore a hole in the floor of the centre section the full width of the fuselage and three feet long. The radio operator's position had a large hole torn out of the fuselage side; both turrets were put out of action and one petrol tank punctured. Three crew members had also fallen out of the aircraft, two of whom survived, one as a POW, the other evading capture. The intercom, all instruments and hydraulics were damaged, the latter allowing the bomb doors and flaps to come down. A fire had started in the rear of the bomb bay but Bancroft managed to keep the Halifax under control while the navigator, P/O Fripp and two other surviving members of the crew, subdued the flames with fire extinguishers. With no compass, Bancroft steered a homeward course using the North Star and landed LV792: E at Hurn airfield[19].

Off-duty crews at Tholthorpe watch as MZ620: T of 425 Squadron taxies out for a sortie, the impressive shield on the nose suggesting that the Canadians were undoubtedly masters of exotic artwork. The signboards on the ground bear the warnings HATCHES and FLAPS, essential reminders before take-off. The Preston-Green ventral gun position visible in this view was a feature on the aircraft of a number of squadrons before H2S became more widely available, although many crews favoured the 0.5-in weapon over the electronic aid. The Browning is in the stowed position partly on the beam, which raised the only small criticism of this added weapon, the end result of nearly 18 months of tests to find a suitable defence for this blind spot. (RCAF)

Summer 1944 and a pair of 420 Squadron B Mk IIIs bask in the sunshine. In the background is LW676: Y, which arrived on the squadron on 29 February 1944 and had 40 operations marked up on its nose when this photograph was taken. It survived to be passed to 1659 HCU on 16 October and was eventually struck off charge on 16 July 1945. In the foreground is LW380: B with just one less sortie marked on its bomb log beside the artwork of a bat-winged buzzard carrying a large bomb with 'The Bird of Doom' written above and 'Achtung! Galloping Buzzard' written beneath in white. Built in late November 1943, it survived its tour of front line operations to be passed first to 1666 HCU, then to 1664 and then back to 1666 before being struck off charge on 5 May 1945. (Public Archives of Canada)

Attacks on marshalling yards had required only part of Bomber Command's forces and some of the remainder had been used in a simultaneous series of raids on enemy aircraft industrial targets, including the French airframe and engine factories, again with considerable success. Every effort was being made to reduce the German potential for retaliation within the immediate area marked for the coming invasion.

In the interim, Bomber Command had not been allowed to neglect its major attacks on German targets. Three weeks after the Nuremberg disaster, an attack against Düsseldorf on 22/23 April marked a return in force to German targets. Night-fighters penetrated the bomber stream to take a fair share of the toll of 16 Halifaxes and 13 Lancasters that were lost from the 596 aircraft sent to the attack, which saw widespread damage confined mostly to the northern suburbs. Two hundred and forty eight Lancasters and 17 Mosquitoes ran a diversion to Braunschweig during which No 5 Group's low-level marking technique saw its first use against a major target by crews of No 617 Squadron. Despite good marking, a thin layer of cloud and faulty communication between the target marking controllers resulted in poor bombing and the attack failed. Strong winds and cloud over Karlsruhe on 24/25th caused the PFF marking to stray too far north, where the only serious damage occurred. Ironically, a smaller force used to split the defences attacked Munich where the target marking was placed right in the centre of the city and much damage caused. To aid both attacks, aircraft from No 165 Operational Training Unit (OTU) carried out a diversionary sweep across the North Sea before turning back 75 miles from the coast while 23 Mosquitoes attacked Düsseldorf and aircraft from 100 Group carried out 11 *RCM* sorties.

Essen and Schweinfurt were next, attacked on 26/27 April by a mixed force, the latter by a smaller force in the developing war of diversion and deceit. Bombing was accurate on the primary target but failed at the second with strong headwinds disrupting the timing for a cost in losses of 9.3% to the all-Lancaster force of 206. The Friedrichshafen attack of the following night in brilliant moonlight was a calculated risk after the Nuremberg disaster in similar conditions. However, the target location was on the fringes of the night-fighter defences and the use of diversionary raids by Halifaxes and Lancasters resulted in a very successful attack on factories producing gearboxes and engines for German tanks. Night-fighters finally intercepted the homeward bound bombers and accounted for 18 of their number, all Lancasters.

During May, two of the largest German military camps were attacked. The first was an all-Lancaster raid against Mailly-le-Camp on the 3/4th while a similar force attacked the camp at Bourg Leopold, in Belgium on 11/12 May. However, the Master Bomber called off the attack due to marking difficulties, and only half bombed. A second attack on the same target by a mixed Halifax-Lancaster force on 27/28 May caused severe devastation for the loss of 9 Halifaxes and one Lancaster. As the time for the invasion drew near the scope of the targets was varied to include the German early warning systems, and during the first week in June, Bomber Command launched attacks on navigational and wireless telephony stations in the intended assault area. These small targets were difficult ones and the enemy's old friend, bad weather, hampered the attacks. Ferm d'Urville, on the Cherbourg peninsula, was headquarters of the German intelligence service in north-west France. Solid cloud shrouded the target and the force of 101 Halifaxes was forced to rely upon sky markers for the bombing. Many crews later expressed doubts as to the success of the operation and their pessimism was borne out by the reconnaissance report. Two nights later, in better conditions, No 5 Group carried out a second attack that successfully obliterated the target.

By 6 June, the German radar and signals network had been sufficiently disorganised to ensure that it would not compromise the element of surprise intended to mark the opening of the invasion. Less successful, however, was the

campaign against the German coastal batteries of Hitler's vaunted 'West Wall'. Although some sites were still under construction, there were 49 gun batteries known to be capable of engaging the invasion forces in the chosen assault area. To avoid any chance of indicating where the invasion might be made, diversionary attacks were also carried out against batteries outside of the prescribed assault area. The main problem was that only 1,000 lb bombs were available and against the heavily armoured guns and concrete casements, they had little effect. However, much of their vital ancillary equipment was destroyed leaving many of the gun sites severely handicapped on the day of the invasion.

The eve of the attack also marked a new phase in the *RCM* war; during the last hours of 5 June and into the opening moments of D-Day, 100 Group carried out its largest operation to date in support of the Airborne Forces who would carry out the opening phase of the landings. Three Halifaxes of 192 Squadron, LW613, LW621: Q and LW624, patrolled throughout the period of darkness along a route between Tonbridge and Yeovil maintaining a *Mandrel* screen to mask the activities of the Airborne Forces (see Chapter Nine). This vital contribution to the invasion planning had had its own moment of high drama a few days prior to the invasion. The entire jamming/spoof cover would be nullified if a single German radar site along the enemy coast was working on a wavelength not covered by the jamming frequencies; ten days before the invasion date, Intelligence sources suggested that there was one, working on a short wave frequency. What followed was just one more remarkable episode in the tireless work being done by the hard-pressed scientists and technicians at TRE. The report arrived on Martin Ryle's[20] desk Thursday afternoon (he was in charge of the countermeasures operation) and by Friday he had replied with three options, none of which could be accomplished in time, plus one that might – identify the site and frequency then hit it with low-level fighter-bomber attack. The latter required an *H2S*-equipped aircraft and a new design of critical equipment. Approval for the required new design was received within a few hours, construction started immediately and by Saturday morning everything was ready and installed and tested later in the day. On Sunday the equipment was test-flown, albeit by a somewhat puzzled and disgruntled Flight Lieutenant, still dressed in white trousers, blazer and wearing spiked cricket shoes (he was about to play for the Defford cricket team). Adding a parachute over it all he flew the Halifax, HX166, with Ryle on board and the equipment worked perfectly. The final cabling and other aspects were then completed and all was ready for a test over the Channel on Monday night; but nature stepped in with violent storms and all flying was cancelled. The test was flown on Tuesday night with two navigators on board but nothing was detected from the enemy coast.

The spoof fleet comprised just eight aircraft and four RAF Air-Sea Rescue boats starting from Newhaven and advancing at a precise speed in long passes parallel to the enemy coast, very precise navigation being called for throughout. Thus, the combination of jamming plus a steady dropping of *Window* produced the desired impression of a vast fleet sailing towards Cap d'Antifer and Boulogne. The men who conducted the operation that night were possibly the most critical players in the entire invasion of Europe.

This success would lead to a much wider exploitation of the *Mandrel* screen and No 199 Squadron's Stirlings would be enlisted to aid these activities. The device jammed German early-warning radar frequencies and was by far the most sophisticated aid available over enemy territory; as will be explained later, if properly exploited, it could protect an entire bombing force. The installation on Halifaxes was distinguishable by six rigid-blade aerials along the ventral centre line, extending from beneath the wireless operator's position, aft to a point just forward of the *H2S* scanner housing. Radio countermeasures was a double-edged sword and while the squadron continued its passive listening watches, it now began a very active programme of electronic jamming in support of the Main Force bombing raids.

CHAPTER ELEVEN

FINAL OPERATIONS IN EUROPE

DURING the night of 5/6 June 1944, Bomber Command launched a series of attacks against ten coastal batteries in preparation for the now imminent invasion. Each was to be attacked by a force of approximately 100 heavy bombers. The first, against Fontenay-Crisbecq, began at 23.35 hrs and was followed 15 minutes later by one against the battery at St Martin de Varreville by the remainder of the No 1 Group force, but both attacks were hampered by solid cloud and rain. The third, carried out by No 6 Group Halifaxes, began at 00.30 hrs but again 10/10ths cloud obscured the target and few of the 16 to 18 500 lb bombs carried by each aircraft hit the target.

The second phase of the attacks began at 03.20 hrs when 101 of the 110 No 4 Group Halifaxes dispatched bombed the battery at Maisy without loss, an Me 210 and Fw 190 being claimed as damaged. The cloud cover, which had plagued the earlier raids, had partly broken up and resulted in a far more accurate attack. However, the No 5 Group Lancasters, which attacked the La Pernelle battery at 03.35 hrs, were not so lucky and the target escaped damage; but in contrast, Halifaxes from No 6 Group successfully attacked the position at Houlgate shortly after.

The four remaining targets were all located within close proximity to the landing beaches and for this reason the attacks were timed for just before dawn to provide maximum benefit to the landing forces. Longues was first, bombed by a Lancaster force, but again weather conditions hampered the attack and damage was negligible. This battery also survived an attack by American bombers at dawn, plus a

bombardment by the naval forces off shore. At 04.35 hrs 101 Halifaxes from No 4 Group bombed the Mont Fleury battery but despite some damage, the single 122 mm gun continued firing until captured later by ground forces. Lancasters carried out the two final attacks against Pointe du Hoc and Ouistreham, but these also met with little success.

Although these attacks failed to achieve their primary objective, the 5,200 tons of bombs dropped, plus those dropped from the 1,361 B-17s and B-24s and the approximately 200 medium bombers that attacked before the actual landings, did much to disrupt the efficiency of the installations and their crews.

While these raids were in progress, a mixed force of heavy bombers was perpetrating an elaborate series of deceptions. Over the sea, 16 Lancasters from 617 Squadron and six *G-H*-equipped Stirlings[1] of 218 Squadron, with the aid of *Window*, created a ghost convoy approaching the French coast between Boulogne and Le Havre. No 100 Group mounted its largest operation so far with 110 of its aircraft on various bomber support sorties; 24 *ABC*-equipped Lancasters from 101 Squadron patrolled the likely night-fighter approaches, their German-speaking crew members ready to issue false orders. Thirty-four other aircraft carried out RCM patrols while the Group's Mosquitoes flew 27 *Serrate* and 25 Intruder sorties.

Over France, Halifaxes and Stirlings simulated airborne landings at various points and even the two Special Duties units were called into play; 11 Halifaxes of 138 and 161 Squadrons, in company with four Stirlings of 149 Squadron, dropped

A Halifax B Mk III passes over a heavily bombed section of the Pas de Calais during the attack on the A-4 (V 2) site at Mimoyecques on 6 July 1944 when a force comprised of 314 Halifaxes, 210 Lancasters, 26 Mosquitoes and a single Mustang used by the Master Bomber, attacked several sites. The only bomber lost during the attacks was F/O R. Bannihr's LW169: L from 424 Squadron, which, hit by flak over Siracourt, crashed 2 km south of St Pol, killing all on board. A second aircraft was also lost following the attacks when Sous Lieutenant (Slt) G. Varlet's LK728: D of the Free French 347 Squadron spun out of control out of cloud to crash 3 miles east of Lindholme airfield in Yorkshire, killing the entire crew. This was the only B Mk V lost by the squadron before it re-equipped with B Mk IIIs and the last B Mk V lost by Bomber Command during operations.

Once the bomb trolleys arrived at an aircraft, a universal bomb carrier beam was fitted to each bomb and both carrier and bomb were then winched up into place from inside the aircraft using a differential winch, as shown here with Canadian armourers loading 500 lb bombs. (Via M. Wright)

Two sizes of bombs being loaded into an unidentified Canadian Halifax. When photographed, a 500 lb bomb was being hoisted by the single cable of the winching system into the main bomb bay. A hand-operated winch lies on top of the nearest group of 250 lb bombs waiting to be loaded into one of the wing bomb cells. (via M. Wright)

dummy paratroops near Yvetot. Fitted with ingenious devices, the dummies landed amidst the sound of machine gun and rifle fire. Three Stirlings of No 149 Squadron made a similar drop near Maltot while a lone Halifax of 138 Squadron and 15 Stirlings of 90 Squadron made another near Marigny.

With the landings established, the Allies were quick to ensure that the immediate German reserves stationed between the Seine and the Loire could not be brought into action on 7 June. While fighter-bombers harassed these forces by day, on the night of 6/7 June 1,065 bombers mounted a series of heavy attacks on key road, rail and communication centres in this same area. Relatively small forces, similar in size to those used against the coastal batteries, were also employed against Vire, Châteaudun, Lisieux, Argentan, St Lô, Caen, Coutances, Condé-sur-Noireau and Achères.

Lancasters successfully attacked Vire just after midnight and two hours later, 107 Halifaxes of No 4 Group bombed Châteaudun with equal success while St Lô, 20 miles behind the beachhead, was also allotted to a No 4 Group Halifax force. No 78 Squadron dispatched 28 for this raid, which was carried out from 3,000 ft. Halifaxes from No 6 Group attacked the bridge at Coutances, one aircraft from 420 Squadron scoring a direct hit while the remainder bombed Condé-sur-Noireau. Low-level tactical support operations brought additional dangers that saw LW337: G from 426 Squadron hit by a bomb while over the aiming point. Fl/Sgt C. Selfe nursed the damaged Halifax back across the Channel but the crew were forced to abandon it over Slapton Sands on the south coast of Devon.

To aggravate the already badly disrupted rail system, four rail centres near Paris, Archères, Juvisy, Massy-Palaiseau and Versailles-Matelet were attacked on 7/8 June. All were heavily damaged but the strong inland anti-aircraft defences – in contrast to the almost negligible ones in the beachhead area – claimed 28 of the attacking 337 bombers. The Archères attack claimed three: LL643: Q from 408 Squadron, NA505: J of 420 Squadron – shot down by a night-fighter – and LV978: K from 427 Squadron. LW128 from 429 Squadron added a fourth to the list but only after a superb effort by the captain and a crew member. S/Ldr W. Anderson DFC had been mortally wounded by flak as the Halifax passed Dieppe and, while still conscious, ordered his crew to bale out, three doing so. At this point, Sgt G. Steere took over the controls and managed to fly the Halifax back across the Channel to reach the Oxfordshire area. There he attached a static line to S/Ldr Anderson's parachute and he and the remainder of the crew abandoned the aircraft. Regrettably, Anderson did not survive.

At Juvisy, 78 Squadron crews pressed home their attacks from 2,800 to 3,000 ft and lost four. After carrying out a successful attack from 5,000 ft, LV868 was badly damaged in a night-fighter attack but F/Lt D. Davies managed to nurse the Halifax back to England for a crash-landing on West Malling airfield. MX568: E is thought to have exploded after being hit by flak, MZ577: O crashed near Lieussant with two of the crew surviving as POWs while the fourth, MX636: Y, crashed near Bretigny-sur-Orge killing all on board. No 466 Squadron lost MZ283: F, which crashed near Montfort-sur-Risie and MZ531: D of 76 Squadron came down near Etampes. The odds of evading capture for those baling out were improving now that Allied forces were gaining ground in France. From the Versailles-Matelet attack, 158 Squadron lost a single Halifax, LK863: C, to flak but P/O I. Seddon and his crew baled out and all evaded capture; but not so lucky were the crew of MX602: U of 431 Squadron, who were killed when their Halifax crashed at Blevy. P/O I. Hamilton and one crew member were killed when LK866: L of 640 Squadron came down at Soulaires and

while four of the crew survived to become POWs[2], the fifth, Sgt L. Devetter, evaded capture.

To widen this state of disruption in France, 16 raids were carried out against rail congestion points between 13 and 30 June. Losses were generally light but the defences, especially on the deeper penetration raids, took a toll of 3.6% of the attacking force.

On 14/15 June, Bomber Command had commenced a series of attacks against troop and ordnance concentrations immediately behind the battle area and although these were sometimes ordered at the last possible moment, for a strategic bombing force, the command coped well with these tactical battlefield demands. Prepared in great haste, the first round of these were well executed with 337 Halifaxes, Lancasters and Mosquitoes attacking troop and vehicle positions at Aunay-sur-Odon and Évrecy, near Caen. Both attacks were successful and no aircraft were lost. Most of the bombing was still nocturnal, but that of 30 June against a road junction at Villers-Bocage was carried out in the last light of evening because two Panzer divisions needed to pass through the junction to attack the line between British and American forces. Mosquitoes placed their Target Indicators accurately and the Master Bomber's instructions were clear and precise for the force of 105 Halifaxes and 151 Lancasters, ordering them to attack from 4,000 ft to ensure that crews could distinguish the markers in the ensuing dust of the explosions. The bombing was accurate with some 1,100 tons hitting the road junction and blocking the German advance. Only a small amount of heavy flak was encountered which died down as the attack developed and only two aircraft were seen to crash, LV782: E of 51 Squadron and a Lancaster of 514 Squadron.

Over German soil however, the defences were stronger. The 28/29 June raid on the railway yards at Metz had met with strong opposition and W/O H. McVeigh's 433 Squadron Halifax was attacked four times. He evaded the first three but, on the fourth occasion, the Halifax was hit while in a corkscrew turn. The starboard fin and rudder were shot off, the starboard elevator damaged and the flap, aileron and wing tip of the starboard wing were smashed. The aircraft went into a tight spin at 13,000 ft and McVeigh ordered the crew to bale out, two members having done so before he managed to regain control and level off at 6,000ft. Shortly after setting course for England, the port inner engine failed but McVeigh managed to nurse LV839: C back to Woodbridge. He was fortunate in choosing this emergency landing airfield with its extra long runway as it was necessary to land the badly crippled Halifax at 155 mph in order to keep the damaged wing up.

Railway yards were still on Bomber Command's target list and 202 Halifaxes, led by 28 PFF Lancasters, had attacked yards at Blainville that same night for a cost of 20 aircraft. The Blainville force was mauled by a combination of night-fighters and flak, which claimed 11 Halifaxes. No 10 Squadron lost two, 76 Squadron three, 77 Squadron one and 102 Squadron five. MZ736: B of 76 Squadron fell to flak and within seconds of being hit the aircraft caught fire inside and P/O I. Weir ordered his crew out, the flight engineer handing the pilot his parachute as he went past. Weir clipped it on, upside down in his haste, but the aircraft exploded before he could get out through the escape hatch. He recovered in time to open his parachute at 4,000 ft, but only after an initial panic looking for the D-ring. F/O Jannings' MZ679: C was lost next, followed by P/O Gramson's MZ539: X, the crew surviving.

Somewhat appropriately, two new squadrons had joined the battle during June, Nos 346 and 347, both manned by French personnel. They commenced operations within a few days of forming, but completed only one operation with their B Mk V Halifaxes, losing just one before being withdrawn for re-equipping with B Mk IIIs.

Another addition to the Halifax force was not so easily discernible. This was the B Mk VII version which, like its predecessor the B Mk III, evolved as an interim model.

*　　*　　*

The Halifax B Mk III had resulted from a need for increased engine power and in most respects was essentially a B Mk II airframe adapted for radial engines. The potential for using more powerful engines resulted in a redesign of the B Mk III airframe to take Bristol Hercules 100 engines, which delivered 1,675 bhp for take-off and 1,630 bhp at 20,000 ft. The fuel system, apart from the tanks themselves, was completely revised and pressurised to accommodate injector-type carburettors. A 150 gallon fuel tank was permanently installed in the optional long-range tank position in the outboard wing bomb cell and the No 6 tank was increased in size and renumbered No 7. The fuel tanks were also grouped with one group per engine and three 230 gallon long-range tanks remained as a standard optional fitting for the bomb bay. Oil tanks, one to each wing, were located between the inner and outer engine nacelles in the leading edge of the wing and were divided in two by a partition, each portion containing 32 gallons.

Externally, there was little to distinguish the B Mk III from the B Mk VI, the latter having only slight variations to the engine cowlings, the cooling gills now being separated by a fixed section in the middle on each side of the engine. A Halifax B Mk III, LV838, was taken from the Handley Page production line and modified extensively to become the prototype B Mk VI. Delivered to Boscombe Down for evaluation and testing on 5 February 1944, it was fitted with de Havilland three-bladed, Type 55/18, semi-flared propellers of 13 ft diameter and underwent climb and level speed performance checks. The more powerful engines allowed an increase in the all-up weight for take-off to 65,000 lb. The tests were quite straightforward and LV838 recorded a service ceiling of 20,000 ft, taking 45 minutes to reach this altitude. The maximum rate of climb was 900 ft/min while the maximum speeds in weak- and rich-mixture cruising were, respectively, 252 mph and 270 mph True Air Speed (TAS).

An attempt was made to better these performance figures by fitting de Havilland experimental three-bladed, Type 55/10, fully flared propellers of 13 ft diameter, but they failed to produce any significant improvement.

The four Hercules 100 engines used in these trials were replacement units and although incorporating minor modifications, differed little from the original Hercules 100 engines. However, a serious setback occurred with a shortage of Hercules 100s and as a stop-gap measure, the modified airframes were fitted with Hercules XVIs. The Air Ministry allocated a new marque number to this version, which became the B Mk VII. A second B Mk VI, LV776, also taken from the original Handley Page B Mk III production batch, was delivered to Bristol's on 29 February. However, apart from these two B Mk VI aircraft, the first production aircraft were not destined to leave the production line until June.

Apart from the differences listed above, the main distinguishing feature between the Mks III, VI and VII was the revised positioning of the engine exhaust pipes. This is easiest to identify if shown diagrammatically; viewed from the front B Mk IIIs had oO oO + oO Oo configuration, the B Mk VIs had Oo oO + oO Oo configuration, and the B Mk VIIs Oo oO + oO Oo.

Meanwhile, production of the interim B Mk VII version continued rapidly and No 6 Group received authorisation to re-equip 426 Squadron with this version as from 15 June. A similar authorisation was given a few days later for 432 Squadron to also re-equip with the type as from 20 June. The last 15 Halifaxes of Handley Page's B Mk III batch – which had also produced the two B Mk VIs – were completed as B Mk VIIs and delivered to 426 Squadron on 16 June. Since the new aircraft were fitted with *H2S*, the squadron crews were a little perturbed at first at losing their B Mk IIIs with the ventral gun position. However, the increased performance of the new aircraft soon overcame their reluctance and within four days the crews were ready for their first operation, a daylight raid on St Harten.

No 408 Squadron, which had relinquished its Halifaxes for Lancasters in July 1943, began to re-equip with the new B Mk VII Halifax just 12 months later. 'B' Flight had completely converted by the end of the month and, apart from a few B Mk IIIs, used the B Mk VII version exclusively for the remainder of the war. With the exception of a few B Mk VIIs issued to 415 Squadron, the use of this particular marque of Halifax was restricted to the three RCAF squadrons mentioned, 408, 426 and 432.

*　　*　　*

Following the Kassel attack of 22/23 December which badly damaged the Henschel works and interrupted V-1 production, only sporadic attacks had been

Having left the Handley Page production line in January 1944, B Mk III LV838 was allocated to the A&AEE for development work, serving as the prototype B Mk VI. Photographed in May, little distinguished the change of engine from the Hercules XVI to the Hercules 100, the primary differences being a section of fixed cooling gills on each cowling extending from the wing leading edge line downward, apparent here by their zinc chromate primer colouring and the change of exhaust configuration, as explained in the text.

carried out against their launching sites. However, this was to change in the weeks following the Allied invasion of Europe. On the night of 12/13 June, Hitler's much-hinted-at secret weapon, the FZG 76 (VI), finally made its appearance but, because of the campaign against its permanent launching sites of the previous months, the start was a dismal failure with only 10 flying bombs launched[3]. That same day, the Chiefs of Staff Committee had met and formulated a directive that would allow Bomber Command to attack these sites as and when bombers could be spared, provided it did not compromise the needs of the Allied forces in France. However, the launching of over 200 flying bombs on the night of 15/16 June led General Eisenhower to issue a more imperative directive on the 16th; flying bomb targets were to be given first priority over everything other than any urgent tactical requirements of the armies in Europe.

Prior to 6 June, the task of eradicating the *Noball* targets[4] had lain with the medium and fighter-bombers of the Allied Expeditionary Air Force (AEAF) and the USAAF Eighth Air Force. Now, the major portion of this task fell to Bomber Command, who diverted a considerable number of heavy bombers to it with the target priorities split into four categories: large sites, supply sites, standard (permanent) sites, and modified (prefabricated) sites. Nevertheless, the Germans held a distinct advantage for, by the time the heavy bombers were committed, the large sites and the permanent sites had lost their significance. Most firings were now carried out from prefabricated sites, which could be erected and removed at relatively short notice. Thus the Allies were forced to adopt the wasteful but unavoidable campaign of attacking all sites. A sustained day and night offensive was instituted to offset the delays caused by the prevailing bad weather.

Eisenhower's directive was but a few hours old when a mixed force of 108 Halifaxes and Lancasters attacked the site at Domleger that night. The solid overcast led to some pessimism about results but reconnaissance photographs later showed that both Domleger and the launching site, attacked under similar conditions the next night, had been put out of action. Bad weather hampered operations for the next two or three days but by 22 June had cleared sufficiently for an attack on the permanent site at Siracourt. This was the first daylight raid of any significance for the Halifaxes of No 4 Group with 15 from 466 Squadron leading the 100-strong force to the target. Heavy flak greeted them and S/Ldr J. McMullen's LW166: X, the only aircraft lost, was shot down just short of the target; four parachutes were seen to emerge, but only two crew survived, one of whom, Sgt C. Dawson, evaded capture. The Master Bomber initially instructed crews to bomb visually but soon ordered the accompanying 105 Squadron Pathfinder Mosquitoes to mark the target. Not many crews saw the Target Indicators and only one from 158 Squadron aimed on them; the rest bombed on *Gee* fixes or the bomb bursts seen through the broken cloud cover. Several of this squadron's Halifaxes orbited the target area trying to identify the site but heavy flak from the defences south-east of Boulogne and a position south of the target curtailed this; five aircraft were damaged.

On the night of 23/24 June, a far more successful attack was made, in good weather for a change, on a supply site near Oisemont. A few hours later, a force of Halifaxes from No 6 Group made an equally successful attack on the site at Bonnetot while No 4 Group Halifaxes attacked the one at Noyelle-en-Chausse. That same night No 4 Group Halifaxes were engaged in an attack on Le Grande Rossignol.

Most crews welcomed the changing emphasis to daylight attacks, as Allied air supremacy was virtually complete. German fighters only ventured into the forward areas at night where they met with some success due to the twilight conditions prevailing at that time of the year. Even so, bomber losses diminished appreciably

After being screened from operations on completion of their tour at the end of June, F/Lt Freeman and his crew were happy to pose with their hard-working ground staff in front of MZ794: W, Winsome WAAF. The occasion had its own brief moment of highlight when, with the crew taking over the Halifax checking it out while the photograph was being arranged, the new navigator accidentally fired off a burst from the Vickers gun in the nose resulting in a spectacular reaction from those below. In the front row, left to right are, F/O T. Walker (navigator), F/O G. Smith (bomb aimer), F/O R. Hughes (WOP/AG). Middle row, unknown, unknown, Fl/Sgt H. Hawthorn (flight engineer), Flight Commander, S/Ldr Simmonds, F/Lt W. Freeman (pilot) and in the back, Sgt D. Donkin (mid-upper gunner) on the right and Fl/Sgt H. Reddy (rear gunner). The Sergeant in charge of the photographic section, previously a commercial artist in Bermuda, painted the artwork on the nose based on a photograph (face only!) of Harry Hawthorn's wife who had flowing red hair and green eyes. Hughes did a further two operations (32), while Donkin, who had only done 28, went to another crew but was killed when their aircraft was shot up. Flying as 'T-Tommy', MZ794 was severely damaged by flak during the attack on Stuttgart on 28/29 January 1945 and attacked twice by a Bf 109, killing Sgt Fenner the rear gunner. F/O Bradshaw managed to crash-land the badly damaged Halifax on A58, an American emergency strip in France but one other crew member was slightly injured. Hughes went on to do a 'rest' tour with 1663 HCU as an instructor before joining 96 Squadron in January 1945. (R. E. Hughes)

with the daylight raids but, while preferred, they could bring home the operational risks in vivid detail. On 9 August 466 Squadron was attacking a flying bomb site at Coquereaux when Fl/Sgt L. Burrow's Halifax was hit by flak five miles west of the target. He continued his run and bombed, but moments later MZ368: X exploded, five parachutes miraculously appearing from amidst the smoke and wreckage with one of the crew evading capture[v] after landing. Unfortunately, Burrows was not amongst the survivors.

Trained for night operations, Bomber Command crews were not generally well versed in formation flying and continued to operate in streams as at night. However, No 76, one of the oldest Halifax squadrons, tried formation flying in Vics of three, spaced at two wing span intervals, and stepped up in line astern. The squadron also pioneered other tactics during the night operations of this period, which primarily consisted of rapid height changes. After bombing from between 17 and 20,000 ft a dive was made to about 2,000 ft in a period of about six to seven minutes at a computed airspeed of over 300 mph. After levelling out near the coast at a level speed of approximately 250 mph, a steep climb was then made to cross over the light flak defences before dropping back down to sea level for the homeward run. Following the first experiments, the squadron diarist noted: *"These tactics had been suggested by the squadron for a very long time against much opposition and it is pleasing to note how successful they are."*

Attack followed attack with some squadrons putting up two raids in one day. The keenness of some crews may be judged by F/O N. Gordon's efforts. No 427 Squadron was part of a force sent to attack the Ferme-du-Grande-Bois site in the early morning of 28 June. Immediately after take-off, at a height of 500 ft, the port inner engine of LV988: P failed, but Gordon continued on to the target. After the attack F/Lt Shannon in MZ757: Y escorted him part of the way back until four Spitfires appeared and took over. Shortly afterwards Gordon's Halifax lost its starboard outer engine, but fortunately he made a safe landing back at base.

At the end of June the permanent sites were removed from the target priority list and attacks concentrated throughout July against the modified sites. The size and nature of these made them extremely difficult to locate in bad weather or at night, even when employing *Oboe*-equipped Pathfinder aircraft.

Among the crews operating at this time was a very special veteran who completed an operational tour with 425 Squadron on 15 July. 'Vickie' was the squadron mascot, a stuffed bunny sent from Ottawa and received on Easter Day 1944. Given the rank of Flight Officer, (after all, she was a female bunny) and made an 'Operational Overseer' she had completed 16 operations by 1 June, with 11 crews booked to take her on future operations. On her 35th and final operation in an attack on Nucourt, she carried a special message for the people of the district. It read, *"14 Juillet, (Bastilles) 1944. France combatante vous envoice par les Canadians Francois de l'Escadrille Alouette, ce symbole de liberation."* Attached to a French flag it was dropped from the aircraft before reaching the target. No 425 Squadron's co-tenant at Dishforth, 426 Squadron, owned a Totem Pole that had a difference of opinion with a Halifax which overshot the runway on 19 July. Damage was fortunately light to both parties.

Some targets required several attacks before they could be definitely declared as destroyed and a far more positive result was achieved against the actual supply dumps that fed individual sites. Typical of this type of operation was a series of five attacks on a suspected supply depot at Fôret de Nieppe. The first of these was a

daylight attack on 28 July by the Halifaxes of No 4 Group. *Oboe*-equipped Mosquitoes led each separate formation in, the first group of six Halifaxes bombing with the leading Mosquito and the next six when they were abreast of the smoke columns that surged up from several large explosions. Early the following morning the same crews repeated the performance, Fôret de Nieppe receiving its fifth and final raid on 6 August.

From the end of July, attacks against modified sites were left entirely to the USAAF Eighth Air Force, while Bomber Command continued its campaign against supply depots and large construction works believed to be associated with the still-to-be-experienced A-4 (V2) rockets. During one of these attacks, against Bois de Cassan on 4 August, F/O R. Simpson of 433 Squadron was leaving the target area when his Halifax was hit by flak, slightly wounding the bomb aimer and severing the rudder control rods. The rear gunner, Sgt D. Brown, found that he could steer manually by manipulating the severed rods, but a more positive form of co-ordinated control was needed for a safe landing. An attempt was then made to repair the rods with wire cut from the trailing aerial, but this proved ineffective and Simpson was finally forced to order the crew to abandon HX275: S, all landing safely.

Destruction of the supply dumps and the means of transportation produced the first positive reduction in the number of V-1 launchings and the campaign proceeded to the next logical step – an attack on the main assembly complex, the Opel factories at Rüsselsheim, near Mainz. On 12/13 August 96 Halifaxes and 191 Lancasters attacked in the face of moderately heavy flak and persistent attention from night-fighters, which appeared in force towards the end of the operation. Damage was light, confined to the storage, loading and dispatch facilities in the south-western area of the complex, but the price was 20 bombers; seven Halifaxes and 13 Lancasters. A second raid, on 25/26 August, completed the task, but the Halifaxes were busy over Brest that night.

With the overrunning of the V-1 sites in the Pas de Calais, the task of the heavy bombers ceased and the campaign ended with a note of appreciation to No 4 Group from the Air Council on 12 September, which read: *"... to convey to you their warm appreciation of the part played by your Command in defeating the enemy's flying bomb attacks on this country. The continuous and heavy bombing of the experimental stations, production plants, launching sites, storage depots and communications which had been carried out by your Command not only imposed on the enemy a prolonged and unwelcome delay in the launching of his campaign but effectively limited the scale of effort which he was able to make. This notable achievement has added one more to the long list of successful operations carried out by Bomber Command."*

*   *   *

Amidst the multiple invasion activities, some crews were still completing their 30-operation tour of duty; getting to that point was often as much a factor of random chance as skill since crews were sometimes split up for one reason or another. Fl/Sgt Harry Hawthorn had crewed up with Fl/Sgt Barry Marshall at 1663 HCU and had started their tour of duty together in May 1943 with 158 Squadron. When Marshall broke his leg playing table tennis in the Mess, Hawthorn was transferred to 51 Squadron at Snaith on 17 January 1944 to a scratch crew being assembled who were short of a flight engineer. He then joined Fl/Sgt W. Freeman's new crew and completed his tour with him. Having recovered, Marshall took on a new crew but all were later killed when LW259: F was shot down by flak during an attack on Kassel on 22/23 October 1943. Four of that crew had survived a serious crash a month earlier when returning from Mannheim on 23/24 September in LW283: V and Freeman had lost all his previous crew when NR721: J '*My Gal Sal*' ran short of fuel returning from an attack on Nuremberg on 10/11 August 1943. After crossing the coast at 8,000 ft on a northerly heading, Freeman had ordered his crew to bale out near Selsey Bill. With the crew gone, he turned the Halifax onto a southerly heading, engaged the autopilot, trimmed for a slow descent and baled out, landing on the beach. The aircraft also landed on the beach after the two port engines cut. Six of the crew were carried out to sea by the gale force northerly wind, the only one to be found alive being F/O T. Walker, the Canadian navigator who was found and picked up by an Air Sea Rescue (ASR) Walrus the following morning.

With the mopping-up of the last vestiges of resistance in the Cherbourg peninsula on 1 July, the Allies had been able to turn their full attention to the problem of relieving the serious congestion of the bridgehead area. The task was not easy since, despite serious handicaps, the Germans stubbornly held fast to a line of well-sited defensive positions throughout the *bocage* country and around Caen. The very nature of the countryside, with its massive banked-up hedgerows providing natural anti-tank obstacles, favoured the enemy and Allied commanders feared that unless a rapid breakthrough was made the whole campaign might be seriously impaired as it had been in Italy. Light and even medium bombers could not deliver a sufficient weight of bombs in a single attack to blast a path through the German defences so Bomber Command was given the task of assisting General Montgomery's frontal attack on Caen.

Originally timed for 04.20 hrs on 8 July, bad weather intervened once more and the mixed force of 467 Halifaxes and Lancasters attacked at dusk on 7 July instead. Escorted by a strong force of fighters, the bombers attacked an area two and a half miles long by one mile deep some 6,000 yards ahead of the foremost British positions. Because of the close proximity of Allied troops, the target area had been moved back, closer to Caen, in an open area and along the northern edge of the city. The only opposition came from the ground defences in the southern sector of the town and bombing was extremely accurate with 2,276 tons hitting the two aiming points. Bomber losses were light. 158 Squadron lost three: MX286: X had crashed into the sea at Barmston two minutes after take-off and two others were lost in the actual attack – MZ703: K was brought down 12 km from Caen with four of F/O B. Garnett's crew surviving as POWs, and F/Lt W. Davies' MZ730: Q crashed in the target area killing all on board. Flak brought down F/Lt J. Cooper's 432 Squadron Halifax NP706: J which crashed with its fuselage on fire; one crew member was killed but six survived with two of them evading capture. This was Cooper's 31st operation. No 578 Squadron lost LK794: Q under mysterious circumstances, the Halifax coming down two miles south of Bisham, in Berkshire, just over an hour after take-off. Fire in or near one of the starboard engines is thought to have been the cause. F/O V. Starkoff had given the order to bale out but only Fl/Sgt H. Sloan had jumped before the Halifax went completely out of control and exploded.

The attack was highly successful from the bombing aspect, but it was later assessed that the original aiming points should have been used as few German troops were killed, although some units were badly shaken up. By the evening of 8 July, British troops had reached the northernmost suburbs of Caen. Unfortunately, the bombing had been a little too effective and the heavy cratering and fallen masonry in the narrow streets halted the armoured forces trying to reach the Orne bridges which the Germans destroyed, establishing a new defensive system in the industrial suburbs of Vaucelles.

While the aims had not been fully achieved, the application had been proven and General Eisenhower approved the subsequent use of Bomber Command and the Eighth Air Force for two similar operations named *Goodwood* and *Cobra* which were designed to smash outlets through the German positions for both the British and American forces in the lodgement area. Some 2,019 heavy, medium and light bombers were committed to *Operation Goodwood*. American heavy bombers were assigned three areas, two to the rear and one on the eastern flank of the enemy positions, while the medium and light bombers of the AEAF were to attack three specific pinpoints. Bomber Command was given the task of attacking five areas on a line directly in front of the Allied positions that were only about one mile away to the north.

At 05.45 hrs on 18 July this highly complicated aerial operation began, with 235 bombers attacking Colombelles from low level, completely saturating the target area in a precision attack. The smoke still shrouded the target area when, 20 minutes later, a second force comprising 232 Halifaxes and Lancasters, swept in for a low-level attack on enemy positions around the Mondeville steel works just south of Colombelles. The Master Bomber, S/Ldr E. Creswell, changed the aiming point from time to time to ensure that the target area was completely saturated and crews were highly confident of the results. Losses were light and not all due to enemy action. No 429 Squadron lost a Halifax when bombs from another Halifax overhead struck LW127: F, completely removing the starboard side of the tail plane, causing it to crash in the target area. F/Lt G. Gardiner and three others survived with one managing to evade capture. No 427 Squadron lost LV985: K on the same target but there were no survivors from P/O T. Kelly's crew.

While the Colombelles attack was in progress, the road and rail junction at Sommerville was receiving the attention of 105 Halifaxes from No 4 Group, accompanied by 125 Lancasters of No 1 Group, who delivered a very concentrated low-level attack. Twenty minutes later, coincidental with the Mondeville raid, a

18 July 1944: Operation Goodwood was in progress when LW127: F, a B Mk III of 429 Squadron, was hit by two 500 lb bombs from another aircraft while attacking Mondeville on the outskirts of Caen. This type of accident was always possible, even with planning which gave each squadron its time and height over target and angle of approach. Severely damaged LW127: F crashed in the target area killing all on board.

mixed Halifax-Lancaster force of 242 attacked Mannerville. Cagny, a strong point to the rear held by the 21st Panzer Division, was the final target for a force of 106 bombers, which attacked successfully at 06.20 hrs. In the remarkably short time of 35 minutes, 5,000 tons of bombs had been dropped for the loss of nine bombers, which included a Halifax from each of Nos 76 and 578 Squadrons.

Bad weather yet again interceded in the enemy's favour and after rapid advances, the ground forces became bogged down when heavy rain fell on the 20th. The same bad weather also hampered *Operation Cobra* but most objectives were taken and the American forces at last gained a foothold in Brittany. This produced a new requirement – to prevent transfer of German reinforcements from the British sector to meet this new emergency. The Second British Army, ordered to make a strong attack in the Caumont area, was to be supported by a force of 692 Halifaxes and Lancasters plus 500 light and medium bombers of the AEAF. As at Caen, *Oboe* marking was used but only 377 aircraft were able to bomb on 30 July because of cloud, which resulted in only two of the six targets being hit effectively for the loss of four Lancasters. Yet even these limited results assisted and within a few days, the enemy had been driven back to Villers-Bocage and Beny-Bocage, thus securing the threat to the American flank.

The next major action by Bomber Command in direct support of the ground forces on 7/8 August called for an unprecedented and daring night attack on five aiming points along the flank of the projected advance, with great care being taken not to endanger the nearby First Canadian Army, which was to make a night assault on Falaise. Low cloud and smoke quickly obscured the target markers and the Master Bomber cancelled most attacks soon after they began with only about 660 of the 1,019 aircraft dispatched actually bombing, for the loss of nine Lancasters. Although the attack on May-sur-Ome by Halifaxes of No 4 Group was curtailed after three minutes, they managed to drop 427 tons of bombs during this brief interlude.

One final close-support operation awaited Bomber Command. On 14 August, General Montgomery gave the order for *Operation Tractable* to begin – the daylight assault that was to cut through the German lines at Falaise and link up with the American Third Army, thus isolating the German Seventh Army. Seven strong points, all within 2,000 yards of the Canadian positions were selected for the force of 805 aircraft comprised of 411 Lancasters, 352 Halifaxes and 42 Mosquitoes. Planning was most careful because of the proximity of the Canadian troops and both *Oboe* and visual marking were employed, with a Master Bomber and a deputy at each of the seven targets. For once, the weather was favourable and visibility excellent, some crews pressing home their attack from as low as 2,000 ft. Most bombing was accurate but part way through the attack some aircraft began bombing a large quarry in which were Canadian troops. Post battle analysis pointed to the use of yellow flares by the troops, which had been confused with the yellow Target Indicators being used by the bombing force. The Master Bomber attempted to stop the bombing but 70 had already attacked, killing 13 Canadians and injuring 53. Three Lancasters were lost from the bombing force, two coming down in the target area and one crashing before reaching the English coast. By 16 August, the Canadians were in Falaise. With the advance mobile once more, Bomber Command's direct assistance was no longer required.

The following day 1,004 bombers were sent to attack nine airfields in Holland and Belgium known to house Luftwaffe night-fighter units. Visibility was excellent and all attacks were assessed as successful for the loss of three Lancasters. That attack marked the end of Bomber Command's current tactical deployment in support of the ground battle and it turned its full attention once more to the strategic night

On 12 October 1944, the Wanne-Eickel oil refinery was attacked again, this time by 111 Halifaxes and 26 Lancasters of No's 6 and 8 Groups, and when this photograph was taken the target was already covered with smoke from a storage tank that had received a direct hit very early in the attack. Unfortunately, this successful hit hindered the remainder of the attacking force and although the German report stated that the attack achieved little damage, the GAVEG chemical factory was destroyed. In this overhead view of a 6 Group Halifax above the target, the standard A Type camouflage pattern applied to Halifaxes is clearly visible. (via M. W right)

offensive. However, before returning to those operations, other tasks that Bomber Command had been pursuing must be recorded.

In addition to the immediate tactical needs of the ground battles, Bomber Command was also called upon to make heavy attacks on the isolated garrisons and strong points left behind in the coastal regions. Some were carried out to meet naval requirements such as the small force of Lancasters and Halifaxes which had bombed the E-boat and U-boat pens at Boulogne in daylight on 15 June. Brest was attacked on 14 September by a force of 53 Halifaxes from No 4 Group, but this time as part of the campaign to sink the block ships being prepared to deny the port facilities to the Allies when they inevitably occupied it.

Delay in securing sufficient harbour facilities had seriously impeded the flow of supplies to the Allied forces and 21st Army Group HQ made an approach to No 4 Group to deliver urgently needed supplies of motor transport fuel to Brussels-Melsbroek airfield. The Halifax's spacious interior was well suited to the task and in eight days from 25 September, Nos 77, 102, 346 and 347 Squadrons transported 431,800 gallons of fuel to Belgium with each of the 70 Halifaxes carrying approximately 165 jerry cans on each flight.

Brest was proving a tenacious obstacle and 334 Halifaxes and Lancasters dropped 1,200 tons of bombs on this target on 25/26 August for the loss of one Halifax and one Lancaster. Despite this and other attacks, it was not captured until 18 September. By Hitler's orders Le Havre, Boulogne and Calais were declared fortresses and their defenders were to resist to the last in the tradition of the Brest defenders. The Le Havre defenders did just that and it took a series of four raids to dislodge them. The first two, on 8 and 9 September, were hampered by bad weather resulting in little damage. The next day a mixed force of Halifaxes, Lancasters and Mosquitoes returned and attacked eight different strong points, each clearly marked by the PFF aircraft. A very successful attack resulted for no loss to the bomber force. The following afternoon a small force of 105 Halifaxes, 103 Lancasters and 10 PFF Mosquitoes returned and delivered another accurate attack, again for no loss. Dust and smoke from the bombing reduced the number to bomb to 171 but it was sufficient; 10 hours later the garrison surrendered to the Allied Divisions assaulting the positions.

The success of the Le Havre battle led to similar requests for assistance from Bomber Command. A mixed force of 742 bombers attacked Boulogne on 17 September and 76 Squadron crews, who were at the tail end of the attack, reported that the target was well and truly hit. Boulogne surrendered on 22 September. Calais received similar treatment between 20 and 28 September with the raid on the 27th being made at low level. Integrated with these attacks were two against the fortified areas protecting the long-range guns at Cap Gris Nez. On 29 September, the garrison capitulated with the garrison at Calais following suit the next day.

The campaign against enemy communications had also continued unabated during this same period with attacks on 18 rail centres in the six-week period from the beginning of July. Lancaster-equipped Groups made the bulk of the early attacks as No 4 Group, as noted below, was preoccupied with attacks against V-1 sites; so the Halifaxes did not participate until 18 July, when they successfully attacked Vaires, heavily cratering the main sidings and severing the Paris-Meaux through-line in

several places. Ground fire was intense, both en route and at the target, and many Halifaxes sustained minor damage. About 15 minutes short of the target area, MZ313, a 466 Squadron Halifax, was severely damaged by a flak shell that burst in the fuselage and F/Lt P. Finley found that he could get no response from either the rudders or the elevator. With every indication that the aircraft might break up at any moment he ordered the crew to bale out, two of the five managing to evade capture. The mid-upper gunner later reported that the Halifax's back must have been broken because he could see the tail unit swinging from side to side as he floated away. P/O R. Evans, the bomb aimer, however remained with Finley and they attempted to get the Halifax back to England. By sheer physical effort, they managed to keep it flying straight and level and had reached the Dungeness area off the English coast when they were finally forced to give up the struggle and baled out just before the Halifax broke up in mid-air. Two other Halifaxes were lost in the target area, LW572: Q and MZ628: Y, both from 431 Squadron.

No 4 Group's next daylight railway target was Hazebrouck on 6 August but it returned to night operations for a very successful attack on Dijon on 10/11 August. Following hard on the heels of this raid, part of the Halifax force returned a few hours later to bomb the railway bridge at Etaples. The intense activity of this period is epitomised by the 429 Squadron diarist who recorded that it was not unusual for the squadron to operate simultaneously against two or three targets with one group of crews taking off while the next were being briefed, etc.

Overlapping all these activities were the oil targets still being attacked on German soil. Two of the three targets hit on 20/21 July were the German oil plants at Bottrop and Homberg, the latter being severely damaged. German sources show that the April figures for aviation fuel production was nearly 6,000 tons per day but had fallen to 120 and 970 tons per day in the wake of raids against oil plants by Bomber Command and the Eighth Air Force. Attacks against such targets were still costly at times, Homberg raid costing 20 Lancasters from an attacking force of 147, 75 Squadron losing seven out of the 25 aircraft sent. Bottrop was a Halifax operation with 149 sent and supported by 13 Mosquitoes and four Lancasters of the marking force; seven Halifaxes and a Lancaster were lost, and 158 Squadron was particularly badly hit with four shot down over enemy territory. F /Lt A. Hope-Robertson's MZ511: M fell to the guns of Major Martin Drewes of the III./NJG 1 and crashed between Oldebroek and Heerd with only two of his crew surviving. F/Lt J. Couture, one of many Americans flying with the RCAF, was killed along with all his crew when MZ617: D was shot down by a night-fighter at Herpen in Belgium; Fl/Sgt K. Hutton's MZ556: P fell to flak 6 km west of Moers, killing him and two of his crew. F/O T. Harrison's MX572: C simply failed to return and was lost with all of its crew. Then fate stepped in with thick cloud over Burn when the remaining Halifaxes returned to base, which saw Sgt W. Davidson's LK834: E colliding with F/O M. Day's MZ696: K as both descended through cloud at 2,000 ft and crashing at Balkholme, killing both crews. No 51 Squadron's MZ851: C also fell at the last moment. Hit by flak over Bottrop, F/O H. Jowett RAAF managed to retain control despite damage to both fins and rudders but soon after collided with another aircraft, but again Jowett managed to regain control and set course for the emergency landing field at Woodbridge in Suffolk – minus four of the crew who had baled out in the ensuing chaos. On approach to the airfield, the Halifax collided with trees and crashed near the runway, killing all those remaining on board. The four who had baled out all came down behind Allied lines and returned to the squadron soon after and were integrated into other crews. Fl/Sgt K. Adams RAAF was killed almost a month to the day when LW538: N captained by F/O W. Quan RAAF, failed to return from the raid on Sterkrade by 234 Halifaxes supported by 14 Mosquitoes and 10 Lancasters on 18/19 August. One Lancaster was also lost but the heavy damage for the loss of just two aircraft was deemed a very good result.

The abrupt shift to daylight operations had produced a new set of markings – daylight tactical markings, applied to the vertical tail surfaces of the Halifaxes and Lancasters of some squadrons. The colours were those available at unit level, used for national markings and squadron codes, the Night Black surfaces providing the contrasting colour, and a multitude of geometric designs appeared using yellow, red and white. Approval for the markings, and their specific form, must have originated at Air Ministry or at least Bomber Command HQ level to prevent duplication between units who chose to adopt them, but no official documentation has yet emerged for historians to check against. Interestingly, not all Bomber Command squadrons used such markings. Of the 21 Halifax bomber squadrons at the time, only nine have been recorded with daylight tactical markings, these being Nos 51, 78, 102, 158, 346, 347, 462, 466 and 640. Nos 51, 158 and 640 Squadrons also used two variations, possibly to distinguish between Flights. The usual RAF squadron structure was based on a three-Flight system A, B and usually C. In a few instances, the C Flight of one squadron became the nucleus of a new squadron; for example, 578 Squadron was formed from C Flight of 51 Squadron. A careful check of the role of those squadrons using such markings, in terms of daylight attacks, provides no specific reason for their adoption of these markings other than for the convenience of the individual squadron. The practice of outlining either the aircraft letter, or squadron codes, or both, thinly in roundel yellow was more widespread across units but equally random, even within a single squadron.

Having received permission to use French Air Force shades of colours for both the fuselage roundel and fin flash, the two French Squadrons had also reversed the usual sequence by using a blue centre for the roundels with a red outer ring, this latter also being the leading colour of the fin flash. This was not the dull, darker red used by the RAF but rather the more crimson shade of the French Air Force and both squadrons also used it for their tactical markings. It is difficult to be definitive about time of introduction but it would appear that these new markings did not appear until well after D-Day. Prior to D-Day, squadrons had not known that they would be used extensively for daylight operations, and permission to adopt such obvious bold markings prior to the invasion would not have been given on security grounds. As mentioned earlier, the black and white band markings used by some of the RAF forces were applied only hours before the first sorties were dispatched – in No 38 Group, they were applied quite roughly with six-inch distemper brushes on some aircraft, just hours before take-off.

* * *

During the period from late May to late July 1944, Bomber Command had not carried out any attacks against German cities. As noted, activities over Germany had been restricted to oil targets in the Ruhr, and some concern was felt over the respite afforded the vast German industrial system, which had already demonstrated a capacity for recuperation. Accordingly, the strategic bombing offensive had recommenced on 23/24 July and by the end of September, 30 major raids had been completed against 18 targets.

The Kiel attack of 23/24 July was the first major assault on a German city for two months. The RAF won the war of deception that night; elaborate spoof attacks and tenuous routing of the bomber stream combined with the surprise return to a German city, to produce very good bombing results for the loss of four Lancasters from the mixed force of 629 aircraft.

Kiel received three more raids and the defences took an increasing but still relatively small toll of the bombers during the second and third attacks. The fourth was more successful and the 490-strong force destroyed large sections of the eastern port area with its naval dockyards, arsenal and marine stores. It was enough – Kiel was removed from the target list for the remainder of the year.

Within a few days of the Normandy landings, both British and American bomber forces had been allocated a new series of priority strategic targets; from July to September, Ruhr synthetic oil plants were given precedence. The only diversion would occur in August, when the fluid nature of the ground battles required attacks on storage depots, dumps and refineries in occupied territory.

Synthetic oil was not a wartime innovation. Pre-war, Germany had recognised the need for careful husbanding of strategically sensitive supplies, including minerals and oil, enforcing this discipline on many areas of German manufacture. Oil industry scientists had responded to the challenge and before the war had perfected a system of synthetic oil manufacture. Thus, this sector of the industry was well established and highly productive and became critical once German reverses lost access to oil fields in formerly occupied or friendly territories.

Lancasters had attacked the first of these targets on 12/13 June and four nights later a mixed force of Halifaxes and Lancasters bombed the Fischer-Tropsch plant at Holten-Sterkrade. Flak and night-fighters provided strong opposition and nature added an additional complication – solid cloud extending from 7,000 to 10,000 ft which quickly swallowed up the Target Indicators, leaving crews to aim on any glow that filtered through. Compounding the problems, the route chosen passed close to the German night-fighter beacon at Bocholt – and the German controller had chosen this beacon as the assembly point for his force. Of the 31 aircraft lost, 21 fell to night-fighters while flak claimed the remainder. The hardest hit were the Halifaxes, of which 23 of their number failed to return. It is clear from the records that many of these were intercepted on the homeward leg and 77 Squadron lost seven of its 23 aircraft. Some savage exchanges took place and not all were one-sided. From 77 Squadron, P/O S. Judd's gunners drove off a night-fighter, which was last seen diving away on fire, but the damage was done, Judd having to ditch MZ705: Q off Lowestoft, the crew being safely rescued near Felixstowe at 06.30 hrs. For their actions, Judd was awarded a DFC and both gunners the DFM. Other crews also had some success against the fighters; an Fw 190 and then a Ju 88 attacked P/O Sargeant's 466 Squadron Halifax causing minor damage, but a third attacker fell to the Halifax's gunners.

Although 149 Halifaxes of No 4 Group made the initial attack on 20/21 July against Bottrop-Welheim, while No 3 Group aircraft attacked the Homberg-Meerbeck plant, not all of the Halifax squadrons were operating at full strength because of the divided commitment to the V-1 campaign. For example, 466 Squadron sent six to the oil target and 12 to attack the V-1 installation at Ardouval

Caught by the camera in F/O Nixon's 433 Squadron Halifax HX268: A, 346 Free French Squadron's MZ737: B passes over the Fôret de Nieppe at 15,000 ft on 3 August 1944. Nixon's Halifax was carrying sixteen 500 lb bombs, the type of load favoured for attacks on V-1 storage sites. HX268: A was the oldest aircraft on the squadron at the beginning of October and had completed 62 sorties. Like other veterans, it was passed to an HCU, in this instance 1659 while MZ737: B, having served previously with 158 Squadron, was eventually struck off charge on 16 May 1945. (via M. Wright)

and while no aircraft were lost at the latter target, German defences brought down seven Halifaxes and a PFF Lancaster at Bottrop-Welheim.

On 25/26 July, 114 Halifaxes of No 4 Group attacked the Krupp oil refinery at Wanne Eickel. Thick haze obscured the target but not the target markers; even so, damage was light with bombs only falling on one corner of the site. However, the bombs that missed were not wasted having hit the nearby Hannibal coal mine, causing production to cease and, although the ground defences inflicted some minor damage and several night-fighters were seen, no combats took place and no aircraft were lost.

Yet over Stuttgart, the night's primary target, things were different and saw eight Lancasters and four Halifaxes brought down out of the combined force of 550 aircraft, 412 Lancasters and 138 Halifaxes, sent to attack the city. This was the second attack of two consecutive nights, the first mounted by 461 Lancasters and 153 Halifaxes, 17 of the former and four of the latter being brought down. The third and final attack in the five-day sequence would be made on 28/29th by 494 Lancasters at a cost of 39 Lancasters or 7.9% of the force. A difficult target situated in a series of narrow valleys, Stuttgart had escaped major damage to date and although losses were high, the city was badly damaged.

That same night Hamburg had been attacked by a force of 107 Lancasters, 187 Halifaxes and 14 Mosquitoes but the ever-present night-fighters successfully penetrated the homeward bound bomber stream to claim 18 Halifaxes and four Lancasters. This first heavy attack on Hamburg in nearly a year was not successful. German estimates put the number of attackers at only about 120 with much of the bombing falling on already devastated areas of the city and the bomber crews paying a savage price for the failure. No 431 Squadron in particular lost five of its 17 Halifaxes. For 408 Squadron it was a double jeopardy as it was making the transition from Lancasters back to Halifax B. Mk VIIs and operated both types that night, losing NP716: P near Heide killing all of S/Ldr G. Latimer's all-Canadian crew and 2.Lt. A. Hauzenberger of the USAAF. The squadron also lost three Lancasters, the squadron's last for the type[6]. The remaining Halifax losses from this operation were all Canadian and by squadron were as follows: No 415 LW595: Q and MZ686: U; No 420 MZ645: N; No 424 LV997: E; No 425 MZ641: K and MZ712: S; No 426 LW202: P and LW208: U; No 427 MZ757: Y; No 431 LK833: R, LK845: J, MZ589: H, MZ597: B and MZ859: A; No 432 NP702: B; No 433 MZ816: W; and No 434 LW347:X and LW596:Z.

Then it was back to flying bomb launching sites, storage sites, and railway yards with the occasional diversion for tactical bombing in support of the Allied ground forces. The diversionary attacks on storage depots ceased with the raid against Ertvelde Reime on 18/19 August. As noted earlier, that same night an attack by Halifaxes on the Sterkrade-Holten plant marked the start of a new series of raids against the Ruhr-based synthetic oil plants.

The Allied advances of August overran most of the German night-fighter bases in France and made the position of those in Belgium and Holland precarious, not only for the loss of these airfields but also their early-warning radar installations along the Calvados coast and the Brest peninsula. Thus, Bomber Command was able to approach northern German targets across the neck of Denmark while using the *Mandrel* screen to conceal its activities. However, the size of the attacking formations presented a problem although this apparent disadvantage was rapidly turned to an advantage. When only minor operations were in progress, the *Mandrel* screen was used in conjunction with a small force carrying *Window*. At an appropriate time, the latter would burst through the *Mandrel* screen and release the *Window* to simulate a larger force on the German radar, resulting in the night-fighters being scrambled to meet it, thus causing confusion amongst the German controllers. The element of doubt created by these spoof raids was perhaps the greatest benefit, for suspicion caused delay while the controllers made certain that the raid was genuine and in turn, cost the night-fighters any tactical advantage they might otherwise have achieved.

Braunschweig was chosen for a bold experiment on 12/13 August when 137 Halifaxes and 17 Lancasters were sent to attack without the use of PFF markings as Bomber Command was interested to see if crews could successfully attack a city using individual *H2S* sets. While the Braunschweig authorities deemed it a heavy attack, no bombing concentration was achieved and towns 20 miles distant recorded damage. The experiment cost 10 Halifaxes and 17 Lancasters. Rüsselsheim was also attacked that night, but using conventional PFF methods.

On 27 August, No 4 Group dispatched 216 Halifaxes to attack the Homberg-Meerbeck plant in Bomber Command's heaviest raid yet committed to a single oil target. It was also the first daylight raid on Germany by British bombers in force since the Cologne power station raid of 12 August 1941. In addition to a strong fighter escort, the force was accompanied by a single Mosquito to make an immediate assessment of the resulting damage. The newly formed 462 Squadron made their operational debut on this raid and for F/O A. Lane it was nearly his last. Having lost the port outer engine before even crossing the enemy coast, he continued on to the target despite being at a reduced altitude. Over Homberg, his Halifax faced the double danger of being singled out by the flak defences and running the gauntlet of bombs showering down from above. Finally, with a second engine put out of action by flak and the main target obscured, Lane was forced to bomb the docks on the east bank of the Rhine. The target was heavily damaged and losses were nil.

On 8 September, a second bomber support squadron came into being when No 171 Squadron was formed from 'C' flight of 199 Squadron at North Creake, leaving the latter permanently reduced to two flights. No 199 Squadron continued to administer the fledgling unit until the official postings of flight personnel were made on 1 October. Although allocated 20 B Mk IIIs it continued to operate Stirlings until the Halifaxes arrived in force and for a while operated both types[7]. Although the new squadron was ready for operations on a limited scale from 9 October, it was not until the 15th that two Stirlings were sent out, completing their sortie successfully. On the 16th, the first of the Halifaxes arrived and conversion training started immediately while the Stirling force continued operations.

The superior performance and fuselage capacity of the Halifax proved far more suitable than that of the Stirling for *Mandrel* operations. While it was intended to standardise on the type for all of 100 Group's operations, the size of some of the equipment ruled this out and led to 214 Squadron, based at Oulton, to retain its B-17s and B-24s[8]. The first Halifax operation proper by the squadron, consisting of one Halifax and three Stirlings, took place on 23 October. On this date, 112

Lancasters carried out a daylight attack on the gun batteries on Walcheren but visibility was poor and the bombing scattered. Four Lancasters failed to return. The following day, 171 Squadron began ferrying its Halifaxes, of which it now had eight, to St Athan for the fitting of *Mandrel* equipment.

Meanwhile Bomber Command had been pursuing its daylight campaign with vigour against synthetic oil plants in the Ruhr. On 11 September 205 Halifaxes, 154 Lancasters and 20 Mosquitoes attacked the Kastrop-Rauxel, Kamen and Nordstern plants. The first two were attacked successfully but the Nordstern plant was partially protected by a smoke screen which hindered the bombing. No enemy fighters were encountered but 5 Halifaxes and 2 Lancasters were lost over Nordstern and a Lancaster was lost from each of the other raids – all to either flak or 'friendly' bombs.

During the first raid, F/O J. Currie's 77 Squadron Halifax was hit by flak five minutes before bombing. The starboard outer engine was damaged and a considerable oil leak occurred, making it impossible to feather the propeller. Despite the subsequent loss of height, the crew elected to continue and bomb as planned. During the final run-up to the target MZ710: E[10] was repeatedly hit by flak, which inflicted some 200 holes, set fire to the dinghy and disabled both the DR and magnetic compasses and radio. Just after bombing, one fuel tank in each wing was punctured and the port inner engine was hit, removing one cylinder. Height was lost steadily down to 3,500 ft, but the Halifax managed to escape the flak at the Dutch coast. This height was maintained across the North Sea, but just before reaching Orfordness, the starboard outer propeller and reduction gear flew off, damaging the starboard inner propeller. Despite the loss of one engine and two others only providing partial power, Currie was able to maintain sufficient height to reach the Woodbridge area, three Spitfires, which had taken up station in the target area, having remained a comforting escort throughout. The endeavour nearly ended in disaster when Currie made his approach, skimming the tops of the trees, on to an experimental runway, but a series of yellow flares diverted him at the last moment and he was able to turn on to the correct one. The port inner engine cut over the boundary fence but the landing was completed safely thus showing that the old Halifax problems of insufficient power and poor asymmetric handling were things of the past.

On 12 September, a force of 412 comprised of 315 Halifaxes, 75 Lancasters and 22 Mosquitoes attacked plants at Dortmund, Schloven-Buer and Wanne-Eickel. The Dortmund attack was successful but smoke screens prevented the observation of results from the other targets. Seven aircraft were lost[11], 3 Lancasters and 1 Halifax from the Wanne-Eickel raid and 2 Halifaxes and 1 Lancaster from that against Schloven-Buer. The following day, a mixed force of Halifaxes, Lancasters and Mosquitoes attacked Nordstern again with large explosions being observed through the smoke screen. Two Halifaxes failed to return[12].

The second series of oil raids, made in late September, were nearly all disrupted by vagaries of weather. Typical of these was the Bottrop attack on the 27th. Solid cloud obscured the target and most crews were forced to make a timed run from a navigational fix. During the long steady run one of 432 Squadron's B Mk VIIs, NP692: K, was hit by flak, wounding the pilot, F/Lt Woodward. He nevertheless held the bombing run steady while the bombs were released, only to have a stick of bombs from above fall past the nose of NP692, barely missing it. The Halifax went into a dive with 30 degrees of bank on and Woodward slumped over the controls. F/O D. McLennon, the wireless operator, managed to pull him out of the seat, while the navigator, F/O C. Hay, brought the aircraft under control again. Woodward's parachute was beyond use and his condition made it impossible for him to jump and as Hay headed for Woodbridge, the rest of the crew elected to stay with the aircraft and assist him. Hay had some difficulty locating Woodbridge at first but finally found it. Woodward revived and attempted to take over for the landing, but his condition was too critical and Hay decided to attempt it himself. The sole B Mk II Series II Halifax, HR756, now attached to the Bomb Ballistics Unit was sent up to guide NP692 in and to assist Hay with instructions. Having formed up with NP692, Hay was talked down to a very smooth landing, but the speed was too high and the Halifax rose again then dropped back heavily and the engines caught fire as it came to a halt. The crew all escaped, but sadly, Woodward succumbed to his injuries the following day.

The Allied breakout from France and the link-up with the forces that had landed in the South of France opened up a surge towards the German frontier and signalled a significant shift in the war situation. The German border had been reached on 10 September, Belgium was liberated earlier in the month and the port of Antwerp seized with its facilities almost intact. Holland was reached on 15 September but the bold plan to seize vital road bridges across the rivers Rhine, Waal and Maas were stalled when ground forces failed to reach the British and American airborne troops at Arnhem. Holland now became a stalemate zone, something that would not change for the next four months. There were also now logistical problems, with few ports to handle the huge inflow of materiel and men. The successes, however, allowed Bomber Command to be returned to the direct control of the Air Ministry, but with the proviso from SHAEF that all future operations were still required to fit into the Allied master plan.

There immediately arose three options for the employment of Bomber Command, each supported by its own strong faction. Synthetic oil production was seen as a key strategic target but during the early period of the war, the Command had lacked the numbers effectively to attack and destroy them. However, with the strength of Bomber Command growing rapidly – it would increase by 50% by the end of the year – that situation had now changed and nine new Halifax squadrons had been added to its strength. The German transportation system was also viewed as a valuable target which offered the possibility of results that would also cripple the German capacity to fight on. The third option was to continue the bombing of German industrial cities. Fewer supported the latter option but Harris was the leading protagonist among them and a man determined to prove his long-standing contention that bombing of such targets would end the war.

On 25 September, a new directive had been issued to Bomber Command and the American Eighth Air Force which clearly demonstrated that the oil strategy had won favour with the strategic planners. This was reinforced with an order to Bomber Command to conduct a maximum-effort offensive against such targets. Despite his objections Harris obeyed, but managed, by careful target selection, to maintain his own policy.

What followed was the final chapter in Bomber Command's wartime history. Its strength was increasing along with its bomb-carrying capacity[13] to which could be added the rising sophistication of its bombing aids and bomber-support techniques. The enemy night-fighter force was in decline, but still deadly, but daylight operations were on the increase. Even so, there would follow a bitter campaign with not insignificant losses.

A part of 192 Squadron's activities centred on the German rocket weapons and during October, special patrols were carried out off the Dutch coast between Walcheren and Texel to try to locate signals believed to be associated with these missiles. A somewhat unusual crew took MZ564: X of 192 Squadron to Walcheren Island to watch the breaching of the sea wall at Westkappelle on 3 October. The captain, W/Cdr Donaldson, was accompanied by Air Commodore R. A. Chisholm, DSO, DFC acting as second pilot, while W/Cdr Willis, DSO, DFC acted as bomb aimer. The purpose of the flight was to record any enemy radiotelephony in connection with the attack by the 252 Lancasters. Three other aircraft accompanied them on this daylight mission, a Halifax and two P-38 Lightnings – the latter temporarily on the Squadron's strength.

The next night, MZ706: P and LW623: S went to Saarbrücken to investigate enemy VHF telephony while MZ795: V recorded VHF and D/F centimetric signals. A fourth Halifax, MZ932: Z, patrolled the Kattegat while Main Force bombers sowed mines off the Danish coast. The job of this particular Halifax, in addition to recording enemy VHF telephony, was to locate the coast watcher[14] stations, for which purpose automatic homing equipment was fitted.

No 192 Squadron continued to specialise in signals investigation and jamming for most of its career but occasionally joined the other squadrons in the Group to perform *Window-Mandrel* operations. It carried out the first of these on 9 October when MZ706 and LK781 went to a point midway between Heligoland and Wilhelmshafen where they dropped *Window* to create a diversion for the Bomber Command force operating that night. Such diversions, however, were few and in November, the Squadron continued with its investigation of the enemy coast watcher stations to try to determine if they were being used in connection with the inland flak bases. On several occasions, radio buoys in the North Sea were also investigated to see if they were associated with the launching of V-1s – perhaps there was something almost prophetic about a lone V-1 that passed over the Squadron's base on 3 January 1945?

The liberation of France now denied port facilities to German U-boats and Norwegian ports had become home to much of this force. Bergen's facilities were being enlarged and German technicians and a large labour force had been moved in to carry out the work. On 4 October 93 Halifaxes of No 6 Group and 47 Lancasters from No 8 Group were sent to disrupt this. While the Main Force attacked the U-boat pens, 14 Halifaxes and six Lancasters went after individual submarines known to be moored in the harbour. Despite what appeared to crews to be a successful attack, which cost a single Lancaster, tragedy was hidden behind the destruction, as civilian casualties, caused principally by two bombs, were high.

During October, weather again proved to be the decisive factor and restricted the number of oil plant attacks to five by Bomber Command and four by the US Eighth Air Force. Bomber Command restricted its attention to the Ruhr and launched a double daylight attack against Schloven-Buer and Sterkrade-Holten on 6 October. The Schloven-Buer raid was carried out using a group formation for the first time and 76 Squadron led the vanguard. A heavy fighter escort, mainly of Spitfires, guarded the second force of 126 Halifaxes detailed to put the refinery out of action. Every effort was made to ensure that the force arrived in a compact group and 33 Pathfinder aircraft were on hand to provide a well-laid and sustained series of target markers. A concentrated attack developed in the face of strong ground defences and reconnaissance later confirmed a high degree of damage to the target. Three Halifaxes were lost from the latter attack and four from the Schloven-Buer raid and 70% of the force suffered flak damage. That night No 6 Group mounted its

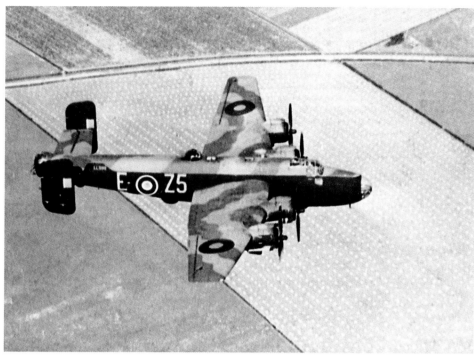

LL599: E of 466 Squadron was fitted with a Preston-Green ventral cupola, its rounder shape easily identifying it from the more often seen H2S radome. It was lost in the daylight attack on Essen on 23 October 1944. En route to its home base after the attack it collided with LM691: O, a Lancaster of 625 Squadron and both aircraft exploded. Only Fl/Sgt J. Grace RAAF from F/O F. Neider's crew managed to bale out, landing safely behind Allied lines. The pilot of the Lancaster, S/Ldr C. Hamilton and only survivor of its crew also landed behind Allied lines. (T. Eagleton)

heaviest operation of the war when 248 Halifaxes and 48 Lancasters took part in an attack on Dortmund by 523 aircraft. Severe damage was caused and despite the clear skies and the notorious Ruhr tag, only two Halifaxes, two Lancasters and a PFF Mosquito failed to return.

The next day No 4 Group were called upon to attack Kleve, a town ahead of the advancing ground forces and the source of a possible threat to the flank of the 21st Army Group following the failure of *Operation Market Garden* at Arnhem.

Bomber Command had already expended some effort in assisting with the final assault on Walcheren, the heavily defended island at the mouth of the Scheldt Estuary and gateway to Antwerp. It lay below sea level and was protected by a massive sea wall and a system of dykes and embankments. The intention was to breach the sea walls and flood out the defenders. The particularly successful raid on 3 October breached the sea wall at Westkapelle, leaving the sea to pour in through a gap 100 yards wide. On 7 October, a second breach was opened at Flushing but a further attack on the 17th produced no significant results despite the accuracy of the bombing. Two more attacks on the 21st and 23rd added no major damage and a larger operation, by 277 aircraft, 155 of them Halifaxes, was mounted on the 28th, this time against the gun emplacements in five places along the rim of the now flooded island. This was more successful at the cost of one Halifax and a Lancaster. The next day, 358 aircraft were sent back, 128 of them Halifaxes, and 11 targets were successfully attacked for the loss of one Lancaster. A final raid the following day was followed by a ground assault and the garrison surrendered on 3 November.

Immediately following the Walcheren attacks came an order for all Groups of Bomber Command and the US Eighth Air Force to prepare for a maximum effort attack on the enemy defences along the River Roer, 30 minutes before the Allied ground offensive opened. Bad weather delayed the operation for five days but, finally, on 16 November, the heaviest tactical bombardment to date broke loose on the enemy. While American heavy bombers attacked the front-line positions, 1,188 Halifaxes and Lancasters attacked the fortified base towns at Heinsburg, Julich and Duren. Halifaxes hit Julich with 1,946 tons of bombs, raising huge pillars of smoke that towered to 8,000 ft. A large portion of the town was devastated and the road bridge across the Roer effectively removed. All three raids were highly successful and losses amounted to a modest four, none of them Halifaxes. Between October 1944 and May 1945 Bomber Command would reach the climax of its strategic bombing offensive. New techniques, new aids, new weapons and an endless supply of well-trained crews gave it a flexibility and striking capability never before achieved. In the last three months of 1944, a greater weight of bombs was dropped than the total tonnage for 1943. During this period was fought the last battle of the Ruhr with some 61,000 tons of bombs dropped during 14,254 sorties. The cost was less than 1% – only 136 bombers were lost.

The Dortmund raid of 6/7 October had been the opening gambit of this winter offensive against the heart of Germany. After Dortmund and Bremen in the same

On 25 October, cloud cover hampered the daylight raid on Homburg by 199 Halifaxes, 32 Lancasters and 12 Mosquitoes, but no aircraft were lost. However, LW386: A almost became a fatality when a 1,000 lb bomb smashed through the port wing between the engines, taking with it the No 1 and No 3 fuel tanks, while a second struck the starboard elevator close to the rear turret. Fortunately, the Halifax remained controllable and F/O V. R. Glover was able to fly it back to their home base where it was landed safely. Having converted from Wellingtons to Halifaxes in January 1944, 420 Squadron began converting to Lancasters in April 1945, so the Lancaster behind LW386: A helps to date this photograph to no earlier than that. The squadron's last Halifax operation was an attack against the German naval base in Heligoland on 18 April. During the 15 months that the squadron flew Halifaxes it took part in 160 bombing raids comprising 2,477 sorties for the loss of just 25 aircraft. (Dennis Davison)

night, Kleve, Emmerich and Bochum, and then Duisburg, received a double blow on 14 October. This was a special operation, part of *Operation Hurricane*, designed to demonstrate to the Germans the overwhelming superiority of the Allied Air Forces. Bomber Command and the Eighth Air Force were to be used in the shortest space of time, in a maximum-effort attack against a target in the densely populated Ruhr. Just after first light a force of 1,013 Lancasters, Halifaxes and Mosquitoes were dispatched, with RAF escorting fighters, 957 attacking to drop 3,574 tons of bombs and 820 tons of incendiaries on Duisburg. Flak was intense and 14 of 158 Squadron's 27 Halifaxes sustained damage, but no losses. Only one Halifax from the 474 dispatched failed to return; 13 Lancasters were also lost. The Halifax, P/O F. Augusta's MZ453: J from 429 Squadron, was hit by flak on the approach to the aiming point, with F/O W. Potts sustaining minor injuries. With the starboard wing on fire, Augusta continued the bombing run, dropped the load, and then headed for Belgium with the wing still burning. Once over the border, the crew baled out over Keerbergen, 26 km from Brussels, all landing safely. They were back in England within four days. This was almost a case of *deja vu* for Augusta and his crew; just days before, during the attack on Bochum on 9/10 October, LV965: J had been hit by flak, puncturing the No 4 tank and, running short of fuel on the return journey, they made their landing at Old Buckenham in Norfolk. The friction nut on the throttle quadrant had, however, become detached and the port engine could not be throttled back, producing a savage ground loop, collapsing the starboard undercarriage leg. Skidding on across the airfield at speed it further damaged itself before coming to rest, whereupon the port outer engine burst into flames but was extinguished by the crew. The Halifax was a write-off, but no one was injured, though shaken up by the wild experience.

The Americans followed up the same day with 1,251 heavy bombers, and 749 fighters as escort, which attacked Cologne for the loss of five bombers and a fighter. That night Bomber Command returned to Duisburg with 1,005 aircraft but this time in two forces, two hours apart. In both cases, a greater weight of bombs was dropped than in any previous attack on a German industrial city. Splitting the force caught the city's civil defences in the second wave of bombing, adding to the spread of destruction and hampering rescue operations. The 941 attacking aircraft dropped 4,040 tons of high explosive and 500 tons of incendiaries. Enemy defences were less active during the night raid and only six aircraft failed to return. Some, however, had harrowing experiences. During a visual inspection after bombing, a hole seven feet by two feet was seen in the bomb doors of a 415 Squadron Halifax. A single 1,000 lb bomb had failed to drop with the rest of the bomb load and parted company during some evasive manoeuvres when the bomb doors were closed.

No 462 Squadron lost a Halifax which crashed at base due to flak damage and could have lost another but for the tenacity of its pilot, Fl/ Sgt Cockerill. Coned by searchlights just short of the target, the Halifax was hit severely and the pilot was wounded in the left eye. Momentarily losing consciousness, he recovered in time to bring the aircraft back on to an even keel and complete the bombing run. The return trip was a nightmare; fire broke out in one engine and at one stage night-fighter flares illuminated the aircraft. Unable to see the instruments, Cockerill had one of the crew call out the readings and he successfully flew the Halifax back to England, where

he made an emergency landing at Manston. Reports came in from many crews of the sighting of jet night-fighters that night and reports of this nature were to increase over the next few months, culminating in a disastrous daylight encounter over Hamburg in March 1945.

While Duisburg was being bombed, a second force of 233 Lancasters accompanied by seven Mosquitoes for marking, attacked Braunschweig. Supporting these dual attacks were 141 training aircraft on a diversionary sweep over Heligoland, 20 Mosquitoes to bomb Hamburg, 16 to Berlin, eight to Mannheim and two to Düsseldorf, while 132 aircraft from 100 Group carried out RCM sorties. *Serrate* and intruder flights were added for good measure.

Essen, a target all too familiar to crews, received two raids in quick succession. The first was a major attack by a force of 1,055 bombers on the night of 23 October, with the returning aircraft landing before midnight. Pathfinders laid sky markers over the heavy cloud covering the target and enabled approximately 90% of the bomber force to attack. Two new records were established that night, for Essen was receiving its heaviest raid to date by the greatest number of aircraft sent to a single target so far. Of the 4,538 tons of bombs dropped, more than 90% were high explosive, a reversal of the earlier area-bombing practice of using a higher proportion of incendiaries. Like so many other German cities, Essen was now considered to have had most of its combustible materials nearly exhausted; the blast effect of the high explosives was to complete the devastation. Times had changed, and losses were less than 1%, although two badly damaged Halifaxes, one from 78 Squadron and the other from 466 Squadron, barely managed to reach base. Of the eight that failed to return that night two, Halifax LL599: E of 462 Squadron and Lancaster LM691: M of 625 Squadron, were lost in a mid-air collision near Aachen, only S/Ldr C. Hamilton, pilot of the Lancaster, surviving. Another Halifax, MZ742: A of 346 Squadron, was lost in a mid-air collision over the Channel. More aircraft were lost in crashes on return; LV872 had been attacked over the target but F/O C. Wenzel coaxed his 78 Squadron Halifax back almost to Woodbridge but a fire broke out in the port inner engine and the crew baled out over Suffolk. No 76 Squadron lost MX691: Q when it was almost home. Power was lost in both port engines and structural failure caused the Halifax to break up and crash near Diss in Norfolk, killing Fl/Sgt L. White and his crew. Weather seems to have been poor in some parts of the country and two other Halifaxes were lost in diversions. The same fate struck several of the returning Lancasters.

On 25 October 771 Halifaxes and Lancasters returned to Essen for a daylight attack through cloud and sky markers once more enabled the Krupp works to be damaged extensively; after this raid, Essen ceased to be one of the most important centres of war production. Again bomber losses were low, two Lancasters and two Halifaxes. Both of the latter were from 158 Squadron, MZ734: U and MZ945: W, and with the exception of F/Lt G. Woodward DFC & Bar in MZ945, both crews survived to become POWs. Such were Bomber Command's resources now that Homberg was also attacked that day, by 243 aircraft, 199 of them Halifaxes. One 420 Squadron aircraft gave an admirable demonstration of the Halifax's sturdy construction. Over the target area F/O Glover's LW386: A was hit by several 1,000 lb bombs, some of which passed between the engines of the port wing, carrying away

Nos 1 and 3 fuel tanks, while another struck the starboard elevator close to the rear turret. Miraculously the Halifax did not go out of control and Glover brought it safely back.

Then it was the turn of Cologne, a triple blow being delivered within the span of four days. The first, carried out by 733 aircraft in two waves late on 28 October, caused enormous damage for the loss of four Halifaxes and three Lancasters. It was during the second raid on the night of 30/31 October that, in addition to reports of jet fighters, a crew from 158 Squadron described how they had seen a rocket projectile come up from the ground and then travel horizontally across the Halifax's track before trailing off. Despite a pessimistic assessment of the bombing accuracy, which had been marked by *Oboe* through cloud, enormous damage had again been done, this time for no loss. More references to jet night-fighters appeared in the crew reports for the following night's raid on Cologne, which again produced much devastation although not on the same scale as the previous two attacks. Two Lancasters were lost from the mixed force of 493 bombers.

MZ954: M, a B Mk III of 425 Squadron, taxies out prior to taking part in the attack on Neuss on the western edge of the Ruhr by a force of 173 Halifaxes, 102 Lancasters and 15 Mosquitoes on 27 November 1944. Seen more clearly here, the Preston-Green mounting has the long barrel of the 0.5-in Browning pointing aft and MZ954's production date of early September 1944 shows that these mountings were still being installed at that late date. The Perspex has twin navigation lights fitted above the Vickers G.O. gun mounting and an open-ended Perspex blister (Mod 904) fitted beneath the bomb aimer's position; both were additions found on late B Mk III aircraft. The chute for dropping Window can be seen below the wireless operator's position although the bomb aimer usually did the dropping until reaching the target area. The truck in the background carries nitrogen-filled cylinders used to top up fuel tanks as a precaution against fire if hit. MZ954 was transferred to 187 Squadron in February 1945. (Public Archives of Canada)

The 31st October had a special significance for 425 Squadron for 'Vicki', that illustrious veteran mascot of so many sorties, had 'given birth' to four offspring in early October, two daughters, 'Mich' and 'Marie' and two sons, 'Gerry' and 'Jos'. All five were posted to 22 OTU, 'Vicki' as an instructor and the rest as sprog aircrew. All were then posted back to the *Alouette* Squadron as sergeants and commenced operations. 'Vicki' received a well-earned DFC and was repatriated to Canada with effect from 12 October, her final words of wisdom being, *"Now get some* [service time] *in, kids."* Four days later the squadron was plunged into gloom when, on 4/5 November MZ831: Z failed to return from the raid on Bochum. Reputedly, Sergeants 'Mich' and 'Gerry' were among F/O D. Smith's missing crew with all but one becoming POWs but they mysteriously reappeared several days later. Another Halifax from the squadron nearly met a similar fate at 18,500 ft over Bochum when a load of incendiaries hailed down upon it, causing 37 holes, but fortunately no injuries. Both wings were severely damaged, as were the aileron controls, flaps, elevators, rudders and tail plane. The oil fuel lines to one engine were severed and it burst into flames but extinguishers overcame the blaze and F/O J. Desmarns nursed MZ621: O back to base where, after being inspected, it was written off.

The French Halifax crews of 346 Squadron were hardest hit on the Bochum raid, losing five out of 16 aircraft. Flak hit NA121: D killing the pilot, Adjutant (Adj) R. Guise and Lieutenant (Lt) E. Dabadie then ordered the remaining crew to bale out but found that the forward escape hatch was jammed. Only two escaped via the rear escape hatch before the Halifax crashed. Sgt G. Roca's NA546: G was lost to an unknown cause, killing all on board. It was possibly due to a night-fighter attack as the remaining three Halifaxes all fell to such attacks. Commandant (Cne) A. Beraud and Lt P. Raffin died when NA549: N was shot down near Pulheim and although all escaped by parachute, only five survived. Adjutant (Adj) R. Hannedouche's NA558: N was shot down leaving the target area, while Cne R. Baron's NR181: J came down just 5 km from the centre of Neuss with three surviving and Lt A. Truchee managing to evade capture. Twelve other squadrons lost Halifaxes. No 10 lost LW716: Z, No 51 lost LW177: N and MZ933: W, 76 Squadron lost LL577: M and LW648: Q, No 78 lost LK838: E, No 102 lost MZ772: Q, 158 Squadron lost LV771: Y, No 408 NP750: F, No 424 MZ896: Q, No 425 MZ831: Z, No 426 lost two, NP775: K and NP800: S, No 433 lost NP992: F, and 640 Squadron lost MZ409: C and MZ930: K.

Badly damaged by a Ju 88 night-fighter, Fl/Sgt E. Stevens' LV819: F from 51 Squadron made it home only to be written off as being beyond economical repair. Two of the seven Lancasters lost were victims of crashes on return to their bases while two of the remaining five raid casualties, ME865: K and NF936: F were from 101 Bomber Support (BS) Squadron and had accompanied the Main Force on *ABC* duties.

Peter Hinchcliffe was part of P/O L. Berry's 158 Squadron crew in MZ933: W, which was caught by a night-fighter while homeward bound at 7,000 ft. His account typifies the continuing potent nature of the Luftwaffe night-fighter force and the swiftness with which an aircraft – and often its crew – could be destroyed. *"...Berry was on his first trip as a commissioned officer.... but still wearing his badges of rank as a Flight Sergeant. We were on our fifteenth operation as a crew* [seven flown in this aircraft]. *The target that night was Bochum, in the Ruhr area, and we were on our way back after the attack. Our route took us to the south of Aachen, and it was soon after that point that we were hit, presumably by a night-fighter using Schräge Musik, the fixed, upward firing cannon that were widely in use at that time. I say 'presumably' because we saw nothing in advance, and the aircraft caught fire in its starboard wing immediately. The skipper gave the order to bale out, and as navigator I was first to go. I saw the machine hit the ground just as I pulled the ripcord, and hit the ground myself, very, very soon afterwards: it*

transpired later that I was about 300 yards or so distant from the spot where MH-W had come down, with my wireless operator, Johnny Davis, in between. The other five of the crew all perished with the machine.

"We were in the small Belgian town of Marche-en-Famenne in the Ardenne hills, and marginally in American-occupied territory; there were German troops ensconced in the woods about two kilometres away. The first house I was taken into was that of the Masson family: M. Masson was a prominent member of the local Résistance.... Johnny and I were rapidly back in England, and we joined up with another crew that had lost its navigator and wireless operator, that of Flying Officer Freddy 'fair-weather', and we did another twenty or so operations with them. The other members of the crew are buried at Hotton, not far from Marche."

Overall, 23 Halifaxes and five Lancasters failed to return from the force of 749 aircraft, night-fighters accounting for most but not all casualties. Two had collided before crossing the Dutch coast and flak took its own toll. No 466 Squadron lost two, NR132: Z and LV936: D, the latter having been hit by flak just after completing its bombing run. Fire began to spread inside the fuselage and F/Lt J. Herman ordered his crew to bale out. When they had all jumped, he undid his seat belt and bent to pick up his parachute pack just as the starboard wing tore away. He braced himself against the canopy and tried to reach for the pack again, but the aircraft blew apart and he found himself falling from 17,000 ft with no parachute. He could see the thin ribbon of a river far below and for a moment wondered if he would fall into it. Next moment he collided with something, which turned out to be P/O J. Vivash, his mid-upper gunner. He now found himself clinging to the gunner's leg and kept a tight grip, but the double load increased the rate of descent and Herman attempted to jump clear at the last moment. However, his timing was off and the two men crashed through the branches of a fallen tree. Both survived. Despite shrapnel wounds that made walking difficult for Vivash, and broken ribs and a fractured hip that impeded Herman, they managed to evade capture for six days. With Sgt H. Knott, the three who baled out were later reported as killed, but all survived as POWs. The raid had been successful and Bochum had received its last major attack.

Many a derogatory remark had been passed concerning the single, hand-operated Vickers gun in the nose cone of the Halifaxes, but it proved its worth to a 429 Squadron crew over Oberhausen on 1/2 November. As the Halifax turned for home, an Fw 190 swept in for a frontal attack on MZ474: B but F/O R. Herbert, the bomb aimer, opened fire with the Vickers gun, sending it down in flames. The flak, however, was deadlier and five Halifaxes and a Lancaster were lost from the force of 202 Halifaxes, 74 Lancasters and 12 Mosquitoes used in the raid. Cloud cover favoured the city and it escaped significant damage.

From the evidence of the crew debriefings, German jet night-fighters also appear to have suffered at the hands of 427 Squadron that same night. Conditions were favourable for the enemy with a full moon and clear skies above a solid layer of 10/10ths cloud. At 20.45 hrs the tail gunner of LV945: F sighted a 'jet fighter' well astern, but it disappeared. A few moments later another, possibly the same 'jet fighter', appeared about 800 yards away and the tail gunner instructed the pilot to

Produced in the second week of March 1944, LV937 was allocated to 578 Squadron and then passed to 51 Squadron, thus reversing the process that had created 578 from the latter's C Flight. Not that this crew were concerned about such matters after completing 'Expensive Babe's' 100th operation (plus one fighter shot down), the attack on Osnabrück on 6/7 December 1944. From left to right the crew are F/Lt R. Kemp, Fl/Sgt A. R. Townsend, W/O R. Williams, Sgt E. Hawkins, Fl/Sgt R. Jackson and Fl/Sgt F. Thwaites. Interestingly, 51/578 Squadron(s) produced three Halifax centenarians and 158 Squadron the other two. In the background is what appears to be the fin of a Halifax painted with a daylight tactical marking of white, rather than yellow. Only two Halifax squadrons used Snaith, Nos 51 and 578, the latter only being in residence during January and February 1944 and before tactical markings were instituted, and LV937: E was photographed at the end of 1944. This suggests that the tactical marking was being used by 51 Squadron, possibly to distinguish between A and B Flights. The final operation tally for this Halifax is unknown, but as it survived past the end of the war to be struck off charge on 1 July 1945, it was probably quite a few more. The small Mod 904 Perspex blister was located further aft on this aircraft, and possibly the entire production batch to that point, although it became more usual to see it fitted over the front edge of the small oblong window fitted in the bomb aimer's position to allow him to follow the track of the bombs. (J. D. Silberberg)

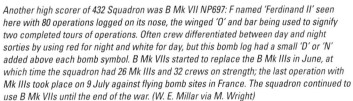

Another high scorer of 432 Squadron was B Mk VII NP697: F named 'Ferdinand II' seen here with 80 operations logged on its nose, the winged 'O' and bar being used to signify two completed tours of operations. Often crew differentiated between day and night sorties by using red for night and white for day, but this bomb log had a small 'D' or 'N' added above each bomb symbol. B Mk VIIs started to replace the B Mk IIIs in June, at which time the squadron had 26 Mk IIIs and 32 crews on strength; the last operation with Mk IIIs took place on 9 July against flying bomb sites in France. The squadron continued to use B Mk VIIs until the end of the war. (W. E. Millar via M. Wright)

It did not need the Maple Leaf emblem to identify this superb piece of artwork as Canadian; NP689: M 'Moonlight Mermaid' had completed eighty operations, marked by stars, when photographed in early 1945. The names of the crew, Mac, Pere, Duke, Lloyd, Pinky and Jack were carried beneath the cockpit while the winged 'O' and bar signified the successful completion of two operational tours. The sheer size and execution of such work is impressive but unfortunately, few of the artists are known, another lost piece of Second World War history. Thomas E. Dunn, the creator of 'Mermaid', was born in Winnipeg in 1912, his sole art training being a correspondence course in lettering and show card writing from where he developed his talent. Having joined the RCAF and trained as a mechanic he was posted to 432 Squadron where his artistic talents quickly became known. His first work, 'Moonlight Mermaid' completed in the spring of 1944 was quickly followed by 'Oscar the Outlaw', 'Old Joe Vagabond', 'Queen of them All', 'Leaside Lulu', two versions of 'Every valley shall be filled and every mountain and hill shall be brought low' and five others, to total twelve in all. (via M. Wright)

dive towards the clouds and opened fire as the range decreased to 600 yards. The glare from the jet increased greatly as it followed the Halifax through the turn. Moments later the glow turned to flames as the rear gunner's fire struck home, sending it spinning down to burst against the ground. The pilot, bomb aimer and flight engineer confirmed its destruction.

At precisely the same time but several miles away, the flight engineer of LW130: U also sighted a 'jet fighter' on the port beam and slightly higher. The pilot put the Halifax into a corkscrew dive towards the cloud cover as the fighter, now identified as an Me 163, closed in, firing as it came. The mid-upper and rear gunners returned the fire with long bursts as the enemy fighter pressed home its attack to approximately 200 ft before bursting into flames and dropping vertically through the cloud. The crew did not see the aircraft hit the ground but considered it as being destroyed. They were quite positive about the identity of their attacker and if they were correct then it is the only known instance of the use of this radical rocket fighter operationally at night. However, from information circulating through the Allied air forces about the potential threat of German jet fighters, eventually a reality in the day fighting, they never, as far as can be ascertained, occurred at night. The Me 163 was dangerous enough when landing in daylight and not operational at this time. The two seat night-fighter version of the Me 262 was eventually only used by one small

unit, the 10./NJG 11, charged with defending Berlin; only seven reached the unit and just four were the two-seat Me 262 B-1a/U1 radar-equipped night-fighter versions. The claims of glare from the jet engines may well have been exhaust glare, especially from single-engine machines. When Bomber Command finally did meet jet fighters, it would be in daylight – and was a very sobering demonstration of what might have been.

No 171 (BS) Squadron, its Halifaxes now fitted with *Mandrel* equipment, began its new role with this equipment on 20 November in support of 183 Lancasters of No 3 Group in a *G-H*-led daylight attack on an oil plant at Homberg. Stormy weather disrupted the *G-H* leaders of what was to be a formation bombing run above cloud and bombing was scattered, five Lancasters being lost. Just four of the squadron's Halifaxes had been scheduled for the operation and while one had aborted with magneto trouble, the remaining three, NA106: X, NA110: Z and LK874: C, carried

Artwork on the tail end of Halifaxes was rare indeed but sometimes no less exotic. Readers old enough to remember the Blondie and Dagwood comic strip will recognize this near life-size rendition of the hero with a parachute on his back and about to jump from an upstairs balcony with the words above stating 'Just Testing' and Dagwood saying, "I know its OK but I want to make sure." Unfortunately, neither the rear gunner nor Halifax is identified, but it belonged to 408 Squadron. (Public Archives of Canada via D. Wadman)

F/O R. Drummond-Hay photographed discussing the tail art of a 424 Squadron Halifax with H. T. Mason of the Victoria Colonist newspaper. A little less flamboyant perhaps, but still relatively unique, 'The Devil's Doorstep' may have been applied to NP945: D, which also carried the nose artwork 'Der Fuehrer's Fate'. If this is correct, it failed to return from Osnabrück on 6/7 December 1944 with F/O D. McCullough and two of his crew dying when the Halifax was brought down over Germany on their sixth operation. (Public Archives of Canada via D. Wadman)

out the operation. LK874 had been attached to 199 Squadron on 22 August for instructional work on the *Mandrel* installation so that those crews going to 171 Squadron would have completed their training in advance. This particular Halifax was also fitted with a multi-*Mandrel* installation and had undergone tests at the TFU at Defford before returning to squadron duty.

Bomber Command had maintained its heavy tempo of day and night raids. Hamburg, Oberhausen, then Hamburg again followed by Düsseldorf, which received its last major attack of the war on 2/3 November. A mixed force of 992 bombers had attacked Düsseldorf for the loss of 11 Halifaxes and eight Lancasters. Significantly, four of the bombers came down behind Allied lines in France and Belgium; crews now had better odds for survival and evading capture. The bomber support crews had their own share of hazardous situations, bombs now added to some of their sorties. No 171 Squadron's schedule for 4/5 December was of the now often multiple sort. W/O J. Philipson RAAF and his crew were out in NA694: H with three targets to cover that night – Kassel, Karlsruhe and Heilbronn – one of 47 RCM sorties for the night. They were on a joint *Window*-bombing operation, carrying 3,500 lbs of bombs but, unbeknown to the crew, one of the 500 lb bombs had hung-up, which was unfortunate as on the way home, the tachometer for the port inner engine failed, followed by the engine. Philipson recalls the events *"When the undercart was selected the down-indicator lights went haywire, and the warning horn didn't operate when throttles were closed. It was a very dark night with crosswind from starboard and I assumed u/c locked down. On touch down tail wheel touched then a clicking sound was heard as the props touched and we were on our belly, sliding off the runway to port and finishing on grass halfway up the runway and 100 yards to port. Crushed bomb doors, H2S dome, three propellers folded back, lower blade of feathered port inner ripped out. When the aircraft was hoisted up a week or so later a 500 lb bomb was found, hung-up and unarmed. The aircraft had 14hrs 36min in its log at the time of landing – brand new on first operation."* Fortunately, the grass area was waterlogged and covered with about eight inches of water.

The list of targets grew longer as the weeks passed and most raids were successful. Essen received its last heavy night raid on 12/13 December. Bombing accuracy was very high and industrial damage, particularly at the Krupp works, extensive. In view of the number of bombers and crews lost attempting to destroy the Krupp works since the earliest days of the war, it must have been a moment of great significance to those taking part. From the force of 540 bombers dispatched, five Lancasters failed to return and two Halifaxes were lost in landing accidents without any loss of life.

Then, out of the thick fog of Saturday morning 16 December, the German 5., 6. SS and 7. *Panzerarmees* burst through on a front stretching from Monschau to Echternach. The Ardennes offensive had begun. The ground fog continued for days and greatly hampered Allied tactical air support and both Bomber Command and the USAAF were forced to attack communications centres at Duisburg, Munich and Ulm, on 17/18 December instead. The Duisburg attack by 523 aircraft, 418 of them Halifaxes, resulted in severe damage at a cost of eight Halifaxes. Munich was an all-Lancaster attack by 280 aircraft with severe damage being claimed around the centre of the old town and the rail yards; four Lancasters were lost in the process. For Ulm, it was a new experience as this was its first and only attack with 317 Lancasters and 13 Mosquitoes carrying out the raid for the cost of two Lancasters. The raid lasted 25 minutes and was very destructive but a decision to evacuate the population hours earlier kept the death toll relatively low.

As weather conditions improved the blows moved closer to the battlefront and Trier was attacked three times in daylight, on 19, 21 and 23 December, each time by a small force of Lancasters. On 21/22 December, 54 Halifaxes, 67 Lancasters and 15 Mosquitoes attacked Cologne/Nippes marshalling yards, which were being used to supply the Ardennes front. Cloud cover made bombing difficult and while few crews claimed to have hit the aiming point, destruction of rolling stock, a repair shop and some of the rail lines was enough to be judged a success. No aircraft were lost.

Other November attacks on communications centres, railroad and waterways were delivered against an elongated strip of land bordered on the west by the Rhine and Hamburg, Hanover, Würzburg and Ulm to the east. The success of this

Delivered from Fairey Aviation on 16 October 1944 and issued to 347 Squadron, B Mk III PN167 is seen here after the change of its original identity letter from 'C' to 'Z'. Beneath the name 'Miquette' is the white Free French Cross of Lorraine superimposed on a red diamond. The Night Black finish was the slightly shiny ultra smooth type introduced in 1944. In a reversal of the old RDM 2A assumption about absorption of light, the new synthetic cellulose finish worked on the opposing principle, which deemed light reflection more effective against searchlight illumination. The matching shade of crimson of the tail marking and that of the fin flash can be seen. The aircraft survived the war to be struck off charge on 28 November 1945. (ECPA)

NR284: Q of 462 Squadron is seen here at Foulsham where the squadron had moved in December 1944 on its transfer to 100 Group. When NR284 was photographed in early 1945, squadron aircraft were being progressively modified for their bomber support role in which they were primarily used for Window-dropping during spoof raids, the additional dispenser chute for which can be seen just aft of the H2S radome. The squadron retained the daylight tactical marking seen on the fin, which it had used when with No 4 Group. Produced in December 1944, NR284 was lost following a forced-landing near Beetley Hall on 17 April 1945 after the failure of both starboard engines. (R. Hines via Wright)

campaign was marginal at first. The Germans had only been able to gather sufficient supplies, equipment and troops together to launch their Ardennes offensive at the cost of civilian and low-priority military traffic, so targets were limited. Despite a poor start, the campaign continued throughout the remaining months of the war and finally achieved its desired effect.

Oil targets, neglected during October, had received increased attention with eight daylight and six night attacks being made during November. The success against this type of target was more readily assessable than for communication centre targets – the impact of this success had a direct bearing on not only the Ardennes offensive but other fronts as well. Production had struggled but made a remarkable recovery during October and November but, by December, it began to taper off and continued to decline rapidly throughout January. The effect would have been achieved earlier, but during December tactical requirements absorbed a larger proportion of Bomber Command's efforts and only two daylight and three night attacks were made.

On 24 December 248 Halifaxes, 79 Lancasters and 11 Mosquitoes attacked two German airfields, Lohausen and Müllheim, in daylight. No record of the purpose has been found but the attacks were most likely to disrupt the movement of supplies to the Ardennes battle area. For once, visibility was good, both targets were heavily damaged, and Hangelar airfield received the same treatment that same night. Two Lancasters and a Halifax, NP781: U were lost in the Lohausen attack, but significantly, FO W. Dunwoodie and Fl/Sgt J. Chaisson not only survived the Halifax loss but also managed to evade capture. Some of the crew members from the three Halifaxes lost on the Müllheim attack[15] were not so fortunate, however, and all were made POWs.

The weather finally broke on 26 December and 136 Halifaxes, 146 Lancasters and 12 Mosquitoes attacked enemy positions at St Vith in the Ardennes. F/O D. Woolf's MZ740: R from 10 Squadron had the nose section shattered by flak and moments later, the aircraft crashed into woods near Nassogne in Belgium, killing all on board.

A second 10 Squadron Halifax, NR246: Y, and its crew were lost when almost back to England, diving into the sea off Margate, possibly a result of damage from the raid.

The rail yards at Koblenz, one of the main centres serving the Ardennes forces, were hit by a double raid on 29 December when 162 Halifaxes, 22 Lancasters and eight Mosquitoes attacked the Mosel yards, while 85 Lancasters bombed the Lützel yards north of the city. Neither force suffered any losses and a local report stated that the whole rail system had been blocked and the cranes in Mosel harbour put out of action. Troisdorf rail yards were attacked that night by a mixed force of 159 bombers but most of the bombs fell wide. While that was taking place, Lancasters raided Schloven-Buer oil refinery using *Oboe*-directed sky marking above the thick cloud cover and causing severe damage. Bomber Command now worked round the clock against multiple targets.

The New Year brought with it the sureness that the end of the war in Europe must be near and during these closing months, 181,000 tons of bombs would be dropped by Bomber Command to equal nearly one-fifth of the total tonnage for the entire war[16]. Collectively, losses remained at less than 1% and far more danger seemed now to arise from mid-air collisions in the congested skies than from the German night-fighters, though the latter would rally dangerously at times. January's weather restricted operations but March heralded a return to intensive day and night attacks against oil, rail, road, canals and communications centres. Middlebrook and Everitt, in their superb *'Bomber Command War Diaries'* make the point that Harris, when opportunity arose, continued attacking cities when the main emphasis had shifted to oil and communications targets but did not do so significantly at the expense of the main directive. Bomber Command's crews have long paid for that historical misunderstanding. The worst example of Government indifference to how crews are remembered historically occurs in Canada, where, at the time of writing, the narrow-minded views of a few and the inaction of the Government Minister responsible, cause unwarranted pain to the survivors who gave so much and never failed to go where ordered, more than 47,000 giving their lives in the process.

A third bomber support Halifax squadron, No 462, had been posted to 100 Group in December, moving to Foulsham that same month.

The intention was for the squadron to operate in the radar countermeasures role and its Halifaxes were to be fitted with the latest equipment designed to jam not only radar transmissions but also wireless and radio-telephony. This naturally involved a considerable amount of modification work that could not be done quickly and as an interim measure, the squadron continued to operate on spoof sorties. These commenced on 1 January 1945 as part of 42 RCM sorties and 59 Mosquito counter night-fighter patrols mounted by 100 Group. Being a former bomber unit, it was not surprising that on this operation its Halifaxes each carried two 500 lb bombs. This practice spread rapidly to the other Halifax squadrons within the Group, which, from February, included 199 Squadron based at North Creake with Stirlings[17], and eventually led to an elaborate deception technique. The *Window* force would simulate a normal bomber attack complete with Pathfinder-type pyrotechnics and a spoof Master Bomber using No 5 Group radio frequencies.

Hanau, an important rail junction, was attacked on 6/7 January 1945, by a mixed Halifax, Lancaster, Mosquito force and, despite some scattered bombing, some 40% of the Hanau complex was destroyed. A smaller, all-Lancaster force raided Neuss the same night and in addition to spoof attacks and minelaying off Baltic ports, 52 RCM sorties were flown in support of the bombers, the latter costing two RCM Halifaxes. F/Lt G. Cox's NA687: A of 171 Squadron was brought down near Rochefort, killing all on board, while P/O M. Rohrlach's 462 Squadron Halifax, MX469: N, fell in Belgium with just one of the crew surviving as a POW.

The extent to which this practice of multiple spoofs and distractions was escalating can be judged from operations on the night of 14/15 January 1945 when 58 RCM sorties were flown in support of attacks on a synthetic-oil plant at Leuna, railway yards at Grevebroich and a Luftwaffe fuel-storage depot at Dülmen, the last two by Halifax forces. The attacks were supported by a bewildering array of other activities; a diversionary sweep by 126 training aircraft over the North Sea, 83 Mosquitoes of the Light Night Striking Force going to bomb Berlin and nine others to Mannheim, plus 54 Serrate night-fighter protection patrols. Additionally, 21 Halifaxes and ten Lancasters laid mines off Oslo and in the Kattegat. No 462 Squadron had scheduled 15 Halifaxes to join the force attacking Mannheim but two aborted and one, LL598: A, crashed 30 minutes after take-off, killing six of the crew and injuring the two who had managed to bale out. This force was carrying *Window* plus 1,000 lb of bombs in each aircraft. Two other BS aircraft, a Liberator and a Mosquito were also lost. Bad weather over England caught the returning Main Force aircraft and several crashed at their bases. One additional Halifax was lost, 578 Squadron's MZ583: S from the Dülmen raid plus 11 Lancasters from the Leuna attack and two more back over England – a bad night all round.

The Halifaxes of the Main Force had opened their New Year with a return to Dortmund on 1/2 January, attempting to attack the coking plant, but bad weather caused the bombing to be ineffective. Better results were obtained at Ludwigshafen on 2/3rd with the I.G. Farben chemical plants being badly damaged for the loss of two Halifaxes which crashed at their home bases following the attack, fortunately

While of poor quality, this photograph shows just how much damage a Halifax could sustain and remain under control. Part of the 51 Squadron force sent to attack Saarbrücken on the night of 13/14 January 1945, MZ465: Y collided from behind with LL590: L of 347 Squadron. Adj E. Jouzier immediately ordered his crew to bale out, but only four managed to do so before his Halifax crashed 10 km south-west of Gisors, the three crew members still on board being killed. In F/O A. Wilson's Halifax, nine feet of the nose section had been destroyed taking with it the navigator, Fl/Sgt T. Whitehouse, and bomb aimer, Fl/Sgt D. Hauber. Perhaps the luckiest man in the nose section was the wireless operator. Despite the massive damage, the aircraft remained controllable and Wilson managed to land it safely at Ford airfield in Sussex. This side view shows just how drastic the damage was compared with C8-T of 640 Squadron standing behind it.

without loss of life. Then, on the evening of 5 January, Hanover received its first major attack since October 1943.

F/Lt R. Sledge of 578 Squadron had successfully attacked but twenty minutes later, at 13,000 ft, another Halifax was seen simultaneously by the mid-upper and rear gunners to be converging on their Halifax from above and behind. Its approach was so rapid that neither gunner had time to warn Sledge and the first thing he knew was the shuddering impact as it hit the port wing outboard of the engines, badly damaging the whole wing section. The port aileron was rendered useless and at the same time, the flaps came down 30 degrees, which did little to assist Sledge as he fought to pull RG367: O out of its spiral dive to port. Eventually, by sheer physical force on the control column, full right rudder and by throttling back the starboard outer engine, he managed to regain control and level out. The only way that he could now keep the aircraft on a rough course for home was by keeping the starboard engines throttled back and varying the settings of the port engines and the rudder trim. Münster provided a warm welcome for the battered Halifax and Sledge somehow managed to turn north, regaining his original track. His troubles were still not over as the Halifax was again hit by flak over Nijmegen and became almost uncontrollable. The end was obviously near and over Maas, the IFF set was switched to distress while the wireless operator tried repeatedly to contact their home base at Burn, but without success. As the Halifax passed south of Antwerp near Ghent, the crew baled out leaving the battered aircraft to crash in a cabbage field at Sleidinge. The other Halifax involved in the collision was MZ693: F flown by Fl/Sgt H. Ball from 76 Squadron. Unlike Sledge's aircraft, his was not badly damaged and he managed to return safely, his aircraft subsequently being repaired and returned to service on 17 February; but Ball was not so fortunate, losing his life in NR121: E in an attack on Worms on 21/22 February. However, Sledge's aircraft was not the only casualty; 22 other Halifaxes and eight Lancasters failed to return from the force of 664 bombers. Hanover had received its first large-scale raid, and a successful one, but the casualty rate of 4.7% was chillingly reminiscent of earlier days.

Saarbrücken, a choke point on the German supply routes to both the Ardennes sector and the southern front, received a significant share of the 7,000 tons of bombs dropped on transport targets in January. Three attacks were made on the city in 24 hours, the first in daylight on 13 January, followed by a night attack the same evening during which the sturdiness of the Halifax was established for all time.

F/O A. Wilson of 51 Squadron had bombed the target and was on the way back when his Halifax collided with another aircraft and had nine feet of the nose section chopped completely off, taking with it the navigator, Fl/Sgt T. Whitehouse and the bomb aimer, Fl/Sgt D. Hauber. Miraculously, the four engines continued to function perfectly despite some propeller damage caused by pieces of wreckage. The aircraft plunged to 1,500 ft before Wilson could regain control and climb back to 11,000 ft. The loss of so much of the fuselage produced a serious trim problem and it was hardly surprising that MZ465: Y should stall and dive again, but Wilson managed to master its idiosyncrasies and was eventually able to hold the Halifax steady at

Displaying its remarkable bomb log, LV920: D was taken on charge by 158 Squadron on 7 March 1944 and had completed 94 operations before failing to return from Düsseldorf on 20/21 February 1945. Sent to bomb the Rhenania Ossag oil refinery installations in Reisholz, it crashed at Drecke Bauernhof, near Fuerde with F/O C. Ramsey RCAF and Fl/Sgt F. Grant perishing in the crash and the rest of the crew made POWs. The artwork consisted of Donald Duck and the slogan 'Git up Dem Stairs' – some stairs! When this photograph was taken, F/Lt H. New and his crew and ground staff were celebrating, possibly at the end of their tour. There are at least 77 sorties recorded here along with a DSO, DFC and two Mentioned in Dispatches. The other very interesting feature of this Halifax is the daylight tactical marking of an all-yellow fin; a second Halifax with the same bold marking is visible to the right. The squadron also used a marking of two diagonal yellow stripes across both fin and rudder definitely still in use at war's end and as with two other squadrons, the dual form of markings may have been to distinguish between Flights. (W. R. Chorley)

7,000 ft. The radio had also remained serviceable and the wireless operator managed to get out an SOS before having to shut the equipment down because of shorting as blue sparks played around the fuselage. The five remaining members of the crew were frozen by the icy blast of air that tore through the fuselage, the few pieces of fuselage skinning bent round over the shattered nose section giving little protection from the elements. Most instruments had been put out of action, including the airspeed indicator and the DR compass, but by a superb piece of airmanship Wilson nursed the battered aircraft back to England and landed safely at Ford airfield without causing further damage. The only loss for the night was a Halifax, Adj E. Jouzier's LL590: L from 347 Squadron which had been struck by Wilson's Halifax. Jouzier and two other crew members were killed in the collision but the remainder of the crew baled out before the aircraft crashed 10 km from Gisors.

The bad weather of January restricted the numbers sent to many targets; Ludwigshafen, Hanover, Hanau, were all attacked in turn and on 16/17 January, Magdeburg received a full-scale attack. The force was composed mainly of Halifaxes, and 76 Squadron, the originator of many new tactics, opened the attack well before the Main Force. The object of the exercise was to draw off any night-fighters from the Pathfinder aircraft following behind and was most successful, but while all of the PFF Lancasters and Mosquitoes returned, 17 of the 320 Halifaxes fell to the defences.

The next and last area raid of the month was an attack on the Zuffenhausen district of Stuttgart on 28/29 January. It was, in effect, a double raid, one portion of the force bombing the jet engine production facilities while the remainder bombed the nearby marshalling yards – thus Harris combined area bombing while carrying out the aim of the main bombing programme. There was a three-hour interval between the two attacks with 226 bombers sent against the railway target while the other 376 attended to the Hirth aero-engine factory. Cloud obscured both targets and sky marking was used, resulting in scattered bombing for the loss of four Halifaxes, six Lancasters and a Mosquito, mostly to flak. F/O J. Brayshaw of 428 Squadron had just bombed when heavy flak started making things difficult and shortly afterwards a Bf 109 attacked the bomber, killing the rear gunner, Sgt R. Fenner. Brayshaw managed to land the badly damaged MZ794: T at an American airstrip in France. These strips would prove valuable to many a damaged aircraft in the closing stages of the war. No 408 Squadron lost two, NP743: K and NP746: E, both crews being killed. A night-fighter claimed W/Cdr F. Carling-Kelly's NP768: Q, he and three others from this 408 Squadron crew surviving as POWs.

The January attacks were dominated by a triple theme that continued for the remainder of the war; industrial capacity, fuel and transport. Emphasis on communications targets also remained high because the shrinking perimeter of German occupation was now virtually confined to Germany itself. Strategic and tactical requirements overlapped and attacks on some cities now fulfilled a double role as the ground fighting encroached on Germany itself. Some cities not previously

included on the list of targets were now because of their new significance. Mainz, not attacked in force since August 1942 because it had no significant industrial capacity, now assumed a new value because of its geographical position in relation to the proposed ground campaigns. The initial raid of 1/2 February was by a force of 293 Halifaxes from Nos 4 and 6 Groups. Lancasters and Mosquitoes of No 8 Group marked the partly cloud-covered target with ground markers and the initial force aimed on these. However, as the attack developed so did the cloud cover and sky markers were dropped to enable the rhythm of the bombing to continue unabated. Ground defences and a few night-fighters were active but to little effect and no bombers were lost but even so, most bombs fell outside Mainz and little damage was done.

During the first week in February while preparations were underway for the new Allied offensive, the Second Tactical Air Force and American light and medium bombers were committed to an intensive series of attacks against enemy rail and road complexes. The aim of these was to deny German forces the opportunity to regroup in the face of the British XXX Corps attack across the German frontier in the area of the Reichswald on 8 February. To precede the heavy artillery bombardment, Bomber Command launched two successful attacks on the night of 7/8 February against the key centres of Goch and Kleve, both cities having been incorporated into the German defensive line.

The Master Bomber at Goch directed the first wave to attack from beneath the 5,000 ft cloud base and a very accurate attack developed, but it was too concentrated as the dense smoke obscured the target marking and the Master Bomber called off the attack. This caused problems for aircraft arriving over the target and F/O J. Beeson was still at 3,500 ft when his 158 Squadron Halifax, NP973: P, collided with Fl/Sgt D. Muggeridge's MZ689: Z from 77 Squadron, which crashed moments later 20 km from the target area, killing the crew. Beeson tried for two minutes without success to regain control before ordering his crew to bale out but unfortunately, only three made it in time.

The Luftwaffe made an appearance over Goch and lost an Me 410 to a Halifax of 466 Squadron for its effort. No 102 Squadron's NA175: Q was not so fortunate and on the return flight, a Ju 88 damaged it so badly that the crew had to take to their parachutes over Belgium but W/O W. Smith appears to have been killed while keeping the Halifax steady for his crew to bale out. Sgt B. Peckham, the rear gunner, was last to leave and saw the enemy night-fighter firing at the crew as they descended so continued to fire his own guns until the ammunition was exhausted, then baled out himself. His hasty exit did not allow him to see the results of his last burst of fire, but the crew later found out that the Ju 88 had been damaged and crash-landed safely on a railway line, but its pilot was killed by a train moments later. A second Halifax from the squadron, LW142: N, was also brought down 12 km from Leuven, killing all aboard. No 347 Squadron lost two crews – Sgt J. Bagot's NA197: H crashed near Veluve, killing three crew-members, but Adc J. Aulens' crew in NA260: G were less fortunate after a night-fighter shot the Halifax down over Asten in Holland with only Cne G. Stanislas surviving after being thrown clear and parachuting into Allied hands. These were the only losses during the attack.

Pölitz was the main target for 457 Lancasters on the night of 8/9 February, which attacked in two waves. Weather conditions were clear and results very good, the synthetic oil plant being so heavily damaged that it never resumed production. A smaller-scale attack was mounted by 200 Halifaxes on the Wanne-Eickel oil refinery while 151 Lancasters bombed the railway yards at Krefeld. In addition to the now usual range of spoof and other activities, 47 RCM sorties were flown for the loss of a single Halifax from 192 Squadron. F/Lt B. Butler's MZ342: B was tasked with duties near Stettin but homeward-bound it collided with Lancaster PD376 of 625 Squadron. The latter escaped serious damage but the Halifax plunged into the sea, taking all its crew with it.

Operation Thunderclap had been before the planners at the Air Ministry for several months, its aim being to produce such confusion and consternation amongst the now hard-stretched German war production and civil administration that it would precipitate an end to the war. Implementation, however, had been held back until the military situation in Germany was deemed critical and now, that moment seemed at hand. Russian forces had swept through Poland in the second half of January and crossed into Germany and German forces were now fighting on home ground but on two fronts, the most critical area in the East. Berlin, Dresden, Leipzig and Chemnitz were all just to the rear of the German defensive lines and all were vital communication and supply centres for the fighting on that front, each now packed with refugees and wounded from the battles to the east. At the Yalta Conference on 4 February, Stalin had asked for attacks of this type to take place. The Air Ministry had already issued its directive at the end of January and the plans were in place, Churchill having taken a direct hand in the planning, which also involved the USAAF. The first attack of the campaign, against Dresden, was to have been carried out by American bomber forces but bad weather caused its cancellation. What followed has become perhaps one of the most controversial actions of the entire wartime bombing campaign. Lancasters carried out two separate attacks against the city, three hours apart, and with great accuracy, the resulting firestorm being estimated to have killed 50,000. Eighth Air Force B-17s attacked the next day using the railway yards as their aiming point, while escorting P51s were ordered to strafe road traffic. The Eighth Air Force bombed again on the 15th to add to the chaos and returned on 2 March. It was a terrifyingly deadly start to *Operation Thunderclap*.

The Halifax force was out, attacking the Braunkohle-Benzin synthetic-oil plant at Böhlen, near Leipzig, on the night of the first attack but bad weather with 10/10ths cloud and icing at 15,000 ft produced scattered marking and the equivalent in bombing results. Just a single Halifax from 77 Squadron was lost, Fl/Sgt A. Simmons' crew all perishing with MZ803: G. Two nights later on 14/15 February, a combined Lancaster/Halifax force attacked Chemnitz, losing eight

Lancasters and five Halifaxes. This was the first major attack on the city by Bomber Command and again the raid was split into two phases, three hours apart, aided by very elaborate diversionary raids. Crews from No 95 HCU carried out a sweep into the Heligoland Bight, 46 Mosquitoes went to Berlin, 19 to Mainz, 14 to Dessau, 12 to Duisburg, 11 to Nuremberg and eight to Frankfurt, while 21 RCM sorties were flown in support of the main attack. A further 87 Mosquito patrols were added along with 30 Lancasters and 24 Halifaxes minelaying in the Kadet Channel, leaving the German night-fighter controllers little chance of making decisions in the face of such deceptions. The minelaying sorties proved almost as costly as the main attack with a single Lancaster and five Halifaxes failing to return. No 10 Squadron lost MZ793: X, 77 Squadron lost MZ924: D, 78 Squadron MZ799: X, while 427 Squadron lost MZ355: W and 429 Squadron MZ865: V. The latter violated Swedish airspace and was shot down by Anti Aircraft fire killing F/Lt R. Charlton and crew. Some squadrons lost aircraft and crews on both the minelaying diversion as well as the main target; No 78 lost MZ791: T and 427 MZ422: N.

Wesel was attacked three times in daylight on the 17th, 18th and 19th but good weather only attended the last attack, which delivered the best concentration of bombs on the railway area. Interestingly, only a single RCM sortie was flown on the last occasion while nine were flown, along with diversionary actions when Böhlen was bombed that night by a small force of Lancasters. Then, on 20 February, a lone RCM aircraft flew the only operational sortie of the night. The following night Dortmund received its last large-scale attack, during which the southern half of the city was destroyed, Lancasters, Halifaxes and Mosquitoes bombing the Rhenania Ossag refinery in the Reisholz district, halting oil production at the cost of four Halifaxes and a Lancaster. A force of 112 Halifaxes, 10 Mosquitoes and six Lancasters attacked the same company's refinery at Monheim with equally destructive results, losing two Halifaxes in the process while a force of Lancasters and Mosquitoes attacked the Mittelland Canal, the raid being abandoned because of cloud cover. The now usual diversionary tactics were employed and 65 RCM sorties were flown for the loss of one Liberator, TS520: J, from No 223 Squadron to a night-fighter attack.

A 192 Squadron Halifax had a harrowing experience during February but survived to deliver some important information. On the night of 19/20th, F/O Dutton was sent to the Bohlen area to search for possible enemy centimetric transmissions in the 3000-4000 megacycle band and while en route, one of the engines of NA242: D failed, but Dutton elected to continue the sortie. When leaving the target area, his Halifax was subjected to 15 attacks over a period of 90 minutes by a number of assailants including a Ju 88, a Bf 109, a 'jet fighter' and others, which were unidentified, but the Halifax survived the attacks and landed safely at Manston. The sortie had been very successful; W/O Coulton, the special operator, had obtained the first reliable information to be gained on enemy centimetric radar transmissions.

German night-fighters may have had better luck during the attack on Worms on 21/22 February even though the flak was intense. A force of 349 bombers, 288 of them Halifaxes, was dispatched for what was to be Bomber Command's first and only attack on this city. Bombing accuracy was very good but the defences took a

The Canadians were masters of artwork with many former professional commercial artists amongst those who created and applied the art. 'Willie Wolf' (sometimes appearing as 'Willie the Wolf') was a popular name and appeared in various forms on several aircraft, including at least one RCAF Lancaster. This example of very high quality adorned a No 408 Squadron RCAF B Mk VII, NP717: Q; instead of the usual girl fleeing the attentions of a wolf, this one featured a very sophisticated wolf in flying boots and Mae West carrying a bomb in one hand and a dinghy in the other. Individual names and nicknames were the other great popular addition, usually applied in white; here it was Banny (bomb aimer), Alec (navigator), Smitty (W/Op), Boss (pilot) and Rhett (flight engineer); there would also have been names beside the mid-upper and rear turrets. Despite its reputation as "...the ropiest kite in the squadron", NP717 survived the war to be struck off charge on 28 May 1945. (via M. Wright)

heavy toll with 10 Halifaxes and a Lancaster failing to return. At the debriefing, a 158 Squadron crew reported seeing a Halifax go down with one engine on fire and explode on the ground and a second Halifax shot down by what was believed to be an Me 410. No 102 Squadron also took part in the raid using 13 of their new B Mk VI Halifaxes.

In the meantime, 462 Squadron continued its spoof activities on 22/23 February with a double 'attack' by eight of its Halifaxes. For this type of operation, the *Window* force came out from the cover of the *Mandrel* screen and dropped sufficient metal foil to stimulate a reaction from the German night-fighter controllers before withdrawing behind the screen again. A little later, as the night-fighters were being recalled, the Halifaxes emerged once more and made another *Window* drop. The resulting confusion disrupted any efforts to present a co-ordinated defence. This operation was part of the night activities designed to keep German industry disrupted and under pressure.

In fine weather, Bomber Command had already made a relatively small-scale daylight attack that day on two oil refineries with 85 bombers sent to Gelsenkirchen and 82 to Osterfeld. That night, 22/23rd, 73 Mosquitoes went to Berlin, six to Bremen and four to Erfurt while three others over-flew various towns as nuisance raiders to trigger alarms. Thirty-five Lancasters bombed the railway viaducts at Altenbeken and Bielefeld, while 23 Mosquitoes carried out patrols. To this widespread activity were added 43 RCM sorties, including the eight by 462 Squadron mentioned above, to create a variety of additional problems for the overstretched German night-fighter control system. The night's operations cost one Mosquito from the Erfurt attack.

Next evening, nine 462 Squadron aircraft, in company with USAAF RCM Liberators, returned to the Neuss area of the Ruhr for another spoof raid, without loss. W/O Philipson's crew from 171 Squadron was detailed to drop *Window* and to bomb the night-fighter airfield at Neuss as part of the cover for the attack on Pforzheim. At Neuss, Philipson was first in to attack, dropping 3,500 lbs of bombs from LW471: H, which hit the aiming point and started fires, but crews from 192 Squadron operating in support of an attack on Pforzheim by Lancasters did not fare as well. It was that city's first and only area bombing attack of the war and produced devastating results, the bombing having been carried out from 8,000 ft and the

Although a little grainy and time-worn, this photograph records S/Ldr T. E. Eagleton, DFC & Bar flanked by his crew in front of LW172: F of 466 Squadron following its 91st operation in March 1945. The crew had just completed their first tour and Eagleton his second. The artwork was Popeye and Olive Oyl with 'Git Up Them Stairs' written vertically, the first letter of each word in white to spell out GUTS with the remaining letters in red. Chalked on the rear section of the fuselage, aft of the letter F was '91 Ops Get some in'. LW172 crashed on return from its 97th operation, killing F/O D. Watson RAAF and crew following the attack on Hamburg on 8/9 April when, while trying to locate Driffield airfield in dense fog, the Halifax hit some trees and crashed at Kirkburn Grange Farm some two miles west of the airfield. For a part of its career, LW172 was flown by the A Flight Commander, F/Lt D. Shannon DFC who later became the squadron CO. (T. E. Eagleton)

resulting conflagration causing 17,000 deaths and massive damage. Twelve Lancasters were lost plus two from 192 Squadron; Fl/Sgt G. Morgan's MZ449: Y was shot down by a night-fighter near Stuttgart with only four baling out in time, while F/Lt W. Mitchell's NA241: O crashed near Holzerlingen with only one of the crew surviving. A secondary attack was carried out by a small Lancaster force against harbour facilities at Horten in Norway which, in part, was supported by the night's minelaying activities in Norwegian waters.

However, the activities of the night of the 24/25th cost 462 Squadron four of its ten Halifaxes, the heaviest losses suffered in its bomber support role. F/Lt J. Rate's MZ447: A had been sent to mingle with a diversionary sweep composed mostly of training crews heading towards northern France and flak brought it down near Boisheim, just over the border from Holland. Only one crew member survived[18]. F/Lt F. Ridgewell's MZ448 operating on the same duties was brought down over Holland in unknown circumstances with four of his crew surviving as POWs but F/O V. Ely and his crew were all killed when MZ641: G simply failed to return, its fate unknown. Similarly, nothing further is known about the circumstances leading to the loss of F/Lt J. Tootal and his crew in PN429: E.

A close watch was kept on the progress of repair work in Mainz and on 27 February, a daylight raid was made by 458 bombers, 311 of them Halifaxes, which systematically devastated the target. Crews reported it as a routine operation, a remark which showed quite significantly that Allied air supremacy had indeed been secured.

Oil targets had not been neglected during this period with over 25% of the Bomber Command effort being devoted to these, with 14,000 tons of bombs being dropped during February. The scope of targets had widened and now embraced not only the synthetic oil plants but also benzol plants and crude oil refineries, which were also attacked along with oil storage depots. The campaign reached its climax during March, when plants not already destroyed were systematically eliminated.

The Fischer-Tropsch synthetic oil plant at Bergkamen, just north of Kamen, received four raids within eight days, commencing with a daylight attack on 24 February. Fairly heavy damage resulted from the first three attacks at a cost of one Halifax and a Lancaster but was insufficient to ensure that production could not be resumed within a few weeks. Accordingly, No 4 Group was ordered to carry out an immediate repeat attack on the night of 3/4 March and sent 201 Halifaxes, 21

Lancasters and 21 Mosquitoes to carry out the attack. The raid was most successful, with good marking and accurate opening bombing, which provided natural aiming points for the remainder of the Halifax force. Opposition was slight with only a single Halifax, NP936: P from 415 Squadron, being brought down, killing all of WO2 L. Russell's crew. Two 578 Squadron Halifaxes, LW587: A and MZ527: D, completed their 100th sorties during this attack[19]. Crews returned feeling satisfied with the accuracy of the raid and no further production came from this plant. German night-fighters, virtually absent over the target area were, however, waiting over the British bases for the returning bombers.

For *Unternehmen Gisela* approximately 200 Luftwaffe intruder aircraft were sent to trail the bombers back to their bases and attack as they were landing. This tactic took the British defences – and bomber crews – completely by surprise and eight Halifaxes of No 4 Group, two Lancasters of No 5 Group and three Halifaxes, a Fortress and a Mosquito of 100 Group, plus two Halifaxes and three Lancasters from HCUs taking part in a diversionary sweep, were shot down. For the attackers it was a success, but at a cost of some 25 Ju 88s, three being lost through flying too low during the airfield attacks[20].

The 22 Halifaxes from 10 Squadron were all diverted to Leeming, Skipton-on-Swale and High Ercall, but HX332: V was intercepted and shot down south-east of Ripon by a Ju 88[21], only three of F/Lt J. Laffoley's crew surviving, although critically injured. No 76 Squadron's NA584: E was on final approach at Holme-on-Spalding Moor when a Ju 88 attacked, killing Fl/Sgt W. Maltby, but P/O P. Oleynik managed to divert to Carnaby where he made a crash-landing. No 77 Squadron diverted four of its Halifaxes, but one was intercepted by a Ju 88 which, closing to within 500 yards, opened fire and severed the intercom and put the rear turret out of action, slightly wounding the rear gunner. The pilot, F/O J. Gaddes, managed to evade any further attacks and returned to the circuit area where, although all lights had been extinguished and Flying Control could not be raised, a landing was attempted in view of the rear gunner's injuries. The first approach was unsuccessful, but F/O Gaddes was able to land NR210: Z safely at the second attempt.

As F/O Strachen made his final approach to land at Lissett, a Ju 88 raked MZ917 with cannon and machine gun fire, causing serious damage and wounding Sgt A. Tait, the rear gunner, but Strachen was able to complete the landing safely. Another of 158 Squadron's Halifaxes, PN437: X being flown by F/Lt C. Rogers, was less

The shattered remains of NA184: W from 420 Squadron lie at Marrow Flat Farm where it crashed due to severe icing 22 minutes after taking off from Tholthorpe on 5 March 1945, killing F/O E. Clark RCAF and three of his crew, the other three baling out in time. P/O R. Sollie RCAF and all but one of his crew also died as a result of the same icing conditions when NA190: U crashed 21 minutes after take-off – the almost identical timing of the crashes identifying just where the deadly icing cell was located. (via P. Canonne)

fortunate. Diverted because of the intruder activity, his Halifax was shot down in flames near Sledmere Grange. Two more of the squadron's Halifaxes were attacked over the Wash, but managed to extricate themselves, though not without difficulty.

The two French squadrons were also subjected to attacks and 346 Squadron lost NR229: D. Attacked by a Ju 88 flown by Fw Günter Schmidt of the IV./NJG 3 at 2,500 ft over Croft, the Halifax gunners returned fire before the Halifax crashed at Hurworth, three miles from Darlington, Cne P. Notelle's crew escaping by parachute. No 347 Squadron lost NA680: H – diverted, it was intercepted and shot down near Cranwell. Cne P. Laucou gave the order to bale out and five managed to do so safely, but Sgt P. Le Masson had been injured in the attack and was unable to help himself; without hesitation Laucou stayed with the Halifax and made a desperate attempt at a forced landing, but unfortunately both died in the resulting crash. Another pilot from the unit died when NR235: O was attacked and shot down at Sutton-on-Derwent, near York. The body of Lt J. Terrien was found near the wreckage but the rest of the crew escaped by parachute.

Eleven of 466 Squadron's aircraft had landed when the intruders appeared over Driffield, shooting down NR179: C and NR250: N, two of six Halifaxes still airborne. P/O A. Shelton in the former had been forced to go round again and, while doing so, the airfield lights had been extinguished. He climbed to 4,000 ft and set course for the alternative airfield when a Ju 88 attacked out of nowhere, bringing down the Halifax at Fridaythorpe, about nine miles from Great Driffield, killing Shelton and three more of the crew. P/O A. Schrank and his crew in the other Halifax were luckier, all baling out safely when it was shot down. A final possible victim of the intruder attacks was P/O P. Manton's NP931: J from 640 Squadron. While trying to land at Woodbridge it crashed just north of the airfield, the time of the incident suggesting that an intruder possibly brought it down.

The Bomber support crews also had casualties on their return. No 171 Squadron's NA107: T, out on *Mandrel* duties was flying at 3,000 ft on the homeward leg when a Ju 88 attacked and S/Ldr P. Proctor and his crew were lucky to all escape, baling out at just 1,000 ft, the Halifax crashing five miles from Diss, in Norfolk. LV955: G from 192 Squadron was caught with its navigation lights on by a Ju 88. The wing tanks were set on fire and both inner engines put out of action, possibly indicating a *Schräge Musik* attack from underneath. The specialist operator F/O R. Todd was able to bale out before the second attack on the now blazing Halifax, which crashed moments later four miles from Fakenham. F/O E. Roberts, the pilot and another crew member were dragged clear but the rest of the crew perished. A Mosquito from No 169 Squadron also out on Bomber Support duties was diverted to Coltishall and was also shot down by a Ju 88. A similar fate awaited B-17 HB815: J of 214 Squadron on returning from *Window*-dropping duties when a Ju 88 attacked and set the aircraft on fire. The B-17 crash-landed at Lodge Farm airfield, killing P/O H. Bennett and all but four of the ten-man crew.

Crews on training flights that night also fell to the intruder attacks, one a Halifax of No 1664 HCU. All of P/O K. Griffey's crew in NA612: S were killed when it was brought down eight miles south of Thirsk in Yorkshire. Four Lancasters, two from No 1651 HCU, JB699: F and ND387: K, and two from No 1654 HCU, LM748: H and PB118: Q, were brought down. Only one crew member in PB118 was killed, but the crews of the three others were all killed.

A few intruders returned the next night and a single Ju 88 shot-up No 425 Squadron's base at Tholthorpe without causing any damage. These last gestures were little more than the death throes of the German night-fighter force and already the Allied Air Forces were beginning a slow reduction in strength in preparation for the end of hostilities. No 578 Squadron would fly its last operation on 13 March as part of a 354-strong force that attacked Wuppertal-Barmen. No aircraft were lost and the target was severely damaged. Over the preceding three-day period, Bomber Command had dispatched 2,541 daylight sorties against Ruhr targets for the loss of five aircraft. Allied air supremacy was now complete.

On 5/6 March Chemnitz was attacked by 498 Lancasters, 256 Halifaxes and 6 Mosquitoes in a continuation of *Operation Thunderclap* but things started out badly with extremely icy conditions bringing down nine of No 6 Group's Lancasters near their home bases soon after taking off, killing all but one of the crews. Two of 426 Squadron's 14 Halifaxes were also victims of the terrible conditions, LW210: Y, which broke up in flight and NP793: H, both coming down over England killing all but one crew member. Five civilians were also killed and 18 injured when an engine hit a local secondary school.

In all 22 aircraft failed to return from the raid. No 10 Squadron lost MZ948: E, which was still fitted with a mid-under gun position, three of the crew surviving and NR131: N which crashed near Stalag IXC. No 346 Squadron's MZ738: H failed to return and the crew of F/Lt W. Mitchell's 415 Squadron crew all survived as POWs when NA204: J was brought down. No 420 Squadron was badly hit, losing NA184: W when it iced up and crashed just over a mile from the airfield, with NA190: U being lost in similar circumstances, while two failed to return from the actual operation. F/Lt V. Glover's NP959: N was brought down over German territory and although all of the crew initially survived, one later died from his injuries. P/O J. Menary's crew was more fortunate; homeward-bound, NR144: H ran low on fuel and the aircraft was headed instead for Juvincourt where an airfield was available. Menary eased the Halifax down through cloud but encountered thin patches of mist and did not see a pole on a hilltop and hit it. The Halifax crash-landed into soft earth moments later, the crew escaping with minor injuries. They were just five miles from their intended destination.

No 425 Squadron also lost MZ454: S to icing, and three of the crew had baled out before it crashed some 22 minutes after take-off, badly damaging the church and Moat Hall at Little Ouseburn and killing the remaining crew members. Within minutes of take-off, MZ845: J collided with PN228: A from 426 Squadron, only Fl/Sgt J. De Cruyenaere from MZ845 managing to bale out in time. PN173: Q was the only one of the three losses to fall over enemy territory with four of the crew becoming POWs. No 426 Squadron's fourth loss of the night, NP799: J, was shot down by a night-fighter with only one of the crew surviving. No 429 Squadron's LV996: K crashed at Halling, in Kent, when nearly home; this was the Squadron's last Halifax loss as it was about to begin converting to Lancasters. LV996 had clocked-up 63 sorties with 427 Squadron before being transferred to its current owner on 17 April. No 432 Squadron's RG475: L was lost in tragic circumstances, falling to AA fire from a coastal battery sited near Walton on the Naze, in Essex. No 578 Squadron lost two at Bovingdon when, low on fuel, both LL559: U and NA173: K landed at that base with LL559 colliding with the second Halifax and writing both

Three of 425 Squadron's B Mk IIIs, MZ454: S, LL596: U with MZ620: T in the background, photographed at Tholthorpe during the winter of 1944/45. Delivered in August 1944, LL596 was later transferred to 1664 HCU and struck off charge 13 December 1946 while MZ454, built around the beginning of October 1944, went first to 424 Squadron, then 431 and finally to 425. The date of construction is valuable as it shows that even in late 1944, some production aircraft were being fitted with Preston-Green cupolas, the long barrel of the Browning 0.5-in machine gun clearly visible here. It was one of several aircraft brought down by freakish icing conditions within less than 30 minutes of take-off for the raid on Chemnitz on 5 March 1945. Uncontrollable, MZ454 crashed at Little Ouseburn, killing all seven of F/O A. Lowe's crew. Lowe was one of many Americans serving with the RCAF and one of his crew, P/O J. Hyde, was 35 years old, well above the average age for Bomber Command. The fact that a crew of seven was on board suggests that H2S equipment may have replaced the Preston-Green fitting by that date. (Public Archives of Canada)

machines off, although no injuries were sustained. The low fuel situation had affected a number of aircraft, and 640 Squadron lost NR120: M through this cause, the crew having to bale out over France on the return flight – all without injury.

The Bomber Support squadrons did not escape loss either. F/Lt N. Irvine's NR180: S from 192 Squadron was badly shot up by a fighter, reported as an Me 262, and in the ensuing chaos, had hit the tail of a Lancaster, which was last seen going down out of control. Able to keep the Halifax flying, Irvine decided to head for the nearest friendly territory – the Russian lines – but the crew were forced to bale out without being certain of their position; most appear to have landed in German-held territory, only two being picked up by Russian forces and passed back to safety. One of the *Mandrel* force on its 48th operation, Stirling LJ617: E of 199 Squadron, was shot down by American AA fire near Thionville with all but the pilot escaping by parachute. This was the last Stirling to be lost by the squadron, which completed its change to Halifaxes on 15 March.

On 7/8 March, while Dessau, Hemmingstedt, and Harburg were collectively attacked by over 1,000 bombers, the usual suite of minor support operations were mounted against numerous targets. All were a part of the confusion factor for German night-fighter controllers with some 56 RCM sorties being carried out and the night-fighter airfield at Münster bombed by some Halifaxes from 171 Squadron. W/O Philipson's NA960: B was on a combined *Window*-bombing sortie and added its 3,500 lbs of bombs to the target. The Squadron lost F/Lt J. Stone's NA111: Y which was tasked with providing a *Mandrel* screen; it was also carrying a large supply of *Window* as well as bombs in support of the Münster attack, but only Stone survived when he was blown clear of the aircraft when it exploded.

The first of 462 Squadron's modified Halifaxes had arrived from St Athan on 15 February but the supply was slow and the first RCM operation was not flown until March. These specialist aircraft were distinguishable by the three tall masts of their

ABC equipment, two above the fuselage and one below the nose section. *ABC* (*Airborne Cigar*) was a jamming device designed to disrupt Luftwaffe radio-telephony control channels in a range of frequencies. It could also be used to jam the navigational aid code-named *Benito*. The operator would sweep the frequency bands for signals and when one was found visually on the cathode ray tube display, he would then listen to it and if it was of German origin, he would tune one of the 50-watt transmitters into it and jam it. This process was continued until all three transmitters were engaged; range was about 50 miles with the receiver in the aircraft being fed by a whip aerial mounted on the top of the fuselage. *Piperack* was the code-name for an American development of the British *Mandrel* system and used to jam radar in the 60-93 MHz range, which included the FuG 220 – Lichtenstein SN-2 – radar carried by the German night-fighters. Its presence in a Halifax was distinguished by two whip aerials on the top surface of each wing near the tip. Only 11 of these Halifaxes were on charge by the time hostilities ceased. The *Window* force was often left to face the repercussions and it was for those circumstances that *Piperack* would have been of distinct advantage.

While Main Force crews attacked the shipyards at Hamburg again on 8/9 March with a mixed force of Halifaxes, Lancasters and Mosquitoes, eight 462 Squadron crews were heading for the Dortmund area on their nightly activities. For F/Lt F. James and his crew, it was a one-way trip. Having survived a crash-landing from operations on 10/11 February, this time they ended up as POWs when MZ370: L was brought down. Yet now, with areas held by the enemy shrinking, one factor favouring crews more and more was the proximity of friendly territory. On 13/14 March, while benzol plants were being attacked at several locations, 462 Squadron had crews out as a part of the 58 RCM sorties flown in bomber support that night. One of its Halifaxes, RG384: M, force-landed at Juvincourt airfield after being damaged by flak, which had also killed the flight engineer and wounded the navigator and wireless operator.

'Willie the Wolf' was a popular slogan that appeared on several aircraft including B Mk VII NP707: W of 432 Squadron RCAF and was yet another example of Sgt T. Dunn's work from July 1944. It had carried out 65 operations when this photograph was taken, marked by red (night) and white (day) sorties and two 30 mission winged 'O' emblems. Many Canadian-operated Halifaxes carried the small white disc with a red Maple Leaf emblem on it, usually marked just below the cockpit. The aircraft survived the war with a total of 67 operations and, although struck off charge in June 1945, its artwork survives as a part of the collection of the Canadian War Museum. At the request of its crew, Dunn painted a second example on B Mk VII PN240: W of 415 Squadron also based at East Moor. That Halifax also survived the war with 42 operations to its credit. Dunn received £5 for each piece of artwork – given the size of some and the fact that he had to search hard in wartime Britain for oil paints to do them, it was good value, and each seems to have carried its own luck. (W. E. Miller via M. Wright)

Not all artwork was humorous or risqué. There were those who put their trust in faith which, as in the case of NP694: R of 432 Squadron, seems to have proved providential, the B Mk VII having already completed 65 operations with another squadron before passing to 432 where the artwork was applied – another example of the talent of Sgt Thomas E. Dunn. When finished it was inspected by the crew who said they wished they had had some artwork, so Dunn removed it and redid the entire work, this time adding a light blue cloud with three yellow lightning bolts, the cross, swastika and factory. A further 13 operations were recorded before the Halifax was flown to 45 MU and struck off charge in 15 August 1947. The text, from the Gospel of St Luke 3:5; "Every valley shall be filled and every mountain and hill shall be brought low", was to prove true by May 1945 when most German cities lay in ruins, 78 contributions having been made by this Halifax and its various crews. (W. E. Miller via M. Wright)

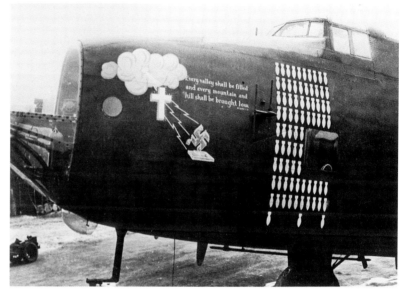

The two tall masts were the transmitting aerials for the ABC jamming equipment, while the four whip aerials, just visible between the mid-upper turret and the rear turret on PN168: R of 462 Squadron, are believed to be the receivers. The additional very large square-sided chute fitted each side with three vents to aid airflow for chaff (Window) dropping is just visible between and below the roundel and letter 'R'. (R. Hines via M. Wright)

In this view, all three ABC transmitter masts can be seen with the third mounted vertically below the nose section. Note that the navigator's triangular window had been blacked out; a small moveable curtain was fitted to Halifaxes at this position but, as seen here, appears to be a solid, internal fitting. (R. Hines via M. Wright)

This ventral view of MZ913: N, while of poorer distinction, shows the additional aerials mounted on the bomb bay doors. Two are mounted on the port side with one forward and one aft, with another on the starboard door set midway between the other two – all three spaced so that when the doors were closed they were almost in a row on the mid-line of the fuselage. Also visible on the original photograph are four short flexible aerials mounted on the port rear bomb bay door section close to the edge that formed the centre line when closed. Three Perspex-covered small rotating aerials were fitted to the midline edge of the port forward bomb bay door. A long-range tank was fitted in the bomb bay, indicative of the extended patrol time required of most Bomber Support aircraft. (R. Hines via M. Wright)

This side view of MZ913: N of 462 Squadron provides a view of the main aerial arrays. The three distinctive masts and aerials associated with ABC jamming equipment were the most prominent (the aft dorsal one here obscured by the wing tip). Two of the three semi-spherical domes fitted to the port bomb bay door can also be seen with the box-like shape of the standard Window distribution chute mounted to starboard, immediately forward of the bomb door leading edge. On the starboard side, just aft of the H2S dome, is the larger angular chute for dropping Window, the volume dropped by these specialist aircraft being far in excess of that dropped by bomber crews during operations. The short rod aerial further aft is understood to be for the Carpet device, which targeted enemy GCI radars. Just visible on the wing tip upper surface are two short whip aerials for the Piperack equipment which, carried above each wing tip, were used for jamming German AI radars. (R. Hines via M. Wright)

Handley Page Halifax, B Mk III
MZ913: N, No 462 Squadron, Foulsham (No 100 Group).

On 15 March, one of Bomber Command's smallest targets, the Mathias Stinnes benzol distillation plant, was attacked in daylight. One of 102 Squadron's new B Mk VI Halifaxes, RG498: N, was badly damaged by flak over the target with the starboard fin and rudder shot off and both elevators jammed, but F/L W. Dick managed to fly the Halifax back to Manston, where he made a forced landing. The aircraft caught fire and was completely destroyed, but the crew escaped unhurt.

The daylight attack on the railway yards and surrounding town of Rheine on 21 March, part of a series of attacks to hinder the Wehrmacht forces nearby, cost a single Halifax from the 150 sent to bomb. No 51 Squadron's MZ348: D had been hit by bombs from another aircraft but F/O J. Paradise and his crew all baled out safely. Paradise was the first to be picked up and was locked in a cell at Dreierwalde airfield, at that time the home to Jagdgeschwader 27[22]. During the course of the raid some of the bombing had hit the airfield killing 40 German and foreign workers. What followed was a black moment in the closing weeks of the war. Later in the day, four other members of his crew were brought in and locked in with him. The following day an escort was arranged to take the five to the nearby railway station for transportation to Oberursel. Heading the escort was Karl Amberger[23], a former wireless operator who had been shot down and captured off Cromer on 17/18 June 1940. Wounded, he was repatriated to Germany in 1943 under the terms of the Geneva Convention as unfit for military duty but rejoined the Luftwaffe. Amberger was vehemently opposed to the Allies and shortly after marching the five along the road to the station, he ordered the escort to shoot them in the back. As the escort cocked their machine pistols, F/O K. Berwick made his escape into the nearby woods

but was hit twice in the leg and, while still managing to escape, was forced to surrender to Army personnel two days later. The Army treated him correctly and he received medical attention before being safely shipped to a POW camp. Further killings of captured airmen occurred on the airfield on 24 and 25 March. The other two members of Paradise's crew, Sgt W. Hood and Fl/Sgt L. Hart, were more fortunate, becoming POWs via other captors.

On 23/24 March the final phase of the land war opened with the amphibious crossing of the Rhine in the Wessel area in concert with the airborne landings of *Operation Varsity* a few hours later. Wessel had been bombed the night before by 195 Lancasters in what was the town's last raid. Destruction was almost complete with about 97% of the town having been destroyed in a string of attacks. British Commandos captured it just after the bombing force withdrew. The RCM crews were kept busy around Wessel; W/O Philipson and his crew were 'on station' in LK868: J, 20 miles west of the target carrying out *Mandrel* and *Window* duties from 21.50 hrs to 23.20 hrs, all jamming stopping at 23.30 hrs. *"Great fireworks display as searchlights lit the crossing, laid horizontal, and 3,500 guns in a barrage followed the bombing which ended at 22.30 hrs."*

On the 24th, Sterkrade, Gladbeck and various benzol plants were also bombed – for the loss of four aircraft. That night only minor operations were mounted but enough to keep the enemy on edge – 67 Mosquitoes to Berlin, eight to Nordheim and two others that bombed both Berlin and Magdeburg supported by 38 RCM sorties and 33 Serrate patrols. Even so, night-fighters remained active and 452 Squadron's MZ308: S was intercepted in the Opaiden area by an Fw 190, which closed to within

Not only Canadians produced large-scale artwork – this one had to be Australian! In addition to the huge kangaroo with a figure (possibly Hitler) draped over the line towing a large bomb marked 'REICH 1000 yrs', each of the 55 operations were recorded by a small, sitting kangaroo symbol, the last five immediately above the name 'MATTHEWS & Co. EXPRESS DELIVERY SERVICE'. Without the numerous aerial arrays, it was unlikely to have belonged to 462 Squadron but may have been a 466 Squadron machine. Equally possible, an RAAF crew within an RAF squadron may have wanted to advertise their identity but, whatever its origin, it must have been the largest work of its kind from a non-RCAF unit. The aircraft letter appears to be 'V-Victor'. (via M. Wright)

Although losses were reduced they continued, made all the more grim when they occurred in broad daylight. This one caught on camera with date and target clearly identified, presents something of an enigma. MZ348: D of 51 Squadron was part of the daylight force sent against Rheine on 21 March when it was hit by flak and went down, wing tanks on both sides blazing; its fall was caught by the camera in F/O Swift's 'Q-Queen' of 426 Squadron, the letter 'D' clearly visible when viewed under magnification. This was the only aircraft lost in the attack; official loss records confirm its identity and crew and the war atrocity investigation which followed, as detailed in the text, makes identification of the crew indisputable. Yet the two broad diagonal yellow tactical bands marked across fin and rudder clearly identifies 158 Squadron. The two squadrons did not share the same airfield and the Halifax was delivered directly from production to 51 Squadron. (via M. Wright)

When 158 Squadron received B Mk III LV907 on 10 March 1944, there was nothing significant to distinguish it at that point. The second B Mk III from Handley Page, it was randomly selected by the A&AEE for routine testing of production aircraft and was test-flown on 2 March, the report concluding with the comment "Performance and handling normal for type." Coded as 'F-Fox' it went on to complete 128 operations, earning a string of decorations for its various crew before finally being struck off charge as Category E2 on 18 May 1945. Christened 'Friday the 13th' it was adorned with a wide range of symbols including a bomb log marked with the usual white bomb silhouettes; the 21st operation distinguished by a key with a Hakenkreuz, the 70th with a blockbuster trailing a spiral and the 100th with a larger than usual bomb lying in an open box or coffin. By the time it was displayed post-war, the log had changed slightly with the 'box' replaced with a single, vertical larger bomb with 100 arranged around the edge of the nose. Nor was the medal count insignificant, comprising a DSO & Bar, DFC and DFM. (via M. Wright)

A display of RAF aircraft was mounted in Oxford Street at the end of the war and amongst those exhibited was LV907: F; this aerial view provides a last testament to a veteran Halifax which was struck off charge on 18 May 1945 and disappeared into the breaker's yard, reduced to scrap. Fortunately, its wonderful record and artwork is preserved to this day. The bold yellow tactical markings on fin and rudder added a touch of colour to the wartime camouflage of all the aircraft present. (via B. Robertson)

Wangerooge was the final mass daylight attack of the war for Halifaxes. two of the 308 dispatched can be seen in this target photograph taken from F/Lt Pitt's aircraft at 9,000 ft, the shadow of the uppermost one can be seen on the clouds below, giving the impression of a third aircraft. (via M. Wright)

400 yards of the Halifax before the rear gunner opened fire, scoring hits, and claiming it as damaged.

The threat from the new prefabricated Type XXI U-boats had been realised late in 1944 and the Admiralty had lost no time in pressing for attacks on the assembly yards. These began in November 1944 and increased in intensity until they reached devastating proportions during March and April 1945. Hamburg and Bremen were the principal recipients and it was during a heavy daylight raid on the former, against the Blohm und Voss shipyards on 31 March, that Bomber Command had its one and only heavy engagement with German jet fighters. A few minutes before 09.00 hrs the last wave of the 469-strong bomber force approached the target. The mixed force of Halifaxes and Lancasters from No 6 Group was late and the fighter escort had already withdrawn when approximately 12 Me 262 fighters from the III./JG7 tore into the formation. The battle lasted 12 short minutes but three Halifaxes and eight Lancasters were later recorded as having failed to return; although not all could be confirmed as victims of the Me 262s, it is highly likely that all but one, a Lancaster, were from that cause.

One of the Lancaster pilots later reported seeing five Lancasters and one Halifax shot down in the space of two minutes. One of 425 Squadron's crews in NR231 also reported seeing rockets used, but possibly not all the Me 262s were fitted with the deadly R4M rockets. This undoubtedly saved the bombers from further destruction, but the effect of the four closely-grouped 30 mm cannon in the noses of the Me 262s still took a grim toll.

Three of the Halifax squadrons each lost a single aircraft, and each was confirmed a victim of the Me 262 attack. The crew of F/O K. Blyth's 408 Squadron NP806: Q all survived to become POWs for a brief time. F/O G. Hyland's crew in MZ922: C from 415 Squadron were not so fortunate, all being killed, and only F/Lt C. Lesesne, the pilot of 425 Squadron's MZ418: C, died while his crew all parachuted to safety and temporary captivity. Four Me 262s were claimed as destroyed but there is no confirmation of these losses and, given the speed of the jets, it would seem unlikely that any fell to the air gunners. This was the last double-digit loss by Bomber Command for an attack on a city.

Hamburg was attacked again on 8/9 April, the next large-scale attack mounted by Bomber Command; 263 Halifaxes, 160 Lancasters and 17 Mosquitoes attempted to bomb the shipyards again, following up an earlier raid in the day by US bombers, but heavy cloud dispersed the bombing. This was Hamburg's last attack of the war.

April marked a further reduction in Bomber Command effort and strategic area bombing ceased as such with only 21 major raids being made in April, a little more

than half of which were night operations. Only 35,000 tons of bombs, about half the previous month's figure, were dropped and the largest single portion of this went on naval targets, harbour facilities and shipping. Railway centres, oil and tactical targets absorbed the remainder. Attacks on oil facilities at Leuna, Harburg, Lützkendorf, Molbis, then Lützkendorf again, and finally Regensburg on 20 April, marked the end of the campaign against such targets.

Kiel was attacked on 9/10th and an accurate raid was carried out aided by 33 Halifaxes on a diversionary raid to Stade while 44 Mosquitoes went to Berlin, 37 to Plauen and 24 to Hamburg. Additionally, 45 RCM sorties were flown in support of this raid and another 37 Mosquitoes carried out night-fighter patrols. Added to all this activity were 70 Lancasters and 28 Halifaxes, which laid mines in Kiel Bay and the Little Belt. Three Lancasters were lost on the main attack and a 10 Squadron Halifax, HX286: R from the Stade attack, the crew baling out safely behind Allied lines.

Bomber support techniques had grown steadily more and more sophisticated and spoof raids had reached a very high standard of efficiency. On 10/11 April, 307 Lancasters, led by eight PFF Mosquitoes, attacked Plauen, while 76 Lancasters and nine Mosquitoes raided the city's Mackau railway yards, which had been bombed only hours before in daylight by a mixed 230-strong Lancaster/Halifax/Mosquito force, losing NA185: B from 415 Squadron and a Lancaster from 433 Squadron to flak. In addition to a range of minor operations arranged to add to the confusion of the dual Plauen/Leipzig rail yard attacks, 462 Squadron was ordered to provide 10 Halifaxes to support the operation against Leipzig's Wahren railway yards. While three operated on RCM duties, the seven-strong *Window* force preceded the Main Force and just before reaching Leipzig, branched off towards Berlin, dropping foil to simulate the Main Force. This was done to raise the enemy night-fighters to the north of Berlin, where Mosquito intruders could engage them and to draw others away from the real target. The ruse was successful in part for the Plauen force escaped losses, but seven Lancasters failed to return. P/O A. Ball's BS Halifax NA240: V fitted with *ABC*, *Piperack* and a *Carpet* jammer as well as *H2S*, was shot down in the Plauen area with only one crew member surviving. With barely 60 miles between the two targets it was not unexpected that a night-fighter would find them.

On 14/15 April, Bomber Command returned to the area around Berlin for the first time since March 1944. Five hundred Lancasters with PFF support went to Potsdam, 20 miles west of Berlin. This was the last major attack of the war on a German city by a large Bomber Command force. It was supported by a diversion of four Mosquitoes to Cuxhaven, 62 more over Berlin and 10 to Weimar, plus 50 more in protective patrols. Additionally 54 RCM sorties were put up. No 462 Squadron fielded 12 Halifaxes, four on *ABC* duties with the Main Force to Potsdam, four on *Window* feint attacks on Neuruppin and the remainder on a similar task over the Jüterbog area. Only one Lancaster was lost from the Main Force, shot down by a night-fighter – a fair measure of the success of this type of operation.

Two nights later Pilsen was attacked by 222 Lancasters and five Mosquitoes of No 5 Group while 167 Lancasters and eight Mosquitoes of Nos 6, and 8 Groups attacked Schwandorf. The usual assortment of support operations were added, including 57 RCM sorties. The spread was now becoming more intensive. No 462 Squadron put up 11 Halifaxes, six going to Augsburg on a feint attack using *Window*, one to Pilsen, one to Prague and two to Schwandorf, while the remainder carried out a protective (*ABC*) patrol. The night's operations cost a Lancaster from each of the main attacks plus three aircraft from 100 Group; a Fortress plus F/O A. Lodder's MZ467: C of 462 Squadron with three crew members surviving and F/Lt P. Jennings' entire crew in LK874: C of 171 Squadron. The latter had collided with a 156 Squadron Lancaster, PB403: E, one of the Markers for the railway yard attack; both crews died in the collision and the remains of the aircraft fell in a wooded area at Mürlenbach on the west bank of the River Kyll.

Rail targets had remained on the list and Leipzig, lying as it did in the path of the Allied ground forces, had a double value. Attacked in the last light of evening on 10 April with a strong fighter escort, opposition was mild, only a small amount of flak being encountered and this was visually aimed. A few isolated jet aircraft were seen in the target area and the crew of NP937: T from 425 Squadron claimed an Me 163 as probably destroyed. The mid-upper gunner had first sighted the enemy fighter attacking a Lancaster 500 yards away and opened fire, whereupon the Me 163 was seen to stall, fall onto its back and descend in a steep dive. Three other members of the crew verified the claim. Encounters with this deadly little fighter were few, but the fact that this encounter was in daylight makes the claim plausible.

It was unfortunate that the B Mk VI Halifaxes should arrive in significant numbers too late to play a major role in the offensive. Nos 346 and 347 Squadrons became fully operational with the type on 4 April and 158 Squadron began operating theirs on the 18th during a mass raid against the military installations and gun batteries at Heligoland. In perfect weather conditions, 617 Lancasters, 332 Halifaxes

No 640 Squadron used yellow squares superimposed on the black camouflage of the fin. All three code letters were thinly outlined in roundel yellow but the aircraft letter was not repeated on the fin as squadrons tended to use some latitude when adding daylight tactical markings and outlining codes. Delivered in early December 1944, B Mk III NA222: O was photographed following the end of hostilities when aircraft were ferried to the various MUs to await disposal. In the background can be seen a 466 Squadron Halifax, distinguishable by its daylight tactical marking of three yellow diagonal stripes. (P. J. R. Moyes)

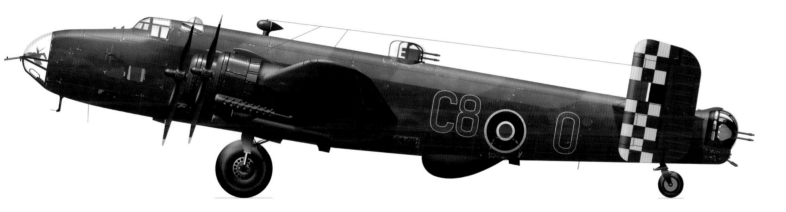

Handley Page Halifax, B Mk III
NA222: O, No 640 Squadron, December 1944.

and 20 Mosquitoes attacked the naval base, small airfield and town situated on this small island producing results mirroring the destructive scenes of the First World War. No 158 Squadron crews, flying in the fifth and sixth waves, reported smoke and flame covering the aiming points and the defences seemed to be overwhelmed. Even so, a flak hit caused another Halifax[24] to explode and damage 426 Squadron's PN226: N but P/O J. Whipple managed to nurse it back to base. There were no survivors from the other two Halifaxes. Me 262 fighters again appeared during this operation and F/O Halle of 425 Squadron was disturbed to find his Halifax, already on three engines, only 700 yards from three of these potent fighters. To his relief they did not attack MZ425: U, possibly being short of fuel or ammunition.

The last major operation for the Halifaxes was another 'naval' target, the coastal gun batteries on Wangerooge Island in the East Frisians.

A mixed force of 482 Halifaxes, Lancasters and Mosquitoes from Nos 4, 6, 8 and 100 Groups was dispatched on 25 April. No 11 Group of Fighter Command provided fighter cover drawn from 10 Spitfire squadrons while *Oboe*-equipped Mosquitoes marked the aiming points. Weather conditions were good with no cloud and visibility was excellent. In spite of accurate and heavy flak from the nearby islands of Spiekeroog and Langeroog and the eastern and western extremities of Wangerooge, a highly concentrated and accurate attack developed. Fighter opposition was restricted to a single, almost prophetic, appearance of a lone Me 262. Of the seven aircraft that failed to return, six were lost in mid-air collisions.

F/Lt A. Ely's 408 Squadron's NP796: M and WO2 J. Tuplin's 426 Squadron's NP820: W were seen by F/Lt A. Rose of 408 Squadron to collide on the way in to the target. Two more Halifaxes, from No 76 Squadron, collided, P/O G. Lawson's RG553: T and WO2 J. Outerson's RG591: A. All but Lawson were killed and he nearly died when he found himself trapped beneath the port wing as his Halifax fell into the target area, pushing himself clear and landing in shallow water. A fifth Halifax failed to return, but NP921: E from 347 Squadron possibly was a victim of the flak, Sgc R. Mercier's crew all being killed when it came down near some military barracks on the island. The two Lancasters lost, KB822: W and KB831: E from 431 Squadron, collided off Norderney; both plunged into the sea and there were no survivors.

For the Main Force crews of Nos 4 and 6 Groups, this was their last operation and it came as something of an anti-climax for many. On 7 May, at 01.41 hrs, German representatives signed the document of unconditional surrender and on the same day, No 4 Group was transferred to Transport Command. No 6 Group began converting Nos 408 and 425 Squadrons to Lancasters as they were to return to Canada with six other squadrons to train as part of *'Tiger Force'* for operations against the Japanese in the Far East. Four other squadrons remained in Bomber Command to serve with the Armies of Occupation, and 426 Squadron converted to Liberators and joined Transport Command.

While the Main Force crews had finished operations, the same had not occurred in the bomber support squadrons of 100 Group. The rapidly approaching end of hostilities had produced a 10-day lull in operations and none of the Halifax squadrons operated during this period. Then, on the night of 2/3 May, Bomber Command launched its last large-scale offensive of World War Two. No 8 Group sent 126 Mosquitoes in two waves to attack Kiel, while a further eight attacked Eggebeck airfield and six others Husum airfield. No 100 Group dispatched a mixed force of 161 Halifaxes, Mosquitoes, Liberators and Fortresses to a wide range of targets for a variety of tasks. Of the four Halifax squadrons, 462 Squadron sent six to the Flensburg area for a *Window* operation and four others to Kiel for RCM duties. Each Halifax carried five 500 lb bombs. The other Foulsham-based squadron, 192, dispatched 14 Halifaxes and five Mosquitoes, six Halifaxes going to Kiel for RCM duties and the other ten dropping *Window* in the Flensburg area.

Both of the North Creake Squadrons put up a maximum effort. 171 Squadron operated four Halifaxes on *Mandrel-Window* operations over Flensburg, 12 more on similar duties, plus bombing operations over Kiel, with two other Halifaxes for the same duties in the Schleswig area. No 199 Squadron put up 21 Halifaxes with two flown by crews borrowed from 171 Squadron. Five carried out *Mandrel-Window* operations in the North Frisian Islands with one returning early due to compass failure. Ten others joined the *Mandrel-Window* bombing operations over Kiel and six carried out a similar task in the Schleswig area. All of the 16 Halifaxes carrying out bombing were each carrying eight 500 lb bombs. Two of this force, RG373: T and RG375: R, failed to return. Both aircraft crashed at Meimsdorf, just south of Kiel and it is thought that they collided on their bombing run. There were only three survivors from the 16 crew members: P/O Crane from F/Lt Brooks' RG373, and two from the other Halifax, F/Lt Currell, the pilot and Fl/Sgt R. Hunter the rear gunner. Along with F/O R. Catterall DFC and his navigator Fl/Sgt D. Beadle, killed when their 169 Squadron Mosquito was shot down by flak, these were the last Bomber Command crews to die on operations in World War Two. The full crew of RG373 was F/Lt W. Brooke, W/O W. Bolton, Fl/Sgt. J. Lewis, W/O K. Gavin, F/O K. Croft, Fl/Sgt D. Wilson, F/O A. Holder DFC, and P/O K. Crane. The crew from RG375 were F/Lt L. Currell, Sgt W. Mackay, Fl/Sgt A. Bradley, Sgt F. Chambers, Fl/Sgt J. Loth, W/O R. Pool, Fl/Sgt D. Greenwood, and Fl/Sgt R. Hunter.

With the cessation of hostilities, the four squadrons carried out routine training flights for a while. One of 462 Squadron's Halifaxes flew members of the Allied Commission to Flensburg and returned carrying several passengers, including a Luftwaffe colonel for interrogation.

On 25 June, *Exercise Post Mortem* began and all four Halifax squadrons participated. The object was to simulate large-scale raids on the former enemy territory so that an assessment could be made of the efficiency of the German raid-reporting system. The exercise continued until early July with aircraft of Nos 1, 3, 8 and 100 Groups participating. All forms of targets were tested with different types of attacking force and bomber support screens; Philipson recorded three in succession between 3rd and 5th July, each over five hours' duration. The first was against Kiel, the second in MZ491: G at Flensburg supporting 250 Lancasters, and the last, in the same Halifax, over night-fighter airfields. The overall results of these extended exercises showed that Bomber Command's techniques had been so successful that in nearly every case plotting of the Main Force was incoherent, scattered and unreliable. The final words of the report were pertinent to 100 Group, their brevity masking a wealth of meaning: *"On the whole there appears no defence against the most effective jamming of the Mandrel and Window forces."*

On this very satisfactory note the Halifax squadrons began disbanding or transferring to Transport Command duties. However, this did not mark the end of the Halifax's service with 100 Group. No 192 Squadron, which disbanded on 22 August 1945, became the nucleus of the Radio Warfare Establishment with the Flying and Servicing Wing formed at Foulsham, while the HQ, Technical Wing and Y Wing were formed at Swanton Morley. An advance party moved to the unit's new location at Watton, in Norfolk, during September. On 6 October the first group of aircraft arrived, 15 Halifaxes, most of them ex-199 Squadron aircraft plus a few from Nos 462 and 171 Squadrons, 10 Mosquitoes, three Fortresses, an Oxford and a Ju 88, albeit that they were three days in advance of the official movement order from 100 Group.

On transfer to Watton, the unit came under No 60 Group, Fighter Command. By mid-October, it had an establishment of 24 Halifaxes, eight Fortresses, 12 Mosquitoes, three Ansons, an Oxford and a Proctor. With such a large number of aircraft three sets of codes were issued; the Halifaxes were allocated V7-A to H, then J to Q, U3-S to Z. The Fortresses were given U3-A to H and the Mosquitoes 4S-0 to Z. Its post-war activities have remained restricted, but the steady advances in electronic warfare, both passive and active, indicate that research continued at a reasonable pace. The Halifax contingent remained until early 1947 and the last four, RG389, PN454, PN452 and PN440, were struck off charge in February. Two more, PN435 and RG387, were sold for scrap on 14 March, but for all active purposes the unit had ceased its Halifax operations by January 1947.

For the Main Force squadrons it had been swifter and they had spent their last days before converting to transport duties dropping now unwanted stocks of bombs in the North Sea. One particular duty was carried out with a distinct air of pleasure, low-level sightseeing tours of the former German targets. Three routes were laid down: route A – base, Emden, Bremen, Hamburg, Kiel, Heligoland, Egmond, Cromer, base, a trip of 859 nautical miles; route B – base, Lowestoft, Rotterdam, Krefeld, Essen, Munster, Egmond, Cromer, base, a trip of 680 nautical miles; and route C – base, Lowestoft, Antwerp, Bonn, Düsseldorf, Dortmund, Munster, Egmond, Cromer, base, for a distance of 745 nautical miles. The bomber support ground staff were similarly rewarded, but with different routes; Philipson carried out one on 12 May in LK868: J taking five passengers on what the squadron described as a Cook's Tour, a 5 hour 40 minute low-level trip starting at West Raynham - Cap Gris Nez - Ypres - Brussels - Maastrich - Cologne - Neuss - Antwerp - Ostend - Dover - West Raynham. Next day he had eight on board NA263: C starting at Margate - Dunkirk - Lille - Brussels - Remagen - Bonn - Cologne - Neuss - Antwerp - Ostend - Dover and back in 4 hours 15 minutes. The last was flown next day with nine on board NA695: D for a 4 hour 40 minute low-level from Margate - Dunkirk - Aachen - Bonn - Cologne - Düsseldorf - Dortmund and then back. The pleasure came not from the sight of the desolation and destruction but rather from the opportunity of showing their passengers, the tireless and oft unsung ground crews, the end result of their years of hard work.

Both French squadrons, Nos 346 and 347, remained under the control of Bomber Command and completed similar bomb-dumping duties, plus some temporary detachments for transport work in France. On 18 June, 14 Halifaxes from each squadron took part in the fly-past over Paris.

Finally, flying officially ceased on 6 October and a few days later both squadrons returned to France, taking with them their Halifaxes, presented to France by a grateful British Government.

After VJ Day, serial numbers were re-introduced beneath the wings on front-line aircraft in the ETO. B Mk VI, PP171, was delivered to 102 Squadron around the end of January 1945 and has its squadron code letters thinly outlined in yellow but not the aircraft letter on both fuselage and fin. The two horizontal bands of its daylight tactical markings were carried on the outside face of each fin and rudder unit in RAF roundel red and the under wing serial numbers applied in white, facing aft on the port wing and forward on the starboard. Handley Page drawing regulation No 6108 stipulated "….black on white under surface or white on black under surface." The markings were to be set at 5 ft 8 in from the wing tip with a height of 5 ft and a width of 3 ft 2 in, the width of each stroke being 7.5 in with a spacing of 6 in between figures. In fact, the drawing shows the forward-most point of the figure nearest the wing tip should touch as close as possible to the leading edge, something treated with a little circumspection on many RAF aircraft of the period. On the Halifax, the line of the plating for the front spar provided a nice straight edge. This particular Halifax became a civilian, sold to the Lancashire Aircraft Corporation and registered as G-AKNL for spares.

CHAPTER TWELVE

OPERATIONS IN THE FAR EAST

PN369: A, one of the modified B Mk IIIs of No 1341 Flight, displays its additional D/F fairing beneath the rear fuselage. Full armament was retained and the aircraft wore the standard RAF night-bomber camouflage with the roundels marked in the alternative blue and white SEAC-type but oddly retaining RAF European Theatre-style fin flashes. Other than the red-painted individual aircraft letter, squadron codes were not applied. In fact, it is not known if unit code letters were allocated to the Flight.

NO 1577 Flight formed in August 1943 to carry out extensive trials with the Halifax Mk V and Lancaster Mk III in India, where it would operate under the control of No 221 Group. Accordingly, on 1 September four crews were assembled at Lyneham under the command of S/Ldr J.H. Leyland DFC & Bar with the remaining three captains, by design or chance, representing a cross section of Commonwealth aircrew: F/Lt Middleton RAF, F/O Richardson RAAF and F/O Stewart RCAF.

The first of the Flight's two Halifaxes, DK254, arrived on 3 September but because of a lack of facilities at Lyneham, the unit moved to Llandow the following day. The two Lancasters, JA903 and JA904, were waiting for them on arrival, but it was another four days before DK263 was available to complete the Halifax contingent.

The engine installations on both of the Halifaxes required a good deal of work to bring them up to the necessary standard and the ground crew worked away at this problem for the next week. A civilian repair team arrived from Handley Page during this period and replaced the original fins on both aircraft with the new 'D'- shaped type[1]. Finally, on 26 September, the flight left for India staging through Portreath, Rabat Salé, Castel Benito, Cairo West and then direct to Karachi. The two Lancasters arrived on 5 October, DK254 on the 6th and DK263 the following morning. All four spent the rest of the month at Salboni undergoing minor inspections and air tests.

On 1 November, the two Halifaxes and Lancaster JA904 took part in a *Bulls Eye*[2] exercise to Calcutta as the start of a series of tests and miscellaneous duties designed to provide information on operational efficiency under tropical conditions. For this reason, most of the tests were kept to normal duties such as meteorological flights. On 3 November, DK254 took off in blazing heat at 15.00 hrs, loaded to an all-up weight of 60,500 lb, and climbed to 19,000 ft. This performance was repeated on 17 December at an all-up weight of 62,000 lb and with the local temperature 5 degrees hotter. The Halifax again performed well, reaching 17,200 ft in just under an hour. Just one week later DK263 was tested at 62,000 lb, taking only 1,200 yards to become airborne, and reached 20,000 ft, a creditable performance.

Unfortunately, the serviceability of all four aircraft was hampered by a lack of spares as the ship carrying these had caught fire and sunk. Even so, the ongoing success of the trials saw the Flight given a more definite role and on 5 December it was notified that it would carry out transport duties but was on no account to undertake combat operations.

The Flight settled down to its new duties but had to operate under some very primitive conditions. F/O Stewart completed the last 700 miles of the return flight from Karachi in DK263 on three engines due to an oil leak in one of the starboard engines. However, not all problems occurred in the air and DK254 along with one of the Lancasters spent an uncomfortable time at Quetta being refuelled from four-gallon cans.

The large 'D' fins fitted to the Halifaxes proved something of a problem in local conditions as the increased fin area caused the aircraft to weathercock quite pronouncedly. Since most runways in India were aligned badly out of wind, most landings were made crosswind, a condition that caused DK254 to come to grief on 3 January 1944. The Halifax had just returned from Bombay and swung badly on landing, hitting a pile of sandbags and collapsing the port undercarriage. This was the flight's first accident in 800 hours of flying.

Far more serious was the accident involving DK263 at Kamptee near Nagpur on 26 January. The Halifax was on a routine flight from Bombay and had a full crew on board plus two ground crew, five passengers and 66 bags of mail. The strip was only 600 yards long but on two engines, F/Lt Middleton did not have much choice. He managed to land the aircraft safely but was unaware of an 80 ft drop into a riverbed at the end of the strip. The Halifax struck a hole with its starboard wheel near the end of its landing run and cartwheeled into the river, landing on its back.

Handley Page Halifax, B Mk III
PN369: A, No 1341 Flight, Digri, India, May 1945.

examination of the wrecked glider showed the basic cause of the accident was failure of an aileron hinge bracket; this led to a more detailed inspection of the other gliders and all were found to be suffering from wood shrinkage.

Early in January 1945, the gliders were supplemented by the arrival of several Hadrian gliders and a solitary Waco CG 13A, KK791[3]. Trials with these new gliders got under way and on 25 January, NA644 carried out a twin Hadrian-towing test. Several record distance flights were made during the next few months; NA642 towed two Hadrians, KH898 and FR767, on the first leg of a trip to Bihta on 24 February. The combination landed at Maharajpin for the night and this was the longest twin Hadrian tow on record. On 9 April NA644, under the command of F/O Bretherton, DFC, towed the CG13A from Mauripur to Bihta non-stop, a track distance of 1,200 miles and believed to be the longest glider tow carried out in India. These trials finished in April, the Halifax, Dakota and Commando aircraft all being found quite suitable for the task and they were now to devote their time to glider ferrying and heavy equipment dropping.

A second Halifax unit, No 1341 Flight, arrived in India in May, but its duties were of a slightly more aggressive nature. The first Halifax of this unit arrived at Digri on 13 May and by the end of the month a total of five Mk IIIs, PN369: A, PN370, PN371, PN381 and PN382, were on strength. Authority had been received during May for 'C' Flight of the Liberator-equipped No 159 Squadron to amalgamate with 1341 Flight. This 'C' Flight consisted of specially equipped Liberators used for investigation of enemy radar transmissions, the same duties for which the Halifaxes were equipped.

The special operations carried out by 1341 Flight were arranged and authorised by the RCM section of Air Command South East Asia (ACSEA) and although relatively few in number, they usually involved long flights in anything but good weather. The Liberators flew three missions during the last week in June making lengthy flights to Bangkok, Sabang and Penang. The severity of the tropical weather conditions[4] may be judged by the fact that F/O Smith was forced to spend five hours of the 20 hr 20 min flight to Penang at 500 ft without the aid of an automatic pilot.

The Halifaxes joined in the four operations flown during July; S/Ldr Hughes flew a sortie to Port Blair on the 21st and F/Lt Morgan visited the same target on the 26th. Although these flights produced no significant new information on Japanese radar, they did serve the additional purpose of providing information on enemy troop movements. Although there was little operational activity the Halifaxes were not idle and were kept busy carrying out transport flights for 159 Squadron to their Liberator detachment based on Akyab Island on the west coast of Burma[5]. The Flight carried out its last sorties on 1 August when F/Lt Morgan and W/O Painter each flew a Halifax to the Port Blair area. For the remainder of the month the Halifaxes and Liberators performed special transport operations as ordered by ACSEA.

With the end of hostilities in the Far East, the Flight turned its talents to a more peaceful occupation, supplying stores, medical supplies and petrol via the 'Hump'[6] route into China but for the crews, the return flights were perhaps the most rewarding, carrying very special cargos of freed POWs. Despite a shortage of spares, the Halifaxes continued to operate under the control of No 117 Wing until the Flight disbanded on 30 October 1945.

No 1577 Flight had also remained active during this period. A detachment at Bihta consisting of one Halifax and one Dakota had ferried 43 gliders over a route of 320 miles during an eight-week period. Two notable tows were achieved during this time when two Horsas, one fully and the other lightly laden, were towed non-stop for 750 and 950 miles respectively.

Even so, such flying duties also had their moments of tribulation. On 6 June 1945, NA644 departed at an all-up weight of 54,000 lb towing a Hamilcar, laden to 26,000 lb, to Chaklala. After 50 minutes a hydraulic failure caused the Halifax's undercarriage to come down, breaking the mechanical locks, but in spite of the additional drag, the combination reached Nawabshah, where they landed safely. After repairs, the combination set off once more the next morning only to have the hydraulic system in the Halifax fail again just as it got airborne. The situation was critical and could easily have ended in disaster but for the skill and cool-headedness of the tug pilot, F/Lt Northmore and the glider pilot, F/O Winnington. Between them, they managed to complete a circuit of the airfield at 50 ft and land safely. After returning to base for repairs NA644 returned to complete the tow to Dhamail on 9 June.

A rare formation shot showing three of the six modified Halifaxes of 1341 Flight airborne together. PN369: A is in the centre with 'B' in the distance.

Nine people were killed but miraculously, the remainder were all off the serious list within a few days. For the time being, the Flight was without Halifaxes until replacements arrived.

On 10 February, the Flight was told that it would be moving to Cawnpore and the aircraft modified for glider towing but on the 15th, told that the move would be to Chakeri instead. Even so, the anticipated move took time and another change of destination, this time to Mauripur, where it arrived on 7 May to carry out glider-towing trials with four Horsa and two Hamilcar gliders provided for the purpose; but these still had to be assembled and it was early June before HH974, the first Hamilcar, was ready for towing trials.

The Flight now expanded to include Dakotas and Curtis Commandos but was still without Halifaxes although action was in hand to fill the gap and on 15 October, the Air Ministry finally allocated two Mk III Halifaxes, NA642 and NA644, for general trials in the Airborne Forces role of glider towing, paratroop- and equipment-dropping. The Halifaxes were ferried out to India by two 38 Group crews with S/Ldr A. G. Norman acting as flight commander and arrived on 10 November, the day after the Lancasters officially ceased their attachment.

No time was wasted and on 15 November, NA644 commenced towing trials with the Hamilcar in which the Halifax responded very well with its engine temperatures remaining well within the prescribed limits despite the high ambient temperatures. The Horsa-towing trials suffered a temporary setback when LH237 crashed from 50 ft on take-off while still on tow behind NA644. Subsequent

The somewhat reluctant NA644 later redeemed itself with a record tow from Nawabshah to Chaklala, a distance of 593 track miles, with a Hamilcar, thought to be the longest tow ever made by this type of combination. The flight also provided some very useful information on cooling and fuel consumption in Halifaxes under tropical conditions where, at 5,000 ft, the average temperature was still 31°C.

After months of waiting an 8,000 lb bomb beam and electromagnetic releases finally arrived at Chaklala on 7 July. They were fitted to NA644 on 11 June and after loading trials with a jeep and gun, the detachment moved to Dhamail to begin dropping tests. The first test was carried out two days later by F/O Bretherton, the jeep and gun being dropped from 1,000 ft at an indicated air speed of 130 mph. Although a parachute malfunction resulted in the gun being destroyed, the jeep made a perfect landing. Further trials using NA642 were quite successful.

Following the cessation of hostilities in Europe, it had been intended to transfer some of the 38 Group Squadrons to the Far East for glider operations against the Japanese. With 1577 Flight having now proven the feasibility of glider operations under tropical conditions, the first nine tropicalised A Mk VII Halifaxes of 298 Squadron left Tarrant Rushton for India on 6 July. A second group of eight Halifaxes left on 13 July followed by a further seven on 18 July. The move cost one casualty en route when S/L R. Smith's PN257: C swung while landing at Shaibah in Iraq collapsing the undercarriage.

All of this Squadron's aircraft were fitted with freight panniers and to facilitate this modification to the new A Mk VII Halifaxes intended for the Far East, a pattern aircraft was loaned to each of the maintenance units at Hawarden, Kinloss and High Ercall. The initial panniers were a flush-fitting type of 3,000 lb capacity and in order to fit them, the bomb doors were removed and stowed in the fuselage. These were soon replaced by the enlarged 8,000 lb capacity, 282 cubic feet type that projected well below the fuselage.

During August, while the remainder of the squadron continued to arrive at Raipur, the Halifaxes undertook their first commitments under the control of ACSEA. These consisted of transporting passengers and freight and collecting the squadron's stores, which required flights to many of the airfields throughout India and Ceylon. The freight varied from stocks of vegetables to medical supplies and miscellaneous equipment, while passengers included members of the 44th Airborne Division, medical teams and various other personnel. In all, during the execution of these duties, some 473 hours flying time was logged and approximately 50,000 lb of freight and 250 passengers were carried.

Weather conditions throughout were typical of the south-west monsoon – chronic! While making its landing approach to Raipur on 9 August, PN264 swung and hit NA357, the latter being finally assessed as beyond economical repair and struck off charge on 6 September.

In mid-September, with the war now over, the squadron began transferring from its airborne duties to transport work, gradually taking over the commitments of 1341 Flight. The squadron used one of the Flight's Halifaxes to fly the 'Hump' run into China from Dum Dum in Calcutta to Kunming on 3 September and returned three days later carrying six ex-POWs. A repeat trip was flown on 10 September using a 298 Squadron Halifax carrying 2,000 lb of freight, in this case petrol, mail packages and six passengers. Several trips were also flown to Singapore and on 30 September, four Halifaxes and six crews moved to Alipore to begin a regular scheduled transport run into China. Four regular trips were made each week using two different routes: Monday and Thursday they flew Dum Dum - Kunming - Chungking - Hong Kong - Shanghai - Hong Kong - Dum Dum; Tuesdays and Fridays they flew Dum Dum - Pigu - Hong Kong - Dum Dum.

During the early part of October and despite the heavy rain and violent tropical thunderstorms, the service never failed to complete a scheduled trip, although some delays were incurred. As the aircraft became due for minor routine inspections three modifications were carried out; the

Photographs of 1341 Flight Halifaxes are rare but inclusion of this somewhat poor quality photograph is warranted as it shows the only known artwork used within the small Flight. The additional D/F loop fitted below the rear section of the fuselage identifies its ownership. (via C. Bowyer)

TR1196 was raised, the hot-air ducting blanked off and a water tank installed in the rear stowage area of the fuselage. All armament, now being superfluous, was removed. Spare parts or lack thereof and the bane of 1341 Flight's existence, continued to make life difficult for the servicing personnel, a situation which was to continue for several months.

October also saw the squadron's scheduled runs increased by the addition of a new route divided into four separate stages. Stage I was from base - Magpur - Dum Dum - Nagpur; stage II was Nagpur - Santa Cruz - Mauripur - Santa Cruz; stage III Santa Cruz - Dum Dum - Nagpur and stage IV, Nagpur to base. A single Halifax left the base every Monday, Wednesday and Friday, Nagpur on Tuesday, Thursday and Saturday, Santa Cruz on Wednesday, Friday and Saturday, Nagpur each Thursday, Saturday and Monday.

Mindful of the increasing passenger needs, the squadron modified NA397: L, one of its A Mk VIIs, during November, stripping the interior of any remaining

Tropicalised A Mk VIIs of 298 Squadron photographed at Raipur, in India; NA356: D in the foreground has an 8,000 lb capacity pannier installed between its main wheels. This Halifax displays some unusual markings with 'City of Dundee' in white on the nose section and the serial number in white, marked above the fin flash on the rudder instead of on the rear of the fuselage in red. The glider-towing rig is still fitted to the second aircraft in the row (just visible framed between the main wheels of NA356) and tail turret armament is still fitted to NA356, indicating that the photograph was taken before October 1945. The small 'DD' code marked on the nose section was a combination code, the first letter being that of the airfield – each airfield had its own specific allocation of identification letters and allocated one to each resident squadron; the second was the individual aircraft letter – handy when walking along a line of aircraft looking for a specific machine. The aircraft letter was repeated beneath the wing tip in white on the Halifaxes of this unit while in India. Changes to markings included over-painting the so-called Type C 1 fuselage roundels and the Type B on wing upper surfaces with the blue and white or blue and pale blue SEAC type. Fin flashes were also replaced to the same dimensions with blue and white or pale blue and blue flashes with the lightest colour always leading. Unit codes were also deleted with only the white-painted individual letter on the fuselage forward of the roundel and repeated beneath the wing tip. NA356: D had a D-type tail turret fitted with armament, plus the standard paratroop-dropping shield and 8,000 lb capacity pannier, which dates this photograph to a period around the end of hostilities. NA356 was among those aircraft struck off charge on location on 31 December 1946. (via S. Coates)

Passengers and packages were the order of the day for 298 Squadron in the immediate post-hostilities period. In this view, 'P-Peter' is being unloaded, the port wheel having sunk into the wet ground, one of the hazards of the tropical location. (N. Gray)

Hot and dusty work; loading rice sacks into the freight pannier on S/Ldr R. Smith's NA393: C at Meiktila, Burma during Operation Famine in March 1946. (S/Ldr R. Smith via G/Cpt D. Richardson)

Halifax A Mk VII NA393: C of 298 Squadron is seen here on the airfield at Meiktila in Burma. With the ending of the Pacific war in September 1945, by October all armament had been removed from the aircraft. Living conditions for this emergency transfer of the squadron were pretty basic, the tents offering little relief from the intense heat and humidity. S/Ldr R. Smith via G/Cpt D. Richardson)

RAF units outside the country. Nos 298 and 10 Squadrons aided by a Liberator squadron were sent to assist, achieving the requirement noted above. On 15 March, the Halifaxes and Dakotas began operating from Meiktila airfield to dropping zones that had to be perched on ridges in what was a carpet of virgin jungle-covered gorges from horizon to horizon; clear approach lines and somewhere to turn away after each drop was critical. The army kept up a stream of rice supplies to the airfield by rail while the Liberators, working out of Pegu airfield, airlifted some 7,000 lbs of rice at a time to the advance air base at Myitkyina.

Each Halifax carried 50 x 80 lb bags of rice in the freight pannier and an identical load in the fuselage. The rice carried in the fuselage was air-dropped at specified dropping zones and the 4,000 lb in the pannier delivered to a central location. By judicious juggling the load was increased and Halifaxes dispatched on 17 March carried 6,000 lb internally plus the usual 4,000 lb in the pannier. Two days later the figures rose by 2,000 lb when it was determined that fuel loads could safely be reduced to 1,500 gallons, thus increasing the amount of rice that could be carried by each aircraft. When the operation ended on 31 March, the squadron had completed 80 sorties lifting 887,415 lb of rice, 360,670 lb of which had been air-dropped. In all, 2,400 tons of rice and 180 tons of salt had been air-dropped. April brought a continuation of the famine and saw Operation Hunger 11 put into effect. The squadron was again committed to these mercy missions, completing 81 sorties and delivering 949,260 lb of rice, of which 456,550 lb was air-dropped.

At the end of this operation, the squadron returned to its normal routine of training with jeep drops but in July, its role changed once more. It was given the somewhat imposing title of Bomber, Airborne Support and Heavy Equipment Dropping Squadron. A dual-control A Mk VII, PP372: W, was allocated to assist with training and practice bombing/equipment dropping until the unit was disbanded in December. Many of the squadron's Halifaxes were then struck off charge locally, which was done by pulling the sump plug on each engine, running it until it seized and then collapsing the undercarriage. This did little damage to the airframe and provided a useful source of airframes and spares when Indian Independence and the creation of Pakistan were declared in 1947[8].

This brought to an end RAF Halifax operations in the Far East. 1577 Flight was disbanded in May and its sole remaining Halifax NA644 was struck off charge locally, NA642 having been returned to the Airborne Forces Experimental Establishment in the UK earlier in the year. However, the Halifax had not disappeared from front line service on the Indian sub-continent, as detailed in Chapter 13.

surplus equipment and fitting seating for 24 people. Thus converted, NA397 was flown to 229 Group HQ at Delhi for inspection and then to Chakiri for further inspection, where it was left. While waiting for approval to carry out further conversions, as an interim measure the squadron removed the armour plating, ammunition boxes and towing gear from the remaining Halifaxes and fitted eight safety straps (four each side) in the rest bay of each aircraft. These interim modifications proved useful when the squadron moved to Digri in December and the Halifaxes transported 800 personnel and 245,461 lb of freight.

Just as the squadron was getting thoroughly organised for its transport duties, a change of command at 228 Group also produced a change of role – back to airborne training. However, on 14 January 1946 they undertook a final major commitment, the transportation of 100 hospital cases from Bilaspur to Mauripur at the rate of 16 a day, for which two Halifaxes were supplied while the remainder of the squadron continued with the training programme.

In March 1946, famine threatened certain areas of India and Burma and the squadron look part in Operation Hunger. For the Kachin[7] people in northern Burma, the famine was heightened by their agreement with British agents dropped into them to deny the Japanese food by destroying their own crops and their rice seeds for the following season. Six thousand tons of rice had to be distributed to the Kachin to save the situation; barely more than half of it could be done by land as much of the population lived in mountainous areas. The only resident RAF squadron available in Burma was about to disband so the call went out for assistance from

CHAPTER THIRTEEN

POST-WAR MILITARY USE

Airborne Forces

WITH the cessation of hostilities in Europe, the Halifax disappeared rapidly from the main bomber force, most squadrons disbanded or transferred to transport duties and re-equipped with Dakotas, Yorks or Liberators. Most of the Halifaxes from Nos 4 and 6 Groups ended up at Rawcliffe or 29 Maintenance Unit at High Ercall, where they languished until broken up for scrap. This began at 29 MU in January 1946 and by June contractors began breaking up some 300 non-effective Halifaxes, mainly Mk II and V airframes, declared obsolete from 14 March 1946. The next to go to the breakers were the B Mk III, GR Mk III and Met Mk III airframes, declared obsolete from 15 August 1946, but their engines were retained and placed in storage.

However, the Halifax was by no means a spent force and its Airborne Forces role potential remained high. Consequently, the end of the war in Europe brought little change in tempo for the four Halifax squadrons concerned and when not engaged in repatriating ex-POWs from the Continent they undertook training exercises or freighting duties.

No 190 (GT) Squadron based at Great Dunmow, began converting from Stirlings to A Mk III and A Mk VII Halifaxes on 4 May 1945 and had completed the task by the 26th. During June, it undertook converting former 620 (GT) Squadron Stirling crews to Halifaxes. Based also at Great Dunmow, 620 Squadron then exchanged some aircrew with 190 Squadron, a high percentage of 620 Squadron's flying personnel being drawn from the latter and the remainder posted in from Nos 295 and 296 Squadrons plus some from various OTUs.

Amidst its work training crews, on 19 June 190 Squadron carried out its first duty, *Exercise Renaissance*, the object of which was to combine the usual glider-towing training with the removal of gliders from Great Dunmow to Thruxton for storage. The exercise was very successful and a second, *Exercise Residue*, was carried out on 30 June during which the remaining seven Horsa gliders were towed to Thruxton, one breaking its tow but landing safely.

At the beginning of July, the squadron was short of aircraft because of the general reshuffle with 620 Squadron, which had finally been brought up to strength with 20 crews. The latter unit had begun operating its A Mk VII Halifaxes on 3 July when five transported freight from Brussels to Copenhagen. Five Halifaxes from 190 Squadron joined it the following day to carry out a similar task. These types of duty were fairly common during the next few months and Nos 296 and 297 Squadrons joined in, ferrying Czechoslovakian repatriates and diplomatic mail to Prague during late July and August, while seven from 190 Squadron performed a similar task to Athens with Greek repatriates. Yet, even ferry flights could be lethal as the crew of 296 Squadron's NA291 found during a ferry test flight on 25 May. The dinghy, stowed in the inner section of the port wing suddenly inflated, deployed on its safety line and wrapped itself around the tail section, causing the Halifax to dive into the ground and burn at the somewhat ironically named Fortune's Farm at Garstow.

One of 190 (GT) Squadron's Halifax A Mk VIIs, NA425: S, is seen here up from Great Dunmow in August 1945. The squadron began converting from Stirlings to Halifaxes in May 1945 and helped convert 620 Squadron to the type before disbanding – on paper – in December to be renumbered immediately as 295 (GT) Squadron. Although white-painted under wing serial numbers were reinstated within Bomber Command in August 1945, they were still absent on this particular Halifax, which retains its red code letters; the retroactive modification process did not happen overnight. (via B. Robertson)

The Air Ministry then started to look further afield for regular use of its transport resources and during October a mobile OTU visited Earls Colne to train Nos 296 and 297 Squadron crews up to the standard required for operations over the Indian Trunk Route, two aircraft from No 296 commencing duties on this run on the 27th of that month. As of November, 297 Squadron joined the scheduled mail run to Dum Dum and Alipore and two routes were flown; the one to Dum Dum went out via Istres, Luqa, Almaza, Shaibah, Mauripur, Dum Dum and returned via Jodhpur, Mauripur, Shaibah, Almaza, Luqa. The Alipore route was via Luqa, Almaza, Shaibah, Mauripur to Alipore, returning the same way.

On 1 November 190 Squadron began its move to Tarrant Rushton from Great Dunmow where all 28 Halifaxes had arrived by the 5th. A fortnight later, the squadron began towing-training with Hamilcars, but these activities were to be short-lived and it was disbanded on 28 December. However, it was resurrected by a policy change on 21 January 1946, albeit under the new identity of 295 Squadron, the latter having disbanded with effect from the same date.

Two other Earls Colne squadrons, Nos 296 and 297, were also marked for disbandment. The former had begun converting from its A Mk Vs to A Mk IIIs in February 1945, using these on the Indian Trunk Route from October. In December, and in line with the other Halifax transport squadrons, it began converting to A Mk VIIs but the post-war cutbacks had begun to bite and 296 Squadron officially disbanded on 23 January 1946. An identical fate overtook 297 Squadron, which had begun conversion to A Mk VIIs in December 1945 and was withdrawn from the Indian Mail Service the same month, three of the squadron's Halifaxes then being

This pair of 620 Squadron Halifax A Mk VIIs were likely photographed at their home base of Aqir in Palestine with PP375: X in the foreground and PP345: T behind. All armament, including that of the D Mk I tail turret, has been removed. Several markings details are visible; the wheel chock in the foreground has 'B Flt' crudely marked in white paint and the tyre 'Cairo West' hand-painted in yellow on its outer surface. The yellow stencil marking visible just below the inboard engine was the standard 24 VOLTS, the white-painted 'LX' on the nose section was the airfield and aircraft code letter combination. The small fixed section between the cooling gills of the outboard engine was a distinguishing feature of the Hercules XVI engine, the more extended fixed section of the Hercules 100 being quite distinct. (B. Robertson)

Looking aft in the A Mk IX from just in front of the main spar shows that the padded centre section rest seats remain as before but two sets of metal utility seats, each for eight paratroops, were mounted either side of the fuselage, aft of the rear spar. The sloping floor between the metal seats held the inward opening 33 in x 59 in paratrooping hatch while the additional Perspex-covered escape hatches in the roof and extra portholes fitted along both fuselage sides provided for better daylight illumination. The door on the left gave access to the tail plane, rear spar and rear turret. The large diameter, asbestos-covered item at the left front of the photograph was the heat exchanger for the internal heating system, the spiral flexible pipe for which can be seen rising vertically to the line of the roof. (The Aeroplane)

stragglers returned during the first week of March, the two from Vienna and NA117 from Bordeaux, where the latter had been stranded awaiting spares since 24 November, arriving just in time for the squadron's disbandment on 1 April. However, the squadron number had no time to be removed from the list of current units with the original 295 Squadron re-forming at Tarrant Rushton on 1 April and re-numbered 297 Squadron. One is left wondering what, other than a flow-on effect, this bewildering game of chess with squadron numbers really achieved.

No 644 Squadron's Middle East Supplementary Mail Service, which normally terminated at Earls Colne, then had to be redirected to Tarrant Rushton from 21 February because of the disbandment of the two resident squadrons.

When 298 Squadron was sent to Raipur in India in July 1945, it had been suggested that 644 Squadron might eventually join it there. However, this was not to be; instead, 644 Squadron was ordered to prepare for transfer to the Middle East along with 620 Squadron. Between August and October 1945 both squadrons gradually re-equipped with tropicalised A Mk VII Halifaxes complete with freight panniers, while their original Halifaxes were ferried to the MUs at Hawarden and Kinloss. No 644 Squadron departed first, sending its 27 Halifaxes, two of them non-tropicalised A Mk VIIs for cannibalisation, out to Quastina in six waves between 26 November and 1 December. The first element of the 30 Halifaxes of 620 Squadron left for Aqir, Palestine on 30 December, flying, as had 644 Squadron, via El Aloine and although bad weather delayed the remainder of the squadron, the move was completed by 4 January 1946.

Both squadrons had barely settled in when, on 16 January, they took part in *Exercise Kick-off II* transporting troops of the 6th Airborne Division. This particular exercise was carried out in several phases over the next month with both squadrons participating. In between there were a variety of duties to be carried out, such as transporting freight and personnel to various points of the globe like Almaza, Kabril, Nicosia, Kasafareet, Habbaniya etc., plus the setting up and operation of a regular mail run to the UK. The first two aircraft for this latter duty were drawn from 644 Squadron and arrived at Earles Colne on 27 and 28 January respectively. On 5 February, both squadrons took part in *Exercise Snatch*, transporting troops to Ramat David and then picking them up again 24 hours later.

There was still an element of danger though, for these were times of great tension in the Middle East, with Jewish nationalists fighting a guerrilla war to establish their assumed right to Palestine. Bombs thrown into cafes killed an injured British serviceman and an attack on the King David Hotel, which housed the British Administration at the time, were part of an escalating series of attacks to drive the British out. Then, at 20.45 hrs on 25 February, a small group attacked the airfield at Quastina causing considerable damage to 23 aircraft with explosive charges. Two Halifaxes were destroyed by fire and eight others damaged beyond repair, among them NA358, NA359, NA362, NA430, NA431, and NA464 of 644 Squadron. The remaining two were possibly PN310 and PN311, which, although barely a year old,

given the task of each taking seven tons of educational books to Vienna. Two left on 23 January but the third was delayed by the non-arrival of its quota of freight while the first two, having reached Vienna, became unserviceable and had to languish there until spares could reach them. Other crews were kept busy ferrying 296 Squadron's Halifaxes away for disposal. However, this did not prevent them from continuing their duties and on 5 February, two of their Halifaxes left Earles Colne for Athens, via Bari, carrying 10,700 lb of Greek currency in 50 packages. Several

RT760, the third production A Mk IX, was delivered to the RAF on 9 November 1945, along with RT759. Hercules XVI engines, as used for the Mk III and Mk VII, were retained for the Mk IX, the continuous ring of cowling flaps identifying them from the Hercules 100s of the B Mk VI and C Mk VIII. This Halifax was eventually sold for scrap to J. Dale and Co. on 1 July 1948, never having flown, part of the post-war economic cutbacks to the armed services and a declining need for military aircraft. (Handley Page)

were struck off charge two months later. While there were no injuries among the squadron personnel, one of the attackers paid with his life. Despite the damage caused by the attack, 644 Squadron flew up to the Elephant Ski Club near Beirut the next day and dropped containers of supplies to relieve shortages due to the club being cut off for several days by heavy falls of snow. As one member of the squadron remarked, *"Just like the old SOE days, shades of Norway!"*

A wide variety of duties were thrust upon both of them and to 644 Squadron fell the responsibility for meteorological flights each morning and evening with two routes being flown, one east and one west, effective from 20 January. No 620 Squadron temporarily took over the duties from 14 February until 644 Squadron resumed the task on 1 March, by which date only the westerly route was being flown, thus reducing the number of daily flights to two, one at 04.00 hrs, the other at 16.00 hrs.

On 3 March 644 Squadron moved its serviceable aircraft from Quastina to a temporary base at Bilbeis in Egypt with two of the Halifaxes each towing a Horsa carrying the necessary supplies, a move that also marked the termination of the squadron's scheduled mail runs to the UK. On the 19th, the squadron moved back to Quastina for *Exercise Larney*, picking up troops and transporting them to Nicosia in Cyprus and in May, both squadrons were involved in a major exercise, *Exercise Gordon*. In conjunction with eight Dakotas of 78 Squadron they transported paratroops from Quastina to Khartoum in the Sudan. Three of 644 Squadron's Halifaxes towed gliders while the rest carried paratroops. A similar exercise took the Halifaxes to Castel Benito a few days later. Ken Russell, then stationed at Khartoum, remembers *Exercise Gordon* and its effects: *"I recall that 32 Halifaxes were used and all available technical personnel were mustered to service and dispatched them back to their home bases. One of the towing aircraft developed engine trouble and had to drop its glider on the return journey; this I believe was subsequently located somewhere between Khartoum and Wadi Haifa by one of our Com-flight Ansons. Unfortunately Operation Gordon proved too much for the runways at Khartoum and for a time it was out of use for 'heavies'."*

His Majesty's birthday in June was celebrated by a fly-past over Jerusalem and 644 Squadron provided 12 Halifaxes with W/Cdr W. H. Ingle, the squadron CO, leading the formation, after which the two squadrons continued their diversified duties. A Halifax from 644 Squadron flew a photo-recce mission to Cyprus on 21 July and the next day, four crews from 620 Squadron ferried the first four of 644 Squadron's A Mk VII Halifaxes back to the UK, carrying as passengers two more 620 Squadron crews. All six crews were to return with the latest version of the Halifax – the A Mk IX.

Handley Page's last production order had been for 200 Halifaxes but the end of hostilities saw this reduced to 150, the first five of which were built and delivered as A Mk VIIs. However, the success of the Halifax in paratroop and glider tug role had prompted Handley Page to explore the possibilities of improving the A Mk VII. RT758 was selected for the redesign work and was fitted with a new rear fuselage section containing a large inward-opening paratroop hatch in the floor some 33 in x 59 in wide, above which was the normal panel with its twin signalling lights operated by the bomb aimer to alert the dispatcher when to start his drop. Two rails for static lines ran along each side of the roof and a winch to retrieve the static lines after deployment was mounted on the rear spar. Handrails were also provided along each side of the fuselage to steady the paratroopers as they moved from the four long bench seats fitted just aft of the rest bay station to the hatch. The seats, fitted two to a side, accommodated 16 fully-equipped paratroopers. The new design received the company designation HP 71 and military designation of Mk IX and like all Halifaxes, it could be used in a complete range of roles.

As with all Halifax A-versions, there was no mid-upper turret, an extra escape hatch occupying the position instead. The rear turret was a Boulton Paul D Mk I type armed with two Browning 0.5-in machine guns, a version already in use on late-production Mk VIs. Late-production A Mk IX Halifaxes were scheduled to be fitted with the Mk II version of this turret and equipped with automatic gun-laying linked to a radar dish slung below the turret.

Trials with a mock-up of this gun-laying radar housing had been in progress for over two years, initiated in May 1943 when W1008, a B Mk II Halifax, had this device attached to its standard E Mk I tail turret. It proved to have very little effect upon the general handling qualities of the aircraft, causing only a very mild pitching motion when the turret rotated. The experiment progressed to installation of a D Mk I turret, complete with Automatic Gun Laying Turret (AGLT)[1] equipment on HX238, a B Mk III Halifax retained for experimental work. The turret balance flaps were fixed open at 40° and a five and three-quarter inch chord deflector plate, also set at 40°, was fitted to the lower circumference of the fuselage immediately in front of the turret.

Flight-testing took place in April 1944 and results showed that while the problem had been partially solved and level flight characteristics found satisfactory, some problems still occurred when the aircraft was dived. Unless properly trimmed, foot loads on the rudder bar were excessive when the turret rotated. At the end of these tests, the scanner housing support brackets were modified and the turret flap angle reduced to 20°. Further flight-testing was undertaken during July, but again the results were not entirely satisfactory and comparative speed measurements with HX226 showed that the deflector plates reduced the top speed of HX238 by 3 mph, which corresponded to a reduction in the cruising ceiling of 250 ft.

Some difficulties were also experienced with the turret itself because severe vibrations made accurate radar-assisted gun-laying impossible. Another B Mk III, LV999/G, was fitted with a D turret and AGLT and an extensive series of trials were

B Mk III LV999/G fitted with the revised two-position fixed deflector plate settings determined in trials with HX238 where the rotation of the scanner housing produced drag in the region below the normal turret bottom line and several settings for the deflector plates were tested. Tests were carried out with this Halifax between September 1944 and April 1945 to try to eliminate turret vibration, during which the metal stiffening ribs for the turret were replaced by Perspex ones to help reduce eye fatigue. It was on this installation that the friction rings taken from the MG 131 mounting of a captured Me 410 were used, reducing vibration considerably. The slim, vertical Perspex panel fitted on either side of the turret could slide down for extra ventilation.

carried out from 9 September 1944 to 10 April 1945. The turret was modified during this period and the metal stiffening ribs replaced by Perspex ribs which, because of their translucency, helped reduce eye fatigue. The oil-damping device was replaced on this particular turret by a series of small-diameter friction rings taken from the MG 131 mounting units fitted to an Me 410 being examined at Boscombe Down and effected a considerable reduction in turret vibration when the guns were fired. Meanwhile, NP834, a B Mk VI had also been fitted with an AGLT-equipped D turret and carried out a series of trials during December and January 1945 testing effects of turret rotation on the auto-pilot and, although the problem was not entirely overcome, the results were deemed acceptable.

Fitting of the D Mk I turret to the A Mk IX Halifax also produced some internal revisions; the rear turret ammunition ducts were shortened and the boxes themselves fitted further aft against the rear bulkhead with a pair of Browning 0.5-in calibre machine guns replacing the 0.303-in weapons. The radio equipment was slightly more extensive than that fitted to the A Mk VIIs and additional radar navigation aids were also provided. The capacity of wing bomb-cell fuel tanks was reduced from 150 gallons to 96, thus reducing the total fuel tankage to 2,772 gallons. Although normal bomb-carrying facilities were retained, the bomb bay doors were removable to allow an 8,000 lb freight pannier to be fitted to the bomb bay. Maximum all-up weight remained the same as for the A Mk VII at 65,000 lb and performance was identical.

Completed in mid-October 1945, RT758 was delivered to the Airborne Forces Experimental Establishment on the 23rd and was followed by the delivery of the first two production A Mk IXs, RT759 and RT760, on 9 November. Two more A Mk IXs, RT814 and RT816, were allocated to the Air Transport Tactical Development Unit (ATTDU) for tactical handling trials, which included range tests with the Short Term Supply Container (STSC), drogue tests and some further work on the dropping characteristics of the STSC. RT814 was also used for gun and jeep drops from 8,000 ft at 170 mph, heavy glider Horsa towing and radio transmitter/receiver fade area trials. On 12 December, S/Ldrs Taylor and Patch of HQ Transport Command (Training) arrived to discuss cruise control charts in respect of the tactical handling trials with the A Mk IX. These trials continued until 1947 and included battle simulation exercises.

In all, almost three-quarters of the A Mk IX production batch had been delivered to RAF storage by the time the first of the type was issued for squadron service. The first two issued, RT845 and RT846, both went to No 1 Parachute Training School in mid-April 1946 and, apart from these, the main batch was directed to the Middle East-based squadrons, with RT880, RT881 and RT882 arriving there on 10 August. Throughout the remainder of the month, the A Mk VIIs were ferried back to the UK and replaced by A Mk IXs.

The squadrons wasted no time in putting them to work and 620 Squadron had two on a paratroop-dropping and glider-towing exercise on 29 August. A change of identity occurred on 1 September 1946 when both 620 and 644 Squadrons were

Delivered to the RAF in February 1944, B Mk III LV876: F went to 517 Squadron, fitted out for meteorological duties. It is seen here after squadron codes were reintroduced for the meteorological squadrons and use of wartime sea camouflage had ceased in favour of standard night camouflage, thus simplifying production. The aircraft codes were applied in white with the individual aircraft letter repeated on the nose and the serial number was repeated in white beneath each wing, thus dating this photograph to late August 1945 at the earliest. This particular Halifax was struck off charge on 20 August 1946 following the disbandment of the squadron in June.

re-numbered respectively as Nos 113 and 47. This had no effect on the training programme and 47 Squadron made its first lift under its new guise on 12 September. Both units then changed their bases, 113 Squadron moving to Kabrit and 47 Squadron going a little further afield to Fairford in the UK on 30 September. No 113 Squadron continued its multiple tasks in the Middle East until reduced to a number-plate basis on 5 April 1947 when the Squadron's Halifaxes and personnel, including HQ 283 Wing, returned to Fairford – which was, with the exception of one Halifax, completed by the end of April.

A diversion in time is needed at this point, back to September 1944 and an Air Ministry conference at which representatives of the Army and RAF agreed that the existing School of Army Co-operation was insufficient to meet the growing scope of combined operations. It was agreed that a School of Air Support[2] would be formed and in December, the Air Ministry laid down a syllabus of training designed to teach a common doctrine to the staff of all three services. The school was formed around two instructional wings staffed by RAF and Army officers, the Offensive Support Wing and the Transport Support Wing. The aim of the Transport Support Wing was to teach airborne assault tactics, air transported operations and supply by air. Offensive Support demonstrations were held at the Westdown artillery ranges near Larkhill and Transport Support demonstrations took place at Netheravon airfield, Halifaxes being used for all heavy equipment and supply dropping.

Still resident at Fairford, 47 Squadron had been very active since its return to the UK but in May 1947 there was a considerable increase in the number of hours flown, with 351 being recorded, well in excess of the normal post-war reduced schedule laid down. During an exercise at Netheravon, they dropped 1,078 paratroopers and later took part in a large demonstration of airborne support work at Fairford, all in addition to their normal glider towing and navigation training exercises. Ground crews were also extra busy that month, stripping excess items from 113 Squadron's Halifaxes before they were ferried away for disposal.

In October 1947, a drastic cut in numbers took place along with a reorganisation of the four Halifax squadrons, Nos 47, 113, 295 and 297. Each was reduced to six aircraft and together they formed the Flying Wing of RAF Fairford. Although reduced in numbers, they managed a collective total of 616 hours flying time during November and although this figure was to drop slightly later, it remained consistent at about 550 hours per month.

Losses through accidents were extremely rare although the occasional narrow escape still occurred. Shortly after take-off on *Operation Demon 51,* the pilot of RT852 reported that the cockpit was filling with smoke and ordered the glider to cast off; the Hamilcar force-landed safely off the aerodrome while the Halifax was put down safely on the main runway. The cause of the smoke was a fault in some electrical wiring. Such faults, however, were few and in July the normal Halifax cycle of 50 and 100 hour inspections and maintenance was extended respectively to 75 and 150 hours.

During August, a further reduction in numbers occurred with Halifax strength reduced to 12 aircraft for 295 and 297 Squadrons while 113 Squadron was disbanded and 47 Squadron prepared to move to Dishforth to surrender its Halifaxes for a new type, the Hastings C Mk I and fittingly, their lineal descendant. Dishforth became the Hastings OTU and in October 297 Squadron moved in to begin its conversion to the new type. Its Halifaxes, along with the remaining Hamilcars and Horsas, had been ferried to 29 MU along with 295 Squadron's aircraft, for the latter squadron had disbanded that same month.

Coastal Command

While the end of the war in Europe had ended Coastal Command's anti-shipping units, squadrons engaged on meteorological duties had remained active. For their crews, the war's end signalled no change of pace or purpose and the sorties continued as before but the repatriation of Commonwealth aircrews, which began the following month, depleted their ranks of experienced personnel for this very exacting duty.

As recorded earlier, Met Mk III Halifaxes had not begun to reach 517 and 518 Squadrons until March 1945 but when they did arrive, the crews, as Cooper Drabble records, welcomed the change from Merlin 22s to Hercules XVIs: *"My impressions of flying the Mk III were very favourable compared with the Mk V. The extra power gave one a great deal of confidence on a fully loaded take-off and of course, its performance significantly improved in all respects. However, we did one trip in RG414: V during which we lost an engine."*

No 520 Squadron, based at Gibraltar, was the next to re-equip, disposing of its Met Mk Vs in May and adding 15 Met Mk IIIs to its Hurricanes and Hudsons, which were used for the continuing *Nocturnal* sorties. In mid-August, 519 Squadron moved from Wick to Tain and gradually began replacing its Fortress Mk IIs with Met Mk III Halifaxes. It moved to Leuchars in November to begin a new meteorological sortie code-named *Recipe*: a straight out and back flight route due north to 78° latitude on what must have been one of the most dangerous patrols ever devised. F/Lt Pullam flew the first of these on 11 November, taking off at one minute past midnight. At 05.22 hrs, he reported hydraulic trouble and was forced to abort the sortie, the Halifax finally running short of fuel and landing at Tain at 08.33 hrs. Although serviceability problems hampered these early flights, the squadron never lost an aircraft on these sorties.

Nos 517 and 518 Squadrons were not so fortunate, their more extensive operational schedule no doubt a contributing factor. Apart from the usual landing accidents, 518 Squadron lost two aircraft; LW170 ditched due to fuel shortage on 10 August and on 8 September, NA142 over-shot at Stornoway while landing and crashed into the sea 30 yards from the boundary of the airfield. No 517 also lost two crews, the first on 10 September when RG380 flew into high ground near Weston Zoyland on approach to land while the second was to be the squadron's last loss when NA248: M simply failed to return from its lonely sortie on 2 October 1945. Its last radioed position was given as north-west of Cape Finisterre on the out-bound leg of an *Epicure* flight. Forced to ditch, the crew were fortunate in that the Halifax stayed afloat for seven hours before being rescued by a passing freighter carrying a cargo of bananas.

The post-war reduction of units did not overlook the meteorological squadrons; while their services were still essential, a scale of economy began to impose itself. Even so, the existing squadrons were about to receive some new equipment in the form of the Met Mk VI Halifax, the definitive Coastal Command version, most of which were fully tropicalised and fully compatible with both meteorological and general reconnaissance/anti-shipping duties.

The first two production Met Mk VI aircraft, RG778 and RG787, came off the English Electric production lines in June 1945. They were eventually issued, albeit briefly, to No 1361 Met Flight along with a C Mk VIII aircraft, PP282, while a second C Mk VIII, PP264, was issued to Aldergrove. Little is known about this Meteorological Flight, but it may also have been stationed at Aldergrove. The combination of their Mk VI and Mk VIII aircraft is also curious. Nos 620 and 644 Squadrons were already flying daily meteorological sorties from Quastina with some of their A Mk VII Halifaxes and there is a possibility that the C Mk VIIIs were being tried in this role, but whatever the original intention, it appears to have been changed quickly. RG778 was allocated to the Flight on 4 February 1946 and RG787 on the 9th, the latter then passing to No 521 Squadron on 16 February with RG778 following on 8 April. The C Mk VIIIs were sold, PP282 on 12 November and PP264 on 7 January 1947.

No 521 Squadron was not to enjoy its new acquisitions for long; already the contraction process was catching up and the squadron disbanded on 31 March 1946. No 517 Squadron was notified of its impending re-equipping with Met Mk VIs but received only four[3] before disbanding on 1 October 1946. The transfer of aircraft now moved on to 518 Squadron, which had moved from Wick to Tain on 8 November 1945. Having received some Met Mk IIIs the previous month, the squadron was informed that it would be converting to Met Mk VIs, but none had been received by the time of its disbandment on 31 May 1946 after having flown its last meteorological sortie the day before. No 520 Squadron followed suit, having its intended conversion to Met Mk VIs cancelled, and left five of its Met Mk III[4] Halifaxes at Gibraltar before disbanding on 25 April 1946.

As the last remaining wartime meteorological squadron, No 518 was soon to lose its identity, but only in name. Although technically disbanded on 1 October 1946 it re-emerged the same day as No 202 Squadron to carry on *'business as usual'* from Aldergrove and Gibraltar with its Met Mk VIs, four being kept on detachment at the latter location. Ground staff have a long tradition of innovation and RG840: M of the Gibraltar detachment had been made serviceable by much effort and cannibalisation of the parts from two other Halifaxes. Thirty-six hours later their toil had been in vain for it ended up in the sea off the end of the runway on 26 November 1946 when it swung on take-off. The Gibraltar runway also claimed two more of the squadron's Halifaxes: ST803 had swung on take-off and burnt out on 13 October 1948 while RG850 had also met a similar fate when it stalled on approach and crashed on 5 March 1949.

The squadron also suffered other casualties when a *Bismuth* sortie claimed ST818 and its crew on 9 July 1949. A large air-sea rescue operation failed to find any trace of the crew or aircraft; all that was known was that the pilot, Tiller, had radioed that he was commencing his climb to altitude 100 nautical miles earlier than planned. Another *Bismuth* sortie ended with RG843 flying into cloud-covered high ground on Achill Island in County Mayo on 16 June 1950 and on 29 December, the squadron lost its last aircraft when ST798, flown by the CO, S/Ldr Cox, was seen crashing into the sea in flames off Barra Head by the crew of a fishing trawler.

Aircraft had changed, but not so flying conditions. The heating system in the Mk VI aircraft sometimes failed and left crews flying in an outside air temperature of -50°F. The climb to 18-19,000 ft also took its toll of engines and three-engined returns were not uncommon, yet the crews never failed to carry out their essential tasks. F/Lt Ignatowski held a dubious double record for the most individual *Bismuth* sorties flown and the highest number of lightning strikes.

In December 1950, 202 Squadron finally surrendered its Halifaxes for the Hastings C I which had started arriving in October. Amongst its Halifaxes, the squadron had had the distinction of operating three former A Mk IXs, RT786, RT798 and RT923, used previously by several squadrons for airborne forces operations, but these were transferred when it converted to the Hastings in October 1948.

It is interesting to see just how much service these three Mk IXs had seen by the time they reached 202 Squadron. Issued to No 47 Squadron on 10 October 1946, RT786 was transferred to 113 Squadron on 11 March 1948 before going to 297 Squadron on 2 September of that same year when all three squadrons were part of the Flying Wing at Fairford. With the disbandment of the Flying Wing in late 1948, the aircraft were reallocated and RT786 went to 202 Squadron on 1 September 1949. RT923 followed a similar path, first to 47 Squadron on 13 November 1946 then to 297 on 28 July 1947 and then to 113, before finally ending up with 202 Squadron on 23 August 1949. RT798 had a less frenetic existence. It started with 47 Squadron on 28 October 1946 and remained there until going to 202 on 14 October 1949. The change of role from glider towing and airborne dropping duties to meteorological duties speaks well of the universal nature of the Halifax design. As there was no manufacturing standard for a Met Mk IX Halifax, it may be assumed that such modifications were carried out on an individual basis. RT923: A hit the BABS[5] van at Aldergrove on 6 September 1949, collapsing the undercarriage and writing the aircraft off. RT786 suffered an undercarriage collapse at Aldergrove on 13 March 1950 and was later scrapped, while RT798 survived to the end before being sold for scrap on 26 January 1951.

No 224 Squadron's association with the Halifax lingered a little longer with taking over the Gibraltar detachment, the waters around Gibraltar collecting RG837 on 16 January 1950 when it ditched on approach after two engines cut. The Squadron continued to maintain the detachment until Shackletons replaced its Halifaxes in July 1951. The last Halifax to leave was RG841, which was flown to 48 MU at Hawarden by F/Lt Finch on 17 March 1952. It was the last Halifax to serve with a front-line RAF squadron. The reason for the disbandment of the meteorological squadrons was technical advancement— data was now available from satellites and intercontinental civil aircraft. It was the end of an era and the end of Halifax operations, altogether a not inappropriate combination.

In all, only 35 Met Mk VI Halifaxes had been issued to the RAF, two of them to the Meteorological Research Flight at Farnborough. RG839 was loaned to Flight Refuelling at Tangmere on 15 May 1946 before being passed on to 224 Squadron at Gibraltar on 13 December 1950. A second, ST801, had also been loaned to that organisation, but at Ford, on 13 August 1946, but was never issued to an RAF squadron, being sold instead to Aviation Traders Ltd to appear on the civil register in 1949 as G-ALOM.

British Military Test Programmes

Post-war, the Halifax was also active in experimental research relating to a wide variety of aeronautical subjects. In January 1945, the Experimental Section and RAF Farnborough merged into one establishment and it was there that various marques of Halifaxes served for several years attached to different sections, i.e. Structural and Mechanical Engineering, Armament, Gas Dynamics, Wireless and Electrical, Instrument Flight, Aerodynamics Supersonic and the Meteorological Research Flight.

F/Lt Finch, who captained RG841 on its journey to 48 MU at Hawarden on 17 March 1952, flew the last official Halifax sortie for the RAF and poses RG841 over Gibraltar for the official photographs of this final sortie. Clearly visible on the nose is the squadron badge, a familiar feature on many RAF aircraft in the 1950s. Interestingly, this Halifax had not received the additional white paintwork added to some of the unit's Halifaxes. (C. Cole)

The Halifax pool was varied. In earlier years, it had had two B Mk IIs, JD254 and JN946, but four B Mk IIIs[6] – a B Mk VI, RG642; a B Mk VII, NP748; a C Mk VIII, PP230; and RG815, an A Mk IX – had now replaced these. Tasks varied widely and the programme of April 1946 is a good example. On the 2nd, NA682 began an investigation by the Instrument Flight into Mk VIII auto-pilot failures, on the 4th RG815 carried out high-altitude tests for the Armament Flight dropping man-carrying parachutes from 26,000 ft, and on the 12th, the Gas Dynamics Flight used NP748 for combustion-cooling trials. RG642 joined the programme next day with low-drag powerplant tests, which continued for most of the year; a part of this programme involved the Aerodynamics and Supersonic Flight, which used this Halifax until it was disposed of to Edzel in June 1947. The same day, LW385 began a long test programme with Goodyear Multi-disc-type brakes for the Structural and Mechanical Engineering Flight; just a year later PP230 would replace it in the test programme. Having completed the engine-surging test programme for the Gas Dynamics Flight, RG431 was flown to High Ercall for disposal on 23 April.

RG815 joined the Telecommunications Flying Unit in late May, finishing its flying clearance with the Wireless and Electrical Flight by the 29th and it received its VHF clearance a few days later, by which time NP748 had joined the Flight's test programme for electrically-operated thermomatically-controlled engine-cooling gills.

In September, a new range of experiments began with a variation on mobile artillery for the Airborne Forces. Using the A Mk IX, a 4.2 in mortar and its jeep were dropped from the forward stowage point of the Halifax's 8,000 lb bomb beam by the Armament Flight, yet it was the Armament and Meteorological Flights that provided the Halifaxes with their most sustained employment. These units moved to Farnborough on 18 August 1946 and spent the next four months re-equipping with personnel and aircraft, the latter comprising two Mk VIs, ST796 and ST817, and two PR34 Mosquitoes. In August 1947, a camera was fitted in the bomb bay of ST796, focused on a point fourteen inches below the aircraft, and brilliantly illuminated from both sides. This equipment was used to photograph raindrops, which appeared as measurable streaks on the negatives; it was then possible to work out the size of the raindrops. ST817 was equipped to investigate the homogeneity of humidity in the lower troposphere, a task that was completed by November 1947. The following month, ST796 began a lengthy programme investigating the sublimation of nuclei at various altitudes with Mr K. D. Palmer of Clarendon Laboratory, Oxford flying with the crew to operate the special instrumentation which had been added on 18 August 1946.

In April 1947, the Universal Freight Container (UFC) was ready for its handling trials and the following month drop tests began using PP350, an A Mk VII Halifax, as the trials aircraft. The UFC enclosed a jeep and 10 cwt trailer, giving a loaded weight of 8,000 lb. Of approximately the same shape but much larger dimension than the standard 8,000 lb capacity freight pannier, it proved to have no adverse effects upon the general handling characteristics of the Halifax. The Halifax was fitted with a fixed camera in a streamlined housing under each wing, several feet in from each wing tip. These provided a record of each release as the UFC cleared the bomb bay while a chase aircraft filmed the drop as it developed near Odstone. Although the crash gear on one side collapsed on initial impact because of a faulty forging, the contents were undamaged and the UFC was easily righted.

Army personnel give a final check to the Universal Freight Container (UFC) loaded into the bomb bay of PP350 prior to a dropping test in March 1951. The sheer size of the container, developed to handle a wide variety of aerodynamically cumbersome loads, may be judged against photographs of a standard 8,000 lb pannier. The reinforced cross-rail on the bottom surface marked the front end of the two longitudinal doors over the shock-absorbing units. A part of the streamlined housing for the starboard wing camera used in these tests is just visible behind the propeller blade. This Halifax had the additional dipole aerial array usually only fitted to the A Mk IX. (C. Cole)

During September, the UFC was modified to carry two observers internally with an automatic observation device fitted to the vents underneath it. This involved a considerable amount of work as intercom, seats, safety harnesses and emergency exits had to be fitted and checked by the stress department. The flight was completed without incident and both observers, Messrs. Merely and Saville, along with the automatic one, functioned correctly. A considerable amount of useful data was obtained, particularly concerning suction on the under surface of the container. The modified crash gear incorporated air bags, which inflated during the descent and projected from the under surface of the container, so suction problems were very relevant. Thus modified it was tested in a live drop in December, the UFC descending beneath eight 42 ft diameter parachute canopies.

The UFC was field-tested during joint battle exercises with US forces run by the School of Land Warfare in March 1951 at Watchfield in Berkshire. Other tests

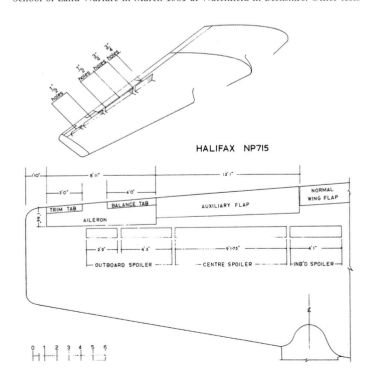

NP715 aileron spoiler control system.

A frame from the film record of the Universal Freight Container dropping from PP350 in March 1951; the drogue chute had just begun to deploy the pack of eight 42 ft diameter canopies and the bottom face of the UFC had opened to deploy two rows of pneumatic shock absorbers. Although grainy, this is the only known photograph showing a UFC being dropped. (via M. Wright)

continued, but changes to battle operations were swinging away from such means of direct field support. The last of the Airborne Forces Halifax squadrons had gone and the Hastings was not designed to carry such external loads. PP350 was struck off charge on 29 May 1952, marking the end of the Halifax's association with Farnborough.

A most unusual Halifax had arrived at Farnborough in December 1947. NP715 was a B Mk VI, which had been extensively modified by Handley Page and was attached to the Aerodynamic Supersonic Flight. Its most pronounced feature was short-span wings of the same dimensions as those fitted to the original Halifaxes. The normal ailerons had been replaced by a very small type fitted with a trim tab and a separate balance tab. An auxiliary flap had been fitted between the aileron and the normal flap while immediately in front of these new control surfaces was a line of four spoilers of semi-circular cross-section linked to the ailerons. The spoilers were very similar to those fitted to the Northrop Black Widow night-fighter. The purpose of the experiment was to gain experience with this type of control system on heavy aircraft with a view to its adoption on future designs.

The tests commenced on 1 December and continued until 22 December, logging some nine hours of actual flying time. Results showed that for normal operations at speeds above 140 mph Indicated Air Speed (IAS) the characteristics of the linked aileron-spoilers were very similar to the conventional ailerons fitted to Halifaxes. Good turns could be made in either direction using only the aileron spoilers, but at lower speeds there was an appreciable increase in the lag in response to control movements; this increased as the stall was approached and the rate of roll was noticeably affected. It was considered that the deterioration was sufficiently bad to render their control inadequate for bad-weather landings, even when allowing for the slight improvement brought about by lowering the auxiliary flaps. In a stall, with all flaps down, the Halifax's normal mild handling characteristics were altered considerably with a tendency for the aircraft to roll. This could not be controlled, even with coarse use of the aileron-spoilers at speeds below about 140 mph IAS with flaps up and at about 100-110 mph IAS with the auxiliary flaps lowered. In view of these results, the experiments were discontinued.

Civil testing programmes

Handley Page retained several aircraft for testing and design purposes; amongst them was one particularly intriguing example, a hybrid conversion of a Mk VII. The late Chris Cole at the Air Ministry had several negatives showing this aircraft and all were marked as Mk VII, and further searching in the individual aircraft records has narrowed the identity to RT757. This Halifax was never issued to a unit, remaining on loan to Handley Page until struck off charge on 4 May 1949. However, looking at the visible features it appears to have been used as a test aircraft, rather than just a revised airframe test bed.

Another Halifax at Khartoum for an extended period was noted by Fl/Sgt Ken Russell: *"During my stay the RAF were carrying out their tropical testing there, and this included a Halifax which, I think, had one engine running on the then new 115/145 grade of fuel. This aircraft had the name The Knocker."* This was NA684, later purchased by the College of Aeronautics at Cranfield and registered as G-AJPG, remaining in use until 1954.

A very much modified Halifax photographed at Handley Page's facility in the immediate post-war period with the HP75 Manx tailless research aircraft just visible in the background. Fitted with the Hercules XVI engines normally used for Mk III, VII and IX Halifaxes, it has a small square window just above the Rebecca/Eureka antennae that was not a design feature of any production, radial-engine marque of Halifax. The two short rod aerials fitted to the upper surface of the nose section and small Perspex sphere added below the fuselage offset to starboard, just aft of the bomb aimer's small rectangular window, were also non-standard features. The pannier has also been modified with its doors sealed and handles deleted and has a large circular window set into its rear lower surface, approximately two-thirds back from the front, and the bomb cell doors are also present in the inboard wing section. (Flight International)

The de Havilland Company also used several Halifaxes. B Mk VI RG820 was delivered to the company on 30 May 1946 and, with the exception of a short period between May 1947 and January 1948, during which time it was returned to Handley Page, it was used for engine de-icing trials.

These started out with a single fixed spray bar rigged to cover the starboard inboard engine with water and then measure the effects of increasing ice accretion. The side of the fuselage immediately behind the cockpit and in line with the propeller rotation plane was reinforced to withstand the impact of ice flung off the blades. The experiments were gradually increased to introduce a multiple spray bar arrangement, which, like its predecessor, was fixed to a central supporting rod mounted in the nose cone. The bracing system used for the 0.5-in Browning machine gun on some wartime Halifaxes was utilised, the rig being strengthened externally with guy wires fitted with turnbuckles for adjustments and each blade was marked with a white Roman numeral for the tests. The Halifax remained at de Havilland's when the tests were completed, the RAF dismantling it for removal in October 1951[7].

Two other B Mk III Halifaxes were loaned to de Havilland, NA683 and MZ956; the former arrived from Farnborough on 2 April 1946 but was disposed of to 45 MU on 9 May due to its poor condition. Built in October 1944, it had been issued to 246 Squadron and according to their records, struck off charge on 15 May 1945. Clearly, it lingered longer and this may account for its poor condition as it was probably stored pending disposal and received little attention. It was replaced by MZ956, which was used for propeller governor tests and, in complete contrast to NA683, remained with the Company until returned to 45 MU on 7 April 1956.

This rear view of the same Halifax (above top) from aft reveals more significant details. The rear fuselage is standard C Mk VIII construction with additional portholes and a tail cone but the base structure and circular flange reveal where the mid-upper turret was removed. This was not a feature of any production C Mk VIII rear fuselage section. All C Mk VIII aircraft were built by Handley Page between the end of March and early August 1945 all of which, excluding those issued to Nos 301 and 304 Squadrons of Transport Command, were all sold to civil operators. Photographs of the few RAF machines show them either in the temperate scheme of Dark Green and Ocean Grey upper surfaces and Medium Sea Grey under surfaces or bare metal, but not standard night camouflage as seen here. Handley Page delivered the last five Mk VIIs, RT753 to RT757 inclusive, on 1 November 1945; the first four were sold for scrap but the company retained RT757, presumably on loan from the RAF, for test work. It remained with Handley Page until struck off charge on 4 May 1949 and suggests, in the absence of any other evidence, that this hybrid may well have been RT757. (Flight International)

A rare bird, NA684 photographed at Khartoum in 1946 where it spent most of a year carrying out engine running tests using the newly introduced 115/145 grade of aviation fuel. The manner of marking the serial number beneath the wing was unusual with the 'NA' portion separated by the outboard engine on the port side and 'NA6' outboard on the starboard side. Despite its production date of late October 1944 and the fact that it was built as a standard B Mk III, it had a day camouflage scheme of Dark Green and Ocean Grey upper surfaces and Medium Sea Grey under surfaces. The presence of the so-called Type C 1 roundels beneath the wings introduced on 7 January 1945 suggests that the airframe may have undergone a repainting of the original night bomber scheme. Although the crest on the nose has been attributed to the College of Aeronautics, which purchased this Halifax in 1947, the obvious discrepancy in dates negates that assumption. It is likely that the name 'The Knocker' referred to its test role and engine performance on the new fuel. (K. Russell)

De Havilland used Halifax A Mk VII PP389 for towing trials with Horsa glider TL349 which had been specially modified and fitted with a mock-up of the Comet airliner nose to determine the degree of visibility, particularly in conditions of rain. John Cunningham carried out the tests in January 1947. Delivered from 29 MU on 17 December 1946, PP389 went to 48 MU on 4 November 1947 and remained there until sold for scrap on 15 February 1949. (de Havilland)

Perhaps the most interesting experiments carried out by de Havilland involved the second A Mk VII loaned to them; PP389 was used for towing tests with a specially converted Horsa glider, TL349, which was fitted with a complete mock-up of the nose section of the Comet airliner design to determine the visibility, particularly in periods of rain. John Cunningham[8] conducted the flying tests in January 1947. The Halifax was flown in from 29 MU on 17 December 1946 and remained with de Havilland until going to 48 MU on 4 November 1947.

On a smaller scale of involvement, A Mk VII PN323 went by a rather roundabout route to its final test use. Built in September 1945, like so many other late-war production aircraft of all types, it was never issued to a unit and remained in storage after delivery to 29 MU on 23 September and was still there when the 1946 Air Ministry census was taken. It was struck off charge in May 1948 to be sold for scrap. Broken down into its major components, it was transported to the Handley Page airfield at Radlett and handed over to Standard Telephones and Cables Ltd who removed the twin fin and rudder assemblies and fitted a single fin and rudder for their subsequent aerial tests for the Bristol Brabazon and Britannia airliner development programmes, the work continuing until 1951. It then fell into disuse and slowly deteriorated until rescued by the Historical Aircraft Preservation Society but, unable to find storage for such a large item, the airframe continued to deteriorate. Finally, in conjunction with the Air Britain Air Relics Research Group and the Forest Gate Branch of Air Britain, the nose section was preserved for restoration, the rest of the airframe being sold for scrap. Unable to raise the funding to carry out the restoration, the nose section was donated to the Skyfame Museum, where it remained until the museum closed, the nose section then passing to the Imperial War Museum where today, renovated, it forms part of the collection.

Sales to foreign Air Forces

L' Armée de l'Air

The RAF had ceased front-line bomber duties with the Halifax immediately after VE Day but the two French Squadrons, Nos 346 and 347, remained under Bomber Command control for the immediate future. They were employed, along with other British squadrons, in dumping unwanted stocks of bombs at sea, but Halifaxes from both squadrons were also detached for transport duties in France. Although planning by the French Government had begun in 1944 with the establishment of a

force capable of assisting with the strategic bombing of Germany and its armed forces, an overall plan for re-establishment of a coherent military force in post-war France was still under examination.

The initial post-war situation in France remained unsettled and argument as to the future requirements of its reconstituted armed forces was split, mirroring to some degree arguments that had threatened the strategic value of the RAF until 1942. Through the service of 346 and 347 Squadrons, the Armée de l'Air had experienced the value of a strategic force capable of independent action at long range. However, the French Army still held to its pre-war position of using air power tactically in support of its ground forces. Future aircraft requirements depended very much on the outcome of the arguments.

Demobilisation of personnel also played a part with the French squadrons understandably keen to return home, most having been absent since 1940. The cost of maintaining the RAF on a wartime footing had been massive; indeed paying for the cost of the war would cripple Britain in the post-war period and it would not be until early in the 21st century that it would be finally achieved. Therefore, Britain was also keen to reduce its military forces and on 6 October all flying by the two French squadrons officially ceased, by which time the French Government had reached a decision to include a strategic bombing force in the Armée de l'Air. The new base for the two Halifax squadrons would be at BA.106 – Bordeaux-Mérignac with Cmdt Puget, the former CO of 346 Squadron, as its first commanding officer. The choice of airfield was ideal from a military aspect because of its existing extensive facilities with large hangars and workshops and long runways. Its location in south-western France also enhanced the decision.

On 24 October small groups of Halifaxes and personnel began leaving Elvington for France, with only one mishap marring the transit flights when, on the 29th, RG561 crashed during a forced landing at Sheep Walk Farm, Deighton, killing two of Lt Wellard's crew. These were the last French losses while serving in England. On 31 October, the two squadrons were removed from the RAF Order of Battle. The following day, le Group de Bombardment n°1 (GB.1) formed at Bordeaux-Mérignac; the title did not last long, being changed to 21éme Escadre de Bombardment Lourd, officially 21.EBL, but remaining records refer only to Group Bombardment Lourd. With this change came also changes to the designation of the two Halifax squadrons, 346 *Guyenne* became GB.2/21 *Guyenne*, and 347 *Tunisie*, GB.1/21 *Tunisie*. On paper though, just as with 21.EBL, the two were referred to only as II/23 and 1/25, their pre-1940 designations. [For clarity of reference for the reader, the terms GBL.1/21 and GBL.2/21 will be used in the following text]. Other things also did not alter, the Halifaxes retaining their daylight tactical markings for some months until finally replaced by the French tricolour fin flash. However, the wartime codes, GB.2/21 alias I/25 as 'H7' and GB.1/21 alias II.23 as 'L8', were retained until close to the final days of the Halifax in French service.

The revived Armée de l'Air was assembling an array of former wartime aircraft to provide for its own immediate post-war needs, including such former enemy aircraft as the Ju 88 for maritime patrol work. The logistics of operating disparate types necessitated some careful training and a School of Mechanics was established at Rochefort during August/September 1945. A French Training Delegation obtained aircraft for ground training at the school with four, possibly six, Mk II and V Halifaxes being transferred to it from RAF stocks. The uncertainty over actual numbers has been compounded for researchers by the fact that only three clear references occur on the actual individual aircraft history cards; JN978 has only reference to its allocation to 614 Squadron plus a 'struck off charge' entry dated

Bordeaux-Mérignac airfield was to be the permanent post-war home of the two Halifax units, the large hangars and other facilities having been used by the Luftwaffe, particularly the Fw 200s and He 177s of KG 40 during the Second World War. Photographed shortly after taking up residence there are, on the right, five of the former 346 Guyenne Squadron Halifaxes with RG607: H7-X and RG510: H7-K nearest the camera. (Via P. Couderchon)

PP165: P of 347 Squadron photographed at Bordeaux-Mérignac after its transfer to the Armée de l'Air in October 1945. It carries both the Moonlit Bison Squadron emblem and Cross of Lorraine on the nose while the aircraft code letters are outlined in RAF yellow with the individual aircraft letter repeated on the fin, superimposed over the hollow red diamond daylight tactical marking. This was the first B Mk VI from the PP165 - PP187 batch delivered between 31 January and 19 February 1945 and the second batch of B Mk VI Halifaxes built by Handley Page. (ECPA)

L8-N taxies in to Bordeaux-Mérignac after its transfer flight from England, each of the two gunners standing in one of the escape hatches and the flight engineer looking on from the astrodome. No armament was fitted to the rear turret. (J. Delmas)

Handley Page Halifax, B Mk VI
RG590: R, formerly of 346 Squadron, after transfer to l'Armée de l'Air in October 1945, and based at Bordeaux-Mérignac.

RG590: R was another of No 346 Squadron's wartime Halifaxes repatriated in October. The markings it carried, other than for the serial number in white below each wing, were those of its wartime service. The effectiveness of the crimson 'trellis' marking on fin and rudder can be appreciated in this view. No armament was fitted for the flight. Built in late March 1945, this Halifax had first been allocated to No 640 Squadron, then transferred to No 466 Squadron and then passed to No 346 Squadron.

This B Mk V Series IA was transferred to the Rochefort site at around the same time as B Mk II Series IA JP327. Although the timing of its arrival remains undetermined it is easily discernible from JP327 by its Dowty lever suspension undercarriage and lack of H2S radome and it had white spinners when photographed. The amount of paint erosion around the lips of the radiator cowlings, the wear on the wing leading edges and the retention of saxophone exhausts indicate that, unlike JP327, this was not a brand new Halifax. There are no signs of code letters or even an aircraft letter on the fuselage or front face of the undercarriage. The lack of a paratroop-dropping windshield suggests that it was a B Mk V rather than an A Mk V – possibly LL483. (P. Couderchon)

16 August 1945. The author, in notations from files examined in the early 1960s, was fortunate to have recorded a reference from another document to the transfer of JP327 and JN978 to a 'French Training Delegation'. Without that accidental discovery, JN978 would have not been positively identified. Additionally, a photograph supplied by French researcher Philippe Couderchon shows an unidentified B Mk V Series IA at what is clearly Rochefort taken at the same time as a second photograph showing JP327. The Mk V LL483 has a card entry 'Fate not known', a euphemism for 'no further details on the aircraft history card' next to it in the Air Britain Publication *The Halifax File*, so this may be the identity of this otherwise unknown Halifax.

Retention of saxophone exhausts, rather than the multi-exhaust variety seen on the JN and JP production series Halifaxes places it close to the condition of the other two positively identified Halifaxes from the LL production series; it had no *H2S* fitting and judging by its appearance, had seen a lot of flying time. An additional unidentified Halifax A Mk II Series IA also appears in a photograph belonging to French collector F. Savoie. In all, there appear to have been at least six Halifaxes at Rochefort. First-hand information from Rochefort is scarce and nothing positive has emerged to give any conclusive information as to actual aircraft holdings, possibly because each airframe was used only for ground instructional purposes.

The four positively identified Halifaxes were transferred from Mediterranean Allied Air Force (MAAF) holdings, all but one being former operational aircraft. The first was a B Mk II Series IA, JP327, a new machine produced in late April 1944. It had passed to 4 Air Preparation Unit (APU) then to 2 Overseas Air Dispatch Unit before being flown out to the Mediterranean on 21 January 1945 and taken on charge by the MAAF the same day. Not issued to a front-line squadron, it was transferred to the French Training Delegation on 13 September 1945.

Two more, JN978: B and LL392, were transferred on 11 October 1945. The first, a Mk II Series IA produced on 4 December 1943, had seen a year's service in the MAAF. It is listed as allocated to 614 Squadron but had a dropping hatch and short ventral metal fin to prevent static lines fouling the tail wheel. There are a number of anomalies between individual aircraft history cards and actual unit records. Some aircraft serving with 148 Squadron are shown as passing to 614 Squadron but the timing of the latter unit's last Halifax operation on 3 March 1945 plus the unexpected continuation of Halifax operations with 148 Squadron until 23 May 1945, negates the transfer data – probably no more than paper entries in the end. The fact that 614 was the PFF unit for MAAF operations makes transfers from an SD unit, which lacked *H2S* equipment, a somewhat fraught process. Conversion could have been carried out but the war was already in its last moments.

LL392, a B Mk V Series IA, also had Special Duties connections having served first with 161 (SD) Squadron as 'W-William' and then 138 (SD) Squadron, before being transferred to the MAAF. The urgent call for replacement crews and aircraft

Left: Another mystery Halifax transferred to Rochefort at the time when the derelict building structures were still present. At first glance, it could be confused with the white-spinnered A Mk V Series IA tentatively identified as LL483 but this is an A Mk II Series IA, its distinctive Messier undercarriage clearly visible. It lacks an H2S radome and has a paratrooping-windshield fitted. Aside from having black spinners, no codes or other distinguishing markings are visible and the paintwork appears to have seen little flying time. It also retains the larger saxophone exhausts, indicative of a production date before the introduction of the final refinements to the Merlin 22 exhaust manifolds. As all Halifaxes passed to the French Training Delegation were from MAAF sources, this particular one may have originated from the reserve aircraft holdings. (F. Savoie)

Right: This brand new, late model B Mk II Series IA, JP327, was photographed at Rochefort (the derelict building structure behind is a handy check for this early period at the School). Its identity is quite clear, the white (rather than usual red) serial numbers clearly visible as are the H2S radome, late model multiple ejector exhaust stubs and Messier undercarriage. This was the first Halifax transferred to the French, the hand over being recorded as taking place on 13 September 1945. (P. Couderchon)

Left: A line up of three of the Rochefort Halifaxes with B Mk II Series IA JN978, White 3, nearest to the camera; it had served for a year on bombing duties with 614 Squadron operating from Amendola in Italy marked as 'B-Baker', the letter 'B' being still visible aft of the roundel. These Halifaxes were each given a simple white identification number starting at 1 and presumably going to at least 5. The next in line is LL392, its distinctive nose artwork still just visible and behind which is an unidentified B Mk V Series IA marked as White 1.

for the disastrous losses incurred by the SD units during the Warsaw uprising in August 1944 had been frustratingly slow. A second urgent request by the Air Ministry was made to HQ Bomber Command on 24 August, for all available surplus Mk V Halifaxes *"... up to a total of ten"* for immediate dispatch, and each was to have *"..a minimum of 90 hours to go before next major inspection: must be operationally serviceable and fitted out to full SD standard."* Ten were found, among them LL392, one of three supplied from 138 SD Squadron. All were delivered to No 41 Group for tropicalisation before being dispatched at the end of the month. Meanwhile the slaughter over Warsaw continued and the ten were insufficient to meet the urgent replacements needed. On 3 September, the Air Ministry signalled HQ Bomber Command for the immediate dispatch of eight more Mk Vs, all to have a minimum tankage of 1,882 gallons, plus one 230 gallon and two 90 gallon overload tanks – such was the operational distance from Brindisi to Warsaw for the supply sorties. They left the same day, and among the eight were LL467 and LL483. This explains the origins of three of the Halifaxes later passed to the French training school. LL467 had served with Nos 138 and 161 Squadrons before going to the Polish 1586 (SD) Flight at Brindisi. It must have been withdrawn from the Flight by 7 November as the

unit was redesignated 301 (Polish) Squadron on that date and LL467's history card shows no change of ownership. It was passed to the French on 18 October 1945. The Halifaxes were each sequentially marked with a white number on the nose and used for training on engines and hydraulic systems, none of them ever flying again after receipt by the school.

The first four months at Bordeaux-Mérignac saw relatively little flying as personnel and equipment were established on a structured basis. The location, while ideal from a military aspect, meant that crews were now far from Paris, a factor that had an effect on recruitment. However, sufficient flying personnel were recruited to form crews that would stay together for much of their service career on the Halifaxes. Initially, air gunners were still part of the crew but, from the winter of 1946, the gradual removal of armament saw the gunners remain as general duties aircrew. The standard crew now comprised pilot, navigator, wireless operator, bomb aimer, flight engineer plus the general duties former gunner.

A small training unit, le Centre de Formation des Equipages de Bombardment Lourd (CFEBL), was also located at Bordeaux-Mérignac to provide the final operational conversion training of new crew members. Formed in England at

Halifax B Mk V Series IA LL392 was transferred to the French Training Delegation on 11 October 1945 and is distinguishable by its nose artwork of a woman in a long dress and high-heeled shoes. Again, four-bladed propellers are fitted but the chipped engine cowlings show that this Halifax had many flying hours to its credit having served with 161 and 138 (SD) Squadrons, probably for only for a few months in each case, before being sent to the MAAF. (J. C. Soumille)

B Mk V Series IA LL467: O had also served with both 138 and 161 (SD) Squadrons before being transferred to 1586 (SD) Flight at Brindisi in late September/early October 1944. It does not appear on the strength of 301 (SD) Squadron after it formed on 7 November, so it probably went into the aircraft storage pool, remaining there until being transferred to the French on 18 October 1945. Positively identified by its reclining female artwork, it is quite distinguishable from that of the walking female figure on LL392. LL467 has its serial number and a white letter 'O' on the front face of the undercarriage, and it also appears to have red painted spinners. (J. C. Soumille)

The final image of what might have been the last complete B Mk VI Halifax available for preservation. White overall camouflage was adopted for some Halifaxes operating on long distance transport flights into tropical areas with black replacing the usual white for code letters. Following its accident and as described in the text, it remained in a hangar at Plumerillo airfield in Argentina until the French government abandoned any interest in it in 1971 after which it was dismantled for scrap. The open dinghy stowage compartment that produced RG874's 'last moment of glory' can be seen in the inboard section of the wing. (SM Roque Varetto via Sergio Bontii and P. Couderchon)

Rufforth, the home of 1663 HCU, it had an establishment of four Halifaxes which used call signs from the F-TKWA to Z allocation. As far as is known to French researchers, no specific codes or any distinguishing badges were carried, pre-existing ones being retained on each aircraft. The last reference to this unit in official documentation ceases at the end of 1949.

Post-war writings about the Halifax in French military service have largely confined themselves to simply stating that after 1945 it was only used for long-range transport duties. Fortunately, that limited perception has been disproven by the research of several noted French aviation writers. While the Halifax did carry out such duties, mostly to French overseas territories, it maintained its military role, the two squadrons having specific duties, GB.2/21 *Guyenne* carrying out long-distance operations while GB.1/21 *Tunisie* performed the meteorological flights and search and rescue duties. The French used a flying control system incorporating a 'civil' call sign procedure, the Halifaxes of GB.2/21 being assigned the series F-RAXA to Z, and GB1.21 F-RAVA to Z. Alternative Tuesdays and Wednesdays were used for navigation and bombing training; for instance, records from 1948 show that a formation of two or four Halifaxes regularly flew training sorties to Algeria and Tunisia where they carried out bombing exercises. RG606 (F-RAXQ) was written off during one of these exercises when it swung on take-off from El Aouina[9] in Tunisia, RG703 being lost in similar circumstances on 9 January 1948. They also took part in joint exercises with the Allied Occupation Forces in Germany.

Accidents, however, were few. RG661 was damaged on 12 March 1946 when a Percival Proctor collided with it, but after repairs at Aircraft Park[10] 2/106, it returned to service. Then, between August and October 1946, a fresh supply of new B Mk VIs arrived[11]. The dates physically received were usually later than the actual date of the transfer of ownership documentation; the dates shown in the end note are those of the aircraft's arrival in France.

Often, some very long pioneering trips were flown as the French Government began regular military and civil passenger flights to its colonial outposts. In addition to the existing seating for eight in the rest bay area between the main spars, 12 more seats were added, providing for a normal capacity of 20. However, on some flights, this arrangement was exceeded and up to 32 were carried on some West African trips and the freight panniers used for a wide variety of items including mail sacks. In the post-war period, France also renewed old cultural and political links with the South American nations but the unremitting expansion of United States commercial and political interests into South America had become dominant and imposed a block on more extensive economic links. As a result, several French official delegations travelled south of the equator. From the aeronautical aspect, some connections took place very early through unexpected occurrences like that precipitated by the 631 victims of a dramatic accident on the Rio de la Plata on 6 November 1945. The French President immediately offered a contribution of a Halifax from its small force of long-range aircraft to assist, an act which was gratefully accepted.

The first long-range flight by GB.2/21 took place in February 1946 to Saigon in what was then still Indo-China, followed by Cairo and the Antilles in November-December and a routine service Bordeaux - Reduction Island - Dakar was opened the following March. Converted Martin Marauder aircraft were also used for transporting families of civil servants to their colonial destinations but, even with its Spartan interior, the Halifax proved more popular for such duties. The start of one such trip was to become legendary when a pilot ordered to carry out a flight on 5 July 1946 damaged RG647 in spectacular fashion. Untrained on the type, a mechanic explained the instrumentation to the pilot and take-off commenced; unfortunately, the pilot was not accustomed to the torque produced by the four engines and a swing to port developed causing the Halifax to ground loop, fortunately without causing damage. On 9 September, this same Halifax carrying out a scheduled flight to Reduction Island, landed without clearance, again without damage; but on 12 November, fate finally caught up with RG647 in a repeat of the original problem of an uncorrected swing during take-off resulting in the starboard undercarriage collapsing. Fire broke out and while

Right: One of the Halifaxes taking part in the 14 July celebration fly-past over Paris in 1947 and although Halifaxes of GB.2/21 still retained their mid-upper and rear turrets, the armament for the latter had been removed when this photograph was taken. The stencilled lettering visible above the crew entrance hatch related to the aircraft data and identity. The RAF serial number (RG86*) is partly obscured, both this and another photograph of the same aircraft revealing all but this last digit, but only three French Halifaxes fit this serial range, RG867, RG868 delivered in May, and RG869 delivered in August, the date of the fly-past eliminating the latter. Thus, as both RG867 and RG868 were on the strength of GB.1/21 at the time it could have been either. However, one more clue may lie in the way that the letter 'C' was applied, as close examination when magnified shows that a letter with two vertical strokes had been over-painted. The right-hand one was still faintly visible, but the left-hand one was more easily detectable where it cut the top horizontal bar of the 'C'; as surviving records identify that RG867 had carried the aircraft code letter 'H', it is highly probable that this is, in fact, RG867. (J. Delmas)

the 14 passengers were safely evacuated, the navigator was slightly injured. Yet, not all was negative and on 14 July, the two Groups carried out a fly-past over Paris.

In November 1946, a diplomatic mission flew to Rio de Janeiro in RG842: F (F-RAVF) of GBL 1/25, the crew enjoying 12 days of relaxation in a distinctly holiday location while General June and his party carried out an extended visit to the Brazilian Academy of Warfare. The round-trip flight took 46 hours and the pilot was particularly pleased with the reliability of the automatic pilot. Navigation was carried out using the *Gee* facilities in France, then radio fixes while transiting Africa and the South Atlantic to Brazil. Astro-navigation fixes and *H2S*, supplemented by the Air Position Indicator[12], which until the trip had been considered of dubious ability in the southern hemisphere, added assistance. The trip provided a wealth of detailed information on weather reporting requirements, radio code handbooks, clothing suitability for travelling between climate zones, the need for de-icing equipment, passport clearance times, etc. For a long time this was recorded as the first crossing of the southern Atlantic between Senegal and Brazil by Armée de l'Air personnel.

However, on 11 November and apparently without full government clearance, a Halifax had departed from Bordeaux-Mérignac for Brazil carrying a small diplomatic mission to oversee the integration of Guyana into the French Overseas Colonies. It reached Dakar without problem but inspection of the oil filter on one engine revealed metal filings and a replacement Halifax was flown out. From there it reached Reduction Island in 5 hours 47 minutes and then Dakar in 7 hours 28 minutes. Then the crew found out it was one oxygen mask short for the sea crossing which was to be flown between 7,000 and 8,000 metres (22,900 to 26,240 ft) altitude at 320 km/hr (198.8 mph). That limited the operating altitude and posed problems with passing through the daily build-up of heavy convection cloud to 10,000 metres (32,800 ft) over the South American coast; so departure was changed to late at night, on the 13 November, when convection would be at its weakest. All went well, accompanied by a spectacular build-up of St Elmo's fire on the end of the wings and propeller tips, and the Halifax landed safely in Brazil next morning. From there a 7 hour 8 minute flight over virgin forest – with no place to force-land – brought them to the wartime Cayenne-Rochambeau landing ground, built by the USAAF in World War Two as part of their staging route for planes and weapons. Sainte-Lucie Island, close to Martinique, where runway facilities were not able to handle such a large aircraft, was the next stop but the crew were surprised when they found their request to land refused by someone with a strong American accent. Permission had been sought and granted by British authorities prior to the trip but they had failed to mention that His Majesty's Government had leased the island to America for 99 years. It would appear that the weather was not the only unpredictable factor but given the location and lack of an alternative, the American controller relented and the Halifax was allowed to land. The Halifax and its crew departed on 5 December

for a military airfield on Antigua, and then on the morning of 7 December flew on to Cayenne, a 5 hour 30 minute flight. The diplomatic duties completed, the Halifax made a fault-free return flight, leaving Cayenne on 14 December and arriving back, via Dakar, at Bordeaux-Mérignac on the 20th. A letter of congratulations from the Minister of Air stated in part."..... *having carried out from 10 November* (sic) *to 19 December* (sic), *1946 a voyage of 23,000 kilometres in the Antilles and in Guyana, 65 hours flying time, in conditions of remarkable regularity and security. This flight being the first of this type crossing the width of the South Atlantic with French personnel."*

On 30 March 1947 an insurrection by nationalist forces broke out on Madagascar, catching the colonial government completely by surprise. Supplies of troops, equipment and ammunition needed transporting swiftly from France and the Halifaxes were called upon for the emergency airlift as the few Dakotas available had insufficient range to load ratio to be effective. Four Halifaxes[13] left Bordeaux on 8 April, each carrying eight tons of freight and 600 kilos (1,320 lbs) of spare parts and tools for their own emergency needs. A refuelling stop was made at Marrakech where 80 paratroopers were added to the load, which now rose from 8.6 tons to 9.6 tons; the Army then requested that four 60 mm mortars with ammunition and wireless equipment also be added to the loads to equal 13.5 tons, very close to the theoretical limit of 4 tons for each Halifax. The heavily laden Halifaxes continued to Tunis but the commanding officer of the detachment refused to risk the next leg of the journey over central Africa with a load in excess of 4 tons, the fuel load being critical, and some surplus materiel was left at El Aouina. Each Halifax crew flew independently over the route from Haden in Libya to Khartoum and on to Nairobi.

From there the final African destination would be Dar es Salaam as no airfield on Madagascar was ready for such large and heavily-laden aircraft. Dakotas would then ferry the loads over the final leg of the journey. RG491 developed hydraulic problems and the third Halifax, having unloaded at Dar es Salaam, flew back and picked up the additional load. A repeat flight by a single Halifax took place on 24 April but a further large lift was required when things became worse on the ground at the beginning of May. On 6 May, RG560 left with 4 tons of ammunition and bombs for the Avro Anson 'bombers' being used in the fighting. The next day, six Halifaxes transferred an additional 20 tons of bombs and ammunition, more than a ton of replacement parts and tools, plus the remaining 48 paratroopers. This was the last phase of the Halifax operations with some 760 hours being flown during eleven sorties. Apart from the problem with RG491, no other problems occurred – at this time lack of spares was affecting the Halifax force at Bordeaux-Mérignac, 23 of the 31 on strength being temporarily unserviceable.

By now, more new B Mk VIs had begun arriving; first RG816 in April, followed by RG703, RG788, RG867, RG868 and RG819 in May, RG828 in June, RG705 and RG821 in July, RG869 and ST797 in August, RG789 in September and the last two,

The last 14 July fly-past to include Halifaxes took place in 1948 when GB.2/21 sent five, RG625, RG821, RG867, ST797 and ST799, to take part. With just the first letter 'R' of the serial number visible, this eliminates two of the five as being the subject shown here, while the E Mk I tail turret points to it being among the earlier Halifaxes transferred to the Armée de l'Air. RG625 had served with 347 Squadron, coded as L8-A, and was among those transferred in October 1945. The photograph clearly shows where the original code letters of 'L8' were painted out, with no attempt being made to restore the sections of upper surface camouflage where this overlapped them. Partially obscured by a propeller blade, the Cross of Lorraine carried on the nose was retained but was a wartime emblem and was not applied to later Halifaxes delivered to the Armée de l'Air. RG867 was received in April 1947 and allocated the aircraft code letter 'H', which it retained until December 1949 and was also fitted with a D Mk I tail turret. RG821 arrived from the UK in July 1947 but no information is available on its initial set of markings other than for it being allocated to GBL.2/21 as 'N' on 5 May 1948 so, based on the available evidence, this would point to H7-V being RG625. Note that the mid-upper turret and all armament had been removed and both a pannier and H2S radome fitted. The national tricolour marking on the rudder had replaced the original RAF-style fin flash in 1947. The colour of the individual aircraft letter matches the crimson of the outer ring of the roundel while the 'H7' code appears to be in a darker shade of red. (J. Delmas)

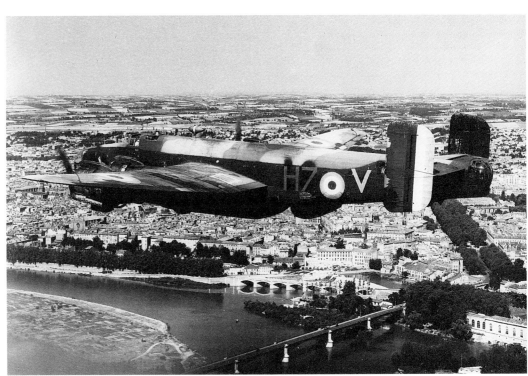

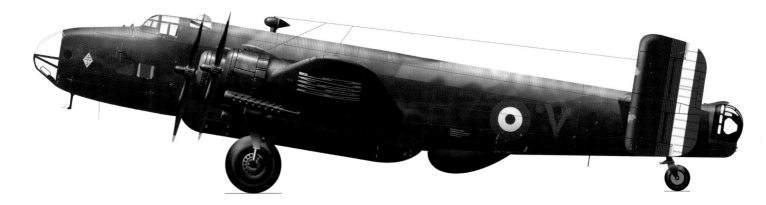

Handley Page Halifax, B Mk VI
RG625: V, of GB.2/21 (formerly of 347 Squadron), during the types last flight with the l'Armée de l'Air, in July 1948.

RG752 and ST799, in October. The latter, transferred on paper on 25 September, arrived on 21 October and was the last Halifax received by the Armée de l'Air.

Meanwhile, GB.2/21 *Guyenne* continued its long-range flights, transporting personnel to Singapore and Saigon in November and December. A circuit of Africa was flown in December via Khartoum, Kano and Dakar and flights to and from Madagascar, having now been established under war conditions, continued over the next four years on a more peaceful basis.

On 14 July 1948, GB.2/21 carried out its last fly-past with Halifaxes over Paris, sending RG625, RG821, RG867, ST797 and ST799. On 20 October a Ministerial Directive changed the role of GB.2/21 to that of a Transport Squadron attached to the Groupement des Moyens Militaires de Transports Aériens (GMMTA). Both squadrons now performed identical duties. These continued into 1949 with regular long-range transport flights to the Far East, its Halifaxes now in a new form of camouflage – uniform green overall with white code letters. The old-style RAF fin flashes had been replaced by 1948, the external trailing edge of each fin and rudder being painted overall in the French tricolour. All personal names and motifs were now banned other than for those on aircraft already transferred to the School of Mechanics at Rochefort, which now included a few of the B Mk VIs.

Captain M. Dauchier, of Group 2/23, the pilot involved with the aftermath of the Rio de la Plata disaster in November 1945, had subsequently flown the relief flights to Rio, accompanied by Lieutenant-Colonel Fourquet. His experience on those mercy flights resulted in him being selected to fly another special journey, this time with a prestigious passenger, the distinguished General Jean de Lattre de Tassigny[14], Inspector General of the Army, who was paying a high-level protocol visit to reinforce economic and cultural ties.

Halifax B Mk VI RG874 had left English Electric's assembly line on 16 May 1945 but remained in storage until received by the French Air Force on 17 August 1946 where it served first with GB 2/23 as H7-N (F-RAXN) until 29 January 1947 when its identity was changed to H7-C (F-RAXC). In order to give the aircraft a little more panache for its high level mission, a few days before departing the existing Dark Earth, Dark Green and Night Black camouflage was repainted with an overall coat of white, but it retained its French Air Force military roundels and tail markings. Capt Dauchier was allocated Asp Gaussin as second pilot for the trip and Adj Chef Jaulin, Anziani and Porque, Asp Kirch as navigator, Sgt Chef Dugast as wireless operator, plus three mechanics. Dauchier was very experienced on the Halifax, having 217 hours day and 47 hours of night flying time in his logbook, much of it gained during the six months flying back and forth to Rio. In addition to the General, there were other distinguished passengers on board.

During the early part of the trip, de Tassigny made several protocol stops for formal appearances, visiting the French garrison at Camp Mayo on 7 October where he gave a press conference. From there next day, a DC 4 of the Fuerza Aerea Argentina (Argentine Air Force) led the Halifax to Cordoba for official engagements. Finally, on 11 October de Tassigny bade farewell to the Argentinian Government at a ceremony attended by President Peron and his ministers during which national gifts were exchanged. Three days later on the 14th, he was flown from Buenos Aires on board a DC 4 to several other stops, ending at Esquel where the Halifax was waiting for him. RG874: C and its VIP passengers left for Santiago, Chile on the 16th for more protocol visits to take place.

The return flight to France began from Santiago on 22 October. They were met at the border by three Argentinian Curtiss Hawk 75s of Grupo 2 de Caza to escort them to El Plumerillo; however, as the Halifax began its approach to the airfield, disaster threatened. Eyewitness accounts stated later that there were personnel on the airfield in line with the start of the tarmac-surfaced landing strip. Dauchier opened up the throttles to extend his approach to clear them, landing some 200 metres down the runway as a result, but too far. He applied the brakes as harshly as possible to try to reduce the landing run before running out of runway but the speed was still too high and after another 200 metres, he cut the throttles. The result was a swing to port and as soon as one wheel hit the unfinished edge of the runway, the aircraft swung further, one side of the undercarriage collapsed and it ended up close to the airport terminal. Fortunately no one was injured other than for some minor injuries to Dugast and Mendoza. De Lattre was generous in his reaction and even publicly thanked Dauchier for having succeeded in avoiding a more serious accident by his competence, but for RG874 it was the end of its flying days. While the protocol visit continued with the provision of a replacement aircraft by the Argentinian Government, the Halifax's part in it was over.

There matters would have remained. A French investigation absolved Dauchier of blame, though in hindsight it would have been better to have aborted the approach and gone round again. The Halifax remained at the airfield and slowly deteriorated, the Armée de l'Air having decided that the cost of repairing it on site would be prohibitive. The Argentinian Government made several requests as to what was to be done with the aircraft and these letters continued until 1971! Given the efforts that went into rescuing W1048 for the Imperial War Museum just two years later, this was an opportunity missed. The Halifax was eventually pulled from its hangar and cut up for scrap but it did not go without a murmur – during the process, one of the workmen, curious as to what a lever marked 'Pull' would do, did just that. A small explosive sound was followed by a panel blowing away from the port wing root area, releasing the dinghy which still inflated itself. Subsequently retrieved, the dinghy joined other artefacts from this last French Air Force Halifax which were kept in the Mérignac Mess.

On 22 May 1949, one of the Madagascar flights had a small crisis when a fire developed in the port outer engine of RG653: M shortly after take-off. Fortunately, Lt Marill managed to land back at Rabat without causing further damage to the Halifax or its passengers, which included Général de la Morlais.

On 12 June, an air display held at Bordeaux-Mérignac included a Dewoitine 520, a de Havilland Vampire, the SO.6000, a Flight of Shooting Stars, and a Halifax flew over to drop the celebrated parachutist Léo Valentine. However, a major restructuring was taking place in the Air Force and eight days later, a Ministerial Directive saw the demise of GB.1/21 as an identity with the creation of Groupe de Transport GT.1/25. The old radio call sign series of F-RASA to Z were surrendered but the last letter for each aircraft was retained. Bordeaux-Mérignac remained the home airfield for the Halifaxes and transport flights continued to the Congo, Madagascar and Tunisia.

A rare fatal accident occurred on 19 September 1949, when ST800 (F-RAVE) carrying some distinguished passengers, crashed in the landing circuit killing all 17 on board. However, 1950 was a year of steady flights with no serious accidents, just two cases of damage on the ground to RG867 and ST797 (F-RASP). Yet age was catching up with some of the Halifaxes and on 9 November RG620 (F-RASH) and RG655 (F-RASD) were transferred to the School of Mechanics at Rochefort. Repairs were now handicapped by a lack of spares and gradually the Halifax units slipped into decline, but two minor accidents give a date range for the last days; on 3 April, RG869 (F-RASN) burst a tyre and was not repaired and on 15 May, RG491 (F-RASB) was damaged in a crash in Colomb-Béchar.

However, other duties now appeared as one or more Halifaxes were seconded to experimental work both mechanical as well as medical, the latter mainly to do with high altitude physiology research.

Of the identifiable experimental flights undertaken in 1948, RG670: K (F-RAXK) was used to tow a Horsa glider at Brétigny, the first flight taking place on 6 April, the trials continuing until the 17th. On 9 April, RG500: H (F-RAXH) joined the trials, towing another Horsa from Bordeaux-Mérignac being joined later by RG821: N (F-RAXN) and RG670 repeating the trial from Bordeaux-Mérignac to Mont-de-Marsan as part of range tests. This was the nadir of glider assault tactics in favour of parachuting troops into the battlefield and, as in Britain, adoption of the heavy glider for the French Army appears to have waned.

Halifaxes also were detached, some for long periods, to the Centre d'Essais en Vol (CEV) research sites at Brétigny and Istres. Among those identified by French

Camouflage changed for the Halifaxes in 1949 with the familiar night-bomber camouflage replaced by an overall green finish. Unit code letters also disappeared at that time but the aircraft retained their individual code letters. This example, its former code of 'V' clearly visible and, more faintly, both the codes of L8 and H7 has been identified in some sources as ST800; however, close examination shows that the last numeral of the serial number is either '3' or '8'. There is little doubt that the last part of the serial number had been over-painted because the distance between the last digit and the small porthole remains standard, something that can be checked against the Halifax in the background which, although coded 'C', appears previously to have been 'O'. The Handley Page Identification Marking Diagram, Drg. No. 6108, which records all changes from the first issue on 22 February 1943 to the last on 21 January 1946, shows no change to the dimensions or positioning of serial numbers. Dimensions are recorded as being set at 8-in high by 5-in wide, with a 1-in stroke width and set at 1.5-in spacing "with the bottom edge set ten inches above the horizontal centre line of the small porthole", the aft-most letter/digit being placed vertically in line with the leading edge of the horizontal tail plane. The rear turret is a D Mk I suggesting a late production B Mk VI but too many possibilities remain to make a definitive identification and surviving records show no instances of a 'V' being replaced with an 'E' on any of the Halifaxes. (C. Boisselon via J. Delmas)

researchers were PP165, RG491, RG500, RG562, RG670, RG821 and RG867, some of which were used for dropping test models of missiles, carrying sections of missiles for airborne aerodynamic measurements, air testing aerofoils, drag parachutes, etc. During 1948 a model of the NC.271 cabin was air-dropped by a Halifax at Brétigny, four separate tests being carried out during which the test model was twice damaged; the suspension points for the parachute attachment failed on one attempt and the second time the wire intended to measure dropping velocity tangled with the parachute.

A more sophisticated series of tests were conducted in 1950; the Matra (Mécanique Avion Traction) missile system had reached the point of aerodynamic testing and PP165 arrived at Brétigny on 29 March to act as the test aircraft. The bomb bay doors, however, required modification to enable accurate measurement of the aerodynamic characteristics around the bomb bay where the missile was to be mounted and the Halifax was flown back to Bordeaux-Mérignac the same day before returning on 31 March. This was necessary if accurate measurement of the angle of incidence of the wing and tail plane of the missile was to be obtained, a fundamental factor for dropping the missile. The modifications were tested and the first airborne tests took place next day, checking stability to a height between 4,000 and 5,000 metres (13,300 to 16,625 ft). After some checks and adjustments, two further flights took place on 12 and 13 April, after which the missile was removed.

Test work also had its difficult moments for the trials aircraft; on 15 May 1950, RG491: B (F-RASB) was damaged in a crash in Colomb-Béchar during experimental work with the Matra missile system. The pilot had more than 1,000 hours on Halifaxes but the problem developed because of the harsh desert conditions and the poor visibility of the actual runway assigned for the landing. The Halifax touched down 350 metres (1,148 ft) past the start of the runway, ran a short distance then rose into the air before touching down again and swinging violently into a ground loop, wiping off the right and then left undercarriage members. The results of the subsequent investigation report recorded that the runway was 'unsuitable for Halifax aircraft'.

On 4 March 1949, airborne test trials had begun at Brétigny with the full-scale model of the Leduc 010 front section. A little over a year later, on 9 May 1950, a second variant was air-tested, again using RG828. It was followed by a third variant test on 17 April 1951 and a fourth on the 18th. The third variant was tested again on 20 March 1952, but by then the Halifaxes had been withdrawn from front-line service. The last public record of a flight from Bordeaux-Mérignac by RG605: J (F-RASJ) was on 8 October 1951 but it is known that several other Halifaxes remained at the airfield, though their fate is not recorded.

Philippe Ricco's research however has unearthed definite proof that RG703 and RG828 continued flying for a further two years, the latter with the Leduc test programme, with flights being recorded during 1953 on 21 and 22 April, 18, 19 and 29 June and 8 and 17 July.

RG703 was reputed to be involved in an air test with a full-scale mock-up nose section for the SNCASO Onera Deltaviex project, a swept-wing experimental single-seat design, but nothing further is known. However, a recent book by Jean-Claude Payer confirms that RG703: N was part of the CEV Halifax detachment but had a

One of the Halifaxes seconded to the Centre d'Essais en Vol (CEV) and used at the Brétigny and Istres research sites. A full-scale mock-up of the Leduc 010 front section is visible suspended from the bomb bay of what was possibly RG828. One of the two longest serving French Halifaxes, it is reputed to have carried out its last test flight in May 1954, as described in the text. (J. Delmas)

short life after crash-landing into the sand dunes at Bargha. RG828 then carried out all the remaining tests with the Matra M.04 missile during 1953 at Colomb-Béchar, two Siebel Si 204 aircraft accompanying the drop tests to photograph the release and check on the deployment of the stabilising parachute. The bomb bay doors had to be cut back for these tests. One minute before releasing the missile at 100 metres (328 ft) above the test height, the Halifax was required to enter a shallow dive to accelerate before releasing the missile, after which the M.04 engine ignited on a signal from the ground station.... One crew had a hair-raising experience when the missile ignited prematurely, still attached, just 30 cm (11.8 in) below the floor of the Halifax, fortunately without damaging the aircraft.

The first drop test took place on 5 February but bad weather delayed the next until the 13th, taking place from just 200 metres (665 ft). A further test was carried out on 13 March from 250 metres and was followed with a final test from 400-450 metres on 13 April 1953. A final altitude test to determine the practical dropping height by a Halifax was flown in May 1954, 6,316 metres (21,000 ft) being determined as the efficient limit.

The Halifax had served the Armée de l'Air well in a wide variety of roles, and outlasted its last RAF counterparts by more than two years.

Royal Egyptian Air Force

Not unnaturally, Britain had sought other overseas military sales in the immediate post-war period, its excess of military equipment and aircraft piling up as industry slowed, which could not be stopped entirely without causing great disruption. The result of this was that some aircraft were completed, flown to an RAF MU and then sold for scrap, never having flown again.

Aviation Traders Ltd sold 22 A Mk IX Halifaxes to the then Royal Egyptian Air Force (REAF), the Halifaxes being granted temporary civil status for ferrying purposes. However, heightening tensions in the Middle East precipitated the 1950 arms embargo and only nine eventually reached their destination. These were, RT846 (1155), RT793 (1156), RT888 (1157), RT787 (1158), RT852 (1159), RT901 (1160), RT938 (1161), RT907 (1162) and RT788 (1163), of which the last to leave was

RT938, the last of 6,176 production Halifaxes to be built. However, prior to the arrival of these nine aircraft, the REAF already had five C Mk VIIIs, these being HB-AIF, HB-AIG, HB-AIH, HB-AII and HB-AIL, their Swiss civil registrations leaving little doubt as to how they were obtained and it is entirely possible that two may have been the two surviving former Pak-Air C Mk VIII aircraft mentioned below.

The A Mk IXs were stripped of their guns before shipment but were later replaced with Brownings taken from former REAF Spitfire Vc aircraft. Primarily used for transportation work, the Halifaxes also carried out morale-boosting sorties with REAF Lancasters during the 1952 disturbances. Three more found their way to the Egyptian Air Force when Payloads Ltd sold three C Mk VIIIs[15] to Air Globe, Geneva. Never used for commercial services they were sold on to the Egyptian Air Force, thus circumventing the arms embargo. By 1955, their number had been reduced to three because the arms embargo extended to spare parts and the other aircraft were cannibalised to keep the rest flying. The ultimate fate of the three is not known, but during the Suez Crisis in November 1956 combat reports on Egyptian aircraft destroyed by strafing included what possibly were some, if not all three, remaining Halifaxes.

Pakistan Air Force

Airtech Ltd, which set up at Thame airfield, was another post-war company that built its business on overhaul, maintenance and conversion of former military aircraft. In 1946, eight B Mk VIs[16] arrived from Stansted for modification to allow them to carry spare Hercules engines in the bomb bay. Five had never been in RAF service and were originally sold to London Aero Motors Service and appeared on the Civil Aviation register; RG782 was the odd one out, having been issued to No 2 Radio School. From there it must have been put up for sale and possibly delivered to Thame under its RAF airworthiness certificate as it did not appear on the British Civil Aviation register. These were sold to the Pakistan Air Force and ferried out to Pakistan in mid-1949 by British-American Air Service crews. Issued to 12 Squadron, they were used for reconnaissance duties, freight-carrying and training. They were supplemented by the surviving two C Mk VIIIs, AP-ACH PP292 and AP-ACG PP323, purchased in 1948 and operated by the civil airline Pak-Air Ltd; these were used as instructional airframes until all the Halifaxes were phased out in 1955.

Seven Halifax B Mk VIs were purchased by the Royal Pakistan Air Force and allocated serial numbers in the M1100 range. Delivered in standard RAF night-bomber camouflage, after arrival in Pakistan they were stripped back to bare metal and the national markings of their new owner applied. These markings consisted of white-centred green roundels and fin flashes of a white crescent and single white star on a green square. All seven were fitted with D Mk 1 tail turrets but no AGLT.

The Egyptian Government had ordered 22 A Mk IXs but only nine were delivered before heightening political tensions precipitated the 1950 arms embargo. All were given temporary civil registrations for the transfer flight, added only on the rear of the fuselage, as shown here by RT901 G-ALVK. Standard Bomber Command night camouflage was retained to which were added REAF identity numbers in Arabic numerals, 1160 in this instance, and military markings. Roundels were green white and green, narrowly outlined in white, with a white crescent and three white stars superimposed on the central disc; fin flashes were in the same colours. Positioning for each marking was as for RAF bombers, with the exception that roundels were marked also on the underside of each wing. This Halifax had been delivered to the RAF in January 1946 and sent to the Middle East, before being purchased by Aviation Traders on 18 August 1949. (A. J. Jackson)

CHAPTER FOURTEEN

SWORDS INTO PLOUGHSHARES

1945-1953

THE Halifax's capacious interior ensured that it was used for other than its intended primary role of heavy bomber. The SOE squadrons were the first to exploit this potential to some degree, with agent and supply dropping sorties over occupied Europe. The temporary detachment of some of their Halifaxes to 511 Squadron for emergency freighting duties in December 1942 has already been mentioned in Chapter Seven; although used only temporarily for this purpose, these Halifaxes had no special modifications other than those required for their more clandestine duties.

A more definitive conversion was made at 144 Maintenance Unit, Maison Blanche. In addition to other commitments, this unit was responsible for maintenance and repairs to Middle East-based Halifaxes, as well as dispatching working parties to locations as far afield as Italy for this purpose. Several time-expired B Mk II Halifaxes that had seen service with Nos 148, 178 and 462 Squadrons were modified as freighters to carry Merlin, Twin Wasp and Hercules engines or a Spitfire fuselage, semi-externally between sheet metal side plates that projected downwards from the bomb bay. These modifications were very much of local origin and inspiration and it is interesting to note that it would not be until April 1946 that official trials were made with a Mk III, NA137 at the AFTDU, fitted with external engine carriage gear.

The first of these conversions was completed around March 1944 and by August four Halifaxes had been so modified and put to good use[1]. During October the first of these had completed 300 hours of flying and was due for a major overhaul, with an almost identical figure being achieved by the combined efforts of all four Halifax freighters during November. The total weight carried to that date amounted to 284,000 lb and included 20 Merlin engines, 13 Pratt & Whitney engines and 93 passengers.

The prototype C Mk VI LV838 photographed in June 1945. Produced in the first week of February 1944 as a standard B Mk III it spent its working life at the A&AEE until struck off charge on 28 November 1946. It incorporated all the recommendations obtained from test-flying with another B Mk VI, TW783, which had its all-up weight gradually increased to 68,000 lb. The 272 cubic feet pannier was also adopted as standard for the new marque. Although used as the prototype for this freight and passenger version, it retained its rear turret complete with Monica dipole aerial.

This closer view of the 8,000 lb capacity freight pannier fitted to LV838 also shows the engine cooling fans tested on this Halifax when it was re-engined with Hercules 100 engines to bring it up to B Mk VI standard. Although subjected to a series of tests, the fan modification was not adopted for production Mk VI aircraft.

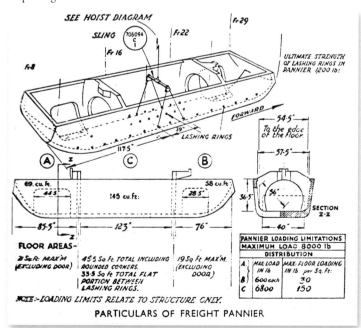

Details of the construction and dimensions of the 8,000 lb freight pannier developed at the Transport Command Development Unit and subsequently used for a wide variety of Halifaxes, both military and civil.

This type of role was not new to Handley Page as the original 1936 specification had listed carriage of personnel, and in 1937 the Company had been asked if the design could also be converted for the carrying of passengers. However, after examination, the design section rejected the idea on the grounds of the, then, power to weight ratio of the existing design. By 1942, the idea of a freight version for carrying equipment had re-emerged within the company and proposals for four variants were examined with some involving an increase in fuselage depth to nine feet. A proposal was submitted to the MAP in January 1943 for a civil version, which was far-sighted given the stage of the war's progress; but perhaps too far-sighted, as no encouragement was offered from official quarters. Undaunted, the Company began a preliminary design under the type designation HP64, which progressed far enough for them to engage in discussions about civil airworthiness standards.

Seen here in April 1945, Halifax C Mk III NA195 was originally issued to 10 Squadron on 29 November 1944 where it was coded first as 'F- Freddie' and later 'R-Robert'. It was transferred to Leconfield on 27 February 1945 and converted to C Mk III configuration and fitted with a flush-fitting 3,000 lb pannier, the streamlined front edge of which projected slightly below the line of the fuselage and is just visible immediately behind the Window-dropping chute. Flush riveting was used throughout and a slightly gloss black finish applied to side and lower surfaces. It was never issued to a squadron in this configuration, apparently suffering damage in an accident and passing to 47 MU on 7 April where it was struck off charge as Category E2 (write-off) on 5 March 1947.

Discussion was already taking place with the specialist committee examining proposals for prospective future and post-war transport conversions and the British Overseas Airways Corporation (BOAC) submitted a paper comparing the Halifax and York designs. By then the Air Staff had already examined the possibility of producing an inexpensive and quickly adaptable interim military transport, designated 'Transport A', and an unarmed version of it termed 'Transport B'. The subsequent rounds of meetings and discussions eventually eliminated the HP64 project in favour of the 'Transport A' concept, which was to be a conversion of maximum simplicity. One result of the discussions was the issue of Specification 15/43, which would eventuate as the HP67 Hastings; the other, immediate decision was a stripped-down version of the B Mk III or B Mk VII. The 'Transport A' idea crystallised as the former, and B Mk III LV838 was used for the trial installation of a bomb bay pannier[2] which had been developed by the Transport Command Development Unit. Two forms of pannier had evolved: a flush fitting 3,000 lb capacity model but LV838 was to trial the second, 8,000 lb, 272 cubic feet model which projected well below the fuselage.

While construction and testing work progressed, the point had been reached where a positive start was being made to exploit this advantage by field-testing the 'Transport A' option, and on 31 October 1944, a signal was sent by No 41 Group, advising 246 Squadron that it was being allocated four Mk III Halifaxes. These had the mid-upper turret and all armament removed but retained the E Mk I tail turret. The squadron had re-formed at Lyneham only days before from the Liberator Flight of 511 Squadron – thus bringing the Halifax connection full circle as it were – and was to be used on the UK - India transport route. The Halifax Development Flight (HDF), however, was to concentrate on developing a UK - Cairo West route and became C Flight, A Flight having Liberators and B Flight Yorks, the latter having arrived at the same time as the Halifaxes.

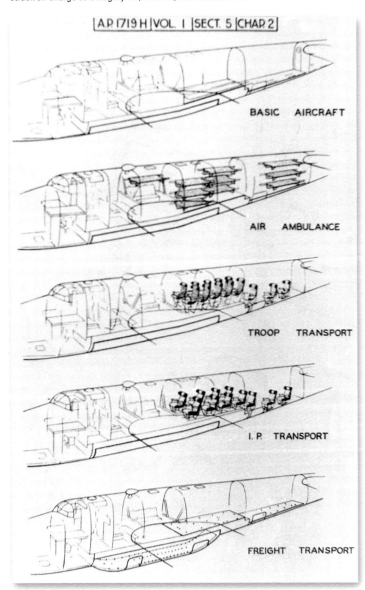

AP. 1719 H | VOL. 1 | SECT. 5 | CHAP 2

BASIC AIRCRAFT

AIR AMBULANCE

TROOP TRANSPORT

I. P. TRANSPORT

FREIGHT TRANSPORT

This illustration shows the five standard options available for C Mk III and C Mk VI transport conversion of the standard bomber version. At the top the standard bomber version, next the ten-stretcher air ambulance, then the thirteen-place troop transport, then the eleven-seat I.P. (Important Person) conversion and finally, the freight version with interior stripped and floor panelling fitted with cargo restraint hard points.

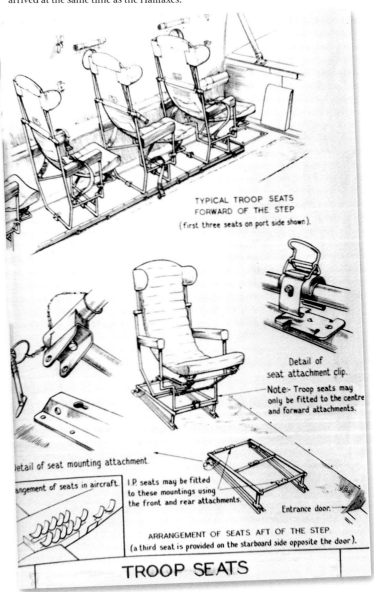

TYPICAL TROOP SEATS
FORWARD OF THE STEP
(first three seats on port side shown).

Detail of seat attachment clip.

Note:- Troop seats may only be fitted to the centre and forward attachments.

Detail of seat mounting attachment.

arrangement of seats in aircraft.

I.P. seats may be fitted to these mountings using the front and rear attachments.

Entrance door.

ARRANGEMENT OF SEATS AFT OF THE STEP.
(a third seat is provided on the starboard side opposite the door).

TROOP SEATS

An illustration of the seating for the standard troop transport configuration showing how seating for the ten sets on the main floor level was attached to twin rails secured to the floor. The remaining three seats in the lower floor section had individual floor fittings and all were quickly and easily removable to turn the aircraft into a pure freight version.

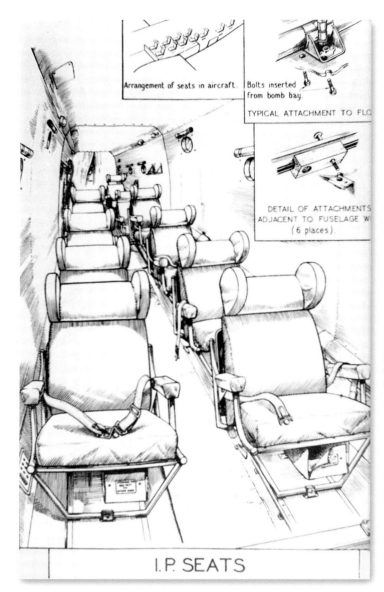

I.P. SEATS

As shown here, the eleven I.P. seating arrangement utilised a more comfortable form of seat made by Rumbolds and the interior of the passenger cabin was lined and sound-proofed. A very similar form of seating, again made by Rumbolds, would be used for the civil version operated by BOAC post-war.

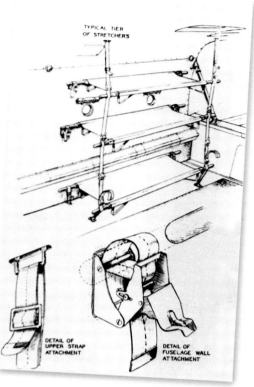

The air ambulance configuration used suspended stretcher attachment webbing, eliminating the need to transfer wounded to a fixed stretcher when loading.

A very interesting sequence of changes of identity and role are captured in this view of LW385: H which, built in November 1943 as a B Mk III, served briefly with Nos 431 and 434 Squadrons RCAF between March and October 1944. After conversion for glider towing and paratroop dropping, it passed to 190 (GT) Squadron in 1945 where it gained its heavy duty tyres. Given that the under wing serial numbers dates the photograph to post-August 1945, the presence of B Mk III RG431 in the background still wearing the 'ZA' code of 10 Squadron suggests that the location may have been an MU where conversion work was carried out. Interestingly, RG431 had been issued to 96 Squadron at the beginning of 1945 when it was allocated an equipment establishment of 26 C Mk III Halifaxes. Within two months, this establishment was revised to Dakotas and the Halifaxes were withdrawn when, presumably, RG431 was refitted as a bomber, such was the versatile nature of the Halifax. No 190 (GT) Squadron only retained its Halifaxes for a few months and LW385 was then allocated to the RAE. (B. Robertson)

During December, a study was made to see what would be the best arrangement for the carriage of passengers and on the 13th NA683 left on a trial trip to Cairo. Although the HDF was still in the experimental stages, on 19 December it was asked to undertake a special flight to India. Satisfied with the results, it began operating regularly in January 1945 when NA683 left Lyneham on the 17th on the UK - Istres - Cairo service. This was the first time that a Halifax had undertaken this scheduled service and the next run, on 21 January, was made by NA679. Two more Halifaxes, LW547 and LW548, were taken on strength, but a third, NA177, was cancelled before it could be physically allotted. Instructions were received for LW547 to carry out an experimental trooping flight to Karachi with 10 passengers and kit plus two Bristol Aeroplane Co. representatives to advise on engine operation. These orders were amended the next day and the Halifax finally left carrying 4,000 lb of freight – the passenger seats were detached and stacked in the fuselage as well.

Just as the flight was settling into an operational routine it was transferred to RAF Merryfield on 12 March; there it became the nucleus of a resurrected 187 Squadron, which had formed on 1 February and was to have had an initial establishment of 25 C Mk III Halifaxes, as the freighter version was now designated. Its purpose was to carry out small-scale trooping to India and the HDF was to be serviced and maintained by the squadron. However, a reshuffling of events overtook the arrangements, with Dakotas being allocated to the squadron before the Halifaxes had barely started their task. F/Lt Wilson had left on 15 March to conduct a Special Survey flight (HEN 291) to India. F/O Kendal then carried out a special flight to Castel Benito (HEN 296) in LW548 on 23 March, NA679 returning to Lyneham the same day from Luqa (HEN 292), having flown out to Malta several days before. The Development Flight Halifaxes continued to operate their runs to the Middle East until the end of March, the unit being disbanded on 3 April 1945.

The second Halifax Transport Squadron, No 96, was officially formed at Leconfield on 30 December 1944 under the authority of Transport Command with the same aircraft establishment as that proposed for 187 Squadron. The reason for placing a Transport Command Squadron at a Bomber Command Group station was justified by maintenance reasons; only 640 Squadron was using Leconfield at the time and the station had accommodation for two squadrons. However, as 96 Squadron was a lodger unit it was intended to transfer it to a Transport Command station at a later date. The 96 Squadron Halifaxes had been converted from standard B Mk III configuration by removing all armament, the mid-upper turret, H2S scanner and housing, the *Monica* set and the tri-cell flare chute. With their interiors stripped bare, each aircraft could handle freight, nine stretcher cases or 14 passengers for whom eight seats could be fitted in the rear of the fuselage with six more in the rest bay benches amidships.

Flying personnel consisted of tour-expired crews from Bomber Command and included a high percentage of RAAF personnel. Training flights began soon after the arrival of the first four Halifaxes, RG422, RG423, RG425 and RG428 on 7 and 8 January, with a further nine, RG371, RG377, RG413, RG420, RG424, RG426, RG427, RG 429 and RG431, arriving shortly after. On 2 February, the squadron was notified that it was eventually to be sent to the Middle East to replace 267 Squadron,

A conversion of B Mk VI, PP225, served as the prototype C Mk VIII, the new marque appearing in Transport Command's temperate sea scheme of Dark Green and Ocean Grey upper surfaces and Medium Sea Grey under surfaces. It is seen here at Boscombe Down during its intensive testing period conducted between 4 and 27 April.

PP217, the first production C Mk VIII, was delivered to the Air Transport Tactical Development Unit on 9 June 1945 for intensive handling and general service trials which continued throughout the remainder of the year. It was damaged in a minor landing accident at Ringway on 30 November, which kept it out of action until 18 January 1946. The red 'X' marking on the rear fuselage related to its testing period as the C Mk VIIIs of both of the two Polish squadrons used conventional post-war white codes in full. This photograph, showing it with the cowlings removed and the tail wheel partly deflated, was taken after it had been struck off charge and put up for sale. Purchased by London & Aero Motor Services it was never placed on the Civil Register and was eventually sold to the Ministry of Civil Aviation Fire School on 2 January 1948.

which had been operating Dakotas since 1943. That same month the squadron received a further two aircraft, MZ458 and MZ464, but lost MZ464 on the 25th when it crashed near Brantingham, three miles north of Brough, killing the crew of four and the two passengers.

On 9 February, the squadron received official authority for transfer to the Mediterranean Allied Air Forces (MAAF) but on 16 March it was notified that its establishment had been changed to Dakotas which would be supplied by MAAF sources. Accordingly, three Halifaxes, RG371, RG413 and RG420, were placed in storage while the remainder[3] were first transferred to 10 Squadron, which was still operating as a bomber squadron, before being sent to 29 MU at High Ercall.

This by no means signified the end of the Halifax as a pure transport aircraft. Testing of a standard B Mk VI Halifax continued at Boscombe Down during January and February 1946 and TW783 was flown at an increased all-up weight of 68,000 lb with the centre of gravity at the aftermost limit. Thorough tests were carried out under all flight conditions and during a full-limit dive the aircraft began pitching and was unable to exceed 300 mph IAS, even when using full nose-heavy trim. The cause was found to be loss of fabric from the starboard elevator; the fabric attachment strings had apparently chafed against the rib flanges through ballooning on the top surface near the leading edge, thought at the time to be an isolated case and not attributable to the increase in the all-up weight. Engine failure at low airspeeds also posed some problems and after trying several flap settings, it was recommended that 20 degrees be used for take-off and that the flaps should not be retracted until a good margin of speed and height had been attained.

The very clean lines of the C Mk VIII can be appreciated in this view in which the doors for the wing bomb cells are clearly visible, the space being retained for extra cargo. Under wing roundels are the so-called C1 type permitted for use on under surfaces where daylight camouflage was applied but no under wing serials were carried as the war in the Pacific was still being fought. (via B. Robertson)

Two modifications were also recommended to improve handling characteristics following engine failure, the rudder balance tab gearing was increased and the rudder trim wheel moved from the left-hand side to the right-hand side of the pilot's seat, making it more accessible.

Both modifications were incorporated on LV838, which, as noted earlier, was serving as the prototype C Mk VI. Additionally, the rudder angular movement outboard had been limited to 18 degrees instead of 20. The same equipment was removed as from the C Mk III version; the bomb bay doors were also removed, and a 272 cu ft freight pannier fitted to the lower fuselage, giving the Halifax a decidedly pregnant profile.

The practicality of fitting such a bulky item stemmed from the early Halifax operations with 4,000 and 8,000 lb bombs and the subsequent test using B Mk II, V9985, fitted with a set of bulged bomb bay doors, which completely enclosed the large bombs. Trials carried out in January 1943 had shown no adverse effect on the handling characteristics. As noted in Chapter 10, 50 sets of bulged bomb bay doors had been ordered before production was cancelled, followed by a discussion for their reinstatement at the MAP planning conference in mid-1943. While production of the doors was never reinstated, the new pannier bore a very close resemblance to them and was almost identical in dimensions and contours. The presence of the new pannier had little effect upon the handling characteristics, which were similar to those of a standard B Mk VI, but asymmetric handling qualities had been improved by modification of the rudder tab gearing. Rudder forces were lighter and allowed reductions in the minimum flying speeds under asymmetric conditions of about 15 mph in the case of engine failure after take-off and about 50 mph in the case of steady flight with two engines dead on one side. The rudder trimmer was very powerful and one full turn of the wrist was sufficient to apply full trim, which in some instances led to over-trimming which was initially mistaken for rudder overbalance, and pilots were cautioned to exercise care. During the dive tests, the elevators again shed some fabric, as had happened previously with TW783. A new set of strengthened elevators was fitted incorporating holding-down plates to prevent the fabric coming away from the metal skin of the nose section, and no further trouble was experienced after this.

Because it was considered that it might prove impossible to jettison the cargo, a series of tests was made with one and two engines cut and showed that the aircraft could be flown straight and level at 160 mph IAS using two divisions of aileron trim. At speeds below this, very mild rudder overbalance occurred but this was easily overcome by exerting a small foot load and by adopting a small amount of bank. Alternatively, by applying 10 degrees of bank from the start, the speed

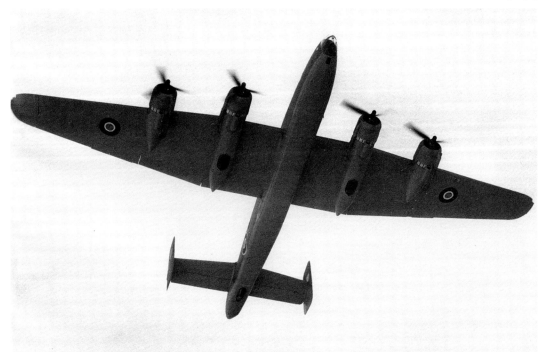

could be reduced to 135 mph IAS without any overbalance occurring, but at this speed full rudder trim, full aileron trim and a medium foot load were required. For general flying over a speed range of 180 to 230 mph IAS, the aircraft was found easy and pleasant to fly.

The Bristol Aeroplane Co., interested in extreme cold weather effects on both engines and airframe, was also experimenting with a B Mk VI and had sent RG814 to Canada for winterisation trials during the winter of 1945/46. The Halifax departed on 9 November 1945, arrived at Dorval on the 11th, and then flew on to Churchill, Manitoba, where the trials were conducted. Exposed to the bitterly cold winds from Hudson Bay, the location was well chosen and while standing at dispersal, the nose Perspex cracked at -35°C. The trials continued and following their completion, RG814 remained in Canada 'on loan' until it returned to Bristol on 30 September 1947 before finally being struck off charge on 5 May 1948.

The 'Transport B' concept took a different course and developed as an unarmed version of the Halifax with a tail cone replacing the rear turret and incorporating the Mod 1377 pannier; the work was coincidental with the C Mk VI prototype trials with PP225 serving as the prototype for what was now designated the HP70, C Mk VIII. This version was to have a carrying capacity for freight or 11 passengers or 10 stretchers plus extra windows in the fuselage forward of the main crew entrance door[3]. With all turrets removed, the fitting of a tail cone increased the overall fuselage length to 73 ft 7 in and the removal of the rear turret required a half a degree reduction in the tail plane incidence to allow for the forward movement of the centre of gravity. The elevator trim range was also decreased, as was downward movement of the elevator from 19 degrees to 17, while the upward range was increased by 2 degrees to 27. The trim tabs were set at 2 degrees upwards relative to the elevators' neutral setting.

Resplendent in Dark Green and Medium Sea Grey camouflage with Light Blue undersides, PP225 began its initial trials at Boscombe Down on 4 April and these continued until the 27th. Handling tests were made at weights of 50,000 lb and 68,000 lb and in most respects, the C Mk VIII as it was now designated, behaved like a standard B Mk VI, except that it proved impossible at either loading to induce a normal stall with flaps and undercarriage up because of the lack of elevator power. Having failed during dive tests, the elevators were replaced with the strengthened type as fitted to LV838 but these in turn failed after eight dives up to speeds of 320 mph IAS. They were replaced by a new set and no further difficulty was encountered. Rudder trouble was experienced under asymmetric conditions but subsequent trials on 25 and 26 May, incorporating the same modifications as applied to LV838, eliminated the problem. However, although this reduced the minimum speeds at which control could be regained following an engine failure at take-off, either clean or with undercarriage and flaps down, speeds were still considered high. It was therefore recommended that if an outboard engine failed on take-off when undercarriage and flaps were down, the corresponding engine on the opposite wing should be cut and the aircraft landed straight ahead.

A top priority order for 100 was placed with Handley Page and subsequently all were built at the Cricklewood plant. It was to be the smallest production run of any marque of Halifax. The first production C Mk VIII, PP217, was delivered to the ATTDU on 9 June 1945 for an intensive series of handling and general service trials. These continued throughout the remainder of the year, but a minor landing accident at Ringway on 30 November subsequently required repairs that kept it out of action until 18 January 1946.

However, the type had already proven itself and in November 1945, 301 (Polish) Squadron, at that time employed on freighting missions to Oslo, Istres, Naples and Athens with Warwick Mk IIIs, was notified that it was to re-equip with C Mk VIIIs with training lectures on the Hercules 100 engines to begin in December. No 304 (Polish) Squadron, its sister unit at Chedburgh, was also notified that its elderly Wellington Mk XIVs would be exchanged for Warwick Mk IIIs in November, but the type replacement was amended on 11 January 1946 to C Mk VIII Halifaxes.

No 301 Squadron, which expressed its pleasure at renewing acquaintance with the Halifax, was given priority and the first 18 aircraft were allotted directly to it, 304 Squadron taking over all the transport commitments during this period. It was intended that re-equipping should take place at the rate of five aircraft a week, but delays held up this schedule. F/Lt K. Twardawa ferried in PP221 from 45 MU on 15 January 1946, a second arrived on the 13th and a third on the 29th. With typical Polish enthusiasm, the squadron began rounding up any pilots and flight engineers with four-engine aircraft experience, their 'bag' eventually including one from No 45 Group who was currently serving at Dorval in Canada. By the end of the month, 33 crews were on strength and fully trained.

An urgent request by HQ No 46 Group produced a further six Halifaxes in February and nine more by the end of March. F/Lt Rusiecki made 301 Squadron's inaugural flight in PP328 to Hassani, a previous attempt having failed because engine

As the first privately owned C Mk VIII placed on the Civil Register, PP336 was converted expressly for the Maharajah Gaekwar of Baroda into what, in BOAC designation, became known as Halton standard, making it the only Halton Mk 2 conversion. The spacious and luxuriously appointed interior included a fixed table and plush seating. Seen here displaying the Maharajah's personal coat of arms on the nose, it was later sold to Alpha Airways who operated it as ZS-BTA until it was scrapped in 1953.

failure forced the aircraft to return. Regular route work began on 15 March with a service to Naples each Saturday and one to Athens each Tuesday and Thursday. However, due to repatriation of personnel and political reasons, an order was issued on 9 April that all flying by the squadron was to cease with effect from 17 April. This was later rescinded and training flights continued, but no aircraft was permitted to land outside the British Isles. Any aircraft currently at continental locations were to be collected only if arrangements had already been made.

No 301 Squadron's operational career with the C Mk VIII was thus virtually stillborn and only 15 flights, including the inaugural one, were made. No 304 Squadron, which had surrendered all its flying personnel with four-engine experience to 301 Squadron, never became operational with the type as its first Halifaxes did not arrive until May. Yet, both squadrons continued a very active training programme with 304 Squadron averaging approximately 140 hours per month. Accidents were few, although PP236 was damaged in a heavy landing after hitting a ditch shortly after being transferred from 301 Squadron in June. One serious accident occurred on 23 August when PP232 stalled whilst banking around the circuit at 900 ft and crashed at Green Farm in Suffolk, killing the crew. Instructions were finally received ordering the cessation of flying from 21 November, both squadrons being disbanded with effect from 10 December 1946.

These two squadrons were the only ones to use the C Mk VIII Halifax and after their disbandment, the task of freight and passenger transportation was integrated into the duties of the Halifax squadrons of No 38 Group. PP285 was retained for further development work by Handley Page and, like other examples produced after VJ Day, it was finished in polished bare metal and retained RAF national markings since technically it was owned by the Air Ministry and still a military aircraft.

However, the C Mk VIII Halifax had by no means disappeared from use. In September 1945, BOAC had requested, and been granted, the loan of three C Mk VIII Halifaxes[4] for a three month period, which produced an anomalous situation as the type was not in service with the RAF at that time. They were flown extensively, carrying freight and mail on an experimental service to West Africa, the objective being to test for maximum utilisation, with inspections and overhauls being carried out at night at their various terminal points. Over a period of two months, the three aircraft logged some 2,000 flying hours, averaging 205 mph on the cruise with an average flying time of 45 hrs 27 min. Comments were submitted to Handley Page by BOAC about weatherproofing, draughts, minor changes to the hydraulic system, some unreliability of fuel contents gauges, sharp projections and rough edges, etc., the latter not surprising since these were military aircraft. Yet the overall results showed them to be suitable for medium-range operations carrying 10 passengers and 3,500 lb of cargo.

The first privately-owned Halifax to appear on the post-war British Civil Register was C Mk VIII PP336, purchased through Thomas Cook and Son Ltd along with a B Mk III on 25 February 1946 and collected from 29 MU at High Ercall. The buyer of PP336 was the well-known racehorse owner, His Highness the Maharajah Gaekwar of Baroda who required a speedy means of transport for his family and staff between India and his new headquarters at Newmarket. The aircraft received a Certificate of Airworthiness (C of A) on 20 March and the British civil registration G-AGZP. Rumbolds carried out interior finishing and furnishing while Handley Page added heavy-duty tyres and wheels fitted with more powerful brakes to bring it into line with the civil Halton standard being established for BOAC. British American Air Services were contracted to crew and service what was, retrospectively, to be known as the only Halton Mk 2; S/Ldr E. A. Hood and a special crew flew the Halifax

G-AGXA Waltzing Matilda photographed after arriving at Mascot airport, Sydney, Australia as the luggage was being unloaded and journalists were interviewing the passengers. With its paint work beginning to show the ravages of time and use, the original 466 Squadron code of HD-T and RAF roundels had been painted over but the artwork and daylight tactical markings had been retained, possibly a useful aid if the aircraft had had to make a forced landing en route to Australia. The turrets and H2S radome were also still in situ. The stencilled yellow block letters above the crew entrance door reads HALIFAX EXHIBITION FLIGHT IN AID OF RAF BENEVOLENT FUND AND RAAF WELFARE FUND. (J. Hopton collection)

Handley Page Halifax, B Mk III
Ex NR169.T, formally of 466 Squadron RAAF (see page 112). This was the first Mk III to join the civil register as G-AGXA and was flown to Australia in 1946.

to Bombay and back in an air time of 56 hrs 30 min for the 10,749-mile round trip.

The B Mk III was privately purchased by former ATA pilot Mr G. N. Wickner to transport both his family and other expatriate Australians home. It was sent to Handley Page's Radlett works in February for a thorough inspection and conversion to civil transport configuration with seating for 15 passengers, plus baggage. Granted its C of A on 16 May 1946 and registered G-AGXA, it became the first of two Mk IIIs to appear on the Civil Register; the other was G-AJPG, alias NA684, used by the College of Aeronautics at Cranfield. Wickner had a dual purpose, one to transport his family back to Australia and the other to exhibit the Halifax as a fund-raiser for the RAF Benevolent Fund and the RAAF Welfare Fund.

Wickner completed his trip to Australia in 71 hours' flying time, leaving Hurn airport on 26 May and touching down at Mascot airport, Sydney on 15 June. The Halifax carried his wife and two children, along with 16 other migrants who could find no other way of reaching Australia. Few internal structural alterations had been made other than putting in some seating and removing the armament from the turrets, thus leaving NR169 in much the same condition in which it had completed 51 operations with 466 Squadron as HD-T. Unfortunately, in the immediate post-war climate of austerity, no financial support was forthcoming for the proposed exhibition flights and the aircraft had to be sold, a group of pilots and engineers purchasing it for air trading in the Far East operating as Air Carriers Ltd.

The final phase for a very rare civil Halifax; registered now as VH-BDT, 'Waltzing Matilda' receives some further attention from the Sydney press corps, including a movie camera, at the launching of the company's new service. The relaxed access to airport areas and facilities makes an interesting comparison with the heavily regimented and security conscious airports of today. (J. Hopton)

All camouflage paint was removed, the existing registration was repainted in black and a cheat line of the same colour marked from nose to tail. The name *Waltzing Matilda* was reapplied, this time to the nose section in script form with the company logo and name also painted along the nose section lower down. It was then placed on the Australian Civil Register as VH-BDT with the wife of the New South Wales Premier, Mrs McGerr, carrying out the launching ceremony at Bankstown airport on 6 March 1947; by coincidence, its new captain, Edmund Hourigan, had flown NR169 on operations with 466 Squadron. However, it made only one trip in June 1947 to Singapore and, suffering a heavy landing en route, limped back to Sydney with the port outer engine feathered. It never flew again and financial problems then saw it sold to a scrap dealer; it languished at Mascot airport until finally gutted by vandals.

Turning back to April 1946, Handley Page had issued a brochure on their HP 70 interim civil transport, a passenger conversion of the C Mk VIII transport. BOAC, encouraged by its experience with the three C Mk VIIIs loaned to the company, decided to go ahead with its programme of using Halifaxes for its West

Below: Looking forward to the steward's doors to the pantry area while on the right-hand side of the photograph can be seen the step-up to the raised floor level, carpeted in dark blue, with its handrail attached to the side of the fuselage. The handrail fitted to the back of each seat could be raised to let the hinged back section fold down to provide a tray unit with an attached, swivelling glass holder. The sign on the back of the upholstery told passengers that their life preserver and oxygen mask were stowed beneath the seat. An elasticised pocket for small items such as books was attached to the wall beside each seat and a non-fume ashtray allowed for smoking. Each square window was fitted with coffee-coloured curtains that passengers could close if required and a clock was mounted on the front cabin wall. The size and comfort of the interior are well illustrated. (Short Brothers and Harland)

A view looking aft towards the entrance door vestibule situated on the starboard side, which, separated from the gangway by a curtain, contained a wardrobe for coats and hats. The carpeting cabin bore the BOAC 'Speedbird' logo. The seating was the RAF Transport Command 'Important Person' design manufactured by Rumbolds Ltd as model J. I. P. 43 and was finished in a dark blue ribbed material. The addition of a 12" x 15" window beside each seat plus an air outlet, a small light and a simple net rack overhead provided quality and comfort for the airline passenger of 1946. The walls were fitted with soundproof quilted fire-resistant fibreglass, which was then covered with 1.5 mm spruce plywood finished off with a covering of two shades of beige Vynide, dark below the window sill line and light above. (Short Brothers and Harland)

Looking forward at the compact installation of equipment fitted in the steward's galley located in the former rest bay area between the main spars. A water heater was fitted above the sink unit with a water pump alongside. Food cupboards are on the right with an open rack to one side while directly above is a wine rack. Flying controls were accessible through the rear section of some cupboards and the fuel distribution cocks were housed under the step to the two small doors above the front spar leading to the flight deck while, out of sight on each side in this view, was a handle for the emergency release of each undercarriage unit. However, the layout seen here did vary slightly between the early and later model Haltons. (Short Brothers and Harland)

G-AHDU was the subject of the official naming ceremony for the BOAC Halton fleet. The BOAC Speedbird emblem, company initials and the individual aircraft name FALKIRK were applied to both sides of the nose with the Union flag placed across the outer face of each fin and rudder assembly. The colour scheme was to DTD Spec 260A of one coat grey primer Type S and one coat of aluminium with all lettering in either BOAC blue or Marine Blue DTD Spec 62A, edged in gold, the anti-glare panel being Night Black DTD Spec 314. The BOAC and Speedbird markings were later repositioned, the latter to the position occupied by 'BOAC' as shown here with two pale stripes extending aft from the emblem with 'BOAC' positioned above and the name Speedbird added beneath. The name FALKIRK was repositioned beneath the circular port on the nose cone.

level with two fitted, one behind the other, on the port side at the same floor level. The fuselage walls were finished in two shades of beige while the seats and carpet were in standard BOAC livery blue. Individual lights, a stewards' call button and oxygen equipment were provided at each passenger position. The main interior lighting came from three roof-mounted fittings while a single window of approximately 12 in x 15 in at each seat position provided natural lighting. A large passenger door was fitted in the starboard fuselage side near the tail plane, a small vestibule for hats and coats isolating it from the main cabin proper. Toilet facilities were fitted in the extreme rear of the fuselage. A well-equipped pantry occupied what had formerly been the amidships rest bay position and was screened from the passenger cabin by means of swinging doors. The metal nose cone was fitted with a door on the port side providing access to a small freight compartment, while the main freight was carried in the 8,000 lb capacity fuselage pannier.

Delivery of the aircraft to BOAC began in July 1946 and the type was officially named 'Halton' during a christening ceremony at Radlett on the 18th, Lady Winster, the wife of the then Minister for Civil Aviation, carrying out the ceremony with G-AHDU and naming it *Falkirk*. The first six, G-AHDU, G-AHDM *Falmouth*, G-AHDW *Falaise*, G-AHDV *Finisterre*, G-AHDS *Fremantle* and G-AHDL *Fitzroy* were received by September but none was fitted with de-icing equipment. A limited service commenced in September 1946 but after six weeks, the aircraft were grounded due to an hydraulic fault and returned to the manufacturer for repair and the fitting of de-icing equipment. As a stopgap measure the Air Ministry loaned eight, now civil-registered C Mk VIIIs to the company: G-AHYH, G-AHYI, G-AIAN, G-AIAO (the anomaly mentioned below), G-AIAP, G-AIAR, G-AIAS and G-AIID – two of which, G-AIAR and G-AIAS, had already flown briefly with the RAF prior to their civil registration. PP272, however, although allocated the civil registration G-AIAO, had flown the route-proving flight to Accra on 13 October 1945. PP325, which appears in some records also as G-AIAO, was loaned to the company for training purposes, but was destroyed in a crash-landing at Aldermaston on 8 July 1946 - prior to delivery of the Haltons.

Finished in the elegant LAMS royal blue and white colour scheme, G-AHZJ was photographed at Stansted prior to the application of its name 'Port of Marseilles'. One of the original six company machines, it was lost in a crash at Bergamo, Italy on 31 July 1947. (R. Riding)

African services to bridge the 12- to 14-month delay before the introduction of its Avro Tudor IIs and issued a contract for 12 modified aircraft. Accordingly, 14 C Mk VIIIs were sent to Short Brothers and Harland Ltd at Belfast for modification to the passenger role after Handley Page completed the necessary structural adjustments. The main external distinguishing refinements were a metal nose cone, a large entrance door on the starboard side, elimination of the crew entrance hatch and the fitting of small square windows to replace the fuselage portholes.

The cabin was fitted with 10 Rumbold (VIP) semi-adjustable seats, (the same type used for RAF VIP transport), eight equally spaced side-by-side on the main floor

Handley Page Halifax, Mk VIII
PP247, G-AHZJ of London Aero & Motor Service Ltd (LAMS), later given the name 'Port of Marseilles'. Crashed at Bergamo in Italy on 31.7.47.

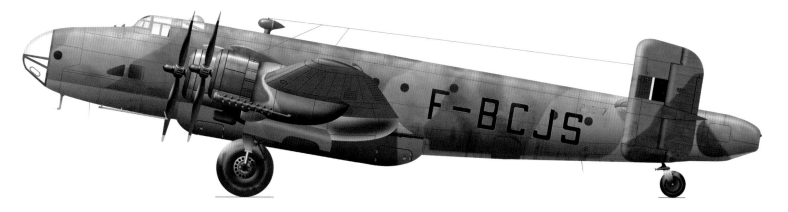

Handley Page Halifax, Mk VIII
Ex PP287, F-BCJS of Aerocargo in 1948. The aircraft crashed on take-off from Casablanca airport 1.12.48.

Purchased by Anglo French Distributors Ltd on 25 October 1947 as G-AGPC, PP287 received its C of A on 20 January 1948. Subsequently sold to Aerocargo, it received its French registration of F-BCJS on 20 October 1948. Seen here, it still wears its RAF day camouflage with the French registration but shows no sign of its British registration, which presumably only appeared on the paperwork for the sale. Its camouflage was later stripped off and replaced by an aluminium dope finish. It crashed on take-off from Casablanca airport on 1 December 1948, killing three of those on board. (J. Delmas)

None of these C Mk VIII aircraft received a formal civil Certificate of Airworthiness and all were returned to the RAF when the six Haltons returned to service. They replaced the Avro Yorks on a twice-weekly service to India, adding a new once-a-week service to Ceylon[5] in July 1947. The West African route also fell to the Haltons the same month when the Dakotas were withdrawn. Meanwhile two more Haltons, G-AHDN and G-AHDP, had joined the fleet in March, followed by G-AHDT and G-AHDX in June, G-AHDR in July and the final aircraft, G-AHDO, in August. In September 1947, the Haltons were transferred to the African and Middle East Division of BOAC and the Karachi and Colombo services were taken over by Yorks, which had now been refitted with additional seating. Halton servicing had now been moved from Bovingdon to London Airport.

Of the other two C Mk VIII Halifaxes delivered to Short Brothers, PP226 was apparently not converted and, according to the company records, PP238 was delivered to the French Air Force on 17 March 1947. This may well have been purely on a loan basis for it carried the civil registration G-AHWM. It returned to Handley Page on 4 July before passing to the RAF. It eventually reappeared on the civil register as G-AJZY.

With the rapid ending of the C Mk VIII's RAF career, Handley Page was able to put a batch of these virtually brand new aircraft up for sale at Radlett in 1946. In July, Dr G. Humby, founder of London Aero & Motor Service Ltd (LAMS), acquired six and the aircraft were ferried to the Company's base at Elstree where they were converted for freight carrying. Elstree was too small for operating the Halifaxes and this part of the company's operations moved to Stansted, which LAMS had now taken over completely. It was the only privately leased airport in England at the time, although other charter operators flew from there under an agreement with the company. The successful utilisation by LAMS led to an order for a further ten aircraft but in the meantime, the original six were reduced to four by the loss of G-AHZN which ditched off Le Zoute, Belgium on 26 September, and the need to cannibalise G-AHZM for spares. This cannibalisation for spares also led to the demise of G-AIWO and G-AIWP, two of the new batch of ten.

Other companies were now buying up surplus Halifaxes, their large interior proving a useful attraction and the immediate post-war boom assured that the Halifaxes of LAMS and other companies were kept busy and business flourished. The soft fruit trade provided a constant source of charters during the summer season and LAMS alone was handling 500 tons a month by mid-1947. The trade was profitable, but it had its inherent dangers: the Lancashire Aircraft Corporation's G-AIHW crashed during a night landing at London Airport on 5 June on its return from Spain with six tons of apricots. Bond Air Services lost G-AIZO almost a year later during a similar freighting operation. It was later established that the cargo of fruit

Another purchase by Anglo French Distributors Ltd was PP287, which received the British registration G-AHVT though clearly that was never applied to the aircraft before it received its French registration. Purchased on 25 June 1947 it is seen here at Gatwick Airport just prior to its flight to France. It was sold to Aerocargo on 21 July and in later service with SANA registered as F-BCJR; it received the name KERLAIN and continued to operate until scrapped in 1951. (J. Delmas)

had shifted in flight causing the Halifax to crash at Studham while inbound to Bovingdon on 23 May.

LAMS' policy was to use the Halifaxes along the same lines as a fleet of merchant ships that took cargoes from anywhere to anywhere. Aircraft captains had authority to trade directly as they went and the aircraft were operated all over Europe, down to North Africa and across to the Middle East, lifting loads of fruit into England and manufactured goods out on point-to-point runs up to 1,400 miles distant. The company concentrated on cargo work, leaving passengers to other operators. With a gross load of seven tons and an all-up weight of 68,000 lb, their carrying capacity made them very competitive at a cost of one shilling and five pence per ton-mile one-way. For a considerable time three of the Halifaxes regularly transported 21 tons of fruit and vegetables from northern Italy to England during the height of the fruit season. The speed of airfreight also overcame the usual one-third loss of perishable goods experienced with the normal combination of sea and rail transport – cargoes were now arriving entirely fresh – and Stansted now had its own resident customs facility.

Amongst the foreign operators of civil Halifaxes and Haltons was the French airline SANA. Purchased by Airtech on 10 September 1947, PP223 was converted and, on 17 August, registered as G-AKGP prior to selling it to SANA on 15 June 1948 when it received the French registration of F-BESE. The French company added the emblem of a bird to the nose and the name KERGOALER in black directly below the cockpit area, both repeated on the starboard side. Damaged by fire while at Blackbushe airport in the UK in 1949, it was scrapped the following year. (J. Delmas)

SANA delighted in using artwork to individualise each of its Halifaxes accompanied by names that all began with 'KER'. This close-up of the nose F-BCJQ 'KEROUAL' taken at Oran-La Sénia in 1947 provides details of the artwork. It was lost in a crash at Aubervilliers, near Le Bourget on 27 July 1948. (J. Delmas)

With demand for aircraft to airlift liquid fuels into Berlin, Airtech Ltd purchased a number of 1,500-gallon lorry bulk fuel tanks and adapted them for installation into the Halifax bomb bay. This close-up of the installation shows the small fixed fairing extending down from the top section of the bomb bay and the bracing struts used hold the tank rigid longitudinally. The sign on the end reads MAXIMUM PERMISSIBLE FREIGHT LOAD IN THIS UNDERSLUNG TANK 12000 LBS. MAXIMUM PERMISSIBLE FREIGHT OIL IN WING FREIGHT TANKS 3500 LBS.

South Africa and Pakistan. In addition to the C Mk VIII and Mk IIIs already released, several batches of Mk VI Halifaxes were also put up for sale, but most were purchased for spares, principally by Lancashire Aircraft Corporation.

By 1948, the boom had passed its peak and many feared that the resulting slump would eliminate many operators. Then, on Monday 28 June 1948, the greatest aerial supply operation in history began. *Operation Carter Paterson*[6], or, as it was more popularly known, the Berlin Air Lift was mounted in an attempt to keep the city of Berlin alive where literally every conceivable item had to be delivered by air. Initially, the brunt of the task was born by the RAF and the USAF for the first three weeks but it soon became obvious that it would require even greater resources than these if it were to continue and succeed. As stocks of available commodities gradually diminished despite the military supply flights, it was at this point that the independent British civil operators were invited to join in the airlift.

The offer was made on Sunday 1 August and an initial force of 12 aircraft – nine Dakotas, one Hythe, one Liberator and one Halton – was quickly assembled. Three days later the Halton, from Bond Air Services, in company with a Liberator from Scottish Aviation, carried out the first of the civil operations into the beleaguered city, landing at Wünsdorf airfield. Within days, other operators had joined in and by 21 September, the civil fleet had doubled in size.

To the civil operators fell the task of supplying the entire liquid fuel needs of Berlin, not only domestic and industrial, but also those for the Allied occupation forces. This was not however, their entire contribution and bulk food stocks such as flour, salt and fish were also carried. The carriage of such a corrosive item as salt required heavy anodisation of the airframe and several Halifaxes and Haltons were specially treated for this purpose.

By far the largest single Halifax operator in the operation was the LAC which, in September, agreed to provide six as freighters and six as tankers for the airlift. The six freighters were actually the company's entire current operational fleet being used to carry milk supplies from Belfast to Blackpool. Extensive overhauls were needed and the first two flew to Wünsdorf on 15 October. The six tankers were developed from standard RAF Halifaxes and required special modification to meet the civil licencing requirements.

The civilian force had grown rapidly and as Wünsdorf could no longer handle it satisfactorily, the various operators began dispersing their aircraft to other airfields. Bond Air Services moved part of its force to Fuhlsbüttel, Hamburg's former airport, where it was later joined by BAAS while LAC moved its Halifaxes to

The company now had a staff of 350 and plans for further expansion. Dr Humby, with Capt Keith Thiele as pilot, flew out to Australia in G-AIWT on a round-the-world training trip. He was also in Australia to negotiate for airport facilities at which to base a fleet of six Halifaxes for seasonal work in the Pacific region, which would expand to a fleet of ten when business expanded. The airfield at Schofield near Sydney was a logical choice, but post-war RAAF requirements remained paramount. (Humby was also negotiating similar facilities for operations from South Africa, a venture which proved more successful.) His intention was to set up an airport for exclusively handling cargo aircraft, a concept well ahead of its time and one that mirrored much of what was happening at Stansted. On 27 May G-AIWT left Mascot bound for Stansted carrying seven tons of edible fats consigned from the Food for Britain Appeal of the New South Wales Section. The dripping was contained in 332 drums and carried free of charge as a goodwill gesture (normal alternate freight charges for this cargo had been quoted at £12,500 per aircraft per one-way flight with an option to pick up fare-paying passengers on the return flight). On the flight home, a stop-over was made in India to try to finalise the acquisition of a further ten Halifaxes for conversion. These could only have been the aircraft left behind by 298 Squadron when it disbanded earlier in the year.

A second LAMS Halifax, G-AIWK, returned to Sydney later in the year and operated into Mascot airport for some months on charter runs, but was damaged by vandals in December and never flew again. It was the end of LAMS' Australian venture, but in other places the future looked promising. In July 1947, BOAC Haltons had commenced a London-Karachi service and on 1 September a trans-Sahara London-Lagos service commenced. Six services a week were operated on the latter route and it was while on this run that the Haltons were finally withdrawn in May 1948 and put up for sale.

The list of civil operators had meanwhile grown to include LAMS, British American Air Services, Alpha Airways, Air Freight, Chartair, Eagle Aviation, Bond Air Services, World Air Freight Ltd, Lancashire Aircraft Corporation (LAC), Westminster Airways, Skyflight and Petair. Overseas they were operated in France,

A mixed line-up of Haltons and Mk IXs of Bond Air Services Ltd is seen here after the Berlin airlift. G-ALOS in the foreground was formerly RT937 while next is ex-BOAC Halton, G-AHDP Fleetwood, another Mk IX, RT763 G-ALON, with Halton G-AHDU Falkirk beside it and finally Halton G-AHDO Forfar. The variation in registration style, even between the Haltons is noteworthy. G-AHDP had been used on the airlift and had suffered an undercarriage collapse at Schleswigland on 4 April 1949 but was repaired the same day, the desperate situation making almost anything possible. It was a Halifax from this company and a Liberator from Scottish Aviation that made the first civil airlift into Berlin.

Schleswigland on 22 November. The latter move to near Kiel was not a particularly popular one as, apart from the size of this dispersed site with two miles separating the parking and loading points from the briefing and canteen facilities, it also lacked the ground-based radar aids so essential for bad weather operations. This meant installing special airborne navigation aids so that aircraft could operate under all conditions — essential also to ensure that they did not stray out of the narrow air corridor and into Russian-occupied territory.

The Foreign Office also made a request during December for all LAC Halifaxes to be used as tankers. Other operators also gradually converted their aircraft for tanker operations and an improved tanker conversion appeared at this time. The Regent Oil Company made available a supply of 1,350-gallon lorry tanks and Airtech

Ltd fitted these directly to the belly of the Halifaxes in place of the standard panniers, with metal fairings used to streamline them into the main fuselage contours. Three 250 gallon aircraft fuel tanks were fitted inside the fuselage and interconnected with the external tank to provide a total capacity of 2,050 gallons with 50 gallons of air space. A pair of 2.5 inch external drain cocks enabled the entire load to be taken on, under pressure, in 14 minutes. Discharge time was approximately the same. This load gave a disposable weight of approximately 14,750 lb of fuel oil and the Ministry of Civil Aviation had already granted a dispensation for the Halifaxes and Haltons to be operated at an increased landing weight of 59,000 lb.

Winter operations with their associated necessity for increased fuel margins in case of diversion, kept the payload down to 1,500 gallons. The onset of winter also

A pleasing view of C Mk VIII LN-OAS (formerly PP328) awaiting delivery at Radlett on 18 August 1947 after being sold along with LN-OAT (PP337) to the Norwegian carrier Vingtor Luftrier. After delivery, LN-OAS was never flown commercially by the company and passed first to D. S. Elliott and then to Petair Ltd who operated it as Sky Tramp until abandoning it at Lydda airport. Its companion went to Eagle Aviation Ltd and carried the name Red Eagle; the company retained the colour scheme and eagle trim but removed the bird emblem on the fin and rudder assemblies and replaced the Vingtor Airways logo with its own name. Originally, LN-OAS was finished overall in red with a stylised eagle's head streaming back in a triple cheat line, possibly of yellow, along the length of the fuselage, cut only by each letter of its registration. A stylised bird emblem with wings curved above its head, and surmounted by a single star appeared across both fin and rudder and the name 'Vingtor Airways' appeared above the cheat line, in the same colour, immediately above the wing.

The Halifax could handle a wide range of seemingly impossible external loads, this one being a two-and-a-half-ton Humber car, airlifted from Bovingdon to Madrid in May 1948 by British American Air Services. The depth of the Humber container was greater than the 8,000 lb pannier and, judging by the unladen extension of the undercarriage once airborne, must have left very little clearance during take-off. There must have been a few anxious moments for the crew, and landing would have required a very gentle touch. There was pleasing resonance to the fact that the Rootes Group who had also built Halifaxes also produced the Humber. (B. Robertson)

removed the previous policy of 'daylight only' operations for the civil operators and gradually a 24-hour schedule was instituted.

A chronic shortage of spares meant that even minor accidents usually resulted in an aircraft being scrapped and nine Halifaxes were lost in this manner during the period of the airlift. Most occurred on the ground at Schleswigland and Tegel. The first was World Air Freight's G-AKGZ, which swung on take-off from Gatow at 17.45 hrs on 8 October 1948. BAAS lost G-AKBB in an emergency landing on 11 February 1949 when the starboard undercarriage failed to retract following take-off from Schleswigland. Four days later the company lost a second aircraft when G-AIOI was involved in a taxiing accident at Tegel. LAC lost G-AJZZ, a tanker, in a crash at 03.00 hrs on approach to Schleswigland on 21 March with three of the crew of four being killed. Westminster Airways lost G-AHDL in a crash-landing on 1 April after it had damaged its undercarriage during an aborted landing at Tegel and the crew chose to make an emergency landing at Schleswigland. World Air Freight's G-AKAC departed Fuhlsbüttel at 22.58 hrs on 29 April for Tegel, but crashed at Nauen in the Russian Zone early next morning; all four crew were killed. Another tanker, LAC's G-ALBZ, collided with the company's G-AHWN on 10 May while landing at Schleswigland when a burst tyre caused it to swerve. On 1 June, G-AKBJ, an LAC tanker, undershot while landing at Tegel and was damaged beyond repair. The final loss was another LAC tanker, G-AHWN, which had already had a close brush with disaster with G-ALBZ. On 6 July, its luck deserted it when its undercarriage collapsed landing at Schleswigland; made airworthy, it was ferried to Bovingdon where it was broken up for spares. It was ironic that in some instances crews who had fought their way through Berlin's notorious defences to destroy it a few years earlier, should now battle to reach the same target to sustain it.

Because of the high priority given to the 'wet lift', LAC, in addition to the 16 aircrews based in Germany, also provided a 100-strong maintenance team. All maintenance other than major overhauls was done on the spot in Germany on a 24-hour basis. Periodically the Halifaxes would return to the company's principal home base at Bovingdon where major overhauls or C of A renewals were done. Part of the work carried out at Bovingdon was the fitting of *Rebecca* sets, which were ruled as mandatory as a homing and approach aid for aircraft on the Berlin run.

On 23 January, LAC celebrated its 100th day on the Berlin airlift by carrying 100 tons of fuel oil into the city. By April, fuel oil supplies carried by the civil operators reached a figure in excess of 400 tons a day.

Finally, at midnight on 11/12 May 1949, 318 days after it commenced, the blockade of Berlin ceased as abruptly as it began and within a relatively short period of time the civil operators were withdrawn. On 12 July, Schleswigland was closed and LAC, BAAS, Scottish Airlines and Westminster Airways ceased to operate. A little over one month later Fuhlsbüttel also closed and with it went BAS, Eagle Aviation and World Air Freight. The following day, 16 August, the civil airlift officially ceased.

The Halifax/Halton operators could look back on their efforts with a considerable degree of satisfaction, having completed 22,576.23 flying hours during 4,653 freight and 3,509 fuel sorties by Westminster Airways, LAC and BAAS's fleet of tanker aircraft. These utilisation figures, which averaged out at 311 tons per day, were the highest of any type used by the British civil operators and included only the flying hours used directly on operations. Individually, some of LAC's efforts serve to give an idea of the intensity of operations achieved. On 3 July the company made 26 round trips into Berlin in a period of 14 hours and in one week, a single Halifax was airborne for 96 hours 7 minutes. Although far higher than normal, it is worth noting that another Halifax averaged 48 hours flying each week constantly over a period of five months. Many of the Halifax crews, both ground and air, produced equally outstanding records.

Throughout the period of the airlift, 41 Halifaxes and Haltons had been used as follows: LAC 13; BAS 12; Westminster Airways four; Eagle Aviation four; BAAS three; World Air Freight three; and Skyflight two. At the time the airlift ceased, the final current Halifax/Halton fleet stood as follows: at Schleswigland were ten of LAC's, two of BAAS's and two of Westminster Airways, while at Tegel, Eagle Aviation had two.

While the airlift had been in progress a few Halifaxes had continued charter operations, principally concentrating on bulk cargo such as the 17 ft ship's propeller shaft carried by World Air Freight Ltd. Weighing more than six tons, it was loaded at Ringway on 10 April using an 8,000 lb bomb beam borrowed from the RAF for the purpose. LAC's station manager at Bovingdon, W/Cdr Collings, borrowed a bomb beam again from the Transport Command Development Unit at Brize Norton to enable one of the company's Halifaxes to carry out an almost identical task in July. World Air Freight, which had moved from Stansted to Bovingdon in late February, managed to obtain similar charters such as heavy mining machinery. There were also lifts of a softer nature. One hundred thousand refugees were without adequate shelter in Palestine in December 1946 and an urgent cargo of 180,000 blankets, donated by the Iraq Petroleum Co, was flown out from Britain. BAAS was granted the charter and began the first lift in January 1947.

However, such charters were relatively few and for many of the operators a decline set in from which most never recovered. There were several reasons and, ironically, the Berlin airlift, which had given renewed life at a critical time, served to produce the circumstances that now brought about their demise.

With the bulk of the heavy charter aircraft committed to the airlift, the contractors had grown accustomed to using the medium class of aircraft such as the Dakota. In addition, Halifax operating costs had risen since the middle of 1948, principally because of the increased cost of engines, which before the airlift had been available for almost the break-up salvage price. Because of the large number of engines used in the airlift, the supply had diminished rapidly and by 1949, a reconditioned engine cost up to £1,200. Many operators had also hoped that the dispensation for the increased landing weight of 59,000 lb would remain in force, but they were to be disappointed and the original figure of 57,000 lb was enforced once more. The increasing emphasis on passenger charters also helped the attrition of the heavy charter force. It was now obvious to most operators that the cost of conversion for such traffic was not a practical proposition because of the increased operating costs as compared to the relatively small number of passengers that could be carried per trip. Westminster Airways did attempt to enter this field with one of its three aircraft fitted with ten seats plus cargo space for approximately 4,000 lb of freight.

With such doubtful prospects facing them, many operators were not prepared to go to the expense of renewing the C of As for their various aircraft. BOAC had also withdrawn its Halton fleet during 1949, replacing it on the West Africa route, six services a week, with Avro Yorks. All 12 were then sold off to Aviation Traders Ltd who resold them to Westminster Airways, Bond Air Services, LAC and the French company Aero Cargo in time for use in the Berlin airlift. By October 1949, the Halifax/Halton fleet had dwindled considerably. LAC had four immediately available, with seven others on stand-by, BAAS had two available, Westminster Airways three, World Air Freight one, Eagle Aviation three and Bond Air Services five, with two stood down.

None of the Halifax/Halton fleet was available when a revival of the soft fruit-carrying charters occurred. A price-cutting war kept a few operating a little longer, charges dropping from the average figure of £85 per hour to about £45 per hour. In the face of direct operating costs of about £40 per hour, this was little short of financial suicide.

The end was inevitable and most of the Halifaxes and Haltons found their way to Squires Gate, Woolsington, Bovingdon and Southend where they suffered the

ignominy of being reduced to metal ingots. A few lingered on and LAC's G-AKEC *Air Voyager* made a final public appearance in September 1950 in the Daily Express-sponsored air race. Capt A. N. Marshall flew it around the course from Hurn airport to Herne Bay at low level to achieve 24th place at an average speed of 267 mph. There were, however, those who still saw some prospects and World Air Carriers Ltd purchased their first and only Halton, G-AHAX, in March 1950. It crashed into Mt Hohgart in the Swiss Alps on 16 April, killing all on board including two directors of the company and marking the end not only of the Halton but also the company. Eagle Aviation continued operating G-AIAP until late 1950 when it met its demise in a take-off crash at Calcutta on 20 November. LAC lost one of its last aircraft, G-AJZY, in a crash near Great Missenden on 8 March 1951. This was the former G-AHWM, which had been converted by Short Brothers in 1947.

An era in civil charter operations had passed and with it the Halifax and its true civilianised cousin, the Halton.

Post Scriptum

Thus, the operational, training and civil career of the Halifax drew to a close within a relatively short time. It had commenced its operational career at a time when four-engine bombers were virtually an unknown quantity and both crews and aircraft had been forced to learn their measure by experience, sometimes at great cost to both. The Halifax, like its contemporaries, was far from perfect initially; it had taken a lot of work and thought before it became an efficient weapon. That it did reach this standard, in spite of its inauspicious beginning, speaks clearly enough for the soundness of the original design. It served in every British theatre of operations and in virtually every type of role, from bombing, glider towing, agent dropping, transport and anti-shipping to meteorological reconnaissance and training: no role was too difficult nor too insignificant. Additionally, it also pioneered the use of equipment and techniques that were later put to good effect by itself and others.

Today three Halifaxes and a nose section remain for posterity, a meagre tribute in terms of numbers. The B Mk II Series I, W1048: S of 35 Squadron, is totally original and, coming from the first RAF squadron to be equipped with the type, could not be a more appropriate acquisition. Recovered from the dark, icy waters of Lake Hoklingen in Norway, it emerged into the sunlight shortly after 14.00 hrs on Saturday, 30 June 1973. It had force-landed on the frozen surface of the lake on 27 April 1942 and sank into 90 feet of water while the crew watched from the shore, never, they presumed, to be seen again. Fortunately, the mud of the lake bed virtually embalmed the Halifax and its contents. Skilful work by a team of RAF sub-aqua

A nostalgic moment as Lancashire Aircraft Corporation's C Mk VIII, G-AKEC Air Voyager, is flagged away in the Daily Express-sponsored air race of September 1950; the end of an era. (Flight International)

The faithfully restored Halifax A Mk VII NA337 of 644 Squadron, now on display at Trenton, Ontario, Canada and a tribute to the very hard work of so many volunteers. Like the Imperial War Museum example on display at Hendon, it was recovered from a Norwegian fjord and fortunately, deemed worthy of full restoration. Having completed an SOE drop on the night of 23/24 April 1945, F/Lt A. Turnbull was heading NA337 for the coast when flak set the starboard wing and outboard engine on fire, forcing him to ditch the Halifax in Lake Mjøsa near the village of Stange, to the north of Oslo. Five of the crew survived, but by morning and clinging to the overturned dinghy, Sgt T. Weightman was the only one left alive when rescued by local Norwegians. (Steve Pomerleau Photography stevepphotography.com)

enthusiasts, working in water temperatures of 4 degrees C, and with torch visibility of about 10 feet, raised the aircraft with the aid of oil drums half-filled with air – but not without some tense moments. The first lift ended with the Halifax on the bottom again, but without causing any damage to the airframe. A second attempt was successful, but the damaged outer section of the starboard wing broke free and the aircraft settled once again on the bottom. The third lift was completely successful and W1048 was towed the three-quarters of a mile to shore. Getting it on to dry land was not easy but, by use of air bags, it was finally accomplished. The aircraft still had fuel in its tanks and inside the fuselage were found the navigator's charts, instruments, flying gloves, first-aid kits and emergency rations. The cockpit light, when tested, still worked. The combined resources of the RAF brought the veteran home for restoration and eventual display at the RAF Museum at Hendon. However, it was not restored but simply exhibited in the condition in which it was found, embodying both the aircraft and its operational risks and consequences, but also denying the type any chance of its former stature.

A second Halifax, A Mk VII NA337: X of 644 Squadron was recovered deep in another Norwegian lake by a Canadian team who encountered their own problems in such deep, cold waters. F/Lt Turnbull had completed an SOE drop on 23/24 April 1944 but his Halifax was hit by flak as he flew towards the coast. With the starboard wing and outboard engine on fire, he put the aircraft down on Lake Mjøsa near the village of Stange, north of Oslo. Five of the crew escaped, but the cold of the lake took four and by morning, only Sgt Weightman had survived by clinging to the upturned dinghy from where he was rescued by two local Norwegians. In the intervening years, through intense work and dedication by a large team of former RCAF Halifax men and volunteers, this Halifax has been brought back to superb condition and today is proudly displayed at the RCAF Memorial Museum at Trenton, Ontario.

A third Halifax was built for the Yorkshire Air Museum under the enthusiastic leadership of Ian Robinson, constructed from a combination of recovered parts and some skilful manufacture of new sections by British Aerospace Engineering Trainees from Brough's training department. The rear section comes from HR792: A, a GR Mk II of 58 Squadron, which made a belly-landing at Stornoway on 13 January 1945. Written off, it was later broken up and the section recovered was used for a hen coop for 40 years on the Isle of Lewis by Robert McKenzie. He generously donated the

section which eventually reached the museum via the generous assistance of a number of people and organisations, including the RAF, which airlifted it, plus other pieces, to Stornoway airfield. From there it came via sea ferry and road.

Work began on restoration in 1985 while the search for other parts continued. A rear turret, with nothing left but its frame, was located and Bernard Jefferson spent 1,500 hours restoring it to original condition. A mid-upper turret was also restored and fitted. A rear fuselage bay was unobtainable, so the Brough trainees built a full assembly jig and produced a replica section using original Handley Page drawings provided by RAF Duxford. The tail plane components were also built from scratch.

The centre section and wings came from Hastings TG536; few people realise that this type, and the Hermes civil variant, was based on the Halifax airframe. One undercarriage leg, loaned by the RAF Museum at Hendon, served as a pattern for two replica units. Four Merlin engines, from another 58 Squadron GR Mk II, JP165: D, were airlifted out by RAF Chinook helicopter from the crash site on the Isle of Lewis. However, the Halifax has been completed as a B Mk III with four Bristol Hercules engines. The Armée de l'Air donated four Series 700 engines while other original Hercules engine components, including propeller hubs, were recovered from a wreck dug up near Nuremberg. These were from the 432 Squadron B Mk III, LW687: Z, flown by F/O E. K. Reid RCAF, shot down by a night-fighter during the fateful raid of 30/31 March 1944, three of the crew being killed. Fry's Metals in Leeds manufactured new propeller blades using an original as a pattern while the main wheels and tail wheel were recovered in good condition from a crash site near Paris in 1988. They came from HX271: V, a B Mk III of 466 Squadron flown by P/O A. L. Smith RAAF, which was shot down during an attack on the Trappes railway yards on 2/3 June 1944. The airframe is a mixture of Coastal Command Mk II and Bomber Command Mk III components – in its own way a unique memorial to both arms of the RAF and its multi-national crews as well as to those who built Halifaxes. It is now on display at the former RAF Station at Elvington from where the two Free French Halifax squadrons operated.

The three survivors provide a tribute to the Halifax and all who were involved with designing, building, servicing and flying the type. The Halifax numbered in the thousands, pioneered much of the equipment and tactics that brought the RAF its final successes, and won a commendable list of battle honours.

A rare example: a B Mk II Series I, possibly of No 28 Halifax Conversion Flight. The early style of fuselage roundel and fin flash remained in use until late 1942, covering the period during which No 28 CF existed before forming the nucleus of 1652 HCU and prior to its absorbing Nos 35 and 158 CFs in October, both of which used their respective squadron code letters. The very stylish '9' marking is distinctive, the only other Conversion Unit known to have used numerals rather than code letters being 1658 HCU; however, that unit's style was very geometrically square. (K. Beetson)

APPENDIX 1: **Training for the Halifax**

The introduction of four-engine bombers into RAF service had produced several difficulties, among them flying training. Initially, this was overcome to some extent by posting experienced operational crews to the first heavy bomber squadrons, and 35 Squadron carried out its own early conversion training as detailed in Chapter 2. However, as more heavy bombers entered service the task grew beyond the practical capabilities of the already fully occupied operational squadrons and the Air Ministry decided to form Conversion Flights (CF) for training crews to handle the new breed of heavy bombers. The normal route for trainees ended at an Operational Training Unit (OTU), where they undertook the last stage of transition to operational types, usually on Whitleys and Wellingtons; but the new breed of four-engine aircraft required an additional layer of training. In October 1941, No 28 Halifax Conversion Flight was formed at Leconfield where it stayed until December, before relocating to Marston Moor. No 26 CF was next, forming at Waterbeach in November to handle Stirling crew conversion. Authority for a further HCF, No 107, to be based at Leconfield was issued in December but no aircraft had been received before the training structure was revised at the beginning of January 1942.

The aircraft for No 28 CF were drawn from Nos 35 and 76 Squadrons. The first arrived in October 1941 but numbers were to be small in the barely four-month life of the Flight, totalling 12 in all, L9486, L9491, L9496, L9509, L9513, L9522, L9525, L9534, L9564, L9565, L9580 and L7245, which arrived on 7 December, allocated to help boost numbers. Front-line operations had priority and replacement aircraft were scarce at the time (No 26 CF received just 18 in its equally brief existence). Using L7245 meant one more production aircraft available for operations; the second prototype had had a busy existence already. Involved in an accident at the A&AEE on 23 December 1940, declared F.A.T. Cat A it was

'O-Orange' of 28 CF viewed from beneath the wing of another B Mk I that had struck the Chance Light, damaging the starboard inner engine and propeller blades and breaking the undercarriage Messier box casting. This unit used only single aircraft letters, no unit code apparently having been allocated by the time it was disbanded and absorbed into 1652 HCU. (E. Marsden)

repaired on site, and returned to test work only to suffer a second accident on 24 October 1941. Declared F.A.T. Cat. B, (damaged beyond repair on site) it went back to Handley Page on 5 November for repair, and then was loaned to the HCF on 17 November; however, the records show that it was removed temporarily before being sent back to the training unit again on 7 December. It survived its time with No 28 CF but would eventually suffer a serious accident on 24 October; declared F.A. Cat. B. Its usefulness, however, continued; converted into a 'synthetic trainer', its identity changed to Instructional Airframe 3474M on 24 December 1942.

No 26 CF kicked off the inevitable losses with two Stirlings written off through undercarriage failure, a mechanical fault causing the first on 17 December and one through swinging to avoid another aircraft after landing the following day. No 28 HCF lost its first and only Halifax in deadlier circumstances on 22 December. F/Lt R. Owen DFC with seven others on board L9522 had left Leconfield at 10.25 hrs in extremely bad weather conditions intending to fly to the Handley Page facility at Radlett. Eyewitnesses reported later that at 11.10 hrs the Halifax was seen flying through mist near the border of Leicestershire and Lincolnshire. Shortly after this, the Halifax crashed into a ridge of ground close to Knipton, ten miles from Melton Mowbray, killing all on board. Owen was a very experienced Halifax pilot, having gained his DFC while with 35 Squadron. Two others killed were also former 35 Squadron personnel, F/O E. Gibb DFM and Sgt S. Mayston DFM. The flight had been authorised by No 4 Group HQ and proved the only fatalities suffered by No 28 Con. Fl. before it was absorbed into 1652 Conversion Unit (CU) on 31 January 1942.

Eric Marsden had moved from 35 Squadron to No 28 CF and his account of the early problems with just the basic requirements to keep aircraft serviced illuminates the situation facing this unit. *"Whilst it was the original training within the Squadron things were OK, because we were still in the squadron, but when we became a separate unit we had to do the full clearance chit business, handing into squadron stores everything that was 35's. This meant that we were tool-less, apart from the kit of our own which many of us carried in our gas mask case or pockets, so as not to be caught out. But of course, the flying programme had to go on. As is the way of the services, unavailability from stores did not mean that toolboxes could not be obtained – when our kites dropped into other stations any toolbox not anchored down was apt to vanish; until Chiefy got wind of this activity and banned it. After that we struggled on for a few more days and then, perhaps initiated by me – one does not like to take credit for what may have been a general move – we staged a sit-down in the hangar, deploring our inability to sign the Form F700 for work we patently could not do because we had not been issued with the basic tools, not even screwdrivers! We were so obviously in the right that no action was taken against us – but we had toolboxes in store in jig time.*

It was when we were at the beginning of the No 35 Squadron Conversion Flight that we were billeted out in what the lads called 'Snake Gulch', old standard huts on the north side of Linton airfield, well outside the perimeter and a heck of a long walk to the cookhouse and NAAFI. The huts had wide verandas facing in the same direction as the adjacent runway. We woke one morning to find the burned-out remains of a Halifax which had run out of petrol on the approach, bellied in and stopped within 20 or 30 yards of our hut, and then burned. Another spoonful in each of the carburettors and we would have had an early awakening ... or perhaps not at all.

My chief memories of No 28 Conversion Flight at Leconfield are seeing a Tiger Moth taxi into our backwash as we were running up a Halifax before going out on to the field for take-off. At the time, I was getting a lot of hours in as a stand-in flight engineer. The incident was unfortunate. We were standing on a dispersal point behind a hedge and a tree or two, which placed our tail at right angles to anything passing. As flight engineer, I checked around behind us to make sure all was clear before giving the pilot the word to carry on with his magneto checks. We got started with me popping up, before each engine was run up, and checking rearwards. I do not recall which engine we had got to when I felt compelled to look out – just in time to see a new-looking Tiger Moth being blown on to its back. What made it worse was that the pilot in it was the Station Master, a Group Captain. What made things even worse was that he was intensely disliked by our aircrew and others on the station for his hard-nosed attitude to people who put aeroplanes U/S after night-flying tests; on one occasion he all but accused a pilot of cowardice after he reported his machine unserviceable two or three times on the same day, although the ground staff could not find a fault. The Group Captain insisted on going on an operation in that machine and was forced to return early when the undiagnosed fault turned up again. He held an inquiry into the Tiger Moth incident which resulted in the Canadian Flight Lieutenant pilot of the Halifax receiving a severe reprimand, although if blame was to be allocated to anyone other than the Group Captain I would have thought that it would have been me."

Although the establishment of a single Conversion Flight each for Halifax and Stirling training would temporarily alleviate the immediate problem, it was obvious to the Air Ministry that the two units could not handle the flow of new crews. Accordingly, in December 1941 it was decided to expand the process by establishing a new system of one Conversion Unit (CU) per Group, plus one CF of four aircraft per squadron. Three were formed immediately and the process of establishing each at its new base began. For No 4 Group, 1652 CU at Marston Moor, Yorkshire on 2 January 1942, for No 3 Group, 1651 CU at Waterbeach in Cambridgeshire with Stirlings and 1653 CU at Polebrook, Northamptonshire. A fourth, No 1654 was formed in May for No 5 Group with a mixture of Manchesters and Lancasters. The existing Nos 26 and 28 Conversion Flights were absorbed into this system at the beginning of January, No 28 going to 1652 CU and No 26 to 1651 CU; for each of them it was a paper transfer as they remained at their existing airfields.

Four-aircraft Conversion Flights were established within each Squadron to handle the transition between the CUs, the 102 Squadron CF forming first in January, followed by the other three Squadrons, Nos 10, 35 and 76, in February. From there on, as each new Halifax

L9509: C of 1652 HCU photographed at Marston Moor while undergoing a 60 or 90-hour inspection. Introduced in July 1942, the so-called C1 type fuselage roundel and narrow white section of the fin flash give an approximate date for the photograph. L9509 served first with 35 Squadron and then passed to 28 CF before ending up with 1652 HCU. It finally came to grief after landing at Marston Moor and running into a ditch following brake failure on 3 April 1943. (E. Marsden)

Squadron formed throughout 1942 it established its own Conversion Flight, this system continuing to February 1943.

The standard training programme at the CUs allowed for approximately 20 hours of instruction and covered all essential aspects, as detailed below:

Familiarisation flight	30 min
Dual circuits and landings	180 min
Solo circuits and landings	30 min
Dual check and overshoot	30 min
Solo 60 min Dual check and three-engined handling	120 min
Solo 60 min Solo	60 min
Dual check and two-engined handling	60 min
Solo climb to 12,000 ft and bomb door operation	90 min
Dual, draining fuel tanks and mid-air changeover	60 min
Solo 30 min Dual instrument flying	60 min
Solo 30 min Dual instrument flying	60 min
Solo 30 min Dual instrument flying	60 min
Dual, take-off with full bomb load, cross-country and tank changeover	120 min
Dual check including three-engined overshoot and landings	60 min

Dual controls were fitted to most of the Halifaxes, greatly facilitating the training. After completing their course, and being posted to a squadron, the *in situ* Conversion Flights then provided final training to new crews. However, experienced pilots were posted in who had never handled the type and the squadron CF had to provide the conversion training. Crews already operational within a squadron were also required to carry out daily routine training between operations, simply to strengthen areas where a Flight Commander thought a crew could do with some extra training; and occasionally operational crews from the parent squadron were attached to the unit's CF for a more extensive refresher course.

Training had its element of danger as would be expected, and the first loss by a CU occurred at 1652 CU on 6 January 1942, just four days after it started operating. At Marston Moor F/O P. Johnson DFC, who had recently completed a tour of operations with 35 Squadron was giving instruction when his pupil realised he was going to overshoot the landing run. Knowing that there was a deep trench at the end of the runway, he attempted to turn L9519 on to the perimeter track, collapsing the undercarriage in the process and damaging the Halifax beyond repair.

However, it did not have to be the newly trained who ended up so ignominiously. The unit's second loss occurred on 10 March when W/Cdr J. Tait was giving dual circuit and landing training to S/Ldr A. Snow in L9513 when a tyre burst as the Halifax touched down and the undercarriage collapsed. More serious events produced more serious results, however, and the following day the unit suffered its first Halifax fatalities; F/O J. Joshua was carrying out general practice flying in L9576: GV-E and had shut down two engines when he lost control and crashed some three or so miles from the airfield. Four pilots were on board, plus five others, three of them ground staff. However, others seemed to have a charmed life; F/O K. Whisken DFC had crash-landed L9509 around 11.00 hrs when the undercarriage jammed. Undeterred, he was airborne again in R9431: GV-K in the afternoon when he had to make an emergency landing with one engine ablaze, at 14.00 hrs – once again without injury to anyone on board the Halifax.

Each squadron's own Conversion Flight also suffered accidents during this period, again often regardless of experience or rank. S/Ldr E. Franklin DFC was practising three-engine overshoots at Linton-on-Ouse in one of 35 Squadron's CF Halifaxes, R9425. Having climbed to 200 ft he commenced another circuit but the undercarriage and flaps failed to retract, reducing speed to a point where Franklin was unable to restart the fourth engine and he had to force-land the aircraft, just off the airfield. This accident resulted in recommendation of a minimum height of 400 ft for circuits on three-engine exercises.

One of the most dangerous aspects of training was two- and three-engined flying and emergency recovery procedures – essential in the extreme because loss of an engine on an operational flight was almost a certainty during a tour of operations. On 11 May 102 CF

This view of 'K-Kitty' of 1652 HCU undergoing a change to propeller to its starboard outer engine provides another look at the seemingly endless work required of the ground staff and the array of equipment needed. The fin flash style places the date after mid-1942. In the right foreground are some Small Bomb Containers (SBCs), a familiar item at the conversion units where the entire range of crew duties was brought to fruition. The SBC could carry a range of small bomb types up to a total weight of 250 lb: twenty 4 lb incendiary bombs, four 30 lb incendiary bombs, three 40 lb General Purpose bombs, or twelve 20 lb F type practice bombs, the two latter types being used for bomb-aiming training. Next to the propeller spinner on the ground is one of the essential toolboxes that resulted in the sit-down strike action at 28 CF described in the text. (E. Marsden)

had V9982 out on what was described in the crash investigation report as "one side flying, port motors feathered." Fl/Sgt C. Harris[1] was having trouble with this exercise because of deteriorating weather and the instructor, S/Ldr P. Robinson DFC commenced to un-feather the two engines, but neither engine picked up power and the Halifax was force-landed some five miles north of Thirsk, in Yorkshire. Restarting an engine required a calm, orderly sequence of actions – and enough airspeed to rotate the propeller once un-feathered; this problem had caught out S/Ldr Franklin, as mentioned earlier.

Operations could still bring crews into front-line service before their training was complete, usually in conjunction with an experienced pilot and, occasionally, extra crew members. The first of Harris' '1,000 bomber' raids had relied in part on using crews from the training establishments to reach the magic number and 1652 CU had contributed 13 to this first attack, losing L9605: GV-Y. Flown by S/Ldr J. Russell DFC with just four others for crew, it was brought down near Tegelen, killing Sgt K. Manley, with the remaining four becoming POWs. Manley, F/O D. Cookson and Sgt R. Tavener had been seconded from 158 Squadron for the night, illustrating how scratch crews had been put together for the raid. This added to the dangers as crews were built on a mutual understanding of every member's abilities and role. The second of these mass raids drew only one from the unit but the last, against Bremen, drew six, fortunately without loss from either attack. The reduced number of crew in many of the second line unit aircraft reflected the fact that Harris had not only had to scour far and wide for aircraft for the attacks but also for sufficient crews. It was also dangerous to put an experienced pilot in charge of a partly trained crew, although that did happen at times during these three mass raids.

The rudder stall problem caught some trainees; on 16 July BB203: Z from 158 CF was out on a training exercise with three pilots and two flight engineers on board. While landing back at East Moor the pilot flying the aircraft overshot his turn for finals on to the duty runway and made the fatal mistake of increasing the bank in an attempt to line the aircraft up with the runway. As the turn tightened up, the rudders stalled and the Halifax crashed at Manor Farm, killing all five. One of the pilots had arrived from 1652 CU on 22 June and the other two six days later, which gives some idea of how far they had all progressed with their solo training.

Yet accidents were not always the fault of the crew under training. No 35 Squadron CF had lost L9568 on 7 May, struck amidships by W1051: C, which swung off the runway on return from a sortie to Stuttgart. Fortunately, the crew of W1051 escaped injury, as did the guard in L9568, but a third Halifax, L9607: Z, was damaged by propeller splinters from

The cockpit set up for dual-control, in this case in a B Mk I or V. The standard blind-flying panel sits immediately in front of the first pilot's position while to the left is the bomb steering indicator with the Beam Approach visual indicator below it. At top right grouped above the throttle quadrant are the four engine tachometers. From left to right, the narrow angled panel contains the pilot's oxygen flow meter, DR compass repeater, flap indicator and a boost gauge for each of the four engines. On the bottom row left are the auto-controls trim pressure gauge (with the call button and its indicator light below again, to the left) and outside air temperature indicator and on the other side of the control column, partly obscured, the port engine ignition switches, the undercarriage indicator lights dial, and then the starboard engine ignition switches. At the bottom is the pilot's bomb-release switch framed between the hydraulic lines leading to the control lever for the twin landing lamps mounted beneath the port wing. The control yoke is fitted with spectacle-shaped brake handles and behind the control column is the standard oil filled P1 compass. (P. Summerton)

This view shows the second set of controls and detachable floor plate. No brake controls were provided for the second pilot's position because that would have required a permanent set of hydraulic fittings. The brass switch at the top of the instrument panel is the landing-light switch. Below the empty compass correction cardholder, set between the lower pair of tachometers, is the vacuum gauge suction changeover switch just behind the left-hand end of the horizontal throttle stop bar for the four throttles with, at the right end, the locking-lever. The friction locking-lever for the four throttles has a black tip. The pitch levers for the Rotol constant speed propellers are at the bottom of the quadrant and below, out of sight, are the supercharger levers and the boost control cut-out with their own friction locking-lever on the right. The red bomb jettison handle – marked 'Jettison Containers First' – is set above the three indicator lights for wing and fuselage bomb bay doors; the red placard states 'Bombs cannot be released unless the light for the section they are in appears. When opening drum switch on selector, switch box must be set on distributor'. Immediately below the placard, partly obscured by the friction lever, is the container jettison button under its spring-loaded red cover and below that, the oxygen flow and contents gauges. The compressed air supply gauge for the brakes is fitted below the engine limitations placard with the W/T visual indicator above to the right. The fuel jettison valves are partly obscured by the head of the control column. (P. Summerton)

W1051. The other two were declared beyond economic repair and written off.

Operations also culled the ranks; the three 1,000-bomber raids in mid-1942 temporarily brought many of the instructional Halifaxes back on to operations; although flown by instructors for the most part, some were crewed entirely by pupils, sometimes with just five on board.

This extract from the pilot's manual shows the additional small panel, common to all marques of Halifax, fitted in the top section of the canopy. The four red-coloured propeller feathering buttons are at the bottom of the panel, with the fuel contents gauges switch above left, landing lights brass switch to the right, with the navigation lights switch above. The Pitot head heater switch is to the right, and the formation keeping lights switch box on the far right. The Beam Approach indicator sits in the bottom of the windscreen frame.

The Cologne raid of 30/31 May 1942 took a heavy toll of OTU crews, plus a Manchester from 49 CF and a Halifax from 1652 CU. F/Lt S. Wright's L9605: GV-Y was brought down near Venlo, in Holland, killing one of the five onboard while the others were made POWs. The unit lost another crew on the second raid against Essen on 1/2 June, when R9372: GV-K lost power on one engine over the target. Unable to maintain height, it was brought down approaching the Dutch coast with F/O H. Williams and his five crew becoming POWs. The third raid, against Bremen on 25/26 June again cost OTU crews dearly, but V9993: GV-U, shot down 6 km from Raalte, in Holland, by Oblt Carsten of the III./NJG 1 was being flown by an experienced pilot, the redoubtable F/O K. Whisken DFC. However, his luck had finally run out and he and one other member of the seven-man crew were killed. No 102 Squadron CF had provided aircraft for all three raids and on the third to Bremen, sent three – one flown by an instructor and the other two by pupils, one of whom had just completed his first solo on the type.

Training accidents at the Halifax-equipped CUs, however, were relatively low, just one in January 1942, one in March, one in April, two in June; but as the number of Halifax-equipped squadrons slowly increased, so also did the tempo of conversion training and accidents would rise in line with the expansion.

Aircraft allotted to Conversion Units were generally not new; Bomber Command was still struggling to expand its heavy bomber force and training units, essential though they might be, were a luxury in many respects. The usual practice was for older aircraft to be passed on to the conversion flights as new aircraft arrived to replace them. This led to some operationally-tired examples finding their way to the training units. It was an unfortunate practice but unavoidable for obvious reasons, and many a station engineering officer shook his head in dismay at the first inspection of a new arrival.

The squadron Conversion Flights were not much better off at times. No 158 CF formed in mid-1942, authority having being issued by Bomber Command on 6 May 1942 for it to be formed at Linton-on-Ouse, with East Moor as its satellite airfield. The next day ground staff were posted to the unit but were employed assisting 35 Squadron, also based at Linton, to gain experience on Halifaxes. On 5 June, F/O D. Wilkinson, with acting rank of Squadron Leader, was posted in from 35 CF to command it. The next day, stores began arriving in a steady stream and, on 7 June, the first Halifax, R9373, arrived. Built near the end of 1941 it had already passed through three squadrons – Nos 10, 76 and 78 – before being passed on from the latter. When the aircraft logbooks were checked, it was found to be three and a half hours off a 4 star (major) inspection. Disheartening in itself, it was worsened by the fact that the CU still did not have any heavy equipment or

R9430, a B Mk II of 1658 HCU photographed while undergoing sink rate tests by S/Ldr P. Dobson DFC AFC to establish the rate of height loss, reportedly starting at 19,000 ft while successively shutting down each engine. With engine failure, the re-start drill required moving the propeller blades from the feathered to course pitch setting to gain the necessary windmilling rotation to start the engine. This required sufficient height and time as the process produced high drag and an increased sink rate. Dobson's report stated that if reduced to a single engine he recommended that the crew bale out rather than attempt a landing. The number 19 appeared on both sides of the fuselage aft of the roundel. The use of numerals in place of letters by this unit continued until at least February 1943 when R9373: 25 was wrecked in a wheels-up landing. Other Halifaxes on strength in May 1942 were using individual aircraft code letters and it is probable that with the aircraft holding having exceeded the 26-letter alphabet, numerals were used initially by one of the Flights. The spinners of R9430 were painted white, suggesting that a colour system was in use to identify each Flight. Some training units adopted a system where a bar was placed either above or below a letter when, out of necessity, it was simultaneously used twice or a small numeral '2' was added after the aircraft letter for the same purpose. However, the loss entry for BB304 in September 1943 records its identity as D23 – possibly a transition between the numeral only and final adoption of full codes when 'TT' and 'ZB were allocated to the unit. Delivered by Handley Page in late January 1942, R9430 had gone first to No 10 CF then to 76 CF and then to 78 CF before that unit was absorbed into 1658 HCU in October 1942. R9430 was eventually converted to an Instructional Airframe, 4162M.

maintenance stands. Despite these shortages, a detailed inspection of the Halifax began next day and revealed two cracked front plates, a cold air intake no longer attached to anything in particular and both main tyres in need of change. The next day's batch included a similar specimen, W1014, again from 78 Squadron, and within seven hours of a 40 star inspection. Even so, not all were such bad specimens; on 16 June, R9388 and W1165 arrived and next day arrangements were made to exchange the latter for BB203, a five tank Halifax from 35 Squadron; both were new aircraft. New or not, some did not last long and BB203 stalled on approach to East Moor, crashing at Manor Farm, Framlingham on 16 June. Problems or not, W1014: X was used by S/Ldr Wilkinson for the attack on Bremen on 25/26 June, but he had to bring back his bomb load as the target was obscured by 10/10ths cloud.

It was not until October that the next CUs appeared, 1656 at Breighton, 1658 at Riccall, 1659 at Leeming, 1660 at Swinderby and 1661 at Skellingthorpe. They were created as the expansion of the training system continued, absorbing some squadron Conversion Flights in the process – 1656 CU absorbed the Flights from Nos 103 and 460 Squadrons, 1658 CU those from Nos 10, 76, 78 and 102, and 1659 CU those from 405 and 408 Squadrons. The remaining two were established from the ground up. The designation of these units changed from Conversion Unit to Heavy Conversion Unit (HCU) on 7 October as the Air Ministry tidied up its system, 1658 HCU forming on the same day. The unit suffered its first fatal accident just two days later when P/O F. Leach, Sgt G. Broughton, Sgt A. Isaac and Sgt G. Buckland were killed in L9574. The Halifax was seen approaching Riccall from the south-east to land when one of the propeller blades flew off; P/O Leach was unable to maintain control and the Halifax crashed 300 yards from Lodge Farm. This type of accident took a heavy toll on pilot trainees as often there were several on board for a single training exercise.

The next round of expansion occurred in 1943 as Bomber Command got into its stride and the aircraft production centres were able to supply an ever increasing number of heavy bombers. In January 1662 HCU was formed at Blyton, followed in March by 1663 at Rufforth, which absorbed 158 CF in the process. No 1665 followed next at Waterbeach in April, No 1664 at Croft in May with two following in June: No 1666 at Dalton and No 1667 at Lindholme. Two more appeared in August, 1668 at Balderton and 1669 at Langar. The last HCU, No 1674 was formed in October to provide conversion training for Coastal Command. Each had Halifaxes of a variety of marques on strength and 1667 HCU eventually became the specialist unit for B Mk V training.

Where possible, HCUs were moved to satellite stations where they would neither impede, nor be impeded by the resident operational squadrons, each Group being allocated a base location and satellite airfields for use by its associated HCUs. For example, the No 4 Group Base Station No 42 was Marston Moor, which housed 1652 HCU throughout the war, while its satellites were Rufforth (1663) and Riccall (1658). A tentative allocation of training unit locations had been set down in a document dated 5 July 1943 which established a Base parent authority to which specific HCUs would now be responsible. No 1 Group had No 12 Base, which had control of Lindholme, Blyton and Faldingworth airfields. No 3 Group had No 32 Base, with airfields at Stradishall and Chedburgh. No 4 Group had No 41 Base with airfields at Pocklington, Melbourne and Elvington; No 42 Base, Marston Moor, Rufforth and Riccall airfields; No 43 Base, Driffield, Leconfield and Lissett airfields. No 5 Group had No 51 Base, with Swinderby, Wigsley and Winthorpe airfields. No 6 Group had No 61 Base, with airfields at Topcliffe, Dalton, Dishforth and Wombelton, plus No 62 Base with airfields at Linton-on-Ouse, Tholthorpe and East Moor.

Mortality rate amongst both aircraft and crews at all training units was not insignificant and it is a sobering thought to realise that a very high percentage of aircrew lost during the Second World War fell victim during their training. This should not be construed to mean that the training programmes or equipment were in any way lacking, but rather that in the pressing needs of wartime both men and machines were trained in huge numbers and required to take calculated risks.

A rather bizarre incident occurred on 25 May 1943, when F/O A. Moir DFC was carrying out a dual check flight with four others on board a 1652 HCU Halifax. A very experienced pilot, he had recently completed a very difficult tour of operations with 76 Squadron. While in the circuit, the port inner engine of L9571: GV-H burst into flames, Moir tried to line up with the runway and land but in doing so the Halifax clipped the roof of Tockworth Vicarage on the eastern side of the airfield and crashed. The CO of Marston Moor airfield at the time was G/Capt Leonard Cheshire VC and he later recounted, most clearly and strongly, that when he reached the crash scene he saw Moir walking towards him, somewhat dishevelled but otherwise unharmed. He was therefore "shaken to the core" when the Station Medical Officer later told him that Moir's body had been removed from the wrecked cockpit. There were only two survivors, Sgts T. King and J. Winchester.

It was not always clear what caused accidents, but usually it involved a human element. A particularly bad accident occurred on 1 October 1943 to one of 1667 HCU's trainee crews. Sent to Swinderby for general flying practice, F/Lt Duxbury DFC had two trainee pilots, three flight engineers, a navigator, an air bomber[2] and a wireless operator on board. The Halifax entered a violent spin, possibly with one of the trainee pilots at the controls, and broke up close to Bardney airfield, killing all of those on board DG275: A.

Yet some remarkable tales of survival also occurred; on 11/12 October 1943, Sgt J. Maher was out on a night cross-country exercise in JB893 from 1659 HCU when problems arose and he gave the bale-out order in the vicinity of Lower Brailes. He and Sgt B. Rowe parachuted to safety, but Sgt G. Conran, in the rear turret at the time, found that he could not rotate the turret to clear the doors at the back. In his panic, he hit his head against the turret structure, knocking himself unconscious, a state he was still in when the Halifax hit the ground, snapping off the entire rear section and hurling it some considerable distance. He was still in the turret when found, head bleeding and one arm fractured, but otherwise unharmed.

While some aircraft succumbed after a brief period, there were always others to prove the exception to the rule. A veteran B Mk I, L9534, originally allotted to 76 Squadron on 15 June 1941, passed successively to 28 CF, 1652 HCU and 1659 HCU before being struck off charge on 20 September 1945. Eric Marsden, a Fitter IIE with the unit, recalls this aircraft well. *"It came to the Conversion Flight from No 76 Squadron and was allotted to my crew. On checking the propeller feathering the fuse blew, and did so each time it was replaced. After two days the electricians discovered that two main cables at the top right of the big Bendix junction box ... had been transposed and the fuse reinforced with silver paper from a cigarette packet to make everything work for the hand-over. This aircraft was also the aircraft on our unit longest without undercarriage doors whilst waiting for the strengthened modified doors, which resisted cracking at the jack anchor points. This led to tail plane buffet, as a result of which two rear anchor bolts on the tail plane became loose during a flight by Wg Cdr Tait, the semi-flying tail plane being restrained only by the tail plane fairings, the elevators acting as servos. This resulted in 'opposite control', undulating flight and a very cross Wing Commander.*

Whilst the undercarriage doors were off, we had to change either a radiator or an oil cooler after every day's flying, a circumstance which had not occurred on the other aircraft in this condition. Despite all this, on operations L9534 was exceptionally fast, and her crew often the first back. If I remember correctly, she was often the choice of Wt Off Holden. It may have been this aircraft which was used for the radio altimeter trials, intended for use at 60 ft, but which proved to be unreliable; though when working it would register sheep and cows.

Bearing in mind the varying qualities of the chaps who flew Halifaxes, and other types, it seems to me that the bad press under which this good aircraft suffered for so long was due to a 'Spitfire' syndrome transferred by journalists to the Lancaster. Certainly after the flying that I did on conversion units in Mk I and Mk II Halifaxes, with some fairly uncertain pupils in the driver's seat, I felt a great confidence in our aircraft – even though they were often squadron rejects."

As production increased, it became possible to supply new aircraft direct to HCUs; DT733, a B Mk II, was one such aircraft. Delivered to 1652 HCU on 21 January 1943, it completed well over 1,000 hours flying time during which more than 250 pupils flew it with varying degrees of skill and, during one 36-hour period, it was airborne for nearly 20 hours. On another occasion, a routine 50-hour inspection was completed on Wednesday and by the following Tuesday it was back for the next 50-hour inspection. Only once was it grounded and then only through a minor accident which caused some buckling to the port main flap shroud. It was finally struck off charge on 26 September 1944. W1046 was

WI005, a well-worn early production B Mk II Series I built by English Electric in January 1942, seen landing at Leavesden aerodrome in 1943. It went first to 102 Squadron and then to 1652 HCU where it served until February 1944, when it ran into a ditch and was written off. Very early production aircraft were to have had their fin and rudder units camouflaged in dark earth and dark green on the upper section and black on the lower portion. Careful examination of the original print shows this earlier scheme bleeding through the worn paintwork, the pre-painted components of which were simply overpainted with black before final assembly. The original roundels and fin flashes had been replaced with the post-July 1942 so-called Type C 1 roundels and the fin flashes by the revised 24 in x 36 in style with the narrow centre white section. Likewise, the serial number had also been reapplied in an unusually low and forward position, possibly when the original unit codes were painted out. (via M. Wright)

another veteran B Mk II, which had clocked up 690 hours flying time by the time it was struck off charge on 12 November 1944 after being damaged beyond economical repair in a heavy landing at Wombelton. It had served on operations with 35 Squadron before passing to 161 Squadron and then on to 138 Squadron for clandestine duties before finally going to 1666 HCU.

Failure of the tail wheel box casting could often cause the tail wheel to collapse and usually at an awkward moment, a not uncommon problem with early marques of Halifax. No doubt, the large number of heavy landings to which training machines were subjected increased chance of this type of failure and it continued, albeit in reduced instances. This is illustrated by an incident from 1943 at 1662 HCU. S/Ldr E. Bell DFC, the CO of 'C' Flight, was giving dual instruction to Sgt Fry; on landing at Wickenby, a violent shimmy developed and before remedial action could be taken, DK118 ran off the runway and into a ditch. The Halifax was recovered but its flying days were over; but not its usefulness for training. Converted to an Instructional Airframe, as 4127M, it was transferred to No 4 School of Technical Training at St Athan.

The handling to which these training Halifaxes were subjected naturally was very varied and did not always stay within the prescribed airframe limits, sometimes with fatal results, as happened to W1009 which crashed on 22 February 1944 through structural failure following violent fighter affiliation manoeuvres. It was not always the case that the resulting structural damage occurred during the actual exercise but rather accumulated over a period of time. One occurrence at 1663 HCU on 6 April 1943 appears to have been due to a more immediate consequence. Delivered in late March, DG413: C was certainly not a victim of age; with twelve on board, comprising the instructor P/O S. Rawling DFC, two trainee pilots, flight engineer, air bomber, wireless operator, five air gunners and one ground staff, it was being used for a fighter affiliation exercise. About 25 minutes into the exercise, while turning steeply at about 6,000 ft, the starboard wing came off, outboard of the inner engine, and the aircraft dived into the ground four miles south of Great Driffield, killing all on board. The Board of Enquiry Report found that the wing attachment bolts had been torn out and recommended that the mild steel units used should be replaced with high tensile steel. This was the first, and worst, loss of life for 1663 HCU.

Others were written off in landing or taxiing accidents. Others fell victim to 'stuffed' clouds such as JD417 from 1656 HCU, which dashed itself to pieces on the Yr Eifel near Trevor, Caernarvonshire on 3 September 1944 while on a night cross-country flight; the crew were all RAAF personnel.

The object of the training was to equip crews with the knowledge and skill to meet the enemy on equal terms, but sometimes the enemy could not wait. On the night of 28 April, BB255 of 1656 HCU was practising circuits and landings when a Ju 88 night-fighter attacked from behind, hitting the starboard fin, wing and outer engine with its cannon shells. Fortunately, the pilot managed to land the damaged Halifax safely. It went on to survive the war, finally being SOC on 1 November 1945. Others had to meet the test in other ways.

A 1658 HCU Halifax, DJ549, was on a night cross-country exercise when everything went wrong in rapid succession. With one engine feathered, one with the propeller constant speed unit disabled, and a third engine running rough, the pilot made an emergency landing at RAF Finmere. Despite the rough-running engine cutting during the approach, he landed the Halifax safely. The same HCU had two cases, one fatal, of propeller failure on its elderly B Mk Is. The propeller blades were suffering from metal fatigue and tended to part company with the rest of the engine, which usually resulted in the reduction gearing being torn out. The unit changed them for wooden-bladed propellers and no further trouble was experienced. A further propeller change, but on a much larger scale, occurred on 17 April 1942 when 1664 HCU began to fit all of its Halifaxes with four-bladed propellers; No 1667 HCU followed suit during the first week in May. Originally it had been intended to fit the four-bladed propellers only to the out-board engines but that decision was rescinded and they were fitted to all four engines.

The aircraft strength of an HCU was usually far in excess of a normal bomber squadron and in some cases the daily average of serviceable aircraft was as high as 40.

Not all Halifaxes used for training succumbed to the often heavy workload and less than graceful handling of pilots undergoing their final conversion training. EB151: R, a B Mk V Series I (Special), seen here just after taking off, was built in May 1943 and allocated to 1663 HCU where it served until struck off charge on 1 November, 1945.

Not surprisingly, turnover in aircraft also was proportionately higher and 1656 HCU's monthly summary for July 1944 is fairly representative of most. BB221 overshot Wrexham airfield after engine failure, crashed and was burnt out. BB261 crashed and burned at Hatfield Woodhouse after taking off from Lindholme in mist; HR837 and JD307 were damaged in taxiing accidents; W7705, W1224 and DT675 were written off due to deterioration beyond repair. Monthly flying times for 1667 HCU reflect the intensity of activity, 2,039 hours being achieved during July and 2,107 hours in August.

When an aircraft was written off, it did not necessarily mean its usefulness was ended; some were converted to instructional airframes and 1666 HCU devised a special series of training aids using portions of time-expired Halifaxes. During September, a Halifax nose section was installed in the Ground Instructional School (GIS). Completely blacked out and fitted with a blackout door at the rear, the Night Vision Section installed lighting representing a full moon and starlight. Bomb aimers under training were then able to do their switch drills under authentic conditions, with a master panel fitted outside the fuselage monitored by an instructor. This project was so successful that the engineering section of the GIS set up a similar nose section to check out flight engineers and pilots. In October, that particular nose section was modified to a B Mk III standard in view of the imminent arrival of this type on the unit.

By December 1944, the length of the training course had increased to five weeks – one week ground instruction and four weeks flying training. Flying hours had doubled compared to the syllabus used by the conversion flights in 1942; total hours now amounted to 41, composed of 7.5 dual and 15 solo by day and 4.5 dual and 14 solo by night. During the summer, 10 to 11 crews a week were posted in but this figure usually dropped to about seven during the winter.

S/Ldr Miller passed through 1659 HCU during this period at the start of his service flying. His comments sum up the varying conditions: *"I arrived at Topcliffe with my crew on 3 September 1944, and left for No 432 Squadron on 12 October. During the intervening time, I flew 44 hours on Mk II and Mk V Halifaxes. I clearly remember the number of accidents during our short stay, due, I believe, to the poor condition of the aircraft. I also remember how impressed I was with the handling characteristics of the Mk III on my first flight at Eastmoor."*

Among the half-dozen Halifaxes were two other ex-TFU machines, W7874 and W7875, passed to 35 Squadron and used for the first *H2S* attack of the war. W7874 eventually passed to 1662 HCU and survived until struck off charge on 22 October 1946. W7875 was not so fortunate, passing to 1656 HCU where it crashed and burned after losing height following take-off from Lindholme on 20 November 1944. Eventually, with No 8 Group's standardisation on to the Lancaster, the Halifaxes and Stirlings were gradually phased out.

Instructors needed their own courses of specialised instruction. The Bomber Command Instructors' School was formed within No 93 Group at Finningley on 5 December 1944; its role was to ensure uniformity of instruction throughout the Command's multiple training establishments, especially at OTUs and HCUs. Staffed by highly experienced instructors, it had an aircraft establishment comprised of Wellingtons, B Mk III Halifaxes[3], Stirlings and Lancasters; losses were few, none of them Halifaxes.

Other specialist units were formed for specific tasks. The TR1335 (Gee) Development Unit had gradually expanded from its early role since forming at Boscombe Down on 14 January 1941, absorbing 1418 Gee Development Flight at Gransden Lodge and changing its name in the process to 1418 Bombing Development Flight on 5 January 1942. In July, its title changed again, to that of Bombing Development Unit (BDU). Equipped with Wellingtons, a pair of Halifaxes and one Stirling and one Lancaster, it carried out service trials with experimental equipment. Its HQ moved to Newmarket in September 1943 where it took on responsibility for Development and Radar Training. The aircraft holding gradually changed and eventually included Wellingtons, Blenheim VIs, Mosquitoes and six Halifaxes – five B Mk IIs and a single B Mk III. In February 1945, the unit moved back to Feltwell.

The only Halifax accident occurred after the war in Europe had ended. On 17/18 July 1945, F/Lt S. Clark DFC RNZAF was flying a night-training sortie with nine on board, in B Mk III MZ369. Returning to Feltwell just after midnight, he elected to abort his first landing approach and go round again but as he opened up the throttles, the Halifax yawed 30 degrees to starboard and, moments later, the wheels contacted the runway. Clark immediately retracted the undercarriage and cut the throttles, making a belly-landing, the Halifax coming to a halt 250 yards later up against a building about 100 yards beyond the airfield. Fortunately, no one was injured.

The unit moved once more, to Lindholme in October, before disbanding in November 1945.

The role of the Bomber Support (BS) units had been crucial to the last phase of the war for Bomber Command and the Radio Warfare Establishment (RWE) had been formed at Watton to train operators for their specialist tasks. The Flying and Servicing Wings had been formed in September 1945 at Foulsham from the disbanded No 192 (BS) Squadron, while HQ Tactical Wing and Y Wing formed at Swanton Morley. This was a large unit, equipped with a variety of aircraft; Mosquitoes, Fortresses, an Oxford, a Ju 88 and 23 B Mk III Halifaxes were on strength by November 1945 and, while the unit carried out specialist trials work, it also trained operators. It was renamed Central Signals Establishment in 1946 and retained its Halifaxes, ten still being on charge when they were withdrawn in January 1947, the last departing the following month.

Perhaps the smallest training unit established anywhere for front-line crews was No 2 Middle East Training School at Aqir, Palestine with three ex-462 Squadron Halifaxes. W1156: Y, seen here at Fayid in 1942, had completed 14 sorties by this stage. A lack of radio navigation aids and night-fighter opposition led to the removal of the Lorenz Beam Approach aerial and exhaust flame dampers. W1156 had a long career, serving with Nos 78, 76 and 462 Squadrons before joining No 2 METS along with W7716 and W7717. It was struck off charge on 1 March 1944. (W/Cdr W. Russell)

Servicing problems were no doubt in part the result of the large numbers of aircraft and the large numbers of flying hours the crews were put through. The same conditions were to be found at most, if not all, HCUs as hard-pressed ground staff fought a battle with time to keep up the expected flow of crews through to squadrons.

The B Mk III version of the Halifax reached the HCUs in late 1944 and was quickly phased into the training programme. All welcomed their greatly improved performance, particularly as B Mk Is and early model B Mk IIs were still in daily use. Of course, this did not make the Mk IIIs any the less prone to accidents and they appeared on the monthly summaries of damaged and destroyed aircraft along with their elders.

Crews posted overseas usually type-trained before being dispatched, but the introduction of the Halifax into the Middle East theatre of operations created an unexpected situation and, in October 1942, a small conversion unit was established at No 2 Middle East Training School at Aqir, Palestine. It received three Halifaxes, W1156, W7716 and W7717, all veterans from the original 10 Squadron detachment via 462 Squadron. W7717 arrived first and was to be the only Halifax lost when on 8 December it was ditched off the coast after an engine caught fire, no doubt a victim of the notorious engine problems of that period. It was replaced by W7697, another former 462 Squadron machine. The other three, however, survived through until March 1944 when, with the focus of the war now rapidly shifting across the Mediterranean, requirements for conversion training no longer existed.

With victory becoming a distinct possibility, a reduction to the already well-stocked overall training programme was reflected by the HCUs, which underwent a major reorganisation on 3 November 1944. Until then, all had been administered by their respective operational Bomber Group; that now changed and No 7 (Bomber - HCU) Group was formed to administer and control all HCUs in Bomber Command, its HQ being set up at Grantham. This resulted in the existing HCU Bases being renumbered, the new designation consisting of the Group number suffixed by the number of the Group to which the Base formerly belonged. Actual HCU numbers, however, remained in force. A decision to retain the Lancaster as the prime post-war bomber saw many HCUs surrender their Halifaxes in favour of the Lancaster but on a smaller scale. No 1667 HCU, which operated a four-Flight system, gave up its large establishment of Halifaxes, but only 28 Lancasters were eventually allotted against an establishment figure of 32. Several other Halifax HCUs, however, soldiered on well into mid-1945, with 1652 HCU, the oldest in No 4 Group, finally disbanding on 25 June.

Among the other specialist training units was the Pathfinder Force Navigation Training Unit (NTU), established on 10 April 1943 at Gransden Lodge to train crews for pathfinder duties. It had received its first two aircraft, a Stirling and a Lancaster, on 10 April and its first Halifax two days later. W7808 was an ex-35 Squadron machine that had also taken part in the *H2S* development programme at the TFU before passing to 35 Squadron and then the NTU. At the time of the unit's transfer to Warboys in June, it had an establishment of six Halifaxes, four Lancasters and four Stirlings.

Only one Halifax was lost during the type's time with the NTU. On 25 January 1944, W7823 was tasked with a TI-dropping exercise but failed to gain height after take-off, crashing through some trees and bursting into flame, killing all ten on board. The pilot, F/Lt B. McSorley RCAF, was an American, one of many of his countrymen who volunteered and remained with the RCAF when the USAAF had entered the war.

Coastal Command

The introduction of Liberator, Fortress and Halifax aircraft into Coastal Command had produced the need for specialist training courses for these long-range tasks. No 6 (C) OTU had a Flight attached to handle the Liberator crews while No 1 (C) OTU had a Flight formed at Thornaby to train Fortress and Halifax crews. However, this was an interim measure and it soon became necessary to form a full HCU to meet the increasing demands; accordingly, 1674 HCU had formed at Aldergrove on 10 October 1943 under the control of Coastal Command. Its mixed establishment of Fortresses, Liberators, Ansons, Oxfords, Martinets and a lone Wellington, reflected the broad scope of its training needs. The Liberator Flight was already resident when the unit was raised, being out-posted and by then under the control of No 1 (C) OTU at Thornaby. With the disbandment of the OTU on 19 October 1943, 1674 HCU moved its collection of aircraft, which now included General Reconnaissance Mk II Halifaxes for crew training for the two GR squadrons, to Longtown near Carlisle. It would return to Aldergrove at the beginning of February 1944. Each course usually lasted about three weeks and comprised 45 hours flying during which special attention was paid to radar aids and Leigh Light techniques.

The varied Coastal Command duties, however, required a much broader spectrum of training and, to overcome the initial bottleneck in meteorological flying training, 518 Squadron at Tiree was screened from duties to act as a conversion unit while managing to continue a small amount of operational flying at the same time. The first Meteorological course commenced on 30 October 1943 at what was now temporarily known as No 1 Meteorological Conversion Unit (MCU). The Halifaxes used were a mixture of 1674 HCU and 518 Squadron aircraft. Cooper Drabble, a Canadian pilot, served with both 517 and 518

Squadrons and his record of the meteorological training gives a good insight into how this temporary unit worked: *"We completed our OTU training at Limavady, Ireland, on Wellingtons and proceeded to No 1 MCU at Tiree. I do recall my consternation when Flt Lt MacQuoid, the instructor, left after only one circuit and landing in Halifax DG302. I believe that operations were being carried out from the station while we were doing conversion training from 13 January to 18 February 1944, but we had no contact with active crews. The training consisted of about 20 hours of flying: circuits and landings, both day and night, air to sea firing and bombing, QGH (approach via R/T instructions by radio fixes from base control) and SBA (Standard Beam Approach) training, plus two navigation exercises, the longest of which was 6 hrs 35 min.*

We proceeded to Brawdy in Wales, posted to No 517 Squadron, after the conversion training and spent a little over a month more in training flights and gaining familiarity with other nearby bases in Cornwall."

Meteorological Halifaxes had two pilots because of the length of operational flights and Glenn Traub, Drabble's co-pilot, had been trained at No 1 Maritime Conversion Unit in the same aircraft and at the same time – a very economical use of aircraft hours.

For navigators, the programme was much longer as accuracy was critical if the meteorological information sent back was to have value. Allen Williamson, who crewed up with Drabble and Traub had already completed the extensive RAF navigator's course before being posted to Prince Edward Island, Canada for a three-month General Reconnaissance course in preparation for a posting to RAF Coastal Command. On its completion he was sent to Limavady: *"The OTU at Limavady was to train crews for night anti-shipping strikes in the Mediterranean, using Wellington aircraft ... However, as the Italians surrendered at this time, we were posted to Tiree in the Inner Hebrides in early 1944. There was a three-month training period at this unit before beginning operations... Incidentally, the navigation training in the RAF was the most advanced of any air force in the world and the standard of navigation the highest."*

By the end of March 1944, 58 fully-trained crews had passed through No 1 MCU and 58 Squadron recommenced full-time operations. New crews posted in were already trained and the squadron retained only one aircraft fitted with dual controls, LL220, which was used for local training of second pilots to first pilot status.

Keith McGonigal, on completion of his first tour (a mixture of work with No 1402 Met Flight at Aldergrove on Hampdens and Halifaxes with No 518 Squadron) was posted as an instructor to No 1674 HCU. He flew with the same unit from September 1944 to April 1945 and recalls the varying qualities of some aircraft. *"I am sure you will agree that aircraft showed near human characteristics at times; our 'own' aircraft at 518 Squadron was, if I remember correctly, LK706. It could be guaranteed to fly perfectly, everything down to the*

By 1945, when this photograph was taken at Rawcliffe, 1674 HCU had reverted to using only individual aircraft letters. DG250: C had previously served with Nos 77 and 58 Squadrons before passing to the HCU. A Mk V Series I (Special), it retained both its tall radio mast as well as the C Mk V mid-upper turret, but had had its Type A fin and rudder assemblies replaced with Type D fins. The rather angular style of the aircraft code letter was a little unusual. (P. J. R. Moyes)

TR9 [radio transmitter] would be spot-on ... Similarly an old black (ex-Bomber Command) Halifax at 1674 HCU was always serviceable and so gentle that it could be persuaded to demonstrate the briefest of stalls [only] with difficulty, and with wheels and flaps down almost refused to stall. I think it was DG304 [ex Nos 460 and 518 Squadrons]. On a less savoury note was a white aircraft whose serial number is forgotten and rightly so. It could fairly be said to be a bastard – it had a built-in cross-wind, would remain trimmed for about half a second and could be trusted for less. I was eventually able to have it grounded and, I hope, made into saucepans."

On 31 October 1944, under Estab. No LWE/CC/4277C dated 29 September, the organisation of RAF Station Aldergrove was amended and 1674 HCU, previously an independent unit, became a Training Wing consistent with an OTU but retained its HCU identity. Many armament experiments were carried out at Lough Neagh Ranges. This was the first bombing range where crews could carry out low-level bombing at night using radar homing and Leigh Light techniques and receive an accurate assessment of their errors. Throughout its career, this unit had a very good safety record and relatively few aircraft and crews were lost. As a Training Wing, it began its move to Milltown in July 1945, the transfer being completed by 14 August.

During its HCU days, it had had remarkably few accidents and even less fatalities; only four of the 11 accidents resulted in loss of life. The first had occurred on 14 February 1944 when BB278 crashed into Morecambe Bay – this was a former Telecommunications Flying Unit aircraft which had then served with 58 Squadron on Coastal Command duties before being sent to the HCU. BB276 swung on take-off at Longtown on 13 March, the undercarriage collapsed and the aircraft caught fire. BB315, an ex-502 Squadron machine, was written off after the undercarriage collapsed during an emergency landing, at the same location, on 11 April. The next day BB310, previously with No 502 Squadron and then one of the original No 1 (C) OTU aircraft, flew into a hillside on Great Dun Fell, ten miles east of Penrith. JD177: J, which had arrived via the same two units, was written off following a fast landing at Longtown on 24 May.

Another fatal accident followed on 29 July when DT642: H, an ex-58 Squadron machine, crashed shortly after take-off from Aldergrove, hitting a wood at Shane's Castle, in County Antrim: there were nine on board. DT683, ex-Nos 58 and 502 Squadrons, was lost on 1 October when the undercarriage collapsed on landing at Aldergrove. The crew of JB963, ex-405 and 77 Squadrons, were less fortunate when it dived into the ground at Dundesert Bridge on approach to land at Aldergrove on 23 October, killing the instructor and four pupils from No 12 course, which commenced on 2 October. Only three crews formed this course, one for VLR training and two for meteorological duties. The next course, No 13, commenced on 25 October with five first pilots to be trained during the three-week course.

1945 saw only three aircraft lost; DT687, ex-58 Squadron and 1 OTU, suffered brake failure on landing at Aldergrove on 28 January and hit a pile of snow, collapsing the undercarriage. DG304 was damaged by pieces of propeller blade that disintegrated in flight during circuits and landing training at Aldergrove on 19 April and, although landed safely, was assessed as beyond economic repair and struck off charge on 30 August. It had travelled a long road by then, first with No 460 and then 518 Squadron before passing to 1674 HCU. The last loss was RG364, an ex-502 Squadron machine that was struck off charge on 4 October 1945 following an accident and was converted to Instructional Airframe 5750M on 27 November. All in all, No 1674 HCU had a remarkable record for any training unit.

*   *   *

Amidst all the military training it should be remembered that ferrying aircraft to front-line units was usually the job of the civilian Air Transport Authority. Aircraft were ferried from factory to MU from where individual aircraft were allocated and delivered to front-line units, some of them overseas. For Halifaxes, 301 Ferry Training Unit was the key unit, which had been formed at Kemble on 1 November 1940 under the title of HQ Service Ferry Pool and incorporating No 7 Ferry Pilots Pool. Staffing was drawn from very experienced private pilots who could be trained to do this vital task, which otherwise would have had to be filled by urgently-needed RAF flying personnel. From this small beginning arose one

Also photographed at Rawcliffe on a raw day in December 1945, was this line-up of seven more Halifaxes with DG250: C off to the left. The first two are JP163: B and BB312: F, both ex-1674 HCU GR Mk II Series IA aircraft fitted with ASV Mk III and reinforced nose cones to take a 0.5-in Browning machine gun. BB312 had previously seen service with 502 Squadron and No 1 (C) OTU but, unlike JP163: C, it was fitted with four-bladed propellers. (P. J. R. Moyes)

of the most talented pool of pilots, who needed to be conversant with multiple RAF types. The unit moved to Honeybourne in November 1941 and was renamed 301 Ferry Training Unit. There, it received two Halifaxes in September 1942 for training Air Transport Auxiliary (ATA) pilots on the type. It moved to Pershore in March 1944 and was absorbed, along with the Servicing Wing from Lyneham, into a new unit titled No 1 Ferry Unit, the Halifaxes remaining on strength.

*   *   *

The value of glider-borne assault forces was still high in the immediate post-war period amidst the rising tensions with Russia and the Halifax played a major role in the continued training for the heavy glider role. No 22 Heavy Glider Conversion Unit (HGCU) at Keevil had been given responsibility for this training since forming in October 1944 and it was intended to add Halifaxes to the unit, but only one, a former B Mk III, LW651, had been received when the allotment was cancelled. Instead, a second HGCU, No 21, was raised at Brize Norton in February 1946 and equipped with Halifaxes and Horsas, moving to Elsham Wolds the same month. No 296 Squadron, at Earls Colne, had just disbanded and 12 of its A Mk III aircraft[4] were transferred to form the initial establishment of No 21 HGCU, all having arrived by 25 February along with some of the 296 Squadron pilots on transfer. When 297 Squadron disbanded in March, ten of its A Mk IIIs[5] were allocated to the unit, plus some surplus and refurbished ex-Bomber Command machines[6].

The HGCU conducted extensive training, including continental cross-country exercises and it was during one of these to Norway, that it lost its first Halifax. NA638 ran into soft ground while taxiing at Gardermoen airfield on 11 May 1946 and, having sustained heavy damage, it was subsequently written off. Overall, operations were remarkably accident-free and only three Halifax tugs would be lost during the intensive flying training. The A Mk IIIs were gradually phased out from mid-1946, the unit receiving brand new A Mk VIIs (NA365, NA368, NA369, NA398, NA371, NA375, NA677, NA422 and NA423); by the end of 1946, it was using this type exclusively having added PP373, PP374, PP377, PP378 and PP383. It lost the first of them when, on 12 July 1946, NA398 had three of its engines cut while on approach to Leconfield, with predictable results. It was almost a year before the last, and fatal, accident occurred. The unit had moved to North Luffenham on 5 December 1946, and PP373 crashed while taking off from there on 17 May 1947. On 3 July, three of the Halifaxes towed three Horsa gliders to Mont de Marsan airfield for *Operation Marsan*, a demonstration for the French Army. The course was base – Cap Gris Nez - Mont de Marsan; an additional combination of Halifax and Horsa placed on standby was not needed.

However, the day of the heavy glider was numbered as new techniques for dropping troops and heavy equipment developed. When 22 HGCU had disbanded in November 1945, it left 21 HGCU to carry out all the training, a role fulfilled until the unit disbanded on 3 December 1947. Its Halifaxes, however, were not re-issued, going into storage instead. Further glider-towing training, although much diminished, was transferred to Upper Heyford under the control of the AOC No 38 Group.

Home-based squadrons were also engaged in military exercises. The School of Air Support had formed in December 1944 from the existing School of Army Co-operation and it was clear to military planners that future land battles would be combinations of both land and air power. As such, senior officers of all arms could no longer remain specialists in their own field. Two instructional Wings were established, the Offensive Support Wing and the Transport Support Wing, which heavily involved the Halifaxes. Their aim was to teach students about airborne assault, air-transported operations and supply by air. Transport Support exercises were held at Netheravon airfield and consisted of paratroop and equipment drops plus glider assault demonstrations by the Halifaxes. Sometimes demonstrations were mounted in Europe; for example, 297 Squadron sent two Halifaxes to Liege in Belgium for an exercise held on 14 July 1946 but the old nemesis, weather, occasionally intervened; that same month six exercises had been planned but one had to be abandoned and two others were made difficult by conditions. High winds on 30 July led to cancellation of the jeep and gun drop section of an exercise – but it was all useful training.

In the developing war of airborne support tactics of 1944, 1332 HCU had been formed at Longtown on 11 August 1944 but remained only until October when it moved to Nutts Corner. Equipped with A Mk III Halifaxes it undertook final training for pilots and Army personnel used for airborne support work. In April 1945, it moved once more, to Riccall, but remained for only a few months before the post-war reshuffle of units and bases saw it moved to Dishforth. It also changed its title in the seemingly inevitable shuffling of such items, to 1332 (Heavy Transport) Conversion Unit but this had no effect on its training role. In July 1946 1665 HCU at Linton-on-Ouse disbanded and its resources, by then A Mk VII Halifaxes and crews, were absorbed into the unit. It eventually received A Mk IXs and was still using these when it was renamed 241 OTU on 5 January 1948, receiving its first A Mk IXs the same day. In its new guise, it continued to use these until they were withdrawn in early 1949.

A second, similar unit had been formed on 26 March 1945 at Leicester East with 107 (Transport) Operational Training Unit being absorbed to form the core of 1333 (Transport Support) Conversion Unit. The supply of Mk VIIs was now becoming more plentiful and A Mk VIIs were issued to the unit. In October, the reshuffle of units saw it moved to Syerston where it remained until July 1947 but with the revised title of 1333 Heavy Transport Support Training Unit (TSTU). It received A Mk IXs and continued to use them when transferred to North Luffenham in July 1947.

A third unit appeared in August 1945, 1383 Transport Support Conversion Unit (TSCU) forming at Crosby, but it lasted only a year, disbanding in August 1946, having used A Mk VIIs. However, as this unit closed down, so 1331 (Heavy Transport) Conversion Unit was formed at Syerston on 14 December 1946, with A Mk VII Halifaxes, the Halifax Training Unit at Dishforth surrendering its resources to the new unit. Its role was the

same, training Army personnel and RAF crews for transport support and battlefield support duties. Unlike its two sister units, it had a settled existence, remaining at Syerston until it also was disbanded. The cutbacks and changing needs of No 38 Group brought an end to such units and on 5 January 1948, Nos 1331, 1332 and 1333 were all disbanded, and as noted above, the resources of the first two were absorbed into 241 OCU.

We must take a small step back in time now to 1944 when the Operational and Refresher Training Unit formed at Thruxton, then moved to Matching where it began equipping with Halifaxes and Stirlings, the intended establishment to be a three-Flight system, two equipped with Halifaxes and the third with Stirlings. ATA pilots ferried the first three A Mk VIIs in on 1 March 1945 and two more arrived next day along with the first Stirlings. Even so, aircraft were slow in arriving and it was not until 30 August that two more A Mk IIIs arrived from Tarrant Rushton, while four crews were sent by coach to Earls Colne to collect four more. However, by this date, a decision was made to equip the unit entirely with Halifaxes and the 14 Stirlings[7] already received were put up for disposal; 12 A Mk III Halifaxes were allotted to replace them. Then came *Operation Varsity*, the Rhine crossing on 24 March and the unit provided 20 of its now remaining 25 Stirlings plus gliders, for this final assault. The Halifax allocation was stalled and all A Mk VIIs were sent to Tarrant Rushton for the operation and all Halifax-screened instructors were recalled to their original squadrons. In their place, 26 Stirlings were delivered and 19 Stirling crews but the Chief Flying Instructor was the only Stirling-screened pilot available to convert them to glider-towing duties. To add to the problem, there was now an acute shortage of essential equipment.

The unit was forced to continue with its remaining A Mk III Halifaxes, three of which were cleared for flying by 2 April 1945. Halifax strength increased to eight on the 16th when two more A Mk IIIs were ferried in from 296 Squadron. Two more arrived the next day and the arrival of the final aircraft the following day brought the total strength to 11 Halifaxes. Meanwhile, the Stirling strength had been reduced once more, in what was becoming a bewildering see-saw scenario, with 15 ferried to MUs for disposal. The remainder, plus the 11 Halifaxes, finally brought the unit up to strength (once more as a mixed establishment) and it was able to commence its training programme. However, within a few days the increase in Halifax crews resulted in the allotment of four Stirlings to Saltby in exchange for four Halifaxes. This fine-tuning process continued and on 11 June two Halifaxes were exchanged once more with Saltby for two Stirlings, with a third exchange taking place the next day. The first long-range cross-country towing exercise with a Halifax, a six-hour flight over France, finally took place on 13 June. Then, the next day, the fourth Halifax in the Saltby exchange was swapped, totally reversing the process begun on 12 May! The A Mk IIIs were now being replaced by A Mk VIIs, of which seven had been received by 21 June.

On 3 July during a night cross-country exercise NA702 collided with a Wellington, LP906 of No 81 OTU, over Werrington, a few miles north of Peterborough, but this was something of an exception, for the general accident rate was low. The unit's aircraft also took part in a wide range of exercises, such as *Comeback*, staged in September – a mass glider-towing exercise – solo and dual towing training, continental cross-country flights, container-, jeep- and gun-dropping, air-to-air firing and fighter affiliation, and DR navigation exercises. Most former Bomber Command crews needed additional training in map reading for the much-reduced heights flown by glider-towing crews. The mass exercises continued under such exotic names as *Doofah* and *Share-out III*, both flown in October. On 15 October, the unit moved to Weathersfield from where it continued to operate, but briefly, before being disbanded in mid-January 1946. It had been a confusing establishment period, but once sorted ou,; the unit had provided valuable training for No 38 Group. Most of its Halifaxes were transferred to existing No 38 Group Squadrons; 644 Squadron received NA336, NA338, NA339, NA340 and NA342, while NA341 went to 297 Squadron; others, such as PN294 and PP339, went to 1385 Heavy Transport Support Conversion Unit (HTSCU).

The last mentioned unit had formed at Weathersfield and received the first of its allocation of Halifaxes in March 1946, to replace its Stirlings, the last of which were disposed of on 1 April. Tasked with teaching the art of supply and heavy equipment dropping plus glider towing, the unit received its first intake of Halifax crews in April, 12 coming directly from 1665 HCU at Linton-on-Ouse. It was decided to use A Mk VII Halifaxes exclusively for training and in May, the A Mk IIIs were ferried to Edzell for disposal. The following month instructions were received for the unit to amalgamate with 1333 TSTU at Syerston. As a result, No 4 course was the last to be trained at Weathersfield and No 5 course was diverted to Syerston when 1385 HTSCU moved in early in July, losing its identity to become a flight of 1333 TSTU. The unit moved to North Luffenham in July 1947 and remained there until January 1948 when it disbanded in another reshuffle of training units.

*   *   *

When the Central Navigation School at Shawbury was renamed the Empire Air Navigation School (EANS) in January 1945, it had been intended that the School should have an establishment of 20 Lancasters. However, a review the same month replaced these with 18 B Mk III Halifaxes, two Lancaster B Mk Is, a Mk XVI Mosquito and a Mustang. Conversion of the school's pilots on to Halifaxes took place on the unit, the first four B Mk IIIs arriving on 6 February. Progress was fairly rapid and No 6 course left for its first navigation exercise to Gibraltar in three Halifaxes on 28 March. P/O Freddie Puttock was a Flight Engineer who had completed a tour of operations with 428 Squadron and was keen to do another tour after a short rest. He tried for a posting to 100 Group but the EANS had a higher priority: "*Twenty-five or so Flight Engineers were posted in to man the 20 or so Halifaxes and they flew some of the Bomber Command and Coastal Command sorties. Here I was finally given a Halifax III and my first trip was on 11 February 1945. For the next three years I had a happy time in Halifaxes, Ansons, Lancaster VIIs and Xs, Stirling IIIs,*

Wellingtons, Lancastrians and a Lincoln, flying to Gibraltar, Iceland, Malta, etc.

There were, of course, the inevitable losses and one of the unit's Halifaxes, RG416, was written off on 10 March. Harry Schwass (a New Zealand pilot) wrote off the undercart when he overshot the runway. He was a big tough chap and as his Flight Engineer catapulted forward, grabbed him by the back of his parachute harness with his right hand while controlling the aircraft with his left. The same pilot plunged in after take-off in PN387 on 8 March 1946, almost a year to the day of the first accident. Definitely a write-off but no fatalities. Excitement was not lacking in these long-range wartime exercises and on 22 April [1945] a crew reported sighting a vapour cloud from a U-boat's Schnorkel device."

The cessation of hostilities allowed a far wider range of exercises and on 30 May, W/Cdr J. C. Halley DSO made a survey trip to Iceland, this new destination, along with Bari in Italy, having been added to the school's curriculum. An additional benefit of the peace also saw approval granted on 1 July to adopt the names of stars for some of its aircraft, *Capella, Polux, Rigal, Wezen, Sirius,* and *Koehal* were used along with *Nath* and *Kitty,* stars of a different nature perhaps?

B Mk III PN441: K named Koehal photographed at Barrackpur, India. In January 1946, it accompanied PN189: L on a liaison flight to Burma and India via Malta and Cairo West, departing on 14 January and returning on 10 February. With the removal of all camouflage, The Empire Air Navigation School marked the aircraft letter in black but in the case of PN441 it only appears to have been applied to the nose section. No roundels were carried beneath the wings.

The Empire Air Navigation School visited Khartoum in 1946 but had to operate from Wadi Saidna, a recent 644 Squadron exercise having damaged Khartoum's main runways. The revised four letter Training Unit codes introduced in the spring of 1946 had not caught up with the EANS when six of its Halifaxes, 'C ', 'H', 'P', 'R', 'U' and 'W', plus a single Lancaster, carried out a training flight to the Sudan between 30 July and 12 June (individual aircraft letters repeated on both the nose and rear fuselage were still in use at this time). Some EANS Halifaxes bore the names of stars painted in white script beneath the cockpit on each side. On the left is R Rigel with NA279: Capella on the right. Post-war, the EANS Halifaxes had their mid-upper turrets and tail and nose armament removed. Rigel had an additional astrodome fitted over the position normally occupied by the mid-upper turret, a feature also of Polux and Wezen. (K. Russell)

Right: Complete with topee, Fl/Sgt Ken Russell poses in full tropical gear, in front of W Wezen as it was being serviced. The code letter was painted in white, and the star name applied in quite elaborate script. The Halifaxes were now fitted with heavy duty treaded tyres as standard issue. (K. Russell)

Although photographs of EANS Halifaxes are, unfortunately, extremely rare, this view from the port side of P Polux and W Wezen clearly shows that the named aircraft carried their star names on both sides of the fuselage. (K. Russell)

The exception often proves the rule; MZ850: U was one of the Mk IIIs at EANS that did not receive a star name. The Shell mobile petrol tanker, complete with white tyre walls, would have provided a splash of colour against the camouflaged aircraft and dun-coloured background of the Wadi. (K. Russell)

Another of the EANS Halifaxes; Mk VI ST814: B Sirius wears the revised coding system introduced in 1946 for Training Command aircraft; prefixed with 'F' for Flying Training Command, with the EANS code 'GF' split by the roundel, followed by the individual aircraft letter 'B'. The heraldic badge of the EANS was also marked on the port side, the name Sirius being applied to both sides of the nose. (J. Halley via B. Robertson)

Some very long-range liaison flights were made by the school's Halifax NA279: C *Capella*. It departed for South-East Asia on 15 June with S/Ldr H. R. Hall DFC in command and returned to Shawbury on 28 July after a very successful trip. The aircraft used for these liaison trips were drawn from No 3 Flight, which maintained two B Mk III Halifaxes, *Capella* and PN441: K *Kitty*, two Lancasters, a Mosquito, two Ansons and a Proctor. No 1 Flight had 19 B Mk III Halifaxes, and No 2 Flight 21 Wellington Mk XIIIs used for advanced navigational training. Because of the rogue characteristics, one of the Halifaxes, NA553, was disposed of to Halton in September to become instructional airframe M5633. The unit's Halifaxes were replaced from time to time, but very few accidents contributed to this turnover; sometimes replacement action was even a little too prompt.

W/Cdr Les Manfield, a highly skilled and decorated navigator who had served with the Special Liberator Flight for agent-dropping sorties into the wilds of wartime Yugoslavia was Course Commander and received instructions to accompany a training flight to Gibraltar and back. *"On 26 September 1945 I took off in a Halifax III (NP952) with F/O Taylor as skipper. We were airborne at 00.45 GMT and expected to land at Gibraltar just*

This starboard side view of Sirius shows the absence of the unit's badge. By the time Sirius reached the EANS, camouflage was no longer required and the aircraft were flown in polished bare metal finish, only the black rubber of the de-icing boots on the fins; the dark leading edge colouring to the wings, air intakes and cowling gills remained, even the Perspex H2S dome was left in clear finish. Under wing roundels were the so-called Type C. (A. J. Jackson)

after first light; but as we were flying over north-western France a 'pot' blew off our port outer engine and we were forced to make an emergency landing at the small airfield of Blagnac, just outside Toulouse. The pilot and his crew had to wait there for a new engine to be flown out and fitted, but I was flown back in the Halifax that brought the replacement." Manfield, who played rugby for both national and international teams, was playing for Cardiff at the time and reached the ground at Cardiff Arms Park just 15 minutes before the kick-off against the famous London club, Wasps. NP952: T remained detached at Toulouse for unspecified reasons for some considerable time and on 14 January, NA162 was taken on charge as a replacement. When NP952 eventually returned to Shawbury, NA162 was put up for disposal as surplus to requirement.

In January 1946, a considerable effort was put into preparing Halifaxes PN441: K *Koehal* and PN189: L for a liaison flight to Burma and India while one of the Lancasters was readied for a flight to South Africa. The two Halifaxes departed at 06.00 hrs on 14 January, going via Malta and Cairo West. They returned on 10 February and both crews spoke highly of their Halifaxes' performance throughout the trip.

Then the school lost two Halifaxes in the space of two weeks. NP952: T crashed while attempting an overshoot on three engines on 21 February, fortunately without loss of life but writing the Halifax off in the process. Then, on 8 March, F/Lt Gilbert's crew of eight were forced to abandon PN387: N *Nath* six miles off Gibraltar. Freddie Puttock was the Flight Engineer: *"I had a dodgy do in March 1946 when flying in a notorious clapped-out Halifax III named Nath but colloquially known as Nuts. After taking off from Gibraltar the 'George' [auto-pilot] went haywire and took control. The aircraft banked at 70° and the autopilot would not disengage. I cut it adrift so that the aircraft could be brought back on a level keel. During this violent period, the ailerons had parted company and we had to bale out. The subsequent report in the Royal Air Force Journal reported the incident as if the engineer had laid about him with the aircraft axe (grossly untrue). I cut the lead pipes to 'George' with a hacksaw and the connecting cables from 'George' to the operating lever.*

Unfortunately, one navigator baled out and ripped his 'chute on the trailing aerial, which should have been wound in. Another, in spite of my effort to stop him, followed an inexperienced ground crew member out through the top escape hatch. Mistakenly I thought that he had made it and as the skipper was getting impatient, dumped my valise through the front escape hatch and followed it.

In actual fact the unfortunate navigator spilled his 'chute and, for some reason, turned his buckle and lost the lot, harness and all; he climbed back in to find that we had all gone. He waited until the aircraft was over water then cut the throttles and the Halifax went straight in and blew up. Miraculously he was picked up by a fishing boat.

I landed near Algeciras and was taken to the Governor-General's Palace where I met the rest of the crew except for the two navigators, one of whom had broken his leg. I had busted up both ankles by landing in a bog. The Court of Inquiry thought that I should have done more to save the aircraft, a view, I am glad to say, not shared by my CO. The Gibraltar Tribunal tested one of their Halifaxes and said it could not have happened. Shawbury tested all 23 of ours and found incipient faults in several of them."

On 26 May, another liaison mission was dispatched, under the command of W/Cdr R.T. Billett to the Middle East and the Mediterranean, returning on 27 June. The purpose of the flight was to enable personnel at the various units to have the opportunity of seeing the Halifax's latest navigational aids and hearing lectures by the various members of the crew. In addition, each leg of the flight was made using pressure pattern flying and grid navigation, two new techniques currently being evaluated.

The success of this flight prompted further tests by six Halifaxes and a Lancastrian, all of which left Shawbury on 30 July and returned 13 days later. Flying via Gibraltar, they went to Castel Benito, over the Sahara Desert to Khartoum, down the Nile Valley to Cairo and then returned via Castel Benito and Gibraltar. The 10,000-mile flight was accomplished using pressure pattern flying and grid navigation. Fl/Sgt Ken Russell was stationed at RAF Khartoum when this liaison visit was made. An earlier visit by No 38 Group had left the runways unserviceable for heavy aircraft and the EANS aircraft had to land at Wadi Saidna, about 15 or 20 miles away, making life interesting for the ground staff who had to maintain the visiting Halifaxes.

These flights provided valuable experience for the school's navigators, who were either Staff Navigators, Navigation Leaders or Specialist Navigators. Policy changes eventually caught up with the Halifaxes and Lancasters had replaced most by May 1947, but a solitary B Mk VI remained on strength until January 1948. This was ST814 *Sirius*, which EANS used for test and development duties under the control of the Air Ministry Flight. On 3 November, F/Lt W. Higgins flew it on Wind Finding Trials to Malta and Gibraltar but this was to be one of the last operational flights. It was disposed of to 45 MU in January 1948, Freddie Puttock noting, *"My saddest duty was to air test Sirius for disposal on 2 January 1948."* But *Sirius* was not yet a spent force, as noted below.

The Halifax served with several advanced flying training schools that ran specialist courses. No 1 Radio School at Cranwell had converted a B Mk II airframe, W1008, to Instructional Airframe 4593M in July 1944, using it as a fixed 'classroom'. In 1946 four modified B Mk VIs were allocated for airborne tuition; PP214: TCAB, RG875, RG876 and ST814. The cutbacks to all flying units saw this training role transferred to the Empire Radio School (ERS) and all but ST814 were disposed of to Maintenance Units to await scrapping. ST814, however, was to have a new lease on life, as detailed below. A second radio school, No 2 Radio School was also formed and received at least two B Mk VI Halifaxes, RG776 and RG782, but nothing further is known about the unit. In view of the cuts to units, it is possible that the decision to equip the unit was cancelled soon after allocation of these two aircraft.

Another of the five 'Empire' schools established under joint sponsorship of the Air Ministry and the Dominion Governments was the Empire Radio School (ERS), which formed at Debden in June 1946. Its mandate was to train Signals and Radar leaders as

then specially modified and equipped as a flying classroom having already been thoroughly tested by the Wireless and Electrical Flight at Farnborough who gave it its flying clearance on 29 May. Equipped with radio and radar installations and heavily modified internally and externally, it had been stripped of all camouflage and the nose cone replaced by a metal fairing with a slightly domed Perspex upper half. The modifications were made under pressure of time and difficulty with obtaining parts, aided by personnel from No 1 Radio School at Cranwell and No 4 Radio School at Madley. The Dominion Liaison Flight departure date planned for this liaison trip had been set for September and, thanks to the efforts of all, it left Debden on time on 18 September 1946 for St Mawgan from where it commenced its overseas flight the next day. En route to Australia and New Zealand it visited Iraq, India, Burma and Air Command South-East Asia in Singapore. The flight was to last 65 days and its objective was to discuss and explain all current practices and policy in radio training in the RAF and to offer advice on radio training techniques. On board were the Commandant of the ERS, A/Cmdr T. Fagan, his deputy W/Cdr D. Rusher DSO, S/Ldr R. Fluke, F/Lt C. Wood, F/O J. Douglas and Dr A. J. Marshall of Training Research. The flight crew comprised F/Lt R. Harrison DFC, F/Lt J. Bowner DFC, DFM, F/O R. Woonton, Fl/Sgt W. Hickson, plus Fitters Sergeants C. Callow and J. Scott. *Mercury* returned on 21 November after a very successful and trouble-free flight, apart from a burst oil cooler and skin cracking on the main planes. After repairs, it set out again for a second liaison tour to the Middle East and South Africa, on 22 January 1947, replacing the scheduled Lincoln aircraft RE414. It returned on 3 March after another very successful trip.

The two Halifaxes continued to fly the major number of sorties at ERS but, in August 1947, the unit records noted that a replacement was needed for RG751, which was disposed of to No 2 Radio School at Yatesbury the following month. RG815 continued its flying training duties until February 1948 when ST806 arrived from 29 MU to help with the workload. Another B Mk VI, ST814 arrived from 45 MU in June still bearing the name *Sirius* from its service with the EANS, but times and needs were changing and in August, ST806 was returned to 29 MU. September proved to be the last month of flying for the remaining two Halifaxes; in October ST814 was sent to No 1 Radio School before being sold to the Lancashire Aircraft Corporation while RG815 went to 34 MU.

The last Halifax used for training purposes served with No 1 Parachute Training School which had used several A Mk IXs for paratroop training, but a shortage of servicing personnel caused them to be replaced by Dakotas. However, when the unit[8] moved from Upper Heyford to Abingdon there was a revival of interest in military paratrooping as opposed to relying purely on assault transports to deliver troops into battle. A few A Mk IXs were taken on charge in January 1950 and RT936 survived its companions to be finally written off in April 1953. With its passing, the Halifax had severed its last connections with the RAF.

No 1 Radio School used at least four B Mk VI Halifaxes for training with one, PP214: B, and possibly all, modified to the same standard as the Empire Radio School's RG815. The modified nose section was identical but had the clear Perspex upper section painted over in Night Black. The code shown here was introduced in 1946 but unlike Sirius of the EANS whose code began with 'F' to indicate Flying Training Command, that on PP214 began with a 'T' to signify Technical Training Command. The second and third letters of the code related to the station, with the letter 'B' being the individual aircraft letter. PP214 retained the standard night bomber camouflage, relieved only by the broad yellow fuselage band behind the roundel. The issue of new aircraft finishing instructions on 15 May 1947 permitted, for reasons of economy, training aircraft to retain their existing finishes until repainting became a maintenance necessity. Training aircraft were also now to carry yellow 'trainer bands' around the main wings and fuselage. The so-called Type D roundel and revised fin flash of three equal widths of colour seen here were also reintroduced in 1947. Little information has survived about the work of Nos 1 and 2 Radio Schools and all of the Halifaxes appear to have been disposed of by 1950, PP214 being sold for scrap on 9 January. (via Chaz Bowyer)

well as wireless operator (air) instructors and pilot signals instructors in addition to providing a radio familiarisation course for General Duties officers. Personnel from any Commonwealth Air Force or other Service, civil aviation or from foreign air forces were also eligible for training.

In June RG751, a B Mk VI Halifax was delivered from 48 MU along with a Lancaster Mk I from Mepal and was joined in July by RG815. Christened *Mercury*, the latter was

A view looking forward inside RG815 Mercury, which was fitted out as a flying classroom with extra seating and equipment fitted in both the rest bay area and aft of the rear spar, the capacious interior of the Halifax providing plenty of room for such modifications. (E. C. Darby)

A Mk IX RT841: E captured on film during a paratroop dropping exercise by No 1 Parachute Training School at Upper Heyford some time after April 1947. This was one of the last training establishments to use the Halifax. Although instituted in 1946, the four-letter training codes appear to have been withdrawn from use by 1947.

A very special Mk VI Halifax of the Empire Radio School, this photograph of RG815 Mercury was taken on 18 September 1946 during its tour of Australia and New Zealand. The standard Perspex nose had been replaced with a metal fairing topped by a bulged clear Perspex dome while the badge, repeated on both sides of the nose, comprised the winged sandal and foot of the god Mercury superimposed on an RAF roundel. The name Mercury, obscured here by the strong sunlight, was painted on the oblong white panel, which was inset with two thin red lines. The finish overall was polished aluminium. The location appears to be Amberley, Queensland. (J. Hopton collection)

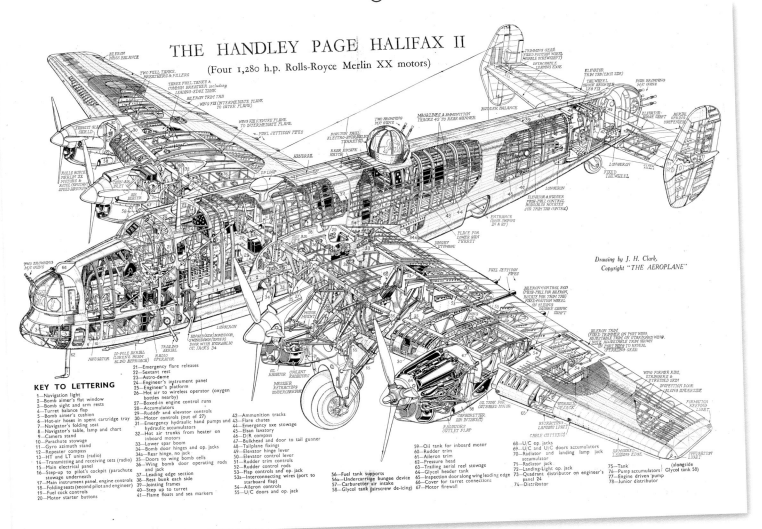

THE HANDLEY PAGE HALIFAX II
(Four 1,280 h.p. Rolls-Royce Merlin XX motors)

Drawing by J. H. Clark,
Copyright "THE AEROPLANE"

KEY TO LETTERING

1—Navigation light
2—Bomb aimer's flat window
3—Bomb sight and arm rests
4—Turret balance flap
5—Bomb aimer's cushion
6—Hot-air hoses in spent cartridge tray
7—Navigator's folding seat
8—Navigator's table, lamp and chart
9—Camera stand
10—Parachute stowage
11—Gyro azimuth stand
12—Repeater compass
13—HT and LT units (radio)
14—Transmitting and receiving sets (radio)
15—Main electrical panel
16—Step-up to pilot's cockpit (parachute stowage underneath)
17—Main instrument panel, engine controls
18—Folding seats (second pilot and engineer)
19—Fuel cock controls
20—Motor starter buttons

21—Emergency flare releases
22—Sextant rest
23—Astro-dome
24—Engineer's instrument panel
25—Engineer's platform
26—Hot air to wireless operator (oxygen bottles nearby)
27—Boxed-in engine control runs
28—Accumulators
29—Rudder and elevator controls
30—Motor controls (out of 27)
31—Emergency hydraulic hand pumps and hydraulic accumulators
32—Hot air trunks from heater on inboard motors
33—Lower spar boom
34—Bomb door hinges and op. jacks
34a—Rear hinge, no jack
35—Doors to wing bomb cells
36—Wing bomb door operating rods and jack
37—Leading edge section
38—Rest bunk each side
39—Jointing frames
40—Step up to turret
41—Flame floats and sea markers

42—Ammunition tracks
43—Flare chutes
44—Emergency axe stowage
45—Elsan lavatory
46—D/R compass
47—Bulkhead and door to tail gunner
48—Tailplane fixings
49—Elevator hinge lever
50—Elevator control lever
51—Rudder trim controls
52—Rudder control rods
53—Flap controls and op. jack
53a—Interconnecting wires (port to starboard flap)
54—Aileron controls
55—U/C doors and op. jack

56—Fuel tank supports
56a—Undercarriage bungee device
57—Carburetter air intake
58—Glycol tank (airscrew de-icing)
59—Oil tank for inboard motor
60—Rudder trim
61—Aileron trim
62—Pressure head
63—Trailing aerial reel stowage
64—Glycol header tank
65—Inspection door along wing leading edge
66—Cover for turret connections
67—Motor firewall

68—U/C op. jacks
69—U/C and U/C doors accumulators
70—Radiator and landing lamp op. jack accumulator
71—Radiator jack
72—Landing-Light op. jack
73—Quadrant distributor on engineer's panel 24
74—Distributor
75—Tank (alongside Glycol tank 58)
76—Pump accumulators
77—Engine driven pump
78—Junior distributor

APPENDIX 2 ; Production and Repair

The Halifax was designed to take full advantage of Handley Page's well-tried and proven split construction and unit assembly methods introduced for its Harrow design, and then utilised for the Hampden production processes. The entire aircraft was divided into a dozen major assemblies, which allowed far more operators to work on each assembly than would normally have been possible. This not only speeded up production but also made transportation and repair far easier.

It was this production technique that enabled Handley Page to utilise the services of other engineering companies, many of them new to the aircraft field. Instructions were received from the Air Ministry on 22 February 1939, to proceed with the necessary planning for the production of 100 Halifax bomber airframes and manufacture of the necessary jigs. That announcement hid a lot of planning and expenditure that now swiftly had to be put into place. The first order meant expanding tooling and jig facilities, expanding the work force and also finding space in which to carry out the manufacturing processes. Co-ordination with engine manufacturers and suppliers of essential sub-components, such as the gun turrets, had to be formalised into a reliable processs. Jigs to produce 50 to 60 aircraft a month would cost between one million to one and a half million pounds. Forward planning was essential if this was to be achieved and between January and June 1939 master jigs were under construction, with templates being prepared by the textile industry work force. The second half of the year saw the shift to jig production. Building the production version of the Halifax was to begin in 1940.

A manufacturing group of companies, the first to be devoted to heavy bomber production, was established with Handley Page as the consultant head. Each member of the group had its own direct contractual agreements with the Ministry of Aircraft Production, Handley Page acting as technical advisers and providing, except in the case of English Electric, the jigs. The first to join the Halifax production scheme was the English Electric Company, already linked to Handley Page by its sub-contracted construction of Hampdens. Unlike the later members of the manufacturing group, English Electric jigged and tooled the Halifax to suit its own production techniques.

An early production B Mk II, its beam gun hatches visible, reaches completion at English Electric's Preston factory. In the left background another Halifax has reached the roll-out stage while, to the right, Hampdens are under construction on a separate production line. All components were painted prior to assembly and transfer to Salmesbury airfield for assembly and flight-testing. The centre section camouflage had a slight misalignment where upper and lower colours met and was characteristic of this production facility. (English Electric)

By November 1939, Air Ministry planning had grown to an expectation of 500 Halifaxes, to be built at a rate of 22 a month, the combined output of both Handley Page and English Electric; but shortages already had the parent company's planning lagging by three to four months. Further revisions followed and by November 1939, Handley Page, seeking extra space, had already occupied the old Nieuport works at Cricklewood. At the outbreak of war, the Government implemented its Shadow Factory scheme to rapidly expand war industry manufacturing. Rootes Securities' new Shadow Factory at Speke was added by inclusion of that firm in the Halifax programme, although it would be

Preston works, but this process was later transferred to the Company's new premises at Low Moor, Bradford. Large magnesium alloy casting had not been used in England, but after acquiring production rights to the Messier design, the process was adapted for the Halifax. Measuring approximately 57 in high by 41 in wide and 17 in deep, the bridge casting weighed 260 lbs and was the largest casting made to that date. The technique required for production was difficult and required very high skills, each casting being done in an individual sand box moulding. The exterior was smooth but, internally, ribs had to be included for both strength as well as attachment points for the hydraulic undercarriage components.

Handley Page's first production aircraft, L9485, had left the assembly line on 11 October 1940, and was test-flown before transferring it to Boscombe Down on the 13th to commence its acceptance checks; it would remain with the A&AEE for its working life, utilised for a series of modifications and tests. English Electric was not far behind, producing its first Halifax just six months later. The main assemblies were transported to the final assembly sheds at Salmesbury airfield on 24 June, 1941, where they were married up and V9976 was test-flown on 15 August. After checking and thorough testing it was ready for delivery on 20 September to the Airborne Forces Experimental Establishment next day; by 31 December seven B Mk IIs had been delivered.

Photographed at an undisclosed production facility prior to February 1942, this view shows the C Mk I nose turret being winched into place on a B Mk II. Each turret was delivered to the production line in a wheeled wooden stand and installed into the nose assembly before the latter was mated to the fuselage centre section. The flared bottom section of the turret is not always apparent when seen on finished aircraft, nor the curved metal fairing between turret and the fixed glazing. (M. Wright)

To help establish the production technique, Handley Page had supplied English Electric with a pattern aircraft, R9538, and the London Aircraft Production Group with

1 April 1942 before their first production aircraft, DG219, would be rolled out. The expanding circle of manufacturers soon included Fairey Aviation Co. Ltd at Stockport and the London Aircraft Production Group. The last-named consisted of the London Passenger Transport Board, Park Royal Coach Works, the Express Motor and Body Works Ltd, Chrysler Motors and Duple Bodies and Motors Ltd; initially they remained responsible to Handley Page, but eventually they became autonomous though still reliant upon Handley Page for detail changes, etc. Changes varied from small detail to larger components; for example, after the first ten Halifaxes from Handley Page the inner nacelle fairings were extended to the trailing edge of the flaps to reduce drag. A more significant change to the jigs occurred with the decision to lock the slats on the wing leading edge; the first 75 aircraft were then produced using the original wing pattern until a revised set of jigs for the outer wing assembly could be introduced into the production cycle. Sometimes it was simply a matter of changing the size of a bolt, or type of rivet used. Ironically, one suggestion made within Handley Page in December 1940, was to extend the trailing edge of the main plane by 35 in where the engine nacelle met it; something that would be explored later in the life cycle of the Mk II airframe.

The original order was followed by a revised one (Contract B982938/39), for 200 Halifaxes, on 30 April 1940. Initially, undercarriages were manufactured at the main

A view inside one of the Rootes Securities' production bays at Speke airport. Assembling the massive front and rear spar assemblies with short aerofoil cross sections and end plates fitted to the outboard and inboard faces each side, created the structural heart of the airframe. A sheet of aluminium was fitted to the top surface and longitudinal plates divided each of the wing bomb cells. The three circular holes on each side were access holes to allow the bomb winch to lower its cable and lift each bomb into its respective wing bomb cell while the sloping black-coloured end plates set the alignment for the wing mid-section dihedral angle. As each section was completed, it was moved back and the upper mid-section, with its two large tubular braces, fitted. At the top of the photograph, upper centre section components undergo assembly before being moved to the next assembly area where they are stacked on end to await installation. The Perspex escape hatch of the upper mid section was aligned over what would become the rest bay area between the spars. (P. Summerton)

Photographed at the Leavesden Transport Depot of the L&PTB in November 1943, a B Mk II Halifax reaches the final assembly stage with aft and rear sections attached. The two long handles attached to the front face of the massive Warren girder construction of the front spar were the emergency hand-operated hydraulic pumps for the undercarriage and flaps. The access panels between the fuselage and first bomb cell in each wing hang open and show their cross reinforcing. The fixed metal side panels of the bomb bay were built as part of the ventral sub-assembly and the leading edge of each wing carried the control rods to the engines as well as the electrical cabling. The various types of bomb beam carriers were attached to the heavy cross-braced bomb bay structure. The difference in construction sequencing and painting processes between various manufacturers is interesting, given that all finished major structural components were identical. (M. Wright)

Completed nose sections, some of which retain the tissue covering over the Perspex noses to protect against scratches, lined-up waiting to be assembled to fuselage centre sections at the Stockport factory. The upper portion of the centre section assembly was pre-painted in the Fairey Aviation assembly sequence with the wing middle section being painted after assembly. Seen on the right, the finished centre sections face in the same direction as the completed nose sections to facilitate assembly. (Fairey Aviation)

R9539 and R9540; all were to be completed to appropriate standard, in addition to the total number of aircraft ordered. To maintain a constant standard of production one Halifax from each one hundred produced by these firms was flown to Handley Page's aerodrome where each was thoroughly test-flown. Any deficiencies were then notified to the firm concerned and necessary remedial action taken.

Production, as already stated, was based on the progressive assembly of major components which were, in turn, constructed into sub-assemblies. The fuselage was built from four sections constructed of light alloy monocoque with 'L' and 'V'-section formers connected by 'L'-section stringers. The nose section, containing the main crew accommodation, joined the centre section just aft of the wing leading edge.

The mid-section built up integrally with the main wing centre section, which extended as far as the inboard engines. The remaining portion of each wing was divided into two sections, the first of which extended to a point just inboard of the outer engines; mounting of the outboard engines on to the final wing section was radical for its time. The third fuselage section extended from the wing rear spar line to a point just forward of the tailplane. The final section carried the rear turret and the attachment points for the cantilever tailplane, which was secured by four bolts. The tailwheel mounting was anchored to the front face of the tailplane spar.

Handley Page had designed its split construction method to speed up production, but its ingenuity was not limited to the final production processes. One of the largest bottlenecks in aircraft production was translation of scale drawings of components into the full-sized article. While in America, Volkert had seen a technique used in naval architecture termed photo-lofting and he adapted it to produce an efficient system whereby the original component was drafted, full size, on to a sheet of half-hardened 16swg aluminium and then photocopied. The 8 ft by 4 ft sheets of aluminium were first coated with four very thin applications of cellulose lacquer, duck-egg green in colour. From the paint shop they were transferred to the layout section on the floor above, an area of 7,500 sq ft. A special silver solder pen point was used to inscribe the detail on the sheets, producing a fine black line. The finished sheets were then passed to the

This view of the full bomb bay and wing bomb cells of EB151, a B Mk V produced by Rootes Securities in May 1943 clearly illustrates their interior details along with those of the bomb bay doors. The rubber seal for the cutout section of the undercarriage doors sealed around the wheels, which still projected slightly when the undercarriage was retracted. The trailing aerial fairlead and aft end of the horizontally mounted Beam Approach aerial are clearly visible immediately ahead of the bomb bay opening. The aircraft identity is stencilled on a primed patch on the wing leading edge with EB on the top line, 151 in the middle and P (for port) below and was also stencilled on the under surface beside the rear end of the wing fairing, a part rarely seen in photographs once an aircraft was assembled. The leading edge section was also similarly marked, hand-written in primer, with the word PORT and the contract number and aircraft contract batch identity number R2/H/...... .
On completion, EB151 was allocated to 1663 HCU until struck off charge on 1 November 1945. (P. Summerton)

With wing outer sections under assembly in the foreground, this broad view of just part of the assembly floor captures the integration of the major component assembly lines feeding into the final assembly area on the left. With space carefully utilised in the giant assembly line processes, while units mounted horizontally were having their final skin attached, the next units, comprising the spar with key ribs already attached, were stacked vertically between the lines, ready to be lifted on to the horizontal work jigs. On the left, finished fuselage aft sections are moving forward with the unskinned frames of the next batch immediately behind. (P. Summerton)

Showing the remainder of the giant assembly shed at Speke, this view provides a panorama of the various sub-assembly processes being carried out simultaneously. To the right, the ventral well sections are under construction prior to being moved forward to have the rest of the structure added, before being turned over and placed in an angled jig to attach the skin and side plates which formed the fixed sides of the bomb bay. In the background, nose sections are under assembly while, just visible at the top left of the photograph, sit completed aircraft fitted with both Type A and D fin and rudder assemblies. (P. Summerton)

The parallel wing outer section assembly lines at Rootes' Speke factory, with LL147 in the foreground, identifiable from the black-stencilled information on the leading edge next to the engine firewall. All components were marked with the production batch, contract number and allocated RAF serial number for the aircraft as they were completed. The stencil markings provide information about the factory identification system used to track and co-ordinate the hundreds of components that had to meet for final assembly. The top line reads SERIAL No. 38308 and the one below, 'No. 373 LL147'. After the gap, the next wing was marked SERIAL No. 38403, and beneath it, 'No. 378 LL152'. The difference in both the contract batch number and Air Ministry-allocated serial number was five airframes. After completion, each wing was fitted with its fuel tanks, two of which can be seen stacked on end in the middle between the two rows; behind them are the fairing panels for the engine-to-wing join on the top surface, the nearest wing already having been fitted with both tank and fairing.
The stencilled information identifies this line of wings as being for the Mk V batch of LL112 - LL153 delivered between 6 November and 12 December 1943. LL152 was eventually issued to 431 Squadron and was written off after suffering damage on landing following the Stuttgart attack on 15/16 March 1944, a hung-up bomb dropping and exploding as it touched down. Completed as an A Mk V and issued to 298 Squadron, LL147 then transferred to 1665 HCU where it survived to be struck off charge on 15 February 1945. (P. Summerton)

The large dimensions of the wing roundel are emphasised by the female paint sprayer applying the dark blue, its outer boundary line marked by a paint resistant material, possibly of a wax composition. This outer wing section has a rounded tip so could have been for either a Mk III or later marque. The fact that the wing was still in bare metal at this stage was a common practice in Rootes Group production but no positive identification can be made. The lines of rivets flushed back to ensure a smooth finish, show as burnished lines against the bare metal surface. (B. Robertson)

The intermediate wing section that fitted between the inner and outer engines shows the depth of the wing at that point, which contained three fuel tanks fitted longitudinally with another fitted spanwise in the leading edge section. (P. Summerton)

Completed sub-assemblies were gathered into a collecting area from where they were issued to a specific section of the production line as needed. In the right foreground, upper right and on the extreme left, are complete tail assemblies, the horizontal planes with the fabric-covered elevators already painted in camouflage, as were the rudders. The metal sections were primed with zinc chromate as were the wing middle sections standing on end in lines, their rivet lines covered in filler and sanded back, creating a patchwork pattern of squares. Two wing outer panels and a single Type D Fin assembly without rudders are visible in the left foreground. (P. Summerton)

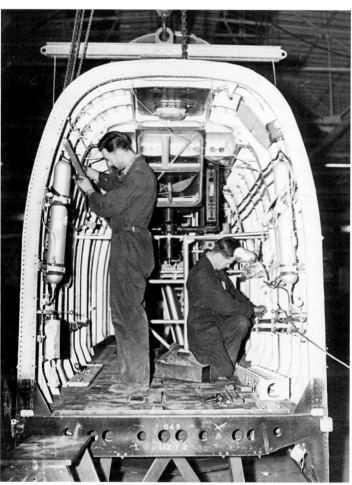

Looking back at the aft section, containing the mid-upper turret, being fitted out. The suspension pillar and attached, dark painted twin turret ammunition boxes are clearly visible; the fixed aluminium ladder was braced to either side of the fuselage with the bottom point bolted to the floor immediately behind the toolbox between the two workers. The hinged dorsal escape hatch frame hanging down shows its deep internal flanges that provided both strength and a foothold for escaping crew. The two vertically-mounted cylinders were the emergency hand pump hydraulic reservoirs for the undercarriage. The torque rods for the elevator and rudder are visible along the fuselage side next to the left knee of the kneeling worker.

The entire rear section comprised two major units; the mid-aft section with its main crew entrance door and fitted with small circular portholes and the rear section holding the tail plane assembly and rear turret, the latter containing a heavy frame built into the front edge to which the horizontal tail plane spar was anchored. Access to the rear turret was under the spar and then through the turret doors, the purpose of the large white 'L' marked on the rear face of the turret is unknown. The centre section assembly to the right has 'Ship 291' painted in white on the end sheet web and 'LK929 G Jig' marked in chalk. After completion, LK929 was issued to 76 Squadron before passing to 1663 HCU where it was lost on a training exercise on 28 June 1945, some of the crew baling out before it crashed. (P. Summerton)

The C Mk V mid-upper turret was assembled on a mobile stand that was used to transport it to the assembly line for installation, the heavy central supporting frame to which the gun cradles were attached being clearly visible in this view. The marked curvature of the lower edge of the Perspex-glazed rear frame gave this turret a distinctly rounded appearance. The '209' chalked on the next turret possibly identifies the aircraft serial number for which it was scheduled; if so, this was from the BB236 - BB285 batch. (M. Wright)

Below: B Mk Vs nearing the end of the production line at the Speke airport facility provide an insight into the mixed state of painting of finished components at this stage of the war. These were part of a batch of 100 produced between April and July 1943. The centre section of the Halifax on the right was fully painted but the aft and rear sections were in bare metal, as were the wing surfaces, while the next Halifax in line had its front section painted but not the centre section; the one behind that, other than for the Tollerton fairing, had a fully painted nose section. The tail assembly, just in view on the left, has only the lower half of the fin painted Night Black while the horizontal tail surfaces were still bare metal, only the fabric-covered control surfaces having been painted beforehand. (P. Summerton)

A Halifax airframe photographed while undergoing assembly at the Leavesden L&PTB factory. After attaching the nose section, the wing outer sections were winched into place; note that all components are fully camouflaged at this stage, something that also varied between manufacturers. (M. Wright)

Fitting the port inboard Merlin to B Mk II JP181 at the Rootes Speke factory, the aircraft being identified by its serial number, painted in white on the engine block as 'JP181 PI', the last part visible just behind the exhaust. Women performed every task in the assembly process after having advanced from their pre-war status of unemployable on male tasks in manufacturing, to being recognised by necessity as capable of any task. JP181 was a Mk II delivered from the L&PTB batch JP159 - JP207 built between 1 December 1943 and 27 January 1944 and was issued to the Polish 1586 (SD) Flight in Italy. It was lost on 4/5 August 1944 during the first of a series of desperate operations to help the Warsaw uprising while the Russian forces massed close by refused help as Stalin saw this as an opportunity to destroy the Polish Home Army. even aircraft were sent from 1586 (SD) Flight and 148 Squadron, who between them lost five aircraft and four crews, amongst which were P/O C.W. Crabtree and crew in JP181: X. (Via M. Wright)

Below: Nearly completed airframes were moved forward on sets of dolly wheels until time came for the attachment of the undercarriage and, after that, installation of the engines. The lower height allowed for the completion of several stages of work without too many assembly platforms being used at the same time. The height of the fairing around the A Mk VIII (Special) turret is clearly visible from this angle. All sub-assemblies and major components for each aircraft were pre-marked with the Air Ministry serial number; this B Mk V Series I (Special) had DG416 in black stencilled on the side of the nose section. Delivered in March 1943 it went to 1663 HCU and was written off on 25 May 1944 when it overshot on landing at Rufforth and swung, collapsing the undercarriage. (P. Summerton)

Left: Turning a little further to the right, the same production line reveals more painting anomalies, with the Halifax on the right showing its aft section painted but not the rear section, the horizontal tail surfaces and fins in primer but the wing surfaces and outboard engine nacelle in bare aluminium. The next in line had a fully camouflaged nose section but with the Tollerton fairing still in primer finish. This mixture of finished and unfinished components suggests that it was at the time when the company was adopting a practice of not painting an aircraft until after its air-test was completed. The Halifax on the right is EB249, its identity recorded handpainted in white on the camouflaged section just visible below the flap. Issued to 76 Squadron and coded MP-E, it was shot down during the Hamburg raid of 2/3 August 1943 and crashed in the woods at Hesedorf, eleven kilometres from Zeven, killing F/O S. Dillon RNZAF and crew. (P. Summerton)

The production line at Speke photographed from the point where airframes were nearing completion. All major components, including engines had been fitted other than for the nose section on these B Mk V Series IA Halifaxes (another photograph of this assembly area shows glazed nose sections being fitted). All had Type A fin and rudder assemblies, with the A Mk VIII (Special) dorsal turret in the high position, identifying these as early production Series IA aircraft. (M. Wright)

The large H2S scanner housing was vacuum moulded from four sheets of Perspex with the sheets first pre-joined and then clamped across a female mould, heated and drawn into the void to create the familiar shape. Lifted out after completion of the moulding process it was trimmed and fitted with a metal collar for attachment to an 'L-shaped' frame riveted to the underside of the Halifax. (English Electric)

A view along the final assembly line at Stockport where the wing sections, engines and propellers were added to finished fuselage and tail sections. In the foreground is B Mk III NA579, its duplicated serial number just visible under the camouflage paint on the wing leading edge inboard of the engine and duplicated in chalk on the cowling ring. Last adjustments were made on this line and NA579 has unpainted fairing panels around the horizontal tail plane roots while the next in line has a strip of skinning removed from just behind the flight engineer's glazing. This was part of the production batch serialled NA543 - NA587 delivered between 9 June and 19 July 1944. Issued to 420 Squadron, NA579 became PT-J during the period when the squadron was converting to Lancasters. Transferred to 1664 HCU, it was struck off charge on 24 September 1946. (Fairey Aviation)

photographic section for recording on quarter-plate glass negatives. These were then reproduced as enlargements on suitably sensitised metal sheets with consistent accuracy. This method ensured that all components were interchangeable, whether produced by Handley Page or any of the other firms.

Another special process was introduced when *H2S* became a standard fitting on the production lines. The large scanner cover was manufactured from Perspex and because of its size began life as four sheets of this material joined together. This composite sheet was then placed on a specially-heated metal table. By covering the Perspex sheet with a felt blanket the temperature was raised to 170°C and the heat was applied until the material became soft and pliable. From the table it was then slid over a female mould and the outer edges securely clamped with a series of wooden bars. The mould was then evacuated until a vacuum of 15-20 in of mercury was reached, slowly drawing the Perspex in until it took the shape of the mould. Within three minutes the completed blister was ready for removal and trimming.

After being test-flown by a company test pilot, Halifaxes were usually delivered to a Maintenance Unit (MU); Air Transport Auxiliary (ATA) pilots usually then flew them to the various squadrons or units. This unique group of pilots had to fly a wide range of aircraft and a class 5 conversion needed to be completed before four-engine aircraft could be flown. The original four-engine aircraft used by the Ferry Pool, which was based at White Waltham, was a Focke-Wulf Condor that had been flown to England when Denmark was overrun. This was later written off in an overshoot and no other aircraft of this class became available until 1942, when a B Mk II Halifax, BB191 (prior to being allocated to No 1652 HCU), was loaned for training purposes. The instructor was Klemens Dlugaszewski, a former pilot with the Polish airline, LOT, and with 20 years' experience. This Halifax had been built at Leavesden and remained there for the period of the ATA conversion training. With production test-flying going on it was not an ideal location for circuits and bumps and it was flown to any nearby airfield that could take it for a training session. It remained at ATA disposal until late in 1942 when winter weather brought the conversion course to a halt for the time being. The course recommenced in February 1943, but under more organised conditions; Pocklington was chosen as the base airfield, which eliminated the search each time for a suitable airfield.

The training flight was under the command of an RAF Squadron Leader and provided conversion training to both ATA and No 41 Group Maintenance Command pilots: the latter were the source of flight test crews at Maintenance Units. R. H. Henderson was sent in as an instructor on behalf of ATA and, by default, took over the training flight with its 30 RAF ground crew. The Halifax was now armed and a gunner was carried on each flight. Lettice Curtis was the first woman to complete the conversion course, on 25 February, and ferried her first Halifax, DG303, two days later. Her account of wartime ferrying duties, *The Forgotten Pilots*, is aptly named. Without this civilian organisation the RAF would have lost

Tuesday, 27 October 1942 and a memorable moment caught on film as B Mk V DJ980 left Fairey's Stockport factory, its major components transported on a series of trailers. This ability to reduce the Halifax airframe to manageable components proved invaluable when recovering damaged aircraft and transporting them to the repair works at York. This particular Halifax served first with 77 Squadron then with 1664 HCU and then with 1666, and survived the war to be struck off charge on 1 November 1945 when the older marques of Halifax were declared obsolete. (Fairey Aviation Co Ltd.)

The rear section of EB148 is seen here being transported on a Queen Mary trailer, open end first in yet another small variation between manufacturers, and shows to advantage the size and shape of the large fairing required by the initial supply of A Mk VIII (Special) mid-upper turrets. Issued to 427 Squadron, it only had a brief operational life, being declared Cat E (FB) on 29 June after sustaining battle damage. Outward bound for Cologne on the night of 28 June, it was attacked by a night-fighter and badly damaged, leading F/L V. Ganderton little option but to jettison his bomb load and abandon the sortie. After re-crossing the East Anglian coast, Ganderton crash-landed the aircraft near Soham, Cambridgeshire, slightly injuring two of the crew. (M. Wright)

thousands of hours of valuable aircrew flying time to the detriment of front-line activities. For delivery to overseas theatres of operations the process usually included an additional step, namely a Ferry Transport Unit. No 301 FTU at Lyneham received its first four Halifaxes, two for conversion training of the ferry pilots and two for dispatch, in September 1942.

Halifaxes passed through regularly during the next two years and very few failed to reach their destination. Among those that did not was DT493, which force-landed in Portugal on 8 October, 1942, through engine failure. Capt J. Stagnes of Ferry Command and his crew escaped unharmed while the aircraft, complete with its secret equipment, was destroyed by fire. Six months later, BB322, en route to the Middle East, force-landed in Spain on 10 April at San Fernando, again without loss of life. Others, however, were less fortunate and BB377 ditched 300 yards off Bournemouth Pier on 6 January, 1944, taking the ferry crew down with it. The unit closed in March 1944 and Halifaxes were then handled by No 1 Ferry Unit at Pershore, this new unit absorbing 301 FTU and its servicing wing.

1942 had marked the beginning of the intensive production programme for the Halifax and the London Aircraft Production Group had delivered their first Mk II in January, while Rootes produced only 12 Mk IIs before concentrating exclusively on the B Mk V variant. Fairey commenced production of the Mk V at its Eastwood Park factory, in Stockport, and delivered its first aircraft on 27 October. Like Rootes, it concentrated exclusively on this marque until introduction of the radial-engine variant. Within 18 months Fairey was producing 34 Halifaxes a month. One production plan that failed to gain favour was the mid-war discussions with the Canadian Government to set up Halifax production.

EB148 was part of a batch of Mk Vs, EB127 - EB160, produced between 12 April and 21 May 1943 by Rootes Securities Ltd. The finished aircraft were transported in sections to the flight-test assembly shed; the smaller trailer unit carrying a prominent Ministry of Aircraft Production sign on its mudguard could adequately handle the front fuselage section. (M. Wright)

Changes to design were fed into the production cycle, but some came abruptly – the product of urgent measures – such as the swift clean-up of the Halifax airframe, the most obvious item being the replacement of the C Mk I nose turret with a Tollerton fairing. This caught some aircraft at their respective manufacturers while awaiting either test flights or delivery, thus allowing the changes to be made before delivery. This Mk II was one such aircraft and, photographed during the replacement of the nose turret, shows the extended horizontal metal support frame for the Tollerton fairing attachment. This provided a strong attachment point with the bottom of the fairing sheet anchored to the horizontal mid-line frame of the lower section of fixed glazing. As a retroactive modification at the point of assembly and although the handrail on the fuselage top and streamlined Perspex blister over the side nose window have been removed, it was not unusual for the C Mk V mid-upper turret and high astrodome to be retained. The engine cowls were pre-painted components and that fitted to the port inboard engine has the outline of the asbestos shrouds that had been part of the problems with failing performance. The only other painted components were the fabric-covered flaps and ailerons; the wing leading edges, tips and sections aft of the rear spar had received a coat of zinc chromate but the rest was unpainted, providing detail of the various panelling patterns. (P. Summerton)

Seen waiting at Speke airfield for their acceptance test flight are these two B Mk Vs, DG398 and DG393. The latter, in the foreground, was delivered to 1663 HCU on 12 March 1943 but was later withdrawn and flown to Canada on 6 July 1944 as a pattern aircraft when consideration was being given to starting Halifax production there. It was accompanied by three others, EB127, EB138 and EB151 of which two, EB127 and EB138, had seen operational service with Nos 161(SD) and 76 Squadrons before being passed to 1663 HCU; the third, EB157, was delivered to 48 MU at Hawarden on 17 May and then issued to 1664 HCU. Their subsequent fates are not recorded on their respective history cards but an entry on an unrelated card shows all four with the cryptic last entry of Obs 2/46 (perhaps standing for 'Obsolete February 1946'?) suggesting that they were perhaps struck off charge or disposed of on that date.

By the mid-war period, aircraft produced by Rootes Securities Ltd were completed and test-flown without receiving their camouflage and frequently seen in a mixture of bare metal and areas in zinc chromate primer with only fabric surfaces painted in camouflage. But, in contrast, the aircraft seen here had no identification marked anywhere on its airframe other than for a roughly applied '167' on the surface of the port wing just forward of the long strip of new primed metal. The fabric surfaces, engine cowlings, some metal panels on each wing and both wing tips were finished in primer – all of which point to a rebuilt airframe from Rawcliffe and not a newly-built production aircraft. It had Hercules XVIs engines but the exhaust orientation of a Mk VII Halifax. Enlargement of the photograph and careful examination of the major components shows that everything aft of the centre section of the fuselage were replacements in bare metal; the wing outer sections, with repaired sections, were also replacements, as were the wing tips and all flying control surfaces. Thus, the extent to which damaged aircraft were rebuilt was virtually unlimited.

Four Mk V Halifaxes were supplied to the Canadian industry as pattern aircraft but the idea finally failed to gain favour.

However, in Britain some idea of the expansion of Halifax production can be gauged from the following extracts from English Electric's production record:

31 July 1942 – monthly output of B Mk II Halifaxes now 36 (double the March figure).
31 August 1942 – 212 Halifaxes delivered, averaging 4.3 per week since first one delivered in September 1941.
26 February 1943 – second order, for 250 Halifaxes completed. Total production now 450.
31 May 1943 – monthly output exactly to programme, namely 60, making 653 against a progressive target of 648.
24 August 1943 – third order, for 350 B Mk Halifaxes, completed. Total production now 800.
31 December 1943 – total Halifax deliveries now 1,006.
8 February 1944 – record production this month. 81 Halifaxes against a target of 54.
30 November 1944 – total of 1,720 Halifaxes reached on completion of sixth order.
9 January 1945 – first B Mk VII delivered.
9 February 1945 – first B Mk VI delivered, the 1,821st Halifax built by the company.

One company that carried out a specialised task has often been overlooked; Cunliffe-Owen at Eastleigh received a contract in 1943 for conversion of Mk V Halifaxes to meet the needs of Coastal Command The Halifaxes were flown in to the company's dispersed site at Marwell Hall by ATA pilots, and conversion work was carried out there. Each was then ferried to St Athan for fitting of the *ASV* equipment. Cunliffe-Owen also produced conversion kits for the meteorological aircraft, and when Mod 814 (D-type fins and rudders) were introduced, they were awarded a contract to produce ten sets a week

While uniformity of parts had been ensured by Handley Page's production methods, the actual production cycle varied between contractors. Perhaps the most easily distinguished was the painting cycle. Most companies pre-painted major components prior to final assembly, but Rootes Securities produced their aircraft in bare metal right through to final assembly, the exception being fabric-covered surfaces, which were fully painted, including camouflage. The actual process of applying the main colour areas of camouflage was done free-hand but within relatively finely prescribed boundaries. This led to minor variations between individual aircraft; while there were also some very minor variations between components that had been pre-painted, the process worked well. Stencils were used for roundels and fin flashes and again there was great conformity of application. Serial numbers tended to vary slightly in location between manufacturers, but again nothing of great significance. This was helped by the fact that most serial numbers were in the form of a pre-printed decal sheet. (The serial number also appeared during the assembly process, stencilled, or sometimes hand-painted on various major components, usually to be covered by the final camouflage. Engines, once allocated, often had the aircraft serial number added in white on the engine block, including the exact positioning, e.g., 'P.O.' for port outer.)

Production alone was not enough; the need for an efficient repair organisation had been foreseen and the on-site repair and modification policy practised by Handley Page

A foggy, wet day at Speke with at least 21 B Mk III Halifaxes dispersed along either side of the perimeter track and all with square wing tips indicating a date no later than early 1944. The Halifax in the foreground awaiting its engine cowlings and propellers appears to be entirely unpainted; another photograph showed that it was devoid of national markings other than fin flashes. Although the aircraft immediately behind was also waiting for engine cowlings to be fitted, the remainder were all finished aircraft awaiting flight-testing and collection. (P. Butler)

With construction and checks completed, Halifaxes were test-flown and then declared ready for collection by ATA crews for delivery to MUs or direct to specific squadrons. Just getting airborne, this B Mk III appears to carry no codes nor are any visible on the blurred images of the Halifaxes in the background, suggesting the possibility that the photograph was taken at the manufacturer's airfield. The H2S scanner cover appears to be transparent but is in fact an illusion produced by the dark oblong of the rear sections of the open undercarriage doors.

in peacetime naturally applied to the Halifax. This was put to the test on 31 March 1941, when L9486 made a wheels-up landing in the middle of Linton-on-Ouse aerodrome. Eric Marsden recalls, *"The aircraft took over six months to repair, and the Handley Page crew quite enjoyed the break from the London blitz, fire watching and other duties."*

But that scale of repair was never going to be sufficient; the Halifax had entered service with Nos 4 and 6 Groups clustered in airfields in Yorkshire, and MAP decided that it required a suitable site for a repair depot in the York area, home also to the RAF's No 48 Maintenance Unit. In 1941 Clifton aerodrome, with its Shadow Factory, was chosen, Handley Page providing the management for what was known as the York Aircraft Repair Depot. Adjoining the civilian airfield, construction began immediately on three runways and two sites. Four hangars were constructed on the north-west side of the airfield, becoming known as Rawcliffe; an additional hangar was eventually added to the complex. The first hangar was ready for occupation in July 1941, albeit roofless, when Mr E. W. Pickston, with 29 staff, arrived from Handley Page's Cricklewood plant. From this very modest beginning with its single 200 ft by 100 ft hangar it was to grow to a complex of six hangars covering an area of some 200,000 sq ft. By the end of 1941 it was apparent that the existing facilities would not be able to cope with the expected increase in damaged aircraft and, with completion of the third runway, construction began on a second repair depot, the Water Lane complex. From similar beginnings to its sister site, it too grew, eventually becoming a complex of nine hangars of somewhat larger proportions than those at the Rawcliffe site. By war's end there would be 16 hangars spread across both sites, the only damage to the complex occurring in 1943, at the Water Lane depot, when a Halifax caught fire, destroying three hangars and nine Halifaxes.

Damaged Halifaxes classified as Category B, not repairable on unit, were shipped to the repair sites by the lorries and trailers of No 43 Group. No 60 MU at Shipton-by-Beningbrough handled the actual transportation as well as sending out working parties to repair aircraft on site (Category A). Already inspected and their degree of damage assessed, the Halifaxes were stripped of damaged components, new parts were fitted and general repairs carried out. Initially aircraft were repaired and reassembled using the original airframe components, but with new engines and propellers. However, it soon became apparent that damage to one aircraft differed from that of another and a faster process could be employed by interchanging major components; this significantly increased the numbers of repaired aircraft flowing back to front-line squadrons. The extent to which a Halifax could be repaired is indicated by the work carried out on LK660. A B Mk V badly damaged over Berlin, it had to have a new port outer mainplane, port tailplane, port inboard flap and a new section in the rear fuselage. If an aircraft was too badly damaged it was dismantled and salvageable components used to reconstruct less badly damaged aircraft as well as being used for spares in production.

Pilkington Bros. of Doncaster carried out the salvage recovery work under the supervision of the York repair depot staff. Ian Robinson, a test Flight Engineer, recalls, '

"At Clifton (York aerodrome) we frequently flew aeroplanes which had major assemblies interchanged. When Clifton first opened in 1941 each aeroplane was reassembled with the same front fuselage, centre section, planes etc; however, the most seriously damage sub-assembly controlled the speed of the completion. When the second factory opened at the Water Lane side of the airfield it was decided to allocate a hangar per section, i.e., all fuselage sections repaired in one section, etc. A department

October 1945 and Chief Test pilot, Sam Moseley, receives the clearance papers from Mr Pinder, Chief of AID at Stockport prior to test-flying Mk VII PN343, the last Halifax produced by Fairey Aviation. As with so many aircraft produced at this time, it had a brief life. Issued to Middle East Command it was never issued to a squadron. Returned to the UK, it was sold to that major purchaser of surplus aircraft, J. Dale & Co. for scrap on 5 January 1949. (Fairey Aviation)

was created to carry out modification checks and complete aeroplanes were re-built from perhaps two or more airframes. Sometimes we would air-test them before painting and a sorry sight they were; an ex-Coastal Command front fuselage on an ex-Bomber Command set of mainplanes and rear fuselage. What of course all this proved was the excellent production method adopted by Handley Page in the first place. A Halifax made by English Electric at Preston could be fitted with the rear bay from a Handley Page-produced aircraft and so on." Robinson had volunteered for flying duties in 1942, but Eric Pickston, Handley Page's manager at Clifton, had asked him to stay on and train as a flight observer, later changed to second pilot/flight engineer; he eventually became Chief Flight Engineer at Clifton.

"As the Halifax became more complex, three crew were used, pilot, second pilot and flight engineer, although I think Radlett stayed with only two crew. During 1942/3 we flew minus radio and intercom and later in 1943 we used intercom but still no radio, and of course the aircraft were unarmed. We carried colours of the day but still used to have everything from Black Widows, Spitfires, Mosquitos, Mustangs and the whole of Nos 4 and 6 Group Halifaxes looking suspiciously at the odd Halifaxes from Clifton. It was a case of even more odd looks when a couple of civilian aircrew drove into Linton-on-Ouse or Tholthorpe, or wherever, to fly an RAF bomber.

The average length of an air test (production test flight) was 45 minutes. Second flights were required for about 50% of the aircraft and these averaged 20 minutes. The main source of problems were instrument failures and engine failures. Most adjustments needed to the actual airframe concerned only the trim. i.e. heavy or light ailerons, and the flight hangar staff would do the adjustments, e.g. droop or reflex an aileron. [The standard test routine comprised a visual ground check, wheel and brake test, straight and level flight during which trim and controls were checked for heaviness or lightness, a stall with wheels and flaps up, a dive to maximum speed and a check on fuel consumption. Each propeller was feathered in turn during which three-engine handling would also be checked.]

Handley Page test pilots from Radlett who visited Clifton, each on a one-month tour, were Jimmy Talbot, the company's chief test pilot (sadly he was later killed flying the prototype Hermes in December 1945); W. G. (Sandy) Sanders; John Marsh – all civilians; a second pilot was S/Ldr T. V. Mitchell, who still wore uniform. Flight engineers at Clifton were myself and John Harding, W/Cdr Mike Renaut, the chap who dropped the first 4,000 lb bomb, came to work for us for a short while. A most likeable guy who wrote 'Terror by Night', in which he recalled that the Halifax Mk III was faster than the Lancaster and had a tremendous rate of climb – he much preferred the Halifax. He went on to command No 171 Squadron in No 100 Group…..

Serious incidents during testing were few. Jimmy Talbot had the habit of banking steeply to port or starboard on take-off, before the wheels were retracted, and on one occasion we suffered 'near aileron overbalance'. Had he lost control momentarily it would have been fatal. Airspeed indicators seemed to fail frequently, thus precipitating difficult landings. Undercarriage lights showing wheels not locked down was another fairly common failure. Rolls-Royce Merlins had a reputation for breaking connecting rods and three-engined landings were fairly common.

Production test-flying was also carried out on rogue service aircraft. We visited most Nos 4 and 6 Group airfields to air-test their aeroplanes to our standard procedure. Rogue aircraft were those on squadrons where a specific Halifax suffered several early returns with different crews. We usually found that poor maintenance was the basic problem. We would submit a report and recommend certain action and then re-fly the aeroplane.

If weather stopped flying I helped out in the modification check department from time to time. Here, if say a rear fuselage was to be substituted, the modification plates and aircraft log book were cross-checked. Some 2000 modifications were introduced between 1941 and 1944. Only Class 1 and 2 modifications were introduced either on site or at the factory, i.e. they were essential. Class 3 and 4 were only incorporated on construction; e.g. Mod 452, Perspex nose, was Class 3 category and was never incorporated other than on factory-built aircraft."

When the Water Lane site commenced in September 1942 final assembly work of the complete aircraft was carried out there, detailed assembly being confined to Rawcliffe. In mid-1941 the depot had employed 100 people with an additional 50 doing on-site repairs at the various bomber stations. The final employment figure rose to 2,700, most of them women, with 350 working on other airfields. The number of vehicles also increased from a modest two, a 5 cwt van and a three-ton lorry, to over 90. In addition to the repair work the depot also undertook certain major inspections. North Africa-based Halifaxes were flown in direct from the Middle East for this purpose and 240 had been received by the end of hostilities. Liaison with the RAF was very close and during one three-month period 11,500 hours were worked by the depot's civilian personnel on RAF maintenance and repair work. In addition to repair work, aircraft were also modified to update them: the B Mk II conversions to Series I (Special) configuration had produced the major workload.

By the end of the war the depot had repaired or overhauled nearly 1,700 and rebuilt 320 more, flight-testing all of them. Its safety record was broken only by two minor accidents, neither of which caused serious damage or injury. On the first occasion a Halifax overran the runway and struck the boundary fence, while the other involved a Halifax that taxied into soft ground and stood up on its nose. No damage was incurred and it was righted and flown away. Approximately 2,000 Halifaxes had been repaired at York or on site. Components damaged beyond repair were 'reduced to produce' by Pilkington Bros at Doncaster, but all serviceable parts recovered in the process were reconditioned and put back into the repair and production process. With completion of the A Mk IX restricted to the Cricklewood plant, the York repair depot was closed in 1948.

During the peak period the collective Halifax production facilities comprised 41 factories and dispersal units, occupying a floor space of 7,500,000 sq ft, supported by 600 sub-contractors and employed 51,000 people. One complete Halifax per working hour was achieved from the group effort, while on an individual basis for example English Electric produced two aircraft per day consistently. For those who appreciate statistics in detail, 254,000 airframe parts were manufactured, inspected and fitted every hour; two-thirds of an acre of light alloy sheet metal, weighing 7 tons, was cut and formed and fitted per hour; three miles of light alloy extruded sections were cut, drilled and fitted. Close to a mile of pipes and three to four miles of cabling were fitted per hour. To that can be added between 600,000 and 700,000 rivets closed every hour.

With the end of the war in sight, production contracts were cut back, in some cases drastically. English Electric's last order (Contracts/Aircraft/3362/C.4(c)) for 350 Mk VI Halifaxes, placed on 22 May 1944, was progressively reduced to 175 in July 1945 and then to 25 on VJ Day. It delivered the last of its Halifaxes in December 1945. As the Halifax order was cut back, English Electric commenced construction of the de Havilland Vampire, delivering the first of these in April 1945. Although a sub-contractor, this firm produced more Halifaxes than any other constructor, including Handley Page. Rootes' contract for 300 Mk VIIs (Contracts/Aircraft/637) was reduced to 121; Fairey's contract for 90 A Mk VIIs (Contracts/Aircraft/891/C4/C) was reduced to 19.

The last Halifax from Rootes Securities' factory at Speke underwent flight tests on 9 July 1945. At the controls was F/Lt J. R. Palmer who had been the resident test pilot since 1939. On 5 October the last of Fairey's 661 Halifaxes left the production line and was delivered on 17 October.

The Halifax continued in production longest with Handley Page, the only company to manufacture the A Mk IX version. Production of this marque commenced in November 1945 and the last delivered to the RAF, RT938, was taken on charge just 12 months later, on 26 November 1946. It had been a distinguished achievement by all production facilities and their countless staff; production had peaked at 1,200 in 1944, two-fifths of all heavy bombers produced in England, comprising two prototypes and 6,176 Halifaxes constructed since L7244 first took to the skies in 1939.

APPENDIX 3 Contracts and Serial Numbers

Handley Page Ltd (199 aircraft)
Contract No 69649/37, requisition 102/E11/37 issued for 100 aircraft, but increased under contract No 73328/40, requisition 24/E11/39 to 199 aircraft. Deliveries commenced 13.10.40 (L9485) and 11.10.41. (L9610).
B Mk I L9485-9534, L9560-9584, L9600-9608
B Mk II L9609-9624, R9363-9392, R9418-9457, R9482-9498, R9528-9540
 Note: These aircraft supplied for pattern purposes to contractors; these to be completed to appropriate Halifax standards and delivered in addition to those aircraft ordered by contract: R9538 to English Electric Co Ltd, R9539 and R9540 to London Passenger Transport Board (London Aircraft Production Group).

English Electric Co Ltd (200 aircraft)
Contract No B982938/39, requisition 116/E11/39. Deliveries commenced 5.9.41 (V9976).
B Mk II V9976-9994, W1002-1021, W1035-1067, W1090-1117, W1141-1190, W1211-1253, W1270-1276.

Handley Page Ltd (200 aircraft)
Contract No B73328/40, requisition 24/E11/39. Deliveries commenced 24.3.42 (W7650).
B Mk II W7650-7679, W7695-7720, W7745-7784, W7801-7826, W7844-7887, W7906-7939.

London Passenger Transport Board (London Aircraft Production Group) (200 aircraft)
Contract No B 124357/40, requisition HA1/E11/39. Deliveries commenced 10.1.42 (BB189).
B Mk II BB189-223, BB236-285, BB300-344, BB357-391, BB412-446.

Rootes Securities Ltd (150 aircraft)
Contract No ACFT/637, requisition HA3/E11/40. Deliveries commenced 1.4.42 (DG219), 12.8.42 (DG231).
B Mk II DG219-230.
B/Met Mk V DG231-253, DG270-317, DG338-363, DG384-424.
 Note: DG223 crashed on factory test flight, not delivered; DG399 sent to Canada as a production model.

Fairey Aviation Co Ltd (150 aircraft)
Contract No ACFT/891/SAS C4, requisition HA 1/E11/41. Deliveries commenced 27.10.42 (DJ980).
B/Met Mk V DJ980-999, DK114-151, DK165-207, DK223-271.

English Electric Co Ltd (250 aircraft)
Contract No B982938/39, requisition 116/E11/39. Deliveries commenced 22.8.42 (DT481).
B/GR Mk II DT481-526, DT539-588, DT612-649, DT665-705, DT720-752, DT767-808.

Rootes Securities Ltd (100 aircraft)
Contract No ACFT/637, requisition HA3/E11/40. Deliveries commenced 12.4.43 (EB127).
B Mk V EB127-160, EB178-220, EB239-258, EB274-276.

Handley Page Ltd (200 aircraft)
Contract No ACFT/1688, requisition HA4/E11/41. Deliveries commenced 21.12.42. (HR654)
B/GR Mk II HR654-699, HR711-758, HR773-819, HR832-880, HR905-952, HR977-988.

Handley Page Ltd (150 aircraft)
Contract No ACFT/1688, requisition HA4/E11/41. Deliveries commenced 11.8.43 (HX147) and 7.9.43 (HX226).
B/GR Mk II HX147-I91, HX222-225.
B/GR Mk III HX226-247, HX265-296, HX311-357.

English Electric Co Ltd (350 aircraft)
Contract No ACFT/1808, requisition HA1/E11/42. Deliveries commenced 21.2.43. (JB781).
B/GR Mk II JB781-806, JB834-875, JB892-931, JB956-974, JD105-128, JD143-180, JD198-218, JD244-278, JD296-333, JD361-386, JD405-421, JD453-476.

London Passenger Transport Board (London Aircraft Production Group) (250 aircraft)
Contract No 124357/40, requisition HA1/E11/39. Deliveries commenced 7.7.43 (JN882).
B/GR Mk II JN882-296, JN941-978, JP107-137, JP159-207, JP220-259, JP275-301, JP319-338.

Fairey Aviation Co Ltd (200 aircraft)
Contract No ACFT/891, requisition HA1/E11/41. Deliveries commenced 13.8.43 (LK626) and 20.1.44 (LK747).
B/A/Met Mk V LK626-667, LK680-711, LK725-746.
B Mk III LK747-766, LK779-812, LK826-850, LK863-887.

Rootes Securities Ltd (480 aircraft)
Contract No ACFT/637, requisition HA3/E11/40. Deliveries commenced 18.7.43 (LK890) and 13.5.44 (LL543).
B/A/Met Mk V LK890-932, LK945-976, LK988-999, LL112-153, LL167-198, LL213-258, LL270-312, LL325-367, LL380-423, LL437-469, LL481-521, LL534-542.
B/A Mk III LL543-559, LL573-615.

Handley Page Ltd (240 aircraft)
Contract No ACFT/1688, requisition HA4/E11/41. Deliveries commenced 2.1.44 (LV771) and 31.5.44(LW196).
B Mk III LV771-799, LV813-842, LV857-883, LV898-923, LV935-973, LV985-999, LW113-143, LW157-179, LW191-195.
B Mk VII LW196-2I0.
Note: LV776 was a B Mk VI (28.2.44.); LV838 converted to B then C Mk VI.

English Electric Co Ltd (360 aircraft)
Contract No ACFT/1808, requisition HA1/E11/42. Deliveries commenced 25.8.43 (LW223) and 19.10.43 (LW346).
B Mk II LW223-246, LW259-301, LW313-345.
B/A Mk III LW346-348, LW361-397, LW412-446, LW459-481, LW495-522, LW537-559, LW572-598, LW613-658, LW671-696, LW713-724.

London Passenger Transport Board (London Aircraft Production Group) (180 aircraft)
Contract No ACFT/2595, requisition HA10/E11/42. Deliveries commenced 31.3.44 (MZ282).
B/Met Mk III MZ282-321, MZ334-378, MZ390-435, MZ447-495.

English Electric Co Ltd (360 aircraft)
Contract No ACFT/2553, requisition HA9/E11/42. Deliveries commenced 11.3.44 (MZ500).
B Mk III MZ500-544, MZ556-604, MZ617-660, MZ672-717, MZ730-775, MZ787-831, MZ844-883, MZ895-939.

Rootes Securities Ltd (340 aircraft)
Contract No ACFT/637, requisition HA3/E11/40. Deliveries commenced 29.8.44 (MZ945) and 4.2.45 (NA311).
B/A/GR/Met Mk III MZ945-989, NA102-150, NA162-205, NA218-263, NA275-310.
A Mk VII NA311-320, NA336-380, NA392-431, NA444-NA468
 Note: Two A Mk IIIs, NA428 and NA452, and a GR III, NA368, in A Mk VII batch.
 Last Rootes-built Halifax, NA468, completed 12.7.45.

Fairey Aviation Co Ltd (180 aircraft)
Contract No ACFT/891, requisition HA1/E11/41. Deliveries commenced 28.4.44 (NA492).
B/A/Met Mk III NA492-531, NA543-587, NA599-644, NA656-704.

Handley Page Ltd (200 aircraft)
Contract No ACFT/1688, requisition HA16/E11/42. Deliveries commenced 16.6.44 (NP681) and 28.9.44 (NP821).
B Mk VII NP681-723, NP736-781, NP793-820.
B Mk VI NP821-836, NP849-895, NP908-927.
 Note: First production B Mk VI, NP748, included in B Mk VII batch.

English Electric Co Ltd (200 aircraft)
Contract No ACFT/2553, requisition HA15/E11/42. Deliveries commenced 31.8.44 (NP930).
B/GR/Met Mk III NP930-976, NP988-999, NR113-156, NR169-211, NR225-258, NR271-290.

Fairey Aviation Co Ltd (150 aircraft)
Contract No ACFT/891, requisition HA1/E11/41. Deliveries commenced 16.10.44 (PN167) and 3.2.45 (PN208).
B/GR/Me Mk III PN167-207.
B/A Mk VII PN208, PN223-267, PN285-327, PN343.
 Note: Only 131 aircraft built as shown, remainder of order cancelled.

London Passenger Transport Board (London Aircraft Production Group) (200 aircraft)
Contract No ACFT/2595, requisition HA10/E11/42. Deliveries commenced 25.11.44 (PN365).
B/GR/Met Mk III PN365-406, PN423-461.
 Note: Only 70 aircraft built as shown (PN461 not built; PN460 last to be constructed, delivered 16.4.45). Remainder of order cancelled.

Handley Page Ltd (200 aircraft)
Contract No ACFT/3294, requisition HA16/E11/42. Deliveries commenced 19.1.45 (TW774), 23.3.45 (PP217), 23.8.45 (PP339).
B Mk VI TW774-796, PP165-187, PP203-216.
C Mk VIII PP217-247, PP259-296, PP308-338.
A Mk VII PP339-350, PP362-389.
 Note: C Mk VIII block included one A Mk VII, PP277, and one B Mk VI, PP225.

English Electric Co Ltd (400 aircraft)
Contract No ACFT/3362, requisition HA5/E11/43. Deliveries commenced 2.12.44 (RG345), 12.1.45 (RG447), 13.2.45 (RG480).
B/GR/Met Mk III RG345-390, RG413-446.
B Mk VII RG447-458, RG472-479.
B Mk VI RG480-513, RG537-568, RG583-625, RG639-679, RG693-736, RG749-776.
B/Met Mk VI RG777-790, RG813-853, RG867-879.

Handley Page Ltd (200 aircraft)
Contract No ACFT/3645, requisition HA16/E11/42. Deliveries commenced 1.11.45. (RT753) and 23.10.45 (RT758).
A Mk VII RT753-757.
A Mk IX RT758-799, RT814-856, RT868-908, RT920-938.

Note: RT786, RT798 and RT923 modified for meteorological duties. RT937 and RT938 last Halifaxes built, both delivered 26.11.46. Only 150 aircraft built as shown, remainder of order cancelled.

English Electric Co Ltd (350 aircraft)
Contract No ACFT/3860, requisition HA9/E11/43. Deliveries commenced 27.9.45 (ST795).
B/Met Mk VI ST794-818.
Note: Order reduced to 175 in July 1945 and then to 25 shortly after.
Only nine B Mk VIs, ST795, 797, 799, 800, 805, 806, 808, 814, 817.

Other contracts reduced or cancelled due to reduced requirements as war entered final stage. (Serial number blocks are known, but precise contract details remain provisional in some instances):

Rootes Securities Ltd. (300 aircraft)
Contract No ACFT/637. Serial numbers allotted 14.8.43.
B Mk III PX534-578, PX591-635, PX648-689, PX703-748, PX763-805, PX818-859, PX873-909.

Rootes Securities Ltd. (300 aircraft)
Contract details not known. Serial numbers allotted 20.3.44.
A Mk VII SV344-388, SV401-435, SV448-479, SV493-535, SV548-583, SV595-638, SV653-695, SV715-736.

Handley Page Ltd (200 aircraft);
Contract No ACFT/4203, requisition HA6/E11/44.
B Mk VI TH186-227, TH241-287, TH302-338, TH351-392, TH415-446

English Electric Co Ltd (350 aircraft)
Contract No ACFT/3860, requisition HA9/E11/43. Deliveries commenced 27.9.45 (ST795).

English Electric Co Ltd (400 aircraft) Contract No ACFT/3860, requisition HA9/E11/43.
Serial numbers allotted 20.3.44. Cancelled 325 airframes.
B Mk VI ST819-835, ST848-890 ST905-946, ST959-999, SV113-158, SV173-215, SV228-269, SV280-315, SV328-341.

English Electric Co Ltd (200 aircraft)
Contract No ACFT/4418, requisition HA7/E11/44. Serial numbers allotted 19.7.44.
B Mk VI TM392-412, TM424-472, TM502-537, TM550-572,
TM584-630, TM650-689, TM702-738, TM752-783, TM796-824, TM840-887, TM902-939.

Fairey Aviation Co Ltd (150 aircraft)
TM944-983, TN101-115, TN130-153, TN166-213, TN225-247.

Fairey Aviation Co Ltd (19 aircraft)
Contract ACFT/891. Serial numbers allotted 27.2.45.
B Mk VII TZ450-468

Total Halifax production 6,176 aircraft plus the first two prototypes.
Breakdown of production:
English Electric Co Ltd 2,145;
Handley Page Ltd 1,539;
Rootes Securities Ltd 1,070; LPTB(LAPG) 700;
Fairey Aviation Co Ltd 661.

APPENDIX 4 **Design Data**

Design data and specifications common to all marques except where noted.

Wing span: 98ft 8in (late Mk III, VI, VII, VIII and IX 103ft 8in)

Height (tail down): 21ft 4in over W/T mast or 20ft in over D/F loop

Length: 69ft 9in (Series IA and all later marques
71ft 7in except C Mk VIII: 73ft 7in)

Fuselage: maximum width 5ft 6in, maximum depth 9ft 6in

Aspect Ratio: short span 7:8, long span 8:4

Aerofoil: centre and inner mainplane NACA 23021, outer NACA 23009

Wing Incidence: at wing root +3° ±15' (late-model aircraft +2°45' ±15')

Dihedral: inner mainplane 0° ±15', outer 2° 25' ±15'

Chord: root 16ft 0in, tip 6ft 1½ in

Sweep Back: inner mainplane 0°, outer 9° 31'

Tailplane Span: 30ft 4in

Dihedral: 0° ±15'

Incidence: +0.5° ±15' (C Mk VII 0° ±15')

Undercarriage Track: 24ft 8in

Areas (gross):
Ailerons: 85sq ft
Tailplane: 223.4sq ft
Elevators: 98.3sq ft
Fin: (each) triangular 59.3sq ft, oblong 88.1sq ft
Rudder: (each) 57.3sq ft
Wings: short span 1,250sqft (nett 1,162sqft), long span 1,275sq ft (nett 1,190sqft)

Note: A Mk X data not included as it did not progress beyond the proposal stage. It was basically an A Mk IX with Hercules 100 engines.

Company Type No	Marque	Weights Maximum	Mean	Light	Tare	Propeller	Engines	Rated bhp	Altitude	Gear
HP57	B Mk I Series I	55,000	46,300	37,590	33,720	Rotol R6/35/1	Merlin X	1,130 1,010	5,250 17,750	M S
	Series II	60,000	49,000	38,000	34,130					
	Series III	60,000	40,500	38,240	34,500		Merlin XX	1,220 1,120	11,250 19,250	M S
HP59	B Mk II Series I	60,000	51,500	39,200	35,800	R7/35/54 R7/35/55	Merlin XX			
	Series IA	60,000	50,000	39,820	35,577		Merlin 22			
HP61	B Mk III	65,000	54,600	42,860	38,322	de Havilland 55/18	Hercules XVI	1,675 1,455	4,500 12,000	M S
	A Mk III	65,000	N/A	41,210	37,630					
	C Mk III	65,000	N/A	39,970	37,700					
HP63	B Mk V Series I	61,500	51,800	39,500	36,400	R7/35/54 R7/35/55	Merlin XX			
	Series IA	61,500	51,800	40,420	36,177	R7/4B5/4	Merlin 22	1,480 1,480	6,000 12,250	M S
HP61	B Mk VI	65,000	54,600	42,900	38,300	55/18 55/19	Hercules 100	1,680 1,465	9,500 21,000	M S
		* 68,000	56,400	43,540	39,000			1,800 1,625	9,000 19,500	M S
HP61	B Mk VII	65,000	54,700	43,130	38,500	55/18 55/19	Hercules XVI	1,675 1,455	4,500 12,000	M S
	A Mk VII	65,000	N/A	41,590	38,010					
	C Mk VII	65,000	N/A	40,390	38,036					
HP70	C Mk VIII	65,000	N/A	40,110	37,760	55/18 55/19	Hercules 100	1,800 1,625	9,000 19,500	M S
HP71	A Mk IX	65,000	N/A	41,960	37,800	55/18	Hercules XVI	1,675 1,455	4,500 12,000	M S

*Post-war figures.

Mark	Take-off (yds)	Landing (yds)	Speeds 1 & 2 Maximum 3 Economic crsg 4 Weak mxtr crsg (mph/ft)	Time to Height (at max wt) (mini ft)	Service Ceiling at Maximum weight (ft)	Stalling Speeds Clean (mph)	Full/flap ulc down (mph)
B Mk I	1,400	850	(1) 255/ 7,000 (2) 262/18,000 (3) 195/15,000 (4) 233/15,000	29.5/15,000	18,000	110	86
B Mk II/V Series 1	1,250	850	(1) 254/12,750 (2) 261/19,500 (3) 190/15,000 (4) 228/15,000	23/15,000	22,000	95	80

Speeds

Mark	Take-off (yds)	Landing (yds)	1 & 2 Maximum 3 Economic crsg 4 Weak mxtr crsg (mph/ft)	Time to Height (at max wt) (mini ft)	Service Ceiling at Maximum weight (ft)	Stalling Speeds Clean (mph)	Full/lap ulc down (mph)
B Mk II/V Series 1A	1,200	850	(1) 250/13,000 (2) 253/19,000 (3) 205/20,000 (4) 210/20,000	43.5/20,000	21,000	98	82
B Mk III	1,150	1,100	(1) 277/ 6,000 (2) 281/13,500 (3) 225/20,000 (4) 227/20,000	45/20,000	20,000	104	90
A Mk III	1,150	1,200	(1) 285/ 6,000 (2) 289/13,500 (3) 195/10,000 (4) 242/10,000	12/10,000	20,000	118	102
C Mk III	1,200	1,100	(1) 290/ 9,000 (2) 309/19,500 (3) 230/20,000 (4) 256/20,000	31/20,000	23,000	118	102
B Mk VI	1,200	1,100	(1) 290/ 9,000 (2) 309/19,500 (3) 230/20,000 (4) 256/20,000	31/20,000	22,000	118	102
B Mk VII	1,150	1,100	(1) 277/ 6,000 (2) 281/13,500 (3) 225/20,000 (4) 227/20,000	45/20,000	20,000	118	102
A Mk VII	1,150	1,200	(1) 285/ 6,000 (2) 289/13,500 (3) 195/10,000 (4) 242/10,000	12/10,000	20,000	118	102
C Mk VII	1,150	1,200	(1) 288/ 6,000 (2) 293/13,500 (3) 195/10,000 (4) 245/10,000	11.5/10,000	20,000	115	102
C Mk VIII	1,100	1,200	(1) 304/ 9,000 (2) 322/19,500 (3) 200/10,000 (4) 258/10,000	10/10,000	25,000	115	101
A Mk IX	1,150	1,200	(1) 285/ 6,000 (2) 289/13,500 (3) 195/10,000 (4) 242/10,000	12/10,000	20,000	118	102

Note: These official figures were averaged for each marque type – considerable variation occurred between individual aircraft, even from the same production run.

Fixed Armament

Marque	Nose	Midships	Tail
B Mk I	Boulton Paul Mk II turret 2 x 0.303in Brownings with 1000rpg Azimuth: 100° port & starboard Elevation: 60° Depression: 45°	Pillar-mounted Vickers GOs 2 x 0.303in each side with 500rpg Azimuth 27° forward, 21° aft Elevation 45° Depression 26°	Boulton Paul E Mk I turret 4 x 0.303in Brownings with 1700rpg, 4000 reserve Azimuth: 90° port & starboard Elevation: 60° (later turrets 56.5°) Depression 50°
B Mk II Series I	As for B Mk I	Beam guns deleted Boulton Paul C Mk V turret 2 x 0.303in Brownings with 1000rpg Azimuth: 360° Elevation: 60° Depression: 45°	As for B Mk I
Series I (Special)	Turret deleted	Turret deleted initially Boulton Paul A Mk VIII turret 4 x 0.303in Brownings with 1160rpg	As for B Mk I

Marque	Nose	Midships	Tail
		Azimuth: 360° Elevation: 74° Depression: 2.5°	
Series IA	Gimbal-mounted Vickers GO 1 x 0.303in with 300 rounds	As above	As above plus 4800 reserve
GR Mk II/IA	As above	As above	As above
Met. Mk II/IA	As above	As above	As above
B Mk III	As above	As above	As above
GR Mk III	As above	As above	As above
Met. Mk III	As above	As above	As above
A Mk III	Nil	Nil	As above
C Mk III	Nil	Nil	Nil
B Mk V	As for B Mk II series	As for B Mk II series	As for B Mk II series
A MK V Srs I(Sp)	Turret deleted	Turret deleted	As above
A Mk V/IA	As above	As above	As above
GR Mk V/IA	As for GR Mk II Series IA	As for GR Mk II Series IA	As for GR Mark II Series IA
Met. Mk V/IA	As above	As above	As above
B Mk VI	As for B Mk III	As for B Mk III	As for B Mk III
Met. Mk VI	Nil	As above	As above
C Mk VI	Nil	Nil	Nil
B Mk VII	As for B Mk III	As for B Mk III	As for B Mk III initially. Late-model aircraft fitted with Boulton Paul D Mk I turret 2 x 0.5in Brownings with 1000rpg Azimuth: 90° port & starboard Elevation: 45° Depression: 45°
A Mk VII	Nil	Nil	As above
C Mk VII	Nil	Nil	Nil
C Mk VIII	Nil	Nil	Nil
A Mk IX	Nil	Nil	Boulton Paul D Mk II turret with radar gun laying. Details as for D Mk I turret

Disposable Loads

Mark	Fuselage	Wings	Total
B Mk I	2 x 2,000lb		
	6 x 1,000lb	6 x 500lb	13,000lb
	4 x 2,000lb	6 x 500lb	11,000lb
	6 x 500lb	6 x 500lb	9,000lb
	9 x 500lb	6 x 500lb	7,500lb
B Mk II/V Series IA	As for B Mk I plus		
	1 x 8,000lb	6 x 500lb	11,000lb
	2 x 1,500lb mine		
	2 x 4,000lb	6 x 500lb	1l,000lb
GR Mk II/V Series IA	8 x 250lb depth charge	Nil	2,000lb
	4 x 600lb	Nil	2,400lb
	5 x 500lb	Nil	2,500lb
*at auw	10 x 250lb	Nil	2,500lb
63,000lb	6 x 500lb*	Nil	3,000lb
B Mk III	As for B Mk II Series IA	As for B Mk II Series IA	

GR Mk III	9 x 500lb	Nil	4,500lb
B Mk VI	2 x 2,000lb		
	6 x 1,000lb	4 x 500lb	12,000lb
	4 x 2,000lb	4 x 500lb	10,000lb
	2 x 1,500lb mine		
	6 x 500lb	4 x 500lb	8,000lb
	9 x 500lb	4 x 500lb	6x500lb
	1 x 8,000lb	4 x 500lb	10,000lb
	2 x 4,000lb	4 x 500lb	10,000lb
B Mk VII	As above	As above	As above

Range with associated load at most economical speed

	With max bomb load	With permanent tanks full	With auxiliary tanks full		Remarks
Fuel carried (gal)	955	* 1,552 †1,640	2,330		B Mk I *With 160gal Hampden tanks in fuselage
Fuel allowance (gal)	220	220	220		†With additional tanks in wing bomb cells
Range (miles)	1,000	* 1,740 †1,840	2,720		
Bomb load (lb)	13,000	*8,500 †7,750	1,500		
Fuel carried (gal)	985 *830	1,886 *1,882	2,576 *2,342	2,572	B Mk II Series I *Series IA
Fuel allowance (gal)	210 *290	210 *290	210 *290	†290	†With three auxiliary tanks
Range (miles)	920 *650	1,900 *1,660	2,650 *2,100	†2,320	
Bomb load (lb)	13,000 *13,000	6,500 *5,250	—— *1,500		
Fuel carried (gal)	900 *760	1,886 *1,882	2,576 *2,342	†2,572	B Mk V Series I *Series IA
Fuel allowance (gal)	210 *290	210 *290	210 *290	†290	†With three auxiliary tanks
Range (miles)	830 *580	1,900 *1,660	2,650 *2,100	†2,320	
Bomb load (lb)	13,000 *13,000	6,000 *4,750	—— *1,000		
Fuel carried (gal)	1,020 * 1,077	1,802 * 1,998	2,492 *2,688		B MkIII *Post-war figures
Fuel allowance (gal)	220 *350	220 *350	220 *350		
Range (miles)	930 *980	1,770 *2,005	2,430 *2,785		
Bomb load (lb)	13,000 * 13,000	7,250 *6,250	—— *500		
Fuel carried (gal)	1,029 * 1,200	1,998 * 1,998	2,688 *2,228		A Mk III *C Mk III
Fuel allowance (gal)	145 *145	145 *145	145 *145		
Range (miles)	1,020 * 1,240	2,190 *2,230	3,080 *2,520		
Load (lb)	15,000 * 15,000	7,900 *9,200	2,100 *7,100		
Fuel carried (gal)	1,090 * 1,530	1,982 *2,190	2,442 *2,880	†2,672	B Mk VI *Post-war figures
Fuel allowance (gal)	320 *300	320 *300	320 *300	†320	†With three auxiliary tanks
Range (miles)	970 * 1,450	1,965 *2,280	2,490 *2,920	†2,745	
Bomb load (lb)	13,000 * 12,000	6,500 *7,000	2,500 * 1,500	†500	
Fuel carried (gal)	1,177 *1,140 †977	2,190 *2,190 †1,890	2,650 *2,420 †2,760	†2,070**	B Mk VII *C Mk VIII †A Mk VII **With two 90gal aux. tanks
Fuel allowance (gal)	350 *145 †145	350 *145 †145	350 *145 †145	†145**	
Range (miles)	1,075 *1,165 †960	2,225 *2,470 †2,050	2,630 *2,780 †3,170	†2,270**	
Bomb load (lb)	12,000 * 15,000 †15,000	4,500 *7,300 †8,300	500 *5,400 * 1,000	†6,800**	
Fuel carried (gal)	1,180	2,190	2,420		C Mk VIII
Fuel allowance (gal)	140	140	140		
Range (miles)	1,190	2,420	2,710		
Load (lb)	15,000	7,600	5,700		
Fuel carried (gal)	927	1,890	2,760	†2,070	A Mk IX
Fuel allowance (gal)	145	145	145	†145	†With two 90gal aux. tanks
Range (miles)	910	2,050	3,170	†2,270	
Load (lb)	15,000	7,900	600	†6,400	

APPENDIX 5 **Halifax Squadrons**

Squadron records do not always accord perfectly with Air Ministry official documentation regarding formation, transfer and disbandment dates. There are instances where units continue to operate past the paper entry date for their disbandment and vice versa, while physical movements usually took place over days rather than the single day shown in official files. The reader therefore will find some information in the main text that varies with Air Ministry dates shown below. The reader also will find that the immediate post-war period witnessed a series of changes to unit identities that can, at best, be referred to as confusing, with some units disbanded and re-formed the same day with a different number while the original number was transferred to another squadron that disbanded, seemingly solely for the purpose of renumbering.

No 10(B) Squadron Codes: ZA
Based at Leeming, Yorkshire (No 4 Group). Converted from Whitleys to Halifax B Mk IIs in December 1941. Moved to Melbourne, Yorkshire, in August 1942. Converted to B Mk IIIs in March 1944. Last operation Wangerooge, 25.4.45. Transferred to Transport Command 8.5.45, converted to Dakotas.

No 35(B) Squadron Codes: TL
Re-formed 5.11.40 at Boscombe Down, Wiltshire (No 1 Group). Received first Halifax 13.11.40. Moved to Leeming (4 Group) 20.11.40. Moved to Linton-on-Ouse (No 4 Group) 5.12.40. Converted to B Mk IIs October 1941. Moved to Graveley (No 3 Group) as part of PFF in August 1942. (Became No 8 Group on 8.1.43.). Converted to B Mk IIIs in December 1943. Converted to Lancasters in March 1944, the last Halifax operation on 1/2.3.44 against Stuttgart.

No 47(GT) Squadron Codes: MOHD
Based Butterworth, Malay, No 47 Squadron was disbanded 21.3.46. Re-formed and renumbered No 47(GT) Squadron 1.9.46 from No 644 (GT) Squadron based at Quastina, Palestine. Equipped with A Mk VII and A Mk IX Halifaxes it moved to Fairford, Gloucestershire 30.9.46. Squadron strength reduced to six aircraft in October 1947 and with Nos 113, 295 and 297 Squadrons formed the Flying Wing of RAF Fairford. Last Halifax relinquished on 1.9.47 and Squadron moved to Dishforth 14.9.47 to convert to Hastings C I.

No 51(B) Squadron Codes: MH (C Flight coded LK, changed to C6 January, 1944)
Based at Snaith, Yorkshire (No 4 Group) and converted from Whitleys to B Mk II Halifaxes in November 1942. Converted to B Mk IIIs January 1944 and No 578(B) Squadron formed from C Flight. Last operation Wangerooge 25.4.45. Reduced to two flights w.e.f. 7.2.45. Transferred to Transport Command 8.5.45. Converted to Stirlings June 1945 and last Halifax departed July.

No 58(GR) Squadron Codes: BY
Based at St Eval, Cornwall (No 19 Group) and converted from Whitleys to GR Mk II Halifaxes in December 1942. Moved to Holmesley South in July 1943 and then to St Davids in December. Transferred to control of No 18 Group and moved to Stornoway, Outer Hebrides, in September 1944. Converted to GR Mk IIIs and began operations with them in April 1945. Squadron disbanded 25.5.45.

No 76(B) Squadron Codes MP
Formed from C Flight of No 35(B) Squadron 1.5.41 and equipped with B Mk I and II Halifaxes: based at Linton-on-Ouse. Moved to Middleton St George, County Durham (No 4 Group), June 1941. Moved back to Linton-on-Ouse in September 1942. Converted to B Mk Vs in April 1943. Moved to Holme-on-Spalding Moor, Yorkshire, June 1943. Converted to B Mk IIIs in February 1944. Began conversion to B Mk VIs in April 1945 and both marques used on final operation, Wangerooge, 25.4.45. Transferred to Transport Command 8.5.45 and converted to Dakotas.

No 77(B) Squadron Codes: KN (C Flight TB)
Based at Elvington, Yorkshire (No 4 Group). Converted from Whitleys to B Mk II Halifaxes in October 1942, but these were recalled and B Mk Vs issued. On 30.11.42 latter were recalled pending issue of modified B Mk IIs. Between 9 and 11 November, 1943, the B Mk IIs were again exchanged for B Mk Vs. Moved to Full Sutton, Yorkshire, in May 1944 and converted to B Mk IIIs. Began converting to B Mk VIs in March 1945 and used both types for last operation, Wangerooge, 25.4.45. Transferred to Transport Command 8.5.45 and converted to Dakotas. Last Halifax departed in August.

No 78(B) Squadron Codes: EY
Based at Croft, County Durham (No 4 Group). Converted from Whitleys to B Mk II Halifaxes in March 1942. Moved to Middleton St George in June 1942 and then to Linton-on-Ouse in September. Moved to Breighton, Yorkshire in June 1943. Converted to B Mk IIIs in January 1944. Began converting to B Mk VIs in May 1945 and used both types for last operation Wangerooge 25.4.45. Squadron reduced to two flights on 10.4.45, surplus B Mk IIIs going to Nos 171(BS) and 199(BS) Squadrons. Transferred to Transport Command 8.5.45 and converted to Dakotas.

No 96(T) Squadron Codes: 6H
Formed at Leconfield 30.12.44 under authority TCSD 155 No 2976/44. Establishment to be 25 C Mk III Halifaxes. On 9.2.45 authority received for Squadron to be transferred to MAAF to replace No 267(T) Squadron. Notification received 16.3.45 to re-equip with Dakotas which were to be supplied from MAAF sources. Halifaxes disposed of to MU and No 10(T) Squadron.

No 102(B) Squadron Codes: DY
Based at Dalton, Yorkshire (No 4 Group). Converted from Whitleys to B Mk II Halifaxes in December 1941. Moved to Topcliffe, Yorkshire, in June 1942 and then to Pocklington, Yorkshire 7 August. Converted to B Mk IIIs in May 1944. Reduced to two flights 25.1.45 and began converting to B Mk VIs in February. Used both types for last operation, Wangerooge, 25.4.45. Squadron transferred to Transport Command 8.5.45 and converted to Liberators.

No 103(B) Squadron Codes: PM
Based at Elsham Wolds, Lincolnshire (No 1 Group). Converted from Wellingtons to B Mk II Halifaxes in July 1942. Began conversion to Lancasters in October 1942; last Halifax operation, against Milan, 24/25.10.42

No 113(GT) Squadron Codes: MOHC
No 113 Squadron disbanded 15.10.45 but was reactivated, No 620(GT) Squadron being disbanded on 1.9.46 and renumbered as No 113(GT) Squadron at its base at Aqir, Palestine. Equipped with A Mk VII and A Mk IX Halifaxes, it moved to Kabrit. Squadron transferred to Fairford in April 1947 along with HQ 238 Wing. Squadron reduced to six aircraft in October and with Nos 47, 295 and 297 Squadrons formed the Flying Wing of RAF Fairford. Squadron disbanded 5.4.47.

No 138(SD) Squadron Codes: NF
Re-formed from the nucleus of No 1419 Flight at Newmarket, Cambridgeshire, in August 1941; Lysanders equipped A Flight and Whitleys B Flight, B Mk II Halifaxes supplementing the latter in October. Squadron under the control of the Directorate of Plans, but its parent station was Stradishall, Suffolk (No 4 Group). Moved to Tempsford, March 1942, where, with No 161(SD) Squadron, it came under the control of ACAS(I). When not engaged on SOE operations it carried out bombing operations with No 3 Group. Last Halifax operation carried out on 11.8.44 and began converting to Stirlings the following month.

No 148(SD) Squadron Codes: FS
No 148(B) Squadron disbanded on 31.12.42 but leaving X Flight, the Special Liberator Flight, still active. The first of several B Mk II Halifaxes received on 18.2.43. On 13.3.43 unit moved from Shandur to Gambut where No 148 (SD) Squadron re-formed on 14.3.43, incorporating the Special Liberator Flight. Moved to Derna on 5.4.43 and then to Tocra on 1.9.43 with detachments to Protville and Cairo West at various times. Moved to Brindisi, Italy, as part of 334 Wing 31.1.44. Lysanders added to strength for clandestine pick-up work and B Mk Vs began arriving in July. Began conversion to Stirlings in November 1944, but ceased when notified in December that it was to receive Liberators instead. Conversion delayed until 23.5.45.

No 158(B) Squadron Codes: NP
Based at Driffield, Yorkshire (No 4 Group). Converted from Wellingtons to B Mk II Halifaxes 1942. Moved to East Moor, Yorkshire, in June 1942. Moved to Rufforth, Yorkshire, in November then to Lisset, Yorkshire, in February 1943. Converted to B Mk IIIs December 1943. No 640(B) Squadron formed from C Flight in January 1944, and strength expanded to three flights once more in March. Began conversion to B Mk VIs in April 1945 and both marques used for final operation, Wangerooge, on 25.4.45. Squadron reduced to two flights on 1.5.45 and transferred to Transport Command 8.5.45 and converted to Stirlings.

No 161(SD) Squadron Codes: MA
Formed at Newmarket on 14.2.42 from nucleus of No 138 (SD) Squadron, for SOE/SIS operations and moved to Graveley 1.3.42 then to Tempsford 8.4.42. Lysanders equipped A Flight, and Whitleys B Flight, the latter receiving its first B Mk V Halifax on 18.10.42. In August 1944 B Flight began converting to Stirlings and last Halifax operation flown on 1.9.44.

No 171(BS) Squadron Codes: 6Y and EX
Formed at North Creake. Norfolk (No 100 Group), on 8.9.44 from third flight of No 199(BS) Squadron under authority of SD 155 No 2033/44. Allocated a UE of 20 B Mk III Halifaxes, but initially equipped with a mixture of these and Stirlings. The first Halifax arrived on 16.10.44. Last Stirling operation took place on 21.11.44. Last wartime operation flown on 2/3.5.45 and Squadron disbanded 27.7.45.

No 178(B) Squadron Codes: Unknown
Formed at Shandur, Egypt (No 240 Wing), on 15.1.43 and equipped with Liberators. Moved to Hosc Raui, Libya, in February 1943. Began converting to B Mk II Halifaxes in May 1943, but decision taken to keep Liberators and Halifax strength reduced in September. Last Halifax operation, against Manduria, on 7.8.43.

No 187(T) Squadron Codes: Unknown
Formed at Merryfield (47 Group) 1.2.45. Unit to have an establishment of 25 C Mk III Halifaxes under Establishment No LWE/AT/2235A of 30.12.44. Halifax Development Flight attached for servicing facilities on 1.3.45. Squadron notified on 14.3.45 of policy change, UE to be 25 Dakotas. Halifax Development Flight disbanded 3.4.45.

No 190(GT) Squadron Codes: G5, L9 and 6S
Based at Great Dunmow, Essex (No 38 Group). Squadron began converting from Stirlings to A Mk III and A Mk VII Halifaxes on 4.5.45. Used to convert No 620(GT) Squadron crews to Halifaxes and did not reach full strength until July 1945. Moved to Tarrant Rushton in November 1945. Squadron disbanded on 28.12.45, but reactivated as No 295(GT) Squadron on 21.1.46. Disbanded 1.4.46 and re-formed same day as No 297 Squadron and based at Fairford.

No 192(BS) Squadron Codes: DT
Formed from No 1474 Flight at Gransden Lodge (No 8 Group) on 4.1.43. Squadron equipped with a mixture of Wellingtons and Mosquitoes. First B Mk II Halifax received on 9.1.43. Moved to Feltwell (No 2 Group) on 5.4.43 and then to Foulsham on 25.11.43. Began operating B Mk IIIs in March 1944. Last wartime operation, using mixed force of Halifaxes and Mosquitoes, 2/3.5.45. Squadron disbanded 22.8.45, renamed Central Signals Establishment.

No 199(BS) Squadron Codes: EX
Based at North Creake (No 100 Group) and equipped with Stirlings. Began conversion to B Mk III Halifaxes in February 1945 and last Stirling operation on 14.2.45. Last operation 2/3.5.45. Squadron disbanded on 29.7.45.

No 202(Met) Squadron Codes: Y3
No 518(Met) Squadron disbanded at Aldergrove on 1.10.46 and renumbered No 202 (Met)

Squadron at same date. Continued to maintain permanent detachment at Gibraltar, Met Mk VI Halifaxes used in both cases. Three A Mk IXs RT786, RT798 and RT923, issued in August 1949 and Squadron operated them until December 1950, having begun converting to Hastings Met Is in October.

No 224(Met) Squadron Codes: XB then B
Squadron re-formed at Aldergrove on 1.3.48 with initial strength of two Met Mk VI Halifaxes plus, in 1951, the five Met Mk VIs of the former No 202 (Met) Squadron detachment at Gibraltar. Moved to Gibraltar 18.10.48 but maintained a detachment at Aldergrove. Squadron converted to Shackleton MR 1s in July 1951. Last Halifax to leave was RG841 on an official sortie, from the Gibraltar detachment on 17.3.52, the last Halifax to operate with a front-line RAF unit.

No 295(GT) Squadron Codes: 8E and 8Z (Post war MOHC)
Based at Netheravon (No 38 Wing), A Mk V Halifaxes began to replace the Whitleys of A Flight in February 1943; completed by 22.4.43. Halifaxes used for bombing operations between duties. Squadron moved to Holmsley South on 1.5.43 for *Operation Beggar*. Began converting to Albemarles in September and last Halifax operation on 10.10.43. On 21.1.46 Squadron disbanded at Rivenhall, No 190 Squadron at Tarrant Rushton re-forming the same day renumbered as No 295 Squadron, equipped with A Mk VIIs. Disbanded 1.4.46 (and re-formed same day renumbered as No 297 Squadron). No 295 Squadron re-formed at Fairford on 10.9.47 and equipped with A Mk IXs. Disbanded 1.11.48.

No 296(GT) Squadron Codes: 7C and 9W
Based at Brize Norton (No 38 Group) it began converting from Albemarles to A Mk V Halifaxes in September 1944, with crew conversion at No 1665 HCU. Converted to A Mk IIIs in February 1945 and in October began transport work on the Indian Trunk Route. Began conversion to A Mk VIIs in December but disbanded on 23.1.46.

No 297(GT) Squadron Codes: L5 and P5 (Post-war MOHA)
Based at Earles Colne (No 38 Group) it began converting from Albemarles to A Mk V Halifaxes from 1.10.44. Converted to A Mk IIIs in February 1945 and in October began transport work on the Indian Trunk Route. Began conversion to A Mk VIIs in December but disbanded on 1.4.46. On the same date the original No 295(GT) Squadron was re-formed at Tarrant Rushton and renumbered No 297(GT) Squadron. Moved to Brize Norton in August. In January 1947 began partial re-equipping with A Mk IXs (six only). In October unit strength cut and with Nos 47, 113 and 297(GT) Squadrons it formed the Flying Wing of RAF Fairford. In August 1948 further reductions occurred and 12 Halifaxes were held against Nos 295 and 297(GT) Squadrons. Squadrons moved to Dishforth in October and began conversion to Hastings C I.

No 298(GT) Squadron Codes: 8A and 8T (as from 20.5.44)
Initially activated on paper as a mixed Halifax/ Whitley unit on 24.8.42, but formation suspended until 19.10.43. Physically formed at Tarrant Rushton on 4.11.43 from Flight of No 295 Squadron, with A Mk V Halifaxes in two flights; 'C' Flight formed 5.2.44 but transferred as nucleus of No 644(GT) Squadron, on 18.3.44. In September began converting to A Mk IIIs and role changed to transport work. Began converting to A Mk VIIs in February 1945. Squadron transferred to Raipur, India (No 238 Wing), 15 July 1945, taking with them tropicalised A Mk VIIs. Moved to Digri on 9 December, maintaining detachments at Alipore, Meiktila and Chaklala. On 20.5.46 moved to Baroda, then to Mauripur 24.5.46 with a detachment at Risalpur. Title changed again in July to Bomber, Airborne Support and Heavy Equipment Dropping Squadron. Disbanded 21.12.46.

No 301(SD) Squadron Codes: GR (Polish)
Re-formed from No 1586(SD) Flight at Brindisi, Italy, on 7.11.44; equipped with Liberators and B Mk V Halifaxes. Last operational sorties *'Starkadder'*, Roverato. 25.2.45. Squadron transferred to Transport Command and returned to UK, stationed at Blackbushe. Began re-equipping with Warwicks in May. Moved to North Weald on 3.7.45 and again, to Chedburgh, on 5.9.45. Began converting to C Mk VIII Halifaxes in January 1946. Overseas flights cancelled as from 9.4.46 and squadron disbanded w.e.f.18.12.46.

No 304(T) Squadron Codes: QD (Polish)
Based at Chedburgh when notified on 2.11.45 to convert from Wellington XIVs to Warwick I and IIIs. On 11.1.45 advised of conversion to C Mk VIII Halifaxes, but due to embargo on overseas flights as from 9.4.46 squadron did not become operational with Halifaxes, first C Mk VIIIs arriving in May and training intensive, losing two in fatal accidents. Disbanded w.e.f. 18.12.46.

No 346(B) Squadron Codes: H7 (F.F.A.)
Formed at Elvington (No 4 Group) on 16.5.44 with B Mk V Halifaxes. Began converting to B Mk IIIs in June. Converted to B Mk VIs in March 1945. Last operation, Wangerooge, 25.4.45. Squadron ceased flying 6.10.45 and personnel, plus portion of Squadron aircraft, transferred to l'Armée de l'Air in October, moving to Bordeaux-Merignac 20.10.45 and transferred to French control w.e.f. 15.11.45.

No 347(B) Squadron Codes: L8 (F.F.A.)
Formed at Elvington (No 4 Group) on 20.6.44 with B Mk V Halifaxes. Began converting to B Mk IIIs in July. Converted to B Mk VIs in March 1945. Last operation, Wangerooge, 25.4.45. Squadron ceased flying 6.10.45 and personnel, plus portion of squadron aircraft, transferred to l'Armée de l'Air in October, moving to Bordeaux-Merignac 20.10.45 and transferred to French control w.e.f. 15.11.45.

No 405(B) Squadron Codes: LQ (RCAF)
Based at Topcliffe (No 4 Group) and converted from Wellingtons to B Mk II Halifaxes in April 1942. Squadron transferred to No 6 (RCAF) Group 1.1.43. Moved to Leeming 13/14 March 1943 and then to Gransden Lodge, on 19/20 April. Transferred to No 8 Group 19.4.43; began converting to Lancasters in August. Last Halifax operation, Modane, 16/17.9.43.

No 408(B) Squadron Codes: EQ (RCAF)
Based at Leeming (No 4 Group) and converted from Hampdens to B Mk V Halifaxes in September 1942; first Halifaxes did not arrive until 11.10.42. Advised on 30.11.42 of impending conversion to B Mk IIs, the first of which arrived 7.12.42. Advised on 14.7.43 of

impending move to Linton-on-Ouse for conversion to Lancasters. Last Halifax operation 2.8.43. Moved to Linton-on-Ouse (No 6 Group) 10.8.43. Began reconverting to Halifaxes (mainly B Mk VIIs but some B Mk IIIs) July 1944. Began converting to Lancasters May 1945, last Halifax and Squadron operation Wangerooge 25/4/45. Began converting to Lancasters May1945.

No 415(B) Squadron Codes: 6U (RCAF)
Based at East Moor (No 6 Group) and converted from Wellingtons and Albacores to B Mk III Halifaxes in July 1944. A few B Mk VIIs taken on charge in February 1945. Last operation Wangerooge, 25.4.45. Disbanded 15.5.45.

No 419(B) Squadron Codes: VR (RCAF)
Based at Middleton St George (No 4 Group) and converted from Wellingtons to B Mk II Halifaxes in November 1942. Transferred to No 6 Group 1.4.43. Began converting to Lancasters in April 1944 and last Halifax operation Montzen, 27/28.4.44.

No 420(B) Squadron Codes: PT (RCAF)
Based at Tholthorpe (No 6 Group) and converted from Wellingtons to B Mk III Halifaxes in January 1944. Began conversion to Lancasters in April 1945; last Halifax operation Heligoland Naval Base, 18.4.45. Began converting to Lancasters April 1945.

No 424(B) Squadron Codes: QB (RCAF)
Based at Skipton-on-Swale (No 6 Group) and converted from Wellingtons to B Mk III Halifaxes in December 1943. Began conversion to Lancasters in January 1945; last Halifax operation Stuttgart, 28/29.1.45.

No 425(B) Squadron Codes: KW (RCAF)
Based at Tholthorpe (No 6 Group) and converted from Wellingtons to B Mk III Halifaxes in January 1944. Last operation Wangerooge, 25.4.45. Began converting to Lancasters in May 1945.

No 426(B) Squadron Codes: OW (RCAF)
Based at Linton-on-Ouse (No 6 Group) and converted from Lancasters to B Mk III Halifaxes in April 1944. Converted to B Mk VIIs in June 1944. Last operation, Wangerooge, 25.4.45. Moved to Driffield on 26.5.45 and transferred to Transport Command. Moved to Tempsford on 26.6.45 and converted to Liberators.

No 427(B) Squadron Codes: ZL (RCAF)
Based at Leeming (No 6 Group) and converted from Wellingtons to B Mk V Halifaxes in May 1943. Converted to B Mk IIIs January 1944, but began conversion to Lancasters in February. Last Halifax operation, mining in Norwegian waters 3/4.3.44. Began converting to Lancasters March 1945.

No 428(B) Squadron Codes: NA (RCAF)
Based at Dalton (No 6 Group) and moved to Middleton St George in June 1943 where it converted from Wellingtons to B Mk V Halifaxes; these were supplemented by B Mk IIs in November. Began conversion to B Mk IIIs in January 1944 but suspended due to impending conversion to Lancasters in June. Last Halifax operation mining Lorient, Brest and St Nazaire, 5/6.7.44.

No 429(B) Squadron Codes: AL (RCAF)
Based at Leeming (No 6 Group) and converted from Wellingtons to B Mk II Halifaxes in September 1943. Began a gradual conversion to B Mk Vs in November but ceased due impending conversion to B Mk IIIs, which began in January 1944. Began converting to Lancasters in March 1945; last Halifax operation, against Castrop-Rauxel oil refinery, 15.3.45.

No 431(B) Squadron Codes: SE (RCAF)
Based at Tholthorpe (No 6 Group) and converted from Wellingtons to B Mk V Halifaxes in July 1943. Moved to Croft in December and began converting to B Mk IIIs in March 1944. Began converting to Lancasters in October; last Halifax operation Cologne, 30/31.10.44.

No 432(B) Squadron Codes: QO (RCAF)
Based at East Moor (No 6 Group) and converted from Lancasters to B Mk III Halifaxes in February 1944. Began conversion to B Mk VIIs in June. Last operation Wangerooge, 25.4.45. Squadron disbanded 15.5.45.

No 433(B) Squadron Codes: BM (RCAF)
Formed at Skipton-on-Swale (No 6 Group) on 25.9.43 and equipped with B Mk III Halifaxes, the first of which arrived 3.11.43. Began converting to Lancasters in January 1945. Last Halifax operation Magdeburg, 16/17.1.45. Began converting to Lancasters January 1945.

No 434(B) Squadron Codes: IP (RCAF)
Based at Tholthorpe (No 6 Group) and converted from Wellingtons to B Mk V Halifaxes in June 1943. Moved to Croft on 11.12.43. Began converting to B Mk IIIs in May 1944. Began converting to Lancasters in December. Last Halifax operation Koln, 21/22.12.44.

No 460(B) Squadron Codes: UV (RAAF)
Based at Breighton (No 4 Group) the squadron was notified in June 1942 to prepare for conversion from Wellingtons to B Mk II Halifaxes. Conversion flight formed but notification received on 25.9.42 for Halifaxes to be withdrawn and replaced by Lancasters. Halifaxes did not become operational; first Lancaster operation 22.11.42.

No 462(B) Squadron Codes: Unknown (RAAF)
Formed at Fayid, Egypt, 7.9.42, from amalgamation of No 10(B) Squadron and No 76(B) Squadron detachments and placed under the control of No 425 Wing, No 205 Group; equipped with B Mk II Halifaxes. Transferred to operational control of No 236 Wing on 27.11.42. Moved to LG 237 (Kilo 40) with detachment to LG 09 then to LG167, Egypt, 17.12.42; to LG 167 Libya, then to LG 237 and back to LG 167 the same month. Moved to Solluch No 1, Libya, in December and then to Gardabia Main in February 1943; to Hosc Raui in May: to Terria in October with a detachment to El Adem in December. The whole squadron moved to El Adem in January 1944 and then to Celone, Italy, in March, where it was renumbered No 614(B) Squadron on 3.3.44.

No 462(B) Squadron Codes: Z5 (RAAF)
Re-formed at Driffield (No 4 Group) on 12.8.44 and equipped with B Mk III Halifaxes. On 22.12.44, screened from operations and transferred to Foulsham (No 100 Group) with a subsequent change of designation to No 462(BS) Squadron. Last operation Kiel, 2/3.5.45. Disbanded on 24.9.45.

No 466(B) Squadron Codes: HD (RAAF)
Based at Leconfield (No 4 Group) and equipped with Wellingtons. On 1.9.43 screened from operations and commenced training with B Mk II Halifaxes on 19.9.43. On 26.10.43 first batch of B Mk IIIs arrived and squadron operational with this marque by 1.12.43. Moved to Driffield in June 1944. Last operation Wangerooge, 25.4.45. On 5.5.45 ordered to dispose of B Mk IIIs and re-equip with B Mk VIs ex-No 640(B) Squadron. Transferred to Transport Command 8.5.45. On 20.6.45 renumbered No 10(B) Squadron RAAF. Moved to Bassingbourne in September and commenced converting to Liberators. Disbanded 26.10.45.

No 502(GR) Squadron Codes: YG and V9
Based at St Eval; signal received 9.1.43 notifying re-equipment from Whitleys to GR Mk II Halifaxes. Moved to Holmsley South on 30.6.43, then to St Davids on 10.12.43. In September 1944 squadron transferred to control of No 18 Group and moved to Stornoway. Began conversion to GR Mk IIIs in late December 1944. Disbanded 25.5.45.

No 517(Met) Squadron Codes: X9
Based at St Eval, No 1404(Met.) Flight, equipped with Hampdens, Hudsons and Fortresses, was renumbered No 517(Met.) Squadron on 11.8.43 and allotted an establishment of 18+6 Met Mk V Halifaxes. On 5.12.43 ordered to move to Brawdy, a satellite of St Davids, via the main station. Move carried out on 1.2.44. Squadron allocated *Epicure* patrols. In March 1945 began converting to Met Mk IIIs and operated them until June 1946, when it began converting to Met Mk VIs, but only received four. Disbanded 1.10.46, the Met Mk VIs transferred to No 518 (Met) Squadron.

No 518(Met) Squadron Codes: Y3
Formed at Stornoway on 6.7.43 and equipped with Met Mk V Halifaxes. Moved to Tiree on 25.9.43 and allocated *Mercer* patrols. On 14.10.43 squadron screened from operations and used to train 58 Halifax crews for meteorological duties. Squadron reduced to 12 Halifaxes, but surplus crews retained for specific operations as detailed by HQ Coastal Command. On 10.11.43 strength increased to 14 Halifaxes. Trial flight of new flight plan coded *Bismuth* carried out on 24.2.44 and thereafter both *Mercer* and *Bismuth* routes used by squadron. Converted to Met Mk IIIs in March 1945 but continued to operate a mixture of both for some time. Moved to Aldergrove 18.9.45 and absorbed No 1402 Flight. Gibraltar detachment of No 520 (Met) Squadron taken over 24.5.46 and Squadron converted to Met Mk VIs. Disbanded 1.10.46 and renumbered No 202 (Met) Squadron same day.

No 519(Met) Squadron Codes: Z9
Formed at Wick from Nos 1406 and 1408 Flights, moved to Skitten 10.12.43, then back to Wick 28.11.44 operating Fortresses and Spitfire VIIs, then to Tain 17.8.45, where it received some Met Mk III Halifaxes in August 1945. Moved to Leuchars on 8.11.45 and commenced *Recipe* patrols. On 11.11.45 notified of impending conversion to Met. Mk VIs but none received before unit disbanded in 31.5.46. Last flight made by Squadron, using Met Mk IIIs, 30.5.46.

No 520(Met) Squadron Codes: 2M
Based at Gibraltar using Gladiators, Hurricanes, Spitfires and Hudsons, Squadron received first Met Mk V Halifax on 6.2.44 and flew first sortie the same day. Squadron allocated *Nocturnal* patrols. A few Met Mk IIIs received in May 1945. Advised of intention to re-equip with Met Mk VIs but none received by time Squadron disbanded on 25.4.46.

No 521(Met) Squadron Codes: 50
Based at Chivenor using Fortresses and Hurricanes. Began converting to Met Mk VI Halifaxes in February 1946 and used them only briefly before disbanding on 31.3.46.

No 578(B) Squadron Codes: LK
Formed at Snaith (No 4 Group) on 14.1.44 from C Flight of No 51(B) Squadron and equipped with B Mk III Halifaxes. Moved to Burn on 6.2.44 and on 30.3.44 P/Off C. J. Barton earned the only 'Halifax' VC of the war. Last operation, against Wuppertal, 13.3.45. Squadron disbanded 16.3.45.

No 614(B) Squadron Codes: Unknown
Based at Celone, Italy, No 462(B) Squadron was renumbered No 614(B) Squadron on 3.3.44; equipped with B Mk II Halifaxes. Squadron role changed to that of PFF target-marking force for No 205 Group. Moved to Stornara in May and then to Amendola in July. Began converting to Liberators in August but progress slow. Last Halifax operation Porto Marhamo, 3.3.45.

No 620(GT) Squadron Codes: D4 and QS, (Post-war MOHC)
Based at Great Dunmow (No 38 group), converted from Stirlings to A Mk VII Halifaxes in May 1945. Squadron posted to Aqir, Palestine; commenced move on 30.12.45 and completed by 14.1.46. Moved to Cairo West on 6.3.46 with a detachment based at Shallufa. Moved back to Aqir 14.6.46. In July began converting to A Mk IXs. Squadron disbanded 1.9.46 and renumbered No 113(GT) Squadron same date.

No 624(SD) Squadron Codes: Unknown
Formed at Blida, North Africa, 7.9.43. Establishment of 14+4 Halifaxes and 2+0 Venturas, these coming from the disbanded No 1575(SD) Flight. Halifaxes mixture of B Mk IIs and Vs. In October detachment sent to squadron's advanced operational base at Protville; also small detachment sent to Malta for operations over Czechoslovakia. 16.10.43 Protville detachment moved to Sidi Amor. In December Squadron moved to Brindisi, Italy, via Tocra, and placed under control of No 334 Wing. Moved back to Blida in February 1944 and operated exclusively over France. Signal received 12.6.44 ordering conversion to Stirlings. Last Halifax operation 13/14 August, Warsaw, JN896 lost.

No 640(B) Squadron Codes: C8
Formed from 'C' Flight of No 158(B) Squadron at Lissett (No 4 Group) on 7.1.44; equipped with B Mk III Halifaxes. Moved to Leconfield in January. Five times squadron won the No 4 Group Bombing Cup trophy, a record for the Group. Began converting to B Mk VIs in March 1945. Last operation Wangerooge, 25.4.45. Disbanded 7.5.45.

No 644(GT) Squadron Codes: 2P and 9U (Post-war MOHD)
Formed from 'C' Flight of No 298(GT) Squadron at Tarrant Rushton (No 38 Group) on 23.2.44 equipped with A Mk V Halifaxes. Converted to A Mk IIIs in October and continued to use them until June 1945 while converting to A Mk VIIs in March 1945. Squadron posted to Middle East, Quastina, move commenced 26.11.45 and completed by 1.12.45. Began converting to A Mk IXs on 10.8.46. Disbanded and renumbered No 47(GT) Squadron 1.9.46.

No 301 (SD) Flight Codes: GR (Polish)
In July 1943 the Polish Flight of No 138(SD) Squadron was redesignated No 301 (SD) Flight at Tempsford; equipped with B Mk II and B Mk V Halifaxes. On 7 November Flight moved to Tunis, North Africa, and placed under control of No 334 Wing. On the 15th moved to Brindisi, Italy and renumbered No 1586 (SD) Flight for security reasons and Liberator VIs added to Unit Establishment. (See **No 1586 (SD) Flight**.)

No 1341(BS) Flight Codes: Unknown
Formed at West Kirby on 21.12.44 and personnel shipped to Digri, India, arriving 14.2.45. First two B Mk IIIs departed for India in March, and five on charge by 31.5.45. Authority received to amalgamate with C Flight of No 159(B) Squadron (equipped with Liberators for radar investigation work) 15.5.45. Last operation by Halifaxes Port Blair, 1.9.45. Disbanded w.e.f. 30.10.45.

No 1418 Bombing Development Flight Codes: Possibly OT
(See **TR1335 (Gee) Development Unit**)

No 1575(SD) Flight Codes: Unknown
Formed at Tempsford on 21.5.43 with an establishment of 3+1 B Mk V Halifaxes and 2+0 Venturas. Crews drawn from No 161 (SD) Squadron. Moved to Maison Blanche, North Africa, in June. On 25.6.43 moved to Blida; operating mainly over Corsica, Sardinia and Italy. Authority for disbandment received 16.8.43, physically disbanded on 22.9.43, all personnel, aircraft and equipment transferred to No 624(SD) Squadron.

No 1577(Trials) Flight Codes: Unknown
Formed under HQ No 221 Group, India, on 9.8.43 for trials work with Halifax and Lancaster aircraft. Equipment drawn from No 313 MU (No 184 Wing). Two B Mk V Halifaxes, two Lancaster IIIs and personnel departed Portreath on 29.9.43. Established in India by 7.10.43. On 5.12.43 Flight notified that it will engage in transport duties only. On 5.3.44 moved to Chakeri and then to Mauripur on 7.5.44, where aircraft modified for towing. Lancasters removed on 9.11.44 and following day two B Mk III Halifaxes received. Moved to Dhamal in December and then to Chaklala in January 1946. Disbanded May 1946.

No 1586(SD) Flight Codes: GR (Polish)
Formed at Brindisi on 1.10.44 from No 301(SD) Flight using Halifaxes and Liberators. Both Grottaglie and Rosignano used as alternative landing grounds. Flight renumbered No 301(SD) Squadron on 7.11.44. (See **No 301(SD) Squadron**.)

No 28 Halifax Conversion Flight Codes: Unknown
Formed at Leconfield (No 4 group) in November 1941, it received first five B Mk I Halifaxes on 28.10.41 (only a single white-coloured aircraft letter carried by each aircraft). Subsequently decided to equip each heavy bomber group with one conversion unit plus one small conversion flight per squadron. Moved to Marston Moor on 30.12.41. On 3.1.42 No 28 CF and (technically) No 107 CF, disbanded and combined to form No 1652 Conversion Unit at Marston Moor. All CUs were renamed HCUs in October 1942.

No 10(B) Squadron (Conversion Flight) Codes: ZA
Formed in January 1942 at Leeming (No 6 Group), moved to Melbourne on 19 August. Disbanded 7.10.42 and absorbed by No 1658 Heavy Conversion Unit at Riccall Common but No 10 Conversion Flight detachment remained outposted at Melbourne until 22.11.42.

No 35(B) Squadron (Conversion Flight) Codes: TL
Formed January 1942 at Linton-on-Ouse (No 6 Group), moved to Marston Moor on 5.9.42, then to Rufforth on 21.9.42. Disbanded 7.10.42 and amalgamated with No 158(B) Squadron (CF) to form part of No 1652 HCU at Marston Moor.

No 76(B) Squadron (Conversion Flight) Codes: MP
Formed January 1942 at Middleton St George. Moved to Dalton on 9.6.42, then back to Middleton St George on 31.8.42, then to Riccall Common 12.9.42. Amalgamated with No 78(B) Squadron (CF) to form No 1658 HCU at Riccall Common.

No 78(B) Squadron (Conversion Flight) Codes: EY
Formed January 1942 at Croft (No 6 Group). Moved to Dalton 12.6.42, then to Middleton St George by 31.8.42, then to Riccall Common by 16.9.42. Disbanded 7.10.42 and amalgamated with No 76(B) Squadron (CF) to form No 1658 HCU.

No 102(B) Squadron (Conversion Flight) Codes: DY
Formed 6.1.42 at Dalton (No 4 Group). Moved to Topcliffe June 1942, then to Pocklington 7.8.42. Disbanded on 7.10.42 and absorbed by No 1658 HCU at Riccall Common but remained outposted at Pocklington until 23.11.42.

No 103(B) Squadron (Conversion Flight) Codes: PM
Formed July 1942 at Elsham Wolds (No 1 group). Moved to Breighton in October and amalgamated with No 460(B) Squadron (CF) to form No 1656 HCU. Became B Flight.

No 107 Halifax (Conversion Flight) Codes: OM
Authority to form unit at Leconfield (No 4 Group) issued by December 1941, equipment to be B Mk I Halifaxes. None believed delivered before unit disbanded on 3.1.42 and combined with No 28 CF to form No 1652 CU.

No 158(B) Squadron (Conversion Flight) Codes: NP
Formed 5.5.42 at Linton-on-Ouse (No 4 Group). Moved to East Moor 7.6.42, then to Rufforth 25.9.42. Disbanded 7.10.42 and absorbed by No 1658 HCU at Riccall Common.

No 405(B) Squadron (Conversion Flight) Codes: LQ
Formed 29.4.42 at Pocklington (No 4 Group) with B Mk II Halifaxes. Moved to Topcliffe 7.8.42. Disbanded 7.10.42 and absorbed into No 1659 HCU.

No 408(B) Squadron (Conversion Flight) Codes: EQ
Formed 16.5.42 at Syerston (No 5 Group) with Manchesters but cancelled 19.6.42. Re-formed 20.9.42 at Leeming (No 4 Group) with Halifax B Mk I, II and V aircraft. Disbanded 7.10.42 and absorbed into 1659 HCU.

No 460(B) Squadron (Conversion Flight) Codes: UV
Formed 22.5.42 at Holme-on-Spalding Moor (No 4 Group), where Unit Establishment (UE) increased from standard 4+0 to 8+0 B Mk II Halifaxes. Next day ordered to dispose of Halifaxes and replace them with a UE of 4+0 Lancasters and 4+0 Manchesters. On 29.9.42 absorbed by No 1656 HCU as A Flight and four Halifaxes transferred to No 460(B) Squadron, followed by two on 1.10.42 and final two the next day.

No 1652 Heavy Conversion Unit Codes: JA and GV
Formed as No 1652 Conversion Unit at Marston Moor (No 4 Group) 3.1.42 from Nos 28 and 107 Halifax Conversion Flights. Equipped with B Mk Is to serve No 4 Group. On 7.10.42 absorbed No 35 (B) and No 158(B) Squadrons' Conversion Flights. Received first B Mk IIIs 3.12.44 and completed conversion by 17.12.44. Disbanded 25.6.45.

No 1654 Heavy Conversion Unit Codes: UG and JR (Lancasters JF)
Based at Wigsley (No 5 Group) and equipped with Lancasters and Manchesters. Manchesters phased out and replaced with Halifaxes to a UE of 32+0 in September 1943. Replaced by Stirlings 1.1.44.

No 1656 Heavy Conversion Unit Codes: BL and EK
Formed 7.10.42 at Breighton (No 4 Group) with Halifaxes from Nos 103(B) and 460(B) Squadron Conversion Flights. HQ moved to Lindholme 26.10.42, followed by B Flight from Elsham Wolds 3.11.42 and A Flight, partly equipped with Lancasters, on 11.11.42. Allocated full Lancaster flight and both types operated until November 1943, when Halifaxes began to be phased out.

No 1658 Heavy Conversion Unit Codes: TT and ZB
Formed at Riccall Common (No 4 Group) 7.10.42 with B Mk I and II Halifaxes from Nos 10, 76, 78 and 102(B) Squadrons Conversion Flights. Received first B Mk IIIs 14.9.44. Disbanded 13.4.45 and absorbed by No 1332(HT)CU.

No 1659 Heavy Conversion Unit Codes: FD, FV and RV
Formed at Leeming (No 4 Group) 7.10.42 with B Mk I and II Halifaxes from Nos 405 and 408 Squadron Conversion Flights. Moved to Topcliffe 14.3.43, satellite airfield Dalton. Converted to B Mk IIIs September 1944. Dishforth became satellite airfield in 1945. Disbanded 10.9.45.

No 1660 Heavy Conversion Unit Codes: TV and YW
Based at Swinderbury (No 5 Group) and equipped with Lancasters and Manchesters. Satellite airfield Skellingthorpe. Manchesters phased out and replaced with B Mk V Halifaxes to a UE of 32+0 in September 1943. Replaced with Stirlings 1.1.44.

No 1661 Heavy Conversion Unit Codes: GP and KB
Based at Winthorpe (No 5 Group) and equipped with Lancasters and Manchesters. Manchesters phased out and replaced with B Mk II Halifaxes to a UE of 32+0 in September 1943; also received some B Mk III Halifaxes. Replaced with Stirlings 1.1.44.

No 1662 Heavy Conversion Unit Codes: PE and KF
Formed 29.1.43 at Blyton (No 5 Group) with a UE of 16+0 B Mk I, II and V Halifaxes and 16+0 Lancasters. Satellite airfield Elsham Wolds. Also received some B Mk III Halifaxes. On 12.2.44 Lancaster Flight moved to Hemswell (Lancaster Finishing School). Disbanded 6.4.45.

No 1663 Heavy Conversion Unit Codes: 00 and SV
Formed 1.3.43 at Rufforth (No 4 Group) with B Mk II Halifaxes from other HCUs, plus some new production aircraft. A UE of 24 B Mk Vs authorised but later increased to a UE of 32+0. Began converting to B Mk IIIs in October 1944. Disbanded 28.5.45.

No 1664 Heavy Conversion Unit Codes: DH and ZU
Formed 10.5.43 at Croft (No 6 Group), five B Mk V Halifaxes having already been received on the 7th, to which were added some B Mk IIs. Moved to Dishforth 7.12.43. Renamed No 1664 (RCAF) HCU on 20.11.44. Began conversion to B Mk IIIs in December 1944. Disbanded 6.4.45.

No 1665 Heavy Conversion Unit Codes: OG (Stirlings FO, MN and NY)
Based at Woolfox Lodge (No 3 Group) and equipped with Stirlings. Received A Mk V Halifaxes in late September 1943. Unit trained crews for No 38 Group. Moved to Tilstock 29.1.44, then to Saltby on 26.3.45, then to Marston Moor on 1.8.45. With transfer of No 4 Group to Transport Command, unit used to train crews for four-engine transports and designation changed to No 1665 Heavy Transport Conversion Unit. Equipped with A Mk III and C Mk VI Halifaxes. Moved to Linton-on-Ouse 7.11.45. Disbanded 15.7.46 and absorbed into No 1332(HT)CU at Dishforth.

No 1666 Heavy Conversion Unit Codes: QY and ND
Formed 5.6.43 at Dalton (No 4 Group) with 32+0 B Mk II and V Halifaxes. Reduced to a UE of 16+0 B Mk IIs. Moved to Wombleton 21.10.43, sharing it with No 1679 HCU (Lancasters), which disbanded 28.1.44: its remaining Lancaster conversion commitments were taken over by No 1666 HCU. Remaining Lancasters transferred to No 408(B) Squadron in April. UE increased to 40+0 B Mk II and V Halifaxes and three- flight system used. Renamed No 1666 (RCAF) HCU on 20.11.44. Received first B Mk IIIs 3.11.44, but allocation cancelled

and Lancasters issued; first course began 27.12.44 and last B Mk V and III Halifax courses completed by the end of January 1945. Last Halifax left in March.

No 1667 Heavy Conversion Unit Codes: GG and KR (Lancasters LR)
Formed 1.6.43 at Lindholme (No 1 Group) with one B Mk V Halifax Flight and one Lancaster Flight. Moved to Faldingworth 8.10.43 and then to Sandtoft w.e.f. 14.2.44. A, B and C Flights formed 1.5.44 and D (Instructors) Flights formed 26.6.44. Commenced re-equipping with Lancasters in November and remaining two Halifax Flights ceased operations in December.

No 1668 Heavy Conversion Unit Code: IG (Lancasters 2K and J9)
Formed 15.8.43 at Balderton (No 5 Group) and equipped with a UE of 16+0 B Mk II and V Halifaxes and 16+0 Lancasters, but re-equipped with Stirlings in November and disbanded 21.11.43, and moved to Syerston to form No 5 Lancaster Finishing School.

No 1669 Heavy Conversion Unit Codes: L6 and 6F
Formed September 1944 at Langar (No 5 Group) with 32+0 B Mk II and V Halifaxes. Began converting to B Mk IIIs in late 1944 but allocation cancelled and Lancasters issued December 1944.

No 1674 Heavy Conversion Unit Codes: OK (Fortresses RN)
Formed 10.10.43 at Aldergrove and equipped with Fortresses, Liberators and Halifaxes. Moved to Longtown 19.10.43; trained crews for meteorological and VLR duties. (On 14.10.43 No 518(Met) Squadron screened from operations and used as interim training unit under title No 1 Meteorological Conversion Unit. First course 30.10.43 and in five months 58 crews trained.) Moved back to Aldergrove 1.2.44. On 31.10.44 unit redesignated No 1674 Training Wing and organised as an OTU. Moved to Milltown 10.8.45 and converted to Met Mk III Halifaxes. Disbanded 30.11.45 and Halifaxes passed to No 111 OTU, which took over training of Halifax meteorological crews.

No 2 Middle East Training School Codes: Unknown
October 1942 small conversion unit established within No 2 Middle East Training School at Aqir, in Palestine. Received three Halifaxes, W1156, W7716 and W7717, all ex-No 462 Squadron. W7717 lost 8 December, replaced by W7697, another ex-No 462 Squadron machine. Halifaxes used until March 1944 when the requirements for conversion training ceased.

No 111 Operational Training Unit Codes: H3, X3 and 3G.
Based at Lossiemouth from 1.8.45 with Milltown as satellite airfield from 1.8.45. Took over training of Halifax meteorological crews from No 1674 Training Wing until disbanded in September 1946.

No 1 (Coastal) Operational Training Unit Codes: unknown
Based at Thornaby from 9.3.43. One Flight established to train Halifax and Fortress crews as interim measure during formation of No 1674 HCU. Training commitment passed to that unit.

Coastal Command Development Unit Codes: Unknown
Formed November 1940. Moved to Angle, satellite of Pembroke Dock, on 5.9.43, then Thorney Island January 1945. UE one B Mk II Halifax, one Liberator, two Beauforts, two Wellingtons and one Proctor. Administered by No 19 Group, it was responsible for trials and development work with all new Coastal Command equipment. No other details.

No 1361 Meteorological Flight Codes: Unknown
Received first two production Met Mk VI Halifaxes, RG778 and RG787, in February 1946, plus one C Mk VIII, PP282. Allocation altered soon after and aircraft transferred to No 521 (Met) Squadron, PP282 withdrawn and RG778 and RG787 transferred to No 521 Met Squadron. No other details.

No 1361 Transport Conversion Unit Codes: Unknown
No details other than allocation of a single C Mk VIII, PP284, on 13.2.46. Possible connection between this title and that of No 1361 Meteorological Flight; allocation of C Mk VIII aircraft to the former may indicate change of intended role to that of Transport Conversion training.

No 1427 Flight Codes; Unknown
Formed Stradishall, Suffolk, (No 3 Group) 2.10.42. Four B Mk II Halifaxes, R9389, R9419, V9990 and V9992 on strength. Absorbed into resident No 1657 HCU on 1.4.43. No other details known.

No 1445 Flight Codes: Unknown
Four B Mk IIs, W7845, W7849, DT486 and DT495. Flight appears to have been connected with the preparation of aircraft for overseas air ferry flights. No other details known.

Central Landing Establishment Codes: Unknown
Formed Ringway 1.10.40 and equipped with Hotspur gliders with Hawker Hectors and Lysanders for towing. Audaxes added. Development Unit established 22.10.40, under establishment WAR/AC/116A, and added to CLE establishment. Whitleys and Halifaxes attached for experimental work.

Airborne Forces Establishment Codes: unknown
Formed at Ringway 1.10.40 and equipped with Hotspurs, Hectors and Lysanders, with Whitley Mk V towing aircraft. Received first Halifax November 1941. Name changed to Airborne Forces Experimental Establishment under authority WAR/AC/168 November 1941. Moved to Sherburn-in-Elmet 1.7.42 and placed under control of Flying Training Command, No 21 Group. Detachments at Snaith and Ringway. Conducted glider towing and parachute-dropping tests with Halifax, Lancaster, Stirling and Boston. No further details known.

Airborne Forces Experimental Establishment Codes: Unknown
(See **Airborne Forces Establishment**)

Airborne Forces Tactical Development Unit Codes: Unknown
Formed 1.12.43 at Tarrant Rushton (No 38 Group) with mixed establishment of Halifaxes, Whitleys, Wellingtons, Albemarles, Dakotas, Horsas and Hamilcars. Moved to Netheravon 9.1.44 and five days later renamed Air Transport Tactical Development Unit (ATTDU) and transferred from No 38 Group to Transport Command. First B Mk III received in October. On 9.6.45 C Mk VIII PP217 arrived for service trials. In September moved to Harwell then to Brize Norton where it absorbed Army Supply and Transport Development Unit (ASTDU). Unit engaged in trials work in conjunction with Transport Command Development Unit (TCDU). Named changed to Army Transport Testing and Development Unit. Ceased flying trials work with Halifaxes late 1946.

Air Transport Tactical Development Unit Codes: unknown
(See **Airborne Forces Tactical Development Unit**)

Air Transport Testing and Development Unit Codes: Unknown
(See **Airborne Forces Tactical Development Unit**)

Transport Command Development Unit Codes: Unknown
Transferred from control of Flying Training Command (No 23 Group) to No 38 Group in February 1945 and HQ TCDU moved from Harwell to Brize Norton February 1945, replacing No 21 HGCU, which moved to Elsham Wolds. Initially unit was to equip with two Halifaxes, (A Mk III NA137 and first production C Mk VIII PP217 delivered between 8th and 10. 8. 45), two Stirlings and two Albemarles, On 3.10.45 report issued favouring Halifax and other two types rescinded in favour of an all-Halifax establishment. In May 1946 Army Airborne Transport Development Centre commenced move in from Amesbury Abbey, completing it by 15th and much cross-testing work done between this units sections and parent unit. Later received A Mk VIIs and eventually two A Mk IXs. Conducted a wide range of trials work, including Tactical Handling Trials for the A Mk IX Halifax. Unit moved all aircraft to Abingdon on the 28.6.49. A Mk IX RT814 transferred from Transport Command Development Unit to RAE 31.5.50, SOC 23.4.51.

Army Transport Testing and Development Unit Codes: Unknown
Flying trials unit for the Army Airborne Transport Development Centre based originally at Amesbury under the designation Army Supply and Transport Development Unit (ASTDU) and equipped with a variety of aircraft, including A Mk III Halifaxes (NA137, NA294, PN259). Moved to Brize Norton in May 1946, and merged with Air Transport Tactical Development Unit.

No 1 Parachute Training School Codes: Unknown
(See **No 1 Glider Training Squadron**)

No 1 Parachute Training Unit Codes; Unknown
(See **No 1 Glider Training Squadron**)

No I Parachute and Glider Training School Codes: Unknown
(See **No 1 Glider Training Squadron**)

No 1 Glider Training Squadron Codes: Unknown
Formed at Ringway and moved to Side Hill, near Newmarket, 21.11.40 and then to Haddenham (Thame) in January 1941. Removed from Airborne Forces Establishment control and placed under No 70 Group 25.11.41. Moved to Upper Heyford 28.3.46. Moved to Upper Heyford 28 March 1946. April 1946 issued with 10 A Mk IXs (RT837, RT838, RT839, RT840, RT841, RT842, RT843, RT844, RT845, RT846) to supplement its Dakotas, plus also C Mk VIII PP227 on 25 May (latter converted to Instructional Airframe 6010M on 16.7.46). Designation changed to No 1 Parachute Training School (referred to in some documents as No 1 Parachute Training Unit), on 1.1.47 renamed No I Parachute and Glider Training School. Continued in this role until activities wound down in 1949. Remnant of unit moved to Henlow, taking over that establishment's parachute-testing role and its two A Mk IXs, RT868 and RT886. The former was SOC 24-10-51 having been replaced by RT936 1.9.50. This was the last Halifax to serve with an RAF unit; written off, Cat 3(R), following accident on 21.4.53.

No 21 Heavy Glider Conversion Unit Codes: FEP, FEQ, FER, FES and FET
Formed February 1945 at Brize Norton as a Horsa glider training unit and moved to Elsham Wolds the same month. Received 12 A Mk III Halifaxes, ex-No 296(GT) Squadron, in February 1946, followed by A Mk VIIs later in the year. Moved to North Luffenham December 1946 and disbanded 3.12.47.

No 22 Heavy Glider Conversion Unit Codes: Unknown
Formed at Keevil in October 1944. Moved to Blakeheath Farm in June 1945. Only one Halifax allotted, A Mk III LW651, before decision taken to concentrate Halifaxes in No 21 Heavy Glider Conversion Unit and aircraft passed to that unit. Disbanded 15.11.45.

No 241 Operational Conversion Unit Codes: Unknown
Formed at Dishforth 5.1.48 from amalgamation of disbanded No 1331 (Heavy Transport Conversion Unit, No 1332 (Heavy Transport) Conversion Unit and No 1333 (Transport Support) Training Unit. Halifaxes appear to have been disposed of in mid-1949. No further details.

Operational Refresher and Training Unit Codes: OX
The Operational and Refresher Training Unit formed at Thruxton, then moved to Matching where it began equipping with Halifaxes and Stirlings. Intended establishment was to be a three-Flight system; two equipped with Halifaxes and the third with Stirlings. ATA pilots ferried the first three A Mk VIIs in on 1 March 1945, and two more next day along with the first Stirlings. Halifaxes and Stirlings seconded for *Operation Varsity*, on 24 March, Halifaxes going to Tarrant Rushton. Unit continued with remaining A Mk III Halifaxes until finally brought up to strength and commenced training programme. Stirlings gradually exchanged for more Halifaxes. First long-range cross-country towing exercise with Halifax 13.6.45 - a six-hour flight over France. A Mk IIIs replaced by A Mk VIIs June 1946. Decision made to equip entirely with Halifaxes, and Stirling holding put up for disposal; 12 A Mk III Halifaxes were allotted to replace them. Halifaxes used in wide range of exercises, mass glider-towing, solo and dual towing training, continental cross-country flights, container, jeep and gun dropping, air to air firing and fighter affiliation, and DR

navigation exercises. On 15 October the unit moved to Weathersfield from where it continued to operate but briefly and is presumed to have disbanded on, or about, 15.1.46.

No 1331 (Heavy Transport) Conversion Unit Codes: Unknown
Formed at Syerston on 14.12.46 from the Halifax Training Unit at Dishforth. Equipped with A Mk VII Halifaxes. Disbanded and absorbed by No 241 Operational Conversion Unit on 5.1.48.

No 1332 (Heavy Transport) Conversion Unit Codes: YY and OG
Formed 11.8.44 as No 1332 (Heavy) Conversion Unit at Longtown, but changed title to No 1332 (HT)CU. Moved to Nutts Corner 7.10.44 and then to Riccall Common on 25.4.45. Equipped with A Mk III Halifaxes it undertook final training for pilots and Army personnel used for airborne assault work. Yorks also used as a finishing school for No 38 Group crews. Moved to Dishforth 7.11.45. Absorbed the nine A Mk VIIs of No 1665 HTCU, all coded OG, which now became a Flight. Redesignated No 241 Operational Conversion Unit on 5.1.48 and received A Mk IX Halifaxes the same day. It continued to operate these until they were withdrawn early in 1949.

No 1333 (Transport Support) Training Unit Codes: CM and ZR. Post war ODY.
Formed 26.3.45 from No 107 (Transport) Operational Training Unit as No 1333 (Transport Support) Conversion Unit, changing its title twice, to No 1333 (Transport) Conversion Unit and then No 1333 (Transport Support) Training Unit, while based at Leicester East. On 25.10.45 moved to Syerston and equipped with A Mk VII Halifaxes, it received its first batch of A Mk IXs in November 1946. Moved to North Luffenham in July 1947. Designation had changed to No 1333 Heavy Transport Support Training Unit in 1946; its function was similar to that of No 1332 (HT)CU. Moved to North Luffenham July 1947. Unit disbanded on 5.1.48 and some Halifaxes, including RT767 and RT848, transferred to No 241 Operational Conversion Unit.

No 1383 (Transport Support) Conversion Unit Codes: GY
Formed August 1945 at Crosby and equipped with A Mk VII Halifaxes. Disbanded 6.8.46.

No 1385 Heavy Transport Support Conversion Unit Codes: Unknown
Formed at Weatherfield April 1946 having already begun receiving A Mk III Halifaxes from 21.3.46 along with No 1 Course personnel. This was a finishing school for crews from normal HCU courses, providing a concentrated six-week course in glider towing, heavy equipment and stores dropping. Duration reduced to four weeks shortly after No 1 Course commenced. A Mk IIIs disposed of in May and replaced by A Mk VIIs. Only four courses completed before unit disbanded on 3.7.46. Its Halifaxes were transferred to Syerston as a flight of No 1333 (Heavy Transport Support) Training Unit on 1.7.46.

Bombing Trials Unit Codes: Unknown
Based at West Freugh and engaged in bombing trials. One or two Halifaxes on charge throughout late war years; only five known to have served with the unit, W7711, LW514, NA280, NP891 and MZ958. Unit believed to have disbanded about June or July 1945.

Anti-Submarine Warfare Development Unit Codes: P9
Based at Gosport and used for trials work. No other details known other than three Halifaxes on charge, a Met Mk III, NA168, a B Mk III, MZ797, which was also used for meteorological duties, and B Mk III, MZ356. Last aircraft on strength, MZ797, March 1947.

Halifax Development Flight Codes: Unknown
31.10.44 signal received from No 41 Group to form the HDF at Holmsley South and allotting four Mk III Halifaxes for purpose of studying conditions under which passengers could be carried. No 246 (T) Squadron re-formed at Lyneham 11.10.44, from nucleus of No 511 Squadron, with a UE of 25 Dakotas, Liberators and Yorks and moved to Holmsley South 1.12.44, absorbing HDF. On 1.3.45 HDF attached to No 187 (T) Squadron for servicing facilities and transferred to Merryfield 12.3.45. Disbanded under authority dated 3.4.45.

No 1 Ferry Unit Codes: Possibly none allocated
(See **No 301 Ferry Training Unit.**)

No 16 Ferry Unit Codes: Unknown
Moved to Dunkeswell from Talbenny 6.8.45. UE three Halifaxes, two Dakotas, three Warwicks, three Oxfords and eight Ansons. Station closed 26.4.46. No other details.

No 301 Ferry Training Unit Codes: Unknown
Formed 1.11.40 at Kemble as HQSFP and No 7 Ferry Pilots Pool. Moved to Honeybourne and renamed No 301 FTU on 11.11.41. Moved to Lyneham 20.3.42 and received two Halifaxes in September. Moved to Pershore 16.3.44 and absorbed, along with the Servicing Wing from Lyneham, into new unit titled No 1 Ferry Unit. Halifaxes retained to complete commitment. Mk VII PP363 on unit strength September 1945. No further details.

No 13 Maintenance Unit Codes: 3J
Based at Henlow this MU carried out all major instrument, airframe and engine modifications for Halifaxes. Using mobile working parties it visited units in all groups, except Coastal Command, and including Halifaxes held at No 29 MU (High Ercall), No 45 MU (Kinloss) and No 48 MU (Hawarden). At least one B Mk VI, RG872:3J-E, still on unit charge in 1946.

Telecommunications Flying Unit Codes: Unknown
Formed at Hurn with four Wellingtons. Moved to Defford May 1942, where it received its first B Mk II Halifax. Unit worked in conjunction with No 1 Bombing Development Unit. A succession of B Mk II, III, VI and VII Halifaxes used between 1942 and 1945.

TR1335 (Gee) Development Unit Codes: OT (from July 1942)
Formed at Boscombe Down 14.12.41. Renamed No 1418 Bombing Development Flight 5.1.42. HQ moved to Feltwell 8.4.42 and renamed No 1 Bombing Development Unit 20.7.42; initial aircraft holding six Wellingtons, two Halifaxes, one Stirling and one Lancaster. Carried out service trials of experimental equipment. HQ moved to Newmarket 13 September and Flying Unit moved to Gransden Lodge in August 1942 equipped with Wellingtons, Blenheims, Mosquitoes and five Halifaxes (B Mk IIs and IIIs). Moved to

Newmarket August 1944 and took on role of Development and Radar Training. 25.2.45 moved back to Feltwell then to Lindholme in October. Disbanded 27.11.45.

Bombing Development Unit Codes: OT
(See **TR1335 (Gee) Development Unit**)

Bomb Ballistics Development Unit Codes: OR
Moved from Martlesham Heath to Woodbridge in late 1943. Engaged on trials work and known to have had HR756, the prototype B Mk II Series II Halifax, on active strength in 1944. No further details.

Radio Warfare Establishment Codes: V7 and U3 (Fortresses also U3, Mosquitoes 4S)
Flying Wing and Servicing Wing formed September 1945 at Foulsham from disbanded No 192(BS) Squadron. HQ Tactical Wing and Y Wing forming at Swanton Morley. On 6-7.10.45 23 Halifaxes, 10 Mosquitoes, seven Fortresses, one Oxford and one Ju 88 were ferried to Watton (No 60 Group), the unit's new base from 9.10.45. Unit engaged in specialist radio warfare trials. Renamed Central Signals Establishment. Ten Halifaxes still on strength when type withdrawn in January 1947. Last Halifax gone by February.

Central Gunnery School Codes: Unknown
Based at Catfoss. Only one Halifax on charge, B Mk III PN446, which was disposed of in January 1948, converted to an Instructional Airframe as 5731M.

Farnborough Research Flight Codes: Possibly none allocated
The Experimental Section and RAF Station Farnborough were merged into one establishment on 22.1.45. The following specialist sections used Halifaxes for trials/research work from April 1946 - Engineering Flight; Armament Flight; Instrument Flight; Wireless and Electrical Flight; Aerodynamics Supersonic Flight. On 18.8.46 the Meteorological Research Flight moved to Farnborough and re-equipped with two Met Mk VI Halifaxes, two Mosquitoes and personnel, reaching full strength on 17.12.46. No further details available after 31.3.48. PP350 still in use for tests in 1951, struck off charge 29.5.52.

Bomber Command Instructors' School Codes: IK and IP
Formed at Finningley 5.12.44 within No 93 Group. 14.2.45 control passed to No 91 Group, soon after unit came under umbrella of No 7 Group, but following disbandment of that Group returned to control of No 91 Group 21.12.45. Initially 22 Wellingtons, 10 Lancasters and five B Mk III Halifaxes (HX319, MZ873, MZ876, RG349 plus one other). Halifaxes operating on 28.12.44, but ceased by 7.5.45, replaced by Lancasters.

PFF Navigation Training Unit Codes: Unknown
Formed 10.4.43 at Gransden Lodge with a UE of 24 Halifaxes and Stirlings. First B Mk II Halifax received 12.4.43. Moved to Upwood and Warboys 11.6.43. Aircraft establishment amended 5.9.43, decreased to nine Halifaxes and nine Lancasters. One Halifax, W7823, lost in crash during take-off from Upwood on 25.1.44. Halifaxes replaced by Lancasters September 1944; all were allocated to HCUs.

Empire Air Navigation School Codes: FGE
The Central Navigation School was renamed EANS at Shawbury in January 1945 and received 18 B Mk III Halifaxes and two Lancasters, a Mosquito and either a P-47 or a P-51, which were additional to its holdings. Unit divided into flights; No 1 Halifaxes, No 2 Wellingtons, No 3 (Special Liaison) two Halifaxes, two Lancasters, one Mosquito, two Ansons and a Proctor. A single B Mk VI taken on charge November 1946, and the bulk of the B Mk IIIs were disposed of over the next three months and replaced by Lancasters. The B Mk VI was finally sent to No 45 MU in January 1948.

Empire Central Flying School Codes; Unknown
Established RAF Hullavington, Wiltshire, 1.4.42. February 1944, B Mk III Halifax delivered to Leeming. Special conversion course for Halifax Mk V conducted using B Mk V LL234. No further details.

Empire Radio School Codes: FGF (F for Flying Training Command; GF was Station code)
Based at Debden, received one B Mk VI Halifax and one Lancaster in June 1946, a B Mk III was added in July but disposed of the next month. The Halifax was equipped as a flying classroom for long-distance flights. Three more B Mk VIs added over the next two years, but all were disposed of by the end of September 1948.

No 1 Radio School Codes: TCA (T for Technical Training Command; CA was station code)
Based at Cranwell, unit converted B Mk II, former A&AEE test aircraft W1008 to Instructional Airframe, 4593M, in July 1944. Unit equipped with four modified B Mk VIs in 1946, PP214:TCAB, RG875, RG876 and ST814. Fitted with C Mk VIII tail cone and front of fuselage faired in on at least PP214. Halifaxes resident from 1946 to 1949.

No 2 Radio School Codes: Unknown

No details known other than unit equipped with two B Mk VI aircraft in 1946; RG776 and RG782. As with No 1 Radio School Halifaxes, these may have received some degree of modification for their specialist duties. Halifaxes disposed of before 1950.

APPENDIX 6: **Civil Halifax Register**

Serial No	Mark No	C of A Issued	Civil Reg	Details of Ownership
PP287	VIII	20.1.48	G-AGPC	Anglo French Distributors: TAI Paris F-BCJS 1947: Aero Cargo, crashed 1.12.48 on take-off from Lyons-Bron
PP274	VIII	1.8.47	G-AGTK	Anglo French Distributors: TAI Paris F-BCJX 1947 Aero Cargo. Damaged beyond repair after over-shooting Bovingdon 13.5.48
NR169	III	16.5.46	G-AGXA	G.N. Wickner: Air Carriers Ltd VH-BDT 1946: derelict 1947, Mascot airport
PP336	VIII	20.3.46	G-AGZP	Maharajah Gaekwar: only Halton 2: British American A/S: Alpha Airways ZS-BTA. Scrapped 1953
PP224	VIII	18.9.46	G-AHDL	Halton *Fitzroy* BOAC: Aviation Traders: Westminster Airways: crashed 1.4.49
PP228	VIII	20.7.46	G-AHDM	Halton *Falmouth* BOAC: Aviation Traders: Westminster Airways. Scrapped 1950
PP234	VIII	24.3.47	G-AHDN	Halton *Flamborough* BOAC: Aviation Traders: BAAS, scrapped 1950
PP236	VIII	13.8.47	G-AHDO	Halton *Forfar* BOAC: Alpha Airways: Aviation Traders: Bond Air Services. Scrapped 1950
PP268	VIII	24.3.47	G-AHDP	Halton *Fleetwood* BOAC: Aviation Traders: Bond Air Services. Undercarriage collapsed Schleswigland 4.4.49 but repaired same day. Scrapped 1951
PP269	VIII	7.7.47	G-AHDR	Halton *Foreland* BOAC: E. Sutton: Aero Cargo F-BECK. Scrapped 1951
PP277	VIII	24.8.46	G-AHDS	Halton *Fremantle* BOAC: Aviation Traders: Bond Air Services. Scrapped 1951
PP308	VIII	4.6.47	G-AHDT	Halton *Fife* BOAC: Aviation Traders: Bond Air Services. Broken up for spares Schleswigland 1949
PP310	VIII	10.7.46	G-AHDU	Halton *Falkirk* BOAC: Aviation Traders: Bond Air Services. Scrapped 1950
PP314	VIII	19.8.46	G-AHDV	Halton *Finnesterre* BOAC: Aviation Traders: Westminster Airways: LAC. Severely damaged at Squires Gate by gale 17.12.52. Scrapped 1953
PP315	VIII	29.7.46	G-AHDW	Halton *Falaise* BOAC: Aviation Traders: Bond Air Services. Scrapped Berlin 1948/49
PP316	VIII	4.6.47	G-AHDX	Halton *Folkestone* BOAC: Aviation Traders: Bond Air Services: World Air Carriers. Crashed on Mt Hohgart, Swiss Alps, 16.4.50
PP309	VIII	21.7.47	G-AHKK	Anglo French Distributors: Aero Cargo F-BCJV. Written off Casablanca 30.7.48
PP278	VIII	29.12.47	G-AHVT	Anglo French Distributors: TAI Paris: SANA: F-BCJR 1947. Scrapped 1951
PP331	VIII	18.5.48	G-AHWL	Angle French Distributors: TAI Paris: SANA: F-BCJT 1947. Written off at Le Bourget 20.5.48
PP238	VIII	NI	G-AHWM	Handley Page Ltd 4.7.47: RAF: became G-AJZY
PP230	VIII	14.9.48	G-AHWN	Handley Page Ltd: RAF: Lancashire Aircraft Corporation *Air Viceroy*. Undercarriage collapsed Schleswigland 6.7.49. Returned Bovingdon and broken up 1950
PP261	VIII	29.10.48	G-AHYH	BOAC: RAF: Lancashire Aircraft Corporation *Air Merchant II*. Scrapped Woolsington 1949
PP311	VIII	NI	G-AHYI	BOAC: RAF: Anglo French Distributors G-AIID: Skyflight Ltd, but not flown. Scrapped 1950
PP247	VIII	18.9.46	G-AHZJ	London Aero & Motor Service Ltd *Port of Marseilles*. Crashed Bergamo 31.7.47
PP246	VIII	15.11.46	G-AHZK	LAMS *Port of Naples*: Skyflight Ltd. Broken up Stansted 1949/50
PP242	VIII	26.10.46	G-AHZL	LAMS *Port of Oslo*. Broken up Stansted 1949
PP260	VIII	NI	G-AHZM	LAMS. No C of A issued because of undercarriage collapse Elstree 16.9.46. Broken up for spares
PP244	VIII	28.8.46	G-AHZN	LAMS *Port of London*. Ditched off Le Zoute, Belgium, 26.9.46
PP239	VIII	24.12.46	G-AHZO	LAMS *Port of London*: Skyflight Ltd. Scrapped Stansted 1949/50
PP271	VIII	NI	G-AIAN	BOAC (used for training only): RAF. Scrapped 1949/50
PP272	VIII	NI	G-AIAO	BOAC (used for training only): RAF. Scrapped 1949/50
PP281	VIII	15.2.49	G-AIAP	BOAC: RAF: Airtech: Eagle Aviation Ltd. Crashed Dum Dum, Calcutta, 20.11.50
PP326	VIII	9.2.49	G-AIAR	BOAC: RAF: Airtech: British American Air Services: loaned to Eagle Aviation Ltd: Chartair Ltd. Sold to LAC for spares 1951
PP327	VIII	NI	G-AIAS	BOAC: RAF: LAMS, but major accident before C of A issued. Used for spares
RG790	VI	NI	G-AIBG	LAMS for spares, but sold to Pegasus Air Transport Ltd: Airtech Ltd. Scrapped 1950
PP222	VIII	25.9.47	G-AIHU	LAC *Air Adventurer*. Crashed into hill near Rhyl 5.12.47
PP262	VIII	10.4.47	G-AIHV	LAC *Air Trader*. Broken up Bovingdon 1950
PP284	VIII	29.4.47	G-AIHW	LAC. Crashed night landing Heathrow 5.6.47
PP294	VIII	7.6.47	G-AIHX	LAC *Air Merchant*. Crashed night landing Squires Gate 3.9.48
PP241	VIII	19.6.47	G-AIHY	LAC *Air Explorer*. Damaged landing Le Bourget 28.12.49. Scrapped
PP317	VIII	NI	G-AIID	BOAC: RAF: Anglo French Distributors Ltd, Skyflight Ltd, but not flown. Scrapped 1950
PP280	VIII	27.10.47	G-AILO	College of Aeronautics: LAC *Air Courier*. Scrapped 1952
PP240	VIII	15.5.47	G-AIOH	CL Air Surveys: Bond Air Services. Crashed landing Barcelona 30.5.47
PP243	VIII	16.1.47	G-AIOI	CL Air Surveys: Bond Air Services. Taxying accident Tegel 15.2.49. Scrapped

Serial No	Mark No	C of A Issued	Civil Reg	Details of Ownership
PP320	VIII	2.12.47	G-AITC	College of Aeronautics: World Air Freight Ltd. Crashed landing Brindisi 20.1.50
PP218	VIII	13.5.48	G-AIWI	LAMS, operated by Skyfreight Ltd. Scrapped 1950
PP286	VIII	15.5.47	G-AIWJ	LAMS *Port of Athens*. C of A cancelled on sale to Ministry of Civil Aviation Fire School, Stansted, 19.12.50
PP295	VIII	21.7.47	G-AIWK	LAMS *Port of Sydney*: derelict Mascot airport, Australia, December 1947
PP291	VIII	NI	G-AIWL	LAMS. Sold Ministry of Civil Aviation Fire School 19.12.50
PP266	VIII	5.12.47	G-AIWM	LAC *Merchant Venturer*. Sold Ministry of Civil Aviation Fire School 19.12.50
PP235	VIII	23.5.47	G-AIWN	LAMS *Port of Darwin*: Payloads Ltd: R. Sanderson: Bond Air Services, operated by World Air Freight. Scrapped Southend 1951
PP290	VIII	NI	G-AIWO	LAMS, used for spares
PP288	VIII	26.1.48	G-AIWP	LAMS, operated by Skyfreight Ltd. Scrapped Stansted 1950
PP245	VIII	NI	G-AIWR	LAMS *Port of Durban*: LAMS (Africa) Ltd. ZS-BUL. No C of A issued in UK. Crashed landing Port Sudan 25.11.47
PP265	VIII	3.4.47	G-AIWT	LAMS *Port of Sydney*. Payloads Ltd. Written off Bovingdon 5.9.47
PP293	VIII	18.8.47	G-AIZO	Southern Aircraft (Gatwick) Ltd: Union Air Services: Bond Air Services *County of Surrey*. Crashed Studham 23.5.48
RG785	VI	NI	G-AJBE	LAMS: Pegasus Air Transport Ltd, but not flown: to Pakistan Air Force 21.10.49
PP264	VIII	11.7.47	G-AJBK	Air Freight Ltd: TAI Paris *Socota* F-BCJZ. Written off France 17.12.47
PP276	VIII	15.9.47	G-AJBL	Air Freight Ltd: Eagle Aviation Ltd: broken up Bovingdon 1949
PP328	VIII	20.8.47	G-AJCG	Vingtor Juftveier LN-OAS, but not flown: D.S. Elliott: Peteair Ltd *Sky Tramp*. Abandoned Lydda
PP259	VIII	NI	G-AJNT	Payloads Ltd: Delivered to Toussus as F-BCQY. No further details
PP279	VIII	8.6.48	G-AJNU	Payloads Ltd: Pak-Air Ltd AP-ACH 1948. No further details
PP292	VIII	NI	G-AJNV	Payloads Ltd: Air Globe Ltd HB-AIF: to Egyptian Air Force 1947
PP296	VIII	27.4.49	G-AJNW	Payloads Ltd: Westminster Airways Ltd. Withdrawn from use, Blackbushe 1950. Used in film 'No Highway' as fictitious 'Reindeer G-AFOH'.
PP312	VIII	30.4.48	G-AJNX	Payloads Ltd: R. Sanderson. Pak-Air Ltd AP-ABZ, delivered 9.5.48. Force landed next day 30 miles north-west Shaibah. Written off
PP322	VII	2.4.48	G-AJNY	Payloads Ltd: Bowmaker Ltd: Pak-Air Ltd AP-ACG, delivered 8.5.48: Pakistan Air Force
PP323	VIII	26.11.47	G-AJNZ	Payloads Ltd: World Air Freight Ltd *Trade Wind*. Crashed into high ground near Port St Mary, IoM, 28.9.48
NA684	III	NI	G-AJPG	Emergency landing Cranfield 1947. Registered to College of Aeronautics. Reputedly did not fly again. Had been used for period at Khartoum as engine test aircraft (named 'The Knocker'). Still at Cranfield 1954
PP263	VIII	15.10.47	G-AJPJ	Chartair ltd: BAAS: Mayfair Air Services: Hired by Idfaf (Israeli Defence Forces) to transport ammunition from UK and flew to Palestine 20.7.48. Emergency landing near Tel Aviv and destroyed in crash, 21.7.48
PP313	VIII	20.8.47	G-AJPK	Payloads Ltd: LAMS: R. Hayes, VIP Services Ltd. Withdrawn from use, Thame, May 1950
RG722	VI	NI	G-AJSZ	LAC. Broken up for spares
RG720	VI	NI	G-AJTX	LAC. Broken up for spares
RG756	VI	NI	G-AJTY	LAC. Broken up for spares
RG757	VI	NI	G-AJTZ	LAC. Broken up for spares
RG824	VI	NI	G-AJUA	LAC. Broken up for spares
RG825	VI	NI	G-AJUB	LAC. Broken up for spares
PP330	VIII	23.6.47	G-AJXD	Anglo French Distributors Ltd: SANA F-BCJQ *Keroual*. Crashed Aubervilliers near Le Bourget 27.7.48
PP238	VIII	18.3.48	G-AJZY	Handley Page Ltd: LAC *Air Monarch*. Crashed Hyde Lane, Great Missenden, 8.3.51
PP334	VIII	8.7.48	G-AJZZ	Handley Page Ltd: LAC. Hit ground on night approach Schleswigland and crashed 21.3.49
PP267	VIII	2.11.48	G-AKAC	Payloads Ltd: World Air Freight Ltd. Crashed Nauen, Russian Zone, inbound to Tegel 30.4.49
PP283	VIII	1.3.48	G-AKAD	Payloads Ltd: BAAS. Undercarriage collapsed Rennes, France, 17.5.48
RG763	VI	NI	G-AKAP	Marked OO-XAB, but not registered in Belgium: Airtech Ltd. Broken up for spares 1947/48
RG784	VI	NI	G-AKAW	LAMS: Pegasus Air Transport Ltd, but not flown: Pakistan Air Force
PP219	VIII	8.3.48	G-AKBA	Airtech Ltd: Sky Taxis Ltd, operated by Alpha Airways Pty Ltd. Swung on take-off Albacete, Spain, causing severe damage 25.5.48
PP237	VIII	16.4.48	G-AKBB	Airtech Ltd: BAAS. Undercarriage failure on take-off Schleswigland 11.2.49. Extensive damage, dismantled and shipped to UK
RG716	VI	NI	G-AKBI	LAC. Broken up for spares
PP233	VIII	8.12.48	G-AKBJ	LAC *Air Ambassador*. Undershot landing Tegel, damaged beyond repair 1.6.49
PP231	VIII	11.1.49	G-AKBK	LAC: *Air Enterprise*. Withdrawn from use 1950
PP289	VIII	NI	G-AKBP	Payloads Ltd: Air Globe Ltd HB-AIL 1947: Egyptian Air Force
PP329	VIII	9.9.48	G-AKBR	Payloads Ltd, intended for sale as HB-AIM to Air Globe, but cancelled and registered in error as G-AKIE: LAMS: Anglo French Distributors: Skyflight Ltd: Eagle Aviation Ltd. Scrapped 1950
PP273	VIII	NI	G-AKCT	Payloads Ltd: Air Globe Ltd HB-AIK 1947: Egyptian Air Force
PP282	VIII	4.2.48	G-AKEC	Henniker Smith & Co: LAC *Air Voyager*. Damaged beyond economical repair, Squires Gate, by gale 17.12.52. Hit G-AHDV
PP333	VIII	25.8.48	G-AKGN	BAAS: Chartair Ltd. Damaged beyond economical repair by gale, Thame 17.12.52
PP324	VIII	NI	G-AKGO	Airtech Ltd. Sold Ministry of Civil Aviation Fire School 2.1.48
PP223	VIII	17.8.48	G-AKGP	Airtech Ltd: SANA F-BESE *Ker Goaler* 1948. Damaged by fire Blackbushe 1949. Scrapped 1950
PP338	VIII	28.1.48	G-AKGZ	World Air Freight Ltd *North Wind*. Swung on take-off, Gatow 8.10.48
PP329	VIII	NI	G-AKIE	LAMS, mis-registered, already registered as G-AKBR
PP217	VIII	NI	G-AKJF	LAMS. Sold Ministry of Civil Aviation Fire School 19.12.50
RG695	VI	NI	G-AKJI	Air Freight Ltd. Delivered to Doncaster. Scrapped 1948/49
RG698	VI	NI	G-AKJJ	Air Freight Ltd. Delivered to Doncaster. Scrapped 1948/49
RT885	IX	NI	G-AKKP	Aviation Traders. Broken up for spares
RT892	IX	NI	G-AKKU	Aviation Traders. Broken up for spares
RG783	VI	NI	G-AKLI	LAMS: Pegasus Air Transport Ltd: Pakistan Air Force
RG781	VI	NI	G-AKLJ	LAMS: Pegasus Air Transport Ltd: Pakistan Air Force
RG779	VI	NI	G-AKLK	LAMS: Pegasus Air Transport Ltd: Pakistan Air Force
RG658	VI	NI	G-AKNG	LAC. Broken up for spares
RG700	VI	NI	G-AKNH	LAC. Broken up for spares
RG717	VI	NI	G-AKNI	LAC. Broken up for spares
RG759	VI	NI	G-AKNJ	LAC. Broken up for spares
RG712	VI	NI	G-AKNK	LAC. Broken up for spares
PP171	VI	NI	G-AKNL	LAC. Broken up for spares
RG736	VI	NI	G-AKUT	LAMS: Pegasus Air Transport Ltd: Pakistan Air Force
RG813	VI	NI	G-AKUU	LAMS: Airtech Ltd. Scrapped 1950
PP220	VIII	29.12.48	G-AKXT	LAC *Air Rover*. Withdrawn from use Bovingdon 1949
PP229	VIII	NI	G-ALBS	Hyland Automobiles Ltd: Hylands Ltd: LAC. Withdrawn from use Bovingdon. Scrapped 1950
PP270	VIII	NI	G-ALBT	Hyland Automobiles Ltd: Hylands Ltd. Withdrawn from use Bovingdon. Scrapped 1949
PP319	VIII	NI	G-ALBU	Hyland Automobiles Ltd: Hylands Ltd: LAC. Withdrawn from use Bovingdon. Scrapped 1949
PP321	VIII	NI	G-ALBV	Hyland Automobiles Ltd: Hylands Ltd: LAC. Withdrawn from use Bovingdon. Scrapped 1949
PP275	VIII	2.2.49	G-ALBZ	LAC. Collided with G-AHWN landing at Schleswigland 10.5.49
ST808	VI	NI	G-ALCD	LAC. Broken up for spares
PP335	VIII	18.11.48	G-ALCX	LAC *Air Regent*. Broken up at Bovingdon 1950
RG719	VI	NI	G-ALCY	LAC. Broken up for spares 1949
RG774	VI	NI	G-ALCZ	LAC. Broken up for spares 1949
RG822	VI	NI	G-ALDZ	LAC. Broken up for spares 1949

Serial No	Mark No	C of A Issued	Civil Reg	Details of Ownership
RG826	VI	NI	G-ALEA	LAC. Broken up for spares 1949
RG827	VI	NI	G-ALEB	LAC. Broken up for spares 1949
RG847	VI	NI	G-ALEC	LAC. Broken up for spares 1949
RG853	VI	NI	G-ALED	LAC. Broken up for spares 1949
RG877	VI	NI	G-ALEE	LAC. Broken up for spares 1949
PP337	VIII	11.10.48	G-ALEF	Handley Page Ltd: Vingtor Luftrier LN-OAT 1948: Eagle Aviation Ltd *Red Eagle*. Withdrawn from use at Luton 1950
RT791	IX	NI	G-ALIR	Aviation Traders Ltd. Broken up for spares 1950
ST801	VI	NI	G-ALOM	Aviation Traders Ltd. Broken up for spares 1949
RT763	IX	1.6.49	G-ALON	Aviation Traders Ltd: Bond Air Services Ltd. Withdrawn from use 1950
RT787	IX	16.2.50	G-ALOO	Aviation Traders Ltd: Egyptian Air Force 1158
RT846	IX	4.1.50	G-ALOP	Aviation Traders Ltd: Egyptian Air Force 1155
RT888	IX	NI	G-ALOR	Aviation Traders Ltd: Egyptian Air Force 1157
RT937	IX	15.6.49	G-ALOS	Aviation Traders Ltd: Bond Air Services Ltd. Scrapped 1950
RT832	IX	NI	G-ALSK	Aviation Traders Ltd. Scrapped Southend 1950/51
RT924	IX	NI	G-ALUT	Aviation Traders Ltd. Scrapped Southend 1949/50
RT879	IX	NI	G-ALSL	Aviation Traders Ltd. Scrapped Hawarden 1950/51
RT848	IX	NI	G-ALUU	Aviation Traders Ltd. Scrapped Southend 1949/50
RT873	IX	NI	G-ALUV	Aviation Traders Ltd. Scrapped Southend 1949/50
RT788	IX	NI	G-ALVH	Aviation Traders Ltd: Egyptian Air Force 1163 post 31.3.50
RT793	IX	NI	G-ALVI	Aviation Traders Ltd: Egyptian Air Force 1156 21.1.50
RT852	IX	NI	G-ALVJ	Aviation Traders Ltd: Egyptian Air Force 1159 28.2.50
RT901	IX	NI	G-ALVK	Aviation Traders Ltd: Egyptian Air Force 1160 13.3.50
RT907	IX	NI	G-ALVL	Aviation Traders Ltd: Egyptian Air Force 1162 31.3.50
RT938	IX	NI	G-ALVM	Aviation Traders Ltd: Egyptian Air Force 1161 27.3.50
RT884	IX	NI	G-ALYI	Aviation Traders Ltd. Scrapped 1950/51
RT776	IX	NI	G-ALYJ	Aviation Traders Ltd. Scrapped Southend 1950/51
RT785	IX	NI	G-ALYK	Aviation Traders Ltd. Scrapped Southend 1950/51
RT837	IX	NI	G-ALYL	Aviation Traders Ltd. Scrapped Southend 1950/51
RT772	IX	NI	G-ALYM	Aviation Traders Ltd. Scrapped Southend 1950/51
RT762	IX	NI	G-ALYN	Aviation Traders Ltd. Scrapped Southend 1950/51
RT759	IX	NI	G-AMBX	R.A. Short. Scrapped Hawarden 1951
RT895	IX	NI	G-AMCB	Aviation Traders Ltd. Scrapped Southend 1950/51
RT836	IX	NI	G-AMCC	Aviation Traders Ltd. Scrapped Southend 1950/51
RT893	IX	NI	G-AMCD	Aviation Traders Ltd. Scrapped Southend 1950/51
RT890	IX	NI	G-AMCE	Aviation Traders Ltd. Scrapped Southend 1950/51
RT935	IX	NI	G-AMCF	Aviation Traders Ltd. Scrapped Southend 1950/51
RT816	IX	NI	G-AMCG	Aviation Traders Ltd. Scrapped Southend 1950/51

CHAPTER NOTES

Chapter 1

1. Following the outbreak of war, Lachmann, a former pilot in the German Air Service during the First World War, was interned under Defence Regulations 18B, and thanks to the obdurate attitude of the Government, to its shame, he remained so throughout the war years, despite determined intercession by Handley Page himself. He was however, allowed to work on basic aerodynamic and structural calculations for the firm, but the full extent of his talents were never fulfilled.

2. The only other successful competitor was A.V. Roe and Company with their Type 679 Manchester, who received Contract no. 624973/37 for two prototypes, serial numbers L7246 and L7247.

3. The vulnerability of Wellington bombers to beam attacks during early daylight raids had highlighted this deficiency; the Handley Page works drawings for this modification were produced in July 1940.

4. This designation was later changed to R6/35/1; some aircraft would be fitted with RXF5/4 units, later redesignated R6/35/2, although there was nothing visible externally to distinguish between the two types.

5. This issue was resolved by the time the Halifax entered service with just a single pilot's position.

6. Subsequent continued Air Ministry failure to ensure this position remained armed would prove critical, not just for the Halifax but for all RAF heavy bombers.

Chapter 2

1. Wireless Telephony.

2. While on 78 Squadron, his Whitley had been hit by flak during an attack on Bremen on New Year's Eve, but made it back across the Channel on one engine. Balcomb, who usually flew as rear gunner had baled out and, thinking he was in France, quickly buried his parachute in deep snow and made his way to a signal box on a railway line – at Kirton Lane; he would experience a repeat performance within months.

3. Like 10 Squadron, No 76 spent a part of the early war period as an Operational Training Unit before re-forming as a bomber squadron.

4. Formed at Linton-on-Ouse on 1 May 1941.

5. Heavily escorted bomber formations designed to bring enemy fighters into combat rather than destroy the target.

6. Balcomb was helped to a local farmhouse, La Grande Lambarde, where he was sheltered while he recuperated and the local resistance were alerted. Henri Mittard then risked his life to help Balcomb escape, providing him with a bicycle but he was captured just a few days later making a dash on it towards the French unoccupied zone. After the war Balcomb was awarded the Médaille des Combattants de la Resistance by a grateful French Government.

7. This was the first ever successful ditching by a Halifax.

Chapter 3

1. MAP had passed all Boulton Paul turret manufacture to this company shortly after the outbreak of war and Lucas' would build more than 20,000, as well as Frazer Nash turrets, by 1945.

2. This ventral blind spot, on all British heavy bombers, was to significantly add to casualties as the air war developed. The other contentious issue, the replacement of rifle bore 0.303in weapons with those of a heavier calibre would also linger until the closing months of the war.

3. On average, only two-thirds of those dispatched.

4. Ten Wellingtons, nine Whitleys and two Stirlings.

5. Became C-in-C Allied Air Forces in India and S.E. Asia in January 1942.

6. Subsequently recovered, it was used as an instructional airframe with the serial number 3161M.

7. Although six aircraft from 10 Squadron were tasked for the mission, one had failed to take off and a second had aborted on the outward leg due to a glycol leak.

8. Motor Torpedo Boat.

9. This ability to fly with partly exposed bomb load would be further exploited in the coming year.

10. Code named *H2S*.

11. However, as time would show, the ubiquitous Wellington never disappeared entirely from front-line service

12. English physicist and astronomer. He was knighted in 1961 for his important post-war contributions to the development of radio astronomy.

13. When this was later extended to include the Lancaster, Roy Chadwick, its designer was also strongly opposed the idea on aerodynamic grounds as both companies had recognised the drag penalty of such a fitting.

14. Immediately after this crash, the Air Ministry tightened up requirements for civilian personnel to carry parachutes during flights in service aircraft – perhaps a most telling point?

15. Although not as high as the German report that only 80 aircraft had attacked for a loss of 52.

16. In all 12 had survived, including, from Kimber's crew, the pilot, Sgt E. Monk, Sgt D. Lemon, P/O E. Bodman and Sgt H. Corbishley RCAF. Sergeants Kimber and Monk eventually exchanged identities with two Army personnel in January 1945 and escaped, hiding on a Polish farm for some days until joining up with the advancing Soviet forces.

17. Chief of the Air Staff October 1940 to 1945.

18. Subsequently repaired, W7712 survived and was eventually written off in 1947.

19. Production B Mk Is had started life with one coat of U.P.5 (primer) and one coat each of D.T.D 308 Type M (for Matt) Black, Dark Green and Dark Earth. However, as operations progressed and ways were sought to counter German defences, the very matt RDM 2A finish had been introduced; it was considered more effective against searchlight illumination, the theory being it reflected less of the light.

20. A firm previously associated with Handley Page through conversion of the Herefords to Hampdens.

21. As early as June 1942 a report on drag trials completed with L7245 had shown, among other things, that reduction of camouflage paint thickness from .002 in to .001 in would reduce profile drag from 3.1% to 1.7%. More significant was the fact that leak drag, caused by gaps around the undercarriage, bomb doors, wing/fuselage joints, etc. produced anything from 3% to 12% of the total profile drag.

22. This experimental installation was duly tested at Boscombe Down early in 1943 and *may* have been the origin of the basic ventral installation briefly used by some Squadrons in 1944.

Chapter 4

1. Modification No. 421.

2. Included in the modifications was the deletion of the knock-out emergency panel used when fitted to the Defiant and Blackburn Roc; in the turret-fighter application, the gunner wore a standard parachute harness with attached seat pack, but in the heavy bombers, crew wore a harness with snap clips for the parachute pack.

3. This marker was known as a Long Burning Target Indicator.

4. This attack saw the first wartime operational use of *H2S* when it was used by Pathfinder aircraft for target marking.

5. The dropping of Target Indicators set to burst just above ground level.

6. A broadband radar jamming system designed by TRE that blinded German early-warning radars by throwing out radio noise.

7. Modification State.

8. These being: W7873: M from 35 Squadron, DT561: K, DT670, DT690: A, and HR729: R from 51 Squadron, DT575: Y, JB800: U, JB870: F and DK165: E from 76 Squadron, JB908: W from 77 Squadron, DT773 and HR659 from 78 Squadron, HR663: T from 102 Squadron, HR758 from 158 Squadron and BB343: X, DT752, JB854: D and JB925: R from 408 Squadron.

9. Amongst those killed was Sgt L. Jonasson RCAF who, at 17 years of age, was amongst the youngest to be killed while on Bomber Command operations when he was killed with the rest of the crew in DT575.

10. The addition of a bulbous leading edge to the rudders and a restricter on the balance tab.

11. HR748, one of the first B Mk II Series IA Halifaxes, underwent normal routine production tests at Boscombe Down in May.

12. By April 1945 No 8 Group would have no less than 19 Squadrons at its disposal.

Chapter 5

1. Known as '*Window*', the British were unaware that the Germans had already thought of the idea – the German equivalent being known as '*Düppel*' – but had not used it for exactly the same reasons.

2. These being Blohm & Voss, Deutsche Werft AG, H C Stülcken Sohn and Howaldtswerke Hamburg AG who between them, produced some 400+ U-boats of various classes.

3. Code-named *Operation Gomorrah*.

4. It is estimated that some 40,000 people died as a consequence of this firestorm, most of them victims of carbon monoxide poisoning when the air was sucked out of their basement shelters.

5. In between these two raids some two-thirds of the population had fled the city, coming close to fulfilling the directive to break the morale of the people.

6. Italy would surrender on 8 September 1943, five days after the Allied landings in the south, but bitter fighting in the north by Italian and German forces would continue to war's end while the majority of Italian forces in the south joined the Allies.

7. The Master Bomber for this raid was G/Capt J.H. Searby of 83 Squadron. Although this was the first major raid to employ the Master Bomber technique, Searby had acted in this role in the attack on Turin on 7/8 August as a trial for the Peenemünde raid.

8. Any attack on Berlin entailed a minimum flight of 500 miles over enemy territory. This initial series of raids was designed to probe the strength and efficiency of the enemy defences before commencing the main campaign.

9. Rumour lingers about a double gun installation, but there is no evidence to support that contention. Confusion produced by eventual introduction of the Fraser Nash FN 64 ventral turret, armed with two 0.303-in machine guns, is the likely source. Fitted to some production Lancasters, several RCAF squadrons received significant numbers of them.

10. Aside from being the Minister of Propaganda, Goebbels also held the position of Gauleiter (district leader/provincial governor) for the city of Berlin.

11. Part of a trial which had been going on since 8/9 September, this was the last RAF night bombing raid in which American aircraft took part, although individual B-17s would occasionally carry out bombing flights in the following weeks.

12. Marker beacons used to flash coded signals leading to each airfield.

13. See Chapter 15.

14. Fog Intensive Dispersal Operation. Aside from Woodbridge, this system would also be installed at many bomber stations.

15. A homing device used to detect radar emissions from German night-fighter radar.

16. Two Beaufighters and 2 Mosquitoes of 141 Squadron inaugurated Bomber Command's *Serrate* operations in patrols near the routes of the Berlin raid. One Mosquito made contact with a Bf 110 and damaged it with cannon-fire. The crew of this first successful Bomber Command *Serrate* patrol was Squadron Leader F. F. Lambert and Flying Officer K Dear.

Chapter 6

1. W1151: H, W1172: Q, W7697: R, W7716: I, W7717: J, W7757: W and W7758: Y.

2. W1170: U, W1171: X, W1176: Z, W1178: T, W7659: F, W7679: C and W7695: D.

3. W7672: E ,W1144: Q. W1156: Y, W1161: O, W1169: S, W7655: C, W7754: F and W7762: D.

4. W7755: A, W1148: P, W1149: R, W1177: G, W1183: M, W7664: T, W7671: H and W7702: L.

5. Landing Ground 09 (El Daba)

6. Bonfire Night or Guy Fawkes Day is held on November 5 each year in the United Kingdom and some other parts of the Commonwealth to commemorate Guy Fawkes and the Gunpowder Plot to blow up the Houses of Parliament in 1605.

7. Comprising two Halifaxes and six Liberators.

Chapter 7

1. Renumbered as 1419 Flight in March 1941

2. No 138 (Special Duties) Squadron.

3. Now the site of Manchester Airport, this was the same airfield where SOE and SIS agents would also receive their parachute training.

4. Special Duties.

5. In Polish aircrews, the navigator was the senior person, not the pilot.

6. Jan Piwnik would become one of the greatest Polish underground field commanders. He was killed in action near Vilnius on 16 June 1944.

7. Like all Czech operations, these were carried out without the benefit of a partisan reception committee on the ground.

8. The Narodnyi Komissariat Vnutrennikh Del (People's Commisariat of Internal Affairs) was the leading secret police organisation of the Soviet Union.

9. In the post-war period, Seth wrote an excellent book about the Airborne Forces entitled *Lion With Blue Wings*.

10. No 138 Squadron supplied W1229: A, DT542: Q, DT543: G, L9618: W, W1002, W1007 and L9613: V while 161 Squadron sent DG244: Y and DG245: W.

11. A valuable currency on the black market, coffee could buy a variety of things, including information.

12. More commonly known as 'Joes'.

13. Mediterranean Allied Air Forces. At the time, Slessor was also C-in-C, RAF Mediterranean and Middle East.

14. South African Air Force.

15. Officially, the squadron ceased Halifax operations on the 31August/1 September when it sent out a mixed Halifax/Stirling force, losing two Stirlings and Halifax JD171, shot down by a night-fighter at Gilze-Rijen on the way in to a Belgian DZ.

Chapter 8

1. Named after its French manufacturer.

2. Almost twice the range at which an airborne operator could detect a submarine with its low profile all but lost amongst the clutter of the sea surface returns.

3. Initially, Halifaxes carried six-250 lb depth charges for their mixture of anti-submarine patrols and convoy escort work.

4. The Leigh Light was a powerful, 24-inch diameter searchlight of 22 million candelas, carried by a number of Coastal Command aircraft and used to illuminate surfaced U-boats at night.

5. Kapitänleutnant (Kptlt.) Manfred Kinzel's U-338 was one of the successful group of U-boats that attacked convoy SC.122, the most southerly of three convoys sent out simultaneously from the New York in early March to run the gauntlet to England. The attack on SC122 developed into the biggest convoy action of the war with some 40 U-Boats involved; by its end, 21 ships had been sunk for the loss of a single U-boat.

6. Korvettenkapitän (KrvKpt.) Heinrich Schmid.

7. Some credible German sources credit the loss of U-663 to Sunderland 'W' of 10 Squadron RAAF.

8. The attack by Halifax S-Sugar of 58 Squadron on 7 May, 1943 in position 46.33N, 11.12W was in fact against U-214 which sustained minor damage.

9. Kptlt. Herbert Engel.

10. Kptlt. Georg von Rabenau.

11. Kptlt. Ralf von Janssen.

12. A credible German source states that the boat was sunk in position 45.28N, 10.20W by depth charges from a Halifax aircraft of 58 Squadron. This brings into question the first operational use of the Mk 24 torpedo, which several naval sources claim was by a Catalina aircraft of VP-84 against either U-640 on 14 May 1943 or U-657 on 17 May 1943.

13. The 0.303-in Vickers favoured by Bomber Command had been replaced in Coastal Command Halifaxes by a 0.5-in Browning in a strengthened fitting, its heavier hitting power a valuable addition in attacks.

14. KrvKpt. Leo Wolfbauer.

15. Oblt. Gustav Borchardt.

16. A call was received from the aircraft at 19.11 hrs stating that it was under attack. No further messages were received and it is entirely possible that it fell victim to fighters from either the III., IV. or V./KG 40 or the I. or III./ZG1.

17. Kptlt. Hans-Martin Scheibe. U-455 was last heard from on 6 April 1944 while in the Mediterranean. Her cause of loss is unknown.

18. The suffix G denoting that while on the ground, as a research aircraft, it had to be under guard at all times.

19. Respectively commanded by Oblt. Heinz-Konrad Fenn, Oblt. Wolf Jeschonnek and KrvKpt. Helmut Köppe.

20. Kptlt. Günther Krech and RK holder, Kptlt. Hans-Hartwig Trojer.

21. U-461, U-462 and U-504 commanded respectively by KrvKpt. Wolf-Harro Stiebler, Oblt. Bruno Vowe and KrvKpt. Wilhelm Luis.

22. This was U-107 under the command of Kptlt. Volker Simmermacher, which was heading to lay mines off the US east coast. Although F/O Davey attacked her in the face of heavy return fire, no damage was done and after completing a successful patrol, U-107 returned to Lorient on 3 October.

23. A hygrometer consisting of a dry-bulb thermometer and a wet-bulb thermometer; their difference indicates the dryness of the surrounding air.

24. S/Ldr Davey was later awarded the DSO but was to die a few months later when he was killed while flying as a passenger in a flight from the Azores.

25. Oblt. Herbert A. Werner. U-415 was sunk by a mine west of Brest on the morning of 14 July 1944.

26. Grant was to succeed W/Cdr J.M.D. Kerr as CO of 58 Squadron in April and would retain that position until March 1945.

27. Oblt. Dietrich Sachse.

28. A Sperrbrecher (Path-maker) was a robust ship of between approximately 5 - 7,500 tons equipped with a degaussing system used to detonate magnetic mines from a safe distance and withstand the force of their explosion. Their main job was to escort surface ships and U-boats to and from port, remove magnetic mines along the route and, with their quite heavy AA armament, give additional protection against air attacks. For this latter duty, they were often equipped with barrage balloons.

29. Oblt. Herbert Brammer.

30. With winter daylight hours brief in these latitudes, attacks were now classified as occurring during the 'dark' period, which included the normal night hours.

31. Naval Officer in Charge.

Chapter 9

1. Established by Army Order on 24 February 1942.

2. The crew of Halifax 'A' were the only survivors from Operation Freshman.

3. The bodies of the murdered four were sunk at a few hundred metres depth off Kvitsøy Island and while never recovered, they are commemorated on the Brookwood Memorial at Brookwood, Surrey.

4. Their bodies were recovered in August 1945 and buried with full military honours at Vestre Gravlund in Oslo.

5. The glider pilots and the servicemen are buried in Eiganes Churchyard, Stavanger.

6. The remains of the crew of this aircraft were recovered by local people in the spring of 1943 and temporarily buried in herring boxes. In December 1945 they were exhumed and laid to rest in Helleland Churchyard.

7. Flown by Hptm Georg Schabert and Oblt Ludwig Progner.

8. The American Dakota-Waco combinations used in *Operation Husky* had also had only a limited period of intensive training and found themselves handicapped to some extent by their limited navigation techniques, which were inadequate for the task in hand.

9. *Operation Ladbroke*, the initial assault on the Ponte Grande Bridge resulted in its seizure by 73 men and the removal of demolition charges. However, day long counter-attacks by Italian forces resulted in the eventual surrender of the force. However, their resistance had permitted forward elements of the British 5th Infantry Division to arrive and liberate the nine survivors of the initial air assault 30 minutes later, Bernard Halsall among them.

10. Lieutenant John Prout and Sergeants Hill and Flynn were rescued later in the day by a ship of the Royal Navy while credit for the 'shooting down' of the Horsa went to Lt Dieter Meister of the V./KG 40.

11. Manufactured by Excelsior Motorcycles, they were known as 'Wellbikes' and were designed for use by Allied paratroopers.

12. Introduced on 5 December 1942, the four black and three white bands had been applied to Typhoon aircraft and a number of Tempest Vs as an identification marking to denote that they

were friendly aircraft so as to avoid being mistaken, as had happened frequently, for Focke-Wulf Fw 190 aircraft.

13. To the tug crews' eternal embarrassment, this cement factory was one of the few buildings left standing when the Allies finally took Caen.

14. This glider was the same one which had broken loose from its 644 Squadron tug on the first day.

Chapter 10

1. This was Mod 930.
2. Leading Aircraftsmen.
3. Many crews would switch the *Monica* set off, as it became an unnerving, almost constant, distraction for the pilot.
4. An aluminium alloy with the trade name Duralumin, it is also known as Duraluminum or Duraluminium.
5. As noted previously, No 433 and 466 Squadrons received their first B Mk IIIs in November 1943 and by the end of the year, both No 4 and No 6 Groups were using them operationally.
6. Formed at Elvington, near York on 20 June 1944, 347 Squadron (Groupe 1/25 *'Tunisie'*) was the second of the two French Air Force heavy-bomber squadrons that served in RAF Bomber Command. In October 1945, it moved to France and passed to the control of the Armée de l'Air on 27 November 1945.
7. Tame Boar.
8. LW627: Q, LW646: E, LW648: A, LW655: V and LW695: M.
9. One such example being MZ954, which was delivered to the RAF in September 1944.
10. No 433 Squadron would eventually record almost 400 sorties without loss early in the year.
11. Arguably the most well known of all Halifaxes, LV907 completed all of its sorties with 158 Squadron. On arrival on the squadron it was placed in the charge of ground crew chief Fl/Sgt Wicks who was told by its pilot F/O Smith at the beginning of his tour, to name the aircraft whatever he liked as he 'was not superstitious'. Accordingly, Wicks or one of his ground crew chose 'Friday the 13th', which was painted on the port side of the nose below the cockpit. At the end of the war, LV907 was put on display in London. Subsequently scrapped without any forethought, all that remains of this aircraft are the panels carrying the bomb tally and nose art, which are currently on display at the RAF Museum, Hendon.
12. The RAF's first RCM/ELINT unit, it was formed at Boscombe Down on 13 June 1940 under the cover designation of the Blind Approach Training and Development Unit (BATDU). It was redesignated as the Wireless Intelligence Development Unit (WIDU) on 30 October 1940.
13. 1473 Flight was absorbed into 192 Squadron on 27 January 1944.
14. Code-named *Corona*.
15. Code-named *Airborne Cigar (ABC)* it would also be carried by the Halifaxes and B-17s of the specialist Bomber Support squadrons.
16. Also known as 100 (Bomber Support) Group it formed the "clandestine" side of Bomber Command whose trade was electronic warfare, radio countermeasures, radar jamming and night-fighter and interdiction activities flying a wide and varied assortment of aircraft, predominantly from airfields in East Anglia.
17. W. R. Chorley's *Bomber Command Losses 1944* notes the two losses may have been LW687 and MZ504 but which aircraft carried the code 'Z' and which carried 'C' cannot be clearly established.
18. On return, the pilot tried an Instrument Landing at RAF Silverstone, Northamptonshire, but in the poor visibility failed to see the masts of the Assisted Safe Landing equipment and crashed into nearby playing fields. The only survivor from the crash was Sgt W.G. Mountford who was injured.
19. Although the aircraft was written off, the instrument panel survives to this day as part of an exhibit in the Australian War Memorial, Canberra.
20. Later to win the Nobel Prize for Radioastronomy, Martin Ryle spent most of the war working on the development of radar at the Telecommunications Research Establishment (TRE).

Chapter 11

1. GH equipment sent radio pulses to two ground stations in Britain, which re-transmitted them back to the aircraft. By measuring the time interval between the outgoing and returning pulses on an oscilloscope display the navigator could direct the pilot towards the target and determine the precise point for accurate bomb-release.
2. F/O H. D. Bastable RCAF initially evaded until captured in Paris on 19 July. He was imprisoned in the notorious Fresnes Prison before being transported to Buchenwald from where the Luftwaffe had him released to be interned in Camp L3.
3. Of the ten V-1s launched on this night, five crashed shortly after launching, one went missing and of the remaining four, one fell in Sussex, and the others near Gravesend, Sevenoaks and Bethnal Green.
4. The code name given to V-1 launch sites.
5. Fl/Sgt G. W. V. Luck RAAF.
6. These being DS634: A, LL725: C and LL687: M.
7. The squadron's conversion to the Halifaxes was not completed until November.
8. Mosquitoes also formed part of the Group, eventually equipping seven squadrons and were used for *Window* dropping and a variety of duties while mixing with the Main-Force bombers and homing onto German night-fighter radar transmissions with deadly effect.
9. A sortie had been scheduled for 21 October by a Halifax of 171 Squadron but was cancelled for undetermined reasons.
10. After being repaired, MZ710 was issued to 21 HGCU post-war, serving with that unit until struck off charge in November 1946.
11. The Halifaxes being NP741: K of 426 Squadron, HX329: Y of 158 Squadron and MZ406: Q of 640 Squadron.
12. MZ337: A of 158 Squadron and MZ912: Y of 640 Squadron.
13. Nearly half the total wartime tonnage dropped by Bomber Command would fall during the last nine months.
14. An approximate equivalent of the British Observer Corps.
15. These being LW168 :O and MZ871: G of 102 Squadron and MZ489: L from 347 Squadron.
16. The 67,637 tons dropped in March was the heaviest weight ever dropped in a single month.
17. The squadron began its conversion to the Halifax in February 1945 during which time and because of the conversion process its operational timetable was somewhat restricted.
18. Chorley notes in his *Bomber Command Losses* that a Bf 109 of the III./NJG 11 may have also been involved.
19. Between them the two aircraft had completed 1,060 flying hours and successive crews had earned two DSOs, 19 DFCs and 14 DFMs.
20. The third of these, Junkers Ju 88 G-6 W.Nr. 620028, D5+AX of the 13./NJG 3 crashed at Sutton upon Derwent near Elvington at 01.51 hrs on 4 March 1945, the last German aircraft to fall on British soil during the Second World War. Hptm J. Dreher RK and his crew of three all being killed in the crash.

21. Possibly the victim of Lt Arnold Döring of the10./NJG 3.
22. An approximate translation is Fighter Wing 27.
23. Amberger was captured in 1946 and tried, along with some of the escort who had taken part in the killings and also officers in charge of the airfield at that time. Seven were executed for war crimes in May but two involved in the shootings escaped the net. It is to the credit of other German personnel at the airfield that they provided critical testimony at the trial.
24. Either 408 Squadron's NP776: R or 640 Squadron's RG564: P, both of which were lost on this raid.

Chapter 12

1. Mod 814.
2. Bombing training.
3. Essentially a scaled-up version of the Hadrian, KK791 was the only one of its type taken on charge by the RAF.
4. The majority of heavy bomber losses in this theatre of war were the result of the violent tropical weather conditions.
5. Now known officially as the Union of Myanmar, it is the largest country by geographical area in mainland South East Asia.
6. The name given by the Allies to the route across the eastern end of the Himalayan Mountains over which resupply flights were flown into China.
7. The Kachin fought a long and bloody war against the Japanese urged on by the British promise that they would be granted autonomy once peace returned. Unfortunately, they are still waiting.
8. On 15 August 1947, India gained independence from British rule while at the same time Muslim-majority areas were partitioned to form the separate state of Pakistan. Chapter 13 refers.

Chapter 13

1. Later given the code name of *Village Inn*.
2. Formerly the School of Army Cooperation and located at Old Sarum on Salisbury Plain, it was renamed as the School of Air Support in late 1944.
3. These were three ex-521 Squadron aircraft, RG833, RG835 and RG873, which were allocated to the squadron on 22 March and followed two days later by RG780.
4. These were taken over by 518 Squadron as a detachment.
5. Blind Approach Beacon System. Essentially a ground-based short-range navigation system that functions as a beacon by emitting pulsed signals to be picked up by an aircraft and contains information about the aircraft's position with respect to the runway on which it is making a landing.
6. HX246, LW385, NA682 and RG431.
7. RG820 was converted to Instructional Airframe 6903M and allocated to No 4 Group on 29 September 1951.
8. A former RAF night-fighter pilot with 20 confirmed victories, John Cunningham had originally joined de Havilland in 1938. He rejoined the company at the end of the Second World War and in 1946, succeeded Geoffrey de Havilland Jr. as the company's chief test pilot. He was heavily involved in the development of the world's first jet airliner, the de Havilland Comet.
9. A location exposed to some very strong winds at certain times of the year as the wartime RAF squadrons based there had discovered.
10. The French equivalent of an RAF Maintenance Unit.
11. August, RG844, RG852, RG874, ST795 and ST800; September, RG823, RG842, RG845, RG846 and RG818; and in October, two more, RG645 and RG609.
12. Located at RAF Shawbury in Shropshire and formerly known as the Central Navigation School, it was renamed The Empire Air Navigation School in late 1944 and had carried out much work with the API to test its efficiency.
13. RG548 F-RAVW and RG818 F-RAVG of GB.1/21 and RG491 and RG594 F-RAXO of GB.2/21.
14. Tassigny was arrested by the Germans in 1942 and imprisoned at Riom, where he remained until its liberation during the Allied advance. He was then chosen to represent the French government at the surrender of German forces outside Berlin on May 7.
15. G-AJNV (PP292), G-AKBP (PP289) and G-AKCT (PP273).
16. RG736, RG779, RG781, RG782, RG783, RG784, RG785 and RG813.

Chapter 14

1. W7671, W7845, W7847 and W7849.
2. Mod 1377.
3. Collectively grouped as Mod 1192.
4. PP325, PP326 and PP327.
5. Present day Sri Lanka.
6. Named for a famous British removal and transport firm, it was also referred to initially in some RAF documents as *Operation Plainfare*.

Appendix 1

1. Later promoted to Flight Lieutenant, Harris went on to complete his training and served with the squadron until he and his crew were lost on a raid to Bremen on 25/26th June 1942 in W7759: L.
2. Usually referred to as a Bomb Aimer.
3. RG349, the first B Mk III, arrived on 6 December.
4. MZ965, NA132, NA128, NA281, NA298, NA304, NA306, NA308, NA638, NA697, NA698 plus one other as yet unidentified Halifax.
5. MZ569, MZ637, MZ745, NA104, NA297, NA299, NA301, NA523, NA640, NA641.
6. NA575 (ex-76 Squadron), NA576 (ex-346 and 347 Squadrons), NA575 (ex-76 Squadron), MZ571 via a chain of units, Nos 51, No 347 Squadrons then 1658 HCU) and MZ710 (ex-102 and 77 Squadrons).
7. The first batch of Stirlings was moved to Weathersfield where they became the nucleus of 1385 Heavy Transport Conversion Unit.
8. Renamed No 1 Parachute and Glider Training Unit from 1 January 1947.

INDEX